36TH CONGRESS, 1st Session. } SENATE. { Ex. Doc. No. 30.

MESSAGE

OF THE

PRESIDENT OF THE UNITED STATES,

COMMUNICATING,

In compliance with a resolution of the Senate, the instructions to, and dispatches from, the late and present Ministers in China, down to the period of the exchange of ratifications of the treaty of Tientsin, and also the instructions to Mr. Parker of February, 1857.

MARCH 13, 1860.—Read.
APRIL 2, 1860.—Ordered to be printed; and that 1,500 additional copies be printed.

To the Senate of the United States:

In answer to the resolution of the Senate, of the 6th ultimo, requesting copies of the instructions to, and dispatches from, the late and from the present minister of the United States in China, down to the period of the exchange of ratifications of the treaty of Tientsin; and also a copy of the instructions from the Department of State of February, 1857, to Mr. Parker, former commissioner in China, I transmit a report from the Secretary of State, and the papers by which it was accompanied.

JAMES BUCHANAN.

WASHINGTON, *March* 12, 1860.

DEPARTMENT OF STATE,
Washington, March 9, 1860.

The Secretary of State, to whom was referred the resolution of the Senate of the 6th ultimo, requesting the President to communicate to that body, if, in his judgment, not incompatible with the public interest, "copies of the instructions to, and dispatches from, the late and present ministers in China down to the period of the exchange of ratifications of the treaty of Tientsin; and also a copy of the instructions from the Department of State of February, 1857, to Mr. Parker, former commissioner in China," has the honor to lay before the President the papers specified in the accompanying list.

Respectfully submitted.

LEWIS CASS.

The PRESIDENT OF THE UNITED STATES.

List of accompanyiny papers.

Mr. Marcy to Mr. Parker, 2d February, 1857.
Same to same, 27th February, 1857.
Mr. Cass to Mr. Reed, with an accompaniment, 30th May, 1857.
Mr. Appleton to Mr. Reed, 22d June, 1857.
Mr. Reed to Mr. Cass, 26th June, 1857.
Mr. Cass to Mr. Reed, 29th June, 1857.
Same to same, 29th July, 1857.
Mr. Reed to Mr. Cass, 9th September, 1857.
Same to same, 10th November, 1857.
Mr. Cass to Mr. Reed, 5th February, 1858.
Mr. Reed to Mr. Cass, with accompaniments, 25th November, 1857.
Same to same, with accompaniments, 14th December, 1857.
Same to same, with accompaniments, 15th December, 1857. Extract.
Same to same, with accompaniments, 16th December, 1857.
Same to same, with accompaniments, 28th December, 1857. Extract.
Same to same, 30th December, 1850,
Same to same, with accompaniments, 13th January, 1858.
Same to same, 14th January, 1858.
Same to same, with accompaniments, 26th January, 1858.
Same to same, with accompaniments, 26th January, 1858.
Same to same, with accompaniments, 1st February, 1858.
Same to same, with accompaniments, 4th February, 1858.
Same to same, with accompaniments, 13th February, 1858.
Mr. Cass to Mr. Reed, 28th April, 1858.
Mr. Reed to Mr. Cass, with accompaniments, 26th February, 1858.
Same to same, with accompaniments, 3d April, 1858.
Same to same, with accompaniments, 3d April, 1858.
Mr. Cass to Mr. Reed, 25th June, 1858. Extract.
Mr. Reed to Mr. Cass, with accompaniments, 10th April, 1858. Extract.
Same to same, 28th April, 1858.
Same to same, with accompaniments, 6th May, 1858.
Same to same, with accompaniments, 15th May, 1858. Extracts.
Same to same, with accompaniments, 21st May, 1858. Extracts.
Mr. Cass to Mr. Reed, 17th August, 1858.
Mr. Reed to Mr. Cass, with accompaniments, 2d June, 1858.
Mr. Cass to Mr. Reed, 3d September, 1858.
Mr. Reed to Mr. Cass, with accompaniments, 15th June, 1858. Extracts.
Same to same, 18th June, 1858.
Same to same, with accompaniments, 30th June, 1858. Extracts.
Same to same, with accompaniments, 1st July, 1858. Extracts.
Same to same, with accompaniments, 13th July, 1858.
Mr. Cass to Mr. Reed, 16th October, 1858.
Mr. Reed to Mr. Cass, with accompaniments, 24th July, 1858.
Same to same, with accompaniments, 29th July, 1858.
Mr. Cass to Mr. Reed, 25th October, 1858.
Mr. Reed to Mr. Cass, with accompaniments, 1st September, 1858.

Mr. Marcy to Mr. Parker.

No. 9.] DEPARTMENT OF STATE,
Washington February, 2, 1857.

Sir: Your dispatch of the 22d of November, with its accompaniments, was received at this department to-day. I hasten to acknowledge them, and to furnish you with a very brief reply thereto, in the hope that my communication may reach England in season to go out in the next overland mail for China. The President has had only time to glance at the papers you have sent, (the report of Commodore Armstrong not having arrived,) he cannot, therefore, at this time, present fully his views upon the occurrences to which your dispatch alludes. When all the documents are received, you will be again addressed on the subject. It appears that previous to the occurrence of the 16th of November the conduct of the governor general of Canton towards Americans had been unexceptionable. Commander Foote states that his professions towards them had "been uniformly courteous, manifesting every disposition to preserve peace with us," (the Americans.) As a precautionary measure, the conflict with the English having already commenced, he wished the Americans to leave the city of Canton, and suggested that our naval forces should be withdrawn. I will not say that the suggestion should have been acted on, but, after this proceeding on the part of the governor general, and the notices given to our consul, Mr. Perry, it does appear to the President that it was not a discreet act to send a boat from the San Jacinto to "sound the river in the vicinity of the forts." This act provoked the fire upon the boat; the origin, as I understand the case, of all the difficulties which subsequently followed. Whether this act of taking soundings in the river while the city of Canton was the scene of actual hostilities between the British and Chinese was justifiable, or that of firing upon the boat under the circumstances was of the aggravated character attributed to it by Commodore Armstrong, and fully justified his subsequent measures, the President will not pronounce a definite opinion until the report of that officer is laid before him. From the cursory reading of the documents which have been received, I think he is inclined to regret that there had not been more caution on the part of our naval force in the beginning, and more forbearance in the subsequent steps. The British government evidently have objects beyond those contemplated by the United States, and we ought not to be drawn along with it, however anxious it may be for our coöperation. The President sincerely hopes that you, as well as our naval commander, will be able to do all that is required for the defense of American citizens and the protection of their property, without being included in the British quarrel, or producing any serious disturbance in our amicable relations with China.

I need not impress upon you the great importance of this object.

The President trusts that, by your prudent acts and counsels, the difficulty which existed at the date of your dispatch has been already settled, and that American interests will not be seriously injured by what has taken place.

There is one transaction not noticed in your dispatch, probably not known to you when it was written, which has excited deep regret. It appears, by the reports of Commander Foote, to the Navy Department, that our flag was unfurled and borne into the city of Canton when the British forces entered after the walls had been breached by the British batteries. I do not perceive that we had, at that time, any cause of complaint which could afford the slightest pretext of justification or excuse for such a rash act.

This proceeding deeply compromitted our neutrality, and, in appearance at least, made us volunteers in a quarrel from which we were bound by every consideration to keep aloof.

It appears, by the various accounts which have reached this country, directly and through the English press, that our consul at Hong Kong had left his post, was at Canton when the British forces attacked that city, and joined them in their hostile proceedings, at the same time displaying the flag of his country.

This statement, though it has not reached this government in an official report, so far as it directly involves our consul at Hong Kong, seems to require the President to take some measures in regard to it. Unfortunately, it is not a matter of doubt that the American flag was displayed in the fight in the city of Canton. Who bore it there? You are directed by the President to ascertain, if possible, that fact. It is important that the effect of such a rash and ill-advised step should be counteracted as promptly as possible. If, as it is alleged, an American functionary was concerned in this desecration of his country's flag, or was a volunteer in the attack upon Canton, or entered the city and participated in the conflict therein, the President is called upon, by a high sense of duty, to manifest his displeasure at such conduct.

There are such grounds for apprehending that the statement in regard to Mr. Keenan may be true, that the President has directed me to place in your hands a letter removing him from office, to be delivered or forwarded to him by you, in case you should ascertain to your satisfaction that he bore the American flag upon the walls or within the city of Canton, at the time the British made their attack upon it, or that he had any agency in displaying our flag on that occasion. If he was then at Canton, and took a part in the military operations upon or in the city, you will, in that case, also deliver the inclosed letter to him. If you are not satisfied that he had an agency in displaying the American flag on the occasion alluded to, or was a participant in the military operations against the city or within it, you will not deliver the letter to him. There will then be no occasion to let him know that the letter has been confided to you, to be used in the contingency I have stated. If Mr. Keenan is not implicated in the grave charge brought against him, (and I sincerely hope it will turn out he is not,) then the imputation will fall upon others, and I trust you will be able to ascertain who they are, and report them to this department. Should you deliver the letter to Mr. Keenan, you are authorized to designate a proper person to take charge of the archives of the consulate and act as consul until the vacancy shall be filled.

When Commodore Armstrong's report of the proceedings of the force under his command shall have reached this government, you will be again addressed on the subject to which this dispatch relates, and furnished with the President's definite views thereon, and instructions for your future conduct.

I am, sir, respectfully, your obedient servant,

W. L. MARCY.

PETER PARKER, Esq., *&c.*, *&c.*, *&c.*

Mr. Marcy to Mr. Parker.

No. 10.]

DEPARTMENT OF STATE,
Washington, February 27, 1857.

SIR: In acknowledging your dispatch of the 22d of November, I stated that the President had only time to glance at it and the papers which accompanied it, and that he was not then prepared (not having Commodore Armstrong's report) to present his views in full upon the occurrences at Canton to which that dispatch related.

In my comments, I find, on reëxamining the case, there was some inaccuracy as to the order of the events, which may, perhaps, to some extent, vary the conclusions of the President thereon. I perceive that the firing into the boat in which Commander Foote was, actually occurred on the 15th, the day previous to that on which Mullen the cockswain was killed in the boat of the San Jacinto. Further dispatches on the subject have been received at the Navy Department since my last communication to you, and it is probable that the President will instruct the secretary of that department to make known his views in regard to the proceedings of the naval forces on that station.

I have this morning received your dispatch No. 34. (I suppose it is yours, though your name is not to it.) I have not yet had time to submit it to the President. As there are but three or four days now remaining of his term, and the pressure of business attendent upon the close of a session of Congress being very great, he will hardly have time to go fully into the considerations presented in that dispatch. The subject has already been submitted to him through the French minister here, and his conclusion thereon communicated verbally to that functionary. The President does not believe that our relations with China warrant the "last resort" you speak of, and if they did, the military or naval forces of the United States could only be used by the authority of Congress. The "last resort" means war, and the executive branch of this government is not the war-making power. There is no obligation, perfect or imperfect, resting upon China to negotiate, in regard to the revision of our treaty, at Pekin or any place in the vicinity of that capital. China has agreed to revise the treaty, but no particular place for doing it is designated. This is the view which the President took, when the suggestion of making a demonstration of force, in order to open the way to Pekin, was made by France. For the protection and security of Americans in China and the protection of their property, it may be expedient to increase our naval force on the China station, but the President will not do it for aggressive purposes.

The documents will, of course, go into the hands of the incoming administration, and it may take a different view of the subject.

Yours, truly,

WILLIAM L. MARCY.

PETER PARKER, Esq., *&c.*, *&c.*, *&c.*

Mr. Cass to Mr. Reed.

No. 2.] DEPARTMENT OF STATE,
Washington, May 30, 1857.

SIR: I have already announced to you your appointment as envoy extraordinary and minister plenipotentiary from the United States to China, and I am now to furnish you for your guidance with the general views of the President upon the subjects connected with your mission. Many of these views are contained in the communication of April 10 last, from this department, to Lord Napier, the British minister, of which a copy accompanies this letter, and to which your attention is specially directed. You will also receive, herewith, copies of several communications from Lord Napier, and of dispatches from the

British government to some of its officers, which disclose the purposes of that government in China, and the measures by which it expects to accomplish them. As to these objects and measures, there seems to be an entire unanimity of sentiment and action between Great Britain and France, extending even to armed coöperation, and you will find from the papers annexed, that the United States have been invited to join the alliance and to participate in its hostile movements. The reasons of the President for declining this participation are sufficiently stated in the communication to the British minister already referred to, together with his opinions as to the extent to which the United States may fairly coöperate with the allied powers in China.

The objects which it is understood the allies seek to accomplish by treaty stipulations are:

1. To procure from the Chinese government a recognition of the right of other powers to have accredited ministers at the court of Pekin, to be received by the emperor, and to be in communication with the authorities charged with the foreign affairs of the empire.

2. An extension of commercial intercourse with China, which is now restricted to five ports enumerated in the treaty.

3. A reduction of the tariff of duties levied upon domestic produce in its transit from the interior to the coast, as the amount now imposed is said to be a violation of the treaty.

On this subject you will be able to ascertain the true state of the alleged grievance when you reach China, and to act accordingly.

4. A stipulation for religious freedom to all foreigners in China.

5. An arrangement for the suppression of piracy.

6. Provision for extending the benefits of the proposed treaty to all the other civilized powers of the earth.

These objects are recognized by the President as just and expedient, and so far as you can do so by peaceful coöperation, he expects that you will aid in their accomplishment. In conformity with this policy, you will communicate frankly with the British and French ministers upon all the points of common interest, so that it may be distinctly understood that the three nations are equally influenced by a determination to obtain justice, and by a desire to procure treaty arrangements for the extension and more adequate protection of their commercial intercourse with China. But on your side these efforts must be confined to firm representations, appealing to the justice and policy of the Chinese authorities, and leaving to your own government to determine upon the course to be adopted, should your representations be fruitless.

Special reference is made to your communication with the ministers of Great Britain and France, not only from our common interest with those nations in the trade of China, and in the means suggested for its extension, but because they alone among the great powers of the world have diplomatic representatives at Canton. It is understood, however, that Russia, which has long been represented in China by missionaries of religion, has attempted recently to secure the reception there of an accredited minister, and you may possibly find this purpose accomplished when you reach your destination. In that event, there is no good reason why you should not have the same friendly relations with the Russian envoy as with the representatives of Great Britain and

France. You are authorized, therefore, to communicate with him as far as practicable upon all subjects of mutual concern, and should his disposition prove favorable, as it is believed it will, his coöperation may be highly advantageous in promoting the objects of your mission. This coöperation is to be expected, moreover, with the greater confidence, because there is nothing in the policy of the United States with respect to China which is not quite consistent with the pacific relations which are understood to exist between that empire and Russia.

This country, you will constantly bear in mind, is not at war with the government of China, nor does it seek to enter that empire for any other purposes than those of lawful commerce, and for the protection of the lives and property of its citizens. The whole nature and policy of our government must necessarily confine our action within these limits, and deprive us of all motives either for territorial aggrandizement or the acquisition of political power in that distant region. During the hostilities which now exist in China, we may be able to avail ourself of this fortunate position, not only for the benefit of our countrymen who reside there, or who have extensive interests there of a commercial character, but in order to facilitate also the general objects sought to be accomplished by a revision of the existing treaties. It is possible even that it may be employed with advantage as a means of communication between the belligerent parties, and tend in this way to the termination of the war. You will therefore not fail to let it be known to the Chinese authorities that we are no party to the existing hostilities, and have no intention to interfere in their political concerns, or to gain a foothold in their country. We go there to engage in trade, but under suitable guarantees for its protection. The extension of our commercial intercourse must be the work of individual enterprise, and to this element of our national character we may safely leave it. With the domestic institutions of China we have no political concern, and to attempt a forcible interference with them would not only be unjust in itself, but might defeat the very object desired. Fortunately, however, commerce itself is one of the most powerful means of civilization and national improvement. By coming into peaceful contact with men of other regions and other races, with different habits and greater knowledge, the jealous system of seclusion which has so long separated China from the rest of the world will gradually give way, and with increased intercourse will come those meliorations in the moral and physical condition of its people which the Christian and the philanthropist have so long and so ardently desired.

In connection with these views, there is one subject to which, from its relation to the internal policy of China, as well as its important bearing upon the intercourse of foreigners with that empire, I desire to call your particular attention. The effort of the Chinese government to prevent the importation and the consumption of opium was a praiseworthy measure, rendered necessary by the prevalent use and the terrible effects of that deleterious drug. All accounts agree as to the magnitude of the evil, and the wide-spread desolation caused by it.

Upon proper occasions, you will make known to the Chinese officers with whom you may have communication that the government of the United States does not seek for their citizens the legal establishment of the opium trade, nor will it uphold them in any attempt to violate the laws of China by the introduction of that article into the country. While desirous that the blessings of Christianity and the benefits of a more advanced civilization should be extended over the empire, and while convinced that free commercial intercourse will become a powerful agent in the accomplishment of these great results, it would be a subject of deep regret and mortification to the American people should these hopes be disappointed by the illegal cupidity of their countrymen.

There are other matters of importance which will engage your attention, and which ought to make part of the proposed modification of the treaty. Among these is the absurd regulation which reduces the true standard of our coin much below its actual value, and does serious injury to our trade. A legal currency ought to be established at its true standard.

Some of the stipulations of the existing treaty have been neglected or violated, and our merchants have suffered by this bad faith. Among these is the provision that American citizens "shall enjoy all proper accommodations in obtaining homes and places of business, or in hiring sites from the inhabitants on which to construct houses and places of business." This engagement has been rendered nugatory, not by the indisposition of the holders of property to dispose of it, but by the interference of the local authorities, who have prohibited the making of such an engagement, and in some instances have actually imprisoned and tortured their unfortunate countrymen who have ventured to violate the prohibition.

The treaty also provides that the government shall examine the complaints of American citizens against Chinese subjects for frauds or debts, and "take the proper measures to compel satisfaction." This stipulation has been rendered useless by the neglect of the authorities to enforce it.

Entire security of persons and property is among the guarantees which this same treaty expressly holds out to our citizens. Practically the engagement is a barren one, for the prompt and efficient interposition of the authorities to protect foreigners from the injuries to which they are exposed is a rare event in the annals of Chinese justice.

In relation to these and other subjects of a similar character, you will be able in China to obtain more exact information than can be furnished here, and you will govern your conduct accordingly. With respect to all your official action, much of course must be left to your discretion.

The empire to which you are accredited is so remote, and its condition so extraordinary, that it is difficult to decide with confidence, upon the particular measures which events may, from time to time, render necessary.

These instructions will indicate to you the general wishes of the President, but as to the best mode of carrying them into effect you may often be obliged to exercise your own judgment; and I am gratified to believe that this authority is vested where it will be safely employed.

The internal dissensions of the Chinese empire will not fail to engage your earliest attention, connected as they may be, in their varying phases, with both the rights and interests of the United States, and with the course you may find it necessary to adopt. It is difficult, with the scarcity of information which reaches this country, to form any definite opinion of the causes and objects of the insurrection, or any probable conjecture as to its issue. We have no other concern as to its progress or result than to take care that our rights are preserved inviolate. We have no reason to believe that one of the contending parties is more favorably disposed towards foreigners than the other, or more ready to extend commercial intercourse with them, while both are bound by treaty stipulations to us and to other powers, and will be held to their faithful observance; but in all that relates to these internal disturbances you must be guided by your own discretion, applied to the circumstances in which you may find yourself placed.

It is important that our consuls in China should act in conformity with your general policy as the representative in that empire of the United States, and a superintending authority over them, so far as regards the exercise of their functions not judicial, has, therefore, been committed to you. A circular letter has been addressed to them, communicating this arrangement, and requesting them to carry into effect your wishes. You will accordingly give them such instructions as you may deem necessary; and should these instructions be neglected or disobeyed, in any instance, you will immediately report the circumstance to this department for the consideration and decision of the President.

By the copy which accompanies this paper of the instructions of the Secretary of the Navy to the commanding officer of our Chinese squadron, you will perceive that our forces in that quarter have been increased, and that their movements have been placed, as far as possible, within your control. The armed steamer Minnesota has been specially assigned for your accommodation, not only on your passage to China, but during your residence there, and the commander of the squadron has also been authorized to charter a small steamer "for the purpose of ascending rivers or entering ports inaccessible to the other vessels of his squadron." It is hoped that these instructions will enable you to have the cordial coöperation of our naval forces for the purposes of your mission. On the other hand, I am persuaded that I only anticipate your own views, when I suggest to you the importance of cultivating the most friendly relations with the officers of the squadron, and especially of maintaining the most unreserved intercourse with its commander.

I recommend also that you confer with the commissioner, Mr. Parker, who will be superseded by your arrival in China. This change, you are aware, is not intended to cast the slightest censure upon him. He has an intimate knowledge of Chinese affairs, has discharged his duties with zeal and fidelity, and is entitled to the thanks of the government. I have already informed him that it has been thought expedient, at this apparent crisis of Chinese affairs, to send from this country, as its representative, a citizen of high public character and consideration, who will be able to carry with him a full knowledge of the views of the President, communicated in several interviews, as well as of the feelings and expectations of the American people. I am satisfied that Mr.

Parker will take pleasure in being useful to you, and that his knowledge of the public men of the country, and of its true condition, will render him a safe adviser.

The Minnesota is understood to be nearly ready for sea; and it is the wish of the President that you embark on board her as soon as her preparations are completed, since it is important that you reach your destination with as little delay as possible. On your arrival you will place yourself in communication with the proper authorities, announcing your official character, and demanding an interview with the imperial commissioners, or with one of the high functionaries specified in the treaty as the medium of communication between the two governments. You will exercise your discretion as to the delivery of the letter of credence from the President to the Emperor of China, confiding it only to an officer of the highest rank, and following, in this respect, the practice which has guided the European representatives as well as our own.

I am, sir, respectfully, your obedient servant,

LEWIS CASS.

WILLIAM B. REED, Esq., *&c.*, *&c.*, *&c.*

NAVY DEPARTMENT,
June 12, 1857.

SIR: Recent events in China have induced the department to increase the squadron under your command, by adding to it the steam frigates Minnesota, Captain S. F. Du Pont, Mississippi, Captain W. C. Nicholson, and the sloop-of-war Germantown, Commander R. L. Page. These vessels are nearly ready for sea, and will soon leave the United States.

The President has appointed the Hon. William B. Reed as envoy extraordinary and minister plenipotentiary to China, investing him with large discretionary powers, and has directed that a passage be afforded him in the Minnesota to his place of destination. On his arrival, you will receive him with his suite, and he will remain on board the Minnesota, and she will convey him to such points as he may designate. All expenses of subsistence will, of course, be borne by himself.

The department has so much reliance on your judgment and disposition to advance in every way the interests of your country, that it deems it almost unnecessary to give you any specific instructions in relation to your coöperation with Mr. Reed to further the objects of his mission. Without intending to interfere with the command of your squadron, the department instructs you to consult freely with the minister as to its movements, and to pay the highest regard to his wishes. If, in his opinion, it should become necessary, in order to accomplish the objects of his mission, that the squadron should be concentrated at any one place, upon his communicating his wishes to you, you will promptly proceed to the point designated and coöperate with him.

Should it be necessary to charter a small steamer of light draft, for the purpose of ascending rivers or entering ports inaccessible to the other vessels of the squadron, you are authorized to do so, on the most reasonable terms, and to retain her no longer than the necessity requires.

I am, respectfully, your obedient servant,

I. TOUCEY.

Flag-officer JAMES ARMSTRONG,
Commandant East India Squadron, Hong Kong, China.

Mr. Appleton to Mr. Reed.

No. 3.]

DEPARTMENT OF STATE,
Washington, June 22, 1857.

SIR: The dispatch dated April 10th last, of which you will find a copy inclosed, is the most recent communication which has been received at this department from our commissioner in China. The previous dispatches to which it refers you have already seen. With reference to the general policy to be pursued in that empire by the representative of the United States, the three propositions which, according to Mr. Parker's report, he has adopted for his guidance, are in conformity with your instructions, and are therefore approved. The subject of indemnity to American citizens for their losses by the late disturbances at Canton, to which he specially refers, will necessarily engage your early attention. The claims already presented for these losses amount to more than a million of dollars, and this aggregate will doubtless be increased. It is desirable that the statements of the claimants should be full and precise, in reference both to the manner and the amount of their respective losses; and you will, of course, take care that the American claims are as favorably treated by the Chinese government as those of any other nation. Since the United States were neutral in the difficulties by which the losses were occasioned our citizens were obviously innocent sufferers for occurrences over which they had no control; and in the consideration of their demands for indemnity this circumstance ought to have great weight. There are other claims of citizens of the United States against the government of China, which you will find among the archives of your mission. Some of them have already been delayed for an unreasonable time, and the parties interested in them are naturally anxious for their immediate payment. In the present condition of Chinese affairs, you may find it impracticable to pursue them with advantage, while the attempt to do so may interfere, possibly, with more important objects; but, in the exercise of your discretion on this point, you will employ your best efforts to have them adjusted at an early day. There can be no doubt that Mr. Parker is right in his judgment concerning the importance of additional accommodations for foreign trade in the neighborhood of Canton, and the President would be glad to see this object accomplished. It is substantially embraced, however, in the several purposes of your mission, for, if you succeed in these, new facilities will be given to commerce, not only at Canton, but in other portions of the Chinese empire.

The bankers of the United States at London have been authorized to honor your drafts on special account for a sum not exceeding ten thousand dollars. Full confidence is reposed in your discretion as to the expenditure. It will of course, however, be expected that the particulars will be specified, and that they will be supported by vouchers when these may be obtainable.

I am, sir, respectfully, your obedient servant,

JOHN APPLETON,
Acting Secretary.

WILLIAM B. REED, Esq., *&c.*, *&c.*, *&c.*

Mr. Reed to Mr. Cass.

No. 1.]

OLD POINT COMFORT, VIRGINIA,
June 26, 1857.

SIR: On the 24th instant, before leaving Philadelphia, I had the honor of receiving your dispatch No. 3, dated the 22d instant, inclosing a communication from Mr. Parker, dated Macao, 10th April, 1857, and memoranda of interviews with the English and French ministers in China. You state that "the three propositions which, according to Mr. Parker's report, he has adopted for his guidance, are in conformity with my instructions, and are therefore approved." On other matters referred to in Mr. Parker's dispatch, you are silent, and I infer their determination, subject to my general instructions, is to be left to my discretion.

There is one point in Mr. Parker's dispatch on which I shall be glad to have the views of the President; unless, as is probable, they have been already communicated, and then I shall find them in the archieves of the legation. The passage in Mr. Parker's letter of 10th April to which I refer is this:

"In view of this state of facts, on the 24th December, I confidentially addressed the British minister, (dispatch No. 36 of December 27, exhibit C 5,) submitting the propriety of the amount of losses thus suffered by citizens of the United States (their accounts having been first duly audited) being included in the sum total to be finally demanded from the government of China by that of England for losses suffered by British subjects, as the same measures necessary to obtain a part will suffice to secure the whole, and ventured the opinion that in a change of circumstances, the same office would be accorded by the government of the United States; and exclusive of this local question, there are numerous others of common interest for the concurrent action of the treaty powers. To this proposition I have specially invited the attention of the department."

Solicitous as I am to secure to our fellow citizens compensation for the injuries they are said to have suffered, I shall not, as at present advised, feel at liberty to adopt the view suggested by Mr. Parker, of soliciting the good offices of the British authorities in including American claims in the sum total to be demanded by them, without express instructions to that effect. It is unnecessary for me to say this suggestion impresses me unfavorably. I content myself with calling your attention to it, and shall be glad to hear the views of the department on a point of so obvious interest and delicacy, if possible, before I sail, or, if that be impossible, on my arrival in China. It is not probable the Minnesota will be ready for sea before Wednesday next.

I repeat that this inquiry may have been already answered in some communication made to Mr. Parker, but none such occurs to my recollection.

I have this morning received your dispatch No. 4, inclosing the copy of instructions from Lord Clarendon to Lord Elgin, and the copy of an additional order from the Secretary of the Navy to Commodore Armstrong, for which I thank you.

I am, very respectfully, yours,

WILLIAM B. REED.

The SECRETARY OF STATE, *Washington.*

Mr. Cass to Mr. Reed.

No. 5.]

DEPARTMENT OF STATE,
Washington, June 29, 1857.

SIR: Your No. 1, dated at Old Point Comfort, Virginia, June 26, 1857, has been received.

In communicating to you on the 22d instant a copy of Mr. Parker's dispatch of April 10, the department expressed its confident expectation that the American claim for losses growing out of the recent difficulties at Canton would be as favorably regarded by the Chinese government as those of any other nation. With the expression of this belief, and under the guidance of your general instructions, the whole subject of these claims was confided to your discretion. It was not contemplated, however, that you would find it necessary to adopt on this subject the course suggested by Mr. Parker, "of including the amount of losses thus suffered by citizens of the United States in the sum to be finally demanded by England for losses suffered by British subjects." The measures employed by Great Britain to obtain the adjustment of British claims may produce a result possibly which will insure the settlement also, upon a just basis, of American claims; but to unite our claims with those of other countries would imply a disposition on our part, not only to let them share the fate of their associates, but to participate actively in all the proceedings which might be thought necessary for their advancement. This, you are aware, is not the policy which has been adopted by the United States in respect to the affairs of China, nor is it the policy which this country has uniformly pursued in its intercourse with foreign nations. While, therefore, you will endeavor, by all proper means, to secure a just indemnity to our citizens at Canton for the injuries they are said to have suffered, you will not feel yourself at liberty to do so by soliciting the adoption and enforcement of American claims by the authorities of Great Britain.

I am, sir, respectfully, your obedient servant,

LEWIS CASS.

WILLIAM B. REED, *&c., &c., &c.*

Mr. Cass to Mr. Reed.

No. 6.] DEPARTMENT OF STATE, *Washington, July* 29, 1857.

SIR: A copy of the inclosed memorial of A. P. Edwards, Esq., of New York, asking indemnication on account of ill-treatment received by him at the hands of the Chinese authorities in the month of November, 1841, was furnished by this department to Mr. Cushing when he was about to start upon his mission to China in 1843. It is understood, however, that after reaching China, Mr. Cushing became erroneously impressed with the idea that the matter had been settled, and that he, therefore, took no steps towards prosecuting the claim against the Chinese government. Subsequently, his immediate successor at the mission, Mr. Alexander H. Everett, was also furnished by this deparment with a copy of the memorial above referred to, which was transferred by him to Commodore Biddle, at the time he was temporarily intrusted by Mr. Everett with the discharge of the duties of commissioner. Commodore Biddle, it would seem, also failed to prosecute the claim, for in writing to Mr. Buchanan from Canton, under date of the 9th of April, 1846, he says: "Among the papers put into my possession by Mr. Everett at Rio Janeiro, was a copy of a memorial to the President from Alfred Pierrepont Edwards. As there is no mention of this memorial in your instructions, I have concluded, from information received here on the subject, not to bring before the Chinese authorities the claim of Mr. Edwards for pecuniary compensation on account of alleged ill-treatment during the last war between Great Britain and China." Here it is believed the matter rested until a day or two ago, when Mr. Edwards called upon the department, and requested that your attention should be invited to the subject of his claim.

You will accordingly make yourself acquainted with the merits of Mr. Edwards's claim, and do whatever in your judgment shall be deemed necessary and proper in the premises.

I am, sir, respectfully, your obedient servant,

LEWIS CASS.

WILLIAM B. REED, *&c.*, *&c.*, *&c.*

Mr. Reed to Mr. Cass.

No. 2.] CAPE TOWN, CAPE OF GOOD HOPE, *September* 9, 1857.

SIR: Before leaving the United States I addressed you (No. 1, 26th June) on the subject of the claims of American citizens on the Chinese government, and on the day of my departure received your dispatch (No. 5) of the 29th, in reply.

I have now the honor to advise you of my arrival at this anchorage on the 7th instant, after a passage of sixty-eight days from the Chesapeake. No further delay will occur here than is absolutely necessary for the supply of the Minnesota with coal and water, as the naval commander is fully impressed with my anxiety to arrive in China at as early a time as possible.

I beg you to express to the Secretary of the Navy my grateful sense of the considerate and unremitting kindness extended to me by Captain Du Pont and his officers during our long voyage. Everything has been done for my comfort that I could desire.

In consequence of the disturbances in India, of which the first news reached me here, the mail steamers have been withdrawn from this line, and there being no American vessels destined to the United States, I avail myself of the offer of Sir George Grey, the governor of this colony, to forward this dispatch through the foreign office in London.

I have the honor to be, very respectfully, yours,

WILLIAM B. REED.

The SECRETARY OF STATE, *Washington.*

Mr. Reed to Mr. Cass.

No. 3.] UNITED STATES LEGATION TO CHINA,
ON BOARD THE MINNESOTA,
In the harbor of Hong Kong, November 10, 1857.

SIR: I beg to advise you of my arrival here on the 5th instant, and to acknowledge the receipt of your dispatch, No. 6, dated 29th of July, inclosing the memorial of Alfred Pierrepont Edwards for remuneration for losses during the war of 1840. It shall receive my early attention, though it is to be feared that the lapse of time since the alleged injury occurred, and the unsettled condition of affairs in this part of the empire, very much diminish the chances of success.

So short a time has elapsed since my arrival, that I do not feel that I should even form an opinion as to the actual state of things here, or the course which, so far as our interests and policy are involved, affairs are likely to take. The Earl of Elgin is the only one of the representatives of what are called the treaty powers now here, the French plenipotentiary being with the fleet at a point about thirteen miles distant. I have direct information from Shanghai that Admiral Pontatin, the Russian plenipotentiary, was at that place at the latest dates, awaiting, as he told my informant, my arrival before he came here or to Macao.

With Lord Elgin and the British admiral, Sir Michael Seymour, my intercourse to this point has been entirely formal, though friendly, and nothing in the shape of official or confidential intercourse, except in the most incidental way, has occurred. There seems, however, to be no reserve as to the intentions of the English. The admiral is only waiting for a few reinforcements to take active measures against the Cantonese; and it may be assumed that, unless some unforeseen interposition occurs, the city of Canton will be attacked or surrendered within the next few weeks. There will be military coöperation on the part of the French. It is, I learn, proposed to concentrate the forces as far up the river as possible within the next fortnight.

Opinion is very much divided here as to whether the Cantonese will surrender the city or stand an assault. For the sake of humanity, it is to be earnestly hoped that as the movement is inevitable, peaceable possession may be taken; and I have no doubt, independently of other considerations, that the British naval and diplomatic authorities are very anxious to avert the discredit which always attaches to the sacrifice of human life in an unequal contest. It is scarcely necessary for me to add that nothing is in any way likely to occur to affect the strict neutrality of the United States.

I cannot but believe—and this impression I derive from a cursory examination of the archives of the legation, and from a brief conversation with Lord Elgin—that a double mischief has been done by the course which my predecessor felt it his duty to pursue. Down to a certain point the ministers of the treaty powers, and especially Sir John Bowring, were encouraged in the most extravagant expectation of coöperation on our part, to the extent even of acquisition of territory; and I am not at all surprised at the disappointment experienced when this delusion was broken. This was the first harm done. The next was, that the moment it was understood that the extreme policy of coöperation was disavowed or discouraged, all suggestions of friendly concert on points of common interest, which the well-known policy of the government authorized, were suddenly repelled. Mr. Parker thought himself somewhat justified in this by the silence of the government at home; and it is a matter of respectful urgency on my part, in the outset, that I may never have this excuse for inaction.

I do not think I shall have the least difficulty in putting this matter right, and making all parties here comprehend distinctly how far in the way of friendly concert we can go, and at what limit we must resolutely stop.

Our fellow-citizens have not merely given me a cordial welcome, but have shown great consideration in not troubling me too soon on the subject of the claims which many of them have for damages recently incurred. Not having yet formally taken possession of the archives of the legation, I am unable to have any opinion as to their merits. I have no doubt some of them are cases of great hardship.

I presume the declaration of Lord Palmerston in the House of Commons, on the 19th of June last, when he was interrogated as to the Greytown affair, and of his view of the rule of public law affecting neutral claimants, has not escaped your attention.

He is understood to have said:

"It was an unquestionable principle of international law that, when one government deemed it right to exercise acts of hostility against any part of the territory of another power, the subjects or citizens of a third power who might happen to be resident in the place so attacked had no claim whatever upon the government which, in the exercise of its natural rights, committed those acts of hostility; when, for instance, it was deemed necessary by us to destroy the town of Sebastopol, although there might have been there Germans, Spaniards, Portuguese, or Americans, none of these parties had any ground whatever upon which to found a claim, either upon the English or French governments, for compensation for the losses they might have sustained. Those who went to a foreign country must abide by the chances which might befall that country. If they had any claim at all, it must be on the country in which they were; but they certainly had no claim upon the government which thought it right to commit the acts of hostility."

It can hardly be questioned that this view has reference to possible claims on his government, arising out of the hostilities last fall against Canton, and I have understood that the British authorities rely confidently on Secretary Marcy's letter, on Greytown, to the Count de Sartiges, to protect them. I have no means of forming any judgment on the subject, having no copy of Mr. Marcy's dispatch, and never having seen it. I shall be glad to be furnished with it at the earliest moment, as well as with your views on the doctrine thus enunciated. There is no knowing at what moment this question of claims may present itself.

Commodore Armstrong arrived here in his flag-ship, the San Jacinto, a few days ago, from Shanghai. He is in very infirm health, and has, I learn, applied to be relieved; in which case, till the arrival of the Mississippi, the command of the squadron would devolve on Captain Du Pont, in whose eminent good judgment and energy I beg to assure the President and the Secretary of the Navy the greatest reliance may be placed. With Commodore Armstrong my relations are of the most friendly nature. I should do great injustice to the naval service were I to omit to say, that I am confident that never have the honor and interests of the country been in safer hands than in those of the commanders of the ships on this station. I hope the squadron will, under no circumstances, be reduced in numbers.

As Congress will be in session when this dispatch reaches the United States, I beg to call attention earnestly to the deficiency of war steamers of light draft. Without at least one there is an absolute certainty of failure of diplomatic intercourse. Sailing vessels, however admirable, cannot be relied on for intricate river navigation where strong tides are running. At this moment it is very desirable that, before active military operations begin on the part of the British, I should be able to go up the river and give the Chinese imperial commissioner an opportunity of an interview, if he desires one. Yet I have no means of doing so. There is a scarcity of steamers for charter, and the expense is very great—so great, that at present I do not feel authorized to ask the commodore to incur it, though I shall do so the moment the necessity arrives. Should negotiations be transferred to the north, the want of such craft will be more sensibly felt. In unison with all my predecessors, I implore the attention, the prompt attention, of the Navy Department and Congress to this matter.

It is my intention, in a day or two, in conformity with my instructions, to announce my arrival to the imperial commissioner at Canton.

I have the honor to be, very respectfully, your obedient servant,

WILLIAM B. REED.

The SECRETARY OF STATE, *Washington*.

Mr. Cass to Mr. Reed.

No. 9.]

DEPARTMENT OF STATE,
Washington, February 5, 1858.

SIR: Your dispatches to No. 3, inclusive, have been received.

No time was lost by me in communicating to the Secrerary of the Navy so much of your dispatch No. 3, of the 10th of November last, as relates to the deficiency of American war steamers of light draft on the China station, and I now transmit to you several printed copies of Mr. Marcy's letter on Greytown, to which reference is made by you.

I am, sir, respectfully, your obedient servant,

LEWIS CASS.

WILLIAM B. REED, Esq., *&c., &c.*

P. S. Since writing the foregoing dispatch, I have received a letter from the Secretary of the Navy concerning the deficiency of war steamers of light draft on the China station, a copy of which is hereby inclosed to you for your information.

Mr. Reed to Mr. Cass.

No. 35.]

LEGATION OF THE UNITED STATES IN CHINA,
Macao, November 25, 1857.

SIR: Nothing decisive has occurred since the date of my last dispatch, and I regret to say the same perplexity exists as to the issue of what, it is understood, will soon be attempted by the belligerent powers, England and France. The French fleet, consisting of two frigates and a number of steamers and gun-boats, are at this anchorage, and, as the admiral informs me, are fully equipped and ready for service. The expected reinforcements of the English have not yet arrived, and the latest news from India is of such a nature as to render highly improbable any military aid from that quarter.

On the 14th instant, Count Poutiatine, the Russian plenipotentiary, arrived at Hong Kong in the steamer America from Shanghai, and anchored very near the Minnesota. I have had with him the most frank intercourse on all matters of common interest. He is more sanguine than I am as to our ability, representing peaceful and neutral powers, "to effect a desirable settlement of the present affairs in China." It seems to me that there is on the part of the English (and perhaps of the French also) a fixed determination, at any cost, to inflict chastisement on the Cantonese; this resolution being the more determined in view of the awkward attitude in which the disturbances in India have placed them, and the relatively small military resources at their command. There is great irritability among them all. They are fretful, not only at their dependence on the French, without whom they could not take a step in advance, but at their inability to involve the United States in their unworthy quarrel, for such, as it now stands, I confess, it seems to me. On the other hand, the Chinese every hour are putting themselves in the wrong, and seem to be willfully blind to any distinction between friends and enemies. With such parties, it is difficult to imagine any opportunity of arresting by friendly offices an actual and I fear a bloody conflict. It is the opinion of the Russian minister, whose opportunities of knowledge of the state of feeling near the imperial court are better than those of any one here, that the fall of Canton will produce no effect at Pekin, and that it will be both a bloody and a barren victory. This view has some corroboration in a curious private communication that has fallen into my hands, and to which I beg to refer you as of especial interest. Its history is this:

Mr. Paul S. Forbes, the senior partner of the American house of Russel & Co., and who is, of course, deeply interested in the commercial tranquillity of China, addressed a confidential letter, in July last, through a channel that appeared to him safe, to Keying, the commissioner who negotiated the treaty of 1844 with Mr. Cushing, and whose favorable disposition to foreigners is well known to you. A copy of this letter you will find hereto annexed, (marked Exhibit 2 *a*) and I am confident you will agree with me in thinking it is extremely creditable to Mr. Forbes. About the 20th of August the answer was received. (Exhibit 2 *b*.) You will find in it much that is interesting, and revelations of some curious coincidences, especially with reference to Russian intervention, though I incline to think, in the true Chinese fashion, it is somewhat overstated. Mr. Forbes thinks that it is really the answer of Keying, though, as you will observe, any such idea is earnestly disclaimed. Assuming the letter to be genuine, it is an entire corroboration of Count Poutiatine's opinion that the fall of Canton will produce little or no effect at Pekin. I may observe here that no one is aware of this correspondence, and there are obvious reasons for its being regarded as strictly confidential.

The history of the recent Russian diplomatic experiment in the north of China is briefly this: On the 22d of April, 1857, Count Poutiatine reached Kiatchka, on the Chinese frontier, and communicated his arrival to the authorities at Pekin, asking for access to the imperial court, and informing them that he should remain there a stated time for an answer. In the interval of six weeks there was some troublesome and impotent ceremonial, but no answer coming, Count Poutiatine pursued his journey eastward till he reached the Amour river, at the mouth of which he embarked in the America for the Peiho. On his arrival there, he was visited on board his ship by some mandarins of high rank, one of whom agreed to forward or carry a new and more earnest letter to the imperial authorities. The Russian envoy was urged to land and remain on shore till the answer should be received. This he refused to do, promising, however, to return in a fortnight, which he did after a visit to Shanghai. This was at the end of August. In the early part of September, he returned to the Peiho, and there found an answer awaiting him. It was a flat refusal, on the old ground that the application to approach the imperial presence was not accompanied with a promise to pay tribute and to perform the kotow. So resolute are these strange people in their perverse exactions. There was great personal civility and quite munificent hospitality on the part of the Chinese officials, but nothing beyond this. It is difficult for me to say whether this refusal was unexpected by the Russian envoy, or how far disappointment influences the very decided judgment which he has that it will be necessary next year to make a strong military or naval demonstration at the north. It seems that he is in expectation of a squadron from Cronstadt, of a frigate, two corvettes, and some light-draft steamers, to be used on this service. I have every reason to believe that Count Poutiatine will remain in the south of China this winter.

On leaving the Peiho finally, he proceeded to Japan, where he succeeded in negotiating, at the instance of the Japanese, a very favorable treaty. He has furnished me with a copy, and I shall make it the subject of a separate dispatch.

I am unable, yet, to say whether my reception as the representative of another friendly nation will be more favorable.

On the 16th instant, in pursuance of my instructions, I announced my arrival and demand for an interview to Yeh, the imperial commissioner at Canton. A copy of my letter is annexed, (Exhibit 1.) It was translated and forwarded, through the Portugese authorities, about ten days ago, and as yet I have received no answer. Supposing that, in the existing state of things, it would be better not to communicate with the Chinese from a British colony, my letter was dated at Macao, and I have come here to receive the answer. I shall return to the Minnesota in a few days. Should any communication come from Yeh before the closing of the mail to-morrow, I shall, of course, apprise you of it. I am very much afraid that either no answer will come, or that it will be a denial of what I ask. In either such a result it will be a new proof of the infatuation of their officials. I hope, however, for the best.

Appended to this dispatch (Exhibits 3 to 6) you will find copies of my official communication of my arrival to the different plenipotentiaries, and their answers. It has seemed to me best under all the circumstances to have the legation permanently on board the Minnesota.

I am not aware of anything further of interest to communicate, unless it be that in conversation with Lord Elgin, before my letter to the imperial commissioner was sent, he endeavored, though with much courtesy, to persuade me not to send it. On two occasions he renewed this dissuasion. Even if I had not been positively instructed to make the announcement at once, I found no reason in his lordship's politic urgency to withhold it. I must not be understood as complaining at all of what Lord Elgin said, or of the manner in which he said it. I am on the most friendly terms, as well with him as with the other plenipotentiaries.

The only other topic referred to in the accompanying documents is that connected with the detention of the duties at Foo Chow by our late consul, Mr. Jones. It had attracted my early attention, and on the 19th instant (Exhibit 7 *c*) I wrote to the acting consul for a report of the facts. I have not yet received it. The day after my letter was dispatched I received from Sir John Bowring a communication on the subject, which, with my answer, is appended.—(Exhibit 7 *d.*)

In the inaction to which I fear I shall be condemned for the next few months, it is my intention to try in some way to correct and systematize the consular administration in this country. It is entirely disorganized now, and I fear will continue to be so until some restraint is put upon a habit which here seems to be inveterate of consuls literally running away from their posts, leaving matters in the hands of irresponsible people, or of nobody. This, as I am informed, has happened at Shanghai, Foochow, and Amoy. Consuls consult their own convenience as to leaving their posts, very often going away at moments of the greatest entanglement, and hurrying home to perplex the government with their murmurings, or their interested speculations. I beg earnestly to impress upon the President the necessity of extreme circumspection in consular appointments in this distant region. I feel I have no right to make any such suggestion to him, but I am painfully struck by the actual condition of things in this region.

I desire to exclude from the censure which I have more than implied, Mr. Keenan, the consul at Hong Kong, who, though very desirous to return home, has delayed his departure till my arrival in order to confer with me as to his temporary successor, and Mr. Perry and Mr. Rawle, at Canton and Macao.

I have the honor to be, very respectfully, your obedient servant,

WILLIAM B. REED.

The SECRETARY OF STATE.

Index to dispatch No. 35, *from W. B. Reed, Macao, November* 25, 1857.

Exhibit.	From—	To—	Subject-matter.	Date.
1	W. B. Reed	Yeh, governor general	Announcing arrival, and asking for interview	Nov. 16, 1857.
2 *a*	P. S. Forbes	Keying	Respecting public affairs between English and Cantonese	July 21, 1857.
2 *b*	Anonymous	P. S. Forbes	Difficulty of meeting English, and resistance at Canton	No date.
3 *a*	W. B. Reed	Cte. Poutiatine	Announcing arrival	Nov. 14, 1857.
3 *b*	Cte. Poutiatine	W. B. Reed	Reciprocating amicable coöperation	Nov. 17, 1857.
4 *a*	W. B. Reed	Lord Elgin	Announcing arrival	Nov. 14, 1857.
4 *b*	Lord Elgin	W. B. Reed	Reply, giving assurance of coöperation	Nov. 19, 1857.
5 *a*	W. B. Reed	Baron Gros	Announcing arrival	Nov. 14, 1857.
5 *b*	Baron Gros	W. B. Reed	Reply, giving assurance of coöperation	Nov. 23, 1857.
6 *a*	W. B. Reed	John Bowring and A. de Bourbelon.	Announcing arrival	Nov. 14, 1857.
6 *b*	John Bowring	W. B. Reed	Reply, giving congratulations	Nov. 16, 1857.
6 *c*	A. de Bourbelon	W. B. Reed	Reply, giving congratulations	Nov. 19, 1857.
7 *a*	T. Dunn	S. W. Williams	Informing him of taking charge of consulate; attack on letter-boat	Oct. 27, 1857.
7 *b*	T. Dunn	S. W. Williams	Pirates on river; wants ships-of-war at Fcoohow	Nov. 9, 1857.
7 *c*	W. B. Reed	T. Dunn	Wishes to know who appointed him, and information respecting keeping back duties.	Nov. 19, 1857.
7 *d*	John Bowring	W. B. Reed	Calls attention to the stoppage of duties at Foochow by Consul Jones, and trouble therefrom to British.	Nov. 19, 1857.
7 *e*	W. B. Reed	John Bowring	Has made inquiry upon the subject, and desires to consult upon the matter after hearing.	Nov. 20, 1857.

Exhibit 1.

LEGATION OF THE UNITED STATES,
November 16, 1857.

I announce to your excellency my arrival here, commissioned by the President of the United States of America as envoy extraordinary and minister plenipotentiary to the Chinese empire. I am charged with messages of friendship and good will. The people whom I represent have always been the friends of China. For twelve years we have been bound by a treaty which has never by us been broken, and which I now wish to renew. This can best be done by frank intercourse. With this object, I announce to you my arrival and ask for an interview, in order that I may place in your hands, to be faithfully forwarded, the letter with which I am charged from the President of the United States to his Majesty the Emperor of China, and to consider, with your excellency, how our friendship can best be maintained.

The undersigned avails himself of this opportunity to wish your excellency health and prosperity, and with sentiments of distinguished consideration, has the honor to be,

Your excellency's obedient servant,

WILLIAM B. REED.

His excellency YEH,
Imperial Commissioner and Governor General of the two Kwang Provinces, &c., Canton.

Exhibit 2 *a.*

TO KEYING, the former Governor of the two Kwangs, (Kwang Tong and Kwang See;) written by the former American consul, Forbes, for Canton province:

SIR: In former times, when you were empowered as governor to superintend all trades in Canton, I had from many times received fruitful words from you. More than ten years have elapsed since you left Canton for Pekin, and consequently after that time I have returned to my country with fixed mind not to come out again to China; but since last year I have heard that Canton is in a state of disturbance, caused by the English demanding permission for the entrance into the city of Canton, which demand, on being refused by the Chinese, has caused wars to be aroused, and houses and properties burned to ashes, souls of both honor and common grade lost on either side, and enmity to the last. All these reports have caused my mind to be deeply agitated! I think much to be useful on both sides, and for the sake of gaining a peace between the Chinese and English, I have made my second appearance in the land of China. When I arrived at Canton, unfortunately, I found it was strictly guarded, and so I was unable to gain a welcome from the general. I know very well that the Cantonese will never hurt me, as most of them faithfully trusted and loved me when I was at Canton before. I then came up to Shanghai with self-confidence of finding a comforter to soothe my mind, but not one was to be found even worthy to be consulted with! Of late I think of you, who was once so good to me in every respect; even when there was a secret thing you never pushed me aside without consulting together; and I am proud now to say within myself that all our doings were done perfectly well, and besides, that we were mutually trustful to each other. I have a mind to obtain a peace between the Cantonese and English in the present trouble, and I think nothing but your excellency's presence and assistance.

But is a great pity that you are now out of service, and live leisurely in your own mansion; and I do not know if you can speak for me to the court of Peking, that the meaning of the English asking entrance into the city of Canton is not for one day; and if they are absolutely refused, their mind will never be satisfied, and so the calamity with their soldiers no one can foresee when it will cease.

On my way out to Canton, Lord Elgin, the English commissioner, was one of my fellow-passengers. He is an officer of high rank, of great power, and straight mind, and very different from that of the former commissioner. I have asked him many questions about his intention to work with the Canton province. His answer is: "That there was an alliance held with the French while he was in England, that their destination to China was not to make war nor to ask for more territory, but chiefly for the residence of an officer in Peking like the Russians, so that, in cases when important business occurs, they can conveniently report up to the royal court, and save any troubles, &c., &c." Lord Elgin also says, that "should their request be refused, and wars at the south insue, and not peace, there is no other course to run but to march directly up to Tien Chin with some ten men-of-war and a number of strong soldiers, there to display his power, &c., &c."

Lord Elgin asks nothing but conciliation, which is much agreed to my destination to China; and I think there is an opportunity of settling the difficulty, if the great Emperor of China would send down a great and noble officer to Canton.

I write this to you because there is no one to talk with, and the privilege is not for one, but for the life of many. I wait for your answer to condole my mind.

Address any letters to me, outside, care of Messrs. Russell & Co., Shanghai.

Exhibit 2 b.

I have received your valued favor on the 9th August, accompanied by the one from his excellency the American consul, and am glad that you do regret the late troubles that have occurred in Canton, and in return I beg you to accept my thanks.

Keying was an associate friend of mine, but owing to our distant separation, with warm weather and constant rains lately, I am prevented from going up to him for his opinion, and an answer to your letter. He is out of public service, living leisurely in his house, and reading his books; so I imagine, though he may receive your letter, yet he can do nothing as requested. Moreover, official rule prohibits outside association, and how can he dare to show a foreign private letter to his majesty the emperor? Therefore, I am quite certain that Keying can do nothing about this; and I would particularly request you to show this letter to nobody, lest some spying mandarins should know and report up to Peking, in which case Keying will have trouble about his life and family.

I have carefully read over the copy of your letter to him, and I find it is impossible to accomplish, otherwise I shall be happy to consult with those great mandarins, and try to finish the thing here; and as my family and property are in Canton, who dare say that I do not wish the difficulty to be settled at once? England, and all other foreign nations, are different from the Russians; Russians had been in Peking since the reign of Hong Hee, emperor one hundred and more years. They are but respectful and obedient sort of people, to be taught and dressed like the Chinese. Their students never meddle outside business. They are not allowed to write any letter to his majesty the emperor, nor to his officers. In case they want to write to his majesty the emperor, their writings have to go first to the high mandarin at Peking, to examine if there be any wrong words used in them. His majesty the emperor liberally allows the Russians only to learn Chinese literature; they are by no means allowed to become mandarins, nor have right to write to the court. The Russians sent their son (prince) for security of their good abode in Peking. They are not allowed to build houses without the sanction of high authority, while the English had so often violated the Chinese law. It is like to the parable of a common man who allows his good friend to go into any part of his house to sleep, eat, and drink with him, but when an enemy meets him, great care will be taken for fear he will be stabbed, or his enemy will create a disturbance in his house, &c.

The only blame is that Yeh had an overtrust upon the treaty; he was not aware of the undulating characters of these foreigners; had too much honesty displayed towards them, and which had lastly caused them (the English) an entrance into the inland. On the contrary, when the quarrel first commenced, if Yeh should have given an order for the people to keep a good look-out at every entrance, I am sure that Sir John Bowring and Admiral Seymour can do nothing cruelly against the braves of the Cantonese and the compactness of our forts, but will soon see the dead bodies of the English everywhere, and not one sail to run away from our waters. Many of our forts are gone now, and many entrances are undefended, yet the Cantonese were able to protect their city, and many English soldiers were killed when coming up our shore; and how much more will the Cantonese kill the English should their forts and entrances be all well kept? The English could do what they chose in the war in the year 1842, but I am sure of our victory by the next battle to come. The Russians had lately written to the court that they will prepare provisions, soldiers, and ammunition to destroy the English; but as the emperor has always a good mind upon the distant foreigners, I can say nothing if he allows them or not. To give entrance into Peking to our enemy, I should say, is more wise to accept the assistance of our good friends to destroy the traitors. We are all born and brought up at Canton, and our hearts have grieved too much on this account. The distance is of 8,000 more lees from Canton to Peking, and though Canton may, perhaps, fall into the hands of the English, it will hurt nothing to this empire of several 10,000 lees wide.

The emperor knows very well the strong minds of the Cantonese, who will never stand with the English, though even Canton city should be lost; this is quite known by our emperor and great mandarins at Peking. We fear nothing about the report that the English want to go up to Tin Chin with some ten men-of-war.

The troubles now existing were wrongfully commenced by the English. Loo Asing, and not the English, is the real owner of the Lorcha. The former found out his boat in the hands of pirates. To cover their own shameness, Sir John Bowring and Admiral Seymour had made the excuse that we pulled their flag down, and I believe you know very well too.

About war, Tin Chin has a very dangerous harbor, and its inhabitants are more strong than our Cantonese. There is no place to anchor ships there; besides, there is sandy ground some hundred lees long; vessels can go in with high tide only. The courageous character of their undisciplined people, show sometimes in the war with the rebels who marched against their boundary, and been terminated in a few days. The emperor praised the conduct of Tin Chin's officers, and since that the Tin Chinese have practiced much about artillery; so I dare say the present war with the English will show a great difference from that of 1842. The Chinese enjoyed a long peace before, and it was very easy to defeat them in 1842, owing to their anger not being very great against the English, but not so in the present case. Great pity I am at Peking, and I am unable to accept the kindness of the American consul for to speak of conciliation; and, moreover, I cannot speak to him face to face, and it is impossible to write to him in the paper all my mind and opinion; therefore I shall wait to see him by-and-by.

I write you this, and I hope you will agree with me in opinion.

I have the honor to be, &c. &c.

Exhibit 3 *a.*

UNITED STATES LEGATION TO CHINA,
On board the U. S. Frigate Minnesota, November 14, 1857.

SIR: I have the honor to announce to your excellency that, under a commission from the President of the United States appointing me envoy extraordinary and minister plenipotentiary, I have assumed the duties of my trust, and that the business of the legation will, for the present, be conducted on board the frigate Minnesota, now lying in the harbor of Hong Kong.

It gives me great pleasure to add, that I am instructed by the President to communicate with your excellency, as far as practicable, upon all subjects of mutual concern, and should your disposition prove favorable, as the President believes it will, your coöperation will be highly advantageous in promoting the object of my mission.

With assurances of distinguished consideration and respect, I have the honor to be, your excellency's obedient servant,

WILLIAM B. REED.

His excellency, the Count E. POUTIATINE,
Envoy Extraordinary and Minister Plenipotentiary of his Majesty the Emperor of all the Russias, in China.

Exhibit 3 *b.*

STEAMSHIP AMERICA, HONG KONG,
November 17, 1857.

SIR: I had the honor to receive the announcement of your excellency's appointment under the commission from the President of the United States as envoy extraordinary and minister plenipotentiary in China, and the assuming of the business of the legation on board the frigate Minnesota.

The instructions of the imperial government bid me to be on the most friendly terms with the representative of the United States in China, and I shall be happy to communicate with your excellency, and to afford my cordial coöperation on any subject of mutual concern which you may deem it requisite to let me know. I doubt not that the good understanding existing between our two governments will materially contribute to a desirable settlement of the present affairs in China.

With assurances of my high consideration and esteem, I have the honor to be your excellency's most humble servant,

C. E. POUTIATINE.

His excellency WILLIAM B. REED,
Envoy Extraordinary and Minister Plenipotentiary of the United States in China.

Exhibit 4 *a.*

UNITED STATES LEGATION TO CHINA,
On board the U. S. Frigate Minnesota, Nov. 14, 1857.

MY LORD: I have the honor to announce to your lordship that, under a commission of the President of the United States appointing me envoy extraordinary and minister plenipotentiary, I have assumed the duties of my trust, and that the business of the legation will, for the present, be conducted on board the frigate Minnesota, now lying in the harbor of Hong Kong.

It gives me great pleasure to add, what I have already personally communicated to your lordship, that I am instructed by the President to communicate frankly with you and the French minister upon all points of common interest, so that it may be distinctly understood that the three nations are equally influenced by a determination to obtain justice, and by a desire to procure treaty arrangements for the extension and more adequate protection of their commercial intercourse with China.

With assurances of distinguished consideration and respect, I have the honor to be your lordship's obedient servant,

WILLIAM B. REED.

The EARL OF ELGIN AND KINCARDINE,
Her Britannic Majesty's High Commissioner and Plenipotentiary.

Exhibit 4 *b.*

HONG KONG, *November* 19, 1857.

SIR: I have the honor to acknowledge your excellency's letter of the 14th instant, informing me that you have assumed the duties of your trust as envoy extraordinary and minister plenipotentiary of the United States, and adding that you are instructed by the President to communicate with me upon all points of common interest, so that it may be distinctly understood that the three nations are equally influenced by a determination to obtain justice and by a desire to procure treaty arrangements for the extension and more adequate protection of their commercial intercourse with China.

I have received this intimation with much satisfaction, and beg to state, in reply, that I am instructed by my government to act, as far as possible, in conjunction with the representative of the United States in the discharge of my duties, and that I shall have much gratification in giving effect to this instruction by communicating in the most frank and cordial manner with your excellency.

I have the honor to be, sir, your excellency's most obedient, humble servant,

ELGIN AND KINCARDINE.

His excellency, Hon. W. B. REED, *&c., &c., &c.*

Exhibit 5 *a.*

UNITED STATES LEGATION TO CHINA,
On board the U. S. Frigate Minnesota, Nov. 14, 1857.

SIR: I have the honor to announce to your excellency that, under a commission from the President of the United States appointing me envoy extraordinary and minister plenipotentiary, I have assumed the duties of my trust, and that the business of the legation will, for the present, be conducted on board the frigate Minnesota, now lying in the harbor of Hong Kong.

It gives me great pleasure to add, that I am instructed by the President "to communicate frankly with the English and French ministers upon all points of common interest, so that it may be distinctly understood that the three nations are equally influenced by a determination to obtain justice and by a desire to procure treaty arrangements for the extension and more adequate protection of their commercial intercourse with China."

With assurances of distinguished consideration and respect, I have the honor to be your excellency's obedient servant,

WILLIAM B. REED.

His excellency M. LE BARON GROS,
Commissioner Extraordinary and Embassador of His Majesty the Emperor of the French, in China.

Exhibit 5 *b.*

[Translation.]

MISSION EXTRAORDINARY OF FRANCE TO CHINA,
On board the Frigate L'Audacieuse,
In the Canton River, November 23, 1859.

The undersigned, embassador of France, sent to China by his Majesty the Emperor of the French, there to regulate, in the capacity of commissioner extraordinary and plenipotentiary, the differences existing between the two nations, and to obtain for commerce and navigation more ample concessions than those which are at this time accorded to them in the Celestial Empire, has received the note which his excellency, Mr. W. B. Reed, did him the honor to write to him on the 14th of this month to announce to him that, appointed by the President of the United States envoy extraordinary and minister plenipotentiary of that power to China, he had entered on the exercise of his functions, and that the affairs of the legation confided to him would be conducted at present on board the frigate Minnesota, moored just now in the port of Hong Kong.

His excellency is pleased to add that he is happy to have received from the President of the United States an intimation to have a frank understanding with the ministers of England and France, in all questions of interest common to those nations, in order that it may be well understood that the three powers referred to desire equally to obtain justice, and to improve and protect, by international conventions, the relations of commerce which now exist between them and China.

The undersigned associates himself completely with Mr. Reed, minister of the United States, in the views expressed by him in his note of the 14th of this month; and his excellency may be assured that the instructions which he has received from his government, as well as the sentiments which animate him, will make it his duty to hold with his excellency the minister of the United States relations as frank as friendly on all questions which shall offer a common interest to the two powers which they represent.

The undersigned embraces with ardor this first opportunity to offer to his excellency Mr. William B. Reed, envoy extraordinary and minister plenipotentiary of the United States of America to China, the assurance of his sentiments of the highest consideration.

BARON GROS.

His excellency Mr. WILLIAM B. REED,
Envoy Extraordinary and Minister Plenipotentiary of the United States of America to China.

Exhibit 6 *a*.

UNITED STATES LEGATION TO CHINA,
On board the U. S. Frigate Minnesota, November 14, 1857.

SIR: I have the honor to announce to your excellency that, under a commission from the President of the United States appointing me envoy extraordinary and minister plenipotentiary, I have assumed the duties of my trust, and that the business of the legation will, for the present, be conducted on board the frigate Minnesota, now lying in the harbor of Hong Kong.

With assurances of distinguished consideration and respect, I have the honor to be your obedient servant,

WILLIAM B. REED.

His excellency Sir JOHN BOWRING,
Her Britannic Majesty's Plenipotentiary, &c., Hong Kong.

The same dispatch sent to his excellency M. de Bourboulon, envoy extraordinary and minister plenipotentiary of his Majesty the Emperor of the French, in China.

Exhibit 6 *c*.

No. 302.]

SUPERINTENDENCY OF TRADE,
Hong Kong, November 16, 1857.

SIR: I have the honor to acknowledge your excellency's communication of the 14th instant, advising me of your appointment as envoy extraordinary and minister plenipotentiary from the United States, and that the business of the legation will for the present be conducted on board the frigate Minnesota in this harbor.

I beg to offer your excellency my cordial congratulations on your arrival, and to assure you that nothing shall be wanting on my part to consolidate the friendly relations which happily exist between our respective countries, and to promote those common interests committed to our charge in these regions.

I have the honor to be your excellency's most obedient humble servant,

JOHN BOWRING.

His Excellency WILLIAM B. REED.
United States Envoy Extraordinary and Minister Plenipotentiary in China, &c., Hong Kong.

Exhibit 6 *c.*

[Translation.]

LEGATION OF FRANCE TO CHINA,
Macao, November 17, 1857.

SIR: I have received the letter which your excellency did me the honor to address to me dated the 14th instant, by which you are so good as to announce to me, that having been appointed by the President of the United States to the post of envoy extraordinary and minister plenipotentiary of the United States to China, your excellency has entered upon its functions and established the seat of the legation on board the frigate Minnesota, at present in the roads of Hong Kong. I am very much obliged to you, sir, for this communication, and beg you to accept my ardent felicitations on your happy arrival in this country, and the assurance of the high consideration with which I have the honor to be your excellency's very humble and most obedient servant,

A. BOURBOULON.

His Excellency Mr. WILLIAM B. REED,
Envoy Extraordinary and Minister Plenipotentiary of the United States of North America to China, &c.

Exhibit 7 *a.*

No. 14.]

UNITED STATES CONSULATE,
Foochow, October 27, 1857.

SIR: I have the honor to inform you that I have been appointed United States vice-consul for this port, and that I have entered upon my official duties.

I am in receipt of instructions from the Department of State directing me to keep you "well apprised of all subjects of public interest" that may occur within my consular jurisdiction. The only event that has called for any direct consular interference was the seizure of an American boat with its Chinese crew by the custom-house authorities on the 14th instant. When the Chinese authorities declared their ntention of levying a duty upon opium, they requested the United

States consul to allow them to search American passenger boats when passing the custom-house at Limpoo, (a place about midway between the anchorage and Foochow.) The consul agreed to this measure on condition that no delay or trouble was to ensue therefrom. On the morning of the 14th instant, while Messrs. Stone & Co.'s post boat, flying the American flag, was passing Limpoo, it was boarded by a Chinese custom-house boat, five of her crew were seized, nearly everything was stolen from the boat, and an English passenger on board received several severe blows. The five men were taken on shore, severely beaten, and then released. The boat, with the passenger and two or three of her crew, was turned adrift upon the river.

So soon as I became aware of these facts, I wrote to the prefect demanding an apology for the insult to the flag, and informing him that for the future I should require him to abide strictly by the ninth article of the treaty in the collection of his import duties. I have received an apology for the insult, and have every reason to believe that my request in reference to his collecting import duties will be complied with.

I am, very respectfully, your obedient servant,

THOMAS DUNN,
United States Vice-Consul.

S. WELLS WILLIAMS, Esq.,
Chargé d'Affaires, ad interim, Macao.

Exhibit 7 *b.*

No. 15.]

UNITED STATES CONSULATE,
Foochow, November 9, 1857.

SIR: I last had the honor to address you on the 27th ultimo, which document I forwarded per schooner Eamont.

I have now to call your attention to the state of affairs existing at this port. For some months past the duties due from American vessels have been withheld from the Chinese government. Of the cause why these duties have been withheld, I presume that you have already been informed. There is now owing to the Chinese government a sum equal to 100,000 taels, and far from their desiring the payment of this sum, they have, in one instance, refused the duties due by an American firm on an English vessel when tendered in Foochow dollars. I am quite at a loss to account for this refusal, knowing, as I do, the poverty of the local government.

I have also to inform you that a report is current that there is at present on the river a band of Canton men (said to number about eighty) who are here with the design of plundering the treasure-boats when on their way from the anchorage to the foreign hongs. This rumor is so current, and so generally believed, that not only the native boatmen but even the Canton compradors are much alarmed. It is useless in this state of affairs to look for any assistance or protection from the local authorities; and I have to request that a man-of-war be sent here as soon as one can possibly be spared.

To this demand I have been repeatedly urged by the Americans residing at this port.

I have the honor to remain, with great respect, your obedient servant,

THOMAS DUNN,
Vice-Consul United States.

S. WELLS WILLIAMS, Esq.,
Chargé d'Affaires, ad interim, Macao.

Exhibit 7 *c.*

LEGATION OF THE UNITED STATES,
On board the frigate Minnesota, November 19, 1857.

SIR: I announce to you my arrival in China as envoy extraordinary and minister plenipotentiary of the United States, and that the business of the legation will be for the present conducted on board this ship, now lying in the harbor of Hong Kong.

I beg to recall to your attention a letter addressed to you or your predecessor by the Secretary of State, dated the 20th June last, by which you are directed, in all cases of emergency, to apply for instructions to this legation, to keep me apprised of all subjects of interest occurring within your consular jurisdiction, and to conform to the directions which you may from time to time receive from me in all matters which have reference to our treaty obligations, or a bearing upon our political relations with China, and pertaining to your consular functions.

In the same letter you are instructed to forward your quarterly reports directly to Washington, but to furnish me copies or extracts, if I desire them.

In my instructions from the Secretary of State the same views are expressed, and in conformity with them, I beg you to give me information on these points:

1. Whether you are acting under an appointment from the President, or as vice-consul; and, if the latter, by whom and when you were appointed, and whether the fact of such substitution was communicated to this legation?

2. If you are acting as vice-consul, whether your principal vacated his post and returned home with the leave of the government?

I am especially anxious to be furnished, with as little delay as possible, with a full report of the action of the consulate at Foochow in relation to the duties which are said to have been withheld from the Chinese government. In a letter—which is on file—from you to Mr. S. Wells Williams, chargé d'affaires, *ad interim,* dated November 9, you say:

"Of the cause why these duties have been withheld, I presume you have been already informed;" and you add, "that there is now owing to the Chinese government a sum equal to 100,000 taels."

I find on the records of the legation no report of this proceeding, and no reason for it; and Mr. Williams tells me he has no information about it. You will see the necessity for my having an immediate explanation of this resort to extreme measures by the consul, and I shall be much disappointed if it is not furnished me at once, and in detail. My attention has already been called to the matter by the representatives of one of the treaty powers.

I will thank you to furnish me with copies or abstracts of your quarterly reports sent to the department.

I am, very respectfully, yours,

WILLIAM B. REED.

THOMAS DUNN, Esq.,
Vice-Consul of the United States at Foochow.

Exhibit 7 *d.*

No. 306.]

SUPERINTENDENCY OF TRADE,
Hong Kong, November 19, 1857.

SIR: I have the honor to call your excellency's early attention to a state of matters which appears to me dangerous to the general interests of the treaty powers in China, and which has caused to myself much anxiety and embarrassment.

I was given to understand by your excellency's predecessor that the stoppage of duties due to the Chinese custom-house, and the exemption of the citizens of the United States from the obligations of the tariff established by treaties, were not powers conferred upon local consuls, without reference to the superordinate authority.

But I am advised that, in consequence of a question as to the discount at which Mexican dollars shall be received at the Chinese custom-house, the United States consul at Foochow has taken upon himself to allow the departure of many American vessels without payment of the duties due.

This state of matters has led to grave and justifiable remonstrance on the part of British merchants; and I have been called upon to release them from the obligations imposed by treaty, and to place them in the same position as that occupied by merchants of the United States.

This I have refused to do; but I have (and that with considerable repugnance) authorized the British consular authorities at Foochow to receive the duties, and to hold them, pending the solution of a matter which I may safely leave to your excellency's sense of justice, and of the claims of good faith.

Nor need I add how important it is, in the present state of our relations with China, that no local action by subordinate officers should interfere with or imperil the friendly relations which happily exist in all the legal ports, with the solitary exception of Canton.

With regard to the general question of the position of consuls towards the plenipotentiaries of the treaty powers in China, I doubt not that his excellency the Earl of Elgin, will call your excellency's early attention to this very important subject.

I have the honor to be, sir, your excellency's most obedient, humble servant,

JOHN BOWRING.

His Excellency W. B. Reed,
United States Envoy Extraordinary and Minister Plenipotentiary to China, &c., &c., &c.

Exhibit 7 e.

Legation of the United States,
November 20, 1857.

Sir: I have the honor to acknowledge the receipt of your excellency's dispatch, dated yesterday, calling my attention to the state of things said to exist at Foochow, and the rumored action of the American consul at that port. I beg to inclose to you a copy of a letter sent on the 19th instant, previous to receiving your dispatch, to Thomas Dunn, Esq., vice-consul of the United States at Foochow, from which you will see that the subject had already attracted my attention, and that I had initiated an inquiry into it. From the same letter (and, with some modifications, it has been sent to the consuls at the other open ports) you will perceive that it is the wish of the government of the United States, and my own determination, to bring consular action under some sort of supervision.

I shall be most happy, so soon as the facts are regularly before me, to confer with your excellency on the course to be taken in the particular instance to which you have called my attention.

I concur in your excellency's suggestion as to the importance of preventing, as far as possible, local action which may interfere with or imperil the friendly relations which happily exist in all the legal ports except Canton, and I cannot refrain from adding that this suggestion presents itself to my mind with great force, in view of the injury to American commerce by the anomaly of a local war such as exists in the Canton river.

I have the honor to be, your excellency's most obedient servant,

WILLIAM B. REED.

His Excellency Sir John Bowring,
Her Britannic Majesty's Plenipotentiary, &c.

Mr. Reed to Mr. Cass.

No. 37.]

United States Legation to China,
On board the Minnesota, December 14, 1857.

Sir: I have the honor to forward you a copy of the new treaty negotiated between Russia and Japan on the 12th of October, 1857. I am indepted for it to his excellency Count Poutiatine, the Russian plenipotentiary to China, who has communicated it to me *confidentially*, and to be transmitted to you with that understanding. His reason for wishing it to be so considered, is that it has not been yet submitted for ratification to the Emperor of Russia. It is rather remarkable that, during a visit which Count Poutiatine made last summer to Japan, this treaty was suggested by the Japanese and signed by him, as he tells me, without any instructions on the subject. I am inclined to believe that his excellency has not communicated this treaty to any of the other of the plenipotentiaries now here. In accidental conversation yesterday, Lord Elgin told me that part of his duty was to visit and treat with the Japanese, and that he meant to go there next summer.

On receiving the draft of this treaty, I submitted it for careful examination to Mr. Williams, the secretary of this legation, who accompanied Commodore Perry on his visit to Japan, and has large experience of these eastern nations. He has prepared a series of remarks which I forward for the consideration of the department.

I make this the subject of a separate dispatch.

I have the honor to be, very respectfully yours,

WILLIAM B. REED.

Hon. Lewis Cass,
Secretary of State.

[Confidential.—Translation.]

Supplementary treaty between Russia and Japan.

In addition to the treaty concluded between Russia and Japan at Simoda on the 26th January, (7th February,) 1855, or of Ansei, first year, twelfth month, 21st day, the undersigned, Count Euphemius Poutiatine, vice-admiral and aid-de-camp general of his Majesty the Emperor of all the Russias, and their excellencies Midzno Tsikogo-no, Kami, controller and first governor of Nagasaki, Alao Iwamie-noKamie, second governor of Nagasaki, and Iwase Iga-no. Kamie, imperial commissioner, came to an agreement, and have stipulated the following articles :

Article 1.

In order to establish commerce and friendly intercourse between Russia and Japan on a more solid foundation, new regulations are hereby enacted for the guidance of the Russians and Japanese in the ports of Hakodadi and Nagasaki.

As to the port of Simoda, it being an unsafe harbor, the former stipulations alone will there remain in force. The new regulations will then be applicable when it is finally decided that Simoda or some safer port is to be opened for foreign trade.

ARTICLE 2.

In future, the number of ships, or the amount of money employed in trade will not be limited, and all commercial transactions will be done by the mutual consent of both parties.

ARTICLE 3.

When a Russian merchant vessel arrives in one of the above-mentioned ports, the captain or supercargo is bound to present, through the Russian consul, or where there is not one, to deliver himself to the local authorities, a declaration comprising the name of the ship, its tonnage, the name of the captain or supercargo, as well as the sort and quantity of goods brought by him.

Such declaration is to be made during the first day, or not later than forty-eight hours. In that space the captain is bound to pay anchorage money, consisting of 5 mace or 42 copecks for each ton, if the vessel is above 150 tons, and 1 mace or 9 copecks for every ton if the vessel is 150, or of a smaller size.

The anchorage money is to be paid even when a vessel has entered a port not for the purposes of trade, but has been staying in it longer than forty-eight hours.

No anchorage money is levied from a vessel coming for repairs, except its cargo, or a part of it, has been discharged on land or into another ship.

The custom-house having received the anchorage money, is bound to give a receipt, and to allow at the same time the unloading of the ship.

ARTICLE 4.

If the captain of a merchantman does not present a declaration during the first forty-eight hours after his arrival in port, he will have to pay a penalty of 65 roubles 50 copecks for each day, which is not to exceed 266 roubles.

In case of a false declaration, the captain will be fined 655 roubles; and for underloading the cargo without license, besides the aforesaid penalty, his goods will be confiscated.

ARTICLE 5.

Russian vessels having paid the anchorage money on their arrival in the first Japanese port, can go into other ports without further payments, if they only produce the receipt given them at the first port.

It is understood that this rule does not apply to vessels which during their voyage, enter and take new cargoes in ports of other nations.

ARTICLE 6.

Boats employed in towing vessels, loading or discharging goods, and all sorts of workmen are to be hired from the number appointed for that purpose by the local Japanese authorities. These boats, as well all others, are to land at fixed places or wharves.

ARTICLE 7.

The goods purchased by Japanese from Russian merchant vessels, as well as those that are sent in return, are to be transmitted through the custom-house. Besides this transmission, the custom-house is not to interfere in any commercial transaction between Japanese and Russian merchants.

ARTICLE 8.

In default of Japanese goods, to be exchanged in return for a Russian cargo sold in Japan, the custom-house will pay for it in silver or gold foreign coin, according to the fixed rate of change.

ARTICLE 9.

The existing duty of 35 per cent. will be levied on the sums realized for goods, sold by public sale or private transaction, till a tariff shall be enacted. For this purpose, the consul or the captain of the merchant vessel is bound to signify, at the custom-house, the payments agreed for the purchase of the Russian goods.

The above-mentioned duty does not apply to the goods purchased by the custom-house.

The exposition of the goods and the public sale may be repeated as often as the Russian merchant desires; and the custom-house cannot limit the number of Japanese merchants coming to that sale.

ARTICLE 10.

If the goods are sold at the public sale, the custom-house is answerable for their payment. In private transactions, it does not take the responsibility upon itself, but will examine and decide any complaints which may arise, together with the consul.

After the goods have been once delivered, neither party can complain about the quality or value of the purchased goods.

ARTICLE 11.

Goods bought by the Russians in Japanese shops will be paid in paper money, delivered by the custom-house, for which it is bound to give real coin to the Japanese merchants immediately on the presentation of the paper money. The Russians will make payment in the same way for hiring boats, purchasing provisions, and other objects; but the pay in Russian or foreign coin is only to be made through the custom-house.

ARTICLE 12.

In settling accounts for purchased goods, and all sorts of objects, the value of the money will be defined by the comparative weight and quality of the Russian or foreign gold or silver with the Japanese gold and silver ichibus, viz: gold with gold, and silver with silver; and after an exact appreciation of their value, a further sum of six per cent. will be allowed for the expenses of recoinage. The settlement of accounts may also be done by reckoning one Spanish dollar equal to two and a half Dutch florins, or one rouble thirty-three copecks; or one Mexican dollar to two Dutch florins, fifty-five cents, or one rouble fifty-five copecks.

The weights, the measures of capacity and length, will be compared and fixed in each of the opened ports, by persons appointed for this purpose by the governments.

ARTICLE 13.

All articles of war are not to be sold to private persons, but to the government alone.

If, in future, the Japanese government finds it necessary to stop the sale into private hands of some imported goods unknown to it, they will be purchased then on account of the custom-house.

ARTICLE 14.

In case Russian vessels shall import opium in Japan, their cargoes will be confiscated, and the guilty will be dealt according to the Russian laws, strictly forbidding that pernicious trade.

ARTICLE 15.

The exportation from Japan of gold and silver, in coin or bars, is prohibited, except gilt objects, or gold and silver manufactured wares.

Copper, all sorts of arms, harness, silk stuff under the name of yamatoni-siki, can only be exchanged for objects purchased or ordered by the Japanese government.

ARTICLE 16.

Rice, barley, wheat, red and white beans, coals, writing paper, called *mino* and *hanci*, books, charts, and copper wares, can only be obtained by purchase from the custom-house; but this prohibition does not apply to persons buying these objects for their own use, with the exception of prohibited books and charts.

In case of scarcity, the exportation of articles of food, vegetable, wax, and paper may be stopped for a time.

ARTICLE 17.

To prevent smuggling, guard-boats may be stationed about merchant vessels by the local authorities; but the expenses on that account are not to be levied on Russian trade.

ARTICLE 18.

For the above-mentioned reason, the crew of a merchantman, and boats loaded with merchandise, may be searched at the custom-house, or at the place appointed as a depot for goods.

ARTICLE 19.

If any loss of goods or other objects belonging to the Russians shall ensue during the transportation in hired boats, a strict examination will be made, and all means taken to recover what was lost; but in this case, as in all similar difficulties, the custom-house, besides making inquiries, will not be responsible for any losses.

ARTICLE 20.

The transhipment of goods from one Russian vessel to another or a foreign one, cannot be done without a previous declaration to the custom-house by the consul or the captain of the vessel. The declaration must contain the sort and quantity of merchandise intended for the transhipment, and in such case the custom-house can send an officer on board to insure that no contraband should take place during the dischargment.

If the transhipment is done without license, the custom-house will make it know to the consul, and when there is not one, will itself stop and seize the transhipped goods.

ARTICLE 21.

When any Russian merchantman is found smuggling in open ports, the goods alone will be confiscated, but if in other places in Japan the vessel also will be seized.

This, however, must not be done before a previous examination and decision of the case shall be made by the Japanese authorities, together with the Russian consul.

ARTICLE 22.

If the captain of a merchantman, or any one belonging to a vessel, desire to make a present to a Japanese, they are to deliver with the donation a note certifying its being made by them.

ARTICLE 23.

During the stay of a vessel in port, all the ship's papers are to be kept at the Russian consulate, and where there is none, they are to be delivered to the local authorities.

The consul or the authorities, at the departure of the vessel, will not give up the ship's papers till all accounts are settled with the custom-house and the Japanese merchants.

Article 24.

Russians desirous to study the Japanese language or any of the Japanese arts, are bound to make their wishes known through the consul or the captain to the local authorities, and proper persons will be appointed for the desired instruction.

Article 25.

All communications of the Russian Government with the Japanese will be done through the highest person representing Russian authority in Japan, and by him transmitted to the local governor. If, from some circumstances, the communication or the letter is brought to a port where there is no consul, it will be presented by the person to whom it was intrusted to the governor of the place, and immediately sent by him to its destination. The answer may be forwarded to the port where the letter was delivered, if the vessel is awaiting it there, or may be sent through the consul, to forward it by the first opportunity to Russia.

Article 26.

The rights of neutrals acknowledged by all civilized nations, oblige two belligerent States not to attack the ships of their adversaries in neutral ports. It is understood that in case of war between Russia and another nation, the Russian ships will not attack their enemies lying in Japanese ports.

Article 27.

Russians residing constantly or temporarily in Japan, have a right to bring their wives and families to live in that country.

Article 28.

If in future it may be found necessary to alter or add any articles to this treaty, each of the governments has a right to demand a revision of it.

The ratifications of this supplimentary treaty will be exchanged in eight months, or as circumstances will allow. The copies in Russian, Japanese, Dutch, and Chinese language, signed and sealed by those who have concluded this treaty, will be now exchanged, and all the articles are binding from the date of the signature, and will be observed by the contracting parties faithfully and inviolably.

Done and signed at Negasaki, the 12th (24th) of October, in the year of our Lord 1857, and the third of the reign of his Majesty Alexander II., Emperor of all the Russias, or of Ansei, the 4th year, 9th, moon, 7th day.

C. E. POUTIATINE,
MIDZNO TSIKOGO-NO, KAMIE,
ALAO IWAMI-NO, KAMIE,
IWASE IGA-NO, KAMIE.

Remarks on the treaty between the Russians and Japanese, signed at Nagasaki 12th October, 1857.

The similarity between this treaty and the draft of a commercial treaty made out by Commodore Perry in February, 1854, which was based on the treaty of Waughia, in many of the particulars is so striking that I am led to infer that the Japanese have taken that scheme for a commercial treaty as the basis of the present, and they are doubtless willing to make a similar compact with other nations, the American and English, and perhaps have done so already with the Dutch.

ARTICLE 1. If Simoda be abandoned, either Kanagawa, a town in the bay of Yedo, about ten miles below that city, or Chosaka, the large port in the center of Nippon, not far from Miako, where the dairi resides, and which is the largest manufacturing city in Japan, should be strongly insisted on. It is not best to urge the residence of foreigners at Yedo or Miako at present, nor until the people themselves are prepared for it, for, in a feudal autocracy like the present Japanese government, foreign consuls would be very likely to get embroiled in the politics of the country, and excite unmeasured jealousy with their movements among the princes and high officials.

Kanagawa is a town near enough to the capital to attract the merchants there, while it is far safer for shipping than Uraga, in the entrance of the bay, about 40 miles further south. Kamakura, a town northeast of Simoda, at the head of the bay of Kadzusa, was mentioned to Commodore Perry with Simoda, but the greater facilities of the latter for coaling steamers coming from San Francisco led to its adoption, and Kamakura was not examined. Its position and size are such as to give it no claims to be taken, even if the harbor is a good one and spacious. Chosaka would be preferable for trade to any other, as it is already an entrepot for Japanese fabrics, and the capital collected there will be immediately serviceable for foreign merchants. At present all the trade likely to be carried on with Japan can be conducted at three ports situated like Nagasaki at the extreme west, Hakodadi at the north, and Kanagawa, or Chosaka, in the southeast, on the southern coast. Not that there are no other large cities where commerce would benefit those who carried it on, but the trade being new, the taste of the Japanese for western products not yet general, and it being doubtful what they can profitably supply us with, even if the Dutch do not manage to get a monopoly of all the government orders, these three ports will be well situated to attract those natives who can labor or furnish articles suitable for foreigners; their present trade is considerable, too.

ART. 2. This article has reference, undoubtedly, to the former long-established restrictions upon the Chinese and Dutch trade at Nagasaki, and it was in fact stated by the Japanese commissioners at Yokohama that such would be the case with the American trade.

ART. 3. The rate of tonnage money is about 75 cents of pure silver for large ships, and about 15 for small vessels, which is the same as is charged in Chinese ports according to the present treaty, and was probably taken from the latter. The paragraph respecting vessels which enter port "not for the purpose of trade," and yet, after 48 hours, must pay tonnage dues, seems to be almost or quite neutralized by the one next to it, allowing vessels to enter freely which come in for repairs.

ART. 4. This article involves a right of search of a foreign vessel in order to prove that there was a false declaration of the cargo, which foreign consuls would be very loth to grant the Japanese custom-house officials, if they are no better than the Chinese. It would be advisable to guard the liberty of search to prove it by some clauses enabling the consul to exercise some sort of supervision.

ART. 5. In the working of this regulation considerable difficulty is likely to be experienced for want of more definite directions about the frequency of returning to the same port; if the Japanese, as the Chinese have done, begin to use foreign vessels and steamers for their own coasting trade, the charge of 75 cents tonnage duty for every entrance to Nagasaki, on the return voyage from Hakodadi, will be a heavy tax, and rather unjust. This needs to be more explicitly stated, and also whether a ship can be allowed to stop outside of the port, as at the Papenberg, off Nagasaki, and discharge anything without incurring tonnage dues and pilotage. The coasting trade in Japan is likely to get gradually into foreign steamers if the authorities show any disinclination to encourage foreigners serving native-owned steamers, and therefore some clauses upon the above points would be desirable.

ART. 6. The stipulation providing for a guild of coolies and boat people, will tend to keep up the high prices which the Japanese have for so many years saddled every thing connected with foreign trade; and yet such is the whole structure of society in the country, that at present, it is probably the safest way of doing all the work connected with loading and purchasing cargo, and the safest is also ultimately the cheapest mode.

ART. 7. The design of this article is to foster the barter trade, which is the only kind of traffic the Japanese seem to intend to allow. They have not forgotten what immense sums were once exported by the Portuguese and others, two centuries ago.

ART. 8. This mode of taking the remainder of a cargo might be avoided by allowing a vessel to take away all the import goods the owners did not wish to sell; if the custom-house bought this remainder, it might not be willing to pay the market price, or perhaps the demand would depend on the arrangement the customs authorities could make with the native traders how the latter wished to pay for the goods. Altogether the provision is one that will not work well, if the ship be required to leave all her import cargo, and will not be necessary if she is allowed to take away unsalable articles; a bonding warehouse would remedy it.

ART. 9. The exhibition of goods at certain intervals is a mode of traffic the Japanese have been so long accustomed to, that they do not yet feel willing to admit free trade between parties at their option. Anything like a duty of 35 per cent. on both imports and exports, will amount to a prohibition of many articles, and stand in strong contrast to the five per cent. of the tariff in China. No specification is made as to ship's provisions and to baggage, both of which, with other points, would doubtless be made clearer when a full tariff is made out. If there is no duty charged by the custom-house, it must either be that it buys all goods itself in bond, or else that its prices are such as to include the duty. The arrangement is a good one for the Japanese authorities, and can be made a convenient mode of nullifying article seventh; for, by holding out an advantage of thirty-five per cent. by selling to the custom-house, no private merchant could compete with them. The whole article may however be so altered by the specifications of the tariff to be made out, that it is not likely to be put in practice as it is, or else the Japanese have rules of these sales, which will make them work easily.

ART. 10. This article is a continuation of the last in reality, and adds another inducement to trade with the government, and continue its paramount influence and interference. Perhaps this is the only way until it is convinced that there is no danger by a different course; and, in some respect, the foreigner is better off by this security against bad debts.

ART. 11. The rate at which the paper money is to be taken by the people from the custom-house, may include the thirty-five per cent.; and thus the apparent freedom of trade with the native merchants is resolved into a mere competition with the same parties in different relations to it.

ART. 12. This arrangement is a good one when compared with the one established by the Japanese at Simoda, in 1854, and is even better than the present mode in China, of nominally reckoning all payments in pure sycee, as it reduces trade to the currency of the country, instead of making a foreign coin the measure. This advantage is owing to the Japanese government being able to maintain a metallic currency in the three common metals used, which the Chinese have not hitherto done.

ART. 13. Where a tariff is made out, the prohibited articles should be specified; the import of revolvers and other fire-arms, is likely to increase among a people used to the sight and possession of arms as the Japanese are, and smuggling is very likely to be the result of any prohibitory enactments as contemplated by this article, if the boat-people and others who come to the ships, are like the Chinese.

ART. 14. One must agree with the Japanese, that if a preliminary prohibition like this can prevent their people from learning to love and use opium, it will be a wise precaution to stop its ingress by the severest enactments.

ART. 15. The preservation of the trade in copper to the exclusive management of the government is partly owing to its apprehension that the native supply will not be enough for all demands at home and abroad upon it. In future, the premium Japanese copper has always brought, from the small admixture of gold in it and its own fine color, may be lessened by the large results of the mines of America.

ART. 16. The importation of food into Japan is likely to be a constantly growing trade, for the same reason it is now in China; and if the Japanese can be induced to make the trade equally liberal with the

Chinese, a large business will gradually spring up in rice, and perhaps other grains too, but not in prepared food, as flour, salt meats, &c. It is not easy to perceive the reason for classing coals with the other articles in this list, for the supply is abundant and not likely to be wanted for exportation at the prices hitherto quoted.

ART. 17. The prevention of smuggling in some way or other will be a difficult thing on the part of the Japanese authorities; and none are so likely to promote it as the guard-boats and their crews.

ART. 18. The carrying out of this article will be likely to give rise to altercation, and a much safer way would be for the custom-house to see what goods went into boats alongside, and after that they would have no need of searching. It will be an earnest endeavor on the part of the Japanese to keep foreigners from rambling about the country at will, and by requiring all ship's boats to land at the custom-house wharf, much will be accomplished towards the object. If the evil conduct of sailors could be restrained by such a regulation, it would be a good arrangement; and it deserves a trial, and even some disabilities, for the [illegible] of attaining such an object. The sailors heretofore resorting to Japan have been kept on board their own ships, and the people ashore would do well to keep them there, if possible.

ART. 19. The precaution of sending responsible persons from the ship or consignees will be the best way to prevent losses in lading or unlading vessels; but the phrase "in all similar difficulties" is too vague. In case of bad debts, non-fulfillment of contracts, thefts, burglaries, and the many other ways in which losses can come or be suffered, there should be something more than a promise to make inquiries; and it is not unlikely that the Japanese would assent to a clearer article than the present, how they were to make compensation for some of the above losses.

ART. 20. The transhipment of the goods in China has been done to a large extent in violation of the stipulations of the treaty, owing partly to the difficulties put in the way by the custom's authorities, especially in transhipping native produce, and partly to their desire to exact new duties, if possible. If the coasting trade should become as considerable in Japan as it is in China, this article ought to stipulate some conditions on this point, in order to facilitate the transhipment.

ART. 21. Smuggling must, to be brought home to the merchantman, be stopped in the very act; and if the guard-boats do their duty, nobody can smuggle besides themselves. The amount of smuggling, the Japanese will find out, will be much greater under a tariff of 35 than under a cheaper one; but if the natives there are like those in China, no regulations will stop smuggling.

ART. 22. The object of this regulation seems to be simply that a native may be able to explain how he came by something for which he paid no duty. When Commodore Perry was in Japan, the presents given to officials and their attendants were put in large trunks, to be kept for the inspection of their superiors, before they used them.

ART. 23. The last clause of this article will prove a means of enabling native merchants to force the payment of their claims; and it is a provision that is much needed where the parties cannot, from ignorance of each other's language, draw up legal contracts. A stipulation of this sort would have saved Chinese merchants many losses in their trade with foreigners.

Art. 24. This seems to us a very unimportant concession, and probably few will ever avail of it, but the Japanese and Chinese have both long endeavored to prevent foreigners learning their language, under the impression that thereby their power to govern them would be much stronger, as they would not then be able to communicate except through interested native interpreters. But the present spirit of the Japanese seems to be very different.

Art. 25. There seems, at present, to be no danger that the same scrupulousness will be manifested by the Japanese which has been shown by the Chinese respecting the modes of address, and the way in which their Emperor and his officers shall be communicated with. Perhaps trouble would be avoided on both sides by having the proper styles of address mentioned in this article, and stating that certain officers would be required to forward all such dispatches.

Art. 26. This singular provision has doubtless a reference to the unnecessary violation of the neutrality of Japanese ports in 1811 by the British frigate Phæton, Captain Pellew, who endeavored to cut out the Dutch merchantmen at Nagasaki, and was the cause of [illegible] Japanese officials committing suicide. The article is proper enough as an intimation that the Japanese are not altogether ignorant of the position of neutral powers.

Art. 27. In connection with this, or some other article, it would be desirable to have some clauses stating how foreigners can obtain land to build their own houses and warehouses upon, how they can hire houses or other property, and what restrictions, if any, are to be put upon their acquiring real estate in the country. The stipulations in the treaty with China have proved inadequate to protect the native against his own authorities, and especially his own neighbors, when he felt inclined to sell or lease to a foreigner, as the charge of traitorous leaguing with them was easily trumped up against him.

In regard to the general provisions of this treaty between the Japanese and Russians, it is a great advance upon their former secluded policy, and it is to be hoped that the Japanese will go on in the path of free intercourse until they are able to visit and trade with other nations in their own vessels, and take a proper stand among the nations of the earth. If another power, in making a commercial treaty with them, could get some of the stipulations in this more clearly expressed, and obtain a few other points more or less involved in those already granted, it would tend to prevent disputes and future altercations. Among these may be mentioned:

Right of appeal to the Emperor or high council at Yedo, by the consul, whenever the local governor refuses to hear or attend to his complaints.

Right to build churches and hospitals at the ports open to trade.

Mode of recovering debts from bankrupt or fraudulent foreigners. In China the natives have suffered much from their ignorance of the mode in which they could recover their debts against their foreign customers.

Perhaps some of the suggestions have already been acted on, and are embodied in the treaty before made with Russia. Perhaps, too, they have, in other cases, been urged and rejected by the Japanese. Now that the matter of valuing foreign coin has been placed on so improved a basis, there are strong grounds for hoping that some trade will spring up. If the Japanese could be led to see the use and benefits of bonding warehouses, they would allow them, at least they might permit that articles sold to foreign ships not the produce of Japan might be reëxported or sold without paying import duties. The plan of levying export duties, adopted by both China and Japan, would make bonding warehouses very difficult to manage.

Probably no one is surprised that treaties made with pagan nations like the Siamese, Chinese, and Japanese are broken by the people of those lands where the obligations of truth are reckoned a good deal by the penalties likely to ensue if it be forfeited; but it is found, unhappily, that the foreigner gauges his own obligation to observe the stipulations of these treaties by the weakness of the government to visit him with the penalties for breaking them, and he excuses himself for his own delinquencies by the wickedness and temptations presented him by the natives. Consequently, it is much more difficult to carry out the safest precautions of trade and intercourse than it is in Christian and strong governments; but none are more ready to cry out against the deeds of these pagan authorities than the foreigner, whose unpunished offenses may have been the slow-moving cause of the visitations he suffers.

Mr. Reed to Mr. Cass.

[Extract.]

No. 36.] LEGATION OF THE UNITED STATES IN CHINA,
On board the Minnesota in the Harbor of Hong Kong,
December 15, 1857.

SIR: In my dispatch (No. 35) by the last steamer, I informed you of my having officially announced my arrival in China to the imperial commissioner. Not receiving any acknowledgment for two weeks, although I had every reason to know my letter had been received, I addressed another communication to him on the 28th ultimo, rather more emphatic in its language, but with no inappropriate expression of anything like irritation or asperity.—(Exhibit 1 a.)

Several days afterwards, and before my second communication could have reached its destination, I received the annexed letter, (Exhibit 1 b,) which will, of course, attract your attention, and which, I imagine, will be the beginning and the end of my communications from him. It is a capital specimen of Chinese diplomatic style, dextrous, disingenuous, but in this instance entirely courteous. In contrast with the tone which Yeh adopted to my predecessors, the deferential style of this letter is remarkable. It is, of course, only a symptom of the effect produced by the hostile pressure upon him. The evasion of my request for an interview, and his denial of the necessity or the right to revise the treaty, are very characteristic. Notwithstanding the occupation of the river by the English cruisers, there would have been no difficulty in a meeting on shore in the neighborhood, the risk being entirely mine, and he would have caused no little embarrassment to all whom it seems his pleasure to annoy, if he had agreed to a meeting at Canton, or on board one of our ships. I have great confidence, had this interview occurred, I could, under existing circumstances, have induced such fair concessions as might have averted the catastrophe still impending, and which I really do the British plenipotentiary the justice to believe he regards with great repugnance.

In the imperial commissioner's denial of the necessity of a revision of the treaty, Yeh has certainly touched the weak point of our case. No one can read the thirty-fourth article without being struck with its very ambiguous terms. It really seems as if those who negotiated it were so grateful for success, and so well satisfied with their work, that they regarded substantial or considerable modifications or alterations in the remote future as highly improbable. This criticism the Chinese commissioner has had the sagacity to make, and he is thus enabled to have a pretext to refuse the chance of revision. Not being willing that he should suppose such sophistry had convinced or silenced me, I have sent him an answer, which, I presume, closes all correspondence between us, (Exhibit 1 c,) and, upon the whole, I am glad it is at an end. I already concur in the received opinion here, that there is nothing which the Chinese like better, or which is practically more unprofitable, than diplomatic correspondence. The point which is to be settled, (and how it will be determined I do not pretend to say,) is whether we shall hereafter meet their public men on terms of equality—on such terms be received and confer. This, of course, involves personal face to face intercourse. This, in my judgment, is far more important than forcing ourselves over the ruins of usage and prejudice of all kinds into the presence of that mysterious being, the emperor, whom it suits this strange people to enshrine and seclude from ordinary contact. Personal intercourse with responsible officers of high rank we are entitled to and must have. I hope the President will approve of the course I have pursued.

The refusal of the commissioner to see me, and my inability to take any further measure to compel direct intercourse, reconcile me to the inaction to which, for the present, I find myself reduced, and to a tacit acquiescence in the course the belligerents are pursuing, taking care to say nothing, or to put nothing on record, which might be construed into a positive approval of the policy of the war.

* * * * * * * *

I have the honor to be, sir, your most obedient servant,

WILLIAM B. REED.

Hon. Lewis Cass, *Secretary of State.*

Exhibit 1 *a.*

Legation of the United States,
Macao, November 28, 1860.

Sir: On the 17th instant, I addressed a letter to your excellency announcing my arrival in China, as the envoy extraordinary and minister plenipotentiary of the United States of America, charged with messages of friendship and good will, and desiring an interview with you. In doing this, I conformed not only to the requisitions of the treaty which recognizes you as the proper medium of communication with his majesty the emperor, but to the high sense I have of international courtesy, and the value of the friendship happily subsisting between us. To this letter I have received no answer, not even an acknowledgment of its having been received. I can only account for this by the fear, in the present disturbed state of public affairs, it never reached your excellency's hands, or the greater fear that, having received it, your excellency, unwisely confounding the United States with hostile powers, does not choose to acknowledge it. This I am most reluctant to believe.

If the letter never reached you and this does, I beg to renew my request for an interview that I may, in person, express to you the friendly feelings of the people and President of the United States, and renew the assurances that we are not parties to existing hostilities.

Your excellency will permit me to suggest that it would be a new misfortune to the government of his imperial majesty, if, at a moment like this, the long-tried friendship of the United States should be interrupted, and my countrymen, instead of being earnest and anxious friends as they now are, and mean to be, should be wholly alienated or become indifferent spectators of the deplorable war now in progress. We would stop it if we could, but it is useless to cherish even the wish, if your excellency withholds that intercourse through which, alone, any good offices could be rendered.

The citizens of the United States have received wrongs at the hands of the Chinese authorities, which must be redressed; but they have been willing to suspend anything like urgency, till the pending hostilities should be determined. But, I beg earnestly to impress upon your excellency, that it will be impossible that this friendly feeling and hesitation shall continue, if the ordinary courtesies of personal and official intercourse are withheld.

I await your excellency's answer before deciding what further steps to take, or to recommend to my government.

Availing myself of this opportunity to wish you health and prosperity, I am yours,

WILLIAM B. REED.

His Excellency YEH,
Imperial Commissioner and Governor-General
of the Two Kwang, &c., Canton.

Exhibit 1 *b.*

NOVEMBER 24, 1857.

YEH, Imperial Commissioner, Governor General of the Two Kwang Provinces, a Baron of the Empire, &c., &c., hereby replies:

I received and read your excellency's dispatch on the 23d instant, from which I learned that you have been appointed envoy extraordinary and minister plenipotentiary to China, and that you have arrived in Kwangtung. On hearing that an officer of the highest fame and reputation, with such kindly feelings as your excellency, had reached China at this time, I was extremely desirous of having a personal interview. My predecessor, Seu, had one with the former minister, Davis, in September, 1848, at the Jinsin hong, (a suburban residence of Howqua;) but in October of last year the English moved up their forces, and attacked the provincial city in an unprovoked manner for successive days with their cannon; and then on the 12th of January of this year they set fire to and burned the houses along the river banks in the western suburb, at which time the Jinsin hong was also entirely consumed. Thus, much as I should like to have an interview, there is really no place where to hold it.

In your dispatch you speak of having a letter from the President, which you wish to deliver into my hands; but as there is no place now for us to meet, I have to request that your excellency will inclose it to me, that I may forward it to court by a convenient opportunity.

In regard to the remark you make that "our two countries have been bound by a treaty for the last twelve years, which has never been broken by the United States, and which I now wish to renew in accordance with the stipulation that after twelve years changes may be made in it," I may quote from the thirty-fourth article of it, which provides that "when the present convention shall have been definitely concluded, it shall be obligatory on both powers, and its provisions shall not be altered without grave cause; but, inasmuch as the circumstances of the several ports of China open to foreign commerce are different, experience may show that inconsiderable modifications are requisite in those parts which relate to commerce and navigation; in which case the two governments will, at the expiration of twelve years from the date of the said convention, treat amicably concerning the same by the means of suitable persons appointed to conduct such negotiations."

It is well known that since the treaty was formed citizens of the United States have carried on trade with China now for twelve years, and among all foreigners they are to be commended for their courteous, peaceful conduct. In carrying on commerce at the ports, and in matters relating to navigation, they have conducted them according to our law, and adhered to one mode. Consequently, if the treaty then settled has proved so very satisfactory and beneficial that your excellency can say that it has never been broken, then there is no necessity of making even these slight modifications in it; and, intelligent and candid as you are, you must clearly see that the old regulations now in force require no alterations.

While making this reply, I take the occasion to express the wish that peace and tranquillity may be yours.

His Excellency W. B. Reed,
Envoy Extraordinary and Minister Plenipotentiary of the United States, in China.

Translated by S. Wells Williams.

Exhibit 1 *c.*

LEGATION OF THE UNITED STATES,
Macao, December, 1857.

SIR: I have had the honor to receive your excellency's letter of the 24th November, and thank you for the friendly sentiments you express. They make me the more regret that you are unable to meet me, for I am sure a personal interview in which we could interchange opinions would convert the professed friendliness into some practical advantage to your countrymen and mine. It is now too late; and I can but regret the decision. As the representative of the United States, I have come here to render friendly offices to the goverment of his imperial majesty, and the opportunity is denied me.

Your excellency refers me to the interview which my predecessor, Mr. Davis, had with your excellency's predecessor, Seu, in 1848. This brings to my mind the fact that since that time, now nearly ten years, no representative of the United States has had the benefit of personal intercourse at Canton with a commisioner charged with the superintendence of the concerns of foreign nations in China, or with a governor general of the Liang Kwang.

In that interval there has been much unpleasant correspondence, and difficulties have arisen which a few honest-spoken words would have removed. I have come here with higher diplomatic rank than many of my predecessors. I have come, too, at a moment when friendliness more than ever is important, and a personal interview has been declined. The want of a place to meet in is not a sufficient reason, for I should, trusting to your excellency's safeguard, have been willing to meet you anywhere on the soil of China, or more glad still to receive you on the deck of my ship, under the flag of my country, which no one would dare or wish to violate. I repeat, I can but regret this. The time is not distant when your excellency may be sorry you have not seen me.

I decline to inclose the letter with which I am charged from the President of the United States to his majesty the emperor. That letter is too important to be trusted to ordinary conveyance. Had your excellency received me, I should have been glad, confiding in your word of honor, to place it in your hands; but I can trust it to no others, especially when I remember that, in 1856, my immediate predecessor forwarded a letter from the President to his majesty the emperor, and it was returned with the seals broken and unanswered. Such an indignity could only be excused by its having fallen into improper hands, which prevented it from reaching its destination.

I retain the letter with which I am charged till I can present it in that mode which is suited to the dignity of the President of the United States.

The treaty of 1844 must be revised. Grave cause has arisen for its alteration.

Your excellency misunderstands me when you attribute to me the remark that the treaty has never been broken. I said, and I say still, it has never been broken by the United States. But even if it had not been broken at all, the lapse of time and change of circumstances furnish grave cause to revise and alter it for mutual advantage. To make that revision properly and safely, requires consultation and friendly intercourse. To such intercourse I have invited your excellency, and you have refused it. I can do no more.

The time has come when the United States, the greatest nation of the western world, must be treated with on terms of equality with China, the oldest civilized nation of the East, and I have come in a conciliatory spirit to claim that right. It is a matter of deep regret that my mission of peace seems to be thus frustrated.

Availing myself of this opportunity to wish you health and prosperity, I am yours,

WILLIAM B. REED.

His Excellency YEH,
Imperial Commissioner and Governor General
of the Two Kwang, &c. &c. &c., Canton.

Mr. Reed to Mr. Cass.

No. 38.] UNITED STATES LEGATION TO CHINA,
On board the Minnesota, Hong Kong, December 16, 1857.

SIR: I have this morning—and only a few moments before the departure of the mail—received the inclosed letter from his excellency the Earl of Elgin. This, I presume, for the present, closed the correspondence, which I think will be productive of good.

You will perceive that his lordship withdraws the intimation that his delay in going north was due to the American refusal.

Being on shore when this communication was received, I have been prevented from sending the copy on dispatch paper. One shall be forwarded by the next mail.

I have the honor to be, sir, your most obedient servant,

WILLIAM B. REED.

The SECRETARY OF STATE.

P. S.—The inclosures in Lord Elgin's letter will be found in the department. They are:

1. Letter from Sir John Bowring to Mr. Parker, 4th August, 1857.
2. Letter from Mr. Parker to Sir John Bowring, 8th August, 1857.

There is not time to make copies.

HONG KONG, *December* 15, 1857.

SIR: I received last evening your excellency's letter of yesterday's date, and, notwithstanding your courteous remark that you do not desire to draw from me at a moment when I must be much engrossed any expression of opinion on the matters on which you have thought it right to explain your views, I consider it due to your excellency that I should answer it forthwith.

I beg to assure your excellency that I believe her majesty's government still entertain the sentiments expressed in the extract which you quote from a letter of Lord Clarendon's, and to add that, in the discharge of my duties, it is my intention to conform, in so far as I can possibly do so, to the principles therein laid down.

I am bound, however, to observe that I hardly think that the paragraph in my letter to your excellency of the 12th instant, in which I referred to my correspondence with Dr. Parker on the subject of a visit to the Peiho in July last, properly bears the construction which your excellency has placed upon it. It was certainly by no means my intention to hold Dr. Parker responsible for the resolution which I ultimately formed, to postpone that intended visit, although no doubt his refusal to accompany me was an important element among the considerations which influenced my final determination on this point. I adopted that determination, however, on my own judgment, and am accountable for it to my own government. What I meant to convey by the paragraph in question was simply this: that on my arrival in China in July last, I proposed to the minister of the United States to accompany me to the mouth of the Peiho, with the view of effecting an amicable arrangement of differences with China by a direct appeal to the court of Pekin; that I made this proposal in the most perfect good faith, and should certainly have held myself bound by it if he had consented to go with me, and that therefore it was not until after I had received his refusal that I deemed the plan open for reconsideration. I referred to this circumstance, however, not with the view of questioning the propriety of Dr. Parker's proceedings in the matter, but in proof of the sincerity of my desire to act cordially with the representative of the United States in China.

As your excellency refers more than once to the present state of affairs in this quarter, I think it right to observe that in addressing to the minister, who is both governor general of the two Kwang, and also charged by the Emperor of China with the direction of foreign affairs, claims of redress for wrongs suffered, or for the violation of treaty rights, and in enforcing those claims by the measures of coercion to which civilized nations are wont to resort, Great Britain and France are adopting a course which is in strict conformity with public law and with the prescriptions of the Chinese government itself. The result of Count Poutiatine's mission to the mouth of the Peiho furnishes abundant proof of the indisposition of that government to listen to appeals addressed to it through any channels except those appointed by itself. The desire of the governments of Great Britain and France that hostile measures should, if possible, be local in the sense of being confined to Canton, and that commerce at the other ports should not be interfered with, does not seem to me a fitting subject for complaint.

As regards the claims alluded to in the latter part of your excellency's letter, I have only to say that any representation which your excellency may address to me on that or any other subject, will always command my most respectful attention; but that until I received this last letter, I did not know to what you referred, as I find no specific mention of them in Dr. Parker's correspondence.

Before closing this letter, I would beg leave to refer to a paragraph in your excellency's letter to me of the 7th instant, which I omitted to notice in mine of the 12th to your excellency. In that paragraph your excellency, after alluding to the correspondence which had passed between Dr. Parker and me on the subject of a visit to Peiho, observes:

"I do not find any further official correspondence between this legation and your lordship from the date of Mr. Parker's note of the 6th of July until my arrival in November, although in that interval had occurred, during your absence, the leading incident of a blockade of the Canton port and river by Sir M. Seymour's authority."

I have conferred with Sir J. Bowring on this subject, and he has furnished me with a correspondence that passed between Dr. Parker and him in reference to the blockade, of which I herewith inclose the copy.

I have only to add, in explanation of my own proceedings, that on my return from India on the 20th of September, I found that Dr. Parker had already left China, and that your excellency was daily expected.

I have the honor to be, sir, your excellency's most obedient, humble servant,

ELGIN & KINCARDINE.

His Excellency Hon. W. Reed,
United States Envoy Extraordinary, &c., &c., &c.

Mr. Reed to Mr. Cass.

[Extract.]

No. 39.] LEGATION OF THE UNITED STATES,
Minnesota, harbor of Hong Kong, December 28, 1857.

SIR: I send with this dispatch copies of two communications (inclosures 1 a, b) I have received from the Imperial Commissioner Yeh, in reply to letters already forwarded to you, which I had addressed to him. They are curious, among other things, in this, that they illustrate the formal punctiliousness of the Chinese officials in answering communications made to them, even at a time when, as now, more pressing exigencies might so well excuse them. There is, in these letters, all the characteristic artifice of Chinese rhetoric.

I beg to impress upon you the necessity in construing such productions of penetrating this surface of plausible courtesy.

That these communications are more respectful and apparently cordial than those which Yeh was in the habit of addressing to my predecessor is true, but the substance of them is precisely the same—refusal to receive me and a refusal to treat. I have little doubt that his tone to the belligerent plenipotentiaries is scarcely less courteous and deferential. Friends and enemies are alike refused, and, if there be now any difference, I do not doubt that the moment the pressure is removed he would resume the tone which was so offensive to my predecessors. I have not answered the last letter, seeing no good in continuing the correspondence, and taking for granted that the crisis at Canton is near at hand. * * * * * *

I have the honor to be, sir, your obedient, humble servant,

WILLIAM B. REED.

Hon. LEWIS CASS,

Secretary of State for the United States, Washington.

[No. 39—Inclosure 1 a.]

Commissioner Yeh to Mr. Reed.

DECEMBER 8, 1857.

YEH, Imperial Commisssioner, Governor General of the Two Kwang, a Baron of the Empire, &c., &c., hereby replies upon business:

On the 7th instant I received your excellency's communication of the 28th ultimo, in which it is stated that, on the 16th of November, you had sent a dispatch to Canton, and that thirteen days had already elapsed without an answer being received. To this I may reply that your dispatch of the 16th of November came to hand on the 23d, and that I sent a reply on the 24th through the subprefect of Macao, whose duty it was to forward it to its address; and that in due course that officer had reported to me that it came to hand at 5 o'clock, p. m., on the 27th, and had been straightway sent to its destination. I am quite unable to explain why it had not been received by you on the 28th, though I think that you must have got it before this time; and you will surely then have learned that it was not because I did not wish to have an interview that I declined to answer your dispatch.

It is observed in the dispatch before me that the citizens of the United States have suffered many wrongs from the rulers and people of China, which have already been made known in communications from your predecessors; but allow me to observe, on the other hand, that since the merchants and citizens of the United States have come to China to trade they have ever been treated with courtesy and kindness, and therefore can have no wrongs to redress. It may be that the former minister, Parker, has given you to understand that some things had happened at Canton which were not agreeable; but he has been recalled, and I am of opinion that your excellency, being clear-headed, and acquainted with the requirements of reason, will not act as he did.

For this purpose I reply, at the same time hoping that you are in the enjoyment of every blessing.

His Excellency, WILLIAM B. REED,

Envoy Extraordinary and Minister Plenipotentiary of the United States to China.

Translated by S. W. Williams.

[No. 39.—Inclosure 1 b.]

Commissioner Yeh to Mr. Reed.

DECEMBER, 18, 1857.

YEH, Imperial Commissioner, Governor General of the Two Kwang, a Baron of the Empire, &c., &c., hereby replies on business:

On the 15th instant I received your excellency's communication of the 12th. In it you remark: "I the more regret that you are unable to meet me, for I am sure a personal interview, in which we could interchange opinions," &c. From this it is plainly to be perceived that your excellency well understands the position of things, and the heartfelt regrets which you express have greatly tranquillized my feelings. In my previous reply there was not a word, not a sentence, which did not express my real wishes and thoughts; and I have not changed since in any respect, nor was this professed friendliness on my part mere talk. Why, then, do you put so much stress on a transient interview in order to render more certain the friendly feelings therein expressed? For instance, two persons who have some knowledge of each other may really entertain a hearty reciprocal liking, and look upon a letter from each other as good as a personal interview; while, if their friendliness is all pretense and they have no real hearty regard, though they should see each other constantly, what avails it if their feelings are estranged as they look one another in the face? Do not, therefore, regard it as doggedness on my part if I decline to have a meeting.

You say, again, in your communication: "Your excellency refers me to the interview which my predecessor, Mr. Davis, had with your excellency's predecessor, Seu, in 1848. This brings to my mind the fact that since that time, now nearly ten years, no representative of the United States has had the benefit of personal intercourse at Canton with a commissioner charged with the superintendence of the concerns of foreign nations in China, or with a governor general of the Liang Kwang. In that interval there has been much unpleasant correspondence, and difficulties have arisen," &c. Now, during the last ten years, there have been no difficulties between our two countries, nor anything which has been unpleasant and jarring, calculated to excite any ill will. The dispatches of your predecessor, Parker, sometimes had remarks in them which were not agreeable and courteous, but I never attached much importance to them in my mind. I heard, however, that the Americans have rather come to the conclusion among themselves that he made a good deal out of little; and now he has been recalled. I am well aware, consequently, that your country fully understands public courtesy, and therefore did not wait for me to speak out more plainly on the subject. Since your excellency arrived in Kwangtung, several communications have passed between us, which have disclosed our hearts to each other and made us better acquainted even than a personal interview would have done.

In the present dispatch you also say: "I decline to inclose the State letter, for it is too important to be trusted to ordinary conveyances," &c. Now the truth is, that all the orders and rescripts of his imperial majesty are sent over the hills and rivers of China in this way; and, if a dispatch be intrusted to any officer to be personally delivered, he must undergo the drudgery and toil of travel to effect it; everything which I myself receive from his majesty comes by the common post, and hitherto there has been no occasion requiring a special messenger to be dispatched. The correspondence between our two countries comes under the same rules; and I request that you will send what you may have in the same way, and it shall be attended to.

Again you observe: "The treaty of 1844 has never been broken by the United States, and the two countries have never revised or renewed it," &c. On this point I have already remarked in full in a previous reply. Our two countries are like two good friends; and, during the period since making the treaty, have not altered, but are still, in every respect, on the best of terms. Let your excellency, therefore, still continue to act according to the provisions of that compact, and it will most plainly evince the harmony between two friendly nations; nor will I obstinately interfere or obstruct that good feeling.

For these reasons I send this reply, at the same time adding the hope that your excellency's happiness will continually increase.

His Excellency W. B. REED,
Envoy Extraordinary and Minister Plenipotentiary of the United States, in China.

Translated by S. W. Williams.

Mr. Reed to Mr. Cass.

No. 40.] LEGATION OF THE UNITED STATES,
Minnesota, Hong Kong harbor, December 30, 1857.

SIR: I send the latest intelligence from the city of Canton, for which I am indebted to the kindness of Captain Edgell, R. N., the naval commander at this anchorage, and of the Belgian consul. I send extracts from their notes to me this moment received.

Captain Edgell says: "Gough's fort and magazine were taken at 5 o'clock yesterday, the city still burning in many places. By evening all must have been in our possession, as its defenses had fallen. We have lost Captain Bate, one of our best surveying officers. The gunboat has only brought Lord Elgin's dispatches. The casualties on Gough's hill we do not know. I hope not many."

My other informant writes: "The forts are all taken. The Kwan-yin hill, inside the city, and the east wall are in our possession. The city was on fire, but it was expected that all fighting would be over before night. The loss has not been severe in numbers, but Captain Bate's death will be much regretted. His death was caused by a gingall shot. He was taken by surprise when reconnoitering. The thirty-ninth regiment lost four men and an officer, (Captain Hackett,) the latter killed when conveying a dispatch or order. The French have one officer killed. The Chinese fired on the French gun-boats from the city, but the fire was soon silenced. The punishment the Chinese are getting is severe, but I fancy most of the quietly disposed have left the place. The admiral's dispatches are down, but the Kestrel is coming with supplementary dispatches, and Captain Bate's body.

The Kwanyin hill referred to in this letter is a hill within the wall, in the northeast corner of the city, and completely commanding it. There is great reason to believe that the city may be destroyed by fire.

I am glad of the opportunity of sending this late intelligence.

I have the honor to be, sir, your obedient servant,

WILLIAM B. REED.

Hon. LEWIS CASS,
Secretary of State for the United States, &c., &c., &c.

Mr. Reed to Mr. Cass.

No. 1.] UNITED STATES LEGATION TO CHINA,
Macao, January 13, 1858.

SIR: The subject of the employment of American ships for the transportation of Chinese laborers or coolies to the Island of Cuba demands your early attention. It has been brought to mind by the accompanying letters from the acting consul of the United States at Batavia, and the master of a vessel engaged in the trade, to which, for particulars, I refer you.

They relate to the case of the Kate Hooper, an American vessel belonging to Baltimore, and commanded by John J. Jackson, which sailed from this port on the 14th of October, 1857, bound to Havana, with six hundred and fifty coolies on board. The registered tonnage of the ship was 1,488 $\frac{76}{95}$ tons.

Thus freighted, she was next heard of at Angier in distress. Her master reported the cause of trouble to be, that the sight of the land around Gaspar Straits excited these poor creatures to such a degree that they rose in mutiny. They were driven below, and kept there. This, it will be recollected, was about three degrees south of the equator. They attempted to burst the hatches, and set fire to the ship below; and the resistance was only quelled after five had been killed, several wounded, and twenty of the others put in close confinement. What punishment was inflicted on these prisoners I do not know; but a rumor has reached this legation that some of them were summarily executed. The American consul at Batavia furnished the requisite assistance to the vessel, with which, I presume, she proceeded on her voyage. My correspondence with the consul is annexed. (Inclosures 1 a, c.)

This is one case of recent occurrence; another, though not so well authenticated, is that of the American ship Challenge, which sailed from Swatow for Havana with coolies. There is a credited rumor here that this ship put into Singapore in distress, being infected with disease, and having lost many passengers. Swatow, as you are aware, is a port about one hundred miles southwest from Amoy, and one not recognized by treaty. A large trade in opium and coolies is there carried on, with the seeming acquiescence of everybody engaged in trade; and the shipping lists belonging to it are regularly published in the Hong Kong newspapers.

Such, I regret to believe, is the almost uniform fate of vessels thus employed, sickness, mutiny, and death in some form of misery, and the number of laborers which reaches the place of destination though large is, after all, but a remnant. It must be remembered too, that the voyages are rarely less than four months with every extreme of temperature and every variety of exposure. The occurrence of these cases has induced me to regard this trade with new and painful interests, and to endeavor to bring it at once, with reference to some early and decisive action, to the attention of the President. This has been already done by my predecessor in different forms.

In March, 1853, (Official No. 9, printed H. R. Doc., page 78,) Mr. Marshall wrote to the Secretary of State fully on the subject, discussing it, however, mainly in relation to the proposed emigration of free laborers to the British West India Islands, and the possible influence on the southern United States. The remedy he suggested was one which, I confess, though I express the opinion with some diffidence, does not seem to be consonant with law, that "if the President desired to manifest the disinclination of the United States to the progress of this emigration, he should issue an order to the American consuls to refuse clearance to any ship under American papers or colors, carrying coolies from China." I do not see how this can be done while the act of Congress providing the terms on which clearances are to be given is in force. Mr. Parker, in 1856, essayed a new mode of prevention by issuing a circular or proclamation denunciatory of the trade as inhuman and unlawful. I entirely agree in the earnest disapproval he expressed. Mr. Parker's proclamation, unfortified by any sanction or penalty, had a good influence in apparently dissuading one American shipper and firm from continuing longer in the trade.

With these ineffectual precedents to enlighten me, I have been constrained to act. I do not consider myself authorized to direct consuls to withhold clearances when the local authorities furnish the requisite certificates. At Swatow, being an illegal port, there is no consul, no clearance, no semblance of law. It is said there is a Spanish consular agent there, an American by birth; his special duty being to supervise this very traffic.

I have no great taste for proclamations, and no confidence that any opinions in this form, however strongly expressed, would deter traders from a course that promoted their interest. I felt, and still feel, some uncertainty as to the application of existing laws, but on full consideration, I thought it best to attempt to arrest this traffic by a warning, if not threat, which it will be for the government at home to carry it into effect.

The fourth section of the act of Congress, of 20th April, 1818, provides:

"SEC. 4. That if any citizen or citizens of the United States, or other persons resident within the jurisdiction of the same, shall, from and after the passage of this act, take on board, receive, or transport from any of the coasts or kingdoms of Africa, or *from any other foreign kingdom, place, or country*, or from sea, any negro or mulatto *or person of color*, not being an inhabitant, nor held to service by the laws of either of the States or Territories of the United States, in any ship, vessel, boat, or other water-craft, for the purpose of holding, selling, *or otherwise disposing of such person* as a slave, *or to be held to service or labor*, or be aiding or abetting therein, every such person or persons so offending, shall, on conviction, by due course of law, severally forfeit and pay a sum not exceeding five thousand, nor less than one thousand dollars, one moiety to the use of the United States, and the other to the use of the person or persons who shall sue for such forfeiture, and prosecute the same to effect; and moreover, shall suffer imprisonment for a term not exceeding seven years nor less than three years; and every ship or vessel, boat or other water-craft, on which such negro, mulatto, or person of color, shall have been taken on board, received, or transported, as aforesaid, her tackle, apparel, and furniture and the goods and effects which shall be found on board the same, or shall have been imported therein in the same voyage, shall be forfeited, one moiety to the use of the United States, and the other to the use of the person or persons who shall sue for, and prosecute the same to effect; and every such ship or vessel shall be liable to be seized, prosecuted, and condemned, in any court of the United States, having competent jurisdiction."

In determining the application of the laws—designed, I am aware for a different evil—two questions only arise: is the Chinese cooly a person of color as distinguished from negro or mulatto? and is the contract under which he agrees to go, goes, and is landed in Cuba, a disposal of him to be held to service or labor?

In the act of 1818 the words "person of color" is used as distinguished from negro or mulatto. In the act of 15th May, 1820, the words "person of color" are omitted. If, instead of the question arising on the modified color of the Chinese, it arose on a cargo of the black sepoys one meets daily in the streets of Hong Kong, or the Malays and Javanese of the Archipelago, there could be little doubt about it. They would be clearly within the act of Congress. The Chinese cooly is, to the sense at least, a person of color.

As to the tenure of labor or service for which these poor people are destined there is still less question. I am not able at this time to furnish you with the contract by which they are held; but accompanying this dispatch you will find the Spanish ordinance under which they are shipped, to which I desire to direct your especial attention. The word by which the cooly is described in this ordinance is equivalent to "laborer" in English, or it may mean "imported laborer." It does not mean "free day laborer," for which another word is used, or slave. They are imported under a contract for a term of years. They are the subject of transfer, with no volition of their own, and no provision is made for return to their native country. To this time none have returned.

All these elements combine to make the Chinese cooly a man of color, to be disposed of to be held to service in Cuba. At all events, I have thought myself authorized to try to arrest this pernicious traffic by a warning that all parties concerned, especially the owners and masters, may expose themselves to the penalties of the law. With this view, in the case of the ship Flora Temple, now in these roads, awaiting a cargo of coolies for Havana, and of the Wandering Jew, said to be loading at Shanghai, I directed (inclosures 2, 5 a) the consuls to advise the Spanish authorities and the masters of the ships that the traffic is, in my judgment, contrary to the laws of the United States. In the case of the ships at Shanghai I am enabled to go further, and by the intervention of the Chinese authorities, probably prevent the clearance of the ship. In that of the Flora Temple the master feels himself bound by the orders of his owners to ship the coolies. He sailed many months ago on a trading voyage to San Francisco, and it was on his arrival there, as I learn, that he found himself implicated in this traffic, the discredit of which attaches to his owners. The answer of the Spanish consul general on the subject is a peremptory refusal. He receives a fee of five dollars for each cooly shipped. My power of intervention here is thus exhausted. The correspondence on this subject is annexed. (Inclosures 5 a to 5 d.)

I have thus considered the trade only in its relations to the laws of the United States. There can be no doubt that it is entirely repugnant to the laws of China, and for the evidence of this I beg to refer you to the decrees and proclamations of the local authorities of this province communicated to the department by my predecessor, Mr. Parker, in 1856–57.

On the 30th of November, the intendant at Shanghai issued a notification renewing a prohibition at that port, a copy of which, as published in the "North China Herald" of the 12th of December, I now forward, (inclosure 6,) remarking incidentally that the spirit which animates this document is in every way creditable, and ought to command the sympathy and coöperation of those to whom it is addressed. I fear, however, such is the indurating influence of illegal traffic in its various forms that it will be of no avail.

Should the interpretation which I have endeavored to put upon the act of Congress not be sustained, and the prohibitions of the Chinese authorities be disregarded, then I hope the subject will attract the immediate attention of the President and Congress, so that, if they agree with me in my opinion of this trade, effective legislation may be adopted. The remedy might be to extend the act of 1818 expressly to the case of Chinese coolies; or, if still more stringent measures are thought expedient, to apply the provisions of the act of March 3, 1819, to the trade, and enable the President to authorize the seizure of cooly vessels at sea and, on capture here, the restoration of the Chinese to their native country. The American vessels engaged in this trade are first-class clipper ships, which must anchor in deep water and cannot evade cruisers. The Flora Temple, at this moment in my sight in the Macao Roads, is within musket shot of the Minnesota, and there, her living cargo will be shipped. I further suggest that either our consul general at Havana, or some special agent be directed to examine and report on the statistics of this traffic, and the actual condition of the laborer in Cuba. The former cannot, with accuracy, be collected here, at least by our consular agents, especially the Swatow trade.

In making these suggestions, I have assumed that the government at home will agree with me in deeming the trade a mischievous one. My duty is done in bringing it to their attention and in expressing my own opinion.

The whole subject of Chinese emigration is too wide and perplexing to be discussed now, and the impressions which the observation and reflection of a few months on what is so intricate and peculiar as the state of society here in any of its relations are worth but little.

They seem, however, I am bound to add, of quite as much value as the judgments of those who have watched longer and studied more thoroughly. No two men in China agree upon any one thing. No generalization is safe—for to one hundred examples proving any result or authorizing any opinion are opposed, a hundred and one that prove the contrary. So of this emigration procees. Starving multitudes; women and female children for sale to save them from destitution; land tilled, if not at its utmost and most minute capacity at least as far as the law, which guards peaceful labor, permits the singular and active industry of this people; their frugality and wonderful economy, by which they so easily subsist; the crying want of labor elsewhere; the cost of a Chinese field laborer, if these contracts be regarded as purchases, being less than one fifth of one in Cuba or the southern States. All these might seem to point to the exhuberance of population, and the transfer of its surplus, as a great means of social relief and benefit to the world at large. But I confess that I am unable yet to contemplate these remote and speculative results. I see in its origin, the violation of the local law and the defiance of treaty obligation; in the process, wretchedness, disease, and death; and, in the result, as far as it is yet developed, a new and illegitimate slavery, the practical enslavement of a distant and most peculiar race. It is in this view a dishonest invigoration of West India slavery.

If, on the other hand, the Chinese are to be regarded as free laborers in Cuba—and it is alleged there are now more than thirty thousand in the island, with every prospect of an enormous increase, for, owing to the fall in freights, and the political disturbances in this country, a great impulse has been given to the trade—then another question will, I am sure, suggest itself to your mind and that of the President; how far the general interests of the United States are to be promoted by this new infusion of strength into the decaying institutions of colonial Spanish America. One of the peculiarities of the trade is that no females accompany the cooly emigrant, and one of two consequences must ensue, either that they will amalgamate with the negro race, and thus increase the actual slave population, or maintain a separate existence, their numbers only to be recruited by new arrivals. The latter is at present the most probable, and then we may look, at no very remote period, to the same result which has occurred at Luzon, in Java, and in Borneo, a vast aggregation of troublesome populace, oppression to them, sanguinary resentment ending probably in bloody massacre, the victims being the party which happen to be weakest.

In 1838, the Dutch government prohibited the immigration of Chinese to Java. They are now shipping them to Surinam. The colonial authorities have done the same thing at Luzon, and the trade is divested to Cuba, so that the spread of the Chinese population in the eastern seas, which seems to be a natural process, is to be arrested, and then forced transportation to the slave colonies of the west is to be substituted.

With reference to the actual condition of the Chinese population in Cuba, and the danger their presence may involve, I beg to call your attention to the following extract from a report made by the British consul general to the foreign office in 1855, which I find in the archives of this legation, communicated to Mr. Parker by Sir John Bowring:

"These laborers come engaged for eight years, so that the contracts of those imported in the year 1847 have expired, but I have not heard that any of them have applied to be sent back to China. No doubt a great number of them have died, so that probably not more than half of those who arrived that year are surviving, and as most of them have risen to posts of trust and confidence upon the estates, I am of opinion that in general they have bettered their condition by coming here, but this opinion I would restrict to those of the Chinese who first were brought over. They are too numerous now to obtain preferments, and as they are treated with very little more consideration than the slaves, I consider that their position now and henceforth, as regards further importations, is and will be exceedingly miserable.

"The estimation in which they are held by the planters is as varied as are the characters of their masters. Upon some estates they are preferred to the Africans, upon others they are not at all prized. They are, however, acknowledged to be superior to the negro in intelligence, but in many instances they have displayed a malicious and vindictive disposition, and have had recourse to incendiarism of the works and cornfields out of revenge for punishment, or what they may have considered ill-treatment of other kinds.

"Their importation has been found to be a profitable speculation hitherto, and therefore it is likely to be continued for some time longer, but I doubt, if their numbers are much increased, that their superiority of intelligence will give rise to claim on the part of the government, the more so as it will hardly be possible to continue to subject them to the severe dominion which is exercised over them by their masters, hardly differing from that which is enforced upon the slaves with whom they are set to work. Some of their superiority of intellect and intelligence will unavoidably pass to their African co-laborers, and if discontent should arise, which may reasonably be anticipated, the consequence would be very serious.

"I understand the expenses attending the engaging and bringing over of these coolies amounts to about $85, and the price paid for transfer of them under the contracts is about $170, and $12 besides, as reimbursements for two suits of clothing, which are furnished to each previous to their sailing from China."

Viewing it in any light as a matter of humanity and policy, I deem it my duty to condense this traffic, and to beg the early attention of the government to its repression, so far at least as it is conducted in American vessels. The best proof as to their complicity can be obtained at Havana.

The answer from the consul at Shanghai shall be forwarded as soon as it is received. I desire to call your attention to the fact that the consulship at Sanghai is vacant, it being understood here that Mr. Murphy does not mean to return. The acting consul is a very young man. I must be excused for renewing the expression of my great solicitude that the vacant consulships in China should be filled by capable men. This one at Shanghai is especially important. If I may indicate a preference as to the professional qualifications of individuals to be named, I have no doubt that a clear-headed lawyer, one unconnected with trade, or even missionary enterprise, would be the best. The emoluments of the post and its growing importance in the estimation of the community ought to enable the President to command a high order of ability and character. The English and French consular corps in this country are very efficient. Ours, I regret to say, is not.

I have the honor to be, sir, your obedient servant,

WILLIAM B. REED.

Hon. LEWIS CASS,
Secretary of State.

P. S.—January, 14. Since writing this dispatch I have received the accompanying documents from the acting consul at Shanghai in relation to the Wandering Jew. The transport of Chinese from Shanghai to Amoy is of course entirely legal. (Inclosure 7.)

I also inclose a copy of the Hong Kong Government Gazette of the 9th instant, containing a return of what are described as emigrant ships cleared from this colony in 1857. (Inclosure 8.)

W. B. R.

Index to Dispatch No. 1, January 13, 1858.

Exhibit.	From—	To—	Subject-matter.	Date.
1 *a*	H. Anthon, jr.	W. B. Reed	Requests advice as to assisting American ships when laden with coolies	Nov. 20, 1857.
1 *b*	John J. Jackson	H. Anthon, jr.	Desires additional crew to enable him to go on	Nov 13, 1857.
1 *c*	W. B. Reed	H. Anthon, jr.	Cannot legally withhold assistance to such ships	Dec. 14, 1857.
2	W. B. Reed	W. Knapp, jr.	Wishes information of "Wandering Jew" loading at Shanghai with coolies	Dec. 28, 1857.
3 *a*	W. B. Reed	S. B. Rawle	Are consular attestations required for coolies shipped to Havana, or elsewhere?	Dec. 7, 1857.
3 *b*	W. A. Macy, for S B. Rawle.	W. B. Reed	None required ; no American ship with coolies has ever applied for a consular certificate.	Dec. 18, 1857.
4 *a*	J. Keenan	W. B. Reed	Incloses copy of Spanish decree about coolies	Dec. 21, 1857.
4 *b*	L. Gutierres	J. Keenan	Furnishes copy of Spanish decree, March 22, 1854. (Translation affixed.)	Dec. 17, 1857.
5 *a*	W. B. Reed	S. B. Rawle	Inform Spanish consul of illegality in cooly trade in American ships, and notify American captains of the penalty.	Jan. 5, 1858.
5 *b*	W. A. Macy, for S. B. Rawle.	W. B. Reed	Incloses replies from Spanish consuls ; inefficiency of prohibitions	Jan. 8, 1858.
5 *c*	N. Cariete	W. A. Macy	Vindicate his allowing coolies in American ships	Jan. 7, 1858.
5 *d*	J. M. Cole	W. A. Macy	Owners require him to carry coolies to Havana	Jan. 7, 1858.
6			Proclamation of See at Shanghai against shipping Chinese to foreign ports	Nov. 30, 1857.
7	F. Jenkins	W. B. Reed	Forwarding correspondence relating to ship "Wandering Jew" with Tautai	Jan. 6, 1858.
8			Hong Kong Government Gazette, containing statement of Chinese emigration	Jan. 9, 1858.

Exhibit 1 *a.*

UNITED STATES CONSULATE,
Batavia, November 20, 1857.

SIR: I inclose you copy of a letter from John J. Jackson, master of the American ship Kate Hooper, of Baltimore, bound from Macao for Havana with some 650 Chinese coolies on board. The twelve men that he required have been sent to Anjier, and I trust that by this time he is out of difficulty.

My object in addressing you is to ask if you can inform me as to the present opinion of our government upon the, as it is called, "cooly trade." Some three years since your predecessor issued a proclamation upon the subject. Unfortunately, I cannot obtain a copy of it at this time, but if I recollect aright, Dr. Parker denounced the trade in no measured terms; and, if I am not very much mistaken, declared that the United States government regarded it as very little different from the traffic in slaves.

I should feel obliged if you would cause a copy of this proclamation to be sent to me, and should it still be in force, would you please inform me how far, in your opinion, a consular officer of the United States can afford assistance to a vessel under circumstances similar to those of the case of the Kate Hooper, and render such aid officially as shall tend to the prosecution of the voyage.

The Harry of the West arrived here a few days since, all hands sick with fever contracted at Mew Bay, and I regret to say that two of the crew have since died.

I have the honor to be, sir, very respectfully, your obedient servant,

HENRY ANTHON, JR.,
Vice Consul United States of America.

His Excellency the Hon. WILLIAM B. REED,
United States Commissioner to China.

Exhibit 1 *b.*

ANJIER, *November* 13, 1857.

DEAR SIR: The ship Kate Hooper, of Baltimore, under my command, arrived here last night in distress. I sailed from Macao on the 16th ultimo with 650 Chinese passengers for Havana.

As the people came on board of their own free will, and as I told them twice publicly that any man who did not come willingly should not be taken aboard, I anticipated no more trouble than with any other passengers.

They have been treated as well as possible, fed well, and allowed much more liberty than is usual, and everything went along comfortably, with one slight exception, until about six days ago, when seeing the land around Gaspar straits excited them to such a degree that they arose en masse to take the ship.

With difficulty we managed to get them below, but when there they began to pull down the bunks and set fire to the ship below, at the same time making a furious attack on the hatches.

The same operation was repeated next day, and in repelling this assault there were five of them killed and several wounded. Since that time, I have succeeded in arresting about twenty of the ringleaders, and have them confined. The balance of the coolies are confined between decks.

As these people are all joined together to take the ship, the greatest vigilance has been necessary, and my people are entirely fagged out. Even now, lying here, we are obliged to be constantly under arms and on guard.

I applied last night to the harbor master here for a guard of soldiers, but he refused to render me any assistance at all, saying that you were the only person that could help me.

I cannot go to sea without at least a dozen more men, and, as there are none here, this is to request you to send them to me if you can.

I have refused absolutely to leave this port with the ship in her present condition, and, unless you can do something for me, I am rendered powerless to do anything for myself.

Let me have your advice as soon as possible. If you can send me the men, I will remit you the expenses immediately. My health is very bad, and I am hardly able to leave my bed, so that I again request that you will give me your advice as soon as possible; and, in the meanwhile, I remain yours, respectfully,

JOHN J. JACKSON.

The AMERICAN CONSUL AT BATAVIA.

Exhibit 1 *c.*

UNITED STATES LEGATION TO CHINA,
On board the Minnesota, Hong Kong, Dec. 4, 1857.

SIR: I have the honor to receive your letter of November 20, inclosing a letter to you from John J. Jackson, master of the American ship Kate Hooper, lying at Anjier.

The subject to which you refer is one of painful interest and some perplexity, and I scarcely know what with precision to say about it. The written law does not seem to be against it, but the spirit of all law which is meant to protect humanity is. The opinion of the government of the United States is adverse to it; and if that be of any value to you, my own judgment and instincts condemn it. But I can do little else than give expression to this opinion. I have but one copy of Mr. Parker's proclamation, and can not spare it, nor do I advise its resuscitation, for though entirely just in sentiment, I do not think proclaimed sentiments unenforced by practical penalties do much good. I am trying to devise some mode by which I can stop at the clearing ports this vile traffic, which is contrary to the laws of China. In order to do so, I shall need precise statements of facts, and if you can furnish me with one in connection with the Kate Hooper I shall be glad. The papers here make out the case worse than you do, bad as your report is. Let me have the truth. I observe in Captain Jackson's letter he says: "*Everything went along comfortably with one slight exception, till*" &c. Can you ascertain what this exception was. It may have been something far more aggravating than the sight of the land around Gaspar? I do not doubt some of these cooly captains have tempers congenial to their trade, though in this instance, Captain Jackson may have done no wrong.

I do not think you would, as consul, be authorized to withhold assistance from a vessel in distress, trading as this vessel was. Everything as to the flag and the papers was, I doubt not, regular. So soon as I get full information, I shall write to the government on the subject.

I am sorry to hear of the ill luck of the Harry of the West. I hope the captain, who seemed a very worthy man, has recovered.

I shall be happy to hear from you at all times on matters connected with public or private affairs, and am, dear sir, truly and respectfully yours,

WILLIAM B. REED.

H. ANTHON, Jr.,
United States Acting Consul at Batavia.

Exhibit 2.

UNITED STATES LEGATION TO CHINA,
Minnesota, December 28, 1857.

SIR: Information has reached this legation that an American ship called The Wandering Jew, is now loading or about to load at Shanghai with coolies for the Island of Cuba. The reputed Spanish agent is a person named Lorenzo Soto.

I desire to interpose to the full extent of my power to arrest this traffic, which is condemned by the laws of China, and being so condemned, is within the prohibition of the treaty with the United States.

I direct you, therefore, at once to ascertain the fact as to the shipment of coolies in this ship, and if you are satisfied of this, to inform the Chinese authorities. It will be for them then to determine whether they will give you the necessary papers for the clearance of the ship.

Before taking this step, I desire you to see the master, or if they be American citizens, the consignees of this ship, and advise them of the views which the government of the United States have on this subject. If they be good citizens, and are desirous to avoid exposure at home, this intimation may suffice.

If, however, it does not, then I direct you to say to the master of the ship, if he is a citizen or resident of the United States, that in case he takes on board his vessel at Shanghai, or any other port of China, Chinese for the purpose of transporting them to the Island of Cuba, there to be held to service or labor, I shall feel it my duty to recommend to the government at home, immediately on his arrival in the

United States, to institute a prosecution for a violation of the act of Congress in such case made.

I beg your immediate attention to this, and request you to report to me at once on the subject.

In relation to the homicide of Fitzgerald, by persons supposed to be connected with the brig Mondego, in August last, the governor of Macao has informed this legation that the two sailors arrested for that crime were tried by court martial on board the ship, and found guilty of riot on shore, but no proof was brought sufficient to convict them of the homicide. One was condemned to five years, the other to three years' transportation to Mozambique, part of them in close confinement.

I remain, respectfully yours,

WILLIAM B. REED.

WILLIAM KNAPP Jr., Esq.,
Vice-Consul, Shanghai.

Exhibit 3 *a.*

LEGATION OF THE UNITED STATES,
December 7, 1857.

SIR: I see a statement in the public papers that there is an ordinance of the Spanish government requiring that to all contracts for the shipment of Chinese laborers, commonly called "coolies" there must be the attestation of the consul at the port of clearance.

Do me the favor to say if there is such a provision of law known to you, and whether and how often you have been called on to comply with it.

Yours, respectfully,

WILLIAM B. REED,

S. B. RAWLE, Esq.,
United States Consul, Macao.

Exhibit 3 *b.*

CONSULATE OF THE UNITED STATES,
Macao, December 18, 1857.

SIR: I have the honor to acknowledge the receipt, on the 17th instant, of your dispatch of the 7th instant to Mr. Rawle, requesting some information respecting the shipment of coolies from this port.

I have the honor to state on his behalf, that it is not known to him that a certificate is required from this consulate when such coolies are carried in an American vessel. But it has been stated that each of the coolies must have a passport from the Spanish consul residing here, and the captain a certificate of compliance with the Spanish regulations.

No American vessel carrying coolies has ever applied for a consular certificate of any description. The vessels have loaded this year for the Havana with these Chinese laborers, and in the absence of any authority to restrain them, they have been simply warned of the consequences as laid down in the decree of Dr. Parker on this subject, and required to furnish evidence that they were not violating the general passenger act. I personally visited the last vessel which sailed from this port, and saw that her accommodations were at least tolerable, although for a voyage of such length, and in the tropics during most of its continuance, the number seemed too great.

I trust some steps may be taken to restrain American vessels from engaging in the business hereafter.

I have the honor to remain, sir, your obedient servant,

WILLIAM A. MACY,
Deputy Consul.

His Excellency WILLIAM B. REED, Esq.,
United States Minister, &c., &c.

Exhibit 4 *a.*

UNITED STATES CONSULATE,
Hong Kong, December 21, 1857.

SIR: Inclosed I send you a copy of the ordinance of the Spanish government in relation to shipment of Chinese laborers for Spanish ports before the consulate at the port of clearance.

You will observe that the attestation is to be made before the Spanish consul, therefore I have never been called upon to perform any such duty. I have, however, at the request of the harbor master of this port, visited American cooly ships with that officer, both inside and outside of the harbor, in order to see that the proper number had been shipped in accordance with their contracts, and the proper arrangements made for them.

My presence upon such occasions was requested rather in order to facilitate the operations of the functionaries on board.

I am, sir, very respectfully,

JAMES KEENAN,
United States Consul.

His Excellency WILLIAM B. REED,
Envoy Extraordinary, &c., &c.

Exhibit 4 *b.*

[Translation.]

CONSULATE OF SPAIN,
Hong Kong, December 17, 1857.

SIR: I shall have much pleasure in furnishing you with a copy of the royal ordinance of colonization of the 22d March, 1854, if you will send to this office a person to make it, as my engagements, and the bad state of my health do not permit me to do so.

The contractors who ship laborers in American vessels for the Havana, observe the ordinance strictly.

L. GUTIERRES.

The CONSUL OF THE UNITED STATES OF AMERICA.

CHAPTER I.

On the introduction of laborers.

ARTICLE. 1. Parties wishing, for their own emolument, to introduce into the Island of Cuba, laborers from Spain, China, or Yucatan, can do so from this date, and during a space of two years, by subjecting themselves to the conditions laid down in this ordinance.

ART. 2. The party about to import the aforesaid laborers shall be obliged to obtain previously the permit of the government, and to solicit this he shall present a certificate or document showing that the vessel destined for the conveyance is in a state to undertake the proposed voyage.

This certificate or document shall be issued if the vessel be anchored in a foreign port, by the Spanish consul there, and if in a Spanish port, by the corresponding naval officer.

ART. 3. None of the aforesaid permits shall be issued unless the person to whom leave is granted binds himself to introduce the number of women which the government shall deem proper, taking into consideration the number of males to be imported in each expedition, their nation, and divers circumstances.

For the women the importers shall pay no fees for passage.

ART. 4. The government, in granting the permit mentioned in the preceding articles, shall have the power to exact from the importers any further conditions which it may deem fit, considering, however, the number, nation, and other circumstances of the laborers about to be introduced.

ART. 5. The contracts between the importers and the laborers shall be written in the language of the latter, and shall be viséed by the consul of her Majesty, if made in foreign countries, or by the governor of the province if agreed to on Spanish territory.

ART. 6. These contracts shall be bound to contain the following circumstances:

1. The age and sex of the laborer, and the country of which he is a native.
2. The time during which he is to remain bound.
3. The wages, and the kind, quantity, and quality of the food and clothing which he is to receive.
4. The obligation of furnishing him medical aid during his illness.
5. Whether the wages of the laborer are to cease when he is ill through some cause which does not arise from his work, or which is independent of the will of his guardian.

6. The number of hours that the laborer pledges himself to work every day, declaring whether the guardian is to be empowered to increase by a corresponding diminution on other days.

7. The obligation of the laborer to indemnify his guardian for the hours of work which he has lost through his own fault.

8. The obligation of the same laborer to subject himself to the discipline of the workshop or establishment where he is to labor.

9. A clause expressed in these terms:

"I, M. N., agree to the stipulated wages, even though it appear that much more is gained by the free day laborers and slaves in the Island of Cuba, because I consider this difference compensated by the other advantages that my guardian is to afford me, and which are those belonging to this contract."

10. The signatures of the laborer, if he can sign his name, and that of the contractor.

ART. 7. The laborer shall receive, and keep always in his possession, a copy of his contract signed by the contractor.

ART. 8. If the laborers are Spaniards and minors, they cannot contract with the importers without the consent of their parents or guardians. If they are foreigners, and under 14 years of age, it will be necessary for them to introduce into their contract some person to whom they shall be bound.

ART 9. The importers of laborers shall not embark in any vessel more than one person for each registered ton in voyages from the ports of Spain, one person for each ton and a half in passages from the ports of China, and in the same proportion, taking into account the shorter distance, in those which are accomplished from Yucatan.

ART. 10. There shall furthermore be an obligation on the part of the importers:

1. To provide the vessels with water and healthy food in a quantity proportioned to the number of persons on board, and to the length of the voyage.

2. To adopt the necessary precautions for maintaining on the aforesaid vessels the cleanliness and ventilation indispensable for the health of the passengers.

3. To provide a physician and a medicine chest whenever the number embarked exceed one hundred.

4. To subject themselves, on their arrival at any port of the island, to the regulations of health and police in force there.

ART. 11. In order insure the observance of this regulation, it will not be allowed to land the laborers at any other than the port of Havana, except in case of shipwreck, or other unavoidable accidents which may oblige an arrival and landing in any other port.

ART. 12. Within the twenty-four hours following the arrival of the vessel or its admission to *free intercourse*, in case of search or quarantine, the importer shall present a list of the laborers whom he shipped, accompanied by their contracts, noting those who have died during the voyage, and the causes which brought on their death.

The governor captain general having examined these documents, and after taking the precautions which he thinks necessary for the prevention of all fraud, shall allow the disembarkation (of the laborers.)

ART. 13. The importers of laborers shall be allowed to transfer them to other *capitalists, men of property, and private persons,* under such conditions as they consider proper, always providing that the latter pledge themselves (are bound) to fulfill the contracts made with the said colonists, and to subject themselves to the regulations of this ordinance.

Those to whom the laborers have been transferred shall possess equal power under the same conditions. Those transfers of laborers shall be void which are accomplished by altering, without the express consent of the latter, the conditions of their primitive contracts.

ART. 14. The importers, as well as the immediate receivers of the laborers, shall render to the government the number they have transferred or received within twenty-four hours after the completion of the contract, specifying the number, sex, and age of the aforesaid laborers, the vessel in which they arrived, the conditions of the contract made with them, the kind of work for which they are intended, and the point where they are to reside.

The government shall then return to the receiver the contracts obtained from the importer relative to the laborers transferred, an entry of their contents having been made in the books which shall be kept for this purpose in the *public archives.*

ART. 15. The residence of laborers cannot be changed from one point of the island to another, unless the government is previously informed of it.

Faithful extract of the royal ordinance of the 22d of March, 1854.

L. GUTIERRES,
Spanish Consul.

Exhibit 5 *a.*

LEGATION OF THE UNITED STATES,
Macao, January 5, 1858.

SIR: Since the receipt of Mr. Macy's letter of the 18th ultimo, written on your behalf, my attention has been again called to the subject of the shipment in American vessels of Chinese laborers, commonly known as coolies, especially to the Island of Cuba.

Full consideration of the matter has satisfied me of the necessity of a resolute effort to arrest a traffic which in its inevitable abuses is repugnant to the instincts of humanity, in contravention of the laws of the Chinese government, and as clearly a violation of the well-settled policy of the government of the United States.

My immediate predecessor, as you are aware, felt it his duty to condemn this trade by a proclamation or circular, in the spirit of which I entirely sympathize. Mr. Marshall, in 1853, made it the subject of earnest remonstrance and of anxious correspondence with the government at home. Neither effort has been permanently successful in putting a stop to it; and learning, as I do, that the trade is in full vigor, not only in some of the northern ports of China, but that American vessels are now loading here for Havana especially, I feel it incumbent on me to try, by a still more precise effort, to prevent it.

How far the transfer of coolies from the Chinese territory to the Portuguese colony of Macao, and hence to an American vessel for transportation, is a violation of the laws of China and the treaty by the American shipper, it is not necessary now to decide.

So far as the citizens and authorities of the United States are concerned, the question of duty and responsibility may be disposed of more easily and precisely.

I am satisfied that the carrying of Chinese laborers (coolies) in American ships, from any foreign ports to any port foreign or domestic, there to be held to service, is prohibited by acts of Congress, and exposes the master to a heavy penalty, and the forfeiture of his vessel on its arrival in the United States, and this whether the laborers be taken to the United States or not.

This being so, there can be no question as to the duty of the United States officers in China, and I now point it out to you.

Understanding that there is an American vessel, (the Flora Temple,) commanded by an American master, now lying in the roads awaiting a cargo of coolies to be carried to Havana, I request you, on receipt of this letter, to address the Spanish consular authorities at this port, either personally or in writing, informing them of the views of this trade entertained by me as the chief diplomatic representative of the United States in China, and that I consider it expressly prohibited by law. I have every reason to hope, from the friendly relations of the government of her most Catholic Majesty to the United States, and of the personal high character of Mr. Cañete, the Spanish consul general, that this intimation will be sufficient to prevent any countenance or official sanction on his part to an illegal, and therefore prohibited trade.

I request you further, to call the attention of the master of the vessel to his responsibility, and to say to him, that if he, being an American citizen or resident of the United States, shall take on board, receive, or transport from this port, or any port in China or its dependencies, any Chinese coolie or laborer, for the purpose of disposing of such person as a slave, or *to be held to service or labor* in the United States or *elsewhere*, he will expose himself, on his arrival in the United States, to a prosecution for a violation of the act of Congress, with the penalty of fine and imprisonment, and the forfeiture of his vessel.

You will further inform him, that in the event of a disregard of such a premonition, given in a spirit of entire friendliness and fairness, I shall feel it to be my duty to inform the government of the facts, and to recommend a prosecution for so clear and deliberate a violation of law. I have no reason to doubt that such a recommendation will at once be regarded.

I desire you further to furnish me with such evidence in the form of consular certificate and affidavit of some competent person of the facts of the shipment in case it be persisted in. There will be abundant time for the authorities at home to anticipate the arrival of any such vessel in Cuba, and to procure complete evidence there, provided you communicate in season the fact of the departure hence.

You will, of course, understand that these directions are not confined to any particular case, but are meant to regulate your official conduct with reference to the prohibited trade generally. Copies of these directions will be sent to the consuls at the other ports.

I have to request that for the future enumeration be made of all coolies shipped in American vessels from this port, and forwarded to this legation. I shall be glad to have a statement of such as have already gone.

I have the honor to be, sir, your most obedient servant,

WILLIAM B. REED.

S. B. RAWLE, Esq.,
United States Consul, Macao.

Exhibit 5 *b.*

CONSULATE OF THE UNITED STATES,
Macao, January 8, 1858.

SIR: In reply to your dispatch of the 5th instant, to S. B. Rawle, Esq., consul of the United States for Macao, relative to the transportation of Chinese coolies in American vessels, from this port, I have the honor to say that your views, as expressed in the said dispatch, were immediately communicated to N. Carĭete, Esq., the Spanish consul general, and to Captain J. M. Cole, master of the ship Flora Temple. Replies have been received from each of these parties, which I have the honor to inclose herewith, (inclosures A and B.) As you will perceive, the remonstrances in both cases have proved quite ineffectual; and having exhausted the resources at present in our power, I do not see that there remains anything further to be done, until either the courts at home decide the question authoritatively, or until it shall please Congress to pass a definite act prohibiting or limiting this traffic, at once nefarious and dangerous. The difficulty of dealing with the matter here is greatly enhanced by the fact that the contracts for vessels are made in the United States, and the masters feel themselves quite unable to turn back after their arrival in so distant a port.

I have the honor to remain, sir, your obedient servant,

WILLIAM A. MACY,
Deputy Consul of the United States for Macao.

His Excellency WILLIAM B. REED, Esq.,
United States Minister, &c., &c.

Exhibit 5 *c.*

[Inclosure A.]

CONSULATE GENERAL OF SPAIN IN CHINA.
Macao, January 7, 1858.

MY DEAR SIR: I have received your communication of yesterday, in which you are pleased to inform me that his excellency William B.

Reed, Esq., minister plenipotentiary of the United States to China, has sent a dispatch to you relative to the transportation of Chinese laborers, in American vessels, to other countries, and especially to the Havana, in the Island of Cuba; requesting you, at the same time, to make me acquainted with his views on this business; for which purpose, you transmit to me two paragraphs of his excellency's dispatch.

Having learned the contents of these, and of the rest of your communication, I have the honor to state, in reply, that, until I receive new instructions from my government, I do not feel myself authorized to refuse my assistance and sanction to all acts which require them in the contract and embarkation of Chinese laborers in ships, no matter of what flag, bound for Spanish possessions; for, should I do so, I should act contrary to the provisions of the royal decree promulgated by my august sovereign, on the 22d of March, 1854, and should furthermore compromise the interest of those Spanish subjects and foreigners who are engaged in this business, which is allowable, just, and legal, seeing that it consists in a contract made spontaneously by one free man with another free man, the one offering his services, and the other accepting them, for a determined space of time and in consideration of a remuneration, and of certain conditions stipulated between them.

Were I to refuse to legalize the said acts, my government, on the one hand, would demand from me a strict account of my conduct; and on the other, the individuals whose interests I should have prejudiced would, with perfect justice, protest against me, holding me responsible for the losses and injuries occasioned by my illegal procedure. Both of these responsibilities it is my duty carefully to avoid.

While obliged here, in fulfillment of the duties of my office, to watch over Spanish interests, and to give them all the support and protection in my power, allow me, sir, to say that it does not belong to me to ascertain whether the American ship-owners and captains, in chartering their vessels, infringe the laws of their country or not. They must answer to their own government, in case of any infraction, and take upon themselves all the consequences thereof; but these must never recoil upon those Spaniards who, in good faith, have made a contract, as formal and as clear in every country in the world, as in the chartering of a ship. Besides, any refusal of mine to sanction the contracts of the laborers, and the other acts of the embarkation, would render this shipment without effect, as the agents of emigration would not venture to send the laborers without the requisite legal formalities prescribed by the above-mentioned decree.

I hope that you will consider as just and reasonable the reflections I have just made, and I flatter myself that I will meet with the like appreciation from the well-known ability and deep penetration of his excellency Mr. Reed.

Wishing you long life, I have the honor to be, &c.,

NICASIO CAÑETE Y MORAL,
Consul General of her most Catholic Majesty.

S. B. RAWLE, Esq.,
United States Consul, Macao.

Exhibit 5 *d.*

[Inclosure B.]

MACAO, *January* 7, 1858.

SIR: Your letter of the 6th instant is at hand, the contents of which are duly noted.

My instructions from the owners of the ship Flora Temple direct me to convey passengers from this port to Havana.

I see nothing to justify me in acting in disobedience to their orders.

I am, sir, very respectfully, yours,

JOHN M. COLE,
Master ship Flora Temple.

WILLIAM A. MACY, Esq.,
Deputy United States Consul.

Exhibit 6.

CIRCULAR.

BRITISH CONSULATE,
Shanghai, November 30, 1857.

At the request of his excellency the Taoutae, her Majesty's consul has to give publicity to the accompanying letter, having reference to the shipment of coolies.

FREDERICK HARVEY,
Vice-Consul.

The BRITISH COMMUNITY,
Shanghai.

SEE, Intendant of the Soo and Tae circuit, sends the following communication:

It having come to my knowledge that certain foreign merchants are about to collect Chinese subjects in large numbers, and, putting them on board a foreign vessel, send them to foreign places, I find on examination that these people are poor and ignorant, and for the sake of a few dollars readily bind themselves to go abroad, leaving their families to starve, and become a burden to all. Now, the government of China is compassionate and careful of its people, and its first duty is to see that the laws of Heaven are respected, and that the children should support their parents and the parents take care of the children. How can this be if the young are tempted to leave their homes and families? It is, indeed, contrary to the laws of Heaven and earth, and it is my duty, as the high local authority, to prevent this evil. It is accordingly proper that I should request you to inform your countrymen that by inducing the people to leave their country they are acting illegally, and in a manner not contemplated by the treaties under which they reside in China.

I have, therefore, to send you this communication, and have now to beg you will issue the necessary orders to your countrymen for their information, in order that they may act accordingly. This is most important; I trust no delay will take place. A necessary communication.

D. M. ROBERTSON, Esq.,
Her British Majesty's Consul.

True translation.

JOHN A. T. MEDOROS,
Interpreter.

Exhibit 7.

UNITED STATES CONSULATE,
Shanghai, January 6, 1858.

SIR: I have the honor to acknowledge receipt of your communication with reference to the American ship Wandering Jew being about to take coolies from this port to the Island of Cuba, in answer to which I have only to state, that after a great deal of trouble, said ship was cleared from the custom-house on the 26th December, 1857, for Amoy, and is at present anchored about eight miles outside of Woosung village, in the Yangtsze Keang.

I beg to transmit for your information copies of the correspondence which passed between Mr. Knapp and his excellency See, superintendent of customs, on this subject.

I have the honor to be, sir, your most obedient servant,

FREDERICK H. B. JENKINS,
Acting Vice-Consul United States of America.

SEE, Intendent of the Soo, Sung, and Tae circuit, sends the following communication:

It having come to my knowledge that certain foreign merchants are about to collect Chinese subjects in large numbers, and putting them on board a foreign vessel, send them to foreign places, I find on examination that these people are poor and ignorant, and for the sake of a few dollars readily bind themselves to go abroad, leaving their families to starve and become a burden to all. Now, the government of China is compassionate and careful of its people, and its first duty is to see that the laws of Heaven are respected, and that the children should support their parents and the parents take care of the children. How can this be if the young are tempted to leave their homes and families? It is, indeed, contrary to the laws of Heaven and earth, and it is my duty, as the high local authority, to prevent this evil. It is accordingly proper that I should request you to inform your countrymen that by inducing the people to leave their country they are acting illegally, and in a manner not contemplated by the treaties under which they reside in China.

I have, therefore, to send you this communication, and have now to beg you will issue the necessary orders to your countrymen for their information, in order that they may act accordingly. This is most important; I trust no delay will take place. A necessary communication.

WILLIAM KNAPP, Jr., Esq.
Vice-Consul, United States of America.

SHANGHAI, *November* 29, 1857.

True translation.

FREDERICK JENKINS,
Interpreter.

UNITED STATES CONSULATE,
Shanghai, December 2, 1857.

SIR: I am in receipt of your excellency's communication of the 29th November, in reference to the shipping of coolies, which should have been replied to before but for the absence of the interpreter. I perfectly agree with you that the inducing, by foreign merchants, of ignorant and poor Chinese subjects to leave their homes and families to go to foreign lands, perhaps never to return, is most illegal, and should be stopped.

I am of the opinion that your excellency would be fully justified in refusing to give a port clearance to any vessel taking these people under such circumstances, and would beg to advise that you should at once give instructions to that effect to the inspectors of customs. I have, as you requested, circulated your communication in reference to the shipping of coolies to all the foreign merchants.

I have the honor to be, &c., &c.,

WILLIAM KNAPP, JR.
Vice-Consul United States of America.

His Excellency SEE,
Intendant, &c.

SEE, Superintendent of Customs, &c., &c., makes the following communication:

I have just received from the inspector of customs a communication informing me that the British merchant, Mr. Connolly, has chartered the American ship Wandering Jew, for the purpose of taking a number of Chinese subjects to foreign ports, which they request me to examine into, &c., &c.

On examination of this affair I find that I have received a letter from your excellency in answer to a former communication of mine on the subject, in which you state "that should foreign vessels be found taking Chinese subjects away to foreign ports you request that I should not issue a port clearance to them," which is on record. Whereupon I ordered the inspectors of customs to dispatch an officer on board the Wandering Jew, and any Chinese subjects found on board, to have them brought to my office, and not issue a port clearance to her; also, I now send this letter to your excellency, requesting that you will immediately order the captain of said Wandering Jew to deliver to the custom-house officers all the Chinese subjects he may have on board; while, on the other hand, examine into the reasons why the said captain is infringing the treaty, and, according to your honorable country's laws, punish him severely, as an example to others.

I await your answer.

WILLIAM KNAPP, Jr., Esq.,
United States Vice-Consul.

SHANGHAI, *December* 11, 1857.

True translation.

FRED'K JENKINS,
Interpreter.

UNITED STATES CONSULATE,
Shanghai, December 16, 1857.

SIR: I have the honor, last week, to receive a communication from your excellency relative to the taking away in foreign ships of Chinese subjects to foreign and distant lands to serve as laborers, and perhaps never to return. I think your excellency will remember that I perfectly agreed with you in the opinion that this kind of business, the "cooly trade," was very bad, and should be stopped. Your excellency then informed me that the British merchant, A. Connolly, had chartered the American ship Wandering Jew to take coolies from this port to Havana. At the time you addressed me to that effect I was of the opinion that such was the case, and that the captain of the ship said that I would not allow him to enter into such business. On yesterday I summoned him to appear before me, and, after a close examination into the matter, I find that he has no intention of taking coolies from here to Havana, but to take Chinese passengers from Woosung to Amoy. He is ready and willing to give me a guarantee or bond to that effect, as is also the merchant, Mr. Connolly. I think that there is no Chinese law to prevent Chinese subjects from going voluntarily from one part of the empire to another, and I have most respectfully to request that your excellency will order the inspectors of customs to give the captain of the Wandering Jew his port clearance, that he may proceed to sea without further delay.

Trusting that you will take the matter into immediate consideration, I have the honor to be, &c., &c.

WILLIAM KNAPP, JR.,
Vice-Consul United States America.

His Excellency SEE TAOUTAE, &c.

UNITED STATES CONSULATE,
Shanghai, December 23, 1857.

SIR: On the 16th of the present month, I had the honor to address you on the subject of the American ship Wandering Jew, being about to take Chinese passengers from this port to Amoy. To that communication, I have as yet received no answer, which is certainly very strange. As I said in my former letter to you on the matter, I have clearly examined, and find that it is not the intention of the master of the ship, or of the British merchant to take Chinese subjects away to foreign lands, but to take passengers from one part of the country to another. I have had a conversation with the inspectors of customs, and they inform me that the business of the ship at the custom-house has been done in the regular and proper manner, and that she is by right at liberty to go to sea. In view of the facts above stated, I can see no reason why you should refuse to grant a port clearance to the ship, and thus distress people engaged in business. I have inquired closely into this matter, and find that you have detained the ship, without any good reason, and I have come to the conclusion, that if a port clearance is not granted before four o'clock, I will give the captain his papers, and allow him to proceed to sea. This is very important, and I trust that your excellency will make no delay in granting the necessary port clearance.

I have the honor to be, &c.,

WILLIAM KNAPP, JR.,
Vice Consul United States of America.

His Excellency SEE TAOUTAE, *&c.*

Return of emigrant ships to which certificates have been granted by the emigration officer during the year 1857.

Date of certificate.	Ship's name.	Tons.	Of what port.	Master's name.	Whither bound.	Adults.		Children.	
						Male.	*Female*	*Male.*	*Female*
1857. Jan'ry 9	Joseph Shepherd	630	London	Robert Barber	Havana	311			
12	Rebecca	250	Adelaide	H. R. Marsh	Guicheu bay	104			
13	Investigator	531	London	W. H. Pryen	Guicheu bay	347			
17	Hurricane	1,338	New York	Samuel Very	California	265			
17	William Miles	1,227	Bristol	Frederick Erwin	Guicheu bay	694			
20	Oracle	1,200	Thomaston, Maine	Albert D. Wood	Guicheu bay	429			
24	Challenge	2,007	New York	J. Kenny	Guicheu bay	924			
27	Siam	324	Singapore	J. D. De Silva	Singapore	52			
Feb'ry 6	J. Godfrey	483	New York	N. B. Grant	San Francisco	68	140	8	7
7	Alfred the Great	575	Glasgow	Peter McIntyre	Guicheu bay	352			
18	Almonde	556	Amsterdam	H. G. Surie	Guicheu bay	313			
20	Sportsman	626	Boston	W. Thompson	Guicheu bay	322			
26	Sultana	588	London	W. Tapper	Guicheu bay	387			
28	Young America	1,961	New York	D. S. Babcock	Guicheu bay	969			
28	Queen of the Seas	1,355	Boston	W. B. Cobb	Guicheu bay	611			
March 3	Annandale	759	Annan	W. Crocket	Guicheu bay	466			
5	Hamilton	438	Hong Kong	James Farr	San Francisco	186			
6	Francis P. Sage	1,400	New York	Thomas Ingersoll	Guicheu bay	725			
6	Jacob Cats	779	Dordrecht	A. Vander Windt	Guicheu bay	440			
12	Kensington	800	Newcastle	William King	Guicheu bay	450			
14	Cold Stream	756	London	George Tickell	Havana	220			
14	Kate Hooper	1,488	Baltimore	John T. Jackson	San Francisco	383			
19	Deva	1,039	Liverpool	A. C. Hawkins	Guicheu bay	454			
20	Pudsey Dawson	762	Liverpool	T. Harrison	Guicheu bay	387			
23	John Mattie	566	Liverpool	J. G. Hunter	Singapore	277			
23	Tuskina	449	San Francisco	W. Crane	Havana	227			
24	Speedy	1,031	Liverpool	J. H. Nightingall	Guicheu bay	615			
25	Eagle Wing	1,174	Boston	R. H. Waters	Guicheu bay	555			
26	Formosa	400	London	C. J. Rollason	San Francisco	100			
26	Archer	1,098	New York	H. N. Osgood	San Francisco	397	6		
26	Generaal de Stnees	749	Alblasserdam	Fokke Fokkens	Guicheu bay	515			
30	Gulnare	1,002	Glasgow	John Wardrop	Havana	326			

RETURN OF EMIGRANT SHIPS—Continued.

Date of certificate.	Ship's name.	Tons.	Of what port.	Master's name.	Whither bound.	Adults.		Children.	
						Male	*Female*	*Male.*	*Female*
1857.									
March 30	Etoile	588	Bordeaux	J. Moyzes	Guicheu bay	442			
31	Maria Hay	980	Sunderland	C. H. Middleton	Guicheu bay	577			
31	Robert Small	655	London	J. W. R. Darke	Havana	240			
April 2	Eranee	735	Calcutta	A. Smith	Guicheu bay	393			
22	Torrent	644	New York	J. S. Copp	San Francisco	301			
24	Konnig Wm. Tweede	800	Rotterdam	H. R. Giezen	Guicheu bay	396			
25	Man-hon	1,113	Macao	Bernadine	Guicheu bay	383			
25	Joseph Peabody	1,198	Boston	E. Weston	San Francisco	445			
30	City of Carlisle	1,099	Newcastle	W. Storey	Guicheu bay	586			
May 1	Caribbean	874	London	J. Winchester	San Francisco	398			
2	Robert Passenger	480	London	E. Sayer	San Francisco	290			
12	Wizard	1,600	New York	S. H. Slate	San Francisco	706			
16	Salsette	756	Newcastle	E. Sivinton	Guicheu bay	415			
18	Winged Arrow	1,052	Boston	F. Bearse	San Francisco	356			
20	Mary Wienholt	1,800	London	J. Weissenhorn	San Francisco	519			
29	Lancashire	985	Liverpool	J. W. Young	Guicheu bay	321			
June 15	Chapman	750	London	R. Harland	Sau Francisco	277	23		
20	Mary Whitridge	978	Baltimore	R. C. Chesbrough	San Francisco	60			
July 9	Eva Johanna	979	Rotterdam	S. Van Bochoene	San Francisco	241	17	2	
August 25	Kensington	500	New York	F. W. Thrane	Sydney	200			
Sept'r 2	Philip Laing	499	London	J. L. Cadenhead	Melbourne	97			
12	Gouverneur Gen. Van Twist	471	Rotterdam	C. E. Hoekmar	San Francisco	8	49	1	
21	William and Jane	489	London	J. Chapman	Melbourne	145			
October 2	Claremont	634	London	W. H. Burgoyne	San Francisco	53	37		
10	Starr King	1,140	Boston	G. H. Turner	San Francisco	10	150		
10	Hebe	600	Rotterdam	Adolphe H. Kiehl	Melbourne	150			
Nov'r 9	Oithona	766	London	William Holmes	Sydney	380			
9	Edwin Fox	892	London	Joseph Ferguson	Havana	310			
18	Alfred the Great	649	Glasgow	Peter McIntyre	Sydney	301	1		
18	Bengal	667	Bristol	W. Summerfield	Sydney	323			
19	Cashmere	640	London	George Pearson	Melbourne	122			
21	Queen of the Seas	1,400	Boston	W. B. Cobb	Melbourne	569			
23	Hindostan	708	London	James C. Boeuf	Melbourne	123			

Dec'r	2	Earl of Eglinton	1,274	Glasgow	John Laughton	Havana	491	...	...	...
	12	Wizard	1,601	New York	J. G. Woodside	Sydney & Melbourne	967	...	...	...
	15	Osborn Howes	1,100	Boston	N. D. Kelly	San Francisco	210	90	...	...
	23	Cornwall	584	London	William Dawson	Sydney & Melbourne	317	...	...	...
	26	Houguemont	455	London	J. H. Dalton	Sydney	455	...	...	...

SUMMARY.

Whither bound.	Adults.		Children.	
	Male.	*Female.*	*Male.*	*Female.*
To Guicheu bay, Sydney, and Melbourne	17,721	1	...	...
To San Francisco	5,273	512	11	...
To Havana	2,126	...	...	...
To Singapore	329	...	...	...
Total	25,449	513	11	...

EDMUND R. MICHELL,
Emigration Officer.

VICTORIA, *Hong Kong*, *January* 1, 1858.

Mr. Reed to Mr. Cass.

No. 3.] UNITED STATES LEGATION TO CHINA,
On board the Minnesota, Harbor of Hong Kong,
January 14, 1858.

SIR: The city of Canton is completely in the power of the allies, and the Imperial Commissioner Yeh, a captive. The outline of what has occurred since the date of my dispatch, (No. 40,) is this: After all efforts on the part of the English and French plenipotentiaries to induce Yeh to yield to their demands or to capitulate, the military commanders took the requisite steps to enforce submission. The northwest end of Honam, and the island known as the Dutch Folly, on which formally a fort stood, were occupied by the English troops, and the gun-boats, and such of the ships of the allies as could float there, were stationed along the line of the river front. On the morning of Christmas, and the next day, proclamations of an admonitory nature were circulated as extensively as possible in the southern and western suburbs of the city. They were eagerly sought for by the inhabitants. During this process, as well as during the military reconnoissances made on each of the land sides of the city, scarcely a shot was fired from the walls, and no interruption given. On Monday, 28th, the bombardment began, and continued for rather more than twenty-four hours, the fire being directed at the river wall, the governor general's yamun inside, and the heights and the fortified positions within, and to the north of the city. The troops and drilled sailors forming the naval brigades were landed under cover of the bombardment to the eastward, or below the city. They encountered some trifling resistance, and before three o'clock in the afternoon, the fort to the east of the city, called Lin Fort, was taken, and the allied troops established in position within less than half a mile of the wall. The fire from the ships and the mortar battery on the Dutch Folly continued during the night. On Tuesday morning, the 29th, the eastern wall was scaled, and was soon in the easy possession of the assailants. The attack was made on this side of the city, no doubt in the belief, probably well founded, that as the assault of Sir Hugh Gough, in 1841 was made on the other side, Chinese foresight would not dream of a change of plan. As soon as the wall was scaled, its whole extent on the eastern and northern side was occupied, as well as a pagoda and a commanding height within the wall, known as the Kwan Yin or Magazine Hill, which the admirals and commanding general with their escort took quiet possession of. There was some fighting on the west wall. On the next day, 30th, the western wall was taken, and thus the city held in complete military control.

In all this time during a fierce bombardment with every opportunity of successful defense, no serious resistance was offered, and no word of supplication or conciliation uttered. It was Chinese throughout. The whole wall on the river front was next occupied and the circuit completed. Lord Elgin and Baron Gros landed a day or two afterwards, and, it is understood, went completely round the city. I have every reason to believe that it was the desire and resolute effort of the plenipotentiaries and of the English admiral to circumscribe the military operations so as to limit the sacrifice of life. The loss to the allies was trifling, but five or six men being killed in the conquest of a walled city of nearly a million of inhabitants, with five or six thousand Tartar soldiers, and many thousand volunteers and bannermen.

The Imperial Commissioner Yeh, it is believed, left the city at one time of the attack, but subsequently returned to it and was captured by a party of sailors under command of Commodore Elliott and Captain Key of the navy. He was seized by the latter officer in an attempt to escape in partial disguise by a back door. At first he exhibited signs of terror, but has since become quite calm and resolute. Nothing of his characteristic insolence has left him. He is now a prisoner in one of the ships-of-war in the river. The lieutenant-governor and Tartar general were taken by different parties about the same time, as well as an amount of treasure, the exact sum of which I am unable to state with accuracy, and all the public documents and diplomatic and official correspondence of the imperial commissioner. Among them, were the English, French, and American ratified treaties in original, they never having left Canton. My informant as to this is Commodore Elliot who tells me he saw the original treaties. It is now understood that a Chinese municipal government of some sort has been or is to be established in the city, under the nominal charge of the late Lieutenant Governor P'ïk Kwei; but how it is to be organized I have no means of knowing. No official dispatches have yet been published, and no communications of any sort made to the Russian plenipotentiary, or to myself. The Chinese rumor at Macao, on which some reliance is to be placed is that in the captured city, a material improvement has already occurred especially in the feeling of the people themselves, that the released mandarins were rendering assistance in restoring order, showing greater aptitude under foreign direction than might have been expected. The common people are said to coöperate cheerfully. The same rumor states that a large fleet of junks from the neighborhood of Falshan is coming to Canton to aid in the suppression of river piracy.

This has been consummated that, to which so much importance has been attached, the punishment and the humiliation of the Cantonese. The great problem now remains, will this severe blow be felt beyond narrow local bounds, or will this bloodshed be vain or a mere satisfaction of resentment? On this I have no opinion to express.

I have no hesitation, however, in saying, now that this result has occurred, that it was a disgraceful surrender, for such it is, without the grace of being voluntarily ; an indifference to the sacrifice of human life ; an obstinate and unreasoning faith in a superiority of race made more absurd by a cowardly dereliction of duty; the insolence of Yeh one day and his neglect of all means of defense, though with abundance of resources, and running out of back doors the next; his refusal to receive the visit of a friendly power, such as he admits the United States to be, at a time when some good offices of mediation might have been rendered—in view of all this, I do not hesitate to say that a new policy towards China ought to be, and, I have no doubt by others, will be initiated, and that the powers of western civilization must insist on what they know to be their rights and give up the dream of dealing with China as a power to which any ordinary rules apply.

With some allowance for peculiar characteristics my belief is that Yeh is but a type of the official class, that he has been the faithful servant of his imperial master, if master he had, (which I sometimes doubt,) that his long career of stern exclusiveness has won for him the confidence of all classes whom he at once enslaved and protected, and that what he has done, or tried to do, at Canton, may be looked for at any point in China where it is the interest of the authorities to maintain a repulsive policy. The impotence of the resistance at Canton at the end of a career of individual butcheries, poisonings, and burnings, such as occurred a year ago, in a cause which was, in some of its bearings, a just one, is illustrative of the pusillanimous ferocity of the race.

I hope in my next dispatch to be able to communicate to you some further information as to the intentions of the allies.

The expected change in the naval command on this station and the departure of Commodore Armstrong, to whose private secretary, Mr. Van Don Huwel, I have intrusted my dispatch No. 1, seems to authorize me to bear my willing testimony to the great good sense and proper feeling with which, under circumstances of peculiar embarrassment, and in feeble health, Commodore Armstrong has discharged his duty. It is an act of simple justice to say this to you, and through you to the Secretary of the Navy.

I have the honor to be, sir, your obedient servant,

WILLIAM B. REED.

Hon. LEWIS CASS, *Secretary of State.*

Mr. Reed to Mr. Cass.

No. 5.]

LEGATION OF THE UNITED STATES,
Macao, January 26, 1858.

SIR: In my dispatch of the 14th January, (No. 3,) I mentioned the fact that, among other important documents found at the capture of Canton, were the original treaties between China and England, France, and the United States, and their ratifications. A few days ago I received a letter from Lord Elgin, confirming this intelligence, and adding that, as these papers were in great disorder and were much exposed to pillage, they had been removed, for safe custody, to the military headquarters and placed in charge of a commission, consisting of the chief secretaries of the English and French missions. Lord Elgin further said that he mentioned this to me in order that, if I had any wish to express regarding the disposal of our ratified treaty, he might be apprised of it.

After a brief hesitation as to whether I should in any way interfere with the possession of these documents or leave them in the hands of the captors, I came to the decision that it was not worth while even to seem to repel a courtesy, and that it was better, under all the circumstances, and in relation to this peculiar people, to ask the British plenipotentiary to send me the treaties, or to allow me to send an officer to receive them; taking care to express clearly the idea that I respected the right of property in the Chinese authorities whenever they should be reëstablished. The correspondence on the subject is annexed.—(Inclosures 1, 2, 3, 4.)

Yesterday, Mr. Bruce, Lord Elgin's brother, and chief secretary, came to Macao, where this legation is temporarily, and delivered into my hands the case containing the original treaty of the 3d of July, 1844, and tariff annexed, signed by Mr. Cushing and Keying; the original powers of Commodore Biddle to exchange ratifications, and the ratification itself with the seal of the United States, signed by the President, Mr. Tyler, and the Secretary of State, Mr. Calhoun. The papers generally are in good preservation, although the box itself has been somewhat injured.

Mr. Bruce informs me that the treaties and other documents were found confusedly packed in trunks in the house where Yeh was captured, and whither they seemed to have been removed from his yamun or official residence. The other papers consisted of diplomatic correspondence, though not of recent date, and imperial rescripts relating to foreign affairs, confirming the idea that practically the foreign office of China had for many years been at Canton. Among these rescripts were some of peculiar interest, described to me as being the imperial orders to the commissioners at Canton, prohibiting all negotiation or revision of treaties or friendly adjustment with any foreign powers. Of these, which, according to the description, must be extremely interesting, I am promised copies.

Lord Elgin desired Mr. Bruce to communicate to me fully and unreservedly his views as to the state of things at Canton, which confirm the impression recently made on me that it is the earnest desire of the allied plenipotentiaries to put an end, as soon as possible, to the existing and anomalous state of things in the Canton river. Before the capture of Yeh, negotiations had been attempted by some of the leading Chinese merchants, with the design of conferring temporary authority, after a pacification, upon Pih-Kwi, the governor, but it failed, even after the fall of the defenses of the city, in consequence of the mysterious dread which Yeh, while alive and at liberty, seemed able to inspire. It is probable, though this I do not positively know, that from these sources the allies learned that Yeh was still within the city. Capture put an end to his influence for evil; and the governor at once, on the terms prescribed, assumed command in the city. His authority has thus far been maintained without disorder.

The allied commissioners have been removed from his immediate residence. The sailors, with the exception of a small detachment of French, have been disembarked, and detached bodies of soldiers are stationed at different points to aid the Chinese police in maintaining the peace.

The confidence of the Chinese traders is gradually but slowly reviving. Some shops are opened, though yet numbers with their families are leaving the city. The Chinese rumor here is that until the emperor's will is known the opulent merchants will not venture to return. Private junks are loading with merchandise, and a plan has been initiated by which armed Chinese cruisers are to coöperate with the allied gun-boats in the suppression of the piracy which now, to an unprecedented extent, afflicts the river passages and the western coasts.

Should the precautionary measures of the allies succeed, and peace and good order be maintained with any prospect of permanence, I have direct assurances that the blockades will be removed and the trade re-opened. The time now indicated for this is the 10th February, which is about the China new year.

No attempt has been made to open any communication with the imperial court. The intelligence of the fall of the city has been circulated through the newspapers, some of which are printed in Chinese, and by the consular authorities at the open ports; but, so far as we know, no popular excitement has been produced by it.

With regard to the general politics of the empire, I have nothing more decided to communicate, especially with reference to the civil war which has been so long waged in the central provinces between the imperialists and insurgents under Tai-ping, than was given in M. Williams's dispatches Nos. 31 and 33. This chief maintains his headquarters at Nanking, and his supremacy on the Yangtsze-kiang, west of that capitol as far as the province of Kiang-si.

His principal general is named Shih-takai, and this man is the only one living of the original corps of chiefs, with whom he left Kwang-si in 1851, all the others having died by violent deaths. This general has a body of troops variously estimated from ten to eighty thousand men, but what is more certain is that he holds the entire province of Kwang-si, except the capital, and has ruled it for about two years, so as to assure the people safety and protection. So far as can be ascertained, this large province (about the size of the State of Virginia) has been more quiet during the last year than for a long time. Shih-takai made some inroads upon the neighboring provinces of Cheh-kiang and Fuh-kien, on the east and south, during the past twelve months, but was not able permanently to occupy any place of note. Tai-ping has not left the vicinity of Nanking. It is in the region of this ill-fated city that the effects of civil war are to be seen, and though it can only be inferred what is the state of the country there from what was seen in the region about Canton during 1854 and 1855, it may be set down as greatly harrassed and depopulated. The Chinese in these struggles give and expect no quarter, but both sides extend a sort of black-mail protection to the peaceful farmers and traders near their armies, from whose property and industry they both expect to draw supplies.

In the vicinity of Nanking the insurgents have lately lost the strong city of Chin-kiang, about fifty miles east of Nanking, on the Yangtsze river, which the imperialists have taken after a siege of nearly five years, the occupants having been starved out. This city was taken by the English in 1842, and commands the grand canal in its passage across the Yangtsze river. Its possession by the imperialists only assures them a quiet traffic on both streams, and communication between Pekin and the southeastern provinces. The base of operations for the insurgents is at present along the Yangtsze river, west of Nanking, and though they have lost the large cities of Wu-chang and Chin-kiang on their extreme eastern and northwestern sides, they still occupy a region fully a hundred thousand square miles in extent, from which the imperialists will not soon be able to drive them. On the other hand, they are perhaps too weak to enlarge their sway.

There is more chance of a composition with these successful insurgents by allowing them to keep possession for the present of their territory, inviting the leaders to a share in the legitimate government. What use foreigners can make of the insurrection to extend trade and intercourse with the Chinese is as much a problem as ever; but there is no doubt that the people in the vicinity of the four northern open ports are constantly learning so much of their fellow-men from abroad that no laws will long prevent them from having more communication and treating them kindly.

The Secretary of the Navy will be apprised of the arrival of Flag-officer Tatnall by the last mail steamer. Commodore Tatnall will, on the departure of the present commander-in-chief, hoist his flag on the San Jacinto. I am happy to say that there is the kindest and most confidential feeling between Captain Tatnall and myself.

I have the honor to be, sir, your obedient servant,

WILLIAM B. REED.

Hon. LEWIS CASS,
Secretary of State.

HER MAJESTY'S STEAM FRIGATE "FURIOUS,"
January 16, 1858.

SIR: I have the honor to inform your excellency that in the yamun, in which the Inperial Commissioner Yeh was captured, a considerable number of official documents were found, and among them the original of the treaty of the United States with China, and the ratification thereof.

These papers were in great disorder, and as, if left in the yamun, they would, in all probability, have been pillaged, it was deemed advisable to seize them and to carry them to military headquarters for safe custody.

They are now under the charge of a commission, at the head of which are the Hon. Frederick Bruce and M. Duchene de Bellecourt, secretaries of the British and French missions.

I have taken the liberty of mentioning this fact to your excellency in order that if your excellency should have any wish to express regarding the disposal of these important documents to which I have referred I may be apprised of it.

I have the honor to be, sir, your excellency's most obedient, humble servant,

ELGIN & KINCARDINE.

His Excellency Hon. W. REED, *&c., &c., &c.*

LEGATION OF THE UNITED STATES,
On board the Minnesota, January, 18, 1858.

MY LORD: I am much indebted to you for your dispatch of the 16th, informing me that in the yamun where the Imperial Commissioner Yeh was captured, the original treaty of the United States with China, and its ratification by the President, were found; and that, as the papers were exposed to pillage, they had been seized and removed to headquarters for safe custody, and placed in the charge of a commission, at the head of which are the Hon. Mr. Bruce and M. De Bellecourt, secretaries of the British and French missions. Your excellency is good enough, further, to say that you mention this to me in order that I may express my wishes regarding the disposal of these important documents.

I beg to say to your excellency that I very highly estimate the courtesy which prompts this communication. I should not hesitate to leave these papers in the custody of the gentlemen who have been appointed commissioners, believing that they would take such care of them as is due to the dignity of the functionaries whose acts they record; but this, I presume, will not be agreeable to them. I shall, therefore, be glad if your lordship will either dispatch some officer of her majesty's service to bring to me these documents, or allow me to send for them a gentleman in the service of the United States.

I have the honor to be, my lord, your excellency's most obedient and humble servant,

WILLIAM B. REED.

His Excellency the EARL OF ELGIN AND KINCARDINE,
&c., &c., &c.

HER MAJESTY'S SHIP FURIOUS,
Canton, January 21, 1856.

SIR: On receipt of your excellency's dispatch of the 18th instant, which reached me this morning, I immediately communicated its contents to Baron Gros, who at once acceded to my proposal that the treaty of the United States with China, and its ratifications, should, in accordance with your wish, be delivered to your excellency.

I have therefore commissioned Mr. Bruce, the secretary of this mission, to proceed to Hong Kong, or to Macao, as the case may be, in order that he may in person hand these important documents to your excellency; and I have to request that you will have the goodness, when he shall have delivered them, to give him a receipt for them.

I have the honor to be, sir, your excellency's most obedient, humble servant,

ELGIN AND KINCARDINE.

His Excellency, Hon. W. B. REED,
U. S. Envoy Extraordinary and Minister Plenipotentiary.

UNITED STATES LEGATION TO CHINA,
Macao, January 25, 1858.

MY LORD: I have had the honor to receive from Mr. Bruce, whom your excellency had commissioned for that duty, the original treaty of 1844 between the United States and his Majesty the Emperor of China, and its ratification by the President, which were found in the yamun of the late imperial commissioner, and taken possession of by the allied forces in the recent capture of Canton. I shall retain these documents until an opportunity presents itself of restoring them to the Chinese authorities, or make such other disposal of them as the President shall direct.

I beg to renew to your excellency my thanks for the consideration shown in this to the United States, as well by yourself as by Baron Gros, to whom I should sooner have made the acknowledgment, had your first communication referred to his intervention.

I have the honor to be, my lord, your excellency's most obedient, humble servant,

WILLIAM B. REED.

His Excellency the EARL OF ELGIN AND KINCARDINE,
&c., &c., &c.

Mr. Reed to Mr. Cass.

No. 6.] LEGATION OF THE UNITED STATES,
Macao, January 26, 1856.

SIR: I have the honor to forward the consular correspondence since the last mail, and am happy to report that it is in every respect satisfactory; the acting consuls seem disposed to second my efforts to establish a proper system of coöperation. I have not yet received an answer from Mr. Freeman, to whom I tendered the post of vice-consul at Shanghai. (Inclosures 1 to 9.)

I have the honor to be, sir, your obedient servant,

WILLIAM B. REED.

Hon. LEWIS CASS, *Secretary of State.*

Index to Dispatch No. 6, Macao, January 26, 1858.

Exhibit.	From—	To—	Subject-matter.	Date.
1	W. B. Reed...	Consul General at Havana.	Notify him of American ships going there with coolies.	Jan. 12, 1858.
2	W. B. Reed...	A. Freeman......	Requests information respecting coolie ships, currency, and inspectorate system..	Jan. 15, 1858.
3	E. Doty.........	W. B. Reed......	Temporary filling of consulate since Hyatt.	Dec. 31, 1857.
4	E. Doty.........	W. B. Reed......	Spanish consul attests all coolies sent thence.	Dec. 31, 1857.
5	W. B. Reed...	E. Doty............	Informs him of penalties in passage law.	Jan. 15, 1858.
6	W. B. Reed...	T. Dunn...........	Requests information about opium trade.	Jan. 15, 1858.
7	C. W. Bradley.	W. B. Reed......	No coolies sent from Ningpo...........	Jan. 15, 1858.
8	J. Bowring....	W. B. Reed......	Acknowledges papers sent him by coolies.	Dec. 31, 1857.

Exhibit 1.

UNITED STATES LEGATION TO CHINA,
Harbor of Hong Kong, January 12, 1858.

SIR: I have had occasion to write to the Secretary of State on the subject of the traffic in coolies between this country and Cuba, in American ships, which, I regret to say has very much increased. Two vessels have lately sailed thus freighted: one from Macao, the Kate Hooper, and one from Swatow, the Challenge. They have been heard of at Anjier and Singapore in distress, the passengers in one of them having mutinied. There are two other American vessels now loading with coolies for Havana: the Flora Temple at Macao, and the Wandering Jew at Shanghai.

It is very important that so soon as these vessels arrive they should be visited by you, and a report as to their condition and the number of surviving coolies in each actually disembarked, be made to the department. I have no doubt the government will be glad to have early information as to the tenure, condition, and value, of this class of population in Cuba. I have solicited their early action with regard to this trade.

I have the honor to be, sir, your most obedient servant,

WILLIAM B. REED.

The CONSUL GENERAL OF THE UNITED STATES, *Havana,*

Exhibit 2.

No. 1.]

LEGATION OF THE UNITED STATES,
Minnesota, harbor of Hong Kong, January 15, 1858.

SIR: By the steamer Yañgtsze, which sailed yesterday, I forwarded to you an appointment as vice-consul of the United States at Shanghai.

With the renewed expression of a hope that you will accept the post, I beg to communicate a few suggestions as to the discharge of your duties to this legation, being sure that you will cheerfully coöperate with me in my efforts to put matters in this country on a proper basis.

I beg to direct your special attention to the circular addressed by the Secretary of State to the consuls in China, dated the 20th June, 1857, which you will find in the archives.

The great defect in the working of the consular system heretofore has been, so far at least as I can judge from the archives of the legation, the want of frequent and reliable correspondence. Things occur at distant ports, and the first intelligence the minister receives comes through some foreign official, tinged very often to the disparagement of the consul by the medium. It is the interest, therefore, as well as the duty of consul to make an early report of what happens. In the present perplexed condition of Chinese affairs, this is more than ever important.

Thus negligent of corresponding, the consuls of the United States have been too much in the habit of resorting to extreme measures of redress for wrongs inflicted or threatened by the Chinese authorities, such as summary stoppage of duties, clearing vessels without due formalities, and other means. All this is wrong and an assumption of authority. Before such action is taken, there ought always to be a report made to this legation, and accompanying it, the formal evidence of the acts of the officials complained of.

There are one or two matters on which I shall be glad to hear from you specially, treating, if possible, (this being a mere matter of convenience,) each subject in a separate letter. One is the much disputed point of the foreign inspectorate at Shanghai, on which my judgment is yet suspended. Any views you may have on this point I shall be glad to receive.

The actual state of the currency at Shanghai is a very interesting subject.

You will see from a letter which I addressed to Mr. Knapp, that I am resolute in an intention to try to put a stop to the cooly trade, especially to the West Indies.

The views there expressed I hope you will, in all cases, carry out. If my opinions receive, as I have little doubt they will, the approval of the government at home, those engaged in this traffic may encounter penalties which they do not anticipate. I beg you to communicate to the Chinese authorities my determination on this point. It is the use of American ships that I can interfere with. The Spanish government is most active in this trade, though it is to be feared the French are about to engage in it.

Now that the Canton question may be assumed to be decided, some solicitude will be felt as to the policy of the imperial court, and official and popular sentiment in the northern provinces. I hope you will keep me regularly advised of any symptoms which may be detected. In this relation, I shall be glad to know what is the extent and course of trade, especially in provisions, from Shanghai and the neighboring districts to the north.

I believe this legation subscribes for a copy of the North China Herald. None has reached me recently.

In your correspondence, to be addressed to me always at Hong Kong, be so good as to use, as far as possible, the quickest steamers. I have no doubt that the English and French men-of-war will, at any time, take charge of dispatches.

Hoping soon to hear from you, I am, sir, your obedient servant,

WILLIAM B. REED.

ALBERT FREEMAN, Esq.,
Vice-Consul of the United States, Shanghai.

Exhibit 3.

No. 2.] CONSULATE OF THE UNITED STATES OF AMERICA AT AMOY,
December 31, 1857.

SIR: I have the honor to acknowledge your dispatch of November 19, and inclosure of December 7, announcing your arrival in China as envoy extraordinary and minister plenipotentiary of the United States. This was received 21st instant. Although not yet officially informed of the fact, I had the pleasure of congratulating on the event in my dispatch to the legation, bearing date December 9, instant, in which I acknowledged the reception of a commission as vice-consul at this port, and my acceptance of the appointment.

You call my attention to a letter from the honorable the Secretary of State, dated the 20th of June last, containing certain instructions referred to in your dispatch. That letter has not been received at this office. I shall have pleasure in attending to your directions as to quarterly reports, and will now say, that for this present quarter, ending this day, there is not an item of any nature upon the consular records in relation to commerce to be the subject of the report.

In reference to your dispatch—

Point 1. I have to refer you to mine of the 9th instant, which will show the source of my appointment and position. I do not regard myself as a substitute to any other person, but simply as filling a vacancy *ad interim* pending the pleasure of the President.

Point 2. Under date of April 1, 1857, I find the record of the appointment of Thomas Hunter, M. D., to act as vice-consul at this port by T. H. Hyatt, Esq., until such authority shall be revoked by the said T. H. Hyatt, Esq., and on the 22d of the same month there is a record of the taking of the oath of office by the said T. Hunter.

Again, I find a copy of a dispatch to his excellency P. Parker, commissioner, &c., by James T. Wilson, Esq., dated May 30, 1857, announcing his appointment as vice-consul by T. H. Hyatt, Esq., for this port; his arrival here on the 29th of May, and his having entered on the duties of office; also, a copy of the oath of office of James T. Wilson, taken before T. H. Hyatt, Esq., at Hong Kong, on the 19th day of May, 1857.

Again, under date of March 4, 1857, I find a copy of a dispatch to the honorable Secretary of State, by T. H. Hyatt, Esq., giving information or notice, that as leave of absence which had been applied for had not been received, that, with the consent of the United States commissioner, and on medical certificates of impaired health and need of change, he, the said T. H. Hyatt, would soon as practicable leave this port for the United States.

I have reason to think the said Thomas Hunter did for a short time act, or profess to act, as United States consul in charge here, although I have found no other than the above-noted records of the fact. The said J. T. Wilson did come to Amoy, and professedly acted as consul in charge. This was for a few weeks only, when he left this place in the American ship Ino, which sailed about June 28 for the United States. Mr. Wilson has left no complete records of his acts. The names of a few vessels are entered as having arrived, but nothing more. The consular archives were left in the house of Mr. Hyatt, on the island of Kolongsee, then temporally occupied by a British subject, Thomas D. Boyd, Esq., whom it appears Mr. Wilson requested to take the archives in charge.

Since the departure of J. T. Wilson, Esq., this consular office was vacant, until I assumed, under commission from the legation of the United States, the duties of office on the 4th day of this present month.

Very respectfully, your obedient servant,

E. DOTY,
Vice-Consul in charge.

His Excellency W. B. REED,
Envoy Extraordinary, &c., of United States of America.

Exhibit 4.

No. 3.] CONSULATE OF THE UNITED STATES AMERICA AT AMOY,
December 31, 1857.

SIR: In reference to your inclosure of date December 7, instant, concerning a statement in the public papers, as regards an ordinance of the Spanish government relating to the shipping of Chinese laborers or coolies, I have the honor to inform you:

1. I cannot learn that there is any such ordinance as you refer to which requires the attestation of the consul of the nation to which the ship belongs on which the said laborers may be shipped.

2. There is an ordinance which does imperatively require such attestation to all contracts with such coolies by the Spanish consul of the port from which the said laborers may be shipped for any Spanish port, without which attestation the said laborers or coolies will not be allowed to land.

Your inclosure has probably a reference to the above, and which you will perceive does not require any attestation, nor allow, so far as I can learn, any interference of a consul of another nation.

With great respect, your obedient servant,

E. DOTY,
Vice-Consul in charge.

His Excellency WILLIAM B. REED,
Envoy Extraordinary, &c., of United States of America.

Exhibit 5.

No. 2.] LEGATION OF THE UNITED STATES,
Minnesota, *January* 15, 1858.

SIR: I have to-day received your letters and their inclosures, for which I thank you. They are very satisfactory, and give me every assurance that I may look forward to the most agreeable relations to you. What I need, and what I am convinced you mean to furnish me with, is detailed and frequent communications of the current affairs at the port at which you are stationed.

I forward you a copy of the circular of 20th June, 1857, to which I referred you.

My attention has been anew called to the painful subject of the traffic of Chinese coolies in American ships, especially those destined to the West Indies.

There is a section of an act of Congress—act of 20th April, 1818—which may reach it, and I have urged upon the government at home to direct prosecutions under that act against all masters of American ships engaged in the trade. If the Executive should take a different view of the law, I have no doubt stringent legislation will be recommended.

Should any American vessel be loading at Amoy with coolies for the West Indies—for it is to this trade my attention is mainly directed—I request you at once to notify the master that in my view the trade is contrary to the laws of the United States, that it is your duty to furnish me with the evidence of such shipment, and that I shall at once forward it to the department. The penalty is a heavy fine and imprisonment, and forfeiture of the vessel.

There is another remedy, more effectual than friendly warnings or threats, which rarely check unlawful adventure. If the Chinese authorities are in earnest to put an end to this exile of their countrymen, they can refuse the certificates or papers on which you give clearances. I hope they will do so. I beg you, if occasion offers, to represent this matter to the proper authorities, and ask their coöperation. They may depend on mine.

It was reported to me, some time ago, that an American ship, called the Wandering Jew, was loading with coolies for Havana at Shanghai. The late vice-consul reported to this legation that this ship was not so employed, but was charted to carry Chinese passengers to Amoy. There is some reason to suspect that Amoy is not her ultimate destination. You will oblige me by making inquiry and taking the requisite action.

I desire every shipment of coolies for the West Indies to be reported to me, and also every case of your success in arresting such adventures.

I am much struck with the remarks in your letter to the department (No. 3) of the 9th January, 1858, as to the increase of trade at Amoy, and the reasons for it. The hope of the complete reopening of Canton is not very distinct, and the increase you refer to may go on.

I shall be glad to have precise information as to the reported legalization of the opium import at your port.

Since the fall of Canton, there is no further intelligence than that the allies are endeavoring, apparently with success, to establish a provisional Chinese government.

I will thank you to forward all your dispatches to me directly at Hong Kong, and not to the care of any mercantile firm.

I have the honor to be, sir, your obedient servant,

WILLIAM B. REED.

E. DOTY, Esq.,
Vice-Consul, Amoy.

Exhibit 6.

No. 1.] LEGATION OF THE UNITED STATES,
On board the Minnesota, Harbor of Hong Kong, Jan. 15, 1858.

SIR: I have this morning received your communications (No. 17) of the 23d December, and (No. 1) of the 7th January, the latter giving me the agreeable intelligence that the duty question is at last settled to the satisfaction of all parties. I shall inform Sir John Bowring that the parties in arrear are the British merchants, whose names you give me. I do not doubt, from what I know of their respectability, that they will pay what is due. For this, some responsibility rests on you, as it was your official act, or that of Mr. Jones, which in the first instance withheld the duties. Be so good as to advise me of what is done, and adhere if possible to the rule you have prescribed for yourself, of never permitting a vessel to be cleared, without paying or absolutely securing the duties, and of always informing me of any emergency which may seem to require action on the part of the United States officers. You may rely on my immediate answer, and that I shall not, in dealing with the Chinese authorities, fail resolutely to assert the rights we have under the treaty.

I shall be glad to hear from you on the state of the opium import at Foo Chow, with reference to the report that it has been legalized by the local authorities, and to any other matter of interest; for you must be aware that, in the present state of our relations to China, and the prevalent disturbances of the Empire, accurate intelligence is much needed. I hope to hear from you by every mail.

Commodore Tatnall, who is to succeed to the command of this squadron, arrived this morning, and will, within a few days, hoist his flag. I shall bring to his attention what you say as to the necessity of an occasional visit of an American vessel-of-war at your port.

I have the honor to be, sir, your obedient servant,

WILLIAM B. REED.

THOMAS DUNN, Esq.,
Vice-Consul, Foo Chow.

Exhibit 7.

No. 3.] CONSULATE OF THE UNITED STATES OF AMERICA,
Ningpo, January 4, 1858.

SIR: To your excellency's note of the 7th December, 1857, this day received, I have the honor to reply, that no ordinance of the Spanish government requiring contracts for the shipment of coolies to be attested by the consul, at the port of clearance, has been promulgated at Ningpo, and consequently that no consular officer of the United States, within this district has been called on for such attestation.

After diligent inquiry, I have not been able to learn that a single cooly has at any time been shipped from this port. Ever since its commencement, the traffic has been carried on at points *south* of this; and for the past four or five years has, I believe, been confined almost wholly to Amoy and Swatau.

I have the honor to be, sir, your obedient servant,

CHARLES WILLIAM BRADLEY.

His Excellency WILLIAM B. REED,
Envoy of the United States, &c., to China, Macao.

No. 1.] LEGATION OF THE UNITED STATES,
Minnesota, Harbor of Hong Kong, January 18, 1858.

SIR: I hasten to acknowledge the receipt of your very precise and satisfactory dispatch of the 4th instant; I thank you for it and beg to assure you that I rely with entire confidence on your ability and willingness to give me information at all times. I hope to hear from you regularly, on all matters of interest.

I have the honor to be, sir, your obedient servant,

WILLIAM B. REED.

CHARLES WILLIAM BRADLEY, Esq.,
Consul of the United States, Ningpo.

Exhibit 8.

No. 337.] SUPERINTENDENCY OF TRADE,
Hong Kong, December 31, 1857.

SIR: I have to thank your excellency for forwarding with your dispatch of yesterday copy of the instructions given by you to the United States vice-consul at Shanghai in reference to the cooly emigration from China to the Island of Cuba.

I take due note of the removal to Macao, for the present, of the United States legation. Wherever that legation may be located, I beg to assure your excellency, I shall be most happy to give evidence of my desire to consolidate and strengthen the friendly relations which happily exist between our respective countries, and to promote our common interests in these regions.

I have the honor to be, sir, your excellency's most obedient, humble servant,

JOHN BOWRING.

His Excellency WM. B. REED,
U. S. Minister Plenipotentiary to China.

Mr. Reed to Mr. Cass.

[Extracts.]

No. 7.] LEGATION OF THE UNITED STATES TO CHINA,
Macao, February 1, 1858.

SIR: In your dispatch (No. 3) dated the 22d of June last, received before my departure from the United States, you called my attention to the subject of the claims of American citizens on the Chinese government, many of which, you truly said, had been too long delayed, and the consideration of all of which have been habitually evaded by the responsible authorities here. You again directed my attention to it in forwarding the claim of Mr. Pierrepont Edwards, in your dispatch No. 6, dated 29th July.

I have examined the subject carefully, and now communicate the result which I have been able to arrive at. I do a simple act of justice by repeating my grateful sense of the consideration shown to me by my countrymen here—those, I mean, who have, or think they have, wrongs to redress—in not unduly pressing their matters upon me, or perplexing me or the government with urgency at a moment when action was out of the question, and the greatest reserve and circumspection needed. Their claims do not on this account less deserve favorable attention.

Annexed to this dispatch you will find a "memorandum," carefully prepared, containing a succinct account of what may be described as the pecuniary claims of our citizens, to which I earnestly beg the attention of the President. There are some cases of extreme hardship, involving, I fear, absolute ruin. As to all, if the view I take of their merits be correct, I am the more solicitous, for at my instance, with the entire concurrence of the department, as expressed in your dispatch of the 29th of June, the plan suggested by Mr. Parker of recovering these claims through the agency of the British authorities was overruled. They must now be recovered through our own vigor or be abandoned, or assumed by the government of the United States, or recovered by the possible though most improbable indirect agency of the English, so far as relates to those connected with the recent hostilities, by their recovering such an amount from the Chinese as will enable them to assume the liability to us. This, I repeat, is most improbable, and certainly I shall not suggest it here.

If, then, the government of the United States has to determine among the other alternatives, it is the more important that the questions involved should be seriously and calmly considered.

I have endeavored to do so without prejudice; but I am free to say that no one can carefully study the records of this legation for the last ten years—certainly from the time of the last official interview, in 1848, in the south of China, where, it now seems, the relations of the western nations (with the exception, possibly, of Russia) are determined, when Mr. Davis in vain urged one of these very claims on the attention of the Viceroy Seu, down to Yeh's frivolous refusal to see me, or to listen to a revision of the treaty—without a feeling kindred to resentment for the wrongs which have been done, and for the pitiless disregard of the individual suffering that has occurred.

* * * * * * * *

I do not desire the reproach of indifference for what I am compelled daily to witness to rest upon me; and I have lost no occasion of assuring such of the claimants as have approached me on the subject that I had no doubt their interests would be most considerately regarded by the President.

Before attempting to classify these claims, especially those arising out of the pending hostilities, I desire to say that I have not been at all insensible to the truth that, in the measurement of justice in commercial dealings, the wrong is rarely, if ever, all on one side; and I have, therefore, invariably observed the rule, in my own analysis, of rigidly excluding, first, on a principle of law, all claims for contingent profits, and of rejecting any claim on the government where the business in which it originated was in contravention of the treaties or well-ascertained Chinese lawful prohibition. Some of these claims, and those the strongest in their appeal on the score of hardship, have no connection with commerce; such, for instance, as arise out of the wanton destruction of missionary property, household furniture, and printing apparatus.

The claims of all kinds are arranged in the following order, generally in accordance with that of time.

I. Those unadjusted claims, dating as far back as 1847, and having no relation whatever to the events of 1856.

II. Those originating in the pending warfare; and these, again, may be divided into these classes:

1st. Those which, though no doubt produced by these hostilites, occurred at a distance from the scene; such as the firing on the American steamer Cumfa, in October, 1856.

2d. Those occasioned by the British bombardment of Canton, on the 26th and 27th October, 1856.

3d. Those produced by the burning of the factories, on the 14th December, 1856, and the coincident destruction of American merchandise in the Honan pack-houses.

4th. The destruction of the American docks and vessels at Whampoa, and the reputed desecration of graves.

For the facts connected with these claims in detail, I refer you to the accompanying memorandum; and for the persistent and earnest way in which they have been again and again urged on the Chinese authorities, and by them evaded, I refer you to the correspondence of my predecessors, and especially Mr. Parker, who never lost an opportunity of pressing them on the attention of the viceroy; and I am bound to say that there is no better specimen of the cool effrontery of the latter than his intimation in his letters to me of the 18th of December last, which no doubt has attracted your attention, that these grievances only existed in Mr. Parker's imagination; that he was in the habit of exaggeration; and that, to use Yeh's own language, because he was *recalled*, no attention was due to what he said.

I find the actual truth quite as real and painful as Mr. Parker described it; and however, according to my judgment, he may have been mistaken in the mode of redress which he counseled, I respectfully suggest that he deserved fully the support and approval of the government, in his proper urgency on the Chinese officials.

When, in February, 1857, (Dispatch No. 7, inclosure 2 *a*,) Mr. Parker called the viceroy's attention to these claims, he sent an answer on the 12th March, 1857, (No. 7, inclosure 2 *b*,) which was a positive denial of all redress; and so it has rested till this time.

Now that the British operations at Canton are supposed to be drawing to a close, the parties interested are naturally anxious, and reasonably inquire what mode of redress the representative of their government proposes to adopt. This inquiry, I need hardly say, is a painful one. They know as well as I the distance which separates the government of the United States from its public servant here, but they do not always estimate justly the restraints and limitations of that servant's powers. The perverse Chinese official sometimes seems to understand better the difficulty of our position, and of course presumes on it.

In the classification which I have attempted of these claims, you will be struck by the distinctions which separate them. Those, for example, arising out of the British bombardment in October, do not seem to me to be strong as against the Chinese, who were the party assailed and not the assailants; and I indulge the hope that some remuneration may be made by the English authorities. The property burned in the factories constitute a more meritorious class as against the Chinese. That they had a perfect right by any means to dislodge a hostile force, and in so doing to destroy the buildings occupied, is very clear. It is equally so that they were not bound to abstain from this mode of annoyance because neutral property stored there might be endangered or destroyed; but if that property is destroyed in order to make defense effectual, the innocent sufferers must look somewhere. The more clear is the obligation of the Chinese to make this reparation, from the fact that, while the viceroy gave notice of his inability to protect the stranger, and counseled him to remove himself and his property, he had instituted and enforced, with severe, and, in Mr. Williams's case, bloody penalties, a discipline which deprived any resident or sojourner, friend and enemy alike, of servants or means of making the removal. Again, still stronger is the claim for property of American merchants stored and left in what are known here as "go-downs" and pack-houses, opposite Canton and beyond the area of military operations. The owners, unable to remove any portion, left it all in the implied guardianship of the Chinese authorities. In one instance, at least, that of James Purdon & Co., this custody was express, the public seals having been put upon the goods in question. It will be recollected that, after the middle of January, 1857, the English naval forces evacuated the river, and from that time till October, when the blockade was declared, everything for fourteen miles below Canton was in the undisturbed power of the mandarins. They allowed no American to come back after his property, and would not protect him if he had done so. Personal safety did not exist on the river or its outlets. Yet stronger still is the case of the American citizens whose property, docks, ship-yards, and timber were wantonly destroyed at Whampoa, when the actual conflict was over. For the details of all, I refer to the annexed memorandum.

The amount of actual indebtedness of China to the United States now amounts, on a rigid computation, to at least eight hundred thousand dollars, and this debt can only be realized in one of these modes:

By a voluntary act embodied in a treaty, should one be amicably negotiated; the payments to be arranged in such a way, in view of a friendly concession, as to make it as little onerous as possible on the Chinese government.

[This, I regret to say, I do not confidently anticipate.]

By a detention of the amount claimed out of duties hereafter to be paid, or a portion of them, leaving a part still payable to the Chinese treasury.

[To this mode there are objections of a grave character, chiefly as it involves our government in some sort of agency for its own protection in the collection of the Chinese revenue.]

By a resolute and peremptory demand, to be enforced by a blockade of some one, or all the ports of China, and this to be made intelligible to the Chinese, not as a mode of offensive hostility, but of reprisal, which even a friendly power has a right to resort to, and which, though reluctantly adopted, must be enforced till justice be obtained.

My judgment tells me that this alone will secure redress. It has the advantage of being direct, and intelligible to those—civilized or semi-barbarous, as they may be—on whom it is meant to operate. It is an appeal to the selfish impulses of this trading nation. It may be so localized as to do little harm to our commerce, or it may be so extended as to make it the interest of other commercial nations to coöperate to induce the Chinese to yield. It raises no questions of neutral rights, for the precedent lately set by the English and French, in blockading the Canton river without a national declaration of war, prevents any querulous whisper in that direction. It may be made to apply directly to the imperial power by a temporary suspension of supplies by the Grand canal, or by arresting the commerce of junks to the north, or a blockade of one of the imperial cities lately recovered from the insurgents, on the Yangtse Kiang. It requires no increase of the naval force here, any one or two of the ships now on the station being able to blockade, though not to enter, any port in China, except at certain brief seasons of the year.

These are the inducements which, if the cause of complaint be adequate, point to this mode of redress. I respectfully submit the whole matter for the consideration of the President, begging you to bear in mind that, in the ordinary course of mail, no answer to this dispatch can reach the south of China before the month of July. Then I hope to be in the north, either alone or in coöperation with others, seeking the friendly access to the imperial court, which has been so long and so steadfastly denied. If, being there, I shall be instructed to coerce in some way indemnity for these pecuniary injuries, there will be time before the closing of the season to do so. If, on the other hand, the President shall think it is either beyond his power or inexpedient to give such authority, I can withdraw from a scene of which I should be a troublesome spectator, and do my best to reconcile my fellow-citizens, who have endured so much and so long, to the hopeless expectation of voluntary justice from China.

I have, as far as possible, limited this dispatch to the pecuniary claims on the Chinese authorities. Those of a political nature are referred to in the accompanying memorandum, and on them I have no other observation now to make than that they painfully illustrate the relations in which the United States have been content so long to stand to the authorities of this empire.

I have the honor to be, sir, your obedient servant,

WILLIAM B. REED.

Hon. LEWIS CASS,

Secretary of State.

Memorandum containing succinct accounts of the claims, &c., on the Chinese government.

Robbery and piracy of the Caldera.

This vessel sailed under the Chilian flag, and her cargo was insured by American underwriters. She left Hong Kong for California, 5th October, 1854, and on the 7th was lost near the island of Kulan, southwesterly from Macao, in the district of Sinning. Her cargo was plundered on three or four successive days by various fishing and piratical boats, assisted by parties from on shore, by all of whom the vessel and everything in her were carried off, and no attempts were made by the Chinese authorities on the mainland to hinder their proceedings; but, on the contrary, proof was obtained that they connived at them. The entire losses were reckoned by the sufferers at about $100,000. The United States vice-consul at Canton brought the case before the governor general, demanding an indemnity for the same; but his excellency replied by quoting the twenty-sixth article of the treaty, and excused himself from making any payment on that ground. In March, 1856, the case was again brought to the notice of the governor general, according to instructions from the department, by Mr. Parker, and pecuniary indemnity to the extent of $100,000 demanded from the Chinese government, on the ground that the piracy was not on the high seas, but within the Chinese dominions. To this dispatch no reply was ever received, and Mr. Parker again brought it to his notice on the 9th December, referring him to his former full representations for all the details. This the governor general evaded by putting the matter upon a trivial issue, saying that the captain of the Caldera should have fired upon the pirates, and not suffered himself to be plundered. Here the matter still remains.

Claim of Rev. J. J. Roberts.

This claim grew out of a riotous attack of a mob upon his house at Canton, in 1847, and the matter was investigated by the Chinese authorities there, and the claim for damages allowed by them, but was never paid. All the commissioners to China have successively and unavailably brought it [to] their notice, and Mr. McLane informed Mr. Roberts in 1854 that there was no hope of getting the money by peaceful remonstrance in the present state of Chinese diplomacy. The latter then presented his case to the government at Washington, in October, 1854, petitioning for relief. The claim originally was fixed at $1,400, which with interest, would now be increased to about $2,800.

Claim of Rev. R. S. Maclay and others at Fuh-chau.

This claim grew out of the interference of the authorities at Fuh-chau, by which the landlord of a piece of land which the mission had rented from him, was compelled to rescind the contract, and the mission lost an advance of $213 46 that had been paid him. Some composition was subsequently made with the landlord by which he bore a part of the loss. The matter was vainly brought to the notice of the proper rulers in the city.

Claim of the owners of the ship Mermaid for $3,125.

The ship was fouled by the Chinese government vessel Sir H. Compton, in the river at Shanghai, in March, 1854. As she drifted by, the two vessels came in contact, and the Mermaid lost her bowsprit and cutwater, and injured other parts of her stem. A board of survey was called, consisting of competent ship-carpenters and masters, which estimated the amount of damages at the sum of $3,125, and this decision was made known to the Taoutae. By advice from Mr. McLane, the settlement of this claim was deferred at the time on account of political troubles; and in May, 1854, he advised the consul to wait till a convenient opportunity offered, and then deduct the amount from the duties. This was not done, however; and though the matter has been since brought to the notice of the authorities at Shanghai, they have never paid the money.

Claim of Sandwith Drinker on Kingqwa, for $1,902 51, *awarded by arbitrators appointed by both parties in February,* 1856, *and decided April* 10, 1856.

This claim grew out of an agreement entered into between Mr. Drinker, in 1854, and a number of the gentry at Whampoa and vicinity, the object of which was to expel a party of insurgents from a fort at Sun-tso, near Blenheim Reach, these insurgents having prevented them from cultivating their fields in that region, as well as harrassing the whole population by every species of oppressive cruelty. Kingqwa was the responsible man on the part of the Chinese, and the enterprise was known to and approved by the provincial authorities, though they gave no other assistance than to furnish Mr. Drinker with a commission in the Chinese service. He received in advance the sum of twenty thousand dollars, all of which was expended in hiring and providing arms and provisions for a lorcha and her crew; and the attack was just ready to be made, when Mr. McLane ordered Mr. Drinker to desist under severe penalties, and disband his followers. This was done, and in afterwards settling the accounts of disbursements, there was considerable dispute, and charges of malfeasance. In consequence of the parties being unable to agree, both consented to an arbitration, and to abide by the decision given. The arbitrators examined the accounts of purchases, &c., and found that the money had been faithfully used. and that a balance of $1,902 51 was due Mr. Drinker according to the terms of the agreement entered into between them at the commencement of the affair. This balance Kingqua declined to pay, alleging that he had already lost $20,000 by the non-fulfillment of the contract, and the stipulation of non-interference on the part of United States authorities had not been observed, a stipulation as binding and as well understood by both parties as any other point in the contract.

Firing into the steamer Kumfa.

This vessel was making a trial trip, and went from Macao towards Canton by the western passage, having on board a company of ladies and gentlemen. When near the town of Hiangshau, she was fired into from a small fort, and obliged to return. Heavy shot passed close to the passengers, leaving no room for doubt of the murderous intent. In bringing the insult to the notice of the imperial commissioner, Mr. Parker showed that the steamer had a right to be there, both by treaty, as the place was within twenty-four hours of Canton, and also from it being one of the common passages from Macao to the city, and as such had been used by foreigners in former years with the consent of the Chinese authorities. The governor general, in his reply, refused to make the apology demanded, alleging that the fort was not a government fortification, but a private stockade and defense to repel pirates and insurgents, and added that the people were afraid that the steamer had underhand designs, and therefore opened fire on her. He quoted the third article of the treaty to prove that the vessel had no business where she was, and finally refused to give any satisfaction or make any apology.

Claims of American citizens for losses from fire in Canton and Whampoa, in 1856, 1857.

1st. On 28th October, 1856, Admiral Seymour determined to bombard the walls of Canton opposite the governor general's office, and force an entrance into it, which he accomplished; but a fire broke out in the suburbs near to the spot, towards night, caused, it is believed, directly or indirectly, by the cannonading, and the dwelling houses of two American missionaries were consumed, with several scores of Chinese houses and shops. These losses of Rev. Messrs. Happer, French, and Preston were not caused by the direct act of the Chinese authorities, but more immediately through the bombardment of the English forces. No formal demand has been made upon the English authorities for indemnification, though they were recently incidentally brought to the notice of Lord Elgin, as a separate claim, resting on a different basis from other losses at Canton and Whampoa; nor has any separate compensation been demanded from the Chinese, nor the peculiar circumstances of these losses made known to their authorities.

2d. The losses suffered by the burning of the foreign factories, on the 14th December, 1856.—These were caused by the direct act of the Chinese rulers, who drove out the English troops intrenched in the precincts of the factories by setting fire to the ruined shops just behind them, on the night of the 14th of December. Previous to this act, the governor general had requested the American consul, as well as all other officials except English, to withdraw from the foreign residences with his countrymen, and stated that he had *no leisure* to protect them during his difficulties with the English. After the burning, he excused himself from all liability for compensation by referring to this oft-repeated request to the consul, and that as the English set fire (which was certainly not true) to the factories, they must pay the sufferers. As soon as the British troops landed at the factories, on 28th October, the shopmen and servants in their precincts all left, from fear of being implicated with their own police and higher authorities.

During the four weeks previous to December 11, Mr. Williams, the American secretary of legation and interpreter, was constantly in Canton, engaged in translating and other official business, and was unable to get natives to assist in removing his property, for they were afraid to venture into the factories. Two servants alone remained with him. On one occasion, the difficulty of preparing the papers to be transmitted to the governor general, in consequence of the absence of native writers, was brought to his notice by the United States commissioner; but he replied that it must be a mistake, for he had no wish to impede business, and had never prevented persons going to the factories if they wished. The linguists, or *tung-sz'*, came to the house of the American secretary of legation to get these documents, to take them into the city to his excellency, and he threatened one of them with death if he ever brought another paper untranslated to him; but neither did this dilemma nor a reference to the eighteenth article of the treaty, which allows Americans to employ native scholars in their studies, induce him to grant a passport to any Chinese to visit the factories. The policemen were on the watch for those who left them, and one lad, whom the secretary sent down the river to deliver a verbal errand, was arrested in the streets, and lost his head the next day. Scores of innocent natives were executed in this manner on the pretense of traitorous collusion, while nothing could have been easier for the governor general, if he had pleased, than to furnish a certain number of natives with passports to assist all others but English in removing from the factories, in conformity to his advice. The linguists, who are accredited officers of government for translating their business with foreigners, and take dispatches to them, repeatedly asserted, in the most explicit manner, that there was no danger of the factories being fired by their authorities to expel the English. The property and household goods of the American residents were shown them, and they were told how inconvenient, if not impracticable, it was to move them, and yet how desirable it was to save things like books and types from destruction; to all which they declared that the governor general had no intention of destroying these buildings. These are the circumstances under which so many Americans, as well as others, combined with the difficulty of finding good locations outside of the port, were induced to remain in Canton, and thus lost their household and other property. Considerable amounts of goods were also stored in pack-houses opposite the factories, which it was almost impossible either to protect or remove, and were left where they were stored. A portion of these stocks has been gradually sold off by the Chinese brokers, who have honorably accounted for their sales to the owners; other portions were ruined by mold and other causes, and some have since been purloined.

3d. The losses at Whampoa.—These occurred in January, after the factories had been destroyed; and Yeh endeavored to follow up his success by expelling the English from the river; in doing which, his soldiers and police carried on their hostile operations against all foreigners alike. It was impossible to get workmen to finish operations on ships in docks, early in November; and by the end of December it was not easy to obtain provisions at Whampoa, from the native boats. On the 8th of January, all the foreigners there went on board her Britannic Majesty's ship Sibylle for safety, (the United States ship San Jacinto having already gone to Hong Kong,) in consequence of an engagement between the Chinese troops and insurgents, which exposed them all to great jeopardy. A German, who was left in charge of some property on shore, under the protection of the American flag, had been murdered in his bed the evening previous, and all others soon after left the reach with the Sibylle. As they left on the 13th January, the Chinese began to take possession, and, by the 16th, had carried off or destroyed everything afloat and ashore belonging to foreigners, among which was an American schooner, Excelsior, going to Hong Kong with cargo, whose Chinese crew was all murdered.

In corroboration of these particulars, the narrative of an eye-witness is given, describing the reckless conduct of the Chinese soldiery at Whampoa, and the circumstances attending the departure of foreigners. Mr. H. P. Blanchard thus writes in the journal, from which the extracts are taken, somewhat condensed:

"January 5. A sloop or lighter, carrying the American flag, called the Excelsior, was captured by mandarin boats, belonging to Tungkwan, near the first bar, while on her way to Hong Kong. She had an assorted cargo of matting, &c. Her crew are still in prison. I have offered to ransom them, but the Chinese authorities refuse their release, chiefly because the master of the sloop is a Chinese, who has been with us many years.

"January 7. I was aroused this morning, about five o'clock, by an alarm of the watchman, who asked me to come out on deck, as there was trouble at a chop near by. It being dark, I could only distinguish lights in each window, as if it was on fire within, but surmised that the German, who was living in it, had been attacked. I instantly manned my gig, though the crew at first refused to go, and, going on board the chop, in a few moments found that my fears had been realized. Blood lay in pools by the bed; and there was evidence that the man had been decapitated upon the window sill, from the hair lying on it, and a pool of blood on the verandah outside of it. The body was not to be found, and had probably been sunk in the river. I was informed that the deed was perpetrated by petty officials, whom the offered reward for heads had tempted down from Canton, and this report was afterwards substantiated by rumors from the city. A piece of iron grating, from the garden at Canton, was found in the room. At daylight, I went and hauled down the American flag, which had been flying all night from the chop, and carried it home with me, together with a cutlass sheath, much hacked, the poor man having probably defended himself with it.

"At nine o'clock, I held a council with Mr. Meers, who lived with me, as to the propriety of remaining any longer at the anchorage; and we decided to get up the anchors and move a quarter of a mile up close to the English frigate "Sibylle," the largest man-of-war in the Reach. It was fortunate that we moved that day, for an action took place the next night, on the same ground, between two hundred boats of the government and one hundred and forty rebel boats; the latter were beaten, and took refuge near the Sibylle; and the danger appeared so imminent, that all the few foreigners remaining went on board of her for their lives, abandoning everything, but returned soon after midnight, as nothing hostile was attempted. Next day they were ordered away from that part of the river, by the officer in charge of the frigate, and went down and joined the government boats at second bar, and received a pardon.

"The English river-steamer, Fei-ma, had recently reached Whampoa from Hong Kong; and I learned from her captain that, on his passage up, he had been attacked, near second bar, by fifty-three junks and snake boats, and, during the twenty-five minutes he was under fire, had received seven shots in the hull, one of them striking the angle of the boiler. He stated that he would not leave Whampoa unless protected by a man-of-war, and added that Admiral Seymour intended to abandon Whampoa. I had already begun to remove our property into the two storeships belonging to us; but, on shore, everything was stopped; not a man could be got to work at the docks; not a boat could be hired to bring mud to close their gates, for the authorities had forbidden natives to work for foreigners, and had posted placards, threatening them with death of they disobeyed.

"January 9. The river steamers Lily and Spark arrived in the Reach, having on board Captain Endicott, Consul Perry, Mr. Robertson, and other Americans as passengers. Captain Endicott having heard that the Sibylle was to leave, and knowing that the San Jacinto was at Hong Kong, had put both his steamers at our service, and came up in them to assist in getting away our property. I had applied to the commanding officer of her British Majesty's steamer Sampson, early in the same day, to tow one of our storeships down the river, and had received a verbal answer, inquiring 'where our commodore was.' I accordingly wrote by her, asking commander Armstrong if he could come up, as our lives and property might be lost. However, the Lily and Spark came that afternoon, each of them having on board a lieutenant and twenty men, whom the commodore had granted at Captain Endicott's request.

"January 10. The two steamers dropped down early this morning, off the dock-yards, and got a storeship alongside the pier, into which we loaded materials up to the 13th. The steamers returned every night to their anchorage off the Sibylle. We paid a dollar a day to coolies, who would only work when protected by the steamers and armed men-of-war's men, and declared that five dollars wages for a night's work would not induce them to run the risk of assisting us. The Sibylle was to drop down on the 13th, and every craft in the Reach made preparation to leave at the same time. At 7 a. m., the Spanish brig-of-war Scipion sailed down and anchored near first bar, followed by an English sloop-of-war towing the British vice-consul's residence, and the Lily towing one of our loaded storeships. The latter left her at first bar, and returned to assist a brig manned by Europeans, who had no help. Lastly, the Sibylle came over the bar, followed by the two river steamers towing our second storeship. Our floating residence was left at its moorings, and was shortly after carried off by the Chinese, with the floating Bethel, to a creek near Canton, where they were destroyed.

"On the morning of the 14th we all crossed the bar together, the Sibylle availing herself of the night tide, and moved down the river, where were to be seen, on both sides, a forest of junks' masts. The Scipion towed an unfinished Spanish war steamer, and there were besides, one English frigate, three merchant steamers, two brigs and a schooner, two storeships with forty or fifty thousand dollars of our property on board, two English hulks, and one Chinese-owned ship in our charge. We all reached Hong Kong at 6 p. m., and the following day breakfasted on Alum's (Esing) poisoned bread, which just about finished all of us.

"For two days after our departure, our dock-yards were crowded by people from the neighboring towns, pillaging them of all that was left, and then the whole place was burned over, the bottoms of the docks destroyed, and the timber lining them dug up, and everything carried off which could be taken. We are assured by natives that government boats from Canton lay near the whole time, and bore a prominent part in the destruction and in firing the buildings. They tore down the American flag which Mr. Endicott nailed to the flag-staff just before he left; and we are told that they violated it in a disgusting manner. While these proceedings were going on at our dock-yard, similar destruction was made of the other docks and houses belonging to foreigners at Whampoa, by the same parties, until everything was carried off or ruined."

4. Losses from Chinese soldiers at Canton.—Two American missionaries, Rev. Messrs. Vrooman and Roberts, whose houses lay near the city walls, below Dutch Folly, were intrusted to the care of responsible servants when their owners were obliged to leave. Some time in January, the Chinese police came to both of these houses in large force, and carried off everything in them. The claims of Rev. Messrs. Ball, Vrooman, and I. J. Roberts, are founded mostly on this violent robbery, which was not less unprovoked than useless.

Desecration of graves at Whampoa.

This charge rests upon the testimony of Chinese traders at Whampoa, who declared to Mr. Blanchard, an American merchant residing there, that the bodies of all the seamen who had died or been killed at the attack on the barrier forts in November, 1856, and afterwards buried on Dane's Island, in the usual place of interment, were exhumed by Chinese during the month of January, and their heads cut off and taken to Canton, to receive the rewards offered by the governor general for them. Though the evidence rests only on Chinese authority, still there is no improbability in the matter, and it is likely to have been actually done by them. The outrage was brought to the notice of Yeh, and only a trivial excuse was given.

Indignity in returning the President's letter with the United States Commissioner's letter of credence.

This letter from President Pierce and the letter of credence were delivered to his excellency Wang, governor general of Fuh-kien and Cheh-kiang, at Fuchau, on the 15th of July, 1856, by Mr. Parker, who referred him to the 31st article of the treaty, which mentioned three officers who were authorized to receive and transmit such documents to Pekin. His excellency received it, and there is no reasonable doubt fulfilled his promise of forwarding the box to court. On the 24th of August the same officer communicated to Mr. Parker the disapproval of his government at the course he had taken in the following words: "As to this matter, it is right it should revert to the imperial commissioner and governor general of the Liang Kwang duly to memorialize the throne, and to manage; and not being a subject which ought to be superintended by the viceroy of the Min and Cheh provinces, it is inexpedient for us (the ministers of the privy counsel) to present it in his behalf. We now take the original box and return it (to the viceroy) to deliver over, which will answer."

The commissioner, in his reply to his excellency Wang, October 27, exculpated him personally from all blame, but showed that, in addition to the indignity of returning a national letter on such a frivolous pretense, the insult was greatly aggravated by the condition in which the dispatch was sent back, the seals of the original letters having both been broken open, as well as those of the translations, though the latter documents fully informed the cabinet of their purport. Few incidents during the present reign have shown more decidedly the unsocial and seclusive policy of the Chinese government than the return of this box in the manner in which it came. No one doubts that all the high functionaries of the imperial court learned its contents, and perhaps, too, submitted the original and translations to foreign inspection for the purpose of verifying them, which renders their return more decisive and discourteous.

Schedule of pecuniary claims of American citizens against the Chinese government.

SECT. 1. PECUNIARY CLAIMS UNSETTLED PREVIOUS TO OCTOBER, 1856.

No.	Claimants.	Nature of claim.	Amount.
1	I. J. Roberts.....	House pillaged by mob at Canton in 1847; damages estimated and allowed by Chinese at 1,000 taels, with interest since accrued..................................	$2,800 00
2	Underwriters of bark Caldera.	Ship and cargo plundered near Kulan, in 1854, by Chinese wreckers, with the connivance of the local authorities; original claim is................................	100,000 00
3	R. S. Maclay, and others.	Loss on advance paid to landlord at Fuhchau, the authorities having interfered and obliged him to rescind his contract; original claim is........................	213 46
4	Owners of the Mermaid.	Loss caused by the Chinese bark Compton running into her; damages estimated by a board of survey and allowed by the Chinese; original claim............	3,125 00
5	S. Drinker........	Balance awarded against Kingqua and others, at Canton, for expenditures in fitting out the expedition against the insurgents in Blenheim Reach fort, by arbitrators appointed by the parties; original balance.	1,902 51
		Total of the above claims................................	108,040 97

SECT 2. LOSSES CAUSED BY THE BOMBARDMENT OF CANTON BY THE ENGLISH FORCES, OCTOBER 29, 1856.

No.	Claimants.	Nature of claim.	Amount.
1	D. Ball............	Furniture, books, &c., burned in conflagration caused by the bombardment...	$409 50
2	J. B. French.....	Furniture, books, and clothing, burned at same time...	1,800 00
3	C. F. Preston....	......do...........do...........do...........do...........do......	774 00
4	A. P. Happer....	......do...........do...........do...........do...........do......	1,315 25
5	Presbyter'n mission.	School-room, furniture, books, and apparatus............	2,472 00
		Total of above claims.....................................	6,770 75

SCHEDULE—Continued.

SECT. 3. LOSSES CAUSED BY THE BURNING OF THE FOREIGN FACTORIES AT CANTON, DECEMBER 14, 1856.

No.	Claimants.	Nature of claim.	Actual losses.	Contingent losses.	Constructive losses.	Total.
1	O. H. Perry, U. S. consul	Furniture, silver-ware, clothing, &c., burned in house or pillaged				$971 00
2	Mission of Am. Board C. F. M.	Stock of books, types, presses, and other apparatus of printing office				14,000 75
3	Medical Missionary Society	Furniture of hospital, frames, &c., with part of stock of medicines				270 00
4	S. W. Williams	Furniture, type, books, clothing, &c., burned	$5,700 00			
		Loss of income during time necessary to replace type and other materials			$3,000 00	8,700 00
5	Wetmore & Co	Furniture, hat-blocks, coral, &c., burned; boat lost	999 50			
		Loss on 1,850 pieces damaged shirtings sold		$1,248 92		2,248 42
6	W. W. Cryder	Furniture and stationery burned	695 54			
		Damage to property removed		200 00		895 54
7	S. Robertson	Furniture, books, stores, &c., burned	578 50			
		Damage to property removed		60 00		638 50
8	King & Co	Goods stored in factory burned	3,654 40			
		Goods stored in Chinese warehouses, perhaps saved		27,440 00		
		Loss in removing furniture			4,296 70	35,391 10
9	Aug. Heard & Co	Furniture, clothing, stores, and office burned in factory	10,853 00			
		Goods stored in other factories, burned	4,542 00			
		House No. 17, in British factories	85,000 00			
		Rent paid when premises were unoccupied			2,175 35	102,570 35
10	P. L. Everett	Cash and furniture, some removed		6,500 00		6,500 00
11	A. J. Case	Furniture, books—partly removed		1,200 00		1,200 00
12	Russell & Co	Furniture, stores, coral, &c., burned	2,250 00			

No.	Name	Description				Total
		Demurrage paid on ship "Napoleon III," for detention		500 00		
		Demurrage claimed on 2 ships			4,500 00	
		Goods in Chinese storehouses, condition and losses unknown		107,850 00		
						115,100 00
13	T. Walsh	Furniture, &c., burned	650 00			
		Goods stored in Chinese hands		43,339 00		
		Loss on contracts, goods ready for delivery at outbreak			10,503 90	
						54,492 90
14	J. Reed Smith	Furniture, samples, and books burned	1,650 00			1,650 00
15	H. S. Grew	Clothing, furniture, &c., burned	400 00			400 00
16	George Tyson	Furniture, books, &c., burned	510 00			510 00
17	W. M. Robinet & Co.	Furniture, stores, and goods burned	7,817 20			
		Loss on contract of 49,994 peculs of rice, which could not be delivered at Canton		27,297 00		
		Loss on contract for sugar			14,500 00	
		Brig Ernani, lost on Chuenpee			17,142 70	
						66,756 90
18	W. C. Hunter	Furniture, books, &c., burned	2,699 00			
		Demurrage on Fly Away, and loss of commissions			4,180 95	
						6,879 95
19	Alvord & Co.	Furniture, silverware, stores, and goods; some burned, some saved		10,500 00		
		Cash advanced on contracts		1,483 05		
						11,983 05
20	Williamette, Capt. Curry	Barricades made on board to protect against Chinese, and extra wages			2,065 00	
		Loss of income for six months on steamers			12,162 00	
						14,227 00
21	Carvalho & Co., for Smith & Lawrence.	Losses on goods contracted for ship Fly Away			18,000 00	18,000 00
22	Union Billiard Club	Two billiard tables, lamps, furniture, and other fixtures of room	1,110 00			1,110 00
23	J. P. Van Loffelt	Furniture, books, &c., burned	119 08			119 08
24	J. Purdon & Co.	Furniture, goods, &c., in factory, burned	10,981 50			
		Factory burned	5,710 00			
		Share in billiard room and bowling alley	190 00			
		Ginseng delivered to Chinese, unpaid		19,004 24		

SCHEDULE—Continued.

No.	Claimants.	Nature of claim.	Actual losses.	Contingent losses.	Constructive losses.	Total.
24	J. Purdon & Co—Continued	Ginseng, 149 casks, and 19 casks of furs stored in Chinese warehouses		$98,507 60		
		Loss of commissions on business			$27,629 80	
		Loss by unfulfilled contracts for silks			4,822 50	
		Ginseng rendered unsalable			255,149 00	
						$421,994 64
25	C. W. Gaillard	Furniture, books, &c., burned	$822 40			822 40
26	R. H. Graves	Clothing, books, and furniture burned	769 25			769 25
27	Southern Baptist Mission	House in street near factories	1,184 44			
		Library belonging to mission	611 70			
		Blocks used for printing S. S	700 00			
						2,496 14
28	I. J. Roberts	House and furniture in suburbs pillaged and burned by Chinese police, January 23, 1857	2,400 00			2,400 00
29	D. Vrooman, and others	Furniture, books, &c., destroyed or plundered by Chinese, same day	200 00			200 00
		Total of above claims				893,296 97

SCHEDULE—Continued.

SECT. 4. LOSSES AT WHAMPOA, CAUSED BY THE PROCEEDINGS OF THE CHINESE SOLDIERS, JANUARY 13, 1857.

No.	Claimants.	Nature of claim.	Actual losses.	Contingent losses.	Constructive losses.	Total.
1	T. Hunt & Co.	Three docks, (one of stone,) sheds, blacksmith and engine shops, office, steam engine, and outhouse, abandoned and burned	$80,000 00			
		Loss of materials, timber, paints, rigging, arms, &c.	53,020 19			
		Two floating dwellings, with their ground tackle, abandoned and carried off	6,200 00			
		Schooner Excelsior, and cargo, taken	4,648 00			
		Expenses of moving, injury to bark, loss of debt, &c.		$9,900 00		
		Time of persons out of employ			$6,200 00	
		Depreciation of materials, and expenses of steamers out of use			29,820 00	
		Loss of business and salaries paid			34,600 00	
						$208,288 19
2	H. P. Blanchard	Loss of fees as vice-consul and marshal at Whampoa; personal inconvenience			3,500 00	3,500 00
3	G. M. Ryder	Docks, materials, chop, and furniture	8,850 00			
		Floating residence and dispensary	5,278 00			
						14,128 00
4	F. Cady	Residence, stores, furniture, &c.	19,817 00			
		Loss of business a year			9,000 00	
						28,817 00
5	W. M. Robinet & Co.	Malavah wood burned	24,000 00			24,000 00
		Total of above claims				278,733 19

Summary of the pecuniary claims of American citizens against the Chinese government, as shown in the preceding lists:

SEC. 1. Claims previous to October, 1856	$108,040 97
SEC. 2. Claims for losses caused by the bombardment of Canton by the English, October 29, 1856	6,770 75
SEC. 3. Claims for losses caused by the burning of foreign factories, December 14, 1856, and subsequently	893,296 97
SEC. 4. Claims for losses at Whampoa, caused by the Chinese authorities, soldiers, and police, January 13, 1857	278,733 19
Total of claims	$1,286,841 88

Of this amount, the sum of $245,129 81 is placed in the column of contingent losses, some of the goods having been since recovered, and other portions may be subsequently found not to have been lost; and the sum of $380,137 90 is placed in the column of constructive losses, as all of them may require to be submitted to an investigation, according to their character; deducting these two sums leaves the direct losses by fire, robbery, and other ways to amount to $661,574 17, or thereabouts.

Mr. Reed to Mr. Cass.

No. 8.] LEGATION OF THE UNITED STATES,
On board the Minnesota, Hong Kong, February 4, 1858.

SIR: I hasten to communicate to you the copy of an important document, which has been sent to me from Canton, where it was found among the viceroy's archives.

It is, in form, a letter from the council of state at Pekin to the imperial commissioner at Canton, and to the governors general of the two eastern provinces. It is, in fact, an imperial decree. It is most significant in its illustration of the views of the Emperor, or those who control him, and especially interesting, as it appears to refer particularly to the action of the United States.

I regret to say, and in this view, I have the concurrence of the secretary of legation, Mr. Williams, whose long experience entitled his opinion to great consideration, that it confirms the most discouraging judgment as to the relation of the viceroys to the imperial court, showing beyond question, that in all that Yeh said and did in relation to the treaty powers, he was a faithful exponent of the imperial will. In his refusal in the dispatches sent to me in November and December last, to listen to a revision of the treaty, he used almost the language, as he certainly expressed the leading idea of this decree, that nothing but "inconsiderable modifications" were to be permitted, though with all the craft of his peculiar diplomacy, he did not disclose an authority to negotiate, even as to minute alterations. He was ordered to refuse to treat on matters of substance, and he obeyed. There is in this rescript the usual dash of falsehood in the assertion that the allied plenipotentiaries in 1854, Mr. McLane and Sir John Bowring yielded the grounds of controversy. They did nothing of the kind. They were tantalized by vexatious ceremonial till they were obliged to retire in consequence of the severity of the season.

It will be seen that this decree seems to have been induced by Mr. Parker's avowed intention to go north in the spring of 1856, which as you are aware, he carried into effect later in the season, by visiting Shanghai, whence the letter of the President was forwarded. It was returned, as you know, with the seals broken, and unanswered.

The reply which Mr. Parker received on this visit, that the governors generals were not competent to enter on a discussion of foreign business, but that everything of the kind was intrusted to the commissioner at Canton, seems to have been honest.

The decree satisfies me that any attempt on my part during this winter to have opened negotiations at Shanghai, or elsewhere, would have been fruitless.

It shows further the extreme anxiety of the imperial court to prevent any access to Pekin, or its neighborhood, and strengthens the opinion which has always and strenuously been expressed by the Russian plenipotentiary, that an actual approach to that neighborhood with a decisive tone and available force, might produce a result, and that nothing short of this will.

Above all, it settles the question as to any distinction being taken among the nations of the West to our advantage. Steadfast neutrality and consistent friendship make no impression on the isolated obduracy of this empire. I never thought that there was, on the part of the officials, any such distinction. I am sure of it now. The only doubt that remains, and this the events of the next two months will solve, is whether the catastrophe at Canton is to produce any distant effect. On this, yet, there is nothing but the vaguest speculation to enlighten us.

It shows, too, that the imperial government at Pekin is far from ignorant of what occurs at distant points. The Emperor, or his council, have accurate knowledge, and give precise directions, which are implicitly obeyed. It shows that at Pekin the contents of the treaties are, according to the gloss the Chinese choose to put upon them, well understood. The real responsibility is with the central authority.

All the authenticated facts are now before the President. I ask for them his most considerate attention. My best judgment on the specific wrongs received by citizens of the United States was communicated in a dispatch written before this imperial decree was known to me. It does not in any way weaken that judgment. I am better satisfied than ever that decisive action is necessary with the officials who rule this people.

I desire to add, that there is no doubt of the entire genuineness of this decree, or of the accuracy of the translation.

I have the honor to be, sir, your obedient servant,

WILLIAM B. REED.

Hon. LEWIS CASS,
Secretary of State.

HER MAJESTY'S SHIP FURIOUS,
January 29, 1858.

SIR: I have the honor to inclose herewith the translation of a document found in Yeh's archives, in which the visit of Dr. Parker to Shanghai is referred to, and which may therefore be interesting to your excellency.

I have the honor to be, sir, your excellency's most obedient humble servant,

ELGIN AND KINCARDINE.

His Excellency Hon. W. B. REED,
U. S. Envoy Extraordinary and Minister Plenipotentiary, &c., &c., &c.

Letter from the Great Council to Yeh, a Secretary of State, (or senior member of the inner cabinet,) and Governor General of the two Kwang; to Iliang, Governor General of the two Kiang; and to Keihonga, Governor of Kiang Su, entitled to wear the insignia of the first grade.

On the 18th day of the 2d moon of the 6th year of Hienfung, (March 24, 1856,) we had the honor to receive the following imperial decree:

Iliang and Keihonga represent that the Mei and Ying barbarians (Americans and English) are about to request some exchange in their treaty regulations. The American chief, Parker, writes to Kiang Su that he is waiting for a ship to proceed to Shanghai to reconsider the treaty, and the English chief, Si Tai Kwoh, (Mr. Lay,) also holds language to the effect that application will certainly be made by every State for a revision of its treaty; that the exclusiveness of the Kwang Tung (authorities) has reached such a point that none of their ministers will hold any further communication with them.

The idea (of the barbarians) is to use their intended visit to Shanghai as a means of pressure, while they make it their ground of complaint that they are so buffed and refused intercourse by the Kwang Tung (authorities.) The thing is plain (now;) though the original treaties under which the five ports were opened, did contain a provision that they should be revised, nothing more was meant than that if, in the course of time, abuses came to exist, or points of difficulty or hindrance (were discovered,) as it was to be feared might be the case, there would be no objection to slight modifications. It was never (contemplated) that there could be any alteration in the substance of their conditions. The demands these barbarians made the year before last at Shanghai and Tientsen were so utterly inadmissable that Tsunghun and his colleagues, in their interview with them, rejected (their propositions) with rebuke; and the chiefs themselves, perceiving their own unreasonableness, (the crookedness of their own reason, the badness of their cause,) did not renew the controversy. They are now going to Shanghai on the plea that the exclusiveness of the Kwang Tung [governor] is past bearing; but the governor general and governor in Kiang Su being in no respect competent to the chief superintendent of barbarian business, and of course unable to accede to what they require, and their refusal certain to bring the barbarians to Tientsin, to the yet greater violation of what is right and proper, let Yeh Ming Chin inform himself of the particulars of the case, and hold in the barbarian securely. If the changes they require be merely on points of small significance, there will be no harm in his considering these with them, and forwarding a representation to us; (which received) some slight modifications may be adopted. If they repeat the extravagant demands of the year before last, he will speak plainly, repel (their advances,) and break off [negotiations.] It is absolutely incumbent on him, by an equal employment of graciousness and awe, to put an end to this project of an expedition northward altogether. Let him not show himself utterly inaccessible, (lit., steep and lofty, refuse to see them,) lest his refusal to receive them be converted into matter of complaint. Let Iliang and Keihunga desire Lan-wei-wan to convey their commands to the different barbarian consuls (at Shanghai,) and inform them that all business concerning the trade of the five ports must be referred to Kwang Tung, (and that the authorities of) other provinces cannot overstep the bounds of their own jurisdiction; that if the barbarians do not choose to have intercourse with Kwang Tung, no other provincial government can properly take cognizance of their business in its stead; that they have in this instance reported the different subjects of [Dr. Parker's] communication to the throne, but that they cannot even now do more than request them to hand these over to the imperial commissioner in Kwang Tung for his disposal, and that as regards the proposed revision, they, the governor general and governor, are not competent to entertain applications regarding it. With gentle words, let them persuade them to sail to Kwang Tung, and to prevent anything else coming of it. This is most important. Let copies of the original papers of Iliang and his colleague be supplied to Yeh Ming Chin for his information; and let this decree be forwarded at the rate of 500 li a day, and communicated in confidence to the different authorities whom it concerns. Respect this. In obedience to his Majesty's decree, [the council] write this note.

[Translated,] Thomas Wade.

Legation of the United States,
Macao, January 3, 1858.

My Lord: I have the honor to acknowledge the receipt of your letter of the 29th ultimo, inclosing the translation of a document found in Yeh's archives, in which the visit of Mr. Parker to Shanghai in 1856, and that of Sir John Bowring and Mr. M'Lane to the Peiho in 1854, are referred to.

I thank your excellency for your kindness in communicating to me this very interesting paper, which I am sure will attract the attention of my government.

I have the honor to be, my lord, your excellency's most obedient, humble servant,

WILLIAM B. REED.

His Excellency the EARL OF ELGIN AND KINCARDINE,
Her Majesty's High Commissioner.

Mr. Reed to Mr. Cass.

No. 9.] LEGATION OF THE UNITED STATES TO CHINA,
On board the Minnesota, Canton river, February 13, 1858.

SIR: I have the honor to forward with this dispatch a correspondence which has recently passed between the plenipotentiaries of the treaty powers in China, to which I invite the early attention of the President. It is comprised in the annexed inclosures, (numbered from No. 2 *a* to 2 *u*.) It is so full and precise, of so recent date, and occurs so near to the time of the departure of the mail, that it is neither necessary nor practicable for me to add any comprehensive comments on it. I confidently hope that the course which I have adopted, and the views which, in my part of this correspondence, I have expressed, in accordance with what I understood to be my instructions, will meet the approval of the President.

He will, I am sure, be gratified to observe the prompt and judicious assistance I have received from the flag-officer in command here.

The squadron has been so disposed as to afford me at this moment every facility in my movements and in conducting my correspondence, and, at the same time, to detail a portion of it on active service of observation.—(Inclosures 4 *c*, 4 *d*.)

My previous dispatches have fully apprised you of the progress of the hostilities in the Canton river of our abstinence from any share in them, and of the course I felt it my duty, with the entire acquiescence of my countrymen here, to pursue with reference to the blockades.

On the 1st February, I received a letter from Sir John Bowring, forwarding a government Gazette extraordinary, (inclosures No. 1 *a*, No. 1 *b*, No. 1 *c*,) with the information that, on the 10th, the blockade of the river and city of Canton would be raised. This has been done.

On the morning of the 6th February, I received from their excellencies the Earl of Elgin and Baron Gros their letters of the 4th, accompanied by the draft of papers to be addressed by them to the imperial court at Pekin, and copies of all the correspondence which, before the attack on Canton, they had with the late Commissioner

Yeh. Nearly coincident with them were their letters of the 6th, (inclosures 2 *r*, 2 *s*,) inclosing the notifications of the temporary retention in a state of seige of the city of Canton, the qualified admission of strangers within it, no distinction being made between nations of the West, and the annunciation that, except for the necessary defense of Canton, all hostile operations against China are suspended, and that the relations of British and French subjects are reëstablished on the basis of treaties declared to be in full force; in other words, as in a state of peace.

This frank communication of the intentions of the allies was not confined to this legation, but was made, at the same time, to his excellency Count Poutiatine, the Russian plenipotentiary, then at Macao, (I being accidentally at this anchorage,) and you will, I am sure, be struck, not only with the prompt coincidence of our views as to what we ought to do, but with the very friendly and considerate manner in which Count Poutiatine delayed sending an answer till he should have an opportunity of conferring with me. I was most happy in return, to have it in my power to facilitate his excellency's wishes in the transmission of his dispatches north.—(Inclosures 3 *a*, 3 *b*, 3 *c*.)

The correspondence between the allied plenipotentiaries and Yeh before the attack on the city is very curious, as illustrative of the relations of parties at a moment where, if ever, the power of the strong might have been abused, and the consciousness of weakness should, one might suppose, have prompted concession or submission. I felt no little curiosity to know, with something like precision, what had been demanded before the blow was struck, and what sympathy was really due to the inevitable victims of such a conflict.

It is impossible, I think, to read the letters of the British and French plenipotentiaries without being impressed by the evidence they exhibit, not only of moderation of demand, but of reluctant resort to arms. That of Lord Elgin refers to but two matters of requisition, the right to enter the city of Canton, which, I am very confident, Lord Elgin himself would desire to guard by some limitations, and pecuniary indemnity for private losses and public expenditure. If yielded, the island of Honan, opposite the city, or a part of it, was to be retained as a material guarantee till a treaty could be negotiated, and then positively to be surrendered. If refused, or an answer withheld for more than ten days, military measures were to be resorted to with a reservation of future demands in this event. The French demands have relation exclusively to the case of the Abbè Chapdelaine, a missionary priest who was brutally tortured and murdered two years ago in the province of Kwang-si. The military notices were equally considerate of the duties of humanity.

On the other hand, it is difficult to comprehend the spirit which animated the singular individual who, unfortunately, for many years has ruled with power so nearly absolute the destinies of this portion of the empire, and to whom, with no other limitation of his will than that of being ordered never to yield to the demands of the strangers, has been intrusted the administration of foreign affairs. His letters to this legation, in December last, turning coldly, if not insolently, away from our reasonable demands for a revision of the treaty, and rejecting an honest offer to serve him, his master, and those whom he seems to care little for his poor countrymen, his replies to the French minister, equivocating as to an act of blood, about the details of which there is no doubt, and for which so easy reparation could be made and would have been accepted, and finally his indecorous answers (for clumsy satire or satire of any kind in such matter is very repulsive) to Lord Elgin's respectful communication, in which he seems to have done his best to incense rather than conciliate, the whole indeed forms an obscure compound of cunning and insolence and folly which sets all analysis of character and conduct at defiance. It should be borne in mind, too, that this man has not been, in a strict sense, a self-willed controller of affairs, but a trusted representative of a superior power, and yet so situated, and at least so far enlightened, that he could not but measure the certainty of a disastrous and bloody result, with loss of power and peculiar fame, and probably life or, has been the case, liberty, in the event of conflict. There is no solution of this puzzle in a want of sagacity or of accurate knowledge. His subtle intelligence is manifest enough, and his means of information as to what was doing near him and at a distance very great. His power over the people was enormous, not only because of these resources, but because it was well known he was the favorite servant of the emperor. If, by chance, any more tractable or gentle depository of power was brought in contact with strangers, as was the case in some of the other provinces, he was either superseded or the trust in him suspended, and all conferred on Yeh. It remains to be seen, I may incidentally observe, whether his fall will produce any favorable result, or whether others, like him and his predecessor Seu may not take his place.

As to the manner in which hostilities have been conducted, I am impelled by the strongest sense of justice to say that I believe everything was done to confine the inevitable suffering within the narrowest limits. Sad as is the appearance of Canton, once a great mart of commerce, (and I have just returned from a visit thither, and speak from personal observation,) with its deserted and ruined suburbs and houses, it is well understood that the loss of life among the besieged was relatively small, the estimate varying from five hundred to three thousand, and that the discipline of the assailants, though the town was taken by actual assault, was very strict. That portion of the ruin which strikes the eye as most complete is the site of the foreign factories. They seem to have been rooted out, not a vestige remaining but a portion of the flight of stone steps at the landing, from which the foreign merchants embarked in January of last year. This was the thorough devastation of the Chinese.

Since the capture of the city, the efforts of the plenipotentiaries, and especially of Lord Elgin, on whom this duty, I infer, specially devolves, has been to establish a provisional Chinese government through the agency of officials who were apparently willing to assume the trust. The late Lieutenant Governor Pihkwei is in nominal charge of Canton; and though, of course, in dealing with the very untrustworthy class of mandarins, it would be unsafe to have too much confidence, it is believed by those who have the best means of information that the experiment will succeed. No one can be sure of this till the pleasure of the Emperor is known, which will be obeyed as heretofore by all, officials and others, with the strange sort of superstitious loyalty which characterizes this nation.

In one respect, the belligerents have shown peculiar consideration for the necessities of the Chinese authorities and the interest of commerce. Lord Elgin assures me that, under no circumstances, will he consent that a dollar of the revenue from imposts or any other source shall be collected by foreign authority or diverted from its proper object, and a Chinese custom-house under Pihkwei's authority, has been or is about to be established at Whampoa. No one pretends to conjecture how far trade will revive.

For its suspension, with the losses it entails, and the ruin and desolation of Canton, the heaviest responsibility rests on the imperial authorities. I ought to state here that, since his capture, Yeh has been kept a prisoner on board a ship-of-war in the river, and has, to-day, as I have been informed, been sent, for temporary safe-keeping, to Calcutta. He exhibits no sensibility to his fallen condition, and expresses no regrets.

Such is the clear judgment at which I have come, with no sympathy with the belligerents in the origin of the war.

With these views, enlightened not a little by the revelations of Yeh's correspondence, I could not hesitate, as to the course to be pursued on receiving the communication of the English and French plenipotentiaries. The peaceful policy of my government and its determination not to be involved in the strifes of others, had been vindicated, not merely by my resolute stand against all influences here, the urgency of my own countrymen, and the natural solicitude of others more directly interested, but in my correspondence with the representative of one of the belligerent powers. The exaggerated expectations of a year ago had subsided into a quiet conviction that, after all, we understood our own interests and duties best. But, beyond this, I was not authorized to hold back. Your instructions expressly directed me to coöperate with the representatives of the treaty powers in all peaceful measures of redress. My dispatches written before I knew that such coöperation was to be solicited, shows that my mind had come to the conclusion that, for the redress of our own wrongs, there was a necessity for vigorous action.

The allied plenipotentiaries made their propositions to me in perfect good faith. All that they asked was that I should, in the name of my own government, address a respectful and urgent letter to the imperial court of Pekin, they having done so; and that the communications should be forwarded at the same moment. They furnished me with copies of their intended letters to the prime minister, or supreme council of state at Pekin, for my perusal, and I, as soon as it was completed, sent mine to them. The Russian plenipotentiary pursued the same course, and thus a friendly coöperation, of the most complete and inoffensive kind, has at last occurred. I heartily rejoice at it. I solicit the attention of the President to the four dispatches sent to Pekin, (inclosures 2 *o*, 2 *q*, 2 *v*, 3 *d*,) and rely confidently on his approval of the course I have pursued, and the views I have endeavored to express.

I have reason to believe that the prompt manner in which we have met and agreed to this proposal of friendly coöperation has given great satisfaction to those who made it; and my personal intercourse with Lord Elgin and Baron Gros, since my answer was given, satisfies me entirely of the conciliatory spirit in which they propose to deal with this China question. Lord Elgin seems especially anxious to avoid further conflict.

I am confident, too, that it forms no part of his policy to take or keep possession of Chinese territory. He may fail in his experiment of permitting the Cantonese to govern themselves, but I am sure he means to persevere as long as there is the least chance of success. He has, I believe, an irksome task in protecting the Chinese against themselves, and maintaining his own opinions against the impatience of military men, and amidst the cavils and criticisms of the querulous merchants around him.

I may here confidently mention that, in conversation with me yesterday, his lordship said, by way of explanation, as it seemed to me, of the tone he had adopted in our brief correspondence in December, that he had not then received the copy of my instructions forwarded by Lord Napier. They had, by some post office mistake, been sent back to England from Singapore, when Lord Elgin went to India. I could not but understand his mentioning this as explanatory, and, perhaps, apologetic. The implication certainly was that, had he known the character of my instructions, he would have abstained from the urgency which he had used. I refer to this as a matter of fact, without meaning to attach much consequence to it.

The united letters from all the plenipotentiaries have been dispatched. Count Pontiatine's and mine were placed in charge of Captain Nicholson, of the Mississippi, which sailed this afternoon for Shanghai. The others go by special messengers in the Peninsular and Oriental mail-boat to-morrow. At Shanghai they will be delivered by the consuls to the Taoutae, and by him are to be forwarded to the governor general of the two Kiang at Loo Choo.

It may be that they will be directly presented to the governor general. Should there be no obstacle interposed by the local authorities, these dispatches may reach Pekin in a month from this date, and an answer be at Shanghai in a fortnight later. I shall proceed thither in this ship about the middle of March.

This will be made the most imposing appeal that has ever been addressed by the western powers to the sense of justice and policy of the imperial court. I feel no little pride in uniting in it as the representative of the United States, for it is entirely consistent with the peaceful attitude we have tried to occupy in the East, and equally so with the decided action in the redress of our own wrongs, which, in my recent dispatches, I have urged. I sincerely hope the appeal may be met in a proper spirit, for I do not permit myself to doubt that, if a plenipotentiary, duly accredited, shall come to Shanghai with even a moderate disposition to do right, satisfactory treaties will be negotiated, and, so far as anything can be settled between parties of so contradictory modes of thought and action, matters be arranged on a safe and, perhaps, permanent basis.

But I should do great injustice to myself, to the character of my country, and to the great interests of our people in China, if I did not call your attention and that of the President to the possible alternative of a persistent and contemptuous refusal to entertain any friendly proposition to afford redress for injuries, or to revise the treaty; or, what is equivalent to these, vexatious delay or evasion. What, then, will be the duty of the representative of the United States, is a question I beg leave, most respectfully, to put? Until I have distinct instructions I am, as to the future, within strict limits, which I certainly shall not go beyond. I consider it within those instructions to proceed with the allied fleets to the north, and try what effect the appearance of force near the seat of the imperial government may produce. But here, unless further authorized, my means of efficiency end. I hope the government will permit me, without entanglement with others, vigorously to assert our own rights. I am happy to observe that, with reference to a remote and semi-civilized power in the western hemisphere, the President in his message has asked from Congress the power to resort to some measures of coercion for the redress of wrongs, and with regard to this empire he uses the emphatic and most appropriate language: "that China cannot long be permitted to withhold the just concessions which the nations of the world have a right to expect." More than this, I need not ask. But the power to exercise that amount of coercion, far short of war, which is the the only intelligible appeal to such a people as this, I do most earnestly ask to be invested with.

I beg to recall your attention to my previous dispatches, prepared before I had any communication with the other plenipotentiaries, and sent by this mail. There is no opinion there expressed that I desire to modify.

I regret that the early departure of the mail prevents me from sending translations of all the documents annexed to this dispatch.

I have the honor to be, sir, your most obedient servant,

WILLIAM B. REED.

Hon. LEWIS CASS,
Secretary of State, Washington.

Index to Dispatch No. 9, February 13, 1858.—Relating to letters to Pekin.

Exhibit.	From—	To—	Subject-matter.	Date.
1 *a*	J. Bowring	W. B. Reed	Inclosing Government Gazette announcing	Jan. 29, 1858.
1 *b*			Raising of blockade of port of Canton	Jan. 28, 1858.
1 *c*	Government	Gazette	Regulations respecting entering city of Canton	Feb. 6, 1858.
2 *a*	Lord Elgin	W. B. Reed	Sending draft of his letter to Pekin	Feb. 4, 1858.
2 *b*	Lord Elgin	Yuching	Letter showing the grievances and demands of English	Feb. 1858.
2 *c*	Lord Elgin	Yeh	Recapitulating the wrongs English have received	Dec. 12, 1857.
2 *d*	Yeh	Lord Elgin	Defends his conduct and wishes trade resumed	Dec. 14, 1857.
2 *e*	Lord Elgin	Yeh	Declares the reply unsatisfactory; hostilities resumed	Dec. 24, 1857.
2 *f*	Yeh	Lord Elgin	Reasserts that no wrongs have been done	Dec. 25, 1857.
2 *g*	Baron Gros	W. B. Reed	Sends draft of letter to Pekin, and correspondence held with Yeh. (Translation appended.)	Feb. 4, 1858.
2 *h*	A. Bourboulon	Yeh	Announcing Baron Gros's arrival	Dec. 10, 1857.
2 *i*	Yeh	A. Bourboulon	Details steps taken respecting Abbē Chapdelaine	Dec. 12, 1857.
2 *k*	Baron Gros	Yeh	Recapitulates grievances against China, &c	Dec. 12, 1857.
2 *l*	Yeh	Baron Gros	Declares that Chapdelaine was not killed	Dec. 14, 1857.
2 *m*	Yeh	Baron Gros	Blames him for not believing him	Dec. 25, 1857.
2 *n*	Baron Gros	Yeh	Closes further correspondence as useless	
2 *o*	Allies	To Canton officials	Conditions of their sparing the city	
2 *p*	Allies	To Cantonese citizens	Declaring why the city was taken, and that they had installed Pihkwei as governor.	Jan. 10, 1858.
2 *q*	Baron Gros	Yuching	Letter stating grievances and wrongs of the French. (Translation appended.)	Feb. 1858.
2 *r*	Lord Elgin	W. B. Reed	Inclosing copy of notification of military occupation of Canton by allies	Feb. 6, 1858.
2 *s*	Baron Gros	W. B. Reed	Incloses copy of preceding notification	Feb. 6, 1858.
2 *t*	W. B. Reed	Lord Elgin	Willingly coöperates in the appeal to Pekin	Feb. 6, 1858.
2 *u*	W. B. Reed	Baron Gros	Thanks him for letter and agrees to coöperate	Feb. 6, 1858.
2 *v*	W. B. Reed	Supreme Council of State.	Setting forth the grievances and demands of United States, with note to Ho and Chan, of Kiangnan.	Feb. 10, 1858.
3 *a*	Cte. Poutiatine	W. B. Reed	Inclines to join in the appeal to Pekin	Feb. 6, 1858.
3 *b*	W. B. Reed	Cte. Poutiatine	Proposes sending Mississippi with letter	Feb. 8, 1858.
3 *c*	Cte. Poutiatine	W. B. Reed	Agrees to the plan inclosing copy of his	Feb. 9, 1858.
3 *d*	Cte. Poutiatine	Supreme Council of State.	Letter stating the grievances and claims of Russia	
4 *a*	S. B. Williams	F. W. A. Bruce	Mr. Reed proposes to send "Mississippi" to Shanghai with letter, and will take English letter coming up.	Feb. 8, 1858.

4 *b*	F. W. A. Bruce	S. W. Williams	Lord Elgin intends sending up Mr. Oliphant	Feb. 9, 1858.
			Requests him to charter a small steamer	Feb. 4, 1858.
4 *c*	W. B. Reed	J. Tattnall	Wishes squadron to be at Shanghai last of March	Feb. 6, 1858.
4 *d*	J. Tattnall	W. B. Reed	Squadron will rendezvous at Shanghai ; has chartered the Antelope	Feb. 7, 1858.
4 *e*	W. B. Beed	W. C. Nicholson	Desires him to take letters to Shanghai	Feb. 10, 1858.
4 *f*	W. B. Reed	A. L. Freeman	Wishes his aid in sending in letter to the Taoutae, after conferring with Mr. Oliphant.	Feb. 10, 1858.

Exhibit 1 *a*.

No. 21.]

SUPERINTENDENCY OF TRADE,
Hong Kong, January 29, 1858.

SIR: I have the honor to forward to your excellency a copy of the Hong Kong Gazette extraordinary, announcing that the blockade of the city and river of Canton will be raised on the 10th proximo.

I have the honor to be, sir, your excellency's most obedient, humble servant,

JOHN BOWRING.

His Excellency WILLIAM B. REED,
U. S. Minister Plenipotentiary, Macao.

Exhibit 1 *b*.

No. 1.—GOVERNMENT NOTIFICATION.—DIPLOMATIC DEPARTMENT.

SUPERINTENDENCY OF TRADE,
Victoria, Hong Kong, January 28, 1858.

His excellency her Majesty's plenipotentiary and chief superintendent of trade, &c., &c., has received a dispatch from his excellency, the naval commander-in-chief, an extract of which, with its accompanying inclosures, are hereby published, for general information.

By order:

GEO. S. MORRISON.

Extract of dispatch from his excellency the naval commander-in-chief, dated at Hong Kong, 28th January, 1858, to the address of his excellency her Majesty's plenipotentiary, &c., &c.:

"I have the honor to transmit to your excellency, in original, a notification from the French admiral and myself, that the blockade of the port and river of Canton will be raised on the 10th February next. I also inclose a second notification, that the city and suburbs will be open to foreigners, under certain conditions, which will be hereafter promulgated, and that they will continue under martial law during their occupation by the allied forces."

We, the undersigned, Rear Admiral Sir Michael Seymour, K. C. B., commander-in-chief of her Britannic Majesty's naval forces in India and China, and Rear Admiral C. Rigault de Genouilly, commander-in-chief of the naval forces of his Majesty, the Emperor of the French in India and China, hereby declare that the blockade of the port and river of Canton, established by our respective declarations of the 3d of August and 10th of December, 1857, will be raised on Wednesday, the 10th of February, 1858.

Dated at Canton, this 25th day of January, 1858.

M. SEYMOUR.
C. RIGAULT DE GENOUILLY.

The undersigned, commanders-in-chief of the allied forces of Great Britain and France, hereby declare that the city and suburbs of Canton will be open to foreigners from and after the 10th February, 1858, under regulations to be hereafter promulgated.

The commanders-in-chief declare, at the same time, that the city and suburbs continue under martial law, and will so continue during their military occupation by the allied forces.

M. SEYMOUR,
Rear Admiral and Commander-in-chief of her Britannic Majesty's naval forces in India and China.

C. RIGAULT DE GENOUILLY,
Rear Admiral and Commander-in-chief of the naval forces of his Majesty the Emperor of the French in India and China.

C. T. VAN STRAUBENZEE,
Major-General, commanding the military forces.

Exhibit 1 *c.*

NO. 3.—GOVERNMENT NOTIFICATION.—DIPLOMATIC DEPARTMENT.

SUPERINTENDENCY OF TRADE,
Victoria, Hong Kong, February 6, 1858.

His excellency, Sir John Bowring, her Majesty's plenipotentiary, chief superintendent of trade, &c., &c., has received from his excellency Sir Michael Seymour, K. C. B., rear admiral and commander-in-chief of her Majesty's naval forces, the regulations which have been adopted by the naval and military authorities of the allied powers in connection with the removal of the blockade and the entrance into the city and suburbs of Canton, which regulations are hereby published for general information.

By order:

GEO. S. MORRISON.

As the blockade of the river and port of Canton is to be raised on the 10th instant, the following regulations are promulgated for general information and guidance during the military occupation of the city and suburbs by the allied forces:

ARTICLE I.

The city and suburbs being under martial law, no foreigner whatsoever is permitted to enter them without a passport signed by the allied commanders-in-chief.

ARTICLE II.

A mixed commission has been nominated by the allied commanders-in-chief to preserve good order, and to inquire into all infractions of these regulations or of martial law, with power to inflict fine or imprisonment, and in grave cases to hand over the offenders to the commanders-in-chief.

ARTICLE III.

Every foreigner wishing to enter the city or suburbs must apply in writing to the commissioners. The commissioners will submit the application to the allied commanders-in-chief, who, if they see no objection, will grant the applicant a pass, revocable at pleasure, which must be visaed by the commander every fourteen days.

ARTICLE IV.

A police force, English and French, is charged with the surveillance of the city and suburbs. The police are directed to require the production of passes, and any person refusing to comply with their demand, being without a pass, or being guilty of any offense against good order, will be taken before the commissioners.

ARTICLE V.

Officers of the allied army and navy, and foreign officers in uniform, do not require passes. Seamen and marines are not to be allowed to land except on duty.

ARTICLE VI.

The gates of the city will be open from sunrise to sunset, and no foreigners will be permitted to be in the streets of the city or suburbs after the firing of the sunset gun.

ARTICLE VII.

No foreigner is permitted to enter the official buildings without special permission from the commissioners.

ARTICLE VIII.

Merchant vessels are not to anchor between the ships-of-war and city walls, or except where directed by the harbor-master.

ARTICLE IX.

The introduction of arms or munitions of war is strictly prohibited.

ARTICLE X.

In all cases of alarm, red flags will be hoisted on the heights of Magazine Hill, and at the commissioners' yamun, followed by two guns, and the beating of the retreat in all quarters. All persons should then immediately provide for their safety, either by leaving the city, repairing to the allied lines, or to the police stations.

CANTON, *February* 4, 1858.

NOT TRANSFERABLE.

Pass for the city and suburbs of Canton and allied lines.

NAME.	NATION.	PROFESSION.	RESIDENCE.

Signature of bearer

M. SEYMOUR,
Rear Admiral and Commander-in-Chief of her Britannic Majesty's Naval Forces.

C. RIGAULT DE GENOUILLY,
Rear Admiral and Commander-in Chief of the Naval Forces of his Majesty the Emperor of the French.

C. T. VAN STRAUBENZEE,
Major General Commanding the British Military Forces.

CANTON, the —— of ——, 1858.

True copy.

H. F. HANCE.

[Confidential.]

Exhibit 2 *a.*

HER MAJESTY'S SHIP FURIOUS,
Canton, February 4, 1858.

SIR: I have the honor to inclose herewith, confidentially, for your excellency's information, the copy of a note which I am about to send forthwith to the prime minister or senior secretary of state of the Emperor of China. The note itself will explain to your excellency the course which I intend to follow in pursuance of the policy which her Majesty's government has directed me to carry out in China, and its inclosures will put your excellency in possession of the negotiations between the late Imperial Commissioner Yeh and myself, which preceded the capture of Canton by the allied English and French forces.

In making this frank and unreserved communication to your excellency, I am acting in the spirit of the instructions which I have received from my government, and I have only to add that, in my opinion, the weight of the representations of the plenipotentiaries of the allied powers, and, therefore, the probability that the government of China may be induced without further coercive pressure, to consent to such arrangements as may obviate future misunderstanding, and tend to develop commercial relations between China and other nations, will be increased if your excellency shall see fit to support the attempt about to be made by his excellency Baron Gros and myself to effect a settlement of these matters by negotiations.

I have the honor to be, sir, your excellency's most obedient, humble servant,

ELGIN AND KINCARDINE.

His Excellency Hon. W. B. Reed, *&c., &c., &c.*

Exhibit 2 *a.*

The undersigned, &c., &c., has the honor to inform the prime minister of the emperor of China that the Imperial Commissioner Yeh, having, in the exercise of the authority delegated to him by his imperial master, refused to grant to the subjects of her Majesty the Queen of Great Britain and the subjects of his Majesty the Emperor of the French their treaty rights, and first compensation for injuries inflicted, the high officers representing the governments of Great Britain and France have been compelled to have recourse to arms. The city of Canton, captured after a brief resistance, is now in the possession of the allied forces, and the imperial commissioner a prisoner in their hands.

The undersigned thinks it proper to inclose a copy of the correspondence between himself and the Imperial Commissioner Yeh, which preceded the occurrence to which he is now referring, lest by any means an incomplete report of it should have reached the imperial throne.

The prime minister will observe from this correspondence, that the undersigned, notwithstanding the many and serious causes of complaint which he had to urge on behalf of his government, and of the subjects of his sovereign, confined himself in his communication of the 12th of December to the Imperial Commissioner Yeh, to the following demands: The complete execution at Canton of all treaty engagements, including the free admission of British subjects to the city; compensation to British subjects, and persons entitled to British protection for losses incurred in consequence of the late disturbances, informing him at the same time if these moderate demands, and those preferred on behalf of the Emperor of the French by his Imperial Majesty's high commissioner and plenipotentiary were frankly accepted by the imperial commissioner within ten days from the date of that communication, the blockade of the river would be raised, and commerce permitted to resume its course; but that the English forces, in conjunction with the forces of the French, would retain the Island of Honan as a material guarantee, until the terms of treaty for regulating these and all other questions pending between the governments of Great Britain and that of China should have been agreed to between the undersigned and a plenipotentiary of equal rank appointed by the Emperor of China to negotiate with him, and until the treaty so agreed upon should have been ratified by their respective sovereigns; but, adding, that if the imperial commissioner met these demands by a refusal, by silence, or by evasive or dilatory pleas, the undersigned would deem it to be his painful duty to direct the naval and military commanders to prosecute with renewed vigor operations against Canton, reserving to himself the right to make, in that case on behalf of the British government such additional demands on the government of China, as this altered condition of affairs might seem in his eyes to justify.

The imperial commissioner disregarding the claims of justice, and the true interest of his sovereign, met these very moderate demands by dilatory and evasive pleas, and thus drew down upon himself and upon the city of which he was the appointed guardian, consequences of which the undersigned had warned him in the most distinct and emphatic terms.

It is the intention of the undersigned, in his present communication to the prime minister, to observe the same moderation and frankness which characterized his communication to the Imperial Commissioner Yeh.

In pursuance of this intention, he has the honor to state, that in concert with his honorable colleague the plenipotentiary of France he has resolved that the forces of Great Britain and France shall continue to occupy the city of Canton military, but that for the present, they shall abstain from further measures of hostility against any part of the Chinese empire, except in so far as such measures may be necessary for the security of their position as masters of Canton.

The plenipotentiaries of England and France will meanwhile proceed in person to Shanghai, where they will be prepared to enter into negotiations for the settlement of all differences existing between their respective governments and that of China, with any plenipotentiary duly accredited by the Emperor of China, who may present himself at that port before the end of the month of March.

The undersigned, however, in making this communication, thinks it proper to apprise the prime minister that he is not only authorized by his government to demand from that of China compensation for the wrongs inflicted on British subjects, and indemnity for the expenses of the war in which his country has been forced to engage by the obstinacy of the Imperial Commissioner Yeh, but that he also holds from his august sovereign, the Queen of England, full powers which enable him to conclude on behalf of his government with that of China such treaties, conventions, or arguments, as may obviate future misunderstandings, and tend to develop commercial relations between the two countries; and that he cannot, therefore, consent to treat with any Chinese embassador who does not hold from the Emperor of China full powers equally extensive.

In his present communication to the prime minister, the undersigned restricts himself to a few general observations on this important branch of his duties, reserving the discussion of details for the time when he shall have an opportunity of conferring personally with a plenipotentiary specially commissioned by the Emperor to treat with him.

Notwithstanding the unquestionable benefits which have accrued under the existing treaties between Great Britain and China—to the latter country more especially—in the increase of the imperial revenue from the duties of customs, and in the enhanced value which the competition of foreigners has given to the products of the industry of the Chinese people, experience has shown that in some important particulars they are defective, and require amendment.

It is probable, for example, that if Peking, the seat of the imperial government, had been accessible to foreign ministers, according to the practice which obtains universally among the great nations of the west, the calamities which have lately taken place at Canton might have been averted.

Again, if foreigners were permitted to circulate in the empire under regulations which would give sufficient security for their good behavior, such occurrences as the barbarous murder of the French missionary, which has led to consequences so serious, would probably be prevented.

The spontaneous growth of an unrecognized trade at ports of the empire not opened by treaty, and from which, therefore, the imperial treasury derives no benefit, proves how vain is the attempt to confine the foreign trade to a few ports named in the existing treaties.

Wherefore, indeed, should the industrious and loyal subjects of the Emperor of China, who inhabit the great cities on the seaboard, or along the course of the great rivers, be prevented from selling the products of their labor to the foreigner who is willing to pay full value for them?

Foreign merchants complain that illegal transit duties are levied on the merchandise which they import and export. For this evil the existing treaties furnish us adequate remedy.

The duties on imports and exports originally imposed in the treaties were just and reasonable, but some of them have become, in process of time, unjust and unreasonable, because they remain fixed, while the price of the articles on which they are levied changes. This is not as it should be. It proves the necessity of a periodical revision of the tariffs.

The prevalence of piracy is an embarrassment to trade, and a frightful evil to the people on the coasts of China. The government of her Britannic Majesty is willing to lend its aid to that of China for its suppression.

Christians, in some parts of the empire, are subject to treatment which is not only opposed to the interests of civilization, but also the precepts of the greatest Chinese sages. But Christians only desire to live at peace, and to do their duty to God and man. Wherefore, then, should they be persecuted?

If, then, a plenipotentiary, duly accredited and empowered by the Emperor of China not only to grant compensation for the wrongs inflicted on British subjects, and indemnity for the expenses of the war in which Great Britain has been forced to engage, but also to treat with the undersigned on the above-mentioned subjects, shall present himself at Shanghai, before the period above specified, the undersigned will meet him in a conciliatory spirit, and with a sincere desire to enter into such arrangements with him as may render a further resort to arms unnecessary; reëstablish harmony and a good understanding between the great nations of Great Britain and China; and the differences between France and China being in like manner settled, enable the allied forces to retire from the occupation of Canton.

If, on the contrary, no plenipotentiary so accredited shall present himself at Shanghai before the end of the month of March, or if any plenipotentiary so presenting himself shall be found to have insufficient powers, or, if having the requisite powers, he shall prove himself unwilling to accede to reasonable terms of accommodation, the undersigned hereby reserves to himself the right of having recourse without further announcement, delay, or declaration, to such measures in vindication of the claims of his country on China as in his judgment may appear advisable to adopt.

ELGIN AND KINCARDINE.

CANTON, *February*, 1858.

Exhibit 2 c.

The undersigned, &c., &c., &c., has the honor to apprise the Imperial Commissioner Yeh, that he is the bearer of letters of credence, accrediting him as embassador extraordinary from her Majesty the Queen of Great Britain to the Emperor of China; and further, that he has been specially appointed and deputed by the Queen of Great Britain as her Majesty's high commissioner and plenipotentiary in China, with full powers under her Majesty's royal sign manual and the great seal of the United Kingdom to settle the differences which have unfortunately arisen between certain of the authorities and subjects of her Majesty the Queen of Great Britain, and certain of the authorities and subjects of his Majesty the Emperor of China, and to negotiate and conclude with the minister or ministers who may be vested with similar power and authority by his Imperial and Royal Majesty the Emperor of China, such treaties, conventions, or agreements, as may obviate future misunderstandings, and tend to develop commercial relations between the two countries.

The government of her Majesty the Queen of Great Britain in appointing this special mission is animated by the sincerest feelings of good will towards the Chinese people and its government. It has observed with gratification the happy results which have followed on the enlarged facilities for commercial intercourse between Great Britain and China, provided under the treaty of 1842. The industrious subjects of his Majesty the Emperor have derived therefrom increased returns for the product of their labor; the duties of customs have supplied timely resources to the imperial treasury; free intercourse has engendered feelings of mutual esteem between natives and foreigners; in a word, at all the ports of China opened to foreign trade, save one, commerce has presented itself with its accustomed attendants, national wealth and international good will.

To this favorable picture there is unhappily one exception. By repeated insults to foreigners, and by the refusal to carry out faithfully the stipulations of treaties, the authorities of the province of Kwang Tung have frequently during the period in question put in jeopardy the peaceful relations of China with the treaty powers. Great Britain, France, and America have successively been compelled to seek by menace or by the employment of force satisfaction for wrongs wantonly inflicted, until finally an insult to the British flag followed by the refusal of the imperial commissioner to grant adequate reparation, or even to meet in the city the representatives of her Britannic Majesty, for the purpose of effecting an amicable settlement, has forced the officers who are charged with the protection of British interests in this quarter to have recourse to measures of coercion against Canton. The contest thus commenced has been carried on by the Chinese authorities in a manner repugnant to humanity, and to the rules of warfare recognized by civilized nations. Acts of incendiarism and assassination have been promoted by the offer of rewards. Under the influence of these provocations, innocent families have been plunged into mourning by the kidnapping of private individuals, and vessels engaged in the peaceful pursuits of commerce, have been treacherously seized, and the European crews and passengers barbarously murdered.

The undersigned thinks it right to remind the imperial commissioner that the government of her Britannic Majesty in its endeavors to terminate a state of affairs which has led to these deplorable results has not confined its efforts to representations addressed to the imperial officers on the spot. In the year 1849, a communication was by the express command of Viscount Palmerston, her Majesty's secretary of state for foreign affairs, transmitted to the imperial government at Pekin, warning it of the consequences that would ensue from the non-fulfillment of treaty engagements, and terminating in these words: "Let the Chinese government well consider these things, and whatever may happen in future between the two countries that may be disagreeable to China, let the Chinese government remember that the fault thereof will lie upon them." And, again, in the year 1854, Sir John Bowring, her Majesty's plenipotentiary urged upon the imperial commissioners who were deputed to confer with him at the mouth of the Peiho the necessity of granting the British subjects free access to the city of Canton. These representations, however, prompted by a spirit of conciliation and humanity have been unheeded, and the result has only served to prove that the forbearance of the British government, has been misunderstood by that of China.

In the conviction that the season for remonstrance is past, Great Britain does not stand alone. The disregard of treaty obligations, and the obstinate refusal to redress grievances which have forced the British authorities to have recourse to arms, have aroused the just indignation of the government of his Imperial Majesty the Emperor of the French. The governments of England and France are united in their determination to seek, by vigorous and decisive action, reparation for past and security against future wrongs.

Under these circumstances, the undersigned thinks it his duty to state distinctly to the imperial commissioner, that he cannot assume the responsibility of arresting the progress of hostile operations against Canton, until the following demands of the British government are absolutely and unreservedly conceded: The complete execution at Canton of all treaty engagements, including the free admission of British subjects to the city; compensation to British subjects and persons entitled to British protection for losses incurred in consequence of the late disturbances.

If these moderate demands, and those preferred on behalf of the Emperor of the French, by his Imperial Majesty's high commissioner and plenipotentiary, be frankly accepted by the Imperial Commissioner Yeh, within the period of ten days from this date, the blockade of the river will be raised, and commerce will be permitted to resume its course. But the English forces, in conjunction with the forces of the French, will retain the Island of Honan and the forts on the river as a material guarantee, until the terms of a treaty for regulating these and all other questions pending between the government of Great Britain and that of China shall have been agreed to between the undersigned and a plenipotentiary of equal rank appointed by the Emperor of China to negotiate with him, and until the treaty so agreed upon shall have been ratified by their respective sovereigns.

If, on the contrary, the imperial commissioner shall meet these demands by a refusal, by silence, or by evasive or dilatory pleas, the undersigned will deem it to be his painful duty to direct the naval and military commanders to prosecute with renewed vigor operations against Canton, reserving to himself the right to make, in that case, on behalf of the British government, such additional demands on the government of China as this altered condition of affairs may seem in his eyes to justify.

ELGIN AND KINCARDINE.

December 12, 1857.

Exhibit 2 *d*.

Yeh, Imperial Commissioner, Governor General of the two Kwang, &c., makes a communication in reply:

On the 12th instant, I received the letter sent to me the same day, and was highly gratified to learn that your excellency had been sent with plenipotentiary power to Canton.

By the commercial relations ensuing on the establishment of treaty between our two countries, the mercantile communities of both have alike been advantaged. The letter under acknowledgment observes that "to the favorable picture presented at the ports of China there is one exception." Now, during more than a century that your excellency's nation traded at Canton, its trade was with Canton alone—no such thing was known as four other ports; they were first opened by the treaties of 1842 and 1844. Canton had had, it is true, its own ways (he means under the Company's Hong) of trade long established. So far, indeed, it differed from the other ports; but its commercial intercourse has been throughout conducted on the same principle as theirs, nor has there been any more at Canton than elsewhere any "insult to foreigners."

As to the question of admittance into the provincial city of Canton, no article whatever relating to this exists in the treaties of 1842 and 1844. It was in March, 1847, that the Plenipotentiary Davis attempted, at a moment's notice, to raise the question. He prescribed a term of two years, within which the right was to be conceded; but before one year had elapsed, the unsatisfactoriness of his conduct in many particulars had been complained of by merchants who returned home for the purpose, and he was recalled. He was replaced by the late Plenipotentiary Bonham, subsequently to whose arrival in Kwang Tung there passed, in 1849, a long correspondence between him and the late Commissioner Seu.

Discussion respecting admittance into the city was finally dropped, and the Plenipotentiary Bonham issued a notice from the government office (at Hong Kong) to the effect that he (the governor) would not allow foreigners to enter the city. On this, I myself, then governor, in concert with Seu, then commissioner, represented to his late Majesty, canonized as the Perfect, in a memorial, that the English had finally dropped the question of admittance into Canton, and we had the honor to receive, in reply, the following imperial decree: "The walling of cities is for the protection of the people; in the protection of the people lies the security of the state. The direction of the popular mind is the direction of the will of heaven. If the people of Kwang Tung are unanimously opposed to the admission of foreigners into the city, can an imperial injunction be laid on them by proclamation so to do, whether they will or no? It is not in the power of the government of China to cross the wishes of the people out of deference to the men from afar. On the other hand, it behooves foreign nations to study the temper of the people to the end that they may turn their capital to the best account. Respect this!"

It is also reported, on the authority of an English newspaper of 1850, that a royal (lit., national) letter from the queen arrived at Hong Kong to the address of the late Plenipotentiary Bonham, to the following effect: "We are informed of everything regarding Tientsin and the five ports of China, as detailed in the representation (of Mr. Bonham.) The governor* in question has, without doubt, shown great sagacity in the course he has followed. He was aware that Seu, governor general of the two Kwang, was secretly devising measures, in which Yeh, governor of Kwang Tung, was also taking part; and that they had, together, moved the Chinese government to send from Pekin a secret expedition of the Solon† vessels of war, for the defense of Tientsin. But, though our vessels of war could have been easily worked (*i. e.*, by pushing and pulling) along the shores, (of the Peiho,) to fight with these, Bonham, knowing what was becoming his own nation, (a government,) and being well acquainted with the purpose of his visit to the ports of China, to an observation of the condition of the country,

---

*Governor, great chief of soldiers. The term used by the common people at Hong Kong
†A Mongol tribe.

prosperous or otherwise. Were we to have fought, the Chinese would have said that our people were entirely in the wrong. It is hence evident that our governor, Bonham, has managed matters very satisfactorily. By no offense against reason (or right) has he caused us anxiety. He is very much to be loved. Let Bonham be rewarded with the title of Wi-li-pa."* (The Queen) also conferred on him a badge of honor, to be borne on his person, very goodly to behold; and the English authorities and merchants at Hong Kong went in their dresses of ceremony to offer him their congratulations.

Thus, the merchants of your excellency's nation (showed that they) thought the Plenipotentiary Bonham right, and the Plenipotentiary Davis wrong. It is doubtless the duty of your excellency, who is come here in obedience to your instructions, to imitate the conduct of the Plenipotentiary Bonham. It is equally imperative that you should decline to imitate the conduct of the Plenipotentiary Davis.

With respect to that passage in the letter under acknowledgment, which say that, "until the terms of a treaty shall have been agreed to between the undersigned and a plenipotentiary of equal rank, appointed by the Emperor of China to negotiate with him," &c., in 1850, the late Plenipotentiary Bonham went in person to Shanghai, and detached thence an officer to Tientsin, to request once more admission into the city. In 1854, the Plenipotentiary Bowring went himself to Tientsin, and entreated with instance† to be admitted into the city; also, that the treaty should be reconsidered. His Majesty the Emperor holding that, whereas the treaties of 1842 and 1844 were ratified by the late Emperor, canonized as the Perfect, there was not, in the agreement so sanctioned by his late majesty, and which was to last ten thousand years, with a view to the preservation of a good understanding forevermore, any place for alterations; and that the order of proceeding that had resulted in those advantages which had from the time the treaties were made accrued to Chinese and foreigners alike, from commercial intercourse, had been in no respect other than what was in accordance with the treaties; was satisfied that these were good and sufficient. The cessation of discussions regarding admittance into Canton was, for his Majesty, a point on which the fiat of his late majesty had been received; and as the treaty of peace for ten thousand years had been in like manner ratified by his late majesty, it would have been equally improper to alter this. Hence, although, on both occasions that (officers) of your excellency's government repaired to Tientsin, imperial commissioners‡ were sent to receive them, no proposition respecting (fresh) regulations (of trade) were allowed to be considered. The officers were desired to return to Canton, and conduct business there in obedient conformance to treaty. (And so) now, no officer of China, be his rank what it may, could venture to act otherwise than in accordance with the sacred will (of the Emperor.)

---

*There is a confusion between Sir G. Bonham's Knighthood of the Bath and his Baronetcy. Wei-li-pa, a Chinese suggests, stands for Ba-li-wei; supposed to be Anglo-Chinese for baronet. It is not a Chinese term.

†The term is one commonly used in closing petitions. The Digest of the Statutes employs it in speaking of Russia's solicitation for a commercial treaty in 1793.

‡There is a little confusion here. An imperial commissioner was sent to meet Sir J. Bowring and Mr. McLane, in 1854. None, of course, came to meet Mr. Medhurst in 1850.

Again, your letter says that there must be "compensation to British subjects and persons entitled to British protection, for losses incurred in consequence of late disturbances." The understanding of last October was caused thus: The Chinese government having arrested some Chinese criminals, Consul Parkes wrongfully gave heed to the unsupported testimony of the captain of the lorcha, who asserted that the government executive, when they came on board to seize the guilty parties, hauled down the British ensign. He was not aware that no flag was seen flying by the executive when they boarded the vessel; that, as stated by the sailors seized, the flag was at the time down in the hold, and that it was consequently plain, beyond a doubt, that no flag was flying at all. The lorcha was built by, and in the employ of Too-Aching, for whom the captain obtained a register. The crew were consequently all outlaws of the Inner Land, (that is, offenders against the laws of China.) The prisoners, Te-Ming-Tae and Liang-Kien-fu, both pleaded guilty to acts of piracy on the high seas. To this Mi-Aching bore witness. It was established that the criminals before-mentioned were notorious pirates. On the repeated representations of Consul Parkes, (however,) I returned the twelve prisoners to him. Feeling* and justice were thus alike satisfied; but Consul Parkes, instead of receiving them, suddenly and without a cause commenced hostile operations, attacked and destroyed the forts along the different approaches, for several days in succession bombarded the provincial city, and on three occasions sent parties of English troops to fire houses and buildings in different directions. Millions of people were eye-witnesses of these things. There is not a native of any foreign State who is not aware of them. At the very commencement, every Englishman and every other foreigner, with a sense of justice, did all that in them lay to dissuade Consul Parkes from proceeding; but he would not listen. He declared, too, that he would be personally responsible for all the loss they might incur, and in January last he went to Hong Kong and made out an account of their losses, with all the merchants who had suffered; which shows that he was taking their compensation on himself. The method of effecting this has long been settled; with it China has in fact no concern. Her merchants, alas! have sustained an amount of injury graver than the losses that have fallen on those of your excellency's nation; (but) the same rules apply to both.† My court is thronged by the gentry and people of the city and suburbs, imploring me to write to your excellency to inquire into the matter and dispose of it impartially. I have not made their petitions the subject of a dispatch, but if you will not believe me, I will inclose copies of them in my next reply for your excellency's perusal and guidance. As to Honan, its gentry and people are fierce and energetic.‡ In April, 1847, when the merchants of your excellency's nation wanted to lease ground on Honan, the gentry and people presented a petition, generally signed, to the Plenipotentiary Davis, who notified to them in his reply that the matter should stand

*Feeling, viz: the feeling of unwillingness to act discourteously towards the authority of a friendly power.

†That is, each must bear its own losses.

‡Intractable.

where it was. Your letter talks of a military occupation of Honan and of the forts along the river; but if you could not proceed once before, even with such a measure as the building and leasing of warehouses there, how should it be possible to station troops on Honan? The forts along the river have been built at the expense of the gentry and people, for their protection against piracy. An attempt on the part of the troops of your excellency's nation to occupy these will, I fear, produce a state of irritation which may grow into a serious misunderstanding. (If it do,) let it not be said that I did not speak in time, or that I did not do all that in me lay to provide for your safety.

The propositions brought forward in your letter have been suggested, it appears to me, by some mischievous person at your side. They are not your excellency's own conceptions. I have long heard of your excellency's great experience and discretion; of the universal esteem in which you are held in your own country. The great trust which you are come to Canton to discharge towards your own government, is naturally the termination of the troubles here existing; not, assuredly, the creation of (fresh) troubles. Your excellency's acts will, I feel sure, anticipate my confidence in your perfect sense of justice and thorough impartiality.

The words, "commerce shall resume its course," in your letter, are additional evidence of your excellency's sense of justice and practical knowledge. Ever since the treaty was made, in all their commercial dealings with foreigners the merchants of Canton have invariably behaved as they ought. It is not from any hindrance interposed by China that no foreign merchant vessel has been here since last October. By your excellency's declaration now made, that "commerce between native and foreigner shall resume its course," you justify to their complete satisfaction the high estimation in which you are held by all classes of your own countrymen; what is more, you enable yourself to meet the anxious expectations of the commercialists of every other country.

To conclude, our two nations have ever considered themselves as on friendly terms with each other; and the continuance of trade between native and foreigner, on its accustomed footing, can, of course, be satisfactorily arranged in correspondence between you and myself.

I accordingly reply to you, availing myself of the occasion to wish your excellency the blessings of the season, comfort, and peace.

A necessary communication, addressed to his excellency the Earl of Elgin and Kincardine, &c., &c., &c.

HIEN-FUNG, *7th year*, 10*th moon*, 29*th day*, 14*th December*, 1857.

Translated by T. WADE, *Chinese Secretary*.

Exhibit 2 *e*.

The undersigned has received the communication which the Imperial Commissioner Yeh did him the honor to address him, under date the 14th instant.

The undersigned has failed to discover in this communication, which he has attentively perused, any indication on the part of the imperial commissioner of a disposition to accede to the moderate demands which, in his communication to the imperial commissioner of the 12th instant, he preferred on behalf of the government of Great Britain.

He is, therefore, reluctantly compelled to recall to the recollection of the imperial commissioner the closing paragraph of that communication which is conceived in the following terms: "If, on the contrary, the imperial commissioner shall meet these demands by a refusal, by silence, or by evasive or dilatory pleas, the undersigned will deem it to be his painful duty to direct the naval and military commanders to prosecute, with renewed vigor, operations against Canton, reserving to himself the right to make, in that case, on behalf of the British government, such additional demands on the government of China as this altered condition of affairs may seem, in his eyes, to justify."

The undersigned has now to inform the imperial commissioner that he has called upon the naval and military commanders to prosecute, with renewed vigor, operations against Canton; and to add that, in accordance with the terms of the intimation given in the words above quoted, he formally reserves to himself the right to make, on behalf of the British government, such additional demands as the altered condition of affairs, produced by the imperial commissioner's refusal to accede to terms of accommodation, may seem, in his eyes, to justify.

The undersigned avails himself, &c.

ELGIN AND KINCARDINE,
Her Majesty's Ship Furious.

CANTON RIVER, *December* 24, 1857.

Exhibit 2 *f.*

YEH, Imperial Commissioner, Governor General of the two Kwang, &c., makes a communication:

On the 24th instant I received your excellency's letter of the same date, and acquainted myself with its contents.

In my answer to your earlier letter I replied to every proposition, point by point, specifically and minutely; [yet,] in the letter under acknowledgment, you say that you have failed to discover, in the communication which you have attentively perused, any indication of a disposition to accede* to the moderate demands preferred on behalf of the government of Great Britain.

I shall endeavor to restate clearly to your excellency what I said before.

To go back: in October, last year, Mr. Consul Parkes, without any cause, commenced hostilities, attacked the forts along the different approaches, and thrice sent troops to fire buildings and dwellings in different directions. The gentry and people had suffered sadly by this;

---

*Accede.—The term by which I had rendered this, in Chinese, is composed of two words, *jang*, amicable concession, as opposed to unyielding tenacity, of which strife is the consequence, and *here*, to promise or undertake performance or compliance. It will be seen below that for his own purposes the commissioner divides the combination and deals with each part of it separately.

and on your excellency's arrival at Kwang Tung last July, as I have heard, presented a petition to you on the subject. No steps having as yet been taken in the case, crowds of gentry and people have come to my court discontented, and imploring me to write to your excellency to make equitable decision therein; and, because I did not address your excellency on the subject, they were going to Hong Kong again to clamor for redress, at your excellency's place, with all their might. By various shifts I have dissuaded them, (from this proceeding,) attributing what happened entirely to Consul Parkes's want of sense on a particular occasion, that your excellency might be spared this trouble (or difficulty.)

This shows the best disposition on my part to be conceding. *

In the next place, ever since your excellency's countrymen began to trade at Canton the merchants of China have, in every instance, conducted themselves towards them with propriety. To the proposition in your former letter, "commerce shall resume its course," I gave the fullest assent. How then can I be charged with refusing. † On the contrary, there is plain proof that I "promised" ‡ (to concede what was asked,) as to the passage in the letter under acknowledgment "if (the commissioner shall meet these demands) by silence," in my last reply I answered every question in its own order; in no wise then was I silent and as to the other passage language of retrocession and refusal. ‖ I shall instance (my remarks on) the late Plenipotentiary Bonham's abandonment of the discussions respecting admittance into the city; my last reply detailed clearly how for his satisfactory administration of that question he was honored by the praises of all classes of your countrymen; in no wise then (did I use) "language of retrocession and refusal."

To conclude, our two nations regard themselves as on friendly terms with each other; this being the case, there can be nothing which makes it impossible for us to consult together and arrange satisfactorily by what means, in the words of your excellency, "commerce may resume its course;" (which declaration made) § what becomes of my "refusal to accede to terms of accommodation?"

Pray let your excellency, who has a sense of justice and an experience of business, once more closely examine and carefully reperuse my last reply.

I accordingly reply to you, availing myself of the occasion to wish your excellency the blessings of the season, comfort, and peace. A ne-

* See note above. The commissioner means, had my intention been the opposite of conceding, I should not have dissuaded the petitioners from a course which boded strife.

† The Chinese here quoted is from that part of the Earl of Elgin's letter of the 12th instant, which was repeated in his lordship's letter of the 24th. "If the imperial commissioner shall meet these demands," &c.

‡ This is the second part of the combination referred to in note 1.

‖ The words translated "retrocession and refusal" are not in the letter sent; they have been substituted for those representing "dilatory and evasive." The characters Yeh employs makes us accuse him of "backing out and definitive refusal." I am not sure that much if anything is intended by the change.

§ The commissioner means to imply "and it was made at the close of my first reply"—the language of which he has employed pretty generally in this.

cessary communication addressed to the Earl of Elgin and Kincardine, &c., &c.

Hien Fung, 7th year, 11th moon, 10th day. (December 25, 1857.)

Translated.

THOMAS WADE, *Chinese Secretary.*

Exhibit 2 *g.*

[Translation.]

MISSION EXTRAORDINARY OF FRANCE IN CHINA,
On board the Primauguet, February 4, 1858.

SIR: I have the honor to send herewith to your excellency, the copy of a note which I intend to send forthwith to Pekin, and which is addressed to the minister, the first secretary of state of the empire. This note will make known to your excellency the course that I propose to follow to give effect to the mission which the government of the Emperor, my august sovereign, has confided to me in this country, the first part of which has just been terminated before Canton.

I append to this note a copy of the correspondence that I have had with the ex-Imperial Commissioner Yeh, before the capture of Canton by the allied forces of France and England, and your excellency will see, on reading these documents, all the moderation of the course pursued by the government of the Emperor in these grave affairs. You will also have the evidence that the use of coercive measures, always to be regretted, has unfortunately been the only means that offered any chance of success. Your excellency will see finally that, forced to painful extremities, the plenipotentiaries of the two allied powers have done all in their power to obviate useless severities, to lessen the evils, and to repair the disasters which are inevitable.

Order is reëstablished in Canton, the blockade of the river and of the city will be raised on the 10th of this month; but the city and the suburbs, which the allied forces must hold until the differences existing between China, France, and England shall be settled by common agreement, will remain in a state of siege under the authority of the commanders of the allied forces.

In making, without reserve, this important communication to your excellency, I only obey the spirit of the instructions given to me by the government of the Emperor. Your excellency will see, in the note addressed to the prime minister, at Pekin, what are the principal concessions which, in a common interest, it would be useful to obtain; and if the demands which his excellency Lord Elgin and myself are going to submit forthwith to the discussion and acceptation of the government at Pekin should receive the support which your excellency could give them, should you judge it proper, these demands would acquire a new weight in the estimation of the Chinese government, and would have, consequently, a greater chance of being acceded to, without its becoming necessary to have recourse to coercive measures.

I congratulate myself, sir, on having to make to your excellency a communication of this nature, and I take the opportunity to offer you the assurance of the sentiments of high consideration with which I have the honor to be your most humble and obedient servant,

BARON GROS.

His Excellency WILLIAM B. REED,
Envoy Extraordinary and Minister Plenipotentiary of the United States of America, &c., &c.

Exhibit 2 *h.*

[Translation.]

MACAO, *December* 10, 1857.

Bourboulon, minister plenipotentiary of France in China, addresses the following official communication to his excellency Yeh, high imperial commissioner, &c., &c.

By my dispatches, dated the 14th of March and 4th of April of the present year, I notified the noble functionary that I had received an order from my august sovereign to claim again the reparation which had already been heretofore demanded by Count De Courcy, chargé d'affaires of France, for the violation of the treaty of Whampoa, in the barbarous execution of the missionary Chapdelaine, which was decreed by the magistrate of Si-Linn; and as many months have now elapsed without this demand being satisfied, and without the noble dignitary having announced that he had transmitted it to the court of Pekin, or even that it was his intention to do so, I have declared to him that if, within a settled period, he did not send me a satisfactory answer on this subject, I should consider his silence or an evasive answer as equivalent to a refusal of satisfaction, and should thenceforward deem myself authorized, by the instructions of my government, to act accordingly.

The noble functionary has been thus duly warned of the grave consequences which the refusal to grant the just reparation at first demanded by the chargé d'affaires of France, and afterwards by myself, in the name of his Majesty the Emperor of the French, might have on the maintenance of the good harmony hitherto subsisting between the two empires. But his answer to my last communication was not more satisfactory than preceding ones, and since then nearly eight months have elapsed without his having thought proper to make known to me anything definite in relation to an affair of such high importance.

I have now therefore to make known to him that his Majesty the Emperor, my august sovereign, justly offended at the refusal of all satisfaction, which is evinced by the dilatory answers or continued silence of the noble dignitary who is intrusted with the management of foreign affairs in the Chinese empire, to his representatives, has determined to send to China an imperial commissioner of a more elevated rank, whose mission will be to put an end to a state of affairs which he regards as violating his dignity; that his Imperial Majesty has confided this high mission to his excellency Baron Gros, who is clothed for this purpose with the character of extraordinary commissioner and embassador of the Emperor of the French in China; that this high functionary has arrived lately in the neighborhood of Canton, and that he intends to enter immediately into communication with the noble viceroy in relation to the grave affairs of his mission, while leaving to me, minister plenipotentiary, the care of continuing to treat, if necessary, on the ordinary affairs of my great empire.

This, noble functionary, is what I have to bring to your knowledge, requesting you to take it into serious consideration, and to accept my wishes for all kinds of prosperity.

BOURBOULON.

A true copy.

BARON GROS.

Exhibit 2 *i.*

[Translation.]

YEH, High Imperial Commissioner of the Ta-Tsing dynasty, &c., &c., makes answer as follows:

On the 26th of the 10th moon, (December 11, 1857,) I received from your excellency a dispatch, dated the 25th of the same moon, (December 10, 1857,) and I have made myself acquainted with its contents.

When I received, on the 10th of the 3d moon, (April 4, 1857,) your excellency's dispatch on the subject of the arrest and death of Chapdelaine, the missionary, which were ordered by the mandarin of the district of Si-Linn, in the province of Kwang-si, I wrote to the sub-viceroy of that province, requesting him to inquire into this affair, and I ordered the criminal judge of Kwang-si to have, on his part, a serious investigation made by his subordinates into this matter.

In pursuance of this step, the criminal judge replied to me that after he received my dispatch he had given formal orders that this affair should be well investigated; and the report which this functionary has received from the magistrate of Si-Linn, whose name is Tchang-ming-fung, is as follows:

"On searching the archives (those of the magistrate) in conformity to the orders which you have given me, I have found in them no indication by which it could be made known that either the priest Ma-chen-Foo, (Mr. Chapdelaine,) or the individual named Pa-ven, or the widow Agnes, had been either arrested, or beaten, or put to death by me on the 19th day of the 1st moon of the 6th year of Hien-fung, (February 24, 1856,) and on that day no person was detained in my prison. But here is what took place during the 2d moon of that same year, (during the month of March, 1856.) I being in the village of Si-kiang for the purpose of defending it, and of opposing the entrance of the rebels into the lower part of this village, the principal man of the town of Yug-Young came to tell me that the rebel Ma-tsu-nung and some others had arrived there, and were there spreading strange reports in order to seduce the people, and to induce them to join the

Society of the Triad; that these individuals were indulging in every kind of excess, committing robbery, violating women, &c., &c., &c.

"On receiving this statement from the principal man of the town himself, I at once set out with him and some soldiers, to hunt for and seize the guilty; but I was only able to arrest Ma-tsu-nung, the other rebels having taken to flight.

"Ma-tsu-nung, on being interrogated by me, stated that he was born at Canton; that he belonged to the same society as Lin-pa and Tau-a-sicou; that Lin-pa and his associates were in the district of Youn-hein, creating disturbance among the people. He also said that he had gone to Si-Linn to gather followers, and to obtain members for the Society of the Triad; and he finally admitted that he had committed robberies, violated women, &c., &c., &c.

"In consequence of this statement of the culprit, and under an apprehension that among the great number of rebels who were trying to excite the people, other revolters might assemble for the purpose of creating still further trouble, I caused him to be executed; and in the report which I forwarded, making known the destruction of the rebels, I spoke of this execution

"As I have been ordered to find out all that took place on that occasion, I must say that I caused to be arrested the guilty Ma-tsu-nung only, and had him executed. But this individual's name not being the same as that of Ma-chen-Foo, which you mention to me in your dispatch, and these two individuals not being either from the same place, I do not think that one can be taken for the other.

"I request you to be pleased to send this statement to his excellency the viceroy of the two Kwangs."

I have, therefore, in consequence of this statement of the mandarin of the district of Si-Linn, which has been transmitted to me by the criminal judge of the province of Kwang-si, to remark to your excellency that there has been no arrest made of the person of Ma-chen-Foo (Mr. Chapdelaine.)

I am of opinion, therefore, that your excellency has been wrongly informed; and consequently I find it useless to speak longer of this affair.

As to what your excellency says to me in your dispatch, that a high functionary named Kŏ, (Baron Gros,) sent expressly by his noble empire, had arrived at Canton in order to treat on an affair of high importance which concerns the honor and dignity of your nation, I have to say to your excellency that if his excellency Baron Gros has any negotiations to enter into, my answer is that I shall keep within the limits of the treaty, and shall act as I have hitherto done.

This is the answer I have to make to your excellency, while wishing you, at the same time, every prosperity.

The foregoing dispatch is addressed to his excellency Mr. Bourboulon, on the 27th day of the 10th moon of the 7th year of Hien-fung (December 12, 1857.)

A correct translation.

BARON GROS.

Exhibit 2 k.

[Translation.]

ON BOARD THE IMPERIAL FRIGATE THE AUDACIEUSE,
Canton river, December 12, 1857.

To his excellency the Governor General of the two Kwangs, the noble Imperial Commissioner Yeh, one of the ministers of the Emperor charged with the foreign relations of the Celestial empire, &c., &c.

The undersigned, appointed embassador extraordinary of his Majesty the Emperor of the French, near the great Emperor of the Tsings, and furnished with letters of credence, which accredit him in this capacity, near the august sovereign of the Celestial empire, bearer likewise of powers which have been conferred on him in the capacity of commissioner extraordinary and plenipotentiary of France for adjusting the differences which exist between the two nations, and for seeking to render more advantageous to the subjects of the two empires the relations of friendship, commerce, and navigation, established between them by treaties and by the progress of civilization, has the honor to announce to his excellency the grand dignitary, governor general of the two Kwangs, minister of his Imperial Majesty, and charged with the direction of the foreign relations of the Celestial empire, that he has arrived in the river of Canton, and that he is ready to receive on board his Imperial Majesty's frigate, the Audacieuse, all the communications which his excellency may be pleased to address to him, in consequence of the attitude which he has been directed to take towards him on arriving in China.

The first step which he has to take, after complying with the formalities, of which he has just acquitted himself, is to call the attention of his excellency, the noble governor general, to the violation of the treaty of Whampoa, and to the impossibility, hitherto, of France obtaining, by ordinary means, the just reparation which ought to have been voluntarily offered to her by the superior authority, when the murder of the unfortunate French missionary, Augustus Chapdelaine, took place.

The refusal of justice, which France has for a long while experienced, and which ought no longer to be continued, has given reason for believing that the great Emperor of the dynasty of the Tsings had not been informed of the complaints and reclamations which the legation of France, at various periods, addressed to the depositaries of his authority. To doubt that his Imperial Majesty would have done prompt justice, if the truth had reached him, would be to be wanting in respect towards him.

The undersigned, therefore, received orders from his august sovereign to repair as quickly as possible to China, and, on arriving there, to proceed to the Peiho, in order to make known the truth to the Emperor, and to request him, at the same time, to be pleased to designate a functionary, of rank equal to that of the undersigned, in order that, on meeting in a friendly manner, the two negotiators might be able to come to an understanding in their endeavors to improve the relations which happily exist between the two empires; but, having arrived too late in these distant lands, the undersigned has been obliged to postpone to another period his journey to the north.

His wish, however, to see terminated a state of affairs which, in the south of the empire, is inclined to become more serious from day to day, induces him to make a last attempt with the noble governor general, to whom he now addresses himself, requesting him, at the same time, or requiring him, if it is necessary, to be pleased to make known to his Imperial Majesty the arrival of a superior diplomatic agent of France in his empire, and the reasons which have determined the Emperor of the French to charge him with the high mission which is confided to him.

The position of the plenipotentiary extraordinary of France being thus clearly defined, he asks his excellency, the noble governor general of the two Kwangs, for permission to recall to his recollection, in a few words, and without manifesting therein the slightest feeling of asperity, the serious grievances of which France complains; the almost insulting silence which, on this subject, has been observed towards her; and, finally, the reparations which she demands.

The second paragraph of article 12, of the treaty of Whampoa, is thus expressed: "If, contrary to the present provisions, any Frenchman whatsoever should penetrate into the interior, they can be arrested by the Chinese authorities, who, in this case, shall be required to have them conducted to the French consulate of the nearest port; but every individual whatever is formally forbidden to strike, wound, or maltreat in any manner, the Frenchman so arrested, for fear of disturbing the good harmony which ought to prevail between the two nations." This treaty, which ought to be considered as one of the laws of the Celestial empire, seeing that it has been ratified by the sovereign, must have been communicated to all the magistrates of Kwangsi by the superior authority of this province, by the noble governor himself.

But in the month of February, 1856, that is to say, nearly two years ago, a French priest, Mr. Augustus Chapdelaine, an apostle of peace and mildness, a man who devoted his life to preaching charity towards the poor, obedience to and respect for the Emperor of the Celestial empire, forgetfulness of injuries, and pardon of offenses, was discovered and arrested at Si-lin-kieng, in the province of Kwangsi, of which his excellency, the noble governor, is the supreme head, clothed with a powerful authority.

The unfortunate Frenchman had, without doubt, been wanting in respect for one of the commands of the treaty; he had committed a fault by going into the interior of the country, nothing is more true; but this very fault had been anticipated by the treaty, for it directed that every Frenchman who should commit it should be arrested and delivered up to one of the consuls of his nation, without "experiencing any injury or suffering the slightest outrage."

Instead of obeying this formal injunction of the treaty, and of thus observing a course of conduct alike conformable to the orders of the Emperor of China and to the sentiments of humanity, the magistrate of Si-lin-kieng had the unhappy Frenchman loaded with irons; had him conducted to his prætorium, where he was stretched upon the earth, struck in the face, crushed with blows, and carried almost dying to the prison of the town. Two days afterwards, the same magistrate made this unfortunate man undergo the punishment of the iron chain; on the next, he had him shut up in the cage of great criminals; and finally, on the 12th of February, he had the head cut off of the pious missionary, who, doubtless, at that critical moment, was praying for the man who, without any cause, had become so cruel towards him. The noble governor general is not unaware that one of the precepts of our sublime religion ordains this course.

This is not all. The magistrate of Si-lin-kieng caused the head of the unhappy Frenchman to be thrown into the street; he gave it up to unclean animals; and, while swine were feeding on it, the executioners of the victim tore out his heart, and in their turn devoured that!

On learning the details of such a horrible crime, on becoming acquainted with the formal violation of the treaty of Whampoa, ought not the noble viceroy, the supreme head of this province of Kwangsi, which one of the magistrates, his subordinates, had dishonored, in the eyes of the civilized world, to have punished immediately the author of these atrocities, and to have voluntarily offered to France the reparation which was so justly due to her? Could he not have done this so much the more easily, as the guilty person was within the limits of his high jurisdiction; and as, in not punishing him, the noble dignitary, the supreme head of the province of Kwangsi, might cause the wicked to believe that he did not disapprove of the conduct of the magistrate of Si-lin-kieng?

To chastise the guilty man, and to offer a reparation to France, would have been to act with as much fairness as spirit and wisdom. It would have been to prove to the world that treaties sanctioned by the will of the Emperor were respected, and that an act of barbarism which human reason refuses to believe possible was energetically stigmatized.

Unfortunately, this has not been the case. The noble dignitary, the governor general of the two Kwangs, charged at the same time with the foreign relations of the empire, has taken no initiatory steps in this matter. He has not answered the urgent reclamations of the representatives of France, except by premeditated delays, by inadmissible pleas in bar, and by ambiguous or dilatory phrases; and for more than a year, the legation of the emperor of the French in China has renewed its protestations, and its requests for reparation, without ever obtaining a satisfactory answer, and, it must also be said, without a single word of regret, of blame, or of reprobation having been addressed to it for the purpose of stigmatizing the odious outrage of Si-lin-kieng.

On the 25th of August of last year, upon the refusal with which the noble viceroy met the intimation that had been made to him on the 26th of July by the legation of France, that he should himself offer to that power the just satisfaction which was due to it, a demand for reparation, the terms of which were mildly drawn up, was addressed to him by the legation of the Emperor in China, but the answer made to it was unfortunately similar to all those which had preceded it.

At length, on the 4th of April of the present year—that is to say eight months later, a new attempt was made. His excellency Mr. Bourboulon, minister plenipotentiary in China, again addressed the noble governor of the two Kwangs, and the answer that he received was as evasive and distressing as the other. Everything leads to the belief even that his excellency has never made known to the court of Pekin, to the Emperor, the just complaints of France; and the last letter which the noble governor general has written on this subject to the minister of the Emperor in China would seem to prove that he refuses to do so, although Mr. Bourboulon had earnestly requested him to lay his complaints at the foot of the throne, whence all justice emanates in the Celestial empire.

There is, therefore, no longer any reason to doubt that the noble governor general of the two Kwangs, charged with the foreign relations of the empire, has taken upon himself all the responsibility of this painful affair; and it is, consequently, to him that the undersigned addresses himself, since he cannot at this time proceed to the mouth of the Peiho.

The undersigned must again, before concluding, call the attention of his excellency the noble governor general, to the last demand for reparations, which was presented to him on the 25th of August, 1856, by the legation of France, a demand which makes known in a precise manner the satisfaction it desired to obtain at that period; but in laying them down anew, the undersigned has some modifications to make to them.

The undersigned demands, therefore, in the name of his government: 1st. The degradation and exile of the magistrate guilty of the murder of the Frenchman, Francis Augustus Chapdelaine—a murder committed in the city of Si-lin-kieng, over which is extended the supreme authority of his excellency the governor general of the two Kwangs. 2d. That an official dispatch should be addressed to him by his excellency, announcing to him that justice has been done. 3d. The insertion in the Gazette of Pekin, in suitable terms, of the punishment which the magistrate of Si-lin-kieng has undergone, and of the reason why it was inflicted on him. 4th. The insertion in the same newspaper, and on the same day, of an article calculated to make all public functionaries understand that they will be liable to a similar punishment to that which the magistrate of Si-lin-kieng has suffered, if they shall be evil enough disposed to act as he has done. 5th. A reasonable pecuniary indemnity for the family of the unfortunate missionary. 6th. For Frenchmen, and persons under the protection of France, a pecuniary indemnity equivalent to the losses which they have experienced, either in consequence of the burning of the factories by the mob of Canton, or in consequence of the refusal of justice on the part of the Chinese authorities. 7th. The full and complete performance of article second of the treaty of Whampoa, which prescribes that Frenchmen shall be admitted into Canton, and be there protected by the local authorities as they are faithfully admitted and protected in the four other ports open to foreign commerce.

These are, noble governor general, the demands for reparation which it is the mission of the undersigned to address to your excellency before proceeding to request the government of his Majesty the great Emperor of the Tsings to be pleased to designate one or several plenipotentiaries, with whom he may have a friendly understanding, in virtue of article thirty-five of the treaty of Whampoa, in regard to the ameliorations to be made in the relations established between the two empires. But it is his duty to make known to your excellency that the time for subterfuges is past. The conduct of the French authorities amid the troubles which have disturbed the Chinese empire latterly, and, in short, more than a year's patience and moderation, ought to be sufficient to convince the Chinese government that it can rely on the good will and friendship of France; but the honor of the latter power demands that the present state of things should cease immediately, and that a just reparation should be granted to it.

The undersigned earnestly requests the noble governor of the two Kwangs to reflect fully on the present condition of European affairs in China. They are entering now into a new phase, the importance of which will certainly not escape the penetrating mind of your excellency.

The government of the Emperor of the French has a right to amends for the grievances which his countrymen have suffered for nearly two years in China.

That of her Britannic Majesty has claimed for a long while, and now still claims, the satisfaction which China refuses to accord to it.

In this state of things, the two governments of France and England, united in their wish to obtain from the Chinese government reparations for the past and guarantees for the future, are also mutually agreed as to the means to be employed to arrive at the end which they wish to attain.

Let the noble governor submit to the evidence, let him yield to France and to England what he must certainly grant them at last, and peace and prosperity will very quickly spring up again among the people who are under his care; let him, on the contrary, despise the course which a skillful policy must counsel him to follow, and irreparable misfortunes, perhaps, may arise out of a violent condition of affairs, which it is only for himself to prevent, or which, in short, he can put an end to.

The undersigned will wait for ten days longer, counting from the date of the present notification, for full satisfaction to be granted to the demands of France, and to those which have been addressed to his excellency the noble governor general in the name of her Britannic Majesty, by the high commissioner and plenipotentiary of her Majesty the Queen of Great Britain; and under this hypothesis the satisfactions granted must be insured by sufficient material guarantees, such, for instance, as the occupation of the island of Honan, and of the forts in the river of Canton by the combined forces of France and England; and this up to the time at which the new treaties, ratified by the two sovereigns, shall give a happy solution to all the questions pending between France and the Celestial empire; but, in order to leave nothing in uncertainty, the undersigned has to say to his excellency that silence maintained towards him beyond the fixed period of delay will to him be equivalent to a formally expressed refusal.

On the other hand, as what has taken place for two years makes the undersigned fear that the denial of justice which France has so patiently borne may be still further prolonged, he is under the necessity of taking measures *at once* that are calculated to hasten the desired solution—a solution which it will depend on his excellency the noble governor general to render easy and amicable, or to which his excellency will give a character the gravity of which the undersigned would so much the more earnestly deplore because it would no longer be possible for him to attenuate the consequences of it, and because he would probably be compelled to add again new demands to those which he has just addressed above to the noble governor general.

The undersigned is anxious to declare, in conclusion, that if, in the long exposition which precedes there is a thought or an expression of a nature to wound the just susceptibilities of the noble governor of the two Kwangs, he disavows it, as being absolutely contrary to the sentiments which animate him. The undersigned wishes still to speak like a friend, but like a sincere friend who has nothing to conceal, and who would be happy if his frankness carried conviction to the mind of the noble functionary, whom he addresses under circumstances quite new, the gravity of which, he wishes to say to him again, it is impossible to disregard.

However this may be, the undersigned embraces this occasion to offer to his excellency the noble governor of the two Kwangs, charged with the direction of foreign affairs of the Celestial empire, the sincere wishes which he makes for his personal happiness, and for the welfare of the great empire which reckons him in the number of its most illustrious children.

BARON GROS.

Exhibit 2 *l.*

[Translation.]

YEH, High Imperial Commissioner of the Ta-Tsing dynasty, &c., &c., addresses the following answer to his excellency Baron Gros, Commissioner Extraordinary and Plenipotentiary of the great empire of France:

On the twenty-seventh day of the tenth moon, (the 12th of December, 1857,) I received from his excellency Baron Gros (Kó) a dispatch dated the same day, and I have looked into it.

I experienced a lively satisfaction when I learned that your excellency had arrived in China, in order there to treat on questions of high importance. As to what your excellency says in his dispatch on the subject of the arrest of the missionary, Ma-chen-Foo, (Mr. Chapdelaine,) by the mandarin of the district of Si-Linn, in the province of Kwangsi, I have already written to Mr. Bourboulon in reply to him, and I sent to that minister the report of the criminal judge of the province of Kwangsi, a report which is thus expressed:

"In consequence of the dispatch in which your excellency has ordered me to make an inquiry in regard to the death of Ma-chen-Foo, I have the honor to say to you that I wrote immediately to the magistrate of Si-Linn on this subject, and that he answered me as follows:

" 'On searching the archives (those of Si-Linn) in conformity to the orders which you have given me, I found no indication by which it could be made known that either the priest Ma-chen-Foo, (Mr. Chapdelaine,) or the individual named Pa-ven, or the widow Agnes, had been either arrested, or beaten, or put to death by me on the nineteenth day of the first moon of the sixth year of Hien-Fung, (24th of February, 1856,) and on that day no person was detained in the prison. But here is what took place during the second moon of that same year, (during the month of March, 1856.) I being in the village of Si-hiang, for the purpose of defending it, and of opposing the entrance of the rebels into the lower part of this village, the principal man of the town of Ing-joung came to tell me that the rebel Ma-tzu-nung and some others had arrived there and were uttering strange reports in order to seduce the people and to urge them to join the society of the Triad; that these individuals were indulging in every kind of excesses, committing robbery, violating women, &c., &c.

" 'On receiving this statement from the principal man of the town himself, I at once set out with him and some soldiers, to hunt for and seize the guilty. But I was only able to arrest Ma-tzu-nung, the other rebels having taken to flight.

" 'Ma-tzu-nung, on being interrogated by me, stated that he was born at Canton; that he belonged to the same society as Lin-pa and Tau-a-sicou; that Lin-pa and his associates were in the district of Youn-hien, creating disturbances among the people. He also said that he had gone to Si-Linn to gather followers there, and to obtain members for the society of the Triad; and he finally admitted that he had committed robberies, violated women, &c., &c.

" 'In consequence of this statement of the culprit, and under an apprehension that among the great number of rebels who were trying to excite the people, other revolters might assemble for the purpose of creating still further trouble, I caused him to be executed; and in the report which I forwarded, making known the destruction of the rebels, I spoke of this execution.

" 'As I have been ordered to find out all that took place on that occasion, I must say that I caused to be arrested the guilty Ma-tzu-nung only, and had him executed. But this individual's name not being the same as that of Ma-chen-Foo, (Mr. Chapdelaine) which you mention to me in your dispatch, and these two individuals not being either from the same place, I do not think that one can possibly be taken for the other.

" 'I request you to be pleased to transmit this statement to his excellency the viceroy of the two Kwangs.'

" This report of the magistrate of Si-Linn, having reached my hands, it remains for me to transmit it to your excellency, in order that you may examine it, and adopt such course as may seem proper to you."

It was after receiving this statement, which was transmitted to me by the criminal judge of the province of Kwangsi, that I wrote to Mr. Bourboulon, as my archives show.

It is a principle of the Christian religion to encourage men in the practice of good. Article twenty-three of the treaty says the Chinese authorities shall be permitted to arrest all those (foreigners) who cross the limits agreed upon, and intrude themselves into the country; and it prescribes that in this case the persons arrested shall be delivered to the nearest consul, in order that he may watch after them. It also prohibits any of the Chinese authorities whatever, or any one of the people, to beat or maltreat these arrested persons; but the subjects of your noble empire often violate this clause of the treaty; many times they have gone beyond the assigned limits, and they have frequently intruded themselves into the interior of the country, in order to preach Christianity there. Thus in the eighth moon of the twenty-sixth year of Tao-Kwang, (in September, 1846,) two missionaries named Ko-pi-io-tso-ko ( ) and Va-ti-su-la, (,) were conducted back from Thibet to Canton. In the twelfth moon of the twenty-eighth year, (in December, 1848, to January, 1849,) another missionary, named Lo-ki-tchen, (Mr. Renou,) was sent from Su-tchouan to Canton; in the eleventh moon of the thirtieth year, (January, 1850,) two missionaries, named Ni-ki-li-li-oua ( ) and Linkali, (,) were conducted back from Mongolia to the province of Canton; in the fourth moon of the first year of Hien Fung, (in May, 1850,) another missionary, named Mong-to, was taken back from Kiangsi to Canton; in the ninth moon of the fifth year, (in November, 1855,) another missionary, named Jacquemain, (Mr. LeTurdu,) was conducted back from Kia-ing-tchou to Canton. Finally, in the fourth moon of this year, (May, 1857,) a French missionary whose name could not be learned from any questions addressed to this individual, was conducted back from Jen-hoa to Canton.

All these missionaries were delivered up to the consuls of their noble empire, proof whereof exists in the archives; and, in thus sending back to their consuls all the French missionaries who had intruded themselves into the country, without any exception, as soon as upon inquiry it was ascertained that they belonged to France, we have given proof of the equitable manner in which we conduct ourselves.

The province of Kwangsi not being open to foreigners, to go into it is to cross the established limits, is to go into the interior of the empire. If Ma-chen-foo, (Mr. Chapdelaine,) when he was arrested, had been recognized as a Frenchman, he would not have failed to be carried back to Canton. But in the report made by the criminal judge of Kwangsi, it is said that the magistrate of Si-Linn had arrested a rebel named Ma-tzu-nung, who had declared that he was from Canton, and not from France, and that this rebel, on being interrogated again, had admitted that he had violated women and committed robberies in the villages. If the rebel Ma-tzu-nung was the same individual as Ma-chen-Foo, (Mr. Chapdelaine,) when he was taken before the court he ought to have stated that he was a Frenchman, and this so much the more willingly as the object of the Christian religion, which he exercised, is to induce men to be good. Besides, as the culprit acknowledged robberies and thefts, acts which cannot be committed by those who profess the Christian religion, it is evident that the person arrested could not have been Ma-chen-Foo.

I conclude, from all which has been herein set forth, that Mr. de Courcy has been wrongly informed in relation to this affair, and I do not think I ought to concern myself about the culprit Ma-tzu-nung.

As to what your excellency says in your dispatch, in regard to reasonable indemnities to be granted by China to the subjects of your noble nation, and to those under its protection, for the losses which they have experienced in the burning of the factories at Canton, on consulting the archives, I have found that in the 9th moon of last year, (in October or November, 1856,) when the English, without being provoked to it, sent forward their troops; they set fire to a very large amount of property near the gate or the western custom-house. Everybody was an eye-witness of this act, and all the foreigners know perfectly well that it was the English soldiers who burnt this property. It is to the English, therefore, that foreigners should address their demands for indemnity, and I have even heard it said that the English consul (Mr. Parkes) had already consented to make reparation for these damages, to which the Chinese government is an absolute stranger.

As to the demand which your excellency makes that, in virtue of article thirty-five of the treaty, his Majesty the august Emperor should be pleased to appoint new commissioners to come to Canton, &c., &c., I have to observe to your excellency, that the treaty signed in the twenty-fifth year of Tao Kwang, (in 1845,) between the two empires, was concluded by the august predecessor of the present Emperor, as being a treaty of peace for a period of ten thousand years, in order to maintain harmony perpetually between the two empires without its being necessary to modify the provisions of it at any time. Since the conclusion of that treaty, the commerce of China with foreign nations has conferred advantages on everybody which are attributable to said treaty. It is evident, therefore, that it has been wisely established; and the reigning Emperor, knowing that this compact of ten thousand years was made and sanctioned by his august father, will not consent to modify it. But since no Chinese functionary, whatever his rank may be, now wishes, or dares to act or think contrary to the will of the Emperor, how would it be possible for me to ask at Pekin that new negotiators should be appointed for the purpose of discussing the august orders of his Majesty? Such is the simple explanation which I have the honor to offer to your excellency on this subject, without attaching to it the slightest mental reservation.

Relative to what your excellency says to me, in regard to the demands of England on China, I have to observe to you that in the ninth moon of the last year, (in October, 1856,) the English, without any cause, instigated a thousand disturbances, fired their cannon on the city of Canton, attacked the forts situated in the neighborhood, and burned a great number of buildings in several places. In thus seeing that China has been attacked without cause by England, the foreign nations may judge for themselves, on which side all the wrong is found.

In the tenth moon of last year, (in November, 1856,) when the Count de Courcy wrote to me officially that he was not going to meddle in the wars which our nation might have with other nations, he gave me a proof of his high intelligence and of his spirit of justice in thus not wanting to interfere in the quarrels with England.

I think, therefore, that your excellency, who ought to comprehend right and justice better than he does, will not employ different language from that of Count de Courcy ; and I trust that your excellency will not lend your ear to the seductive (in the Chinese, meaning also intriguing) words which you may hear from persons approaching you, (the English,) words which might induce you to act in a manner that would not be altogether conformable to the sentiments of rectitude which distinguish your excellency.

In regard to the Island of Honan, as it is inhabited by a crowd of insubordinate persons, and as the forts around it have been built with the money of the people, in order to defend them against pirates and robbers, if the troops of your noble empire were to establish themselves on the island and in the forts in question, I should fear that serious disturbances might result from it. I warn your excellency thereof, for your excellency must not be able to reproach me with not having notified you beforehand, and with not having used all my efforts to protect the subjects of your noble nation.

I have heard it said that in your excellency's noble empire, it is customary to adore the God of Heaven, (the Celestial Spirit,) and that on every seventh day thanks are rendered to Him, which is the reason that your empire has enjoyed for many years a great reputation for justice and honesty.

Finally, when your excellency tells me that if in the dispatch which you have written to me, there is a word or a thought which seems to wound me, you declare that it is absolutely contrary to your intentions, you prove to me your wish to maintain the friendship and good harmony which exist between China and France; and I, the high dignitary, not having any other ambition than that of preserving that peace and good harmony between the two nations, if any affairs which are connected with their common interest are brought forward to be treated on, I shall have no difficulty in engaging in them as it shall be proper.

I shall esteem myself fortunate if your excellency does not allow yourself to be beguiled by vain words which can never lead to anything but painful differences.

This is what I have to reply to your excellency, while wishing you at the same time, every kind of prosperity.

The above dispatch is addressed to his excellency Baron Gros, (Kó,) commissioner extraordinary and plenipotentiary of the great empire of France, on the 29th day of the tenth moon of the seventh year of Hien-Fung. (The 14th of December, 1857.)

Exhibit 2 *m.*

[Translation.]

YEH, High Imperial Commissioner of the Ta-Tsing dynasty, replies as follows:

On the 9th day of the 11th moon, (December 24th, 1857,) I received a dispatch from your excellency, dated the 8th day of the same moon, (December 23, 1857,) and I have made myself acquainted with its contents.

The question of Ma-chen-Foo (Mr. Chapdelaine) has already been on my part clearly explained to your excellency in my last reply, in which I inclosed to you the report which the criminal judge of the province of Kwangsi had sent to me, making known to me that the magistrate of Si-Linn had neither arrested, nor beaten, nor put to death Ma-chen-Foo (Mr. Chapdelaine.)

Your excellency tells me in your last dispatch that I have used evasive expressions, and that it would be useless to discuss this affair longer. You further add that, when Ma-chen-Foo was arrested, although he stated the nation to which he belonged, the magistrate (of Si-Linn) wanted to exact from him 400 taels, in order to set him at liberty, or at least 150 taels, as he had not the sum at first demanded. On seeing this dispatch, I remarked that it was entirely different from all those which I had previously received from M. de Courcy and M. de Bourboulon.

In the notes which they addressed to me for the purpose of making known to me the details of this affair, they never told me that the magistrate of Si-Linn had exacted money from Ma-chen-Foo (Mr. Chapdelaine.) Nor did your excellency say anything to me about it in your previous note. How happens it, then, that you now cite to me this demand for money addressed to Ma-chen-Foo (Mr. Chapdelaine?) It may be seen from this fact, which clearly proves it, that your excellency is often wrongly informed. Besides this, when the Chinese government has to do with an affair, it does not act lightly. If the act had really taken place, I should not have kept in office a magistrate so venal and so dangerous to the country. On finding now, after inquiries, that the act did not take place, how could I admit it as true?

In your dispatch of the 27th day of the 11th moon, (the 12th of December,) your excellency tells me that you do not wish to leave me in uncertainty; but I perceive that even yourself, not being absolutely certain of the act, cannot consider it as real. Why, then, should I employ subterfuges and evasive words?

I request your excellency to be pleased to reflect that if the individual arrested was not one of those Frenchmen who exhort men to the practice of good, but, on the contrary, was a malefactor born at Canton, who violated women and committed robberies, there is no reason why we should grant reparations which are not provided for in the treaty; and still less so as the malefactor was born in the country.

As to what your excellency tells me in your dispatch, that my blindness does not permit me to yield to demands, (of the two powers,) I have the honor to reply to you that, as your excellency wishes to continue in good harmony and at peace with China, it seems to me that you will not wish to use such expressions in your dispatches, and that you will not permit such to be used; that you will, moreover, wish the writer to be more careful and more accurate.

This is all that I have to say to your excellency, wishing you, at the same time, the earliest happiness.

The 10th day of the 11th moon of the 7th year of Hien-Fung, (December 25, 1857.)

Exhibit 2 *n.*

[Translation.]

The undersigned commissioner extraordinary and plenipotentiary, sent to China by his Majesty the Emperor of the French, received on the 15th of this month the letter which his excellency the noble governor of the two Kwangs, charged with the foreign relations of the Emperor, did him the honor to write to him on the 14th, in answer to the note that the undersigned had addressed to his excellency on the 12th of the same month.

On reading with the greatest attention the answer which he has just received from his excellency, the undersigned has been greatly afflicted at the levity with which the present grave affairs are therein treated; and he has been troubled, he admits, to conceive how a document of such a character could have been sent to him.

However this may be, and without entering into a useless discussion in regard to the contents of the note which he has just received, the undersigned deems it his duty to pause at one single fact, and he desires, in calling attention to it, to take the gauge of all the others.

The noble governor, in speaking of the magistrate of Si-Linn, who caused to be executed *publicly*, in front of his court, a poor French missionary, who had uselessly invoked his nationality, and whose head the magistrate had had cut off, because the unfortunate Frenchman could not give him the four hundred taels which were at first exacted of him, nor even the one hundred and fifty, with which the magistrate would have been satisfied at last not to put him to death, is bold enough to say to M. de Bourboulon, in the dispatch which he wrote to that minister, on the 12th of this month, that the said magistrate (known by everybody as the murderer of the missionary in question) having been interrogated on this subject, and having stated that he did not commit this murder, it was evident that the murder had not taken place! And to this incredible assertion, the noble governor adds, that, "consequently he is of opinion that the minister of France has been wrongly informed, and thinks that he, the governor general, should thenceforward not concern himself any more about this affair."

Since when, then, and in what country is the denial of a crime by him who has committed it the *evident* proof that there has been no such crime? All reflection on this subject is useless.

However, the whole note of the noble governor general being only a derisive document, which answers nothing, and which, it must certainly be said, is unworthy of the high functionary from whom it emanates, and still less of him to whom it is addressed, the undersigned has to limit himself to calling the attention of the imperial commissioner to the following passage, extracted from the note, which his excellency received on the 12th of this month: "The French plenipotentiary has to say to his excellency that silence observed towards him, or an evasive or dilatory answer made to him, will be equivalent to a clearly expressed refusal."

The reply of the governor general, received on the 15th of this month, not being serious, and only containing evasive language, without coming to a decision on the demands of France, it is equivalent to a formal refusal; and hence it is the duty of the undersigned to inform the governor general of the two Kwangs, that from and after to-day, the 23d of December, the day on which the period of delay fixed for receiving a satisfactory answer that has not arrived has expired, the solution of the present question is placed in the hands of commanders-in-chief of the allied forces of France and England, who can, as soon as they deem it proper, adopt rigorous measures to obtain at last the just reparation, which in his blindness, the noble governor general has been unwilling to grant to the two powers, so long as they only spoke to him in conciliatory and friendly language.

The undersigned embraces this opportunity to renew to his excellency the governor general of the two Kwangs, the assurance of his distinguished sentiments.

A true copy.

BARON GROS.

Exhibit 2 *o.*

[Translation.]

The undersigned have the honor to make known to their excellencies, Yeh, governor general of the two Kwangs, Pih-kwei, governor of Canton, Shanghi, general of the Mantchoos, and Kwang-lin, general of the Han-kinns, that their excellencies, the plenipotentiaries extraordinary of France and England, having made known to them that the negotiations which they commenced with the Imperial Commissioner Yeh had terminated without leading to a satisfactory result, they have requested them to make the necessary arrangements to occupy the city of Canton by the forces under their orders.

The undersigned, wishing to spare as much as possible the lives and property of the inhabitants of Canton, have determined to wait forty-eight hours longer before proceeding to attack the city, and they grant this delay to it in order to give the military authorities, and the Tartar and Chinese soldiers of every class, time to evacuate the city. It can thus be occupied by the allied troops without bloodshed, the lives of the inhabitants will not be jeopardized, and their property will be respected.

If the high authorities, to whom the undersigned address themselves, think proper to accede to the propositions which are made to them, they will act wisely by making known their consent to the undersigned by means of a letter, which must be sent to them within forty-eight hours after twelve o'clock of to-day, and by stating at the same time into what place, distant not less than thirty miles from Canton, and by what route it is the intention of those military authorities and soldiers to retire.

The functionary who brings the reply of their excellencies shall be informed in what place and at what hour the officers of the allied forces are to be in order to receive the keys of the city, and the measures which may be useful in maintaining peace in the city, and in protecting it, shall also be indicated to him.

If the conditions above proposed are not accepted and carried into effect, the city shall be attacked.

[Here the titles of the two admirals, French and English, and those of General Straubenzée.]

A true copy.

BARON GROS.

Exhibit 2 p.

[Translation.]

Kö, (Baron Gros,) High Imperial Commissioner, appointed by the great Empire of France Embassador Extraordinary, furnished with full powers, and hereditary Baron:

Gö, (Lord Elgin,) High Imperial Commissioner, specially appointed by the great Empire of England Embassador Extraordinary, furnished with full powers, and Earl of Elgin and Kincardine:

Sy, (Admiral Seymour,) Vice-Admiral, Commander-in-Chief of the forces of her Britannic Majesty in the seas of Indo-China:

Ly, (Admiral Rigault de Genouilles,) Rear Admiral, Commander-in-Chief of the Naval Division of France in the seas of Indo-China:

Szu, (General Straubenzée,) Major General, Commander of the forces of her Britannic Majesty in the expedition to China:

Make the present proclamation known to all persons.

The high dignitary Yeh, having managed affairs very badly, as the archives prove, and we being placed under the painful necessity of making our troops act, and the admirals of the two empires having united their forces and attacked the city of Canton, we have decided that this city shall be surrendered to the competent authorities as soon as the existing questions between the Chinese government and France and England shall have been lawfully deliberated upon, and have received a proper solution; and, although we have arrested and have kept in our hands the high dignitary Yeh, because we are unwilling that he should exercise public authority, yet, as in establishing ourselves in the city, we sincerely wish that the persons and property of all its inhabitants may be respected and not receive the slighest injury, and as we also wish that, in the measures to be taken to reach this end, nothing may be changed in the manners and customs of the people, and that they may not experience any constraint or difficulty, we make known by this proclamation, to all the inhabitants inside and outside of the city, that we wish his excellency, the high dignitary Pih, to continue to exercise his functions as governor of the province, and to assist the present government when circumstances demand it; and to this end, we have determined that all affairs which only concern the Chinese shall be adjudicated by the said governor, and that those in which foreigners only are interested, or which shall take place between Chinese and foreigners, shall be adjudicated in concert by the authorities whom the high functionaries and the admirals have appointed for this purpose, who shall reside in the palace of the governor for the better dispatch of business.

Let everybody be informed of these regulations, and not contravene them in any manner, which we formally ordain by the present proclamation.

The 25th day of the 11th moon, of the 7th year of Hien-Fung. (10th of January, 1858.)

A true copy.

BARON GROS.

Exhibit 2 *q.*

[Translation.]

Baron Gros to the Prime Minister at Pekin.

MISSION EXTRAORDINARY OF FRANCE IN CHINA,
Canton, February, 1858.

To his Excellency the Prime Minister of the Emperor of China at Pekin:

The undersigned, embassador extraordinary of his Majesty the Emperor of the French, to the great Emperor of the Tsings, and furnished with letters which accredit him in this rank near the august sovereign of the Celestial Empire, bearer likewise of the powers which have been conferred on him as commissioner and plenipotentiary to regulate the differencies which exist between the two nations, and to endeavor to render still more useful to the subjects of the two empires the relations of amity, commerce, and navigation, established between them by treaties and by the progress of civilization, has the honor to announce to the great dignitary, his excellency the prime minister, &c., that he arrived in the Canton river sometime since, and that after receiving from the French authorities in this neighborhood all the information which he needed in order to understand the state of things, and to learn if, at last, the vice-roy of the two Kwangs had acceded to the just demands for reparation which France had long ago presented to the Chinese government, he had learned, with the most lively regret, that dilatory answers or a prolonged silence had always been opposed to the moderate reclamations of the French minister by the Imperial Commissioner Yeh, charged by the Emperor with the foreign relations of the Celestial Empire.

In this state of things, wishing yet to give to China a proof of the conciliatory spirit which animates the government of the Emperor of the French, and of the desire he has of maintaining peace between the two empires, the undersigned addressed himself to the Imperial Commissioner Yeh, because the season, too far advanced, did not permit him to proceed to the Peiho, where he had orders to present himself; and in writing to Yeh to make known to him the objects of his mission, he did not allow him to remain ignorant of what would be the inevitable consequences of his silence, of his refusal, or of the evasive answers which he might give to the notes sent to him.

In order that the noble prime minister, &c., may know exactly the facts which preceded and followed the capture of Canton, and that he may have no doubt on the cause of the grave events which have just occurred, the undersigned sends him herewith a copy of the correspondence which has taken place between him and the Imperial Commissioner Yeh, as well as a copy of the summons and proclamations of the commanders-in-chief; documents which it would be of the highest importance to place before the eyes of the august sovereign of the empire, to whom the whole truth should be known.

Yeh, having, by the derisive answers which he has given, obstinately refused to give satisfaction to the just and moderate demands which were addressed to him by France and England, it being decided between them as to the means to be employed to obtain justice, and the term which had been assigned to him for acceding to them having expired, the French forces, united with those of England, attacked the city on the 28th December, of last year, and took possession of it on the 29th.

The first care of the plenipotentiaries and of the commanders of the allied forces, the prime minister already knows, without doubt, was to protect the lives and property of the inoffensive inhabitants sacrificed to the foolish pride of him who should have been their protector. A few days after the taking of the city, Yeh, the governor Pih-kwei, and the Tartar general, were themselves captured by the allied forces and no harm done to them; Europeans place no price on the heads of their enemies. All the attentions due to the misfortune and the rank of these high dignitaries have been granted them; but Yeh, the first cause of all the evil, has been removed from the empire, where he will not return till the court of Pekin shall have granted the reparations which it owes, and shall have consented to reëstablish, on bases still broader than those which now exist, the official relations between China on the one part, and France and England on the other; relations which the blindness of Yeh has compromised in so lamentable a manner.

The yamun of Yeh exists no longer; a portion of his archives, the treasure, the arsenals of Canton, are in our hands, and the vice roy now mourns in a temporary exile the unwise conduct which has caused so much evil to his subjects.

As to their excellencies the governors Pih-kwei and the Tartar general whom Yeh had deceived, in not letting them know either of the just demands of the allies, or of their summons, or of the time which they granted to the principal authorities of Canton, to find means of entering into an arrangement, these two high dignitaries, inspired by a feeling of patriotism which does them honor, have consented to aid the commanders-in-chief of the allied forces in maintaining order in the city, in restoring confidence, in saving it from pillage, and in seeking thus to preserve it uninjured until the time when the allies will be able to restore to the hands of the representatives of the emperor. These high functionaries have been restored to liberty, and reëstablished in their yamuns where they administer justice, and whence they maintain order in the city.

Tranquillity being restored, the blockade being raised, commerce bringing back its treasures, and the inhabitants already becoming accustomed to see with pleasure and profit to themselves, the foreigners who love them and treat them well, will not be long without seeing that they have been mistaken in representing them as their enemies, and that so far from fleeing from them and fearing them, as they have been ordered to do, they have everything to gain in establishing with them most friendly relations.

In this state of things, the plenipotentiaries of France and England have considered that the time has come to give effect to the mission which they have to fulfill, and the undersigned, together with his honorable colleague of England, wishing still to do everything in his power to prevent the evils, always entailed by the use of coercive measures from spreading to other provinces of the empire, has, in concert with the plenipotentiary of her British Majesty, taken the determination to suspend hostilities, and to make a direct application to the court of Pekin, that it may be willing to nominate diplomatic agents of a rank equal to that of the plenipotentiaries of the two nations, and to order them to repair to the city of Shanghai at the end of March of this year, there to meet the plenipotentiaries of France and England, who will be there at the same time, or not long afterwards.

But to leave nothing in doubt, and to act towards the high dignitary, the prime minister, &c., &c., with the same loyalty made use of towards Yeh, the undersigned ought to say to his excellency that the high dignitaries appointed by the Emperor must be furnished with the full powers necessary not only to accord the reparation which the Imperial Commissioner Yeh has refused to give, and which, so far as France is concerned, might be slightly modified if necessary; but also to regulate the indemnities for the expenses of the war as well as those which Yeh has obliged the allies to incur, and which, as has been already remarked, ought to be charged to the imperial treasury, since the allies have been forced to make use of their arms. It is necessary, finally, that these same dignitaries should be able to turn their attention as well to certain ameliorations indispensable for the resuming of the legal relations interrupted by the events that have taken place, relations which the undersigned doubts not, will not fail to take a new start to the great advantage of the respective populations.

Let your excellency reflect seriously on the events that have just occurred. If, as is the case in all the empires of the West, an officer of an honorable character, and enjoying the confidence of his sovereign, had resided in the capital city as minister plenipotentiary of France or of England, or if he had been able, when he judged it proper or useful to go there to present respectfully his complaints to the Emperor, and to demand justice, the fall of Canton would not have taken place, the Emperor would have known the whole truth, peace would never have been disturbed, and one of the greatest cities of the empire would not be at present held by European troops. It is then, for the interest of the Chinese government even more than for that of foreign nations to remedy so dangerous a state of affairs, and it would act wisely in placing itself in this respect, on a level with the civilized powers of the west, by allowing the complaints and reclamations to go directly to the throne of the Emperor, by the interposition of honorable men resident at Pekin, or at least having the power of presenting themselves there, when grave interests required it. This question must be settled.

The example of Shanghai and of the ports open to commerce, where the Chinese and the foreigners live on good terms, esteem and love each other more as they become better acquainted, ought not to be lost, and the considerable advantages of which these cities, their inhabitants, and their territory derive the profit, can be granted to other populations worthy of enjoying it.

The illegal commerce which is carried on upon a vast scale in the ports unopened to foreign commerce proves to the detriment of the imperial treasury, which derives no benefit therefrom, how useless is the attempt to restrict commerce to the five ports named in the treaties.

Your excellency knows that, notwithstanding the formal prohibition imposed on foreigners from penetrating into the interior of the country, it is almost impossible to execute this clause of the treaties, and that all the foreigners who enter clandestinely into the empire ought, without any ill-treatment, to be placed in the hands of the consul of their country whose residence is nearest to the place where they have been taken. From this often result, grave complications, and, when it happens, as the undersigned has unfortunately a sad example to cite, a prevaricating magistrate, such as the one of Si-lin-kieng, who has tortured and put to death, with a barbarity without parallel, a missionary of peace and charity, and that the Chinese authorities refuse to punish this guilty magistrate, lamentable catastrophes occur, and Canton offers an example which ought not to be forgotten.

Were it allowed foreigners to travel in the empire for commerce or for improvement, on condition, however, of being necessarily furnished with passports delivered by their consuls and legalized by the Chinese authorities on payment of a small sum to the imperial treasury, the result would be a great benefit to the country, and the Chinese authorities would have a guarantee against the reprehensible acts of certain foreigners whose conduct is reprobated by all honest men. This question is one of those which it will be useful to resolve.

Liberty of conscience, an efficacious protection for those pious and charitable men who expose their lives and abandon all they possess in order to assist the poor and infirm, and who exhort men to the practice of good and to the respect of the laws, the authorities, and the Emperor, ought to find place among the friendly relations to be established.

Why should not each producer in his province and each industrious man in the empire be able to sell directly to foreigners, furnished with passports according to rule, and even at the places of production, the fruits of their labor or of their industry? Their interests would be no longer injured, as they are at present by unfaithful or unscrupulous agents who enrich themselves at others' expense.

Why not forbid the illegal levying in the provinces of transit duties or merchandise and produce which leave the country or which are imported into it, and which have already paid the contributions or the duties imposed by the tariffs?

Such, your excellency, are nearly the principal questions to treat, the definitive solution of which, obtained at the same time with the required reparations, will restore peace to the country, and will allow the French and English plenipotentiaries to restore the city and suburbs of Canton to the hands of the representatives of the Emperor. But without wishing to use language like that which it was necessary to employ to the Imperial Commissioner Yeh, the undersigned must nevertheless make known to your excellency that the most intimate concord reigns between the plenipotentiaries of France and England, a proof of which is furnished by the two flags that float above Canton, and that if, at the time designated, that is towards the end of March, the undersigned does not find at Shanghai, where he will be, proper plenipotentiaries vested with sufficient powers to accord the desired reparations and to decide the questions just mentioned, and those of less importance which will arise, he will feel himself forced, though reluctantly, to take the measures demanded by circumstances, in order to put an end to a state of things which ought not to be prolonged.

The undersigned ardently desires that the demands of his government and those of the government of her Britannic Majesty be favorably received at Pekin, and he would be happy to sign his name to the complete and sincere reconciliation of France and China, to the advantage of civilization and of the well-being of the populations of the two empires.

The undersigned offers the most ardent wishes that prosperity may ever accompany the great and noble dignitary to whom he to-day addresses this important communication.

Exhibit 2 *r.*

HER MAJESTY'S SHIP FURIOUS,
Canton, February 6, 1858.

SIR: I have the honor to inclose herewith the copy of a notification respecting the military occupation of Canton, and the suspension, until further notice, of hostile operations against China, which is about to be issued by his excellency Baron Gros and me for general information.

I have the honor to be, sir, your excellency's most obedient, humble servant,

ELGIN AND KINCARDINE.

His Excellency Hon. W. B. REED, *&c., &c., &c.*

The undersigned, high commissioners and plenipotentiaries of their Majesties the Queen of Great Britain and the Emperor of the French, deem it proper to state for general information that Canton, having been captured by the allied British and French forces, the city and suburbs are in military occupation, and under martial law.

Tranquillity being reëstablished, the commanders-in-chief of the allied forces have already declared that the blockade of the river and port of Canton will be raised on the 10th instant, and have made public the conditions under which persons other than the Chinese desirous to visit the city or suburbs will be permitted to do so after the blockade shall have been raised.

Under these circumstances, the undersigned declare that the city and suburbs will continue in military occupation and under martial law until further notice; but that hostile operations against China, except such as the commanders-in-chief of the allied forces may consider it necessary to adopt for the security of their military position in Canton, are for the present suspended.

Beyond the limits of the military occupation, the relations of British and French subjects, and of persons entitled to British or French protection, with the Chinese, are regulated by the provisions of the existing treaties.

ELGIN AND KINCARDINE,
BARON GROS.

CANTON, *February* 6, 1858.

Exhibit 2 *s*.

[Translation.]

EXTRAORDINARY MISSION OF FRANCE IN CHINA,
On board the Primauguet, February 6, 1858.

MR. MINISTER: I have the honor to send herewith to your excellency a copy of the notification which, in concert with his excellency the high commissioner of her Britannic Majesty, I deem it my duty to publish, with a view of making known the present state of affairs in China, and the position which the allied plenipotentiaries now adopt to carry into effect the mission which has been confided to them by their respective governments.

It is with pleasure, Mr. Minister, that I have the honor of making this communication to your excellency, and I embrace the occasion to offer you anew the assurance of my sentiments of high consideration.

BARON GROS.

His Excellency WILLIAM B. REED, *&c.*, *&c.*, *&c.*

[The English version of this document will be found in the preceding inclosure of Lord Elgin, marked Exhibit 2 *r*.]

Exhibit 2 t.

LEGATION OF THE UNITED STATES,
Minnesota, February 6, 1858.

MY LORD: I have had the honor to receive your excellency's dispatch, marked confidential, of the 4th instant, accompanied by copies of the correspondence with the late Imperial Commissioner Yeh, and of a note forthwith to be sent to the prime minister or senior secretary of state of the Emperor of China. I beg to thank you for the frankness and unreserve of this communication.

It is in perfect consonance with the spirit and letter of my instructions for me, as the representative of the United States, to support the attempt about to be made by his excellency Baron Gros and your lordship to induce the government of China to consent to such arrangements as may obviate future misunderstandings, and tend to develop commercial relations between China and other nations. There is nothing in the views which you have done me the honor to communicate of the course to be pursued by Great Britain and France which the United States cannot cordially support, and I beg to add the expression of my personal sympathy with the feeling which animates your excellency's plan of action.

The government of the United States has already, in communications addressed to the British minister at Washington, recognized the justice of the causes of complaint which both England and France have against the Chinese, and I am very sure that in the conciliatory course which your excellency proposes to pursue, the President will find new reason to be satisfied with having instructed me peacefully to coöperate with you.

The United States, as you are aware, have grave causes of complaint against China, and it is a matter of regret, if not surprise, that the forbearance which it has been our duty and policy to exhibit towards a power of relative weakness has produced little or no effect. I now cherish the hope that the thorough and complete concord of the western powers which your excellency desires to initiate may render unnecessary such coercive measures on the part of the United States as I have recently felt it my duty to recommend.

I shall at once address to the imperial authorities at Pekin a communication defining very distinctly the attitude and intention of the United States, and shall be most happy to forward it by one of the ships of this squadron to Shanghai, at the same time that the letters of your excellency and Baron Gros are sent. The United States frigate Mississippi will be ready to proceed to Shanghai on this mission early next week.

I shall have the honor to forward to you a copy of my letter to the imperial court, as well as of my correspondence with the commissioner at Canton, as soon as they can be prepared.

I have the honor to be, my lord, your excellency's most obedient humble servant,

WILLIAM B. REED.

His Excellency the EARL OF ELGIN AND KINCARDINE,
Her Majesty's High Com'r and Plenipotentiary, &c., &c., &c.

Exhibit 2 u.

LEGATION OF THE UNITED STATES,
Minnesota, February 6, 1858.

MONSIEUR LE BARON: I have had the honor to receive your excellency's important communication dated the 4th instant, with the accompanying documents, informing me of the course of action which you propose to pursue in conjunction with his excellency the Earl of Elgin in your future relations to the government of China. I am further indebted to your excellency for the exposition you have done me the honor to make of the studious efforts on the part of the representatives of France and Great Britain to limit the sacrifice of life and property in the progress of the coersive measures which were adopted at Canton. I did not need this to convince me of the extreme reluctance with which you, as the representative of his Majesty the Emperor of the French, resorted to his hostilities against such an adversary as you found at Canton. The good order which your excellency informs me is established in the captured city, and the prospect of the early resumption of peaceful commerce under the regulations made by the allied powers, (a rough sketch of which your chief secretary, M. De Bellecourt, did me the honor to show me this morning,) are matters which will be viewed by all with great contentment.

In relation to the future I beg to say promptly to your excellency that I concur entirely in the plan of action proposed, and shall be most happy to give to it all the support in my power. In this I not only gratify the wish I have always had for frank and unreserved intercourse personally and officially with your excellency; but conform with the spirit of the instructions under which I act.

I shall at once address to the imperial authorities at Pekin a communication defining very distinctly the attitude and intentions of the United States, and shall be most happy to forward it by one of the ships of this squadron to Shanghai, at the same time that the letters of your excellency and Lord Elgin are sent. The United States frigate Mississippi will be ready to proceed to Shanghai on this mission early next week.

I shall have the honor to forward to you a copy of my letter to the imperial court, as well as of my correspondence with the commissioner at Canton, as soon as they can be prepared.

I have the honor to be, Monsieur Le Baron, your excellency's most obedient humble servant,

WILLIAM B. REED.

His Excellency, MONSIEUR LE BARON GROS,
Commissioner Extraordinary and Embassador of his Majesty the Emperor of the French in China.

Exhibit 2 v.

The undersigned, envoy extraordinary and minister plenipotentiary of the United States of America, bearing letters of credence from the

President of the republic to his Majesty the Emperor of China, with full powers, under the seal of the United States, to consult and negotiate with any minister or ministers of equal rank who may be deputed for that purpose by his Imperial Majesty, addresses this urgent communication to the supreme council of state.

He asks for it the respectful consideration which the President and the high authorities of the United States would gladly give to any communication which the representatives of his Imperial Majesty might address to them.

The undersigned arrived in the dominions of his Majesty, in the province of Kwang Tung, on the 5th of November, 1857.

He found the provincial city of Canton threatened by actual warfare, the great western powers of England and France having been compelled, for the redress of wrongs done to them, reluctantly to resort to arms. The United States were no parties to these hostilities. Pursuing a policy of peace and neutrality, which the traditions of the country and the precepts of the great founders of the republic consecrated, they had refused to become parties to a war on any part of China. Deeply aggrieved as the citizens of the United States had long felt themselves, by imposition on lawful commerce, harassed and alarmed by indiscriminate attempts at poison and massacre on their lives and those of their families; aggrieved as the representatives of the United States for years have been, by a contumelious refusal of the local authorities charged with the administration of foreign affairs in the south to hold personal and official intercourse with them; still more justly dissatisfied with the manner in which, within the last eighteen months, an original letter, signed by the great chief magistrate the President of the United States, to his Majesty the Emperor, had been sent back unread and with the seals broken; the undersigned, remembering the many years of former peaceful intercourse, was willing not only to postpone the claims of his government and countrymen for redress, but to interpose his mediation to avert the miseries which war inflicts even when mercifully conducted. The undersigned would have had a rich reward in the support of his countrymen and the approval of his own conscience had these peaceful intentions been consummated.

In this spirit and with these hopes, in the months of November and December last he addressed, in vain, several earnest representations to his excellency the imperial commissioner and governor of the Two Kwang, soliciting an interview, in order that he might place in his hands the letter with which he was charged from the President of the United States, to be transmitted to Pekin, and frankly confer with him on matters of common concern. The interview was refused. The offered mediation was frustrated. In one of those letters, the undersigned used these words: "The time is not distant when your excellency may be sorry you have not seen me."

The time has come when, through the obdurate indifference of the high functionary who, unfortunately for all, and most so for his Imperial Majesty, had charge of these foreign relations, the evils of war have fallen on the empire; the city of Canton, after a brief resistance, is in the power of strangers, and the imperial commissioner a prisoner in their hands.

Of all that has occurred in this neighborhood the undersigned has been an anxious spectator; and it is due to the cause of truth, too long concealed from the immediate councils of his Imperial Majesty, to him to say that the warfare which the representatives of Great Britain and France have waged has been in every act the warfare of conscious and magnanimous power; has not been prolonged a moment beyond the line of a moderate necessity, and that the treatment of a city taken by assault, and of a high functionary captured, as the imperial commissioner was, in the fresh excitement of conflict and with the sight of the misery he had occasioned all around them, will be regarded by the civilized world as illustrative of the highest humanity.

That warfare is now over. The safety of the city of Canton depends entirely on the will of its own inhabitants. Peaceful commerce is resumed by all who choose to partake of it, and the high functionaries representing the august sovereigns of France and Great Britain have again resolved on an experiment of peaceful negotiation, and on another more solemn and direct appeal to the imperial court, in order to avert difficulty in the future.

In that effort, so worthy of Christian powers, the undersigned on the part of the United States, and the representative of his Majesty the Emperor of Russia have been invited, and have agreed to join. We have not only been invited to join in the general effort at pacification, but we have been unreservedly informed of the specific objects which the allies have in view, and the undersigned on the part of the United States expressly says, that in the promotion of these objects, he and his government cordially concur.

The undersigned to bring to the view of the supreme council of his Majesty a clear idea of the exact relations of the United States to the other powers with which we mean peacefully to coöperate, and to China to whose highest authority this last appeal is made. The nearest neighbors among the great powers of the world, which the Chinese have, are the empire of Russia on the north, immediately contiguous, and in a direct line across which, washes the shores of both, the republic of the United States of America. Between Russia and the United States there has been, and is yet, notwithstanding a difference of political institutions, cordial friendship. They have always been, and are yet the friends of China. With Great Britain the relations of the American republic are not less intimate. The bond of a common language, and a common ancestry connects us closely; in addition here, we have the interests of a great commerce, which we have enjoyed together so long, and which we so much desire to increase and perpetuate. To the French nation the people of the United States have relations of ancient and uninterrupted friendship, proved in times of adversity. In the effort now made by his Majesty the Emperor of of the French to secure protection to the humble ministers of a religious faith, which inculcates charity and peace, by asking redress for the inhuman massacre of a Christian missionary, my countrymen and my government will recognize a new proof of his statesmanlike sagacity and power.

It is the consciousness of these intimate and friendly relations which now leads me as the representative of the United States, cheerfully to concur in the great and probably last peaceful effort to be made to approach nearer to the throne of his Imperial Majesty, and make audible our words of friendly warning. The hope of peace to be established on a new basis, and by revised treaties between China and each of the western powers, encourages me to share in the movement proposed.

The first fruit of such a peace will be what the United States and its representatives have always had at heart, the integrity of the Chinese empire in all its parts, from its center to the extremities. Foreign spoliation and civil disturbances are alike deplored by us. The undersigned believes this ancient empire would find a new element of vigor in the permission to foreign commerce to enter its great rivers and all its ports; for it was well said by one of his predecessors, when years ago, he was seeking access in vain to the imperial court, that when commerce licensed by authority, and paying into the imperial treasury taxes drawn from its encouragement, shall cover the rivers and coast of China, western nations will not permit rebel chiefs or pirate adventurers to interfere with its successful pursult. Freedom of trade is the best security of those who make it free.

The undersigned does not deem it necessary or expedient to enter now into further details as to what the government of the United States desire to embody in the revised treaties, which he is instructed to demand. In one respect foreign nations cannot be separated. No one asks or ever will ask peculiar privileges. The United States agreeing to the ends proposed by the other western nations, have special claims for redress, which at a proper time will be presented and resolutely urged. Among them is compensation for the losses which their citizens have incurred whilst pursuing lawful commerce (for none other does the undersigned or the United States desire to countenance) or other mode of peaceful occupation, both in years past and recently, when their resolute neutrality did not seem to give them protection from outrage. This must be adjusted.

In conclusion, the undersigned informs the supreme council of his Majesty the Emperor, that he shall at once proceed to the treaty port of Shanghai, and there hopes to meet an imperial commissioner, or such other plenipotentiary or plenipotentiaries of equal rank with the undersigned, and clothed with equal powers, as may be duly accredited for the purpose of negotiation and deputed by his Majesty the Emperor. The undersigned proposed to remain at Shanghai till the last day of March, for the purpose indicated. He desires, however, to be distinctly understood that any effort to remove the place of negotiation, as was formerly attempted, to the southern provinces of China, or to any place further removed than Shanghai from the imperial court at Pekin, will be regarded, if not as an evasion which the undersigned would be sorry to impute to the supreme counselors of the Emperor, certainly as a refusal to accede to the wishes now earnestly and respectfully expressed for friendly negotiation. In such a result, which the undersigned repeats he should be sorry to say he anticipated, he shall feel at liberty, without further announcement, delay, or declaration, either alone or in conjunction with the other western powers, to approach still nearer to the imperial city of Pekin, or take such other course as the President of the United States may direct him to pursue.

The undersigned forwards to the supreme council at Pekin copies of the letters which were exchanged last autumn between him and his excellency the imperial commissioner at Canton, and with them the assurance of his distinguished consideration.

WILLIAM B. REED.

Dated at Macao, the 10th day of February, in the year of our Lord 1858.

CANTON, *February* 11, 1858.

The United States minister has the honor to request that their excellencies Ho Kweitsing, governor general of the two Kiang, and Chow-Teh-Cheh, governor of Kiang-Su, will have the goodness to forward the inclosed dispatches to the address of his excellency Yuehing, senior secretary of state, &c., &c., &c., to his Majesty the Emperor of China.

The history of late events at Canton cannot be unknown to their excellencies; and the United States minister trusts that, convinced as he feels they must be, of the serious evil which any delay of the letters inclosed may inflict upon the interests of the State, they will employ every means in their power to insure its speedy transmission to the capital.

The United States minister requests their excellencies to accept the assurances of his distinguished consideration.

WILLIAM B. REED.

Envoy Extraordinary and Minister Plenipotentiary U. S. A.

His Excellency Ho, *the Governor General of the two Kiang;* and CHAN, *Governor of the Province of Kiang-Su.*

Exhibit 3 *a.*

MACAO, *February* 6, 1855.

MY DEAR SIR: When this arrives you will probably have received the invitation to join the plenipotentiaries of the allied powers in their demands to be addressed to Pekin, which were forwarded to me yesterday night by Lord (Mr.) Bruce and M. de Bellecourt.

Having well considered my instructions, I find that I could not well desist from coöperating with them as far as negotiations alone can go; but before sending them a reply, I would be very happy to communicate with your excellency, and to know the views that you will adopt in the present circumstances.

If you have postponed your visit to Shanghi, I would be glad to know if you intend coming back to Macao, or prefer remaining at Hong Kong. In the latter case, I would have come to see you by one of the private steamers, as the America being just painted, will not be able to start.

With assurances of great consideration, yours faithfully,

E. POUTIATINE.

His Excellency W. B. REED, *&c., &c., &c.*

Exhibit 3 *b*.

LEGATION OF THE UNITED STATES,
Macao, February 8, 1858.

SIR: Understanding in our recent conversation that it is your excellency's intention to unite with me in the plan of action and proposed negotiation suggested by the plenipotentiaries of Great Britain and France, and as a preliminary means to address a formal annunciation to the imperial authorities, I have the honor to inform your excellency that the United States steam frigate Mississippi, Captain William C. Nicholson, will probably be dispatched on Wednesday next, in order to carry my dispatch for Pekin to the port of Shanghai. It gives me great pleasure to say to you that I am sure Captain Nicholson will feel much honored by being the bearer of any communication your excellency may desire to send to the north.

I have the honor to be, sir, your excellency's obedient servant,

WILLIAM B. REED.

His Excellency COUNT E. POUTIATINE,
Envoy Extraordinary and Minister Plenipotentiary of his Majesty the Emperor of all the Russias in China.

Exhibit 3 *c*.

MACAO, *February* 9, 1858.

SIR: The frank and friendly intercourse which has existed between us since I had the honor to meet your excellency, gives me great pleasure to unite with you in the present important annunciation to be made to the imperial authorities at Pekin, in consequence of the invitation sent to us to that effect by the representatives of France and Great Britain.

I shall be much indebted to Captain Nicholson for taking charge of my note to the supreme council of state at Pekin, and delivering it at the port of Shanghai to the proper Chinese authorities, or else if found more proper, of forwarding it through the medium of the plenipotentiaries of the western powers, as you have proposed.

I herewith inclose a copy of that note for your perusal, and do not enter into any explanations, since everything is known to you from our recent conversation on the subject.

Assuring you of my high consideration and esteem, I have the honor to be your excellency's most humble servant,

E. POUTIATINE.

His Excellency Hon. W. B. REED,
Envoy Extraordinary, &c., &c., &c.

Exhibit 3 *d.*

NOTE TO THE SUPREME COUNCIL OF THE EMPIRE OF CHINA.

The court of Pekin ought to be informed, from the communications made to it last year, as well as from verbal explanations that I had with the Chinese dignitaries Wen and Tsian, during their visits to me at the mouth of Peiho, how much the Russian government has at heart that the Middle Empire should be in peace and good understanding with all nations having any political or commercial intercourse with it.

In all those communications I endeavored to point out the difficulties to which the empire of China in its present state will be exposed, if it resists the demands of civilized States who desire to alter the form of their intercourse with it. There is no doubt that the main reason of all the discords that have happened might have been averted if foreign governments could have communicated directly with the high authorities in the capital. Not considering this, the cabinet of Pekin has not only shown no desire to amend its relations with foreign powers, but undoubtedly has given orders to the local authorities in other parts of the empire to adhere to their former rule, in either refusing to accept any representation, or, after accepting it, to keep a total silence, or, as in some instances, giving a decided refusal without refuting the question raised, and usually referring to circumstances having little or no concern at all with the main object. This form of procedure has been the occasion of ruptures, and of all the evils that have befallen China in consequence of them; and but lately the court of Pekin, undervaluing the friendship of so long a date between Russia and China, refused, in order to keep to its immutable custom, though against a clear stipulation of the treaty of Kiakhta, to receive the envoy sent by his Majesty the Emperor of Russia to Pekin. Now, all the well-intentioned governments, considering their own interests not less than the real welfare of China, can rightly unite their efforts in putting an end to this order of things.

The extraordinary embassadors of France and England, sent lately to China, after several unsatisfactory communications with the viceroy at Canton, appointed to have relations with foreign ministers, were at last obliged to have recourse to arms, but, not wishing to spread the horrors of war, in which thousands of innocent persons suffer for a small number of guilty ones, have resolved to open direct negotiations with the highest authorities at Pekin, and have invited the ministers plenipotentiary of the United States of America and Russia to take a part in them. During my stay at the river Peiho I informed the dignitary Wen that, even if a refusal should be sent by the cabinet of Pekin to my proposals, it would not make me leave the shores of China, but that I would continue to make new efforts to reopen negotiations with the high Chinese authorities.

Availing myself of the present circumstances, and finding that the general demands of the representatives of England and France are conformable in substance to those that I have received, the imperial order to propose to the Chinese government, I, conjointly with them and the representative of the United States of America, address myself to the supreme council of state, requesting it to make a representation to the Throne to name one or more high personages vested with full powers to decide everything concerning the demands hereafter mentioned, and to order those plenipotentiaries to repair to Shanghai and open negotiations with us there not later than the end of the month of March.

The principal demands relating to the general interests of all the States consists:

1. In a free and unobstructed intercourse with Pekin, whenever one of the governments may find it necessary to send there an accredited person to consider and to come to an agreement on any matter.

By this direct intercourse, the representation of any matter or circumstance would be made in its proper and not in an inverted light, as has often been done by local authorities afar from the central power, and this alteration alone would very much consolidate the good understanding between China and the foreign powers. Besides expediency, it is right that China should adopt a mode of international intercourse similar to that maintained among civilized nations, who do find no evil arising from it.

2. In spreading and granting new facilities to the commerce of all the nations in the open ports, as well as in other places which by mutual consent may be made accessible to foreign trade.

Every Chinese who has visited the towns where foreign trade has been established must perceive the beneficial effect it produces on national industry. The impossibility of stopping contraband trade where it is convenient and profitable to carry it on, ought to incite the Chinese government to open a greater number of towns for lawful trade, which has been found to be one of the most important sources of state revenues.

3. In an entire liberty to profess the Christian religion by all foreigners resident in China, as well as by those Chinese who have embraced Christianity, or are willing, by their free consent, to become Christians.

The greatest part of the Chinese who are conversant with Christianity know that this religion enforces charity, obedience, esteem of authorities, and everything that is good. One of the best emperors of China bore witness to its excellence; therefore, the government of China has no reason to oppress men who annunciate it, as well as those who, through their own conviction, have adopted the teachings of Christianity, and are blameless in other respects.

Besides the demands of general importance, it is requisite for the representative of Russia, a neighboring State to China, to take into consideration, with the plenipotentiary sent from Pekin, the frontier questions and the burning and pillage of the Russian factory at Tarbagatæ, which are all well known to the Chinese government.

To refute these demands the Chinese government will not fail to point out the eternal immutability of its regulations, and of its instituted order in China. To this one might reply, if the regulations in China were really immutable, and if the appointed order were everywhere punctually observed, the refutation might have some grounds. But when, on the contrary, one sees everywhere government regulations violated, and a total absence of order and good arrangement, it is difficult to find out in what consists this immutability. It is known that the wisest rulers of China made new regulations suitable to time and circumstances, and the sage most highly honored by Chinese has left a rule in one of his classical books, where, among the nine virtues proper to a wise sovereign, are numbered the endeavor to attract to his dominions all persons who excel in arts and useful professions, and the reception with benevolence of foreigners and embassadors of other princes. Therefore, every one who really wishes prosperity to China must see with pain that, in the present time, those wise, ancient maxims are not followed at all, and that the morals of the people, notwithstanding their many excellent qualities, as well as most of the fine old institutions, are falling to decay.

Let, however, the government of China consider attentively and without prejudice the actual state of China, and the demands now addressed to it by foreigners, and it will arrive at the conviction there is danger and imprudence in thwarting and arousing against itself a number of powerful civilized nations; and, on the other hand, that there is no reason to fear any bad consequences from the measures proposed to be adopted. A flat or evasive refusal will show spite and distrust towards all who have presented their demands, and will in no way be to the interest of China; but, on the contrary, may lead to consequences more disastrous than the present.

Requesting the supreme council of state once more to lay before his Majesty the considerations here expressed, I trust that the great Emperor, in his wisdom, will find it indispensable to the welfare of his subjects to appoint, without loss of time, some high personages, accredited with full powers to open the expected negotiations at Shanghai.

COUNT POUTIATINE.

FEBRUARY, 1858.

Exhibit 4 *a.*

LEGATION OF THE UNITED STATES,
Macao, February 8, 1858.

DEAR SIR: I am requested by Mr. Reed to say to you, and through you to Lord Elgin, that in suggesting the dispatch of the frigate Mississippi to Shanghai, with his (Mr. Reed's) letter to Pekin, he did not mean to interfere with any arrangement Lord Elgin might think more conducive to the general interest. If Lord Elgin and Baron Gros think all the communications had better go in an English or French man-of-war, Mr. Reed will be glad to send his in that way; otherwise, he can easily dispatch the Mississippi. Count Pontiatine's letter (he being accidentally here) will accompany Mr. Reed's in any mode thought best.

It is Mr. Reed's intention to come up the river on Wednesday as far as the draft of water of the Minnesota will permit, and he will be very glad to learn then what Lord Elgin's views are. The Mississippi is quite at the service of the British and French ministers, if they desire to use her for the dispatch of any communication.

I remain, dear sir, yours obediently,

S. WELLS WILLIAMS,
Secretary of Legation, U. S. A.

The Hon. F. W. A. BRUCE,
Secretary to Legation H. B. M. to China, Canton.

Exhibit 4 b.

OFF CANTON, *February* 9, 1858.

DEAR SIR: In reply to your letter of the 4th instant, I am directed by Lord Elgin to state he and Baron Gros think it desirable that their communications should be forwarded to Shanghai in vessels bearing the flag of their respective nations, and that they should be presented simultaneously to the Chinese authorities, in order to insure their transmission to Pekin by the same opportunity.

Mr. Oliphant will proceed either to-morrow or the day after to Hong Kong, and embark thence for Shanghai with the least possible delay, with instructions to await the arrival of the communications addressed by the other plenipotentiaries of foreign powers who join in this course of proceeding.

It is hardly necessary to add that the sooner these communications reach Pekin the better.

I remain, dear sir, yours obediently,

FREDERICK W. A. BRUCE.

S. WELLS WILLIAMS,
Secretary of Legation of the United States in China.

Exhibit 4 c.

LEGATION OF THE UNITED STATES,
On board the Minnesota, February 4, 1858.

SIR: I have the honor to inform you that, anticipating the exigencies of the public service during the coming season, it is, in my opinion, absolutely necessary for the accomplishment of the objects of the mission which the President has intrusted to me to charter a small steamer of light draught.

It will no doubt be necessary for this legation to go to the north so soon as the season will permit, probably about the 1st of April, at which time I shall be glad to have the assistance of such steamer.

I make this communication in accordance with my instructions, and with the letter of the 22d June, 1857, from the Secretary of the Navy to Flag-officer Armstrong, then commander-in-chief of the United States naval forces.

I have the honor to be, sir, your obedient servant,

WILLIAM B. REED.

CAPTAIN TATTNALL,
Flag-officer and Commander-in-chief of the
U. S. Naval Forces in the East Indies and China Seas.

Exhibit 4 *c.*

LEGATION OF THE UNITED STATES,
On board the Minnesota, February 6, 1858.

SIR: In consequence of important dispatches received this morning from the British and French plenipotentiaries at Canton, I find it necessary to relinquish my intention of visiting Shanghai at present. The same intelligence, however, compels me to ask the assistance of a portion of the squadron in another direction. I desire on Wednesday next, the 10th instant, to proceed in this ship from Macao, where the legation is temporarily established, as far up the Canton river as her draft of water will permit.

I have concluded to address to the imperial court at Pekin a communication of a grave and important nature in conjunction with the plenipotentiaries of Great Britain, Russia, and France. Such a communication must go by the way of Shanghai, to which port, I desire (if you think it consistent with the interests of your command) to send it in a national vessel. My letter will be ready by Wednesday next, and I shall be glad to have one of the ships at my command for that duty.

The change which has thus unexpectedly taken place in the action of the foreign powers induces me so far to modify the suggestions of my official letter of the 4th instant, as to request you for the purpose of this mission to charter a steamer of light draft at once, instead of deferring it until the 1st of April, and that such steamer may accompany me up the river.

I have already, confidentially, submitted to you the dispatches sent to me by the allied plenipotentiaries, and my views as to the course to be pursued by the United States. In the same confidence, I beg more formally to say to you that I desire to proceed to Shanghai, either directly or by way of some intermediate port, so as to arrive there on or about the 1st of March. It is my intention to remain at Shanghai or in its immediate neighborhood till the last day of March.

After that time, should there be no negotiation at Shanghai, I shall be glad to have the United States squadron concentrated at that port, or at some convenient place in its vicinity, with a view to ulterior action.

I have the honor to be, sir, your most obedient servant,

WILLIAM B. REED.

Captain TATTNALL,
Flag-officer and Commander-in-chief of the
U. S. Naval Forces in the East Indies and China Seas.

Exhibit 4 *d.*

FLAG-SHIP SAN JACINTO,
Hong Kong, February 7, 1858.

SIR: I have the honor to acknowledge the receipt of your communication of the 6th instant.

In order to advance fully your views and wishes therein expressed, I have directed Captain Du Pont, of the Minnesota, to convey you in that ship to such points connected with your mission and at such times as you may designate. I have, also, in accordance with your wish, directed Captain Nicholson, of the Mississippi, to hold himself in readiness to convey to Shanghai in that ship, at such time as may suit your convenience, the communication you refer to.

The squadron shall be concentrated at Shanghai by the last of March, as you suggest.

In regard to your requisition on me for a steamer of light draft for the convenience of your mission, I have, with authority from the Secretary of the Navy, furnished me in view of such a contingency, made arrangements to charter the steamer "Antelope," owned by the house of Russell & Co., of Hong Kong, for six months, at the rate of $5,250 per month. I shall attach her to the Minnesota as a tender, subject to your sole use and order. Captain Du Pont shall be furnished with particular instructions regarding her.

I have the honor to be, sir, your obedient servant,

JOSIAH TATTNALL,
Flag-officer Commanding-in-chief.

His Excellency WILLIAM B. REED,
Minister Plenipotentiary-to-China.

[Confidential.]

Exhibit 4 *e.*

LEGATION OF THE UNITED STATES,
On board the Minnesota, Canton River, February 10, 1858.

SIR: I have the honor to forward to you two dispatches addressed to the imperial court at Pekin—one from this legation, and the other from his excellency Count Poutiatine, the plenipotentiary of his Majesty the Emperor of Russia. I request you, in consonance with orders already communicated to you by the flag-officer commanding in chief the naval forces of the United States, to proceed at once to the treaty port at Shanghai, and to deliver these dispatches to such of the Chinese authorities as may be designated to you by the vice-consul of the United States, or to the vice-consul himself, for immediate transmission to Pekin. Dispatches of a similar nature from the British and French ministers are about to be forwarded to Shanghai, and it is very important, if you reach Shanghai before the vessels which carry them have arrived, that you should remain there till their arrival, as it is desired that these communications should be simultaneously presented to the Chinese authorities.

I have the honor to be, sir, your obedient servant,

WILLIAM B. REED.

Captain WILLIAM C. NICHOLSON,
United States ship Mississippi, Hong Kong.

[Confidential.]

Exhibit 4 f.

LEGATION OF THE UNITED STATES,
On board the Minnesota, February 10, 1858.

SIR: Captain Nicholson, of the United States ship Mississippi, is the bearer of very important dispatches from this legation and his excellency the Russian minister to the imperial court at Pekin. Dispatches of the same character are sent by the English and French ministers. I have requested Captain Nicholson to hand these dispatches to you, and I shall be obliged to you if you will put yourself in communication with Mr. Oliphant, one of the secretaries of his excellency Lord Elgin, who proceeds at once to Shanghai, and deliver these dispatches to him to be forwarded with the others; or, if he prefers that you should officially present them for transmission to the local authorities, that you do so. I rely on your attention to this, and on your discretion in treating this communication as strictly confidential.

I have the honor to be very respectfully, yours,

WILLIAM B. REED.

ALBERT FREEMAN, Esq.,
United States Vice-Consul, Shanghai.

Mr. Cass to Mr. Reed.

No. 11.]

DEPARTMENT OF STATE,
Washington, April 28, 1858.

SIR: Your dispatches Nos. 1, 2, 3, 35, 36, 37, 38, 39, and 40, of 1857, and those numbered from 1 to 9, inclusive, of 1858, have been received.

You were fully justified by your instructions in joining the envoys of Great Britain, France, and Russia, in their recent representations to the Emperor at Pekin, and the result of this combined movement is awaited with much interest. If it should fail to produce its intended effect, the President readily appreciates the importance of your inquiry with reference to the course which, in that event, you ought to pursue. Great Britain and France are already at war with China, and should their reasonable overtures be refused, they will doubtless continue to employ coercive measures. With the United States, however, the case is different. Although we have serious causes of complaint against that empire, it has not been thought wise, for reasons which we sufficiently mentioned in your instructions, to seek redress of our injuries by a resort to arms. It is possible that this alternative may yet be forced upon us, by the continued refusal of China to do justice to our citizens, or in the possible but improbable contingency to which you allude, that the Chinese authorities should decline to admit the United States to an equal participation in such privileges as may be granted to the belligerents at the close of the present contest. But in the event of such an exigency, it will be necessary for the President to ask from Congress the authority and the means, without which, you are aware, no war can be undertaken by this government. At present, he is not prepared to make this request, and you will continue to be guided, therefore, by the instructions which you already have.

The President observes with great satisfaction the industry and intelligence with which you have sought to improve the condition of our consular establishment in China, and your suggestions on this subject will receive careful attention. The vacancy in the consulate at Shanghai has been already filled by the appointment of William L. G. Smith, Esq., of New York, who will start for his destination in a few days. Mr. Hyatt, the consul at Amoy, will probably return to that post, and he, also, is understood to have nearly completed the necessary arrangements for his departure. It will be endeavored, as far as possible, to prevent the frequent absence of consuls from their posts in China, of which you justly complain, and your efforts will also be supported, to secure among them a greater uniformity of action in respect to their judicial and other duties than seems hitherto to have existed. On the subject of these duties, you are doubtless furnished with a printed copy of the opinion of the late Attorney General of the United States, Mr. Cushing, which discusses, to some extent, the questions referred to in your dispatch No. 36, of the 15th December last. In compliance with your suggestion, this question has been, also, referred to the present Attorney General, and, lest you may accidentally be without Mr. Cushing's opinion, I send a copy of it by this mail.

The claims of our citizens against China have very properly received your early attention, and it is earnestly hoped that some early opportunity may be offered for securing their adjustment.

I am, sir, very respectfully, your obedient servant,

LEWIS CASS.

WILLIAM B. REED, Esq., *&c.*

Mr. Reed to Mr. Cass.

No. 10.] LEGATION OF THE UNITED STAES,
On board the Minnesota, Harbor of Hong Kong,
February 26, 1858.

SIR: Nothing of special interest has occurred since the date of my last dispatch. Canton remains under the quiet control of the allies, and trade is partially resumed. The consuls are at Whampoa. We have a rumor as to a communication with the imperial court to the effect that the Pihkwei, after his capture, but before he was installed as temporary governor, wrote to the Emperor that he had succedeed in getting the English and French completely in his power, and held them at his mercy; that he could, if intrusted with the function, better than any other person, treat with them; and that there was a probability the appointment of imperial commissioner might be conferred on him. There is so much falsehood involved in this as to make it quite probable.

Another is, that a commissioner specially appointed is on his way to Canton to attempt negotiations. In either case, it will be unsuccessful; for no negotiation could take place with a man in the attitude of Pihkwei, or at any point further from Pekin than Shanghai. I annex to this dispatch a copy and translation (inclosures 1 *a* and 1 *b*) of a letter received from Baron Gros. Lord Elgin has left Canton finally, and is now here preparing to go north next week. The French and Russian ministers go about the same time.

I forward the consular correspondence of the last mails. It relates to various topics of interest, (inclosures from 2 *a* to 2 *z*.)

1. To the case of the Wandering Jew, the facts of which are disclosed fully in the correspondence between this legation and the consulates at Shanghai and Amoy. (Inclosures 2 *b* to 2 *p*.) To this I have nothing to add, beyond the renewed expression of my opinion that this cooly trade to the West Indies is a traffic of the most pernicious kind, morally, socially, and economically. During the year 1857, upwards of six thousand were shipped from Macao alone to Havana. Accompanying this dispatch is the copy (inclosure 2 *q*) of a printed circular which I have addressed to the various consuls on the coast, and with this my ability to interpose ends. In this connection, I send a copy (inclosure 2 *r*) of a government Gazette of the 20th, containing an act of the Australian legislature on the subject of Chinese emigrants, from which you will see that even on those who come voluntarily, returning when they please, a capitation tax of ten pounds is imposed; and for a voyage of a few weeks, with no great alternations of temperature, the proportion of passengers to tonnage is strictly limited. Our ships carry coolies, without a chance of return, on a voyage of five months, in every variety of climate, and have no restrictions imposed on them as to numbers or discipline. A large clipper ship, called the Norway, belonging to a firm in the city of New York, has just arrived at this anchorage, armed and equipped for carrying coolies to Cuba. She is now loaded with coal on government account; and, so soon as she discharges this cargo, it is understood to be the intention of the master to proceed to Macao or Swatow to take, it is said, two thousand coolies on board.

2. In the correspondence of the Fuhchau consulate, you will find the local decrees legalizing, under certain limitations, the sale of opium.

Financial necessity has at last come to the assistance of the unprincipled mercantile and political combination which has so long besieged this empire, and I have every reason to believe that the local action at Fuhchau is but an entering wedge of success for the great experiment which it is known the British government has so much at heart—the unrestricted import of opium. You will find in the government Gazette, which I annex to this dispatch, (inclosure 2 *r*) a new revelation of the policy of the colonial authorities on this subject. (Inclosures 2 *s*, 2 *t*, and 2*u*.)

I am compelled to be a spectator of the careless participation of many of my own fellow-citizens in this trade, and am obliged to limit my action to efforts to prevent any official countenance being given to it. On this subject, I refer to the accompanying correspondence with Mr. Perry, the consul at Canton. (Inclosures 2 *v* and 2 *w*.)

3. I have no further information as to the Mexican dollar question than is contained in the correspondence, and in the imperial decree directing the payment of the troops in that coin; which I have the honor to forward. (Inclosures 2 *x*, 2 *y*, and 2 *z*.)

4. Soon after my arrival in China, observing how much diplomatic action here was affected by the disturbances in India, I thought it best to put myself in correspondence, informally, with some of our consular agents in that empire.

I annex two brief letters, received in reply from the vice-consuls at Singapore and Calcutta, and venture to call your attention to the suggestion in the communication of the latter gentleman as to the expediency of one of this squadron, when the public service permits, visiting that port. Any one of the vessels returning home in the winter season by the way of the Cape of Good Hope, might easily visit both Calcutta and Bombay. (Inclosures 3 *a*, 3 *b*.)

Annexed to this dispatch (inclosure 4) is a letter from the American mercantile house of James Purdon & Co., on the subject of their claim for the loss of property at Canton.

As there is every reason to suppose either that negotiations will be begun and successfully consummated at Shanghai during this summer, or that some other decisive action will be taken and lead to some result this season, I solicit the President's attention to my request for permission to return to the United States on the signature of a treaty, or, at the furthest, on the expiration of a year from the time at which I arrived in China. The current business of the legation can safely be confided to Mr. Williams, the secretary of legation, till my successor shall arrive. Indeed, such is my conviction of the advantage of personal intercourse, and so unlimited my confidence in Mr. Williams, that I should hope the departure of any successor whom the President might select would be delayed till I could meet and confer with him at home or in Europe. Be this as it may, I respectfully and urgently ask for permission to return at one of the periods designated. I need hardly add, it would be a matter of great personal gratification if I could be conveyed in this ship either as far as Aden, so as to take the overland route, or direct by the Cape of Good Hope. As this dispatch will not reach you until the month of May, and an answer cannot be returned to me in the north before August, I beg your immediate attention to it.

I shall sail to-morrow for Shanghai, by the way of the Phillippine Islands, hoping there to meet Commodore Tattnall and confer with him as to the disposition of the naval forces during the summer.

As an illustration of the extremely friendly policy of his excellency the Russian minister, I forward copies of a private correspondence, which has just passed between us, simply remarking that he is mistaken in supposing such a thing as a general blockade is contemplated by anybody, and as to my having any diplomatic relations to Japan.

I have found Count Poutiatine a most earnest friend throughout. (Inclosures 5 *a*, 5 *b*.)

I have the honor to be, sir, your obedient servant,

WILLIAM B. REED.

Hon. Lewis Cass,
Secretary of State, Washington.

Index to Dispatch No. 10, *February* 26, 1858.—*Relating to current business of Legation.*

Inclo'rs.	From—	To—	Subject-matter.	Date.
1 *a*	Baron Gros	W. B. Reed	Acknowledges receipt of Mr. Reed's letter of the 6th, and of copies of his correspondence with Yeh, and of his note to Pekin.	Feb. 18, 1858.
1 *b*	Baron Gros	W. B. Reed	Translation of the same	Feb. 18, 1858.
2 *a*	A. L. Freeman	W. B. Reed	Declines appointment of consul at Shanghai	Jan. 22, 1858.
2 *b*	A. L. Freeman	W. B. Reed	Accepted the consulate. Case of cooly-ship Wandering Jew	Jan. 26, 1858.
2 *c*	W. B. Reed	A. L. Freeman	Reply to the preceding	Feb. 6, 1858.
2 *d*	A. L. Freeman	W. B. Reed	Case of the Wandering Jew	Feb. 6, 1858.
2 *e*	A. L. Freeman	Captain Carleton	Coolies on board the Wandering Jew	Jan. 26, 1858.
2 *f*	A. L. Freeman	See, Taoutae	Wandering Jew	Jan. 28, 1858.
2 *g*	See	A. L. Freeman	Reply to preceding	Jan. 31, 1858.
2 *h*	D. B. Robertson	A. L. Freeman	Wandering Jew	Jan. 26, 1858.
2 *i*	A. L. Freeman	D. B. Robertson	Wandering Jew	Jan. 26, 1858.
2 *j*	A. L. Freeman	D. B. Robertson	Wandering Jew	Jan. 29, 1858.
2 *k*	D. B. Robertson	A. L. Freeman	Wandering Jew	Jan. 30, 1858.
2 *l*			Report of interpreter on the Wandering Jew	Jan. 26, 1858.
2 *m*	E. Doty	W. B. Reed	Duty on opium at Amoy	Jan. 22, 1858.
2 *n*	W. B. Reed	E. Doty	Reply	Feb. 1, 1858.
2 *o*	E. Doty	W. B. Reed	Arrival of the Wandering Jew at Amoy	Feb. 5, 1858.
2 *p*	W. B. Reed	E. Doty	Reply	Feb. 15, 1858.
2 *q*			Circular on cooly trade	Feb. 18, 1858.
2 *r*	Government Gazette		On cooly trade in Australia	Feb. 20, 1858.
2 *s*	T. Dunn	W. B. Reed	Duty on opium, and the suspended duties at Fuhchau	Jan. 21, 1858.
2 *t*	Sub-prefects		Decrees on opium	June, 1857.
2 *u*	Prefects		Decrees on opium	June, 1857.
2 *v*	W. B. Reed	O. Perry	Location of consulate	Feb. 17, 1858.
2 *w*	O. Perry	W. B. Reed	Reply	Feb. 18, 1858.
2 *x*	T. Dunn	W. B. Reed	Duty question at Fuhchau	Jan. 22, 1858.
2 *y*	W. B. Reed	T. Dunn	Reply	Feb. 1, 1858.
2 *z*			Governor general's decree on Mexican dollars	Aug. 18, 1857.
3 *a*	T. Biddle	W. B. Reed	Affairs at Singapore	Jan. 15, 1858.
3 *b*	J. E. Amory	W. B. Reed	Affairs at Calcutta	Jan. 23, 1858.
4	James Purdon	W. B. Reed	Claim on Chinese government	Feb. 15, 1858.
5 *a*	W. B. Reed	Cte. Poutiatine	Inquiry as to northern navigation	Feb. 22, 1858.
5 *b*	Cte. Poutiatine	W. B. Reed	Reply	Feb. 22, 1858.

Inclosure 1 *b*.

[Translation.]

MISSION EXTRAORDINARY OF FRANCE TO CHINA,
On board the Primauquet, February 13, 1858.

SIR: I received on the 9th instant the letter which your excellency did me the honor to write, in answer to the one which I addressed to you on the 6th, informing you of the course that I intended to pursue in concert with my honorable colleague, the English plenipotentiary, to give effect, after the taking of Canton, to the mission which the Emperor has confided to me in China, and to put it in your excellency's power, if you have thought it expedient, to unite your efforts to mine, in order to obtain from the Chinese government the concessions which, in a conciliatory spirit, I have demanded, in the name of the government I have the honor to represent.

The government of the Emperor cannot but congratulate itself on seëing that your excellency duly appreciates the moderate and humane conduct which it has, under existing circumstances, adopted; and it will learn with pleasure that your excellency, as well as the plenipotentiary of his Majesty the Emperor of Russia, is about to unite your efforts to those of the high commissioners of France and England, to induce the cabinet at Pekin to listen to language which, though conciliatory, cannot fail, when held by the representatives of four great powers, to be taken into serious consideration by the imperial government of China.

I have also received, a few days later, a copy of the correspondence of your excellency with the Imperial Commissioner Yeh, and of the note which you proposed to send to the council of the empire, at Pekin, simultaneously with that which I have addressed to the prime minister.

These important documents, of which I have caused a translation to be made, have been sent to my government, and it is quite unnecessary to your excellency for me to say that they will be received with all the interest they deserve.

On my part, sir, I congratulate myself on seeing the friendly relations which were established between us on our first interview about to become still more intimate, and on learning that, in uniting with the plan of action proposed, your excellency conforms not only to the desire you have always expressed, to have with me the most frank and unreserved communication, but to the spirit of the instructions you have received from your government.

Accept, sir, the new assurances of my sentiments of high consideration.

BARON GROS.

His Excellency WILLIAM B. REED, *&c., &c., &c.*

Inclosure 2 a.

SHANGHAI, *January* 22, 1858.

SIR: I had the honor to receive your valued communication of the 13th instant, with accompanying documents, appointing me vice-consul at the port of Shanghai, and regret that business engagements render it impossible for me to accept the office.

I have the honor to be, sir, your obedient servant,

ALBERT L. FREEMAN.

His Excellency the Hon. WILLIAM B. REED,
United States Embassador to the Court of China.

Inclosure 2 b.

No. 1.] UNITED STATES CONSULATE,
Shanghai, January 26, 1858.

SIR: Referring to my letter of the 22d instant, in which I informed you of my being obliged to decline the appointment as vice-consul for the United States at this port, and also to a portion of the contents of a private letter under the same date, informing you that under the peculiar circumstances in which the appointment found me I felt it my duty to transfer the official duties of the vice-consul at this port over to Mr. Paul S. Forbes, I beg now to lay before you a brief statement of the events which have transpired since that date.

Without recapitulating the reasons that led me in the first place to transfer the office, I will only say that had I known, at the time the transfer was made, that Mr. Forbes would have left this port by the Antelope, I would never have surrendered to him the trust which your confidence placed in my possession.

You will have doubtless heard of what was generally supposed to be an additional transfer on the part of Mr. Forbes, in favor of Mr. Thomas Walsh, a partner in the firm of Messrs. Russell & Co.

On the 23d instant, it was known that Mr. Forbes had sailed in the Antelope. In the morning of that day a committee of gentlemen, consisting of the heads of the other American houses in the place, waited upon me to know the facts of the case. I stated to them all that I was conversant with, and that I had heard it rumored an hour or two before that Mr. Walsh had received the transfer from Mr. Forbes. On their representing the matter in the light that certain documents deposited in the consulate might by such a transfer be made use of so as to be detrimental to their interests, and their requesting me to reassume the office until your pleasure could be made known in the matter, after fully considering the matter, in connection with the question that might arise as to the legality of such a transfer, I resolved in my own mind to attempt the recovery of the powers which I had transferred.

I accordingly called to see Mr. Walsh, requesting some information respecting Mr. Forbes's departure, and learned from him that nothing more than a verbal transfer had been made to him.

He was willing that I should assume the office, and returned me the written transfer given by myself to Mr. Forbes.

In assuming the duties of the office until your pleasure is made known in a new appointment, I have to crave your indulgence, and trust that the mantle of charity will be thrown over the irregularities which have thus occurred. No one can regret more than myself the first step which led to them.

The Taoutae of this place being at present absent on a visit to Soochow, I have not as yet paid my respects to him in person, but shall shall take the earliest opportunity to do so on his return. I have, however, apprised him, in a written communication of yesterday's date, of my appointment as vice-consul for the United States at this port, conveying to him the renewed assurance expressed in your letter of the desire of the United States and their representatives to cultivate and maintain the most friendly relations with the authorities of this place.

I have also to inform you of my having called upon the consuls of the treaty powers, and have been recognized by them as the vice-consul for the United States at this port.

I have to own the receipt of your letter, dated January 15, 1858, which reached me this day, per steamer Formosa. The suggestions contained in it shall have my attention and support. I find in the archives of the consulate your views communicated on the subject to Mr. Knapp, conforming to those expressed in your letter now under reply.

I regret to find that the views entertained by yourself on the subject applying to the case of the American ship Wandering Jew have not occasioned a more prompt and decisive attempt on the part of my predecessors to put a stop to it.

It is under somewhat embarrassing circumstances that I shall undertake to interpose the authority invested in me to stop further proceedings on the part of the captain of this vessel. A brief statement of the case will, perhaps, be of service by way of preface to the step which I am about to take in the matter.

It will be needless to go over the ground which must have been already stated in order to have drawn forth your opinions on the subject as conveyed in your letter to Mr. Knapp; suffice it to say, that this vessel received her port clearance from the Chinese authorities on the assurance of Mr. Knapp that he had obtained from the captain and consignees of the ship a guarantee, (amount not stated,) the same to be forfeited in the event of her loading with coolies for the purpose of transporting them to Cuba. This guarantee, if any such existed, is not to be found. Mr. Jenkins knows nothing of such a paper. A day or two after, Mr. Knapp gave the ship her papers, and she dropped down the river to an anchorage outside of Woosung, some twenty miles from this, where she now lies. During the past five or six weeks she has been engaged in loading with coolies. It is currently reported and believed that the delay she has experienced has been caused by the interception of some three hundred coolies by the local authorities ere they were put on board.

It having become a public report that illegal and unjustifiable means are being taken by the captain and officers of this vessel in order to obtain coolies, such as stealing, kidnapping, and the various forms of false pretences, I shall, to-morrow morning, go down the river, in company with our interpreter and a mandarin, sent by the Taoutae, to institute an investigation of the matter, and I shall then convey to the captain a written expression of your views, warning him against this violation of the law, and informing him that should he proceed to sea with coolies on board for the purpose of transporting them to Cuba, there to be held to service or labor, steps will be taken to lay the matter before the law officers of the United States government, immediately on his arrival in the United States, to institute a prosecution for a violation of the act of Congress in such cases provided.

Not being able to anticipate the facts which may appear in the investigation, I can only assure you, in the interval which will elapse between the receipt of this and that of my next communication on the subject, that I shall endeavor to use all necessary caution and prudence in the matter, and trust that the demands of justice and humanity will be satisfied without being obliged to resort to a strenuous execution of the law. I shall avail myself of the first opportunity to inform you in regard to the matter.

Regretting that time will not allow of my touching upon some other subjects mentioned in your letter, I remain, sir, your obedient servant,

ALBERT L. FREEMAN.

His Excellency the Hon. WILLIAM B. REED,
United States Embassador to the Court of China.

Inclosure 2 *c.*

UNITED STATES LEGATION, MINNESOTA,
Hong Kong, February 6, 1858.

SIR: I duly received your interesting letter of the 26th ultimo, in which you informed me you had resumed the vice-consulate at Shanghai at the solicitation of some of the merchants whose correspondence you forwarded. I am extremely glad of your decision, though I cannot help saying that the alarm excited by what was done so innocently and carelessly by Mr. Forbes and Mr. Walsh seems to me very exaggerated.

I entirely approve of your course as to the Wandering Jew, as reported in your letter. Much prudence as well as energy is needed in such emergencies.

I beg to say to you, in confidence, that one of the vessels in this squadron, probably the frigate Mississippi, will leave this port for Shanghai during the next week, carrying important dispatches for the Chinese government. I rely on your best exertions in connection with the French and English consuls, to have them forwarded according to their address.

I am, sir, very respectfully yours,

WILLIAM B. REED.

ALBERT FREEMAN, Esq.,
United States Vice-Consul, Shanghai.

Inclosure 2 d.

No. 2.] UNITED STATES CONSULATE,
Shanghai, February 6, 1858.

SIR: On the 26th ultimo, I informed your excellency that I was about to make an investigation in regard to the coolies on board the ship Wandering Jew. I had made arrangements for going down to the ship on the following day, but was prevented from doing so through an interference of one of the foreign inspectors at the custom-house in detaining the cutter Halcyon, which had been placed at my disposal by the acting Taoutae.

I accordingly laid the matter before his excellency, and requested the use of the Chinese steamer Confucius, which was readily granted.

I left Shanghai early on the morning of the 28th ultimo, accompanied by Mr. Interpreter Jenkins, the United States marshal, and an official sent by the Taoutae.

I found that the vessel had moved from her anchorage during the night, and had dropped about five miles further down the river.

When the steamer reached the vessel, every sail was spread, and the men on board were getting her anchors, evidently intending to put to sea at once.

The Confucius anchored a short distance from her, and I then proceeded on board in company with the above named.

At the gangway I met Captain Carlton, and Mr. Connolly, the consignee of the vessel, and after stating to the captain the object of my visit, I requested an interview in which I could more minutely detail the plan I should pursue in an investigation of the condition of the coolies on board.

I then made arrangements for the examination, having previously stated to the captain that if it was found that there were any on board who were detained against their own free will and consent, I should insist upon their being taken out.

In the examination that followed, I found sufficient evidence to convince me that illegal means had been used in procuring these coolies. Many of them stated that a Chinaman in the employ of Mr. Andrew Connolly, the consignee of the vessel, had promised to give them three dollars providing they would go on board the foreign ship to work for a few days; others stated that they were to receive three hundred cash per day to come to Shanghai to serve as soldiers; others were to form a part of a mandarin's retinue. Nearly every one was questioned in regard to the conditions under which he came on board, and not one was found that came on board with any idea of going to a foreign country. Many of the coolies, upon being informed that they were to be taken to a foreign country, begged to be allowed to go on shore, as they had wives and families dependant upon them. Out of two hundred and thirty-six (236) coolies on board, one hundred and seventeen (117) were found to be there against their own free will and consent.

These I caused to be taken out and placed on board the Confucius, and afterwards brought to Shanghai and delivered over to the Chinese authorities.

Those that remained on board, one hundred and nineteen in number, had their situation clearly explained to them, and expressed themselves as being desirous of proceeding in the vessel. The most of these were beggars, who had no connections or ties to bind them to China, and who took the choice of two evils, dying by starvation in their own country, or dragging out an existence in an untried and unknown land.

Before leaving the ship I placed in the hands of Captain Carlton a written warning, containing an expression of your views in regard to the cooly traffic, as contained in your letter of instructions to Mr. Knapp, dated December 28, 1857. A copy of this document you will find in this inclosure. (No. 1.)

Not being able to anticipate the state of affairs on board, nor the reception I might meet with in visiting the ship, I prepared this document before leaving Shanghai. The latter part of it, in reference to persons being detained on board against their own free will and consent, was of course nullified by the action of the captain in surrendering such persons up.

Before leaving the ship I was informed of the captain's intention to take in more coolies and proceed to Amoy, for the purpose of completing the number required by the charter-party. I then stated to him distinctly that, should he take another cooly on board at this port, I should demand his papers and hold them until your excellency could be heard from in the matter.

The peculiar circumstances connected with this case somewhat perplexed me as to the course I ought to pursue, as the Taoutae had stated to Mr. Jenkins a few days previous that in the present instance those who were found on board desirous of going might go in the ship, thus rendering the law that prohibits the cooly trade somewhat indefinite.

On returning to Shanghai I immediately wrote to the Taoutae, representing to him that the consignee or agent of the ship was intending to take more coolies on board, and requested him, in order that the law which forbids the cooly traffic might remain clear and distinct, to communicate to me a refusal on his part to allow any Chinese subjects other than those then on board to proceed to sea in this ship.

I took this precaution in order to have some stand-point to guide me in any future action I might be compelled to take in the matter.

A copy of this letter, together with his excellency's reply to the same, you will find in this inclosure. (Nos. 2 and 3.)

The captain and consignee seemed to be in doubt as to what course to pursue until the 30th ultimo, when the captain informed me that he had concluded not to take any more coolies on board at this port, and that he should proceed to sea on the following morning.

He left Shanghai the same evening, and on the 31st ultimo the ship sailed out of the river.

From information obtained from the captain, I am led to believe that his first destination is Amoy, and that it is the intention of the captain and agent of the vessel to fulfill the agreement of their charter-party by taking coolies on board at that place and proceeding to Cuba.

I inclose copies of correspondence (A, B, C, D) between her Britannic Majesty's consul and myself in relation to this affair.

I am happy to inform you that measures were taken at once to bring the consignee or agent of the ship to justice. He was summoned to appear before the British consul on the 30th, and was fined two hundred dollars.

I also inclose you a report of an investigation made by Mr. Jenkins, the interpreter of the consulate, on board of the ship Wandering Jew on the 23d ultimo.

The statements contained therein were verified by the investigation of the 28th ultimo.

I took occasion to inquire of the captain if he had given to Mr. Knapp a guarantee that he would not take coolies from this port at the time the port clearance was withheld by the custom-house authorities. He replied that he had never given anything of the sort.

I have to inform you that I paid an official visit to the Taoutae of this place on the 3d instant, he having just returned from a visit to the north. He expressed himself as being well satisfied with the course that had been pursued in the case of the coolies on board the Wandering Jew, in taking a portion of them out.

He seemed to be somewhat desirous of obtaining information respecting the present state of affairs in and around Canton, and made inquiries as to when your excellency might be expected in Shanghai.

In this visit his excellency communicated to me his intention of issuing a proclamation to the effect that, on and after an early date, merchandise of all descriptions might be landed on any part of the American grounds, or shipped therefrom.

This portion of the foreign settlement, more particularly known as "Honiker," and upon which the American consulate is situated, is rapidly increasing in the number of foreign settlers, and is being continually improved by the holders of land. The restrictions which have thus far been placed upon it in regard to the landing or shipping of goods being thus removed, will doubtless be of great benefit to this particular portion of the foreign settlement.

The events which have occurred of late in and around Canton have, so far as anything apparent is concerned, produced but little feeling on the part of the natives of this place. The few Cantonese residing here, computed to number between five and six thousand, manifest but little interest in the news that comes from the south.

Generally speaking, the Chinese at this place are as little concerned in regard to the Canton question as they could be in any dispute appertaining to the internal affairs of our own country.

I have, in accordance with your request, directed that the North China Herald be sent to the legation regularly.

With sentiments of respect, I am, sir, your obedient servant,

ALBERT L. FREEMAN.

His Excellency the Hon. WILLIAM B. REED,
United States Embassador to the Court of China.

Inclosure 2 e.

No. 1.]

UNITED STATES CONSULATE,
Shanghai, January 26, 1858.

SIR: It having been represented to me that the American ship Wandering Jew, now under your command, is loading with coolies within the jurisdiction of this port, in violation of the laws of China, thereby conflicting with the treaty regulations existing between the United States and China, I do hereby warn you against such violation, and that, should you proceed to sea with coolies on board, for the purpose of transporting them to Cuba, there to be held to service or labor, steps will be taken to lay the matter before the law officers of the United States government, immediately on your arrival in the United States, to institute a prosecution for a violation of the act of Congress in such case made.

It having also been represented to me that you have on board of your vessel Chinese subjects who are there against their own free will and consent, having been placed on board through illegal means, I do, in accordance with the power invested in me as the representative of the United States at this port, and also in accordance with a petition of the Taoutae of this place, demand that said Chinese subjects be released and taken from your vessel immediately, on penalty of incurring the execution of the law in such cases provided.

I am, sir, respectfully,

ALBERT L. FREEMAN,
Vice-Consul U. S. A.

Captain CARLETON,
American ship Wandering Jew.

Inclosure 2 f.

No. 2.]

UNITED STATES CONSULATE,
Shanghai, January 28, 1858.

I have the honor to inform your excellency that, in company with your official, I have this day proceeded on board the American ship Wandering Jew to make an investigation, in accordance with your request.

On examination of the coolies on board, I found 117 had been placed there through illegal means. This number I caused to be taken out and brought to Shanghai, in the steamer Confucius, and handed them over to your officers. The conditions under which those now on board remain is in accordance with your excellency's wishes.

I have to convey to your excellency the assurance of his excellency the honorable W. B. Reed, envoy extraordinary and minister plenipotentiary from the United States to China, of his intention to administer justice, with an impartial hand, in all such cases.

Information having reached me that the consignee or agent of said [ship] is intending to put more coolies on board, I have to request that your excellency will communicate to me a refusal, on your part, to allow any Chinese subjects, other than those now on board, to proceed to sea in said ship.

I have the honor to be, &c.,

ALBERT L. FREEMAN,
United States Vice-Consul.

His Excellency SEE, *Taoutae, &c.*

Inclosure 2 g.

No. 3.]

See, intendant of Soo, Soong, and Tai circuit, makes the following communication:

I am in receipt of your excellency's communication, in reference to having, in company with my officer, proceeded on board of the Wandering Jew, and taken 117 Chinese subjects out of her, which have been handed over to the district magistrate. You also inform me that you have heard that they intend to place more Chinese on board of her, and request that I shall forbid them from going on board, &c.

According to your request, I shall issue orders to the district magistrate to have the persons who have been the instruments of enticing coolies on board of the Wandering Jew arrested and severely punished, and also issue a proclamation to the people, warning them not to allow themselves, by their covetousness after gain, to be enticed on board of the Wandering Jew.

At the time the Wandering Jew was cleared, the captain distinctly stated that he did not intend to take coolies to foreign ports, but merely take a few passengers to Fuhkien, which is on record.

On examination, over 100 persons were found on board of this ship against their will, and without the slightest intention of proceeding to foreign ports. From this, it is evident that the captain's intention was to take coolies from here to a foreign land. I therefore have to request that your excellency will, in accordance with the tenor of your last communication, deal with him according to the laws of your honorable country, and thus demonstrate the desire of his excellency the American commissioner to administer justice with an even hand.

May the day's happiness be yours.

ALBERT L. FREEMAN, Esq.,
United States Vice-Consul.

Hien Fung, 7th year, 12th month, 17th day. (January 31, 1858.)

A true translation.

FREDERICK JENKINS.

Inclosure 2 h.

A.]

BRITISH CONSULATE,
Shanghai, January 26, 1858.

SIR: Referring to the conversation I had the pleasure of having with you yesterday, respecting the coolies on board the American vessel, the Wandering Jew, when you announced your appointment as United States vice-consul at this port, I beg to say his excellency Sir John Bowring, her Britannic Majesty's plenipotentiary, has communicated to me the dispatch of his excellency the United States commissioner, which you read; and it would afford me much satisfaction to know what steps have been taken to release these people from a confinement which, I understood you to say, the United States interpreter had ascertained to be compulsory upon them, and, according to the Chinese authorities, illegal by the law of China.

I am aware this is a matter strictly appertaining to your jurisdiction; but the unanimity of the high officers in China, of our respective nations, to put a stop to this traffic, warrants me, I trust, in seeking for information on the subject.

I have the honor to be, sir, your most obedient, humble servant,

D. B. ROBERTSON.

A. L. FREEMAN, Esq.,
United States American Vice-Consul, Shanghai.

Inclosure 2 i.

B.]

UNITED STATES CONSULATE,
Shanghai, January 26, 1858.

SIR: In reply to your letter of this date, requesting information as to what steps had been taken in regard to the coolies on board the ship Wandering Jew, I beg to state that I intend going down to the vessel to-morrow morning, in order to make a further investigation in the matter; and the measures I may feel it my duty to employ will depend much upon that investigation, the result of which I shall take an early opportunity to inform you.

I am happy to learn that the views of his excellency Sir John Bowring, her Britannic Majesty's plenipotentiary, coincide with those of his excellency Mr. Reed, the American commissioner, in regard to putting a stop to this traffic.

I have the honor to be, sir, your obedient servant,

ALBERT L. FREEMAN,
Vice-Consul United States America.

D. B. ROBERTSON, Esq.,
Her Britannic Majesty's Consul.

Inclosure 2 j.

C.] UNITED STATES CONSULATE,
Shanghai, January 29, 1858

SIR: I have the pleasure of informing you that I have been on board the ship Wandering Jew, and made an investigation in regard to the coolies on board. I found that out of 236, 117 had been placed there through illegal means, and were there against their own free will and consent. These persons I caused to be taken out and brought to Shanghai.

Those that remained on board, 119 in number, had their situation clearly explained to them, and were desirous of going in the ship.

Before leaving the ship I placed in the hands of the captain a written warning against taking Chinese coolies for the purpose of transporting them to Cuba, stating to him that he would be liable to be prosecuted on his arrival in the United States.

I am led to believe that a person properly belonging to your jurisdiction is the great offender in this matter. I allude to Mr. Andrew Connolly, who was on board of the ship at the time I visited it, and was conspicuous in the investigation as the most interested in this shipment of coolies.

I have the honor to be, sir, your obedient servant,

ALBERT L. FREEMAN,
Vice-Consul United States of America.

D. M. ROBERTSON, Esq.,
Her Britanic Majesty's Consul.

Inclosure 2 k.

D.] BRITISH CONSULATE,
Shanghai, January 30, 1858.

SIR: I have the honor to acknowledge receipt of your dispatch of yesterday's date, informing me that you had been on board the ship Wandering Jew, and made an investigation in regard to the coolies on board, and that you had found out of the number (236) 117 had been placed there through illegal means, and were there against their own free will and consent. These persons you caused to be taken out an brought to Shanghai, leaving 119 on board, who, after having thei situation clearly explained, were desirous of going in the ship. That you had also warned the captain of his liability to prosecution; and that you are led to believe that a British subject, Mr. Andrew Connolly, who was present, is the most interested in this shipment of coolies.

In reply, I beg to tender my thanks for your obliging communication, and to express the great satisfaction it has given me to hear of your prompt and effective interference in this matter, and I have little doubt that our joint endeavors to put a stop to this inhuman traffic will meet with the happiest results, and the approbation of our respective governments.

As regards Mr. Connolly, it will be my duty to take all legal measures against him.

I have the honor to be, sir, your most obedient humble servant,

D. B. ROBERTSON.

A. L. FREEMAN, Esq.,
United States Vice-Consul, Shanghai.

Inclosure 2 l.

Report of an investigation made by me on board the American ship Wandering Jew, in relation to the condition of some 200 or more coolies:

In accordance with the instructions received from the acting vice-consul, I proceeded down the river on the 23d ultimo, and found the Wandering Jew at anchor about six miles outside of Woosung. I proceeded on board, and requested the captain to muster the coolies between decks, which was done. I then questioned them in regard to where they were going, and what inducement had been made to them for coming on board of the ship.

After questioning seventy or eighty, one old man got down on his knees and begged to be taken on shore, as he had a wife and three children at home who were almost starving; he said that he had been enticed on board by the payment of three dollars, and if they would let him go, he would get some of his friends to refund the money.

I found that the majority were totally ignorant of their condition, and when it was stated to them that they were going to a foreign country, many of the coolies begged to be allowed to go on shore, as they had families who were dependent on them for support.

My opinion is that, out of some two hundred or more coolies on board of the Wandering Jew, not over thirty understand that they are going to a foreign country, and that all on board of this ship have been enticed there by the payment of a few dollars in hand and the promise of more after their arrival on board. The leading idea with most of them is that they are coming to Shanghai to serve as soldiers.

The Chinese official, who was to have gone down with me to the ship, did not go on account of his not making his appearance in season.

FREDERICK JENKINS,
Interpreter United States Consulate.

JANUARY 26, 1858.

Personally appeared before me Frederick Jenkins, and swore to the truth of the accompanying report.

[SEAL.] ALBERT L. FREEMAN,
United States Vice-Consul.

SHANGHAI, *January* 26, 1858.

Inclosure 2 m.

No. 5.] CONSULATE OF UNITED STATES OF AMERICA,
Amoy, January 22, 1858.

SIR: On the 19th instant, I had the honor to receive your favor of the 15th, and inclosures.

If circumstances should occur at this port requiring my attention on account of any American vessel being employed in the cooly trade, I will do my best to arrest proceedings, in accordance with your instructions. Your suggestion that the Chinese authorities might refuse the usual custom-house clearances looks feasible, and I would be inclined to urge it if any necessity should arise.

The Wandering Jew of which you make mention has not been at this port to my knowledge. That she could have been chartered to carry Chinese passengers from Shanghai to this place, is not in the least probable, unless it were to transfer them to some cooly ship, bound elsewhere.

You may not be aware that for some time past, compared with former years, very little has been done in the cooly business at this place. I have no means for a positive statement, but think not more than three or four vessels were dispatched from this port during the past year. Among these, I am happy to say, not one was American. They were mostly, if not all, British, and my impression is, all bound to Havana.

There is now one British ship here to load with coolies for that destination, so I am credibly informed. Of our merchants here there is only one firm that has at this place anything to do with the traffic. There is great difficulty to obtain men to go. This doubtless is the chief reason why so little is done.

As regards your inquiry concerning the legalization of the opium traffic, the facts of the case, as I have learned from good authority, are:

1. A duty has been for some weeks past, perhaps six, or two months, and is now levied, of $50 each chest. This is collected from the Chinese purchaser, not from the European merchant or agent who sells it.

2. The collector of ordinary customs has nothing to do with the business. A special officer has been appointed to attend to the matter, with a police force organized specially for this purpose.

3. The governor general of this and the Chih Kiang provinces originated the plan here, to raise funds to meet the expenses of the military operations against the insurgents, who have been giving his excellency so much trouble for a year or so past.

The governor general thus memorialized the Emperor on the subject, but no reply has as yet been received.

You will thus perceive this act of the officials here, by authority of the governor general, can scarcely be regarded as legalizing the traffic, as they take no cognizance of the drug until they find it in the hands of their own people. Indeed what is now done has been in principle done for I know not how long a time. Formerly $2 a chest was levied for local military purposes. There has been simply an increase from

$2 to $50 in the amount required to be paid. There may be another difference. The $2 was, perhaps, a levy made by authority of the local officers, while now they act by command of the governor general, and doubtless expect the imperial sanction.

I remain, very respectfully, your obedient servant,

E. DOTY.

His Excellency WILLIAM B. REED,
Envoy Extraordinary and Minister Plenipotentiary, &c.

Inclosure 2 n.

No. 3.]

UNITED STATES LEGATION,
Macao, February 1, 1858.

SIR: I have duly received your letter of the 22d ultimo, and thank you for it. I have since the date of my last dispatch ascertained that the Wandering Jew is, or was recently, at Woosung waiting for a cargo of coolies for Havana, and that the information I received as to her destination to Amoy was erroneous. I hope to be able to adopt measures to detain this ship. The shipper is an English subject, of the name of Connolly.

It is probable, though not yet absolutely certain, that Commodore Tattnall will within the next few weeks dispatch one of the ships-of-war to Amoy. I may go on board, and have the pleasure of your personal acquaintance. Do not, however, on this account omit your regular correspondence with this legation, which, as heretofore, I beg you to address to me at Hong Kong.

I am, sir, very respectfully,

WILLIAM B. BEED.

E. DOTY, Esq.,
United States Vice-Consul, Amoy.

Inclosure 2 o.

No. 6.]

CONSULATE OF UNITED STATES OF AMERICA,
Amoy, February 5, 1858.

SIR: The Wandering Jew arrived at this port on the 3d, and reported at this consulate on the 4th instant. She is a fine clipper ship, of over eleven hundred tons, and her master, G. H. Carleton, appears to be a gentlemanly person, of correct feelings and bearing. There are 130 Chinese on board, from Shanghai. The ship has stopped here to take in provisions, and thence will proceed to Swatow, and thence to Havana.

I have had a full and free interview with Captain Carleton, as regards the business in which he is engaged, the doubtfulness of its legality, and his danger, and gave full notice of your views and my duty and intention to report to you.

He informs me that every man on board of his ship is so by his own voluntary act; and that an officer, deputed by the Taoutae of Shanghai, and a Mr. Jenkins, interpreter of the United States consulate, examined them, man by man, explaining particularly where they were to go, what to do, and the nature of the articles of agreement which they signed. Of somewhat over 250 persons who had been collected together, upon full information given, only 130 persons were willing and wished to go. All the rest were at once sent by steamer to shore. Afterwards, of those thus sent ashore, large numbers, in companies of fifteen or twenty persons, came back to the ship and begged Captain Carleton to allow them also to go, but that not one of such persons were received back again.

Captain Carleton further states that the Taoutae of Shanghai expressed his full approbation to the shipping of such persons as were without families, and who acted voluntarily, remarking that it would be better, both for the country and also for themselves; and verified the sincerity of these views by taking the oversight, by deputy, of shipping every Chinaman now on board the ship.

All the facts of the case may, and probably will, be fully verified to you by the vice-consul in charge, at Shanghai, as Captain Carleton states to me that he requested them to do so.

Under such circumstances, I do not feel myself authorized to take any further steps in this case, and hereby refer the matter for your further consideration.

With consideration, your very obedient servant,

E. DOTY.

His Excellency William B. Reed,
Envoy Extraordinary, &c.

Inclosure 2 p.

No. 4.] Legation of the United States,
On board the Minnesota, February 15, 1858.

Sir: I am in receipt of your letter of the 5th instant, (No. 6,) relative to the Wandering Jew. After what occurred at Shanghai, where, but for the prompt interference of the authorities, and especially of Mr. Vice-Consul Freeman, many of these poor creatures would have been decoyed into virtual slavery, I confess I have little confidence in any statement or promise of those who control the movements of this ship. Nor does it make the least difference, in my opinion, in a legal point of view, whether the coolies go voluntarily or not to Havana, provided they are shipped under a contract "to be held to service."

I desire you, therefore, at once to give formal notice to the master of the Wandering Jew that, if he pursues this voyage, his case will be at once reported to Washington; and that he exposes himself to a severe penalty, and the property of his owners to forfeiture. And his conduct will not be less censurable if he proceeds to Swatow, (a port not opened by trade,) a trade with which is thereby prohibited.

I beg you, also, to give the local authorities notice that you are instructed to give them assistance in enforcing the laws against such emigration, and to refuse clearance to a ship, if they will withhold the usual certificate, or if it appears on the face of the papers that the ship's destination is to Swatow, or any illegal port.

I am resolute to do all in my power to put an end to this infamous traffic, in this instance carried on in defiance of all admonition, by a most discreditable combination between an American master and lawless British shippers.

I have the honor to be, sir, your obedient servant,

WILLIAM B. REED.

E. DOTY, Esq.,
United States Vice-Consul, Amoy.

Inclosure 2 *q.*

LEGATION OF THE UNITED STATES TO CHINA,
February 18, 1858.

SIR: I am directed by his excellency the minister of the United States again, and most earnestly, to call your attention to the *cooly traffic* in American ships, and the necessity of resorting to all legal measures to arrest it. The view taken of the trade by this legation is, that what constitutes the breach of the laws of the United States is the contract for labor or service under which the cooly is shipped. Hence, it is quite immaterial in point of law, whether the cooly goes with or against his will, if, on his arrival, he is to be "disposed of to be held to labor or service." Of course, there is a greater offense to morals and to the laws of this empire, if, as is generally the case, the cooly is kidnapped, or seduced, or entrapped. The employment of American ships in carrying Chinese coolies to be held to labor is illegal. It has been so represented to the government at Washington, and will be so regarded by it. It is a trade in which, as revolting to humanity in its processes and results, no respectable American citizen will participate. It is a trade which endangers the lives of the mariners engaged in it, and, of course, involves terrible suffering and mortality among its principal victims, the coolies themselves.

The American minister, in order to do all in his power to put an end, or as far as possible, to circumscribe this traffic, instructs you, besides giving as much publicity to this communication as you may think conducive to the ends you have in view, to adopt the following course in all instances:

1. Whenever you ascertain, or have good reason to believe, that an American ship is about to be loaded with coolies for Havana, Surinam, or any other place, under contract for labor or service, you shall at once inform, verbally and in writing, the master, owner, or charterer, of the views of this legation, and of the liability to punishment and forfeiture which he or they incur.

2. Whenever such shipment is about to be made from a British or Portuguese port, you will at once give notice to the superintendent of trade or governor, that the trade is regarded as a violation of the laws and treaties of the United States, and that this legation will regard any countenance given to it as a most unfriendly act. The same notice is to be given to the consular authorities accredited here by the country to which the shipment is made.

3. Whenever such shipment is about to be made from one of the treaty ports in China, immediate notice is to be given to the local Chinese authorities, so that they may withhold the "grand chop" or port clearance. Whenever the local authorities desire the aid of the consul to visit vessels in order to give relief to any Chinese detained against their will, it is to be given promptly. The refusal of the local authorities to give a clearance to an American ship, unless Chinese subjects so shipped are discharged, is a "lawful requisition" of the local authorities, which the consul must respect.

4. Particular attention must be paid by you to the shipping articles of the seamen in such vessels, for it is believed that, in many instances, frauds on seamen have been perpetrated by interlineations and erasures, and other alterations of shipping articles. In such case, where you are satisfied of the fact of the alteration, you will give such relief to the mariner as is authorized by law, and retain the papers till the decision of this legation is known.

5. If it be known to you that the intermediate destination of such ship is to some port not open to trade by treaty, for the purpose of there shipping coolies, you will, if practicable, give notice to the local authorities of the place of this fraudulent design, and warn the master that such trade is a still grosser violation of law, and involves the same penalties.

6. Whenever you have reason to believe that any ship, designed for this or any other trade, is about to sail from Hong Kong or Macao to a port in China not opened by treaty, you shall forthwith give notice to the superintendent of trade, or governor, of the fact.

7. All cases of shipment of coolies in American ships, under contracts to be held to labor or service, must be reported in detail to this legation, and, if possible, the facts verified by the affidavit of some third person.

Every case of such shipment of coolies, with the names of owners, master, and charterers, will, without delay, be reported by this legation to the Department of State, so that all parties engaged in this traffic may be exposed and brought to justice.

I am directed to repeat that you may give such publicity as you deem expedient to this communication, it being the sincere desire of the American minister that, without resort to ulterior measures, his fellow-citizens may be deterred from any further participation in a trade so revolting to humanity and discreditable to the parties concerned.

He hopes and believes that this admonition, meant to be an earnest and respectful one, will have its influence with respectable commercial establishments, shippers, and masters. Should it fail, he has no other resource than to expose the individual ignominy which a share in such a trade involves, and to bring the guilty parties to punishment. This shall be done thoroughly.

S. WELLS WILLIAMS,
Secretary of Legation.

The CONSUL OF THE UNITED STATES OF AMERICA.

A copy of the above sent to the consuls at Shanghai, Ningpo, Amoy, Fuhchau, Canton, and to Sir John Bowring.

Inclosure 2 r.

No. 3.]

AN ACT to make provision for levying a charge on Chinese arriving in South Australia. (Assented to, November 19, 1857.)

Be it enacted by his excellency the governor-in-chief of South Australia, by and with the advice and consent of the legislative council and house of assembly of the said province in this present Parliament assembled, as follows:

1. In the interpretation of this act, the following words shall, unless inconsistent with the context, have the respective meanings hereby assigned to them—that is to say: the word "master" shall be held to apply to any person in command of any vessel; the word "ship" shall mean any sea-going vessel; the word "tonnage" shall signify tonnage according to the registry of the ship, if British, or according to the measurement fixed by the merchant shipping act of 1854, if the ship be not British; the word "Chinese" shall mean any native of China or its dependencies, or of any islands in the China seas, or any person born of Chinese parents; and the word "passenger" shall be held to mean or include any person on board of any ship not being borne upon the ship's articles as one of the crew thereof, or who shall be discharged from or leave such ship during her stay in any part of the said province.

2. The master of every ship, upon arrival at any port in the said province, having passengers on board, shall deliver to the collector, or other chief officer of customs at the port of arrival, a statement in writing, under the hand of such master, of the number of Chinese on board of such vessel.

3. If any ship shall arrive in any port or place in the said province having on board a greater number of passengers, including the master and crew and cabin passengers, than in the proportion of one person to every ten tons of the tonnage of such ship, and more than one sixth of such passengers shall be Chinese, the owner, charterer, or master of such ship, shall be liable, on conviction, to a penalty not exceeding ten pounds for each passenger so carried in excess.

4. On arrival at any port in the said province of any ship having any Chinese passenger on board, before making entry, the master

shall pay to the collector or other officer of customs, the sum of ten pounds for every Chinese passenger arrived in such ship, and no entry shall be deemed to have been legally made, or to have any legal effect whatever, until such payment shall have been made; and if any master neglect so to deliver such statement, or to pay such sum within the time aforesaid, or shall land or permit such Chinese passenger to land at any place in the said province, with the intent of evading the payment of any such sum, he shall, on conviction, be liable to a penalty not exceeding twenty pounds for each Chinese passenger, in addition to the amount of such sum.

5. All sums of money by this act made payable may be recovered, and all proceedings under this act may be had and taken before two or more justices of the peace, in a summary way.

6. All sums of money received or levied by virtue of this act, shall be paid to her Majesty, her heirs, and successors, for the public uses of the said province, and in support of the government thereof.

7. This act shall come into operation from and after the 1st day of December, which will be in the year of our Lord one thousand eight hundred and fifty-seven.

Inclosure 2 s.

No. 2.]

UNITED STATES CONSULATE,
Foo-Chow, January 1, 1858.

SIR: I have the honor to acknowledge the receipt of your dispatch of 28th December, inclosing copy of your letter to Mr. Jones.

In regard to the duty upon opium, I have to inform you that this consulate having refused to have anything to do with the levying of said duty, the authorities addressed a letter to the foreign merchants relative to the matter, and posted proclamations upon the walls for the information of traders generally. I inclose copies of these. As far as I can ascertain, the duty on opium is collected thus: A custom-house spy is put over the foreign godowns to watch if any opium is carried in or out. Whenever a sale is made, the spy follows the opium to the house of the native purchaser, who is immediately reported to the custom-house, and compelled to pay the duty. It is quite evident that by such a system as this, the authorities cannot collect the whole revenue upon the import. The combined cunning of the buyer and seller proving more than a match for that of the spy.

As Mr. Jones must have left Shanghai prior to the arrival of the Yang-tze, I will endeavor to give you some information relative to the points referred to in your letter to him.

1. I now inclose copies of all the proclamations that have been issued relative to the Mexican dollar question.

2. In reply to that part of your letter referring to the agreement on the part of the authorities to receive Mexican dollars at two per cent. discount, I have to inform you that the agreement was an informal one, and that it was merely a "conversational understanding."

3. My letter of January 7 informs you that there were no obligations taken for the duties withheld on American ships.

4. The "formidable obstacles" referred to in Mr. Jones's letter of April 24, 1857, came, as he supposed, from the British consul. The opposition consisted in a want of coöperation on the part of her Britannic Majesty's consul, and in the vacillating course pursued by him. There was a rumor current at the time that her Britannic Majesty's *vice*-consul had told the Haikwan to stop American tea-boats on their way to the anchorage. The foundation for this report was based upon some hints thrown out by the Haikwan, in conversation with Mr. Jones. There is no connection whatever between this "opposition" and the opium duty alluded to in Mr. Jones's letter of May 5th.

5. In reply to your last inquiry, I must confess my inability to tell you "what it all means?" I can, however, inform you that your information in regard to Mr. Jones's action in September, 1856, is quite correct.

I trust that you will excuse me, if the information I have endeavored to give you is not full and satisfactory. You will bear in mind that most of the matters alluded to took place before I entered upon the duties of vice-consul. The records of this office are rather bare of *evidence* relative to the duty question, and I am forced to derive much of my information from such conversations as I have had occasionally upon this subject with the American merchants resident here.

You will note that I make no mention of the progress made in the payment of the back duties. I shall await your reply to my dispatch of January 7, before addressing you further upon that subject.

I remain, very respectfully, your most obedient servant,

THOMAS DUNN,
United States Vice-Consul.

Hon. W. B. REED,
United States Commissioner, &c., &c., &c.

Inclosure 2 t.

LI and HÚ, expectant sub-prefects, with Yeh and Tsin, titular under-prefects and expectant district magistrates, specially deputed to the opium office, in Nantai, in Fuh-Chow, hereby promulgate directions upon the business.

We have had the honor to receive the following orders from the commissioners in charge of the commissariat: "The seditious banditti from Kiangsi having made a foray into this province of Fuhkien, we have received orders from their excellencies (the governor-general and governor) to call out the troops to destroy them, but the expenses on this account are so enormous, that it is necessary to adopt some scheme to provide funds to meet the deficit." It appears that the prefect of Fuh-Chow and other officers have held a joint consultation on the subject, and have proposed that a tax be laid on opium temporarily to aid the revenue; they presented the plan to their excellencies, who looked it over and gave orders for drawing up some regulations concerning it at the same time reporting the same to the throne. They also appointed two of us, Hu and Yeh, to attend to the general office in Nantai, and the other two, Lé and Tsin, to open the office at Linpú for examining the drug, each to be furnished with proper seals to use in their duties. We have also conferred with the prefect of Fuh-Chau and other functionaries, and drawn up certain regulations, which have been submitted to their excellencies.

On the 7th of June, 1857, an office for receiving the opium duty was opened on the island of Chung-Chau, in Nantai suburb, and a toll-house at Linpú, on the same day, where it is to be examined. Hereafter those chests which contain forty balls are to pay a duty of one dollar on each ball; large chests, weighing one hundred catties, or small chests of fifty catties, which contain the drug in mass, are to pay four dollars for every catty—the dollar to be seven mace two candareens weight in silver; and two candareens agio to be levied on each dollar as a fee for the office expenses. Only three sorts of opium chests come at present, but if other sorts are brought in future, one of them shall be opened, its balls counted or its contents estimated in catties, the chest measured, and then a proportionate rate levied upon it.

You merchants from Canton living in the foreign hongs, and you native dealers, all of whom have alike lived on the soil and eaten the produce of our common country, you ought, when the troops are called out on such an emergency, and the demand for supplies is pressing, assist in relieving the public necessities by willingly conforming to this mode of aiding the present difficulties. As soon as a clean riddance has been made of these brigands, trade will revive, and no longer be interrupted, and both state and people alike get the benefit of peace.

Having received orders to attend specially to this business, we shall devote our whole attention to it, sparing no trouble to make it efficient. The offices are now open, and all the regulations are written out, in conformity to the orders given; and we now communicate them to the persons living in the foreign hongs, for their full knowledge of the temporary measure now adopted to increase the revenue and furnish supplies to the army by levying a tax on opium.

Having also received commands from the commissioners in charge of the commissariat, the same having been also reported in a memorial by their excellencies, we now make them known, that when foreign opium has paid the duty, no officer will prevent its being used; when it passes the toll-houses, the military and civil officers there, on seeing the receipt from this office, will let it pass without hindrance. Let all therefore strictly comply with the regulations, carefully attending to every particular, reporting what is received for duty and what for office expenses. Let no one triflingly disregard them, so that the revenue suffer loss by embezzlement and peculation, lest they bring punishment on themselves. Most peremptory are these orders.

Appended are the regulations and a copy of the seal to be used.

JUNE, 1857.

Inclosure 2 u.

YEH, the prefect of Fuh-Chau, CHUNG, the sub-prefect, with HWANG and TSAI, the district magistrates of Min and Haukwân, hereby conjointly issue clear commands concerning the collection of a duty on opium, in order to assist the military expenses:

Whereas seditious banditti from Kiangsi having made a foray into the limits of this province of Fuhkien, we received orders from their excellencies (the governor general and governor) to call out the troops to suppress them, and it will not be difficult to set the day when they will be destroyed. Already have the soldiers and braves been assembled in great force, and the outlay for their equipment is so enormous that it is necessary to adopt some scheme to provide funds to meet the expense. We, therefore, together, examined the list of imports, and found that the article of opium had lately come into very general use as a preventive against the bad effects of malaria, but it had never been inserted in the list of dutiable articles. The request was made that each ball of the drug should be taxed one dollar, and when it came in the mass that the rate of duty should be four dollars for every ten catties—the dollar to weigh seven mace and two candareens of silver, and the duty to be temporarily applied to meet these pressing demands. We have had the honor to receive from the commissioners who have charge of the commissariat the notice that they have examined this, and have requested from their excellencies, who have duly memorialized the throne upon the subject, and have received orders to establish a special office for the purpose of levying this tax, and to issue the necessary commands to make it known through us.

Wherefore, we now accordingly make known these orders: Let all the people and merchants within our jurisdiction know, that henceforth opium is to be taxed to furnish revenue, and the subordinate officers are to allow it to enter for consumption. Stamped tickets will be issued from the special office, and when they are shown at the toll-houses and guard-houses the article will be allowed to pass; nor will the officers be allowed to detain it or extort money from the owners. If it be on board passage or other boats on the river within our jurisdiction, whenever these boats have been examined at the custom-houses they are permitted to go into the country wherever they please; nor shall any officer or subject be arrested or punished for having it. But if merchants or small dealers dare to smuggle the drug, they shall, on detection, be subjected to severe punishment, according to the laws, and no favor be shown. Let all, therefore, tremblingly obey these special orders without any demur or delay.

JUNE 15, 1857.

Inclosure 2 v.

MACAO, *February* 17, 1858.

MY DEAR SIR: In our conversation the other day I understood, and the note from Mr. Blanchard confirms it, that you meant to establish the consulate and hoist your flag on board the Democratia or some other vessel of the kind. Permit me to inquire whether in such vessel opium or any other contraband article is likely to be stowed for disposal up the river or anywhere in China? In such case I object strongly to such location of the consulate. I will in no event agree to it. I would rather a thousand times there should be no consulate than such contamination. If this wish be disregarded, (I beg you to understand I don't expect it will,) I shall at once report the fact to Washington.

Truly, yours,

W. B. REED.

O. H. PERRY, Esq.

Inclosure 2 w.

HONG KONG, *February* 18, 1858.

MY DEAR SIR: I duly received your note of yesterday in reference to my locating the consulate on board the Democratia, or some other vessel of the kind, and requesting me to inform you whether in such vessel opium or any other contraband article is likely to be stored for disposal up the river or anywhere in China. Upon its receipt, I immediately wrote to Messrs. Thomas, Hunt & Co., the owners of the Democratia, upon the subject, and they, in reply, state that it is not, neither has it been, their intention to embark in any contraband trade at Whampoa. A copy of my note to them and their reply I herewith inclose. If, after this response of Messrs. Thomas, Hunt & Co., you shall desire that I shall find other quarters, I shall most certainly do so; but I think that it will be very difficult for me to find proper quarters immediately. I have had a conversation with Dr. Winchester, her British Majesty's vice-consul and acting consul, who is to be located at Whampoa, and he informs me that he has been unable as yet to hire a vessel on which to hoist his flag, although he has been negotiating for one of Thomas, Hunt & Co.'s chops; but in case he is unsuccessful, he is in a more fortunate position than I am, having a man-of-war to fall back upon, and which is the case with the French consul.

I beg leave to add that I am in every way most anxious and desirous to carry out fully your wishes and instructions.

Understanding that you intend to return to Hong Kong on Monday next, I shall remain here to await your arrival and consult with you on the subject.

I have the honor to be, sir, your most obedient servant,

OLIVER H. PERRY.

His Excellency WILLIAM B. REED,
United States Minister Plenipotentiary, &c., &c.

Inclosure 2 x.

No. 3.] UNITED STATES CONSULATE,
Foo-Chow, January 22, 1858.

SIR: I last had the honor to address you on 21st instant, and have since received your dispatch of January 15th.

I regret to inform you that many of the British firms here have not paid their duties due upon shipments per American vessels. I have given to her Britannic Majesty's consul a statement of the case, requesting him to use his authority in settling this unfortunate affair. Her Majesty's consul has written, I believe, to Sir John Bowring for instructions.

I note that you consider "some responsibily" as resting upon *me* in regard to the withholding of duties due upon American vessels. I do not understand how you arrive at this opinion. From 1st October, 1857, to 31st December, 1857, I acted under the orders of a principal, who was during that time in China, and with whom I was in constant correspondence. It appears to me that prior to Mr. Jones's departure *he alone* was responsible for any official acts issuing from this consulate.

I should feel obliged if you would give me your opinion as to the right of a consul to grant either a sailing letter or American flag to vessels not built in the United States, but owned by citizens thereof.

I am, sir, very respectfully, your most obedient servant,

THOMAS DUNN,
United States Vice-Consul.

Hon. WILLIAM B. REED,
United States Commissioner, &c.

Inclosure 2 y.

No. 2.] UNITED STATES LEGATION,
Macao, February 1, 1858.

SIR: I duly received your letter No. 2, of 21st, and No. 3, of 22d ultimo. In saying that a responsibility of some kind rested on you as to the duties withheld or unpaid by the English merchants at Foo-Chow, I did not mean to pass any censure. On the contrary, your official conduct, following the course prescribed by Mr. Jones, was approved fully by me; and yet, anxious as we both are that the Chinese treasury should not be deprived of a dollar belonging to it, and as the amount in arrear, though due by English merchants, was withheld in consequence of what you did, I meant rather to stimulate you to renewed efforts to secure its payment rather than to find any fault.

Sir John Bowring has promised me to do his best to persuade the delinquents to pay the amounts withheld, and unless I learn from you by the next mail that it has been done, I shall call his attention again to the subject.

In answer to your inquiry as to vessels not built in the United States, but owned by their citizens, I beg to refer you to chapter 23 of the Consular Regulations prescribed by the President on the duties of consular officers, in respect to American owners of foreign-built vessels, where you will find the rule prescribed.

Any specific inquiry I will answer with pleasure. Direct all letters as usual to Hong Kong, where my agents are James Purdon & Co.

I am, sir, very respectfully, your obedient servant,

WILLIAM B. REED.

THOMAS DUNN, Esq.,
Vice-Consul, Foo-Chow.

Inclosure 2 *z.*

WANG, governor-general of Fuhkein and Chehkiang, deputy censor and superintendent of the provincial revenue, with KING, governor of Fuhkien, deputy censor and commander of the provincial forces, hereby issue their orders for the circulation, [of dollars,] that the people may be benefited.

Whereas the English and American consuls having requested that new and old foreign dollars may be taken in traffic according to one and the same rule, we communicated on the subject with his excellency Baron Yeh, the governor-general at Canton, who has replied as follows:

"In 1853, Mexican and other sorts of foreign silver coins were brought to Canton, and the various shops and mercantile houses repeatedly requested to have them come into general circulation. I accordingly directed that they should all be received on the same principle; but if their intrinsic value should be found to differ, then they should be carefully distinguished and their value fixed. At present, they all freely circulate in this port; and it would be well to have the same rule apply with you."

Further, it also appears that the tea merchant Ching Pau-shu, and the foreign merchants Messrs. Russell & Co., have together petitioned as follows:

"All merchants doing business in Fuh-chau have heretofore paid the duties to government in sycee or in Carolus dollars, rated according to the market discount to make them equal to it. In all mercantile transactions, sycee and chop dollars have been taken at option. But lately, all the foreign merchants have brought Mexican dollars, the silver of which is fully equal to the other, while, too, they are bright, round, and clean; and it seems highly desirable that they should pass currently in the same manner. We therefore request that they may pass here, as at Canton with the chop dollar, so that all silver coins in the market may be equalized."

Again, all the brokers and shroffs within and without the city walls have presented a petition to the prefect, stating that the silver coins brought to this port are unlike; that Spanish dollars have been commonly used in the market, but they also vary among themselves in value, some of them being light and injured, while those which were reckoned by weight and not by number, as the chopped dollars, were most widely circulated. Mexican dollars have lately been brought here, and are not so generally taken; but we have been deliberating upon the propriety of receiving them at the same rates; and we now humbly beg that you will communicate to the English and American consuls, and that commands may be issued to the foreign hongs, directing how they shall pass in relation to other silver coins, and injunctions given to all the officers within the jurisdiction that they receive all on the same principle, treating all parties alike, and putting no obstacle in the way of the free circulation.

The prefect of Fuh-chau, Yeh Sking-shau, having received the above petition, assembled the district magistrates, to deliberate with them upon the matter, and their report has been presented. It appears that the Spanish dollars come altogether from foreign countries, and though they are not quite pure silver, they circulate among the common people at different rates of discount, just as the market value happens to fluctuate. Mexican dollars have only recently been brought to Fuh-chau, and the traders, seeing their effigies were new, have doubted about them and declined to receive them freely. The foreign merchants, fearing that the common people would not be inclined to receive them willingly, and it would cause at last great obstruction to trade, have been much annoyed and disappointed, and both parties have been ready to blame each other. Now, both sorts pass without hindrance at Canton, and as they circulate from one place to others more remote, how can we be sure that they will not find their way everywhere? As to fixing the rate of discount [from sycee] upon the various kinds of coin, let that be settled by the market rates, for it is useless for the magistrates to deliberate upon such a matter; it will rather hinder business.

While issuing the necessary orders to all the prefects within this jurisdiction, that they take measures to have the coins circulate everywhere among the people, and informing the English and American consuls of the same, we now further issue these plain commands. Let all officers, all merchants, and every class of people throughout the province of Fuhkien know clearly that Spanish, chopped, Mexican, and all smooth dollars, whether now in circulation or brought from abroad, are all to pass current with Carolus dollars and sycee silver, and are to be received without hesitation. But if any of them should not be of the proper standard, then they are to be taken at a proportionate discount, such as the market rate may be at the time. The shroffs and bankers will not be allowed to interfere at their will to alter the rate, or to demand an extortionate discount for quality of metal, nor shall they combine to impede their circulation as they choose. The foreign merchants and those who deal with them shall also receive and pay them at the same rate, not declining to receive them after they have paid them out. In this way all classes of natives and all foreign traders will be alike convenienced in their business, traffic will daily increase, and the revenues of the State and the sustenance of the people will also be improved. Let all, therefore, scrupuously obey, without perversity, lest they involve themselves in unpleasant inquiry.

A special order, promulgated August 18, 1857.

Second edict on the same subject.

WANG, governor general of Fuhkein and Chehkiang, &c., &c., with KING, governor of Fuhkien, commander of the provincial forces, &c., &c., hereby again issue their orders respecting the circulation (of dollars) that the people may be benefited.

(The previous proclamation is here repeated down to the last paragraph, after which it reads as follows:)

We had already issued orders to all the prefects under this jurisdiction to comply with the above regulations, in order that these several coins might come into general circulation; and the prefect of Fuhchau had likewise informed the English and American consuls of the same; and express proclamations had also been promulgated that the same rules for receiving them should be observed throughout the province, and no one be allowed to obstruct their circulation, or extort on the ground of their being debased. All this had been done when the tea merchant, Nieh-tai-kwa, and the tea broker, Ching Pau-shu, with the foreign merchants Russell & Co., presented a petition to the following purport:

"The silver in the Spanish and Mexican dollars is really of the same kind, and there is no reason why the shroffs and bankers should, to further their own selfish ends, charge a rate of discount on the latter coins from eighteen to eight per cent., injuring people very much, and putting great obstructions in the way of trade, so that the Mexican dollars do not circulate freely. We beg that strict orders may be issued forbidding it, and injunctions sent throughout the province to all, informing them that both of these kinds of dollars have been assayed, and found not to differ intrinsically. At Canton, all kinds pass current by one rule, and not above one or two per cent. discount is there charged by the bankers for the difference of assay from pure sycee. It is very wrong and unjust for the bankers in Fuhchau to act so presumptuously in obstructing business as they please, and paying no regard to the assay made of the coins, in order that they may get their own profits by charging a high discount."

Accordingly, we issue these orders to the assayers or money shops, and to all the bankers in Fuhchau, to require them to receive the Spanish and Mexican dollars in their business on the same basis, charging no more discount for one than the other, and also make this plain proclamation: Let all shopkeepers, bankers, merchants, and business men of every kind in this province, know fully, that Spanish and Mexican dollars having been found by assay not to differ, and being also taken at Canton according to one rule, are henceforth to pass according to one and the same rule. Let there be no further discussion respecting the rate of discount you should charge. Foreign merchants will also pay them out and receive them by the same rates, nor shall any one decline capriciously to receive them in payment. The revenue of the country and the business of the people will then both increase. On the appearance of this second proclamation, let all classes of people receive these coins by the same standard. If the bankers pretend to obey, but secretly refuse and resist it, and scheme how they may clog the wheels of traffic for their own selfish extortion, there will be but one law for them all, and they will subject themselves to a strict examination and punishment, in which no leniency will be shown. Let every one therefore obey without opposition.

OCTOBER 15, 1857.

Edict from the Prefect of Fuhchau.

Chung, acting prefect of Fuhchau, Tsai, expectant prefect and acting collector of customs of the port and sub-prefect, Hwang, district magistrate of Min, with Tsin, acting district magistrate of Haukwan, hereby jointly issue these orders respecting the circulation (of dollars) that the people may be benefited.

(Here the previous edict of the governor general and governor is quoted and promulgated.)

Dated August, 1857.

Inclosure 3 a.

CONSULATE OF THE UNITED STATES,
Singapore, January 15, 1858.

SIR: I have the honor to forward you the last advices from India. I would particularly draw your attention to the last paragraph of the extract from "The Friend of India," (a very ably-conducted periodical,) which may somewhat foreshadow coming events. Oude and its capital will probably witness the close, as they did the outbreak of rebellion.

The peace of Singapore and the Straits' settlements remains undisturbed. During the past year rumors of impending dangers from disaffected Asiatics have caused temporary alarms, but our insulated position, mixed population, and untiring vigilance will preserve tranquillity, whilst the importance and prosperity of the port is daily increasing.

I am, very respectfully, your obedient servant,

THOMAS BIDDLE.
United States Consul.

His Excellency the Hon. WILLIAM B. REED, &c., &c., &c.,
Legation of the United States to China.

Inclosure 3 b.

UNITED STATES CONSULATE GENERAL,
Calcutta, January 23, 1858.

SIR: I take the earliest opportunity of replying to your favor dated December 23, 1857.

We have few matters of interest to Americans, except such as relate to mercantile affairs. Troops continue to arrive daily from England, and the upper provinces are gradually becoming more settled and peaceable. The commander-in-chief is still at Fultyghur, which it is supposed he will make his headquarters for the present. The main army of the mutineers is concentrated at Lucknow, but has the means of escape, the British army not being strong enough to surround them, Oude being still in open rebellion.

The King of Delhi is to be brought to court-martial on nineteen charges, and will most probably pay the penalty of his crimes.

As the country becomes tranquillized, affairs are assuming a more healthy tone, and produce is gradually rising in value. Freights continue rather low, but exchange rules high, owing to the difficulty of knowing whom to trust.

We have now thirty-eight American ships in the Hooghly, mostly of large tonnage, whose destination will be shown by a reference to the annexed circular. We have, however, no men-of-war, nor have they for some time visited this port, notwithstanding the magnitude of the American interests here, and the fact that we have the best docks and docking facilities in India. We have quite a fleet of English men-of-war here, under command of Commodore Watson, consisting of the Chesapeake, Pearl, Himalaya, Pelorus, Assurance, Mohawk, Pylades, Megœra, and Roebuck.

Having no further matter of interest to communicate, I have the honor to be, sir, your faithful servant,

JOHN E. AMORY,
United States Vice-Consul General.

Hon. William B. Reed,
United States Commissioner to China.

Inclosure 4.

Macao, *February* 15, 1858.

Sir: With reference to the claims of James Purdon & Co. for losses caused by the hostilities between the English and Chinese, and more particularly for that portion of them relating to the property in store in our pack-house on Honan, in October, 1856, as per sheet D in the list of claims of James Purdon & Co., I beg to state that on the day of the raising of the blockade of Canton, 10th instant, I proceeded thither, having been kindly furnished by yourself with a passage in the United States chartered steamer Antelope, and on arrival off Canton at 3 p. m., on 11th instant, I immediately took a boat and, in company with Dr. S. Wells Williams, secretary of legation, who kindly offered to accompany me, landed at the pack-house.

We found the gates both of the court-yard in front and of the pack-house wanting; the wooden partitions between the divisions in the pack-house carried off; the whole building as open and exposed as any thoroughfare could be, and not a particle of the former contents remaining. In the two rear compartments of the pack-house were some forty-three empty ginseng hogsheads.

On seeing us land, a few of the Chinese of the neighborhood collected together, and, to questions addressed to them by Dr. Williams, replied that the greater part had been pillaged in the first and second Chinese months of last year. This corresponds with the information we received at that time, as mentioned in James Purdon's & Co's. letters of February 5, 1857, to his excellency Dr. Parker, United States commissioner, and to Mr. Perry, United States consul. They also stated that, after that plunder by the Chinese soldiers, thieves had broken in and carried off what had been left, the neighborhood having moved away from the place.

In passing the pack-house in the steamer I pointed it out to your excellency, and you could see there were neither doors nor windows remaining.

In conclusion, I have to say that I do not address this communication to your excellency with the object of more pressingly urging our claims, which I am well aware have received, and are receiving from you, all the attention their magnitude and hardship call for, but to recapitulate circumstances which were immediately communicated to you verbally by Dr. Williams and myself, and to place upon record the result of a visit to the pack-house, made directly upon the removal of the blockade, which has taken away all hope of recovery of any of our property stored therein at the time of the breaking out of hostilities, in October, 1856.

Referring to the statements inclosed in the letter of James Purdon & Co. to the United States consul, Mr. Perry, dated January 26, 1857, for the fullest particulars of our property and claims therefor, I remain, with much respect, your obedient servant,

JAMES PURDON.

His Excellency Hon. W. B. Reed,
Envoy Extraordinary and Minister Plenipotentiary to China.

Inclosure 5 *a.*

Legation of the United States,
Minnesota, Hong Kong, February 22, 1858.

My Dear Sir: It may be necessary for me, before I leave here, to prepare for the commodore some suggestions as to the disposal of the squadron in case our negotiations at Shanghai fail, and we have to go to the north. In this I shall be guided very much by your judgment, on which, as well as your disposition to assist me, I have entire reliance.

Do me the favor briefly to say what your advice is, supposing that we leave Shanghai early in April.

Which is the season when I understood you to say, from rain, &c., operations would have to be suspended, and when can they be resumed?

Where ought coal ships to rendezvous? Would it be desirable, on leaving Shanghai, for me to have the squadron concentrated at Nagasaki, or defer a visit to Japan until weather drives us there?

It is not likely that our relief squadron, or, at least, the commodore's flag ship, the Powhatan, will be here before the middle of April.

I shall be glad to hear from you, if you have time to write, before I leave here, which will not be before Thursday. The Antelope follows me to Manilla with the mail.

There is nothing new here. Lord Elgin arrived on Saturday, but, except in church, I have not seen him. Yeh goes to-day to Calcutta.

My dear Count Poutiatine, truly yours,

WILLIAM B. REED.

Inclosure 5 b.

MACAO, *February* 22, 1858.

DEAR SIR: Your letter reached me this evening, and I hasten to rèply to your excellency's questions.

My movement from Shanghai, if the negotiations prove a failure, will mainly depend on the new instructions I am expecting from St. Petersburg, and the arrival of our ships from the Baltic. However, if the forces of the western powers and your squadron move to the Gulf of Pecheli early in April, I will follow them; in the contrary case, it would be useless for me to proceed with a single ship to Peiho, and I will wait the arrival of our squadron at Shanghai.

The best months for operations on shore in the Gulf of Pecheli are April and May, when the weather is, for the most part, clear, and the heat is not intolerable. In the month of June, and especially in its latter part, the air is rarified to such a degree that it is difficult for weak persons to breathe, and this continues until the rainy season sets in, which is usually about the beginning of July. The rain comes then in torrents, and the low, flat grounds become almost impassable. All this applies properly to Pekin and the country about it; but, from their vicinity to the sea-coast, the same state of weather at that time must be expected to prevail in the Gulf of Pecheli. This rainy season lasts for six or seven weeks, with light southeast winds, and, at the end, is accompanied by violent thunder storms and a change of the wind to the northwest. About the last days of August the periodical rains cease, and the month of September, with the greatest part of October, are the healthiest and the best for the renewal of any operations on land. If a blockade of the coast is intended to be enforced, to be effectual it must be established not later than the beginning of April, and ought to be continued during the prevalence of the southern monsoon in the Chinese seas.

The most convenient place for the rendezvous of coal-ships is the anchorage in the Strait of Mia-tao, between an island of that name and another called Chang-shau. These islands are inhabited, are only one hundred and fifty miles from the river Peiho, and present a good shelter from easterly and northerly winds.

Nagasaki is one of the finest harbors in the world, and, being about seven hundred and fifty miles from Peiho, is not much further from that river than Shanghai. Your squadron may be concentrated there for any operations in the north; but negotiations with the government of Japan, to avoid delay, ought to be carried on at Simoda, which is close to Jeddo.

I intend to be at Hong Kong on Wednesday morning, and will be very glad to give you any further details on the above-mentioned subjects.

Assuring your excellency that I shall be happy to assist you in every way that is in my power, and requesting you to consider me always at your disposal, I remain, dear sir, yours truly,

E. POUTIATINE.

His Excellency the Hon. WILLIAM B. REED,
&c., &c., &c.

Mr. Reed to Mr. Cass.

No. 11.] LEGATION OF THE UNITED STATES,
Shanghai, April 3, 1858.

SIR: I have the honor to inform you of my arrival at this port on the 24th ultimo, after a brief visit to Manilla, at which place I met Commodore Tattnall, and concerted with him the measures necessary for the early concentration of the squadron under his command in the north of China. The San Jacinto, flag-ship, is now here, the Powhatan and Mississippi being hourly expected. The Minnesota is at anchor off Woosung, her draft of water preventing her from passing the bar in the river.

On my arrival, I found I was in advance of all the other plenipotentiaries, except Count Poutiatine. Lord Elgin, however, arrived on the 26th, and Baron Gros two days ago.

In my last dispatch, (No. 10,) I informed you that letters, respectfully and urgently asking for an opportunity of negotiation, had been simultaneously addressed to the supreme council of state at Pekin, and forwarded through the governor of this province resident at Su-chaw. Copies of these letters you have already. They were dispatched by special messengers from this city; my letter being in charge of the acting consul of the United States and his interpreter, and the letter of the Russian minister inclosed in the same envelope with mine. The English and French dispatches were intrusted to the secretaries of the respective legations and the consuls. I annex the reports of the consul of the United States describing their reception. (Inclosures 1 to 16.) They succeeded in entering the provincial capital of Su-chaw, where no foreign official had ever been before, though a dexterous effort was made to keep them out, and, when once inside, were treated with courtesy by the governor. He promised the messengers to forward the dispatches to Pekin, and addressed me a letter to the same effect. (Inclosure 1 *c*.) The letters were received at Su-chaw on the 26th of February.

When I arrived at Shanghai on the 24th ultimo no answer had been received, but intelligence of an interesting character reached me through the public journals.

On the 28th of January, as soon as the news of the fall of Canton reached the capital, there appeared an imperial decree, (inclosure 2 *a*,) degrading Yeh from office, subjecting Pihkwei and the other inferior officials to what may be described as a court-martial, and conferring the post of governor general and imperial commissioner on Hwang Tsung-han, who was ordered to proceed immediately by express to perform the duties of his station, and "manage the affairs of the barbarians." Appended to the decree you will find some notice of the antecedents of the commission, which are thought to be reliable.

On the 15th February, 1858, a decree was issued directing the casting of seals for the new official—a matter considered of much moment among oriental functionaries—and on the 21st of February, (the date being important as showing that the imperial commissioner had not then left the capital or its neighborhood,) a memorial was presented by him praying for the appointment of a certain Peih Ching-chaou as a secretary, his recommendation being that he had been on the coast, and was acquainted with foreigners, and further asking permission to go to Canton by the sea-board route, through this province and city, so as to have the means of conferring on foreign affairs with the local authorities. This was granted by the Emperor. (Inclosures 2 *b* and 2 *c*.)

Though it is apparent the new commissioner had left Pekin before our letters reached the capital, there is no doubt that he was at or near Su-chau at the time, or soon after they were received at that city. The governor of Kiangsu was one of the persons whom, on his way, Hwang desired to consult on the affairs of foreigners, and it was he to whom the letters were delivered, and by whom they were forwarded.

It was in this state of affairs that, after the arrival of Lord Elgin, Count Poutiatine and myself, on the 26th ultimo, through the agency of the Taoutae or intendent of this city, answers were received by all except Count Poutiatine, to whom only a message was sent in the letter to me. I append translations of the answers to myself and the British minister. (Inclosures 3 *a* and 3 *b*.) That to Baron Gros I have not yet seen, there not having been time for translation.

To the answer addressed to me I beg leave to call your attention, simply remarking, on its general purport, that there is no substantial difference between it and the letter to Lord Elgin, these perverse officials seeming to be insensible to any distinction between friends and enemies.

You will observe the same tone of apparent courtesy exhibited here as marked the letters of Yeh last winter; the same unmeaning profession; the same dexterous sophistry; and, what is more material, the same passive resistance, the same stolid refusal to yield any point of substance. On my arrival at Canton, I asked for an interview, and it was refused, because there was pending war and no fit place in which to receive me. I have come to Shanghai, and am ready to go to any designated place in the neighborhood, where all is peace, and prosperity, and contentment; and I am told, in language hardly courteous, that my proper place is Canton, there to attend to my duties.

Assuming that the appointment and dispatch of the new commissioner to Canton, before my letter was received, is a justification of the court for referring me thither, there is not a word in the whole letter to show that his instructions as to personal intercourse, and my reception, are different from those of Yeh, or that he has anything like full powers, or any powers, to revise a treaty, or to do more than to settle the local difficulty at Canton, which, whatever importance may seem to be attached to it from its having generated a war, has relatively little interest for the United States. The fact that the functions of governor general and imperial commissioner are united, (the former being much more important in Chinese estimation than the latter,) confirms this view that, in reality, the adjustment of the local difficulties is the aim of his mission. When Keying made the treaty of Wanghia, he was imperial commissioner, and not governor or governor general. I have no doubt that if, deluded by the thin profession of friendliness which these Chinese officials habitually use, I were to go to Canton, I should degrade myself in the estimation of the Chinese, and be rejected by Hwang, as three months ago I was by Yeh. It is due to myself to say that no such idea ever entered my mind. I had, besides, precluded it by saying, in my letter to Pekin, that I should regard any suggestion for a removal of the proposed negotiation further from the capital than Shanghai as a refusal.

I beg to call your attention to another part of this answer—the denial of our right to correspond directly with the high authorities at Pekin. It is very explicit, and is put upon the ground that it is not according to the organic rule of the empire for such correspondence ever to be tolerated. But this view can only be sustained by asserting that what is called the ancient custom or law is to prevail over a treaty ratified by the Emperor; for nothing can be clearer than that, both by the English and French treaties, the right and the duty of correspondence directly with Pekin is expressly secured. Had the chancellor (as this functionary at the capital is denominated) made any distinction between the United States and England and France, as respects this right of correspondence, there might be an inference that some regard was had for treaties, and that they were at least the subject of criticism. No such distinction is attempted; but, treaty or no treaty, the right to correspond with anybody at the capital is denied.

I have no doubt that, under the very letter of the treaty, we are entitled to the privilege; if for no other reason, because it was conceded to the French in a treaty of later date than ours, and because, by the second article of the treaty of Wanghai, it is provided that if additional privileges, of whatever description, should be conceded by China to any other nation, the United States, in its political capacity as distinguished from its citizens, should be entitled to full participation in the same.

On general principles, I should be sorry to believe that the United States would be willing to acquiesce in a construction, or that the distinguished citizen who negotiated the treaty meant to adopt a form of words capable of it, which would exclude us from a privilege conceded to others.

On every ground, therefore, I considered the reply as evasive and unsatisfactory.

This view, which I formed on the first inspection of the dispatch from Su-chau, I am happy to say, is concurred in by the other plenipotentiaries; and the determination is common to all not to return to Canton, but to advance nearer to Pekin, and still more urgently and impressively to make an effort for peaceful negotiation. I inclose copies of the answers of his excellency Lord Elgin and myself, those of the French and Russian plenipotentiaries not being yet ready.

These answers, prepared without the least concert, differ in form and tone, but not in substance. Lord Elgin chooses to treat the refusal to correspond at Pekin as an indignity, and returns the letter to the governor. I am very doubtful whether returning a letter will not be misunderstood by Chinese intellectual perversity, and may not be understood as a concession that it is unanswerable. But, be this as it may, I see no objection to my answer being less peremptory in its tone, though I hope, in substance, equally decisive. Copies are sent herewith. (Inclosures 4 *a*, 4 *b*, 4 *c*, 4 *d*, and 4 *e*.)

They reveal our decision without further delay to renew the experiment of negotiation nearer to the capital. The correspondence between this legation and that of her Britannic Majesty shows the reasoning which leads to this result. (Inclosures 5 *a*, 5 *b*.) Every effort is now making to expedite the departure of all. I have every reason to hope, that through the active exertions and zealous coöperation of Commodore Tattnall, the American legation will be able set out first.

What course of action will be adopted on our arrival in the Gulf of Pecheli, it is difficult to foretell with anything like precision. Should the action of Great Britain and France be peaceful, though decisive and urgent, I shall unite in it thoroughly and completely. If hostilities recommence, obeying the spirit and letter of my instructions, I shall either continue a passive spectator of what is doing, or what is more consonant with my own feelings, retire till a chance of peaceful interposition presents itself, awaiting any further directions which I may receive from home.

In this inaction I shall, as heretofore, have the countenance of the Russian minister, who has recently, much I think to his surprise, and unaccountably to every one here not in the secrets of his government, received new and positive instructions to abstain strictly from any measures of hostility, except in cases of extremity. He informs me that, reserving for his own use a single frigate, which he hourly expects, and the small steamer America, on board of which he now is, he has sent orders to the rest of his squadron to repair to Japan and the northern ports in Russia. You will observe that in Count Poutiatine's note to me of the 29th ultimo, he specially refers to his instructions to further the demands of the United States. (Inclosures 6 *a*, 6 *b*.)

This attitude of Russia, in the existing complication of affairs, is of course very agreeable to me, as relieving me from the solitude of inaction, and supporting the peaceful policy I am instructed to maintain. It may well be doubted whether such instructions would have been given if the Court at St. Petersburg had known that the letter of its envoy would be so absolutely unanswered, and a mere message sent referring him to the north, as I am to the south.

Still the President will fully understand that the plenipotentiaries go to the north in perfect accord of opinion and intention, and in the hope common to all that the necessity of hostile action by any one or two may never arise, but that the mere appearance of force and earnest intention may suffice. So hopeful of this seem the English and French ministers, that I have every reason to believe they do not mean to await the arrival of naval or military reinforcements. Lord Elgin's language in reply to an address received from the English merchants a few days ago, was this: "In my communications with the functionaries of the Chinese government, I have been guided by two simple rules of action: I have never preferred a demand which I did not believe to be both moderate and just, and from a demand so preferred I have never receded. These principles dictated the policy which resulted in the capture and occupation of Canton. The same principles will be followed by me, with the same determination, to their results, if it should be necesessary to repeat the experiment in the vicinity of the capital of the Emperor of China.

"It is matter for me of the highest gratification, to know that, in pursuing this policy of combined moderation and firmness, I can count not only on the hearty coöperation and active support of the representative of his Imperial Majesty the Emperor of the French, but also on the good will and sympathy of the representatives of other great and powerful nations interested with ourselves in extending the area of Christian civilization, and multiplying those commercial ties which are destined to bind the east and west together in the bonds of mutual advantage."

I think it best, however, to take with me all the available force I have, if it be only to show the Chinese that it is not the want of means which compels the United States to abstain from measures of hostility. I refer you to the accompanying correspondence with the flag-officer in command as illustrative not only of the steps I propose to take, but (as I have had occasion to say before) of the earnest friendliness with which he supports me. (Inclosures 7 *a*, 7 *b*, 7 *c*.)

I hope the President and Secretary of the Navy will approve of Commodore Tattnall's course, wholly unsolicited but most gratefully appreciated by me, in putting me on an equality with the European envoys as to the use of a flag.

The pressure of the correspondence on the leading subject at this moment, prevents me from making any further communication to the department on the current business of the legation. There is nothing however of moment pending.

I have the honor to be, sir, your obedient servant,

WILLIAM B. REED.

Hon. Lewis Cass,
Secretary of State.

1 *a*.

UNITED STATES CONSULATE,
Shanghai February 23, 1858.

SIR: I have the honor to acknowledge receipt of your letter of the 10th instant, containing instructions relating to the despatches by the Mississippi, which reached me on the 21st instant.

In accordance with those instructions, I immediately communicated with Mr. Oliphant in regard to their transmission to the Chinese authorities.

At a meeting of the consuls of the treaty powers, in connection with the secretaries of their excellencies Lord Elgin and Baron De Gros, it was thought advisable that the dispatches should be forwarded together, and that to insure their safety, and perhaps facilitate their transmission to Pekin, it would be better to place them in the hands of the viceroy of the province in person.

With this intention, the English and French consuls and myself have arranged to accompany Mr. Oliphant and M. D. Contrades in their journey to Suchau, the capital of this province.

A communication has been made to the viceroy under cover of one to the Taoutae of this place, informing him of the intended visit.

We leave Shanghai to-morrow evening. I have arranged with Mr. John A. Wheelock to act as consular clerk during my absence, which I now anticipate will be about five days.

I will write you again on my return, informing you as to the success of this visit.

I have the honor to be, sir, your obedient servant,

ALBERT L. FREEMAN.

Hon. WILLIAM B. REED,
United States Minister to China, &c.

---

1 *b*.

SHANGHAI, *April* 3, 1858.

SIR: Referring to my letters of February 23 and March 5, in relation to the dispatches received by the frigate Mississippi, I beg to give you, in accordance with your request, a brief account of the journey to Loo Chow, and the interview with the governor of this province, to whom the dispatches were delivered for transmission to Pekin.

In company with the secretaries of their excellencies Lord Elgin and Baron Gros, the French and English consuls, I left Shanghai on the 24th of February, in a native boat.

On starting, the flags of the different nations represented were hoisted upon the several boats composing the party.

We sailed up the Wangpoo river some twelve miles the first evening, and came to an anchor. Early on the following morning we again started, and during the day entered upon the canal leading to the Manhoo.

We crossed the lake in the early part of the same evening, and entered upon the canal which forms the water communication with the city of Loo Chow.

About nine o'clock in the evening, being some six miles in advance of the rest of the party, we were hailed by persons upon a boat coming in an opposite direction, one of whom represented that he was a messenge sent by the governor, who was waiting at a place called Knanshan to hear any communication we might have to make.

Knowing that the governor's readiness to receive us at Knanshan (which place was some sixteen miles this side of Loo Chow) had more to do with a Chinese policy manifested on a similar occasion, to prevent an entrance into the city of Loo Chow, I immediately communicated to him through Mr. Jenkins, my interpreter, a message for the governor, to the effect that we were bound for Loo Chow, and could not change our route for any other place.

The official immediately left us with the intention of proceeding to Knanshan to inform the governor of the message.

At sunrise the following morning, we came to an anchor under the walls of Loo Chow. At about seven o'clock all of the boats connected with the expedition had arrived with the exception of the English consul's, which had not been seen since the previous evening.

We waited about an hour for him, but seeing no signs of his speedy arrival, and as it was important to obtain an entrance inside the city before it became noised abroad that we were in the vicinity, we determined to push for the water gate which led into the city.

We proceeded up the moat which surrounds the city walls, until we arrived at one of the gates.

On entering the arch, the gate keepers seeing that we were foreigners, attempted to close the gate, but not succeeding in their attempt, we passed through into the inner moat. We made our way up this moat about half a mile, and came to an anchor.

At about ten o'clock, a. m., a messenger arrived stating that the governor had arrived, and was waiting outside the walls to receive us. Word was sent to him that we were inside the city, and would call on him at his official residence within the walls, at any hour he might name, also requesting him to send sedans for our conveyance to his residence.

Some little time was consumed in receiving an answer, and about ten o'clock, Mr. Lay, the British inspector at the custom-house in Shanghai, who had accompanied Mr. Oliphant, was sent for by the governor, and on his return stated that sedans would be at the landing at three o'clock, p. m., to convey us to the governor's residence.

About four o'clock we started from the landing place, and after a journey of two miles through the city, we arrived at the gates and were received with a salute of six guns.

We were then introduced by the interpreters, and Messrs. Oliphant and Contrades delivered a dispatch requesting the governor to forward the inclosures with all possible speed to Pekin, also to forward our acknowledgment of their receipt to us, open, in order that we might see that the style was correct.

After having partaken of refreshments, we proposed receiving the governor outside of the city on the following morning, and immediately returned to our boats and proceeded outside the walls.

On the following day, at eleven o'clock, the governor's approach was announced at the place agreed upon for an interview. We then extended to him the courtesies of the occasion, and after wishing him rapid promotion and the etceteras of a happy official life, we returned to our boats and started for Shanghai, were we arrived on the following evening.

I have the honor to be, sir, your obedient servant,

ALBERT L. FREEMAN.

Hon. WILLIAM B. REED,
United States Embassador to China.

---

1 *c.*

Ho, Governor General of the Two Kiang, &c., &c., and CHAON, Governor of Kiang, &c., &c., sends a communication in reply, as follows:

FEBRUARY 27, 1858.

On the 26th instant, I received a dispatch from your excellency, handed to me by Mr. Secietary Oliphant. I immediately opened and read it, and found it to inclose two communications for Yu, minister of state. On the same day, I gave intimation of the above to the governor general, and also inclosed the several dispatches received, which I forwarded to Pekin without delay or fail. I have now to give you this reply, and take the opportunity to wish you all happiness and felicity.

Further, the governor general being at present at a distance, at Changchow. I am only able to attach his name, but not his seal to this dispatch.

A necessary communication.

His Excellency Mr. REED,
Commissioner of the United States of America to China, &c., &c.

True translation.

JOHN A. T. MEADOWS,
Interpretor.

Imperial Edict.

[From the North China Herald, February 27.]

Muhkitenar and Pehkwei, in a joint memorial forwarded by express, have reported to us that the barbarians have rushed into their provincial city, &c., &c.

Holding the office of imperial commissioner for the direction of the affairs of the barbarians, Yeh Mingchin ought to have devised means to keep in check the said barbarians, if their demands were indeed so unreasonable and extravagant that they could not be granted; also, he ought to have conferred with the commandant, the governor, and other officers of the city, so that measures for soothing and controlling them might have been seasonably adopted.

But while the said barbarians did twice address communications to the commandant, (Tartar general,) the governor, (Pehkwei,) and the major general of Canton, the said governor general, Yeh Mingchin, never once associated them with himself in council or in action; nay, many things that were contained in the communications (from the barbarians) he kept secret and would not divulge. Thus, day after day, for a long time, he dallied with, and put off the barbarians, till excited to wrath, they suddenly entered the provincial city.

So very self-sufficient and obstinate was he, perverse and reckless, utterly disregarding the duties of his high commmission.

Let Yeh Mingchin, therefore, be immediately degraded from his office.

To the other provincial officers of Canton, Muhkitenar, the commandant, Pehkwei, the governor, Chwangki and Chwanking, major-generals, Hangki, the commissioner of customs, Kiang Kwohlin, the commissioner of finance, and Chau Kipin, the commissioner of justice, though all, more or less guilty of a dereliction of their duties in affording protection, (to the city,) yet, inasmuch as they were not in the council of the said governor general, some indulgence may be shown; and instead of dealing with them rigorously, according to the full measure of their guilt, as they have requested, let them be delivered over to the board of punishment. This is from the Emperor.

Imperial Edict.

JANUARY 28, 1858.

Let the governor generalship of Kwang Tung and Kwangsi be given to Hwang Tsunghan, and let him proceed immediately by express to perform the duties of that station; also, let him receive and hold the seals of imperial commissioner, that so he may manage the affairs of the barbarians.

Until he shall have reached and entered on the duties of that station, let whatever appertains to the office of the imperial commissioner and that of the governor general of Kwang Tung and Kwanksi be taken charge of by Pihkwei; and let the office of governor of Kwang Tung be temporarily filled by Kiang Kwohlin. This is from the Emperor. Dated 12th moon, 14th day.

NOTES.

The antecedents of some of the above-named officers are very well known, and need not here be noticed.

Hwang Tsunghan is a native of the province of Fuhkien. In 1851 he held the office of provincial judge, or commissioner of justice in the province of Chehkiang; and in 1853 was treasurer or commissioner of finance in the province of Kansah. He is now, if we mistake not, holding the office of governor general of Szeehuen. To which of the two great political parties he adheres we do not know ; we are inclined to think, however, that he is opposed to the liberal party, of which Kiying and Muhehangah were leaders, and if so, he is probably a leading man in the present hostile party that upholds the old exclusive policy.

Muhkitenar is a Manchu, and so also is Chwangling ; Pehkwei is a Mongolian, as is likewise Chwangki ; Hangki is a member of the imperial household ; Kiang Kwoohlin is a Chinese, a native of Szee-huen ; and Chow Kipin is a Chinese, and a native of the province of Kweichau.

In the two edicts given above, there is nothing to indicate the date of the memorial on which they are founded. The report of the commandant and governor may have been made, and probably was sent off for Pekin, prior to the time these two officers were made prisoners.

---

2 *b*. 2 *c*.

Extracts from Pekin Gazettes.

[Dated February 15, 1858.]

EDICT.

We now command you, the president of the board of rites, to cast two seals—one for the post of governor general of the two Kwang, and another for the post of salt commissioner of the two Kwang—and when finished, you will hand them over to the privy council, that the president may dispatch them to Kwang Tung. These are our commands.

I, the president of the board of rites, memorialize your Majesty, praying that your Majesty will command that I be furnished with the form of the seal of the governor general of the Two Kwang.

[Dated February 21, 1858.]

MEMORIAL.

I, Hwang-tsung-han, governor general of the two Kwang, and imperial commissioner for foreign affairs at Canton, humbly memorialize your Majesty to give certain commands.

I beg to state, that when I had the honor to receive your Majesty's commands, appointing me governor general of the two Kwang and high commissioner for the transaction of barbarian affairs, I memorialize, stating that I had found, on examination, that Peih-ching-chaou, commissioner of finances of the province of Ganhwuy, had, while stationed on the seaboard, filled the offices of magistrate, prefect, and intendant ; that he had always transacted his public business while filling these posts in the most able and successful manner ; that he had always been able to gain the hearts of the people by his upright conduct ; that when on these posts on the seaboard he has transacted the business of the barbarians; and that he was, consequently, a suitable officer to accompany me.

I also memorialize your Majesty, stating that if I proceed to Canton from Chihle by way of Shantung, Keangnan, Chikeang, and Fuhkeen, that as there were many fast vessels continually running between the ports of Shanghai, Ningpo, Fuh-Chau, and Amoy, I should, after passing Looc how, be able to learn in this manner the real state of affairs at Canton sooner; and respecting the barbarian affairs at each of the ports, I should also be able to see personally the governor general and governors of Kiangnan, Fuhkeen, and Chekeang, to arrange such more satisfactorily.

Should your Majesty be pleased to approve of my proceeding by the above-mentioned route, I have humbly now to request your Majesty will also be pleased to issue commands giving permission to Peih-ching-chaou, the commissioner of finances, to start with and accompany me. I shall be extremely grateful. I wait your Majesty's commands. I pray your Majesty to cast a glance on my memorial.

A respectful memorial.

His Majesty has granted the request of Hwang-tsung-han.

HO KWEI-TSING, Governor General of Kiang-su, Kiang-si, Ngau-hwui, &c., &c., &c.; and CHAU-TEH CHEH, Governor of Kiang-su, make this communication:

Your excellency's communication of February 10, was duly received on the 26th of the same month, with one addressed to Yu, chancellor of state, covering two dispatches, which, under a new envelope, were at once forwarded to the capital.

A dispatch from Chancellor Yu has now come to hand, acknowledging the receipt of those two, and signifying his thorough knowledge of their contents, declaring:

That at the present time, England and France being engaged in military operations, America has in no way implicated herself therein, but has firmly adhered to the former treaty, and ever preserved good faith and integrity.

That Russia has never hitherto had commercial intercourse at the five ports, Canton, &c.; that last year, on account of investigations regarding border-lines made by the Russian minister, Count Poutiatine, an imperial decree was given, appointing a minister to repair to the Black-dragon river, (the Amour,) to unite with him in the investigation; and that now, whatever subjects may come up for deliberations should be, as usual, through the foreign office, and communicated by the Sa-na-teh Ya-mun, in conformity to the old regulations, so as to sustain peace and good will.

That Yeh, late governor general of Kwang-tung and Kwang-si, not having managed well, has already, by the imperal pleasure, been degraded and deprived of all rank, and Hwang tsunghan appointed imperial commissioner as his successor, to proceed at once to Canton, there to investigate and direct public affairs in a just and equitable manner; and that, therefore, the American minister ought to be at Canton, waiting to perform his incumbent duties.

That hitherto our imperial commissioners have never repaired to Shanghai to direct and control in the transaction of public business.

That under the administration of the Celestial Court, each office has its appropriate functions, and every one holding authority in our middle kingdom must vigilantly attend to the duties of his own station, and had no right to intermeddle with aught beyond his proper sphere; and therefore

That it is inconvenient (for me the chancellor) to take it upon myself to make a communication in reply, (to the American minister.) All that relates to the above items, however, may be transmitted (in my stead) by your excellencies the governor general and governor, for I would not (seem to) lay aside his case, and give him no answer.

The above having been received by us, and we having ascertained that when your excellency's dispatch left Canton you were not aware that our great and august sovereign had already appointed Hwang to be the new governor general of Kwang-tung and Kwang-si, and fill the office of imperial commissioner, and that he had post-haste proceeded to Canton, there to investigate and direct public affairs, therefore your dispatch having come into our hands, and now Hwang, as imperial commissioner and governor general, having already proceeded on his way to Canton, it is proper for us to communicate for your excellency's examination and action, so as fully to meet present exigencies, (be at your post in Canton.)

Moreover, your excellency will please communicate (for us) with the Russian minister, for his examination and guidance, that he may await a communication from the foreign office.

We avail of this opportunity to offer our best wishes, &c., &c.

May this communication reach him to whom it is addressed.

His Excellency WILLIAM B. REED,

Minister Plenipotentiary of the United States of America, &c., &c.

MARCH 21, 1858.

P. S. The governor general being absent at Chung-chua, writes his official title, but does not affix his seal of office.

---

3 *b*.

[Received at Shanghai, March 26, 1858.]

Ho, Governor General of the two Kiang, &c., in China, and CHAU, Governor of Kiangsu, &c., make a communication:

On the 26th of February we received your excellency's communication of the 10th February, together with that addressed to the secretary of state, Yu, (Yuching,) which we immediately transmitted to the capital in a sealed cover.

We are now in receipt of a letter from the secretary of state, Yu, to the following effect:

"I have perused the letter received (from your excellency,) and have acquainted myself with all that it relates to. In the ninth moon of the year before last, (October, 1856,) the English opened their guns on the provincial city, (Canton,) bombarding and burning buildings and dwellings, and attacked and stormed its forts. The gentry and the people of both the city and suburbs thronged the court of Yeh, imploring him to make investigation, and take order accordingly. These are facts of which all foreigners are alike aware. The seizure of a minister, and occupation* of a provincial city belonging to us, as on this occasion has been the case, are also (facts) without parallel in the history of the past. His Majesty the Emperor is magnanimous† and considerate. He has been pleased, by a decree which we have had the honor to receive, to degrade Yeh from the governor generalship of the two Kwang for his maladministration, and to dispatch his excellency Hwang to Kwangtung, as imperial commissioner in his stead, to investigate and decide with impartiality; and it will of course behoove the English minister to wait in Kwangtung, and there make his arrangements. No imperial commissioner ever conducts business at Shanghai. There being a particular sphere of duty allotted to every official on the establishment of the Celestial Empire, and the principle that between them and the foreigner there is no intercourse being ‡ once ever religiously adhered to by the servants of our government of China, it would not be proper for me to reply in person (to the letter of the English minister.) Let your excellency, therefore, transmit to him all that I have said above, and (his letter) will in no way be left unanswered."

In accordance with this, we have to observe that, when your excellency wrote from Canton, you were not aware that his Majesty the Emperor had dispatched another imperial commissioner to Kwangtung, in the person of Hwang, the new governor general of the two Kwang, to investigate and decide (all matters;) and that you sent the letters under acknowledgment in consequence. It is now our duty to advise your excellency that Hwang, imperial commissioner and governor general of the two Kwang, is already on his way to Kwangtung, that, on the information, you may take that course which will be certain to bring about an amicable solution (of existing differences.)

We avail ourselves of the occasion to wish that your prosperity may daily increase.

The governor general has to add, that he is at Changchau, a place too far (from the governor) to admit of both their seals (appearing on this letter,) which runs in the name of both.

A necessary communication addressed to the Earl of Elgin and Kincardine.

Hien Fung, 8th year, 2d moon, 7th day. (March 21, 1858.)

Translated by THOMAS WADE,
Chinese Secretary.

---

* There is here an erasure. The character employed has probably been substituted for another, nearly resembling it in form, but implying unlawful violence in the act referred to.

† Magnanimous, liberal, or forgiving towards us; considerate towards the Chinese.

‡ Article 13, of the treaty of Nankin, provides the form under which there shall be intercourse between the British minister and high officers of China, both at Pekin and in the provinces.

4 *a.*

To Ho Kwei-tsing, Governor General of Kiangsu and Kiansi and Nganhwui, &c., &c., and Chau Teh-cheh, Governor of Kiangsu the minister of the United States makes this communication:

He has received your excellency's letter of the 21st March. It is wholly unsatisfactory.

The supreme council of state of his Majesty the Emperor of his excellency Chancellor Yu should have directly answered a communication respectfully addressed to them by the representative of a friendly power such as the United States has been and desires to be. The ministers of England and France are by solemn treaties authorized to correspond with Chinese high officers at the imperial capital at Pekin, and the United States of America have the same rights and mean to insist upon them.

Nor is the answer of their excellencies the governor general and the governor in itself satisfactory. It is true that America is in no way implicated in the military operations at Canton, and for that, among other reasons, the undersigned has come away from the place where those operations occurred, in order to meet an imperial commissioner for friendly conference at a place where there is no war. When he was in Kwangtung, in November last, the Imperial Commissioner Yeh would not receive him or listen to him, and there is not one word in the communication of Chancellor Yu to lead the undersigned to believe that if he were now to go to Canton his excellency Hwang would see him or listen to him. The same suggestion was made to the predecessors of the undersigned, and when they went to Canton, out of a great desire to preserve friendly relations, they were refused an audience.

Besides, the undersigned distinctly announces to their excellencies the governor general and the governor, and through them to the imperial council, that he shall proceed to the gulf of Pechele, and to the mouth of the Peiho, there to demand a revision of the treaty between the United States and China, and a settlement of the claims of citizens of the United States aggrieved in various parts of the empire, if he finds a commissioner of equal rank with himself, and clothed with full powers.

If he does not, it is the intention of the undersigned to proceed nearer to the imperial capital, and lay the claims of his government and fellow-citizens before his Majesty the Emperor.

He further informs the supreme council that in this course it is his intention to act in friendly and thorough concord with the plenipotentiaries of England, France, and Russia, whose interests in China entirely harmonize, and whose action, since the hostilities at Canton have been suspended, is strictly coöperative.

The undersigned renews to your excellencies the assurances of his distinguished consideration.

WILLIAM B. REED.

Shanghai, *April* 3, 1858.

4 *b*.

LEGATION OF THE UNITED STATES,
Shanghai, *April* 3, 1858.

The undersigned, envoy extraordinary and minister plenipotentiary of the United States, has received from Ho, governor general of the two Kiang, and Chau, governor of Kiangsu, a letter containing what is described as a message from his excellency Chancellor Yu, stating that it would not be proper for him to reply in person to the undersigned, but directing the governor general and governor to communicate his views. This cannot be recognized by the undersigned as right and proper, or according to the treaties which his Majesty the Emperor has ratified, and which the United States mean to insist on.

The undersigned, therefore, treats this message as no answer at all, and means to go at once to the Gulf of Pechele, and mouth of the Peiho, accompanied by the great ships of his nation, and there demand access to the imperial court, or the high officers who are bound to correspond with him.

WILLIAM B. REED.

---

4 *c*.

[Confidential.]

SHANGHAI, *April* 2, 1858.

SIR: With reference to my letter of yesterday's date, I have the honor to inclose herewith, for your excellency's perusal, the draft of letters which I propose to address to the governor general of the two Kiang and the governor of Kiangsu, and to the prime minister of the Emperor of China, respectively.

I have the honor to be, sir, your excellency's most obedient, humble servant,

ELGIN AND KINCARDINE.

His Excellency the Hon. W. B. REED,
&c., *&c.*, *&c.*

---

4 *d*.

Draft of a note to their excellencies the Governor General of the two Kiang and the Governor of Kiangsu.

The undersigned cannot accept from their excellencies Ho, governor general of the two Kiang, and Chau, governor of Kiangsu, a reply to the letter which he addressed directly to an imperial high officer at the capital, because, in doing so, he would compromise the dignity of his sovereign. He therefore returns herewith the letter which their excellencies did him the honor to address to him on the 26th ultimo, and incloses at the same time a further communication to the prime minister of the Emperor of China, which their excellencies will oblige him by forwarding to its destination.

---

4 *e.*

The undersigned has received from Ho, governor general of the two Kiang, and Chau, governor of Kiangsu, a communication which purports to convey the reply of his excellency the prime minister of the Emperor of China to the letter addressed to him by the undersigned on the 10th of February, and which contains, among other things, the following statement: "There being a particular sphere of duty allotted to every official of the Celestial Empire, and the principle that between them and the foreigner there is no intercourse being one ever religiously adhered to by servants of our government of China, it would not be proper for me to reply in person [to the letter of the English minister.] Let your excellencies, therefore, transmit to him all that I have said above, and [his letter] will in no way be left unanswered."

But the treaty between Great Britain and China states: "That it is agreed that her Britannic Majesty's chief high officer in China shall correspond with the Chinese high officers, both at the capital and in the provinces, under the term 'communication.'"

By refusing to correspond directly with the undersigned, the prime minister has set this provision of the treaty at naught. The undersigned has, therefore, returned to the governor general of the two Kiang and the governor of Kiangsu their communication, as he cannot receive it without compromising the dignity of his sovereign, and he will proceed at once to the north, in order that he may place himself in more immediate communication with the high officers of the imperial government at the capital.

---

5 *a.*

LEGATION OF THE UNITED STATES,
Shanghai, April 2, 1858.

MY LORD: I thank you for the translation of the letter from the governor and governor-general which you have been so good as to furnish me, and which seems generally to correspond with that which I have received from the same officials, a translated copy of which I had the honor of sending to your excellency some days ago.

I am indebted also to your lordship for the information contained in your note of the 1st instant, as to the course you intend to pursue in consequence of the refusal of the imperial court to accede to the reasonable and respectful demands of the representatives of the treaty powers, and, in acknowledging it, beg to say in addition that, on reference to the instructions which I received at Washington, and under which I yet act, I am satisfied that my government will expect me to adopt the same course, and repair as soon as possible to the Gulf of Pechele, and the waters of the Peiho, there still more impressively to demand access to the imperial court, or an interview with a duly accredited representative, in order to a satisfactory negotiation. I shall do so as soon as the naval commander-in-chief informs me that the squadron is ready to accompany me. What limitations are imposed on my action in the north, or elsewhere, your excellency is well aware of. What further instructions I may receive in answer to dispatches already sent to my government I do not venture to conjecture. But I am aware of nothing to prevent a cordial and unreserved interchange of opinions and concert of action in the existing state of things, if such a course be thought conducive to the ends we have in view. I certainly regard it as most important, and beg your excellency to believe that the same feeling animates me as did when I united with your excellency in the representation made to the imperial court.

I certainly concur in the view your excellency takes of the treaty obligation, securing to the representative of her Britannic Majesty the right to correspond with the authorities at the capital. The treaty of Wanghia, between the United States and China, while it contains no such express stipulation, does contain a clause giving to the United States, as well as their citizens, a complete equal and impartial participation in all privileges which might be conceded to any other nation ; and as the privilege of correspondence with the high officers at the capital, as well as in the provinces, was conceded to the government of France in a treaty later in date than that with the United States, there can be no question of the literal obligation of the officers at the capital to receive any proper communication addressed to them by the representative of the United States. I certainly regard a refusal to correspond with me as a just cause of offense to the government of the United States, more serious, as every attempt to correspond on terms of equality elsewhere has, for more than ten years, failed.

I have never for a moment thought of returning to Canton, for not only is there no assurance of a more favorable reception there than my predecessors formerly met with, but I have every reason to infer, from the combination of the functions of imperial commissioner and governor general, that the new officer has no authority beyond that which may enable him to settle a pending provincial difficulty.

I desire also to communicate to your excellency the rough draft of a reply which I propose to send as soon as possible to their excellencies the governor general and governor of the province.

I have the honor to be, my lord, your excellency's most obedient servant,

WILLIAM B. REED

His Excellency the Earl of ELGIN AND KINCARDINE,
H. B. M. High Commissioner, &c., &c., &c.

5 *b*.

SHANGHAI, *April* 1, 1858.

SIR: I have the honor to inclose herewith a translation of a communication, which I have received from the governor general of the two Kiang, and the governor of Kiangsu, purporting to convey the reply of the prime minister of the Emperor of China to my letter to him, of which the copy was inclosed in my dispatch to your excellency, of the February last.

I avail myself of the opportunity to submit a few remarks with reference to the course which I deem it proper to follow, at this conjuncture, in pursuance of the policy which I am directed by my government to carry out in China.

As the month of March has now expired, and the government of China has omitted to send a properly accredited plenipotentiary to treat with me, at this place, I conceive that I have recovered the liberty of action, of which I voluntarily deprived myself, for a specified period, by the terms of my letter to the prime minister of the Emperor above referred to.

The prime minister has further given just cause of offense to the government of her Britannic Majesty, by declining to correspond directly with me, although the treaty between Great Britain and China states that "it is agreed that her Britannic Majesty's chief high officer shall correspond with the Chinese high officers, both at the capitol and in the provinces, under the term communication."

As the communication which I have received from the governor general of the two Kiang, and the governor of Kiangsu, makes no reference to the specific points on which, in my letter to the prime minister, I intimated my desire to treat, I have no assurance that the imperial commissioner sent to Canton possesses the requisite full powers.

Under these circumstances, I am of opinion that the objects of my mission would be seriously compromised by my return to Canton; and I have accordingly resolved to proceed to the north without delay, in order that I may place myself in more direct communication with the imperial government at the capital.

I have the honor to be, sir, your excellency's most obedient, humble servant,

ELGIN AND KINCARDINE.

His Excellency the Hon. W. B. REED.

---

6 *a*.

SHANGHAI, *March* 29, 1858.

SIR: Your excellency has been aware that I was expecting additional instructions from St. Petersburg. They were brought to me by the last mail, and I am able now to inform you of their contents.

The imperial cabinet is animated with the greatest desire to see the complications which have arisen in Chinese affairs settled in a satisfactory way; and I am empowered to apply all moral means in furthering the demands of general interest that would be made at the court of Pekin by the plenipotentiaries of other powers, and especially by the representative of the United States. At the same time, the imperial cabinet, faithful to its former pacific intentions, desires not to employ any coercion against the Chinese government, and bids me not to have recourse to arms, except in cases of extremity.

I have also to communicate to your excellency that the Emperor, my august sovereign, has been pleased to confer on me the title of imperial commissioner and commander-in-chief of the squadron destined for the China and Japan seas.

With assurances of high consideration, I have the honor to be your excellency's most humble servant,

E. POUTIATINE.

His Excellency the Hon. W. B. Reed,
Envoy Extraordinary, &c.

---

6 *b.*

Legation of the United States,
Shanghai, March 29, 1858.

Sir: I have the honor to acknowledge the receipt of your excellency's letter, dated to-day, and thank you for the information it contains as to the views of the imperial cabinet with reference to the complications which have arisen in Chinese affairs, and to the course of conduct you are directed to pursue. I beg you to believe that I most highly estimate, as I am sure the government of the United States will, this new proof of friendly confidence and unreserve; and I am glad to find that, in the revelation which you have made of the policy of the imperial cabinet, there is nothing to weaken the strong sympathy which has influenced our respective nations in their treatment of this peculiar people.

Permit me to offer you my sincere congratulations on the new and deserved honors conferred on your excellency by his Majesty the Emperor, and, with renewed assurances of my most distinguished consideration, to remain, your excellency's most humble servant,

WILLIAM B. REED.

His Excellency the Count Poutiatine,
Imperial Commissioner and Commander-in-chief, &c.

---

7 *a.*

Flag-ship San Jacinto,
Shanghai, March 26, 1858.

My Dear Sir: I find that, by authority of the French government, their minister has followed the example of Lord Elgin, and hoisted the French ensign at the main of the ship in which he resides.

I send you the copy of an order I have addressed to Captain Du Pont on this subject, which I hope may comport with your views.

Yours, very truly,

JOSIAH TATTNALL.

His Excellency WILLIAM B. REED.

---

7 *b*.

FLAG-SHIP SAN JACINTO,
Yan-tse-keang river, March 26, 1858.

SIR: You are authorized, should our minister, Mr. Reed, desire it, to wear (within the waters of his mission) an American ensign at the main of the Minnesota.

The object being to designate the ship on board of which the legation is established, this flag is only to be worn when Mr. Reed is actually a resident on board, and is to be struck whenever he shall have been absent over twenty-four hours.

Hitherto, the ensign at the main has never been worn in our service but in honor of the President of the United States and commander-in-chief of the navy; and the privilege is tendered to Mr. Reed, without waiting for instructions from the government, in view of his high and peculiar mission, and from a desire to place him, so far as depends on myself, on an equal footing of honor and dignity with the foreign representatives with whom he is at present associated.

I am thus particular in stating the object of this deviation from the usage of our service, that it may not hereafter be drawn into a precedent.

Very respectfully, your obedient servant,

JOSIAH TATTNALL,
Flag-officer East India Station.

Captain SAMUEL F. DU PONT,
United States ship Minnesota.

---

7 *c*.

LEGATION OF THE UNITED STATES,
Shanghai, March 29, 1858.

MY DEAR SIR: I have the honor to acknowledge the receipt of your note of the 26th instant, inclosing the copy of an order given to Captain Du Pont, directing him to wear an American ensign at the main of the Minnesota, in order to designate the ship in which the legation is established. For this new mark of friendly and most considerate attention, I sincerely thank you, and I beg you to believe that I appreciate the reasons not only of this deviation from the usage of the naval service, but for your wish that it may not hereafter be drawn into a precedent. I make this formal acknowledgment, placing a copy of it in the archives of the legation, in order to prevent any misunderstanding hereafter of the precise import of this most agreeable distinction of the high and peculiar mission with which the President has intrusted me.

I avail myself of this opportunity to add that, in consequence of the very unsatisfactory replies received by the diplomatic representatives of the treaty powers to their respectful and friendly solicitation for the appointment of an imperial commissioner to conduct peaceful negotiations at or near this place, it will probably be necessary, at an early date, for me, as the representative of the United States, to repair to an anchorage near the mouth of the Peiho. In order to give due effect to the peaceful urgency I may feel it my duty to apply to the imperial government, it will be necessary that as large a portion of the naval force of the United States as can be spared from other duties should accompany me to the north. I shall be glad if you will give the necessary orders to this end. It will be a matter of great moment that the Minnesota and the other ships should be ready to go to sea at the same time as the forces of the other powers; and, though I am unable until the arrival of Baron Gros to speak with precision as to their exact intentions, my impression is that in a fortnight their arrangements will be completed.

Should the urgency to be resorted to continue to be peaceful, I am authorized to take part in it even to the extent of the landing at the mouth of the Peiho, and proceeding with the other plenipotentiaries to Tientsin, or, should it be necessary, even to the capital itself. In such case, I shall need the assistance of the naval commander in providing facilities for a landing, and protection by an adequate escort. During such operations, I hope it will be consistent with your views of duty to give me the benefit of your presence and of your intelligent counsel.

If the measures resorted to by the plenipotentiaries of Great Britain and France be of a hostile nature, and there be such active or passive resistance on the part of the Chinese as to renew the scenes which have occurred near Canton, it will, under the instructions which I have received, be my duty to withdraw from the neighborhood of such a conflict; and it has occurred to me that the treaty port of Nagasaki, Japan, would be the most convenient place, in the event to which I have referred, for the legation to retire to. This, however, I submit to your better judgment, merely adding that I wish to be in a position to enable me to return to the mouth of the Peiho after such hostilities shall be determined, or, in the event of my receiving further instructions, to be where I can threaten such coercion as the government may think themselves authorized to adopt, to enforce our rights against the Chinese.

In this connection, I inclose you a letter received by me a few weeks ago from his excellency Admiral Count Poutiatine, from which you will observe, in his opinion, the only months for efficient action in the northern waters of China, are the months of April and May, September and October.

I also send you the copy of a dispatch received by me yesterday from Count Poutiatine, containing some new revelations of the policy of his government. I do not know that any such communication has been made to Lord Elgin. In sending you this paper, which I do confidentially, you will understand that I seek your friendly counsel in the strange complication which this most peculiar people force upon us, and that I mean to have no secrets from you.

I have the honor to be, your most obedient servant,

WILLIAM B. REED.

Captain JOSIAH TATTNALL,
Flag-officer and Commander-in-chief, &c., &c.

Mr. Reed to Mr. Cass.

No. 12.] SHANGHAI, *April* 3, 1858.

SIR: I have an opportunity of sending by this mail the accompanying correspondence of Mr. Consul Perry, descriptive of the state of things at and near Canton. I am happy to observe the improved appearance of commercial affairs.

Since my dispatch of this morning (No. 11) was sealed, we have intelligence of the arrival at Woosung of the United States ship Mississippi.

This enables me to be ready at once to set out for the north.

I have the honor to be, sir, your most obedient servant,

WILLIAM B. REED.

Hon. LEWIS CASS,
Secretary of State, Washington.

UNITED STATES CONSULATE OF CANTON,
Whampoa, February 24, 1858.

SIR: I have the honor to inform your excellency, that in obedience to your instructions, I have hoisted my flag and established the consulate at Whampoa, on board of a small vessel chartered by myself.

The French consul, Mr. Le Baron de Tranqualhe, has hoisted his flag in Newtown, on the Island of Whampoa. He has a guard of French sailors stationed at his consulate for his protection.

The British vice-consul, Mr. Winchester, has hoisted his flag on Danes Island, on a tract of land leased by the English government, upon which I am informed he intends building a British vice-consulate and jail. Mr. Winchester at present lives afloat.

The general impression amongst the foreign merchants is, that trade will very soon be reopened; it will, however, be necessarily limited at first.

Everything here is apparently very quiet. I have been on shore several times, and have walked about a good deal, and have thus far found the Chinese civil and anxious to go to work and do business. No doubt there are some discontented ones ready to create disturbance and trouble, but I think that such a feeling, if it really exists, will gradually wear off when trade is fairly in its old channel.

I have the honor to be, sir, your most obedient servant,

OLIVER H. PERRY.

His Excellency WILLIAM B. REED,
United States Minister Plenipotentiary, &c., &c., &c.

UNITED STATES CONSULATE OF CANTON,
Whampoa, March 9, 1858.

SIR: I have the honor to inform your excellency that Mr. Le Baron de Tranqualhe, the French consul, and Mr. Charles Winchester, the British vice-consul, called upon me on the afternoon of the 2d instant, and stated that since their arrival at Whampoa, the conviction had been forced upon them that the consular functions with which they were invested could be exercised at Whampoa to much less advantage than at Honan, in the vicinity of Canton; that they had observed facts which left no doubt in their minds that a considerable settlement of the foreign community would speedily spring up in that locality; that at Whampoa it would be difficult for the consular officer, either to protect the interests or control the conduct of the parties under his jurisdiction; that at Whampoa, it was next to impossible to obtain the commercial and general information it falls within the province of a consular officer to furnish; that they expected to see in no long time, the attempt made by the mercantile consuls of non-treaty powers to hoist their flags and exercise consular functions at Honan; that they intended to address their respective chiefs, Lord Elgin and Baron Gros upon the subject, and ask permission to remove their consulates to Honan, and they hoped that I would join them and remove my consulate also to that locality, so that the three treaty consular flags might be displayed in one place.

I agreed entirely in the opinions expressed by these gentlemen, but told them I could not give them a positive answer at that time; that, although my instructions from you directed me to locate the consulate at Whampoa, still they were not of such a positive nature as to preclude my removing to Honan, should such a course become advisable or necessary, yet, in your absence, I should prefer consulting with Mr. Williams, the secretary of legation, before binding myself to any particular course in the matter.

I have consulted with Mr. Williams, and he agrees with me that it would be better to remove to Honan, should the English and French consuls remove, and has authorized me in case they do, to locate my consulate there also, should I still deem it advisable.

Lord Elgin, unfortunately, left Hong Kong for the north, on the very morning Mr. Vice-consul Winchester's dispatch was written, and consequently, it has not yet reached his excellency.

Baron Gros's reply to Mr. Consul Tranqualhe, is to the effect that the French having little trade at Canton, he does not care, in the absence of Lord Elgin, about taking the initiative step in the matter, although he has no personal objection to the French consulate being removed to Honan. I have reason to believe, however, that Sir John Bowring will authorize Mr. Consul Winchester to locate his consulate at Honan. In that case, the French consul will remove also.

I have informed Mr. Consul Tranqualhe and Mr. Vice-consul Winchester that I had authority from Mr. Secretary Williams to remove to Honan, should it become advisable so to do, but that I should not do so until they also had received authority to the same effect.

In connection with this subject, I would remark that the merchants complain of the hardship of being obliged to travel a distance of twelve miles and back, to obtain certificates required by law, such as certificates to invoices, certificates to enter and clear vessels, &c.

I have the honor to be, sir, your most obedient servant,

OLIVER H. PERRY.

His Excellency WILLIAM B. REED,
U. S. Minister Plenipotentiary, &c.

UNITED STATES CONSULATE OF CANTON,
Whampoa, March 12, 1858.

SIR: I have the honor to inform your excellency that it is reported, and generally believed here, that an imperial dispatch from Pekin has been received at Canton, and that Yeh has been degraded, and that Pihkwei, although reprimanded, has been promoted to the governor generalship of the province of Kwang-Tung. It is also rumored that a new imperial commissioner, named Hwang-Tsunghan has been appointed.

I have not the least doubt that these rumors and reports are true, as the guard that was stationed at Pihkwei's yamun has been withdrawn.

Foreigners are fast returning to Canton, and are locating themselves at Honan, on the side of the river opposite to Canton, and immediately opposite the site of the old foreign settlement. There they are free from the annoyances and restraints naturally resulting from martial law. All the habitable houses fronting on the river, and many in the rear, have been rented at exorbitant rates.

There is little trade as yet at Canton, but large shipments of tea and cassia, heretofore locked up in the pack-houses, in the vicinity of Canton, are being shipped by Chinamen to Hong Kong and Macao; in fact, all the steamers for those places leave full, the principal portion of the cargo being tea.

The Chinamen continue to reman quiet at Canton, as well as at this place.

I have the honor to be, sir, your most obedient servant,

OLIVER H. PERRY.

His Excellency WILLIAM B. REED,
United States Minister Plenipotentiary, &c.

LEGATION OF THE UNITED STATES,
Shanghai, March 29, 1858.

SIR: I am in receipt of your several letters directed to me at this place, where I arrived on the 24th instant. I entirely approve of the removal of the consulate further up the river than Whampoa. Lord Elgin informs me that he has written to Sir John Bowring to the same effect with the concurrence of Baron Gross who arrived here to-day.

Be so good as to continue the transmission of intelligence from Canton and its neighborhood. I am especially anxious to know where the new governor general is, and what has been his reception. I hope to set out for the north before long, but all letters may be addressed to me here.

I am, very respectfully, yours,

WILLIAM B. REED.

OLIVER H. PERRY, Esq.,
Vice-Consul of the United States, Canton.

Mr. Cass to Mr. Reed.

[Extract.]

No. 12.]

DEPARTMENT OF STATE,
Washington, June 25, 1858.

SIR: Your dispatches, to No. 12, have been received. The whole series has been read by the President with much gratification. Your views of Chinese affairs are interesting, and your suggestions entitled to much consideration. So impressed is the President with the value of your services to the country, under present circumstances, that it was with regret he learned it was your desire to return. Your wish, however, is so urgent that he assents to it, leaving the time to your own discretion, with this understanding, that he desires you would not leave until it is ascertained that no reasonable hopes of a prompt accommodation can be entertained. Prior to your departure you will of course transfer the archives of the legation to Mr. Williams, the secretary, who will act as chargé d'affaires till the arrival of your successor.

Our last information from China induces the belief that the results expected from the movement to Shanghai have not been realized, and that the squadrons are to be transferred to the Peiho river. You are already possessed of the views of the President respecting your coöperation with the representatives of the other powers, and those views are unchanged. It is understood that the instructions of the Russian minister correspondent in this respect with those you have received. The movements of your squadron along the Chinese coast are entirely within your discretion, taking care that it abstains from all hostile acts, except in case of self-defence, or in the protection of American citizens.

Your views of the commendable conduct of Commodore Tattnall, and your suggestions respecting his flag have been communicated to the Secretary of the Navy. I inclose a copy of the letter I addressed to him.

I inclose also a copy of the letter I wrote him, stating the wish you had suggested that you should be permitted to take passage in the Minnesota for Aden or the Cape of Good Hope, and expressing the hope that your application should be granted.

I have not yet received an answer from the Secretary to either of these applications, but I trust they will both be answered before this dispatch is closed, in which event, they shall be communicated to you.

I have delayed writing you for some time, expecting to receive the decision, submitted to the Attorney General, respecting the legality of the cooly trade, but the pressure upon the time of that officer has been such that he has not yet been able to furnish me with his opinion. As soon as it is received it shall be forwarded to you.

* * * * * * * * *

I am, sir, your obedient servant,

LEWIS CASS.

WILLIAM B. REED, Esq., *&c.*, *&c.*

Mr. Reed to Mr. Cass.

[Extract.]

No. 13.] LEGATION OF THE UNITED STATES,
Shanghai, April 10, 1858.

SIR: I am obliged by my approaching departure for the north to anticipate the next mail, and to send this letter in continuation of my dispatches, Nos. 11 and 12. The Mississippi is ready for sea, and I hope to sail in her day after to-morrow for the mouth of the Peiho. The frigate will be accompanied by the chartered steamer Antelope, and be followed, as soon as some necessary repairs are completed, by the Minnesota. The flag-officer sailed a few days ago in the San Jacinto for Hong Kong, where he hopes to meet the Powhatan and Germantown, and intends with them to join me in the north. Count Poutiatine sailed hence on the 7th, Lord Elgin goes to-day, and the French plenipotentiary follows as soon as the coaling of his ship is completed.

Mature consideration since the last mail went induced me to change the style of my replies to the provincial governors and the council of state at Pekin, and I now send copies of the papers actually transmitted, which I desire to be substituted for those accompanying my dispatch No. 11. (Inclosures 1 *a*, 1 *b*, 1 *c*.) With this you will receive also translations of the Chinese letters to Baron Gros, and of his reply, and that of Count Poutiatine, which they have communicated to me. In order to save time, trouble, and expense, they have all been forwarded through the Taoutae or intendant of this city. (Inclosures 2 *a*, 2 *b*, 2 *c*, 2 *d*, 2 *e*, 2 *f*, 2 *g*, 3 *a*, 3 *b*, 3 *c*, 4.) That functionary, a few days ago, sent me word through the consul that, if it was agreeable to me, he would pay me an official visit. On full consideration, under existing circumstances, I thought it best to decline to receive him; for I can see no advantage (certainly none ever accrued to my predecessors) from any facility of intercourse with these subordinate officials, while those of higher rank so persistently refuse to receive me. This decision was communicated by the consul in courteous though explicit terms, and I have heard nothing on the subject since. (Inclosure 1 *d.*)

* * * * * * * * *

I have the honor to be, sir, your obedient servant,

WILLIAM B. REED.

Hon. LEWIS CASS,
Secretary of State, Washington.

Exhibit 1 *a.*

To their Excellencies the Governor General of Kiangsu and Kiangsi and the Governor of Kiangsu, the Minister of the United States makes this communication:

He has received your excellencies' letter of the 21st March. It is wholly unsatisfactory, and he now incloses a reply which he desires your excellencies at once to forward to the supreme council of state of his Majesty the Emperor or his excellency Chancellor Yu.

WILLIAM B. REED.

LEGATION OF THE UNITED STATES,
April 1, 1858.

Exhibit 1 *b.*

LEGATION OF THE UNITED STATES,
April 1, 1858.

The undersigned, envoy extraordinary and minister plenipotentiary of the United States of America, has received from Ho, governor general of the two Kiangs, and Chau, Governor of Kiangsu, a letter containing what is described as a message from his excellency Chancellor Yu, stating that it would not be proper for him to reply in person to the undersigned, but directing the governor general and the governor to communicate his views.

This cannot be recognized by the undersigned as right and proper, or according to the treaties which his Majesty the Emperor has ratified and which the United States mean to insist on.

The undersigned, therefore, treats this message as no answer at all, and means to go at once to the Gulf of Pechele and mouth of the Peiho, accompanied by the great ships of his nation, and there demand access to the imperial court or the high officers, who are bound to correspond with him.

The undersigned further says that an indignity was done to a great and friendly power, in not sending to the representative of his Majesty the Emperor of Russia a direct and written answer to a respectful communication, and begs to add that hereafter he must not be asked to make a verbal communication to the minister of Russia, or any one else who has claims to more respectful consideration.

He further informs the supreme council that in the course he has prescribed for himself it is his intention to act in friendly and thorough concord with the plenipotentiaries of England, France, and Russia, whose interests in China entirely harmonize, and whose action, since the hostilities in Canton have been suspended, is strictly coöperative.

WILLIAM B. REED.

Exhibit 1 *c.*

NOTE TO THE TAOUTAE.

Desiring to deliver you an official letter addressed to the governor general of two Kiangs, I request you to receive to-morrow, at twelve o'clock, one of your officers, who will attend on you with the aforesaid letter.

I avail myself of this opportunity to express to you the wishes of continual happiness.

WILLIAM B. REED,
Envoy Extraordinary, &c., &c.

TAOUTAE'S ANSWER.

I have received the communication in which you, the honorable envoy and minister plenipotentiary, acquaint me that to-morrow, at twelve o'clock, you intend to send an officer to deliver me an official letter.

In consequence of this, I consider it my duty to wait at the appointed time the arrival of that officer.

I avail myself of this opportunity to wish you an uninterrupted happiness.

Exhibit 1 *d.*

SEE, Intendant of Soo, Sung, and Tai circuit, &c., makes the following communication:

In a conversation with you a few days since, you informed me that his excellency the minister plenipotentiary had arrived at Shanghai. I then requested you to address his excellency as to what day I would call and pay my respects; receiving no answer from you, I have to request that his excellency will name a day, and if you will communicate the same to me, I will be pleased to call on him.

UNITED STATES CONSULATE,
April 5, 1858.

I have the honor to acknowledge the receipt of your excellency's letter requesting me to appoint a day for you to call in person to pay your respects to his excellency Mr. Reed.

In answer to which I beg to state, that as his excellency Mr. Reed is so much pressed with official business at present, and expects to leave this in a few days, I shall have to postpone appointing a day until some future period.

I avail myself of this opportunity to convey to your excellency my best wishes for your happiness and prosperity.

I have the honor to be, very respectfully, yours,

GEORGE B. GLOVER,
United States Vice-Consul.

His Excellency SEE,
Taoutae, &c., &c.

Exhibit 2 *a.*

[Translation.]

SHANGHAI, *April* 3, 1858.

MONSIEUR LE MINISTRE: I have the honor to send herewith to your excellency the translation of a dispatch which the viceroy of the Two Kiang and the governor of this province have written me, in order to communicate to me the reply which the prime minister of the Emperor at Pekin has charged them to make to my dispatch of the 10th of February, a copy of which I then had the honor to send to your excellency.

In my dispatch to the prime minister, I demanded that a commissioner should be sent to Shanghai clothed with full powers to treat and to settle the questions to which I called his attention; and I intimated to him that if such a commissioner, having these powers, was not in Shanghai before the end of the month of March, I should then take such steps as appeared to me proper for the interests of the mission which is intrusted to me.

It is now the 3d day of April, and your excellency will see by the viceroy's dispatch that the contingency which I had hinted at has unfortunately been realized. I may remark to your excellency, further, that the Prime Minister Yu, in declaring that the laws of the empire forbid him to communicate directly with me, has, of his own private authority, annulled the 33d article of our treaty, which confirms in the most formal manner the right of the "high French authorities to correspond with the high Chinese officers in the capital or elsewhere, under the form of a dispatch or communication."

Under these circumstances, it becomes my duty immediately to repair to the north, in order there to be in more direct communication with the court at Pekin.

I shall inform the viceroy of the two Kiang and the governor of this province of my determination, and shall say to them that I prefer still to regard this indirect reply of the prime minister as a nullity and of no account, so as not to have a new subject of complaint against the Chinese government, which appears to make a mock of its most solemn engagements. I shall write in the same manner to the prime minister at Pekin, announcing my intended approach to the waters near the capital.

Such is the course of action which I propose to follow, and I hasten to make the same known to your excellency, as I shall also do to his excellency the imperial commissioner and commander-in-chief of the Russian naval forces in the China and Japan seas.

Be pleased, sir, to receive the assurances of my high consideration.

BARON GROS.

His Excellency WILLIAM B. REED,
Envoy Extraordinary and Minister Plenipotentiary of the United States of America.

Exhibit 2 b.

[Translation.]

The Governor General of the two Kiang to Baron Gros, in answer to his note sent to Pekin. Translated from Chinese into Portuguese, by M. Marquez, and from Portuguese into French.

Ho, by authority of the Great Tsing Dynasty, Second Guardian of the Heir Apparent, President of the Board of War, Governor General of the two Kiang, &c., &c., with CHAU, by authority of the Great Tsing Dynasty, Vice-President of the Board of War, Governor of Kiangsu, &c., &c., hereby make the following communication:

On the 23d day of the first moon of the eighth year of the reign Hien Fung, (February 26, 1758,) we received the dispatch of your excellency, dated 28th day of the twelfth moon of seventh year, (10th February, 1858,) accompanied by another dispatch addressed to the Minister of State Yu, which was placed under another envelope, and immediately forwarded to Pekin. We have now received a dispatch from the minister, in reply, to the following effect:

"I have examined the communication that you have sent me, As to the affair in the district of Si-lin, in the province of Kwangsi, the criminal judge of that province has, in pursuance of the orders received from the Imperial ex-Commissioner Yeh, made inquiry upon this matter, and has learned that the prisoner (the missionary Chapdelaine) was one of the Canton rebels named Ma-tsu-nung, who had been guilty of robbery and outrages, and was not the missionary Ma-cheu-fu. Besides this, there are foreign missionaries constantly found in the provinces, and they have all been transmitted to their consuls. If the said missionary has really been maltreated and actually put to death, how is it that, previous to this, there has never been an instance in which similar bad treatment has been inflicted?

"Since the late viceroy of the two Kwang, Yeh, has managed badly, a decree has been promulged degrading him, and appointing Hwang to the post of imperial commissioner, with injunctions to repair to Canton. Furthermore, it has never been the usage for imperial commissioners to go to Shanghai for the purpose of treating on any affair. The officers of the Celestial Empire have each their appropriate duties to perform, and none of them have violated the law which forbids them to hold communications with persons from abroad, which will explain why I cannot answer the French imperial commissioner directly, but through the medium of your excellencies. It is important that he should be made acquainted with what I have remarked. If I act in this manner, it assuredly is not with the intention of not replying to him."

Having thus referred to this dispatch, it is proper also to observe to your excellency that when the communication to which it is a reply was sent from Canton, it was not there known that his Majesty the Emperor had designated Hwang, the new viceroy of the two Kwang, as imperial commissioner, who had received his orders to proceed to Canton, there to inquire into and arrange affairs; and it was to apprise you of this decision that the dispatch [of the prime minister] was written. As the imperial commissioner and viceroy of the two Kwang has already left for Canton, it behooves us to inform your excellency of it, that you may know how to act in consequence, and that we may go on to obtain the result sought.

We desire at the same time to wish your excellency every possible happiness.

As I am at this time in Changchau, I have inserted only my official titles in this dispatch, not being able to affix my seal to it.

A special communication.

The foregoing dispatch is addressed to his excellency Kó (le Baron Gros,) high imperial commissioner, specially appointed from the empire of France embassador extraordinary invested with full powers, a hereditary baron.

Hien Fung, eighth year, seventh day of the second moon, (21st March, 1858.)

Exhibit 2 *c.*

LEGATION OF THE UNITED STATES,
Shanghai, April 5, 1858.

MONSIEUR LE BARON: I had the honor of forwarding to your excellency, a few days ago, under a blank envelope, a translation of the letter received by me from the governor general of the two Kiang, and the governor of the province.

I have since received your excellency's note of the 3d instant, covering a translation of a dispatch addressed to you by the same functionaries, and explaining the course which you mean to pursue.

I now send to you copies of the letters which I have addressed, in reply to the governor general and the governor, and the minister Yu, or the supreme council of state, and from them your excellency will perceive my view of the present complication of affairs; and it is a matter of great gratification to me, as I am sure it will be to the President, that there is so close a concurrence of opinion and intention between us.

I beg further to remark to your excellency, what may not be without its interest to you, that the right of direct correspondence which I claim with the high officers at Pekin, is a derivative one from the treaty between France and China, negotiated by Monsieur de Lagréné, in October, 1844, and the article (article 2) of the treaty of the United States, which provides that, if additional privileges, of whatever description, should be thereafter conceded by China to any other nation, the United States shall be entitled to a complete, equal, and impartial participation in the same.

Indebted, therefore, as I feel my country to be to some extent to the agency of France for this right under the letter of treaties, I have especial pleasure in uniting with you as the representative of his Majesty the Emperor, in an urgent claim for their honest fulfillment.

I beg your excellency to accept anew the assurance of my most distinguished consideration and regard.

I have the honor to be, Monsieur le Baron, your excellency's most obedient servant,

WILLIAM B. REED.

His Excellency M. LE BARON GROS,
Commissioner Extraordinary and Embassador of His Majesty the Emperor of the French in China.

Exhibit 2 *d.*

[Translation.]

Shanghai, April 6, 1858.

MONSIEUR LE MINISTRE: I have received the letter which your excellency did me the honor to address me, inclosing copies of the communications which you proposed to send to the governor general of the two Kiang, and to the governor of Kiangsu, as also of that to the Prime Minister Yu, or to the supreme council of state, in answer to the communications your excellency had received from those high functionaries, of which you had already sent me translations under cover.

I thank your excellency for these important documents; and I am sure that my government will perceive with the same satisfaction that I have myself had, that your excellency joins your efforts to ours in order to obtain from the court of Pekin the faithful execution of treaties.

I hasten, on my part, to transmit to your excellency a copy of the replies which I have this day sent to the high Chinese officials in question; and I shall be ready to start for the north as soon as the frigate "l'Audacieuse," which arrived yesterday at Wusung, shall be ready for sea.

I have the honor to be, sir, your excellency's very humble and obedient servant,

BARON GROS.

His Excellency WILLIAM B. REED,
Envoy Extraordinary and Minister Plenipotentiary of the United States of America to China.

Exhibit 2 *e.*

[Translation.]

SHANGHAI, *April* 6, 1858.

Baron GROS to the Governor General of the two Kiang and to the Governor of Kiangsu.

The undersigned, high commissioner of his Imperial Majesty the Emperor of the French in China, &c., &c., has received the communication which their excellencies Ho, viceroy of the two Kiang, &c., and Chau, governor of Kiangsu, &c., have done him the honor to address him, on the 21st of March last, in order to transmit the reply which his excellency the prime minister wished to make, through their mediation, to the dispatch which the undersigned had addressed to him directly, on the 10th of February last.

This mode of procedure constitutes a flagrant violation of the thirty-third article of the treaty with France, in which it is said "that hereafter the official correspondence between the officers and the functionaries of the two countries shall be regulated according to their rank and respective position, upon the basis of entire reciprocity; and that this correspondence shall be conducted between the high officers of France and the high officers of China, at the capital and elsewhere, by the term dispatch or communication."

The undersigned desires, however, in a spirit of conciliation, at present, simply to declare that he formally refuses to accept from the prime minister the indirect answer that has been transmitted to him, and that he regards it as a nullity and nothing worth, (*non avenue et de nulle valeur.*) At the same time, he begs their excellencies to do him the favor to forward to the prime minister of the Emperor, at Pekin, the inclosed dispatch, in which he informs him that the undersigned, having waited in vain for a Chinese plenipotentiary to reach Shanghai before the 1st of April, there to treat amicably with him, as he had demanded in the name of his government, intends to repair to the north immediately, there to communicate with more ease and quickness with the high officers at the capital.

The undersigned avails himself of this opportunity to wish their excellencies the highest happiness.

BARON GROS.

Exhibit 2 *f.*

[Translation.]

SHANGHAI, *April* 6, 1858.

Baron GROS to the Prime Minister of the Emperor at Pekin.

The undersigned, high commissioner of his Imperial Majesty the Emperor of the French in China, &c., &c., has received from their excellencies Ho, the viceroy of the two Kiang, &c., and Chau, governor of Kiangsu, &c., the communication which they have done him the honor to address him, on the 21st of March last, in order to convey to him the reply which his excellency the prime minister of the Emperor of China has deemed it proper to make to the dispatch which the undersigned addressed to him directly, on the 10th of February last.

If his excellency the prime minister will have the goodness to reperuse the thirty-third article of the treaty with France, he will there see "that the official correspondence between the authorities and functionaries of the two countries is to be regulated according to their respective ranks and positions, on the basis of entire reciprocity; and that this correspondence shall be conducted between the high officers of France and those of China, at the capital or elsewhere, under the form of dispatch or communication."

In the face of such a formal stipulation, and one obligatory upon all Chinese functionaries, how is it possible for his excellency the prime minister to refuse all correspondence with the undersigned; and how has he been able to bring himself to declare that it is from a principle, religiously observed by Chinese officers, which forbids them to hold communication with strangers, that he has not found it proper to answer the undersigned directly? Without wishing to qualify a course of action which the undersigned does not comprehend, he here confines himself to a formal declaration to his excellency the prime minister, that the reply which he has deemed proper to have transmitted to him is regarded as a nullity and nothing worth; but that still, in a spirit of conciliation, he does not intend to bring it up as a new grievance, for which he shall demand redress.

The undersigned further remarks that the date of April 1, which had been fixed by him as the limit for receiving a satisfactory reply to his communication of the 10th of February, having passed by without any Chinese plenipotentiary having reached Shanghai to negotiate and settle in a friendly manner the differences now existing between the two empires, as the undersigned had demanded in the name of his own government, he regains immediately his liberty of action, and shall repair to the north, there to be able to communicate directly and without loss of time with the high officers of the imperial government of Pekin.

The undersigned takes this opportunity to wish his excellency the prime minster every happiness.

This communication is of great importance.

BARON GROS.

Exhibit 2 *g*.

LEGATION OF THE UNITED STATES,
Shanghai, *April* 7, 1858.

MONSIEUR LE BARON: I have the honor to acknowledge the receipt of your excellency's letter of the 6th, with its inclosures. I beg you to accept my thanks for them.

I hope to be ready to proceed northward on Saturday next, in the United States ship Mississippi, to be followed in a short time by the rest of the American squadron.

Your excellency's dispatches for the consulate at Hong Kong were duly forwarded.

I have the honor to be, Monsieur le Baron, your excellency's most obedient servant,

WILLIAM B. REED.

His Excellency M. LE BARON GROS,
Commissioner Extraordinary and Embassador of His Majesty the Emperor of the French in China, &c.

Exhibit 3 *a.*

SHANGHAI, *April* 5, 1858.

SIR: Our frequent and unreserved communications dispense me from making any comments on the note which has been prepared by me to be sent to the dignitary Yu, at Pekin, in answer to his notification contained in the letter addressed to your excellency by the governor general of Kiangnan, and to inform you of the course I am going to pursue in consequence of it.

Having the honor to inclose the aforesaid note for your perusal, I remain, with assurances of my high consideration and esteem, your excellency's most humble servant,

C. POUTIATINE.

His Excellency the Hon. W. B. REED,
Envoy Extraordinary, &c., &c.

Exhibit 3 *b.*

Draft of a note to be addressed to the dignitary Yu.

SHANGHAI, *April*, 1858.

The decided persistence of the supreme government at Pekin in refusing to give becoming answers to the communications made to it by the representatives of foreign powers, induces the Russian plenipotentiary to address that government once more, and to insist on altering this usage, offensive to other States, and contrary to the best interests of China itself.

The council of state, or properly its senior member, the dignitary Yu, leaving without a direct answer the letter sent by the undersigned, and adopting a method of communicating with him through the governor general Kiangnan, and then in a letter addressed to the American minister, has not acted according to the rules observed by civilized nations in their intercourse with each other.

In referring the Russian plenipotentiary to proceed to the river

Amoor, and pointing solely to the frontier question, the dignitary Yu keeps a total silence on the other demands made by the undersigned, conjointly with the representatives of America, France, and England, for forming more solid and closer ties with China, and thus leaves the principal question without any answer.

In consequence of this, the Russian plenipotentiary finds it necessary to declare that in endeavoring not to break up the friendly relations so long existing between Russia and China, he will, however, conjointly with the plenipotentiaries of other States, firmly insist on adopting by the Chinese government in their principal features the three articles mentioned in the former communication made to the supreme council of state.

Therefore having now come to an understanding with the Representatives of the three other powers, the undersigned will proceed immediately to the north, in order to come nearer to the capital, and to put himself in more direct relations with the supreme government at Pekin.

Exhibit 3 *c.*

LEGATION OF THE UNITED STATES,
Shanghai, April 7, 1858.

SIR: I have the honor to forward to your excellency drafts of the letters which I propose to send to the governor general of the two Kiang, and the governor of Kiangsu, and to the council of state.

I avail myself of the opportunity to say that I hope to be able to proceed on Saturday next to the north, in the United States steamer Mississippi, leaving the Minnesota here to complete some repairs, and to follow me after the arrival of the next mail from the United States.

If your excellency can make any use of her in bringing your letters north, I am sure it willgive Captain Du Pont great pleasure to promote your wishes.

I have the honor to be, sir, your excellency's most obedient servant,

WILLIAM B. REED.

His Excellency the COUNT POUTIATINE,
Imperial Commissioner and Commander-in-chief, &c.

Exhibit 4.

LEGATION OF THE UNITED STATES,
Shanghai, April 7, 1858.

MY LORD: I had the honor to communicate to you last week the drafts of two notes which I proposed to send to the governor general of the two Kiang and the governor of Kiangsu, and to the council of state at Pekin.

I was led, on mature consideration, to change the form of these letters, and I have now the honor to send to your excellency copies of those I have subtituted, and which I shall to-morrow send to the taoutae of Shanghai.

I avail myself of the opportunity to say that I hope to be able to proceed on Saturday next to the north, in the United States steamer Mississippi, leaving the Minnesota here to complete some repairs, and to follow me after the arrival of the next mail from the United States. If your excellency can make use of her in bringing your letters north, I am sure it will give Captain Du Pont great pleasure to promote your wishes.

I have the honor to be, my lord, your excellency's most obedient servant,

WILLIAM B. REED.

His Excellency the Earl of ELGIN AND KINCARDINE,
Her Britannic Majesty's High Commissioner, &c.

Exhibit 5 *a.*

[Translation.]

SHANGHAI, *April* 9, 1858.

MY DEAR SIR: I send you herewith the two documents of which I spoke to you; and, as I have no duplicates of them, I beg of you to have the goodness to return them to me when you have made a copy or a translation of them, if you desire to do so.

I need hardly remark to you that there would be some inconvenience in making them public, and that I send them to you confidentially.

With many compliments, very truly,

BARON GROS.

MR. REED.

N. B. The two documents referred to are merely duplicate translations, only one of which is now forwarded.

Mr. Reed to Mr. Cass.

No. 15.] LEGATION OF THE UNITED STATES,
On board the Minnesota, Gulf of Pechele, April 28, 1858.

SIR: The Mississippi anchored here on the 17th instant, and I have remained on board of her until to-day, when the legation has been again removed to this ship. I am much indebted to Captain Nicholson and his officers for great kindness.

A large portion of the English and French squadrons is now at this anchorage. The Russian, English, and French plenipotentiaries have arrived.

This afternoon a communication has been forwarded to me announcing the appointment of an imperial commissioner for the purpose of negotiation, and his arrival near the mouth of the Peiho. He has asked an interview on shore with Count Poutiatine to-morrow, and with me the next day. No positive answer has yet been sent, in consequence of an informality in the address of the letter which I am advised must not be unnoticed. Lord Elgin and Baron Gros have absolutely refused to receive those addressed to them. I thought it best to return the letter, and request that what I chose to consider a clerical error should be corrected. I believe it will be done.

I regret that the very sudden dispatch of the British steamer prevents me adding to this letter copies of one or two documents properly belonging to it. They are, however, of little interest, and shall be forwarded by the next mail.

I have the honor to be, sir, your obedient servant,

WILLIAM B. REED.

Hon. LEWIS CASS,
Secretary of State.

Mr. Reed to Mr. Cass.

No. 16.] LEGATION OF THE UNITED STATES,
On board the Minnesota, Gulf of Pechele, May 6, 1858.

SIR: In my last dispatch (No. 15) I informed you of my having reached this anchorage, and that it was believed an imperial commissioner had been appointed with powers to treat. I now give you the details of what has occurred from the time of my arrival until now. They are interesting, and may be important, though I fear the immediate results, in consequence of the course of policy which the representatives of England and France seem to think it their duty to pursue, may not be such as I hoped for. They are, however, yet too undeveloped to authorize me to express an absolute opinion.

On my arriving off the Peiho, on the 17th of April, I found Count Poutiatine and Lord Elgin here. No other available military force had come than the British steamer Furious, the frigate Pique, the Cormorant, armed dispatch vessel, and one gun-boat. On the 20th, the Audacieuse, with Baron Gros on board, accompanied by a gunboat, and on the 24th the Calcutta, a line-of-battle ship, carrying the flag of Admiral Seymour, and a steamer, came in, and on the next day the French squadron of one frigate and five steamers. On the 26th the Minnesota arrived.

Until the 23d, although our personal intercourse was friendly, and as constant as the state of the weather permitted, nothing of an official character passed between the English and French plenipotentiaries and myself, and little in the way of conversation on public affairs.

On the 23d, Lord Elgin and Baron Gros simultaneously addressed to Count Poutiatine and myself notes, (inclosures 1 *a*, 1 *b*, 1 *c*, 1 *d*, 1 *e*,) informing us that they meant to send another communication to the authorities at Pekin, demanding the appointment of a minister duly authorized to treat at Takoo, a place just within the mouth of the Peiho, and allowing six days as the limit of time for that purpose. Baron Gros merely announced to me that he meant to send such a demand. Lord Elgin said that if I thought fit to adopt the same course, it would, in his opinion, add to the weight of the representations. I did not hesitate, but prepared and dispatched a similar communication to Pekin. (Inclosure No. 2 *a*.) Count Poutiatine did the same thing, though you will observe in his letter (inclosure 2 *c*) earnest expressions of anxiety that no new obstacle should be interposed by the Chinese to preliminary negotiation, and a reference to the fact that high functionaries of some sort had arrived—a fact, in consequence of our distance from the shore, not before known to either Lord Elgin, Baron Gros, or myself.

On the 26th, I received a communication (inclosure No. 3 *d*) from Tsung Lun and Wu, two high officers, advising me of their arrival at Tientsin, deputed by the Emperor "to investigate and manage," acknowledging the receipt and dispatch of the letters of the 24th, but deferring any further action till on them the imperial will was known. This seemed proper, and no answer was sent or needed. Tsung Lun was the imperial commissioner who received Mr. McLane and Sir John Bowring in 1854.

From the 24th to the 30th, the six days fixed by the letters, not one word passed between the English and French plenipotentiaries and myself, and the time expired without conference of any kind. It was not for me to suggest it, though I began to feel that such reserve had its inconveniences.

On the 28th, a letter came addressed to each of the plenipotentiaries, announcing the appointment of a special imperial commissioner. It was observed by those familiar with Chinese forms, that in the address of the communication there was a derogatory informality in the word *China* being unduly elevated above the nation addressed, which, it was suggested, ought not to pass unnoticed. Count Poutiatine thought it best to pay no attention to it, and received the letter. The French and English ministers absolutely rejected theirs ; but my secrecary of legation, Mr. Williams, in whose judgment on such matters I have great confidence, and to whom it was brought during my accidental absence from the ship, thought best to read the letter, and then return it, with a direction that the clerical mistake (as he thought it best to consider it) must be corrected, or no notice would be taken of its contents.

On the 30th it was brought back in due form and received. (Inclosure No. 4.) You will observe that appended to it is a postcript, by which the idea of clerical mistake was adopted with great facility.

Down to this point of time, the morning of the 30th, I had, as I have said, received no intimation of the intentions of the English and French, though on the previous day their whole available force, consisting of six light draft but heavily armed steamers, several of which had arrived in the interval, had crossed the bar and anchored close to the Chinese batteries. Count Poutiatine, whose ship was anchored much nearer in than the others, had landed, and met the new imperial commissioner on the 29th, and was in actual conference with him when the armed ships came in. He describes the scene as one of great excitement, mingled indignation, and alarm; and it was only through the Russian minister's earnest intercession that the Chinese were dissuaded from the madness of firing on the ships, and beginning hostilities, of which, of course, they would be the first victims.

The invasion of the men-of-war, you will observe, was within the six days allowed to the Chinese. Of all this I was, I confess, an anxious and by no means contented observer.

Had I no other reason for approaching still nearer to the place designated for negotiation, I found ample ones in the rank of the new commissioner, the highest of the governors general, and of the second of the nine official ranks in the empire, and in the perfectly courteous and respectful tone of his communication, and also in the fact that I had said I should come on this day. I took for granted it was the intention of the English and French ministers to go in, and did not dream of the new scruple as to the technical full powers of the commissioner not being exhibited in advance.

I left the Minnesota at two o'clock in the afternoon of the 30th, and embarking with my suit and a small escort on board the chartered steamer Antelope, crossed the bar; that ship anchoring in the river as close to Takoo as the position of the English and French steamers admitted.

In view of the peculiar state of things around us, the Russian minister, who entered the river at the same time with me, and I had exchanged letters of mutual explanation, the tone of which, so far as I took part in it, I hope the President will approve. You will find a number of letters between us, which, though some of them were originally private notes, too well explain our views to be omitted. (Inclosures No. 5, 11 *a*, 6 *a*, 6 *b*, and 6 *c*.)

You will observe that in the communication of his excellency Tau, the new commissioner, he courteously expressed a wish that I should notify him of the time for an interview, "in order," he says, "that the minister of the United States may be properly received." Early on the next day, two Chinese officers came on board the Antelope, desiring to know my pleasure as to the time of reception, and urging that it might not be delayed. My answer addressed to the commissioner is inclosed. (Inclosure No. 7.)

That answer reveals some of the perplexity which I felt at the apparent want of concert and confidence (and it applies with equal force to the Russian minister) on the part of Lord Elgin and Baron Gros, and at finding the ship, on board of which I was, in the close neighborhood of others whose threatening intentions could not be mistaken. Still, determined that no want of courtesy should be attributed to me, I gave the answer to the commissioner, and at once sent a copy to the English and French ministers. On the same evening, and I believe only in consequence of my letter, I received from Lord Elgin and Baron Gros their communications. (Inclosures No. 7*b*, 7 *c*, and 7 *k*.)

From them, I learned the new difficulty which had arisen as to the absence of a proffer of what, in the language of western diplomacy, is known as "full powers," by the Chinese plenipotentiary. I had no hesitation as to my own course, and was gratified to find that, in the view which I took of the duty imposed on me as the representative of a friendly and neutral power, I had now the thorough concurrence of Count Poutiatine, to whose earnest and honest efforts to avert difficulty I can hardly do justice. I forward, with this dispatch, notes addressed by him to the allied ministers, copies of which he furnished to me, which show his feelings and opinions on this subject. (Inclosures 6 *a*, 6 *b*, and 6 *d*.)

It seemed to me that, when an officer of high rank announced himself as specially deputed by his sovereign "to deliberate seriously concerning the affairs" at issue, it would have been a mischievous punctilio that prevented me from at least meeting him, and then ascertaining the precise extent of his functions. I had not, last year, asked Yeh for the production of "full powers" antecedent to the interview which I demanded, and I saw no reason for making it a condition precedent to an interview now. Besides, I could not persuade myself that the technical rules of western diplomacy should be asserted against this strange people.

The circumstances attending the ineffectual conference of Mr. McLane and Sir John Bowring, in 1854, to which Lord Elgin referred, were different. Then, powers of any kind were disclaimed. Here, at least, modified full powers are claimed.

Taking this view of my duty, I landed at the Takoo forts on the afternoon of the 3d, accompanied by Mr. Williams, the secretary of legation, my interpreters, and a number of officers from the Minnesota and Mississippi. I will not trouble you with the ceremonial details of this conference, but need only say that, according to the testimony of the gentlemen accompanying me, who were familiar with Chinese ceremonial, every courtesy was extended, and every form complied with that was due to my position and rank.

I send a summary of the interview, (inclosure 8,) prepared by the secretary of legation, which is substantially correct. The results were these: that, while technical full powers in writing were not delegated to Tau, he had power to discuss and agree to a treaty, to be referred in the aggregate, though without signature, to the capital. Of course, in admitting this to be sufficient as a preliminary, I assumed that he told the truth. But, in this assumption, and to guard against the probable disingenuousness that characterizes Chinese diplomacy, I thought it best to exact some evidence that the commissioner had what he professed—direct official relations to Pekin. I therefore demanded that my letter to the imperial government, from the south of China should be produced, and some assurance given, in an official form, that the letter of the President to the Emperor would be properly, and on terms of equality, received and acknowledged. Both these assurances were given, and five days agreed upon for that end. I announced to his excellency, at the expiration of that time, my intention to meet him again. The interview, though in some measure of the character of an introduction, was satisfactory. At all events, it put me in personal relations to the highest accredited representative of the empire. (Inclosures 8 and 12 *c*.)

I returned to this ship at the outer anchorage the next day, and my first duty, as it seemed to me, was to address to the ministers of Great Britain and France as earnest a dissuasive as I could with propriety send them of a precipitate resort to hostilities.

Such hostilities I especially dread. I have seen enough already of war in China to make me think of it simply with disgust. It is the bloody warfare of the strong and the weak. It is war which afflicts individuals, disturbs trade, and produces no results. Limited to any extent, and I yet believe, as at Canton so here, there will be no willful aggravation of inevitable suffering, it is very dreadful; and the idea of forcing access to Pekin by the exertion of military power is to me utterly repulsive. I fear as a matter of strategy it will be a failure. The letter which I have addressed to Lord Elgin and Baron Gros (inclosure 9 *a*) is meant to be an appeal from any rash judgment which the perversity of this peeple may have precipitated. It is written, I trust, in a spirit of friendliness, and, as you will observe from the answers just received, (inclosures 9 *b*, 9 *d*,) is so acknowledged.

The English and French plenipotentiaries have made a new demand and allowed a further suspension of hostilities. (Inclosures 9 *c*, 9 *e*.)

Coincident with this, the Chinese have made a direct effort to secure the good offices of the Russian plenipotentiary and myself to bring about a settlement. The correspondence on this subject, so far as it has gone, explains itself. (Inclosures 12 *a*, 12 *b*, 12 *c*.)

I repeat the expression of the earnest hope that the President will approve the effort we are making to avert further troubles from this afflicted and disorganized empire.

I have the honor to be, sir, your obedient servant,

WILLIAM B. REED.

Hon. LEWIS CASS,
Secretary of State, Washington.

Inclosure 1 *a*.

HER MAJESTY'S SHIP FURIOUS,
Gulf of Pechele, April 23, 1858.

SIR: I inclose for your excellency's information the copy of a note which I propose to send to-morrow to the prime minister of the Emperor of China, and the copy of a letter to the governor general of Chihli, through whom it is my intention to transmit the former to its destination.

I have reason to believe that Baron Gros is about to make a similar communication to the prime minister; and should your excellency see fit to adopt the same course, it will no doubt add to the weight of our representations.

I have the honor to be your excellency's most obedient, humble servant,

ELGIN AND KINCARDINE.

His Excellency the Hon. W. B. REED,
&c., &c., &c.

Inclosure 1 *b*.

HER MAJESTY'S SHIP FURIOUS,
April 24, 1858.

In a letter bearing date the 1st instant and written from Shanghai, the undersigned had the honor to apprise the prime minister, &c., that the prime minister having, by refusing to correspond directly with the undersigned, set the provisions of the treaty between Great Britain and China at naught, the undersigned had resolved to proceed at once to the north, in order that he might place himself in more immediate communication with the high officers of the imperial government at the capital.

He has now to state that in pursuance of the above intimation he has arrived off the mouth of the Tientsin river, and that he is prepared to meet at Takoo, either on board of his own ship or on shore, a minister duly authorized by the Emperor of China to treat with him and to settle by negotiation the several questions affecting the relations of Great Britain with China, which are detailed in a letter of the undersigned to the prime minister bearing date February 11.

If before the expiration of six days from the date of the present communication a minister so accredited shall not have presented himself at Takoo, the undersigned will consider this pacific overture to have been rejected, and deem himself thenceforward at liberty to adopt such further measures for enforcing the just claims of his government on that of China as he may think expedient.

HER MAJESTY'S SHIP FURIOUS,
Off the Port of Takoo, April, 1858.

The undersigned has the honor to request that his excellency Tau, governor general of the province of Chihli, will transmit to the capital, at his earliest convenience, the inclosed dispatch to the address of his excellency Yu, senior chief secretary of state.

Compliments.

FURIOUS, *April* 23, 1858.

MY DEAR MR. REED: I intend to dispatch Baron Gros's note and mine from this ship to the shore at eight a. m. to-morrow morning. If you like to avail yourself of that opportunity, I shall be happy to forward with them any letter which you may send on board the Furious before that hour.

Yours, very faithfully,
ELGIN AND KINCARDINE.

His Excellency Mr. REED, *&c., &c.*

Inclosure 1 *c.*

[Translation.]

ON BOARD THE AUDACIEUSE,
Off the Peiho, April 23, 1858.

MR. MINISTER: I have the honor to send herewith to your excellency a copy of the note which I propose to write to the prime minister at

Pekin, and which I shall transmit to him through the medium of the governor general of the province of Chihli, to whom I direct it.

This note will bear date the 24th of this month, and the time allowed for answer to be made to it will expire on the 30th.

I embrace this occasion to renew to your excellency the assurance of my sentiments of high consideration.

BARON GROS.

His Excellency Mr. WILLIAM B. REED,
Envoy Extraordinary and Minister Plenipotentiary of the United States of America, in China, &c.

[Translation.]

ON BOARD THE AUDACIEUSE,
Off the Peiho, April 24, 1858.

The undersigned hastens to announce to his excellency that, conformably to what he had the honor to write to him in a dispatch forwarded from Shanghai on the 6th of this month, he has just arrived at the mouth of the Peiho, there to await the plenipotentiary of rank equal to his, and furnished with sufficient powers, whom it may please his Majesty the Emperor to appoint, in order to treat and to arrange amicably the differences which unhappily exist between the two empires, and which both have a powerful interest in causing to disappear.

The negotiations could take place at Takoo, either on board of one of our vessels, which would go there, or on shore in the place in which there might be a plenipotentiary duly accredited by the Emperor of China.

The undersigned will wait six days longer, counting from the date of the present communication, for a satisfactory answer to be made to him; but, if at the expiration of this delay a Chinese plenipotentiary shall not have come to meet him, he will consider himself as having experienced a refusal, and will adopt thenceforward such measures as may appear to him suitable for causing to be allowed at last the just claims which the Empire of France has addressed to the Chinese government.

Let the supreme council of the empire not deceive itself. It is no longer at Canton that negotiations can take place. The imperial commissioners who have been sent thither have never presented to the supreme government of the empire in their true light affairs relative to the great foreign powers, and it is to their interest, as it is to that of China, that, after the example of the great civilized nations of the West, the representatives of foreign sovereigns should be able to communicate directly with the supreme government of the empire. This is the best means of reëstablishing good harmony between the two nations and of maintaining it forever.

The present events would not have taken place if this measure of high wisdom had been adopted long since.

The undersigned embraces this occasion, &c.

His Excellency YU,
Prime Minister of the Emperor, at Pekin.

Inclosure 1 *d.*

[Translation.]

AUDACIEUSE, *April* 23, 1858.

MY DEAR MR. REED: I send you a copy of my note to the prime minister. It will leave to-morrow at eight o'clock with that of Lord Elgin. M. de Bellecourt will go to-morrow morning at eight o'clock with my note on board the Furious, and will attend to its delivery. Lord Elgin requests me to notify you, as on his part he notifies Count Poutiatine; and, if you wish to profit by this opportunity, he will send your note with pleasure. It would be well, I think, that all four should arrive together, no matter how.

A thousand earnest compliments on the part of your affectionate servant,

BARON GROS.

Inclosure 1 *e.*

MISSISSIPPI, *April* 23, 1858.

MY DEAR LORD ELGIN: I had accidentally, in the course of the day, heard of your intention to send another note to Pekin, and told Baron Gros in the afternoon that, if my concurrence in this step were desired, there should be no delay on my part. Not hearing from you till a late hour, I made an arrangement of boats with Count Poutiatine, and am therefore unable to avail myself of your kind offer.

Very faithfully yours,

W. B. REED.

Inclosure 2 *a.*

UNITED STATES STEAM FRIGATE MISSISSIPPI,
Off the Peiho, April 24, 1858.

The high authorities at the capital of his Majesty the Emperor of China, having refused to correspond with the minister of the United States, as by treaty they were bound to do, or to send a plenipotentiary to Shanghai to meet him, no alternative has been left to the minister but to come to the mouth of the Tientsin river, and, meeting no plenipotentiary there, to endeavor to approach still nearer to the presence of the emperor himself. He is now here with that intent. But, anxious to be the means of averting trouble from the empire, and to offer anew his good offices, he again addresses his excellency, and urgently asks for the immediate appointment of a plenipotentiary to arrange all matters fit for negotiation. If on or before the last day of this month such a plenipotentiary shall present himself at or near Takoo, where the undersigned means to be, there will yet be room for peaceful preliminary negotiation. If not, the undersigned shall regard the refusal as indicative of a hostile feeling on the part of the imperial authorities, which will preclude all good offices, and leave the government of the United States and its representative at liberty to seek redress by other means, and to approach still nearer to the capital if he deems it expedient to do so.

W. B. REED.

UNITED STATES SHIP MISSISSIPPI,
April 24, 1858.

The undersigned has the honor to request that his excellency Tau, governor general of the province of Chihli, will transmit to the capital at his earliest convenience, the inclosed dispatch to the address of his excellency Yu, senior chief secretary of state.

Compliments,

WILLIAM B. REED.

His Excellency TAU,
Governor General of Chihli.

LEGATION OF THE UNITED STATES,
On board the Mississippi, April 24, 1858.

MY LORD: I have the honor to acknowledge the receipt of your excellency's note of 23d, and to inclose to you the copy of a note which I have to-day addressed to the prime minister and council of state at Pekin.

I am, my lord, your excellency's obedient servant,

WILLIAM B. REED.

His Excellency the Earl of ELGIN AND KINCARDINE, *&c., &c., &c.*

The same note to Baron Gros.

Inclosure 2 b.

LEGATION OF THE UNITED STATES,
United States Ship Mississippi, April 24, 1858.

MONSIEUR LE COUNT: I have the honor to inclose to you the copy of a note addressed by me to the prime minister and high council of state at Pekin, and forwarded this morning. This, as you are aware, has been done in accordance with a suggestion made by their excellencies Lord Elgin and Baron Gros, in which, though the course was decided on without conference with either of us, it was your opinion we had better acquiesce. My own impression is, that had their excellencies, who unfortunately occupy a quasi-belligerent attitude, been as well prepared for action as we believe ourselves to be, this suggestion would not have been made, but the first occasion seized of entering the river and personally demanding the presence of a plenipotentiary. Still, I entirely agree with your excellency that it is best for us to continue to act in concord when a course that our judgment approves even seems to be prescribed to us. I need scarcely say how much more satisfaction I have—and it is a feeling which I am sure will be shared in by my government—in the "really frank and unreserved confidence" which exists between us.

I was much gratified to learn yesterday from Baron Ostensacken, that a proposition of some kind for conference with your excellency had been made, or was about to be made, from the authorities on shore. It is the first symptom of a proper policy on the part of the Chinese, and some indication that they distinguish between those who have been friends and those who have not. Should a proposition for negotiation be made, and it assume the form of separate conference, it occurs to me that a precedence may well be claimed and yielded to us, as the representatives of strictly neutral and pacific governments.

I have the honor to be, Monsieur le Count, your excellency's most obedient servant,

WILLIAM B. REED.

His Excellency COUNT POUTIATINE,
&c., &c., &c.

Inclosure 2 c.

Translation of the note addressed to the senior member of the supreme council of state, the dignitary Yu, on the 24th of April, 1858, steamer America, at the mouth of the river Peiho:

The plenipotentiary of Russia has received with pleasure the information conveyed to him yesterday of the arrival of two high functionaries from Pekin, for the purpose of opening negotiations with him. On his own part, he is ready without loss of time to enter into communication with the aforesaid functionaries, but finds it needful to apply once more, with a request to the dignitary Yu, that an immediate appointment should be made of some high personages duly accredited to treat on subjects of general interest with the representatives of all the powers that have made known their demands to the cabinet of Pekin.

By mutual consent of all the plenipotentiaries, the place of Takoo has been found convenient for the preliminary negotiations, and the term of six days from this date is accounted sufficient to await the arrival of the expected high dignitaries from Pekin.

The undersigned, moved with a sincere desire to ward off the calamity that threatens China, earnestly requests the dignitary Yu to induce his government to accept the proposal of the representatives of the four great powers, and to comply speedily with their present demand.

Compliments.

COUNT POUTIATINE.

Inclosure 3 *a.*

APRIL 26, 1858.

TSUNG, Superintendent of the Granaries at the Metropolis, with Wú, an Under Secretary of the Privy Council, both high officers of the Ta Tsing Empire, hereby communicate on business.

Whereas, your excellency having made an application to proceed to the capital, and the local officers at this place not being qualified to memoralize the throne, have, on their part, announced the matter to the governor general of the province of Chihli, that he should lay it before the court, his Majesty's commands have in consequence been received to the following purport:

"His Majesty's commands have been personally made known to us, appointing Tsung, the superintendent of granaries, with Wú, under secretary of the privy council, to proceed to the mouth of the river of Tientsin, to investigate and manage. From the Emperor."

In accordance with this we left the capital and have reached Tientsin, from whence we now address you this letter.

On the 24th instant, Tsien, the treasurer of this province, had an interview with your country's interpreter, at which time were brought the dispatches of several countries, each of them one; but, since those dispatches were addressed to the governor general of this province, they have been forwarded by Tsien, the treasurer, to him, that the latter may in due order memorialize respecting them. It will be proper, therefore, to await his Majesty's commands issued on receipt of his (the governor general's) memorial, as to the manner of action in the premises, when we will again communicate with you and appoint a time for an interview.

An important communication sent to his excellency William B. Reed, envoy extraordinary and minister plenipotentiary, United States of America.

Translated by S. W. WILLIAMS.

Enclosure 3 *b.*

[Translation.]

ON BOARD THE AUDACIEUSE,
Gulf of Pechele, April 28, 1858.

MR. MINISTER: I have received the letter which your excellency did me the honor to address to me on the 24th of this month, transmitting to me a copy of the new note which you designed for the prime minister at Pekin, and which was delivered to the authorities at the forts that defend the entrance of the Peiho, at the same time as mine and as those of our honorable colleagues of England and Russia.

In sending you my thanks for that communication, I embrace the opportunity to renew to you, Mr. Minister, the assurances of high consideration with which I have the honor to be your excellency's very humble and very obedient servant,

BARON GROS.

His Excellency W. B. REED,
Envoy Extraordinary and Minister Plenipotentiary of the United States of America in China.

D. S. of April 29, 1858.—A delay which has occurred in sending this dispatch permits me to annex to it a translation of the official communication which I have received from the two high functionaries Tsung and Wú, recently arrived from Pekin.

BARON GROS.

Inclosure 3 *c.*

[Translation.]

COMMUNICATION FROM THE IMPERIAL COMMISSIONERS SENT TO THE PEIHIO.

April 26, 1858.

TSUNG, High Imperial Commissioner of the Tsing Dynasty and General Superintendent of the Public Granaries and Salt-works, and WU, High Imperial Commissioner of the Tsing Dynasty and Minister of the Council of the Interior, make the following communication:

The noble envoy (see note 1) having already presented an application to obtain permission to go to Pekin, (see note 2,) and the officers of this district not being authorized to write to the court for orders on this subject, they have addressed the governor of Chihli, in order that he might, in their behalf, write a memorial to the throne; and, in consequence of this step, a verbal order has arrived from the august Emperor appointing us, Tsung, superintendent of public salt works and granaries, and Wú, minister of the council of the interior, as imperial commissioners, and we have been directed at the same time to go to the mouth of the river Tientsin and there examine into and treat on affairs.

Carrying this order into effect, we have now arrived at Tientsin, and we send you in advance this dispatch in order to inform you thereof.

On the eleventh day of the present moon, (April 24, 1858,) Tsien, the treasurer, saw your interpreter. Your noble nation (see note 3) and the others have each delivered to him a dispatch; and, as those dispatches are representations (see note 4) to the viceroy, they have already been transmitted by Tsien, the treasurer, to the viceroy of Chihli, in order that on seeing them he may present a memorial to the court.

As soon as the august Emperor deigns to decree how affairs must be treated, we shall write to your excellency again, and we shall appoint a day for the interview to take place. Consequently, we send the present dispatch to your excellency.

A special communication.

The above dispatch is addressed to Kó, high dignitary and plenipotentiary of France, on the 13th day of the 3d moon of the 8th year of Hien Fung, (April 26, 1858.)

Notes.

Note 1. The character *Chê-tchen*, although signifying "envoy of a nation," is, however an expression somewhat ignoble and ambiguous, as it also signifies a mere "official messenger," a name given to the envoys of tributary countries. The mandarins of Canton have employed the characters *Kwei Koun Chê*, or *Kwei-ta-tchen*, "the noble public envoy."

Note 2. The character *chang*, representation, has been here employed, which term is only used in requests addressed by an inferior to his superior, as may be seen in the dictionaries of Gonzalves, Medhurst, Csu-Kivé, and others. This manner of acting is not only contrary to the provisions of the treaty, but it is in disagreement with the dispatch of the French plenipotentiary, since he never asked for *permission* to go to Pekin. Another proof that this character has been unusually employed is, that further down, in speaking of the officers of the district addressing a request to the governor general to be pleased to send a memorial to the court, this same character, *chang*, is made use of, one always humbly employed by an inferior who is addressing his superior.

Note 3. The character *kwei kwoh*, "his noble kingdom, or, "his noble nation," is here placed in the middle of the line, and scarcely the space of a letter has been left blank between it and the character which precedes it, instead of its being put at the head of the column which follows, as it would have been proper to do, more especially as it was the first time the functionaries Tsung and Wû were addressing the embassador. It was requisite, besides, to make some difference between them and his excellency, and yet, after the characters which indicate these officers and the treasurer, the interval of a letter has been likewise left blank, which is quite plain, as Tsung and Wû were only speaking of them or of their officers, but which is unbecoming when it concerns a high functionary.

Note 4. In this dispatch the titles of Baron Gros are not enumerated, as they should have been; instead of copying, as the high Chinese functionaries always have done, the formulary used in the dispatches of the ambassador, that is to say, "Kó, high imperial commissioner, specially appointed by the great Emperor of France ambassador extraordinary, furnished with full powers, and hereditary Baron," in the present dispatch it is only "Kó, high functionary and plenipotentiary of the great empire of France."

Inclosure 3 *d*.

HER MAJESTY'S SHIP FURIOUS,
Gulf of Pechele, April 27, 1858.

SIR: I beg to thank your excellency for the translation of a communication from the Chinese officers on shore with which you have furnished me, and to inform you that I have received from the same quarter a letter couched in the same terms.

I have the honor to be, sir, your excellency's most obedient humble servant,

ELGIN AND KINCARDINE.

His Excellency the Hon. W. B. REED,
&c., &c., &c.

Inclosure 4.

APRIL 29, 1858.

TAU, Imperial Commissioner of the Ta Tsing Empire, President of the Board of War, Junior Censor of the Censorate, Governor General of the Province of Chihli and its dependencies, General of Tsz 'King, Mihyun, and other passes, [leading beyond the great wall,] and Superintendent of the Provincial Revenue and affairs of the transit, hereby communicates on business:

Whereas, I was on a circuit of inspection of the provincial troops, when I received your excellency's communication, I immediately took the dispatch, and forwarded it to the Prime Minister Yu, who having presented the matter to the throne, in a memorial, has now received his Majesty's commands, specially designating me to proceed forthwith to Takoo, and in conjunction with the previously appointed Imperial Envoys Tsung, superintendent of the granaries, and Wú, under secretary of the privy council, to see their excellencies the honorable foreign ministers, and there seriously to deliberate with them concerning the affairs mentioned in the letters of their several nations. The proper days for having interviews with each [foreign minister] can be decided on after consultation, in order more conveniently to discuss with them the several points.

As is meet, I send now this communication to your excellency that you may designate on what day you will come into the mouth, [of the river,] where I can have an interview; and it is desirable that the day may be previously notified by a communication, that I may be able to receive you properly.

A necessary communication addressed to his excellency William B. Reed, envoy extraordinary and minister plenipotentiary of the United States to China.

NOTE.—The clerk who wrote out the former dispatch had never had practice before in writing papers to foreign countries, and had no formula before him; but the present dispatch is written out in a more correct manner.

Translated by S. W. WILLIAMS.

Enclosure 5.

LEGATION OF THE UNITED STATES,
On board the Minnesota, April 27, 1858.

SIR: In our repeated conversations, I have explained fully to your excellency the precise relations, which in obedience to my instructions, in the present condition of affairs in China, I desire to have to the Chinese government and to the treaty powers. I believe I understand your excellency's position. But in view of the silence which the plenipotentiaries of France and Great Britain seem to feel it their duty to maintain as to their intended movements, and the complications which may arise, should hostilities occur on or after our entrance into the Peiho river, I think it best to put in writing my views, and shall be glad to know in the same form if they coincide with yours.

It is my determination, as heretofore, to maintain a strict neutrality. Having united with your excellency and the other plenipotentiaries, in letters dated the 24th instant, asking anew for the appointment of a plenipotentiary to meet us within six days, at or near Takoo, a point within the forts at the mouth of the river, it is my wish to go there. But I have no intention of forcing my way, in case of resistance, into the river, or even of going so far as to invite aggression on the part of the Chinese. It is our understanding, as representatives of peaceful powers, that we shall go in company, ready to negotiate, if opportunity occurs, and peaceful measures be pursued, and should unfortunately hostilities occur, either by the act of the Chinese or the English and French, to be at hand to interpose our good officers to mitigate the suffering which must ensue, and to try to arrest a conflict, the process of which may be very bloody and disastrous.

If, as I believe you do, you concur in these views, I need hardly say I shall be most happy to coöperate with your excellency, and at this apparent crisis of affairs to strengthen those relations of confidence and cordiality which we have throughout maintained.

I have the honor to be, sir, your excellency's obedient servant,

WILLIAM B. REED.

His Excellency Count POUTIATINE, *&c.*, *&c.*, *&c.*

Inclosure 6 *a*.

STEAMER AMERICA,
At the mouth of Peiho, April 30, 1858.

SIR: I beg to be excused for not answering your letter of the 27th April sooner. My interview, first with the two functionaries sent from Pekin, and then with the governor general of Chihli and other provinces, who invited me to meet them on shore, has taken up all my time during the last days.

With the views and the mode of action that have been considered by us together, and which are now stated in your excellency's communication to me, I concur perfectly, and believe them quite proper to be adopted by us in the present circumstances. Representing two neutral States in the conflict which may be expected every moment to arise again between China and the western powers of Europe, we ought to be ready on the spot of action, to try by good officers to prevent, or at least to diminish the effusion of the blood that may ensue. This will be an act of humanity, and will no doubt serve our interests as well. I inclose herewith a copy of the communication sent by me yesterday to Baron Gros and Lord Elgin, for your excellency's perusal, and, begging leave to assure you of my high consideration, I have the honor to be, your excellency's most humble servant,

C. POUTIATINE.

His Excellency, the Hon. W. B. Reed,
Envoy Extraordinary and Minister Plenipotentiary, &c., &c.

Inclosure 6 *b*.

Letter to Baron Gros and to Lord Elgin.

[Translation.]

On board the Steamer America,
In the Gulf of Pechele, April 29, 1858.

I had the honor to notify your excellency, by my letter of the 24th April, that I should make it my duty to communicate to you the results of my interviews with the Chinese functionaries who have arrived from Pekin.

Having yesterday received an invitation from the governor general of Chihli, to come ashore to have an interview with him, I did not hesitate to go. In that interview, I thought it my duty to call his attention to the sad consequences which might follow the transmission of the notes which he had addressed to the three plenipotentiaries, as these notes were not written in the respectful manner which is due to the elevated rank of the representatives of the great powers interested in the affairs of China. In consequence of these representations, the governor general consented to put the refused letters in the desired form, and promised me that he would send them thus corrected to-morrow morning, to all four of the plenipotentiaries. I then tried to make him comprehend the necessity under present circumstances of recognizing our collective claims, and of undertaking nothing which could lead to hostilities. I also spoke to him of affairs which concern Russia, especially, and I insisted on the right of being received at Pekin, according to our treaties, and in regard to the urgency of a final solution on the spot of the questions of limits between Russia and

China. He promised to refer them to Pekin, and to make thereon his report to the Emperor, which would prove that his full powers are quite restricted.

It is fortunate that the Chinese made no resistance to the vessels of war entering the river. In this way, the shedding of blood has been avoided, at least for the present, and perhaps altogether, which would entirely agree with your excellency's sentiments that are full of humanity.

Be pleased to accept, &c.,

CT. POUTIATINE.

A true copy.

Baron FR. D'OSTENSACKEN,
Secretary of the Mission.

Inclosure 6 *c.*

[Translation.]

LETTER TO BARON GROS.

I have received the letter, with its annexes, which your excellency has done me the honor to address to me, and I hasten to express to you my sincere thanks for all the information which you have been pleased to convey to me. Believing that you have confidence in the sincerity of my wish to see China open herself to the beneficent influence of Christian nations, by employing violent measures as seldom as possible, I take the liberty of submitting to you some thoughts which have occurred to me during the reading of the documents that you have transmitted to me.

It is scarcely possible to exact at this time from the Chinese government that it should follow and conform itself to the usages which are adopted in the relations between Christian States; and it seems to me that the decree exhibited by the governor general of Chihli contains all the full powers which the cabinet of Pekin could give to its plenipotentiary in view of demands that are so important, and, at the same time, to it not very comprehensible. In previous relations the Chinese functionaries declared, most generally, that it was impossible for them to report to the Emperor demands of much less importance; governor general Tau has not had recourse to such a subterfuge. It is beyond doubt that, if the seat of conferences was at Canton, or even at Shanghai, there would be great inconveniences in the necessity of referring continually to Pekin; but in the Peiho, any communication with the capital would barely take four or five days of time. Besides, it is hardly possible, even in Europe, that a diplomatist, who should find himself in a position as critical as that of Tau, would not be obliged to request that time be granted him to ask for new instructions from his government.

These considerations, and still more the desire of not having recourse to arms except in the last extremity—a desire essentially conformable to the magnanimous sentiments which have always distinguished the

French nation—will perhaps determine your excellency to consent to open negotiations with Tau. It is at the same time to be taken into consideration that, in view of the immense demands which are made by the four nations, without minute explanations, and of the uncertainty of any concessions being possible on our side, the Chinese government might fall into despair, and, by a prolonged resistance, though an ineffectual one in its final results, compromit the advantageous position in which the representatives of the nations that want to open China now find themselves.

I request you, Mr. Baron, &c.,

COUNT POUTIATINE.

Inclosure 6 *d.*

LETTER TO THE EARL OF ELGIN AND KINCARDINE.

I have had the honor to receive your lordship's letter of the 2d instant, with inclosures, and I offer you my thanks for it. If I dare to give my opinion, I would now add that we could not expect fuller powers to be granted to a Chinese plenipotentiary in the pressing difficulties to which China is now exposed; nor do I think that great inconveniences may ensue from references to Pekin, which will not require more than four or five days for answers, though it would have been of immense consequence if negotiations were conducted at Shanghai, or at Canton. In my belief, I consider that the Chinese government has acceded to our last demands in sending a proper person for negotiations to the appointed place, and for the term fixed by us for his arrival.

I must apologize in making known my views on this subject, though they differ with those of your lordship; but I thought it would be better to do so than not to disclose them.

With assurances, &c.,

COUNT POUTIATINE.

Inclosure 7 *a.*

LEGATION OF THE UNITED STATES,
On board the Antelope, Peiho River, May 1, 1858.

The undersigned (with titles) received yesterday your excellency's letter of the 29th, informing him of your appointment as imperial commissioner in conjunction with Tsung and Wú, and that you had arrived at Takoo, and was desirous to have a time appointed for an interview; and the undersigned, having arrived within the bar of the Peiho, has received this morning a friendly inquiry by your messengers, desiring that he should fix a time for an interview. This the undersigned is, at this time, unable to do, being anxious to confer with their excellencies the ministers of Great Britain and France before he designates further any time or place. As he has already informed the imperial authorities, there is, in the course of policy now pursued, entire concord of feeling between the ministers of the four powers, and the undersigned thinks that any separate action on his part, when there is an opportunity of consultation, might be regarded as an unfriendly act. He is in hourly expectation of the arrival of Lord Elgin and Baron Gros, and will be ready on Monday, at the latest, (to-morrow being a day of rest,) to give a positive answer as to a time of meeting.

The undersigned takes this occasion of expressing an earnest hope that if the place of reception be on shore, as he presumes it will be, that there shall be such accommodations provided as are becoming the hospitality of the imperial commissioner and the dignity of an interview between representatives of high and equal rank of great nations.

WILLIAM B. REED.

His Excellency TAU,
Imperial Commissioner, Governor General.

Inclosure 7 b.

LEGATION OF THE UNITED STATES,
On board the Antelope, Peiho River, May 1, 1858.

MY LORD: I have the honor to inform your excellency that, besides the request contained in the letter yesterday received from the imperial commissioner that I should designate a time for an interview, two Chinese officers have to-day been on board this ship and urgently repeated the request. I beg to inclose to your excellency a copy of the answer which I have sent to the letter and to the request.

I have the honor to be, my lord, your excellency's obedient servant,

WILLIAM B. REED.

His Excellency the Earl of ELGIN AND KINCARDINE,
Her Britanic Majesty's High Commissioner.

Inclosure 7 b.

LEGATION OF THE UNITED STATES,
On board the Antelope, Peiho River, May 1, 1858.

MONSIEUR LE BARON: I had the honor yesterday, just before leaving the Minnesota, to receive your excellency's letter of the 28th ultimo, with a copy of the communication of Tsung and Wú, with annotations. I beg to thank you for them.

About the same time, as your excellency is probably aware, I received a communication from Tau, the newly appointed imperial commissioner, requesting that I should fix a time for an interview with him. This morning I have received, through two Chinese officers, an urgent message to the same effect.

I beg to inclose to your excellency a copy of the answer which I have sent to the letter and to the request, and beg you anew to receive the assurance of my high consideration.

I have the honor to be, Monsieur le Baron, your excellency's humble servant,

WILLIAM B. REED.

His Excellency BARON GROS,
High Commissioner and Embassador, &c., &c.

Inclosure 7 c.

HER MAJESTY'S SHIP FURIOUS,
Gulf of Pechele, May 2, 1858.

SIR: I have had the honor to receive, by the hand of Count Poutiatine, a copy of your excellency's letter to me of yesterday's date. The original has not yet reached me.

I beg now to inclose for your excellency's information the copy of a correspondence which has passed between the Imperial Commissioner Tau and me. Judging from what has happened before in similar cases, and more particularly on the occasion of the visit of Sir John Bowring and the Hon. Mr. McLane to this place, (1854,) I fear that the nomination of a minister, with powers so limited as those held by Tau, does not argue on the part of the government of the Emperor of China any intention to discuss seriously, and with a view to their final and satisfactory settlement, the questions brought under its consideration by the representatives of the great powers.

Your excellency will observe that it is my intention to address a further communication to the imperial commissioner. As soon as it is prepared, I shall have the honor to send a copy of it to you.

I have the honor to be, sir, your excellency's most obedient servant,

ELGIN AND KINCARDINE.

His excellency the Hon. W. B. REED, *&c., &c., &c.*

Inclosure 7 d.

TAU, Imperial Commissioner, Governor General of Chihli, &c., makes a communication:

I received your excellency's letter whilst on my tour of military inspection, and having, as in duty bound, submitted for you to the throne your letter addressed to Yu, chief secretary of state, have had the honor to receive a decree from his Majesty the Emperor, commanding me to proceed as imperial commissioner to the port of Takoo, hard by, and there, in concert with Tsung, director general of granaries, &c., and Wú, under secretary of the cabinet, already appointed commissioners, to meet your excellency, and enter upon negotiations with him.

I have decided, upon due consideration,* that for the discusssion and disposal of the questions contained in the letters of the different governments, it will be best to receive [their representatives] on separate days. It is my duty, therefore, to write to your excellency to choose the day on which you will meet me at the port, and I hope that you will give me notice that I may be in readiness to receive you.

A necessary communication, addressed to the Earl of Elgin, &c.

Hien Fung, 8th year, 3d moon, 16th day, (April 29, 1858.)

Postscript.—It is my duty to add, that my copyist's unacquaintance with the forms of correspondence with your excellency's nation was the occasion of certain errors in my letter sent before. They have been corrected in this.

Translated by THOMAS WADE,
Chinese Secretary.

Inclosure 7 *e.*

April 30, 1858.

The undersigned has the honor to acknowledge the receipt of a letter from Tau, imperial commissioner, &c., informing him that he has received the commands of his Majesty the Emperor of China to meet the undersigned at Takoo, and to enter upon negotiations with him.

In a letter addressed on the 10th of February last to the Chief Secretary of State Yu Ching, to which, as yet, no answer has been received, the undersigned expressly declared himself authorized by his sovereign to discuss and determine various questions therein set forth in general terms.

The imperial commissioner is now requested to inform the undersigned, explicity and positively, by letter, this evening, whether his Majesty the Emperor of China has conferred on him corresponding powers, and such as render him competent to independent discussion and to the conclusion of negotiations.

On the receipt of an answer in the affirmative, the undersigned will appoint to-morrow for a conference with the imperial commissioner; but should the imperial commissioner send no reply, or should a reply sent by him declare that he has not the required authority, the undersigned will regard his pacific overture for the appointment of a duly qualified officer as rejected by the imperial government.

A copy of the letter addressed by the undersigned to the chief secretary of state on the 10th of February is inclosed, and the officer charged with the transmission of this is instructed to wait two hours for a reply.

ELGIN AND KINCARDINE.

---

* This may imply one's own resolve individually formed, or formed on consultation with others.

Inclosure 7 f.

TAU, Imperial Commissioner, Governor General of Chihli, &c., makes a communication:

I have to state that the decree of his Majesty, which I have had the honor to receive,* detaches me specially to Taku, there, in concert with the Imperial Commissioners Tsung, director general of granaries, and Wú, under secretary of the inner cabinet, to receive the envoys of the different governments, to enter into negotiations, to report to the throne, and request instructions as to the steps to be taken.

Being now in receipt of a letter from your excellency, it is my duty at once to appoint the 18th instant (1st May) as the day on which I and my colleagues, Tsung, director general of granaries, and Wú, under secretary of the inner cabinet, will meet you, (and learn) from you in person the different matters you have to discuss. I write this to inform you accordingly.

A necessary communication addressed to the Earl of Elgin, &c., &c.

Hein Fung, 8th year, 3d moon, 17th day. (April 30, 1858.)

Translated by THOMAS WADE,
Chinese Secretary.

Inclosure 7 g.

MAY 1, 1858.

The undersigned begs leave to acknowledge the imperial commissioners' letter of yesterday. As that letter contained no satisfactory answer to the question put by the undersigned, in his letter of the 30th ultimo, he did not meet the commissioner as intended to-day.

The imperial commissioner will presently hear more at length from the undersigned.

ELGIN AND KINCARDINE.

Inclosure 7 h.

[Translation.]

EXTRAORDINARY MISSION OF FRANCE IN CHINA,
On board the Audacieuse, May 2, 1858.

MR. MINISTER: I have the honor to send herewith, to your excellency, a copy of the letter which I have written to the new imperial commis-

---

*Were this not in answer to the letter addressed, I should have translated the passage simply, "I have had the honor to receive a decree," &c. The word rendered "decree" is, literally, the will or pleasure of majesty; but technically, the placet or rescript issued by the Emperor when announcing an appointment made, or instructions given, on receipt of information submitted to him.

sioner, Tau, to the end that he should be pleased to explain himself categorically on the subject of the powers with which he says he is clothed; and your excellency will see that the answer which I have received is not satisfactory.

I am at this time preparing the dispatch which I think of sending to Governor Tau, and I shall have the honor of transmitting to your excellency a copy of it as soon as it is finished.

I embrace this occasion, Mr. Minister, to renew to you the assurance of the high consideration with which I have the honor to be your excellency's very humble and very obedient servant,

BARON GROS.

His Excellency W. B. Reed,
Envoy Extraordinary and Minister Plenipotentiary of the United States of America, &c., &c., &c.

Inclosure 7 i.

[Translation.]

TAU TO BARON GROS.

May 1, 1858.

Tau, high imperial commissioner, has the honor to say to your excellency that he has received an imperial decree which orders him to proceed to Takoo, and there, in concert with the Imperial Commissioners Tsung and Wú, to have an interview with the envoys of the various nations, in order to deliberate with them and to refer respecting it to the court of Pekin, that he may have instructions; and having received the dispatch which your excellency has addressed to me, it would be proper to designate a day on which we might meet for the purpose of learning what we are to treat about.

A correct translation.

BARON GROS.

Inclosure 7 j.

[Translation.]

BARON GROS TO TAU.

April 30, 1858.

The undersigned received this morning the dispatch which his excellency Tau, &c , did him the honor to write to him on the 29th of this month, and he hastens to answer it.

The undersigned will be very happy to proceed promptly to meet his excellency, but he wishes beforehand to have a piece of information which the noble governor can give him. His excellency Yu, the prime minister, in not answering the letters of the undersigned, notwithstanding the provisions of the treaty which make it his duty to do so, has left him in an uncertainty, which should cease.

The undersigned is furnished with the necessary powers to treat on all existing questions between France and China, and he will have the honor of transmitting a copy of these full powers to his excellency.

The noble governor doubtless knows that the principal questions to be resolved are:

The reparations which France asked of the ex-Commissioner Yeh, and which she has never been able to obtain.

The opening of the principal ports of the empire to foreign commerce.

The liberty of conscience, and an efficient protection to be granted to Christian worship.

The residence of ministers plenipotentiary of France at Pekin.

The possibility of Frenchmen traveling in the empire by means of sufficient passports.

The indemnities to be given to France for the expenses of operations against Canton.

The power for Frenchmen to buy what they want directly in the place of production or manufacture.

A useful revision of the tariffs, &c., &c.

Has the noble governor the necessary powers to treat on and to resolve these questions with the undersigned? It is necessary for the latter to know by a categorical answer; for, if the powers of the noble governor do not extend that far, it would be useless to lose valuable time, and the present position would become still more serious than it is.

The undersigned therefore requests the noble governor to be pleased to answer him immediately, and to make known to him, yea or nay, whether he is authorized to negotiate and to resolve the questions which are referred to.

The undersigned eagerly desires that a fortunate solution may intervene for the happiness of two empires whose populations are formed for reciprocally esteeming each other.

The undersigned, &c.

A true copy.

BARON GROS.

Inclosure 7 k.

[Translation.]

EXTRAORDINARY MISSION OF FRANCE IN CHINA,
On board the Audacieuse, May 2, 1858.

MR. MINISTER: I have received the dispatch which your excellency has done me the honor to write to me, sending me a copy of the answer that you made on the 1st of this month to Governor General Tau, who had asked for an appointment with you, and I thank your excellency for this communication.

I hasten to make known to you, at the same time, that I have merely sent to that high dignitary an acknowledgment of reception of the last letter which he wrote me, and a copy of which I have already transmitted to your excellency. I expect to be able to answer Governor Tau in the course of to-morrow.

I need not say to your excellency that I shall have the honor of transmitting to you as quick as possible a copy of the answer which I am preparing for the new imperial commissioner; and I think it useless to tell your excellency that the last letter which I have received from this high functionary seems to me to be very unsatisfactory.

I have the honor to be, Mr. Minister, your excellency's very devoted servant,

BARON GROS.

Inclosure 8.

Notes of an interview held at the Takoo forts, May 3, 1858, between his Excellency Mr. REED, United States Plenipotentiary, and the Imperial Chinese Commissioner, TAU TINGSIANG, with his colleagues, TSUNG and WÚ, (or the full names TSUNGLUN and WURGUNTAI:)

Mr. Reed was received at the door of the marquee by Tau and his colleagues, and conducted to a seat on his left hand, the other two commissioners being seated outside of them both. Captain Du Pont was placed on the left hand of Tsung, and Mr. Williams, secretary of legation, next to him, with an overseer of the transit last. Two officers of rank—Tsien, the provincial treasurer, and the colonel of the forces in the encampment—sat on the right of Wú. The other gentlemen of the suite, who were seated in due order, were Major George H. Terrett, marine officer, and Mr. Francis B. Blake, midshipman of the Minnesota; Lieutenant Roger N. Stembel, Surgeon John L. Fox, and Acting Master George Bacon, of the Mississippi; and Mr. Bradley, United States consul at Ningpo, and Messrs. W. Martin and Jenkins, interpreters.

Mr. Reed opened the conference by assuring the commissioners of the good disposition of the United States towards China, and its desire to cultivate friendly relations with it.

Tau. By their commencing hostilities at Canton, the English have violated the principles of justice and propriety; but I am aware that the Americans took no part therein. I regard them with the strongest feelings of consideration and friendship.

Mr. Reed. Is your friendship sufficient to induce you to enter on the negotiations relating to the revision of the treaty of the United States?

Tau. It is. The treaty signed at Wanghia with the United States was called a treaty of peace for ten thousand years; the Chinese government has never broken it; but the English and French have violated their treaty obligations in commencing hostilities at Canton.

Mr. Reed. I did not come here to discuss the conduct of the English and French, but to consider certain modifications which require to be made in the treaty with the United States, and its revision; for there is grave and just cause for so doing.

Tau. Our great Emperor treats all nations with benignity; and, having a special regard for the United States, he will no doubt graciously receive any proposition that is reasonable.

Mr. Reed. The President of the United States has appointed me to be his minister plenipotentiary in China to negotiate and sign a treaty with the empire, and has given me credentials for that object. Have you any written evidence of your having similar full powers?

Tau. I am the governor general of the province of Chihli, and my jurisdiction extends over all its civil and military affairs.

Mr. Reed. Have you powers to enable you to negotiate and sign a treaty?

Tau. I am an officer of the highest grade, and have equal powers with Kiying, who negotiated your treaty at Canton; and I and my colleagues are deputed by the Emperor to meet you for this purpose.

Mr. Reed. Are you empowered to sign a treaty?

Tau. The rules of our country in this respect differ from those of yours, whose ministers are sent abroad to a great distance, and for a long time, and are, therefore, allowed greater discretion, and have powers given to them. We are within the limits of our own country, and near the court, to which we can speedily refer any important questions for his Majesty's decision.

Mr. Reed. If you cannot sign, can you negotiate a treaty?

Tau. I can, and will be pleased, if the points to be considered can all be reduced to writing, so that they can be carefully examined.

Mr. Reed. Will it be necessary to refer each article to Pekin, or only the treaty as a whole? for if the former mode be required, I shall decline to commence negotiations.

Tau and colleagues. Only the whole, for too much time would be consumed by separate references. Have you prepared the points of discussion?

Mr. Reed. It is inexpedient to enter upon the discussion of them this afternoon, as there is not time, but at as early a day as may be convenient to both parties; and before I leave I will place a summary of them in your hands. Previous to doing so, however, I wish to inquire whether my letter, sent to the Prime Minister Yu, from Canton, ever reached him?

Tau. If you refer to the letter written in the twelfth Chinese month, it was received and presented to his Majesty, and afterwards given to Hwang, when he was appointed commissioner to proceed to Canton.

Mr. Reed. That cannot be, for Hwang must have left the capital before that letter was received there.

Tau. Hwang had it when he was sent to Canton, or at least got it before he reached that city.

Mr. Reed. Can a copy of it be procured from Pekin and produced; and how long will it take to receive it?

Tau. It can, and I will procure a copy.

Mr. Reed. I have also here an important document, a letter from the President of the United States to his Majesty the Emperor of China.

Tau. When will the letter be brought, and what does it contain?

Mr. Reed. It contains good wishes and expressions of friendship from our Chief Magistrate. Here is the original, (showing the address.)

Tau. I am unable to read the letters of your honorable country, but there are men in the colonial office, at Pekin, who are acquainted with foreign languages. Was it written by the prince of your country? (Mr. Martin, the interpreter, here requested the commissioner not to call our Chief Magistrate "prince," but "President," which is his proper title.)

Tau. It is a foreign title to which I am not accustomed.

(Mr. Martin: "Then call him '*Hwangti*,' Emperor, as we do your sovereign, for the United States is not inferior to China." This he did during the remainder of the interview.)

Mr. Reed. It bears the autograph signature of the President.

Tau. May I see a translation of it? (It was then shown to the three commissioners, who perused it, and said at the same time: "We can send it; we can send it.")

Mr. Reed. I have to complain of a grave offense on the part of the Chinese government. Here is a letter from the President to the Emperor, sent from the United States, and placed by my predecessor in the hands of Wang, the governor general at Fuhchau, to be transmitted to Pekin. It was afterwards returned unanswered, and in this condition, (showing the mutilated seal.) This was an insult to my country; and, should it at any time be repeated, it certainly would create enmity between the United States and China.

Tau. That is a by-gone affair of which I have no knowledge; but I can assure you, that in the present case the letters will not be treated with disrespect.

Mr. Reed. What guarantee shall I have that it reaches the hands of his Majesty?

Tau. An acknowledgment from the colonial office.

Mr. Reed. But I desire something from the vermilion pencil—from the Emperor himself—addressing the President of the United States in terms of equality.

Tau. All correspondence with foreign States is referred to that office.

Tsung. The addition of the imperial *placet* with the vermilion pencil to a document from that office, so far from being a token of equality, would, on the contrary, indicate the inferiority of the party addressed. (Mr. Martin here remarked that *li-fau-yuen*, the term used for colonial office, signified the office for controlling the foreign *dependencies* of China.)

Mr. Reed. I will have nothing from that office—nothing but from the Emperor himself. Will his Majesty answer the President's letter in his own name and in terms of equality?

Tau. I can send a memorial to-morrow and ascertain the imperial will on that head. In the meantime, you will perhaps place in our hands a summary of the points of the treaty which require discussion.

Mr. Reed. No; not until you have both obtained from Pekin a copy of my letters to the prime minister, and also ascertained whether the Emperor will answer the President's letter.

Tau. The imperial rescript and the letters will both be here within five days or less.

Mr. Reed. I regret the difficulties with Great Britain and France, and the Russian minister and myself are ready to use our good offices to bring about a better understanding.

Tau. We highly appreciate your kind intentions, and indeed it was out of regard for you, the neutral powers, that we refrained from firing on the English and French vessels when they entered the rivers and took up a position in front of our batteries. We shall be glad to have the plenipotentiaries of both countries act as mediators in the pending difficulties.

Mr. Reed. I am well acquainted with the plenipotentiaries of both England and France, and I know them both to be good and upright men.

Tau. The British minister was not, I am aware, concerned in commencing the strife at Canton, and, indeed, he is hardly to be blamed for his course. Our Emperor treats all nations with kindness; but, when wantonly attacked, he cannot but change countenance towards them. Nevertheless, out of regard for you, the neutral powers, he is willing to hear what the English and French have to say.

Mr. Reed. Would it be agreeable to you for the Russian minister and myself to meet you in joint conference?

Tau. I shall be happy to meet you either separately or together, as may suit your convenience.

Mr. Reed. Which do you prefer, that we should come single or both together?

Tau and colleagues. To meet both at once would be a saving of time.

Mr. Reed. As you have expressed orally a wish for the mediation of the United States and Russia, it is necessary that we should have that request committed to writing in a formal communication.

Tau. I shall to-morrow address a communication to that effect to the plenipotentiaries of both nations.

Mr. Reed. It must be expressed to be altogether spontaneous, and contain no allusion to any proposition made by me.

Tau and colleagues. (Smiling that they should be thought to need any prompting on that score.) It will be entirely voluntary on our part, and due care will be taken not to implicate you.

Mr. Reed. When the imperial rescript and a copy of my dispatch from Canton are received, I shall be ready to meet your excellencies again and to enter on negotiations for the modification of our treaty.

Tau. The desired documents will be here in five days or less time, when we can begin the consideration of the treaty. Your country has always been on good terms with China. It is the wish of his Majesty that those relations of friendship may be perpetual, and whatever may conduce to your advantage without implying injury to us, his Majesty will certainly not refuse to concede. To-morrow I shall attend to three things: first, to memoralize his Majesty with respect to the letter of your Emperor; second, to apply for a copy of your excellency's letter to the prime minister; and third, address a communication to your excellency and the Russian minister, on the subject of mediation.

Mr. Reed. I am willing to use all my influence in the way of conciliation, but I cannot guaranty success. (The interpreter added, by way of explanation, as the Chinese proverb says, "To devise is with man; to accomplish, with Heaven.")

Tau. I feel assured of that. We regard Heaven in all we do, and would not dare to say what is false.

Mr. Reed here remarked that it was growing late, and prepared to take leave. The high commissioner accompanied his excellency to the outside of the tent door, and the two assistant commissioners requested that their compliments and good wishes should be communicated to Mr. Reed, at the same time expressing their regret that they were unable to address him in his own language.

Inclosure 9 *a.*

LEGATION OF THE UNITED STATES,
On board the Minnesota, May 4, 1858.

MY LORD: I had the honor, on the evening of the 2d instant, to receive your communication dated on that day, with its inclosures. On the afternoon of the 1st, my letter of that date was put on board her Majesty's ship Nimrod, to be forwarded to your excellency, and the copy which Count Poutiatine kindly exhibited was one which I had furnished him in the ordinary course of our friendly correspondence.

To some extent, your excellency's letter of the 2d instant relieved me from the painful state of uncertainty as to your views and those of Baron Gros, in which I had been since the dispatches demanding the appointment of an imperial commissioner. In the course then suggested I gladly acquiesced, as I have done in every other which has been intimated, though I am bound in candor to say that it occurred to me at the time that the limitation of six days was rather a strict one. Still, having the greatest confidence in your excellency's peaceful intentions, and your desire to give to the Chinese every chance of friendly negotiation, and no opinion being asked of me, I gave none, and did exactly what you did.

In my note of the 24th April to the prime minister at the capital, (a copy of which is in your excellency's hands,) I said: "If on or before the last day of this month such a plenipotentiary shall present himself at or near Takoo, where the undersigned means to be, there will yet be room for peaceful preliminary negotiation." On the 28th, Tau, the governor general, sent me a communication, which on account of an informality in the address, was returned. On the 30th, I received in due form a letter from Tau, announcing his appointment, in conjunction with two other envoys, "to meet and deliberate concerning matters" mentioned in my previous letters. The tone of the communication was perfectly courteous and respectful. I have the honor to inclose a copy of it. I should have done so sooner, had I not at the time had every reason to suppose letters of a similar tenor were simultaneously received by the other plenipotentiaries.

In my judgment, the course for me to pursue was perfectly clear, and I did what in my letter of the 24th April I said I should do. I entered the river on the 30th, and repaired as near Takoo as the position of the English and French ships at anchor permitted me to do. I took for granted—though in this it seems I was mistaken—that on the same or the next day I should have had the pleasure of seeing your excellency and Baron Gros. I beg to assure you, and I am sure you will appreciate the sincere friendliness of the remark, that my disappointment in this respect, when there seemed to me a ray of hope that peaceful negotiations might begin, was very keen. What occurred immediately after my arrival within the river, your excellency knows from the letter to Tau, which I had the honor of forwarding on the 1st instant. I beg to repeat a single passage from this note, as expressing as strongly and as earnestly as I could my deference to your views and those of Baron Gros, and my desire for unreserved confidence:

"This [the fixing of a day] the undersigned is at this time unable to do, being anxious to confer with their excellencies the ministers of Great Britain and France before he designates further any time or place. As he has already informed the imperial authorities, there is in the course of policy now pursued entire concord of feeling between the ministers of the four powers, and the undersigned thinks that any separate action on his part, when there is an opportunity of consultation, might be regarded as an unfriendly act. He is in hourly expectation of the arrival of Lord Elgin and Baron Gros, and will be ready on Monday at the latest (to-morrow being a day of rest) to give a positive answer as to a time of meeting."

On that evening I received your excellency's note informing me that you considered the communications of the imperial commissioner unsatisfactory, and that you had determined not to meet him for any purpose unless he should categorically, and in writing, state that he held what in the language of other nations are known as full powers.

This information, whilst, as I have said, it relieved me from all uncertainty as to your excellency's intentions, left me at liberty to pursue the course my own judgement dictated. I regret that my having said to the Chinese, who expressed so earnest and friendly a desire that I should meet their high officers, that I should give an answer on Monday at latest, as well as my own convictions of duty, prevented me from waiting longer for the further communication which your excellency informed me you meant to send to the Chinese authorities. As to what under the circumstances I ought, and my government would expect me to do, I had no doubt whatever. Peace is too important to the relations subsisting between China and the United States to be imperilled by my adherence, in a preliminary correspondence, to the strict rules of western diplomacy, and I was content to run the risk of ultimate or even preliminary failure on a point which, according to circumstances, might become either substantial or merely technical.

Accordingly, I landed yesterday near the Takoo forts, and had a long and interesting interview with their excellencies the imperial commissioners, the result of which is a clear conviction on my part that it is at present inexpedient to insist on the production of full powers in writing, but that the high commissioner is clothed with ample authority to negotiate, and that the only reference to the capital that he needs or will make is not of each proposition separately, but of the whole treaty or other form of negotiation, after it is completed. This is so nearly assimilated to a reference for ratification, that I am willing to agree to it, and have announced to the high commissioner my intention to begin negotiations with him, or at least to submit the points of negotiation for his consideration and our consultation so soon as he exhibits to me the originals or copies of my correspondence of February last, which he asserts are in the proper department at the capital, and also gives me a direct assurance that the letter of the President to the Emperor shall be received and acknowledged on terms of equality. This his excellency promises me, and five days from yesterday have been agreed to for this purpose. It is my hope then to meet the commissioner again.

Obvious considerations of propriety operated to prevent me from encouraging any references to the matters of difference between China and Great Britain and France; they were frequently introduced, but always and positively discouraged by me. Towards the close of the conference, I felt it to be my duty to try so far to improve the friendly feeling expressed to the United States, as of my own accord to say a single word on this delicate subject. I ventured to give an earnest warning against anything like a contumacious refusal to accede to what I understood to be the demands of Great Britain and France, and a hope that they would share with me the confidence I had in your excellency's moderation and kind feeling towards the Chinese. The reply of the commissioner was very earnest and precise; and, as far as one can judge, the words or acts of this peculiar people, cordial, that he believed that your excellency entertained the opinions I attributed to you, and, to use his very words, that he knew that you were not at Canton when the troubles began, and had nothing to do with them. Beyond this I did not feel at liberty to go, or to permit the subject of your relations to be talked of.

I have thus unreservedly laid before your excellency all that has transpired since I last had the honor of addressing you, and, in conclusion, venture to express the earnest hope that all chances of peaceful adjustment are not at an end. I am quite aware how little confidence is to be placed in the assurances and professions of Chinese officials; but, so anxious am I for peace, and a bloodless settlement of difficulties, so fearful of a renewal of such a state of things as without any agency on the part of your excellency has occurred in the south of China, that I feel I should not discharge my duty by seeing hostilities begin in the north without an effort to avert them.

I have the honor to be, my lord, your excellency's obedient servant,

WILLIAM B. REED.

His Excellency, the Earl of ELGIN AND KINCARDINE,
Her Britannic Majesty's High Commissioner.

Inclosure 9 *b*.

HER MAJESTY'S SHIP FURIOUS,
Gulf of Pechele, May 5, 1858.

SIR: I have had the honor to receive your excellency's letter of the 4th instant, and I beg to thank you for the very full statement which it contains of the views entertained, and of the proceedings adopted by you at this conjuncture.

I must beg to remind your excellency that, in my letter to "Yu," of the 11th February, of which a copy was transmitted to your excellency in my dispatch to you of the 4th of that month, from the terms of which, except in respect of the concession of further delay, I have not departed in any of my subsequent communications to the court of Pekin, I used the following language: "If, on the contrary, no plenipotentiary so accredited shall present himself at Shanghai before the end of the month of March, or if any plenipotentiary so presenting himself shall be found to have insufficient powers, or if, having the requisite powers, he shall prove himself unwilling to accede to reasonable terms of accommodation, the undersigned hereby reserves to himself the right of having recourse, without further announcement, delay, or declaration of hostilities, to such measures in vindication of the claims of his country on China as in his judgment it may appear advisable to adopt."

I can assure your excellency that I am as desirous now, as I have ever been, to arrive at a settlement of the differences existing between Great Britain and China, without further bloodshed, and that I would be most willing to give up any point of form, in order to obtain this consummation; but I fear that, in departing on a fundamental principle from a condition laid down in terms so precise, I should only lead the Chinese government into error as to the determination of Great Britain to assert her claims upon that government, and thus become the means of ultimately bringing down upon it great calamities.

Your excellency will permit me to observe that, not having received from "Yu" any reply to the letters which I have addressed to him, I have no evidence, beyond that which Tau's powers furnish of the view taken by the imperial government of the demands which I have preferred on behalf of Great Britain, and when I ask Tau to inform me of the extent of those powers, he answers in effect, that he is only authorized to engage in discussions with me, and report on the same to his own government for instructions—a proceeding which manifestly does not bind the latter to anything.

The court of Pekin declines to permit the representatives of foreign States to communicate directly with the ministers of the Empire at the capital. The Minister "Yu" has lately reasserted this principle in the most offensive form, by declining to answer the letters addressed to him by the representatives of the great powers from Canton and Shanghai. But, at the same time, while it puts forward this pretension, it informs us that the customs of the Empire preclude it from delegating to any diplomatic functionary authority similar to that which is known in western diplomacy by the term "full powers."

I ask your excellency, in all earnestness, is it possible that international relations can subsist under such a system?

Nevertheless, with the view of reconciling, in so far as it is possible to do so, the course which I feel it my duty to follow with that of your excellency, and also of giving to the court of Pekin another proof of the conciliatory disposition with which I am animated, I have resolved, with Baron Gros's concurrence, to enter into negotiation with "Tau," if he can procure from the Emperor of China powers identical with those which the late Emperor gave to Kiying when he negotiated with Sir H. Pottinger, in 1842. I inclose the copy of the note in which I have informed "Tau" that I will grant him a delay of six days to enable him to procure the powers in question.

I have the honor to be, sir, your excellency's most obedient, humble servant,

ELGIN AND KINCARDINE.

His Excellency the Hon. W. B. Reed, *&c.*, *&c.*, *&c.*

Inclosure 9 *c.*

NOTE TO TAU.

May 6, 1858.

The undersigned has already apprised the Imperial Commissioner *Tau* that the letter addressed by him to the undersigned on the 30th of April, was entirely unsatisfactory. Holding as he does, from her Majesty the Queen of Great Britain, plenipotentiary powers, he cannot consent to treat with a representative of the Emperor of China who is only authorized "to enter on negotiations, to report to the throne, and to request instructions as to the course he is to pursue."

The undersigned finds, on consulting the records that, when his late Majesty appointed Kiying and Ilipu his commissioners for the settlement of pending questions with her Britannic Majesty's plenipotentiary, Sir H. Pottinger, the powers conferred on the high officers were fully set forth in a confidential decree bearing date July 27, 1842, a copy of which is inclosed.

The undersigned has now to intimate to the imperial commissioner that he has determined on according a delay of six days from the date of this letter, in order to enable him to obtain powers similar to those granted to Kiying and Ilipu.

The undersigned has only to express his sincere hope that this additional evidence of his desire to avert the evil which persistence in an evasive policy cannot fail, sooner or later, to entail upon China, may be duly appreciated by the imperial government.

ELGIN AND KINCARDINE.

Inclosure 9 d.

[Translation.]

EXTRAORDINARY MISSION OF FRANCE IN CHINA,
On board the Audacieuse, May 5, 1858.

MR. MINISTER: I have received the letter which your excellency did me the honor to write to me on the 4th of this month, and meanwhile, until I can answer it, I hasten to send to your excellency a copy of the note which I shall transmit to-morrow morning to the Imperial Commissioner Tau.

I deem it my duty to make one more conciliatory attempt with the Chinese government, and I eagerly desire that it may be appreciated at its just value.

I have the honor to be, Mr. Minister, your excellency's very humble and very obedient servant,

BARON GROS.

His Excellency W. B. REED,
Envoy Extraordinary and Minister Plenipotentiary of the United States of America in China, &c., &c., &c.

Inclosure 9 e.

[Translation.]

NOTE TO TAU.

ON BOARD THE AUDACIEUSE,
May 5, 1858.

The undersigned, &c., &c., has received the dispatch which his excellency, &c., &c., has done him the honor to write to him in answer to the one which the undersigned had addressed to him on the 30th of April last, asking him to be pleased to make known to him whether he was furnished with the necessary full powers to enter into negotiations with him.

This rather unsatisfactory answer does not permit the undersigned again to ask for an interview with the noble governor, since he, furnished with full powers from his sovereign, which authorize him to treat on and resolve all the questions pending between the two empires, would find himself in presence of the noble governor, who would only have power, on his part, to listen to what the undersigned should say to him and to transmit his words to Pekin.

The undersigned thinks, therefore, that his excellency might and ought to write immediately to Pekin, asking for powers similar to those which the Emperor Tao-kwang gave to the Imperial Commissioners Kiying and Ilipu in 1842 and 1844—powers without which it is impossible to enter into negotiation. Six days, counting from to-day, are more than sufficient to obtain an answer from Pekin, and, if before the expiration of this period the undersigned has not received notice that these full powers have arrived, he will find himself obliged, much to his regret, to suspend diplomatic action and to place affairs in the hands of the French admiral.

The undersigned doubts not that the Imperial Commissioner will see in this new delay granted to the Chinese government an additional proof of his spirit of conciliation, and the sincere wish which he entertains of putting an end to a state of things that is contrary to the interest of the two empires.

The undersigned, &c., &c.

A true copy.

BARON GROS.

TAU, *&c., &c.*

Inclosure 10 *a.*

MINNESOTA, *May* 6, 1858.

MY LORD: I thank your excellency for the information contained in your letter of yesterday, and sincerely trust that, within the further time allowed to the imperial commissioner and his colleagues, such concessions may be made as to secure what I am confident you desire as earnestly as I do, a peaceful adjustment of pending difficulties.

Should I, as is probable, in the interval have further personal intercourse with the Chinese authorities, I shall continue, if agreeable to your excellency, that unreserve towards you which is most congenial to my own feelings, and, so long as the present state of things continues, completely in accordance with my instructions.

I have the honor to be, my lord, your excellency's obedient servant,

WILLIAM B. REED.

His Excellency the EARL OF ELGIN AND KINCARDINE,
&c., &c., &c.

Same to Baron Gros.

Inclosure 10 *b.*

HER MAJESTY'S SHIP FURIOUS,
Gulf of Pechele, May 7, 1858.

SIR: I have had the honor to receive your excellency's letter of yesterday's date, and beg to thank you for your offer to supply me with information respecting anything which you may learn in personal intercourse with the Chinese authorities.

I have the honor to be, sir, your excellency's most obedient servant,

ELGIN AND KINCARDINE.

His Excellency the Hon. W. B. REED,
&c., &c.

Inclosure 11 *a*.

STEAMER AAMERICA,
In the River Peiho, *May* 5, 1858.

SIR: It is with great satisfaction I read your letter to Lord Elgin, which you did me the honor to communicate, and feel most grateful for the support your excellency gave by it to the notes I have addressed on the same subject to Lord Elgin and Baron Gros. I have no doubt it is the noble attitude maintained by you to the representatives of France and England, as well as the friendly understanding that exists between us, which has been the principal cause of the withdrawal of the order for recommencing hostilities by the western powers. I do not now despair that further bloodshed might be stopped, and that, by God's blessing, the attempts to settle by peaceful means the difficult affairs between China and the four powers may be brought to a successful end. It will be my duty to inform the imperial cabinet that your cordial coöperation has given weight to my representations, and has arrested, at least for the moment, the application of violent measures contemplated by England and France.

I have seen to-day a Chinese official, who came to explain the meaning of some phrases in the letters addressed yesterday to us by the Chinese Commissioner Tau. His interpretation was, that if we undertook to arrange the differences pending now between them and the allies, Tau will then endeavor to settle to our satisfaction the affairs that properly concern us. I did not consent to this proposition, but replied that, conforming to the instructions of my government, I made, before getting their application, exertions, as far as it was feasible, to prevent collision between China and the western powers. I have prepared a short letter to this effect, in answer to the above-mentioned communication, and before making [up] my mind to send it to the Commissioner Tau, inclose it now for your excellency's consideration.

With assurances of high consideration and great esteem, I have the honor to be your excellency's most humble servant,

C. POUTIATINE.

His Excellency the Hon. W. B. REED,
Minister Plenipotentiary, &c., &c.

STEAMER AMERICA, *May* 6, 1858.

MY DEAR SIR: I informed you yesterday that I should write to Tau, and having received the communications of Lord Elgin and Baron Gros, sent to-day to the Chinese plenipotentiary, I wrote in consequence, and forward you the copies of my letters to Lord Elgin and Tau, that to Baron Gros being much the same as Lord Elgin's.

I am, my dear sir, sincerely yours,

C. POUTIATINE.

Hon. W. B. REED.

Inclosure 11 *b*.

[Translation of French version from the Russian.]

NOTE TO COMMISSIONER TAU AND HIS COLLEAGUES.

ON BOARD THE STEAMER AMERICA, *May* 6, 1858.

The plenipotentiary of Russia has received from the plenipotentiaries of France and England a communication, in which it is said that a delay of six days is granted to Commissioner Tau to ask the court of Pekin for full powers, similar to those which the Emperor Tao-kwang gave to the Imperial Commissioners Kiying and Ilipu, in 1842 and 1844, on sending them to the south to negotiate with the plenipotentiaries of England and France. The undersigned requests Commissioner Tau and his colleagues to address their government immediately, and to solicit it to send to Takoo, within the fixed period of delay, full powers written in the exact terms which have been designated to them by the representatives of the allied powers. The plenipotentiary of Russia deems it his duty to urge the Commissioner Tau to take this demand into serious consideration, and to notify him that by satisfying it the Chinese government will avoid hostilities which might otherwise ensue therefrom.

The undersigned embraces this opportunity, &c., &c.,

COUNT POUTIATINE.

Inclosure 11 *c*.

COPY OF A LETTER TO LORD ELGIN.

MAY 6, 1858.

I am much indebted to your lordship for the last communication you did me the favor to address. In allowing time to reconsider at Pekin the present intimation, your lordship has shown great unwillingness to employ violent measures; and no one can deny the propriety to insist on producing credentials of the same form, by Commissioner Tau, as have once been given by the court of Pekin to a Chinese plenipotentiary. I am aware that without firmness and threats there is no possibility to arrive at a satisfactory result in dealing with the Chinese government; but perhaps those means will succeed as well, or even better, than hostile operations.

I am sending to the same effect a short note to Commissioner Tau, thinking that by doing so I am acting agreeably to your lordship's intentions.

COUNT POUTIATINE.

Inclosure 11 *d.*

MINNESOTA, *May* 5, 1858.

MY DEAR SIR: I have this moment received the inclosed letter from Lord Elgin, which I send for your perusal, and which I beg you to return by the bearer, who will return early to-morrow or some time to-night. I have no time to make copies. The dispatch to Tau is dated to-morrow, and will then go in. I think it all important that the Chinese should give the powers *now* demanded. As soon as the Slaney comes in, you may infer the dispatch has arrived. Can you not see Tau, and impress this upon him? Nothing else will avert hostilities, and six days hence *the gun-boats will be here.* No one, of course, knows of my sending this intelligence to you; but my anxiety to avert hostilities will justify this seemingly irregular course. I am glad to find our resolute attitude is at last making its impression.

Very truly, yours,

WILLIAM B. REED.

His Excellency the COUNT POUTIATINE,
Imperial Commissioner and Commander-in-Chief, &c., &c., &c.

Inclosure 12 *a.*

MAY 4, 1858.

TAU, the Governor General of Chihli; TSUNG, the Superintendent of Granaries; and WÚ, under Secretary of the Privy Council, hereby send a communication:

We were very highly gratified with the interview we had yesterday with your excellency. You have come here simultaneously with the English and French. We are desirous to have a meeting with you, that you may then talk reason with [the envoys of] those two nations on our behalf respecting their affairs. Then most probably the other matters [between ourselves] can be settled [or prepared] for negotiation.

For this purpose, we now send this communication.

His Excellency WILLIAM B. REED,
Envoy Extraordinary and Minister Plenipotentiary of the United States to China.

Inclosure 12 *b.*

MINNESOTA, *May* 6, 1858.

MY DEAR SIR: I have concluded to answer Tau's letter, asking mediation, and send you a copy of what I have sent. The answer goes by this conveyance, or it can wait till yours is ready, whichever you think best. Lord Elgin and Baron Gros's letters went in this morning. My boat will come out in the morning.

Truly yours, in haste,

W. B. REED.

Count POUTIATINE.

Inclosure 12 *c.*

LEGATION OF THE UNITED STATES,
United States Ship Minnesota, May 6, 1858.

The undersigned has the honor to acknowledge the communication made on the 4th instant by the High Commissioner Tau and his colleagues, requesting him to mediate between China and the allied powers of England and France in the difficulties that have arisen between them.

The undersigned is doing all in his power to arrest further hostilities, but he frankly says to the imperial commissioners that his efforts will be fruitless, unless the preliminary demands of the English and the French ministers are met and acceded to in a proper spirit. They have now (as the undersigned understands) made a new and most reasonable request that your excellency shall within six days be furnished with and prepared to exhibit similar powers as by a confidential decree of July 27, 1842, were conferred on Kiying and Ilipu for the settlement of difficulties then pending. The undersigned earnestly hopes this may be done, and then there will be a chance for good offices and amicable settlement.

The undersigned expects the same powers to be exhibited to him, as well as the other papers promised by his Excellency Tau, and expects further, that matters of negotiation with the United States shall proceed promptly.

WILLIAM B. REED.

His Excellency TAU,
Imperial Commissioner, Governor General of Chihli, &c.,
With his colleagues Tsung and Wú.

Inclosure 13 *a.*

FLAG-SHIP, SAN JACINTO,
Off Shanghai, April 2, 1858.

SIR: I have the honor to acknowledge the receipt of your communication of the 29th ultimo, and am glad to learn that my order to Captain Du Pont to wear the American ensign at the main of the Minnesota is satisfactory to you in all its bearings.

I regret that the reply of the Chinese imperial court to your friendly communication is such as to call for the presence of the squadron at the mouth of the Peiho with a view to further operations.

Should you have occasion to land at Tientsin, and go from thence to the interior, I will, with great pleasure, afford you all the aid in my power.

The Minnesota is under the necessity of unshipping and reconstructing her rudder, which is very defective, and has been condemned by a board of survey. This, I fear, may detain her three weeks or a month.

The Mississippi is expected from Hong Kong daily. The San Jacinto and that ship shall be got ready for sea immediately; and you may, I think, calculate on their services by the 12th instant, the time specified by you.

The disposition of the squadron, when the climate shall cause a suspension of operations on the coast of China, depends on so many contingencies that I can arrive at no conclusion in regard to it at present. The Minnesota and Antelope shall be placed under your direct control, to remain with you within the limits of your mission, or to convey you with a view to health to Japan, or any other neighboring point that may better suit your convenience.

During the suspension of operations on the coast of China, I think it advisable to employ the other ships in the accomplishment of such other objects embraced in my instructions as may not interfere with their concentration on the coast of China at such point and at such time as you may designate.

I have the honor to be, sir, your obedient servant,

JOSIAH TATTNALL,
Flag-officer Commanding-in-chief.

His Excellency WILLIAM B. REED, *&c.*, *&c.*

Inclosure 13 *b*.

LEGATION OF THE UNITED STATES,
Minnesota, April 29, 1858.

SIR: In the absence of the commander-in-chief of the United States naval forces, I have the honor to inform you, as the senior officer, what my plans are for putting myself in communication with the Chinese authorities. I have received from his excellency Tau, governor general and imperial commissioner, an intimation, which will no doubt be put into more regular form in the course of to-day, that he will meet me on shore to-morrow, at or near Takoo, at such time as it may suit my convenience.

It is my intention, therefore, to go in the chartered steamer Antelope as far as her draft of water will permit. I have requested Captain Du Pont to accompany me, together with Major Terrett and Mr. Blake, of this ship; and, if agreeable to you, I shall be very glad to have the company of Lieutenant Stembel and Surgeon Fox, of the Mississippi.

Any other facilities you may think important to me, I shall be glad to have, though none occur to me at this time.

I avail myself of this opportunity to express to you and to your officers my sincere gratitude for your unvarying and considerate kindness to me during my sojourn on the Mississippi.

I have the honor to be, sir, your obedient servant,

WILLIAM B. REED.

Captain WILLIAM C. NICHOLSON,
United States ship Mississippi.

Inclosure 13 *c.*

UNITED STATES STEAM-FRIGATE MISSISSIPPI,
Anchorage off Peiho river, April 29, 1858.

SIR: I have the honor to acknowledge the receipt of yours of this date, informing me of your plans for communicating with the Chinese authorities on shore, and I am much gratified with your expression of satisfaction of my ship and officers.

Any wish of yours will be a command to me.

I am, sir, very respectfully, your obedient servant,

W. C. NICHOLSON,
Captain.

His Excellency WILLIAM B. REED.

Mr Reed to Mr. Cass.

[Extracts.]

No. 17.] LEGATION OF THE UNITED STATES, ON BOARD THE MINNESOTA,
Off the Peiho river, May 15, 1858.

SIR: Whatever may be the result of the pending preliminary operations here, I am very anxious that the course which I have felt it my duty to pursue—involving a difference of opinion with the plenipotentiaries of England and France—should be perfectly understood by the President. Being understood, I have the strongest confidence it will be approved.

The question has been this: the English and French plenipotentiaries insist that, having demanded the appointment of an imperial commissioner with full powers, they have a right to exact in advance, before they meet him, an exhibition of those powers. There was nothing, it will be observed, in the first letter of the Imperial Commissioner Tau to Lord Elgin and me to exclude the idea of his having full powers; and it was only on a sort of cross-examining correspondence which ensued that he in a certain sense disclaimed them. I attached great importance to personal intercourse, such as I asked last fall from Yeh, at Canton, and was and am of opinion that a moderate concession of a preliminary form, where no principle is involved, could do no substantial harm. I had, too, every reason to believe that the personal intercourse of the plenipotentiaries with the Chinese authorities would have promoted early and peaceful negotiations. They have thought differently; and the effect seems to have been that, whatever thus far has been accomplished in the way of conciliation and concession, has been done by Count Poutiatine and myself, and that the moderately kind feeling which, as I stated in my last dispatch, the imperial commissioner expressed towards Lord Elgin, has given place to a vague dread of him as some mysterious enemy who keeps aloof for purposes of evil.

My last dispatch explained more in detail the motives which influenced me to waive the preliminary scruple and meet the commissioner on the 3d. From him I learned that his powers enabled him to arrange at least the basis of a treaty, and then refer it in the aggregate to the capital. These certainly were not "full powers," in a technical sense; but the reference to Pekin of a treaty, after conference and negotiation, not signed by either party, (for I certainly did not mean to sign unless the Chinese plenipotentiary did,) but agreed to, was a process, which I described in my note to Lord Elgin of the 4th of May, as so assimilated to a ratification as to reconcile me to the experiment of a meeting. On this theory, I felt myself entirely justified in acting. I was content, as every one must be in dealing with these orientals, to take the risk of their not telling the truth.

In an interview, which I subsequentiy had on board this ship with his lordship, I found that we were reasoning from entirely different premises. He had adopted the doctrines of European public law, which make the full powers of a minister evidence of an ability to bind the sovereign; nor did he seem willing to comprehend the distinction which my American training enabled me to take between such full powers and those, for instance, which I had—their exercise subject to ratification by the President or Senate—or those which the Chinese claimed to have, of negotiating and then submitting their acts in the aggregate for the sovereign revision. I do not, of course, mean to say that there is more than an assimilation; but that assimilation is reasonable, if there be, as is alleged by those familiar with the Chinese idiom, a difficulty of rendering the term "*full powers*," or even "plenipotentiary," into a correlative. The word used may as well mean "*almighty*" or "*all-powerful*," as plenipotentiary; and it is not necessary to say that, while etymologically these words in English are identical, they have a very different signification in ordinary use. Besides, the principal reason for Lord Elgin's insisting on this condition precedent was the refusal of the authorities at the capital to correspond directly with us. It was that refusal that seemed to give point to his appeal to me in his letter of the 5th of May, when he asked me, "in all earnestness, how is it possible international relations can subsist under such a system?" Now, when the Chinese explicitly yield the privilege of direct correspondence, there would be no difficulty in answering his lordship's earnest appeal. It may not be as convenient as personal access to Pekin, but it is better than anything we have ever had before, and even this concession would not have been known to us if all the ministers had been equally punctilious.

On the very day when Lord Elgin called on me, guardedly to express his dissent from my views and disapproval of my course, (though it was communicated in the most respectful manner,) I received from

Baron Gros his letter of the 7th of May. (Inclosure 1 *a*.) I was unable to see the justice of the criticism on my conduct which his excellency, the French minister, thought fit, though in the most courteous terms, to pass, and wrote him my answer of the 8th. The effect of which, as revealed in his note of the 10th, and his relations to me since, I am happy to say has been most satisfactory. (1 *b* and *c*.)

Confirmed, on full reflection, in my confidence that I was pursuing the course which would promote, what I had most at heart, pacification and successful negotiation, I had a second interview with the imperial commissioners, at the Takoo forts, on the 10th. At my first interview I had required of them to produce, before I would see them again, a copy of my letter to the prime minister written from the Canton river on the 10th of February last. I thought its production would show that my letter had reached the capital, and that these officials were in communication with the ministry. This was done, and I have it in my possession. An instance of friendly disposition on the part of the Chinese occurred in the interval of my interviews, which had great weight with me. The Russian minister had said to the Chinese officials that he should regard it as an evidence of a friendly spirit on the part of the imperial authorities if they would permit the resident Russian missionaries at the capital to come to Takoo to meet him and their other countrymen on his ship.

The missionaries had been eight years in their exile of Pekin. This, too, was granted; and, after a three days' journey, two members of the Russian Missionary College arrived at Takoo. They represent the capital in a state of deplorable distress and disorganization.

Everything thus conducing to friendly intercourse, on the 10th instant I went again on shore and had a long and interesting interview with their excellencies the commissioners. There was the same courtesy and ceremonial as before; and, with not a little unmeaning conversation, an approach to some results, which were significant. The formal details of the interview I do not care to trouble you with, but the results were these: that they rejected my proposition for a resident or even occasional minister at Pekin, and the free navigation of the rivers of China; but agreed to direct correspondence under seal between the United States and the privy council and prime minister; the opening of seven new ports, including (what I deem of great importance) two in Formosa, viz: Tai-wan and Ton-shui, and five on the coast, viz: Kiungchaw-fu, (capital of the Island of Hainan,) Tienpeh, and Cháu-chau-fu, in Kwangtung; Tsiuenchau-fu, in Fuhkien, and Wanchau, in Chehkiang; the absolute toleration of Christianity and missionary conversion; a modification of the tonnage duties to the advantage of American bottoms; and a stipulation in the broadest and strongest terms that in the event of any other or greater privileges, political or commercial, being either voluntarily or under pressure conceded to other nations, they should *ipso facto* inure to us. I have no doubt, had I been satisfied with this, and felt myself entirely independent of the action of others, I could, on these terms, have made a treaty, which would have been ratified at Pekin and sent back to me in forty-eight hours.

On the subject of our claims, they spoke doubtfully, but adversely, and seemed indisposed to entertain any discussion so long as Canton remained in the possession of an enemy; nor did my assurance, that I desired no final action till Canton should be restored, seem to affect them. As the interview was strictly preliminary, I did not press matters further.

Confident as I was that a treaty to this limited extent might be made, and that in it, as I have said, I could embody an article giving us the benefit of any stipulation which others might exact, I was too sensible of the obligation which even the partial and unsatisfactory concert I had had with the English and French plenipotentiaries created, of perfect frankness and unreserve, to think for a moment of making terms with the Chinese without letting the other plenipotentiaries know what had occurred. I felt my duty to be clearly prescribed, which was to decline further negotiations till I could again confer with the other ministers, and let them know how far the Chinese authorities were willing to go. (Inclosures 2 *a* and 2 *b*.)

For suspending the negotiations I had a fair pretext in the doubt which yet existed as to the reception and acknowledgment of the President's letter, as to which I insisted on a distinct and authoritative assurance that it would be received and acknowledged on terms of perfect equality. I therefore suspended further correspondence, and have not resumed it since, taking the first opportunity on my return to this ship to communicate all that occurred to Lord Elgin and Baron Gros.

On the 14th instant, I received a communication from the commissioner as to the President's letter, (inclosure 3 *f*,) in which there is a distinct assurance that it will be answered, and that there in no pretense that the United States are tributaries of China. Absurd as this disclaimer may seem to us, it is not without its significance.

In all this course of action on my part, waiving mere form and consenting to personal intercourse, no word escaped my lips to induce the Chinese to imagine there is the least difference of opinion between the representatives of the western powers. I lost no opportunity of urging the commissioners to yield any preliminary point as "to powers" to attain the greater good of meeting the plenipotentiaries. My last communication to Tau (inclosure 3 *e*) was as decisive on these points as if I agreed thoroughly with Lord Elgin and Baron Gros as to their importance.

In all that I have done, I have had the hearty concurrence of his excellency Count Poutiatine, to whose integrity of purpose throughout this unpleasant complication I can hardly do justice.

Our reward has been, that down to this time we have averted hostilities. I think, too, we have made a favorable impression on the Chinese. You will observe that Lord Elgin gives as one reason for delaying active operations his desire of reconciling, as far as possible, his course with mine; and I have no reason to doubt it is so. A very large, and, by the recent arrival of the gun-boats, a very available force has now been here for several days, and I have every confidence that it is no longer the want of means that defers action. I repeat, that it is a high pleasure to feel that I have contributed anything to defer, even for an hour, the great misery and discredit of a new Chinese war.

This effort, whether in the end it succeeds or fails, I hope the President will approve of.

* * * * * * * *

Anxious as I am, and as I believe the government at home is, that I should secure diplomatic access to the capital and the thorough revision of the treaty, I know that they only wish it accomplished by peaceful means as prescribed in my instructions. I recognize fully the doctrine asserted to my predecessor, that "there is no obligation, perfect or imperfect, resting upon China, to negotiate as to the revision of our treaty at Pekin, or at any place in the vicinity of that capital," and I do not believe that the civilized and Christian world will justify a war or any share in hostilities for the mere purpose of securing new political or commercial privileges.

Should all our efforts at pacification fail, and hostilities assume the form of an elaborate campaign on the part of the English and French, I still adhere to the course indicated in my dispatch of 15th December last, of withdrawing the legation and the squadron from a scene of conflict in which I have no disposition to participate, and where there are no material interests to protect. Of course, such decision may be modified by circumstances, and will not be finally made till I shall confer fully with the Russian minister.

* * * * * * * *

I have the honor to be, sir, your obedient servant,

WILLIAM B. REED.

Hon. LEWIS CASS,
Secretary of State, Washington.

Exhibit 1 *a.*

[Translation.]

EXTRAORDINARY MISSION OF FRANCE IN CHINA,
On board the Audacieuse, off the Peiho, May 7, 1858.

MR. MINISTER: I have received the dispatch which your excellency did me the honor to write to me on the 4th of this month, with the view of making known to me that, on the evening previous, you had had an official interview with the newly-appointed imperial commissioners, and of stating to me the reasons which have determined you to act separately under these circumstances.

I thank your excellency for the details which you have been pleased to give me in relation to the interview which you had with the Chinese commissioners—a subject full of interest; and I confidently hope that the advice you gave to those high functionaries, not to refuse what you believed to be the demands of France and Great Britain, may be taken into consideration.

Your excellency is pleased to say to me that the communication which I made to you on the 2d of this month—a communication which simply consisted in announcing to you that the answer which I had received from Governor Tau, on the subject of the powers that he ought to have, was not satisfactory—*had relieved you from the painful state of uncertainty in which you had been,* in regard to my intentions and those of Lord Elgin, since dispatches were sent to Pekin asking of the Chinese government the appointment of suitable plenipotentiaries duly authorized to treat with us. Let your excellency be pleased to permit me to remind you of the very *clear* position which I took from the first moment of concert with my honorable colleague of England, and in which your excellency cordially concurred, without, however, being able, as you were pleased to say to me, to exceed the limits which were prescribed to you by your entirely pacific instructions. Your excellency has in your possession a copy of the note which I wrote to the Prime Minister Yu, on the 12th of February last, and your excellency can therein see that, after stating to that minister the demands of France and the reparations which she exacted, except that if it was requisite some modifications might be made to them, I terminated my note with these very precise words: "If, at the period designated, that is to say, at the end of the month of March, the undersigned does not find at Shanghai, whither he is going to proceed, a suitable plenipotentiary, *furnished with sufficient powers* to grant the desired reparations and to resolve the questions which have just been spoken of, &c., the undersigned will be compelled, much to his regret, to adopt such measures as circumstances may demand, to put an end to a state of things which ought not to be prolonged."

It was therefore evident that if, on the 1st of April of this year, I did not find at Shanghai a plenipotentiary furnished with full powers to treat with me, I would have the right to resort immediately to the employment of force, if, in concert with my honorable colleague of England, we should judge it necessary; and your excellency, I trust, will do me the justice to believe that I would *never* have adopted a resolution of this character without previously having made it known to your excellency, who had been so completely associated in our pacific steps.

It is useless to recall to your excellency what has taken place at Shanghai. No Chinese plenipotentiary has presented himself there in the name of the government at Pekin, either before or after the 1st of April; and since that day I have had the right to act in a hostile manner against the Chinese government, if I judged it necessary. But, although having *received an answer which was not satisfactory,* animated then, as I am still, by the sincere wish not to come to painful extremities unless forced into them, and desiring also to afford to your excellency, as long as possible, the means of not yet separating your action from ours, I had the honor to make known to you that, in accord with my honorable colleague of England, I was going to proceed to the Pechele, thus granting a *second* delay to the Chinese government; and I sent to your excellency a copy of the note which I wrote to the Prime Minister Yu, announcing to him my early departure for the north.

Arrived off the Peiho, and not having received any communication on the part of the Chinese, it was agreed between Lord Elgin and myself that, instead of acting in a hostile manner, we would accord a *third* delay to the government at Pekin, and, as always, I had the honor to notify your excellency thereof.

At length, the arrival of the two imperial commissioners at Takoo, followed soon by that of the governor general himself, having been announced to us, it was incumbent on me, before making known to your excellency the determination which I might be led to take, to ascertain correctly whether this step of the Chinese government was *serious*, and whether, as I had demanded of it in terms which did not admit of any ambiguity, these commissioners had the necessary powers to treat with me on the questions which had been submitted for a long while to the court of Pekin. It was requisite, therefore, for me to address a note on this subject to the Imperial Commissioner Tau, and I sent a copy of it to your excellency. Tau answered me that he was here to learn what was to be treated about, and to refer in relation thereto to Pekin. On the 2d of this month I transmitted this answer to your excellency, expressing to you the idea that it was not satisfactory, and announcing to you that as soon as my rejoinder to the governor should be ready, I would send it to you. I need not say to you that a decisive course to be taken under circumstances so grave certainly required a profound examination.

On the following day I learned, from a report addressed to Admiral Rigault de Genouilly, that on that very day, that is to say, on *the 3d*, you had been officially received with great ceremony by the Chinese commissioners; and on the 4th, your excellency, in making known to me the determination which you had taken and carried into effect the evening previous, ascribes it to *the uncertainty which had ceased to exist* in your mind on the subject of my intentions and those of Lord Elgin, and to the impossibility of your acceding beforehand to a correspondence relative to the formulas, more or less strict, of western diplomacy. I can here, Mr. Minister, only recall the facts, and whatever might be the cause of them, it is indubitable that, before the diplomatic action of the four plenipotentiaries had ceased to have a common agreement towards a pacific end, an isolated and *official* act could make the Chinese believe, perhaps, that the understanding so happily existing at that time between the four plenipotentiaries was not so intimate as they had feared it was.

I trust, Mr. Minister, that your excellency will only see in this exposition, which your dispatch of the 4th leads me to lay before you, the desire that I entertain of thoroughly convincing you that I never had the idea of leaving your excellency a single instant in uncertainty, so long as I was not in it myself; and I earnestly request you to believe that if, through an involuntary cause, I have been able to give rise to the slightest of it in your mind, I sincerely regret it.

However this may be, I call your excellency's attention to the note which I have transmitted to Tau, and a copy of which I have already sent to your excellency. This again is a *fourth* delay granted to the Chinese government. I do not ask it, as your excellency might have supposed, to conform to European usages on the subject of full powers to be given to its commissioners; I only claim of it what it has already done, in 1842 and in 1844, for the Commissioner Kiying. Tau, in my opinion, at least, and according to the declaration which he has made to me, has no power to treat with me; and if I were to go and meet him, I should find myself in the *unacceptable* position that, not being able to be received at Pekin, for the purpose of there entering into negotiations, I would be placed in presence of high functionaries who had no power to treat, and who would have nothing else to do but to listen to me in order to repeat at Pekin what I have already written to the prime minister of the Emperor at that capital.

The note which I have sent to Governor Tau is a new attempt, made in the hope—a very feeble one, I admit—of arriving by it at any amicable solution with the Chinese government; and I shall hasten to make known to your excellency the answer which I receive from that functionary, as also the course which it will be my duty to determine on, in concert with my honorable colleague of England, if unhappily it should still be requisite to resort to the employment of coercive measures.

Your excellency is convinced that the imperial commissioner has all the necessary powers for negotiating and settling with you the questions which you have indicated in your correspondence with the prime minister of Pekin, and that he will not have to refer respecting them to the supreme government, except to ask for the final sanction to the treaty agreed on. I earnestly wish that it may be so, and a few days will now be sufficient, in order to ascertain whether the facts upon which I base my conjectures have not the bearing which I have thought I found in them, and whether the confidence which your excellency places on the words of the new envoys is well founded.

I need not say to your excellency that I should be happy if my fears were not confirmed.

I have the honor to be, Mr. Minister, your excellency's very humble and very obedient servant,

BARON GROS.

His Excellency W. B. REED,
Envoy Extraordinary and Minister Plenipotentiary of the United States of America in China, &c., &c., &c.

LEGATION OF THE UNITED STATES,
On board the Minnesota, Gulf of Pechele, May 8, 1858.

MONSIEUR LE BARON: I hasten to acknowledge the receipt of your excellency's letter of the 7th, which came to my hands this morning. The courteous spirit which animates it, so entirely consistent with the cordial friendliness of our personal relations, and the desire I have that no act of mine should ever for a moment be misinterpreted, combine to induce me promptly to reply to it. In order to do so, I may find it necessary to recur to details very familiar to you, but which I desire to present in a proper collocation.

I flatter myself that I can convince your excellency that I have never desired, still less determined to act isolatedly (*isolément*) in the unpleasant circumstances in which, by no act of ours, his excellency the Russian plenipotentiary and myself have lately found ourselves; that what I have thought it my duty to do, has been the result of as careful a consideration (*examen ap profondi*) as I have been able to give it, and that there is as little danger from what your excellency erroneously terms "*un acte isole,*" such as I have adopted, as from any other direct step towards a people so peculiar as the Chinese. If I fail to do so, I beg to say to you, with a sincerity which my high personal esteem for your excellency insures, that I shall most deeply regret it. I do not think, however, when the matter is properly presented, there can be any misunderstanding.

Your excellency's frankness enables and requires me to be equally frank in return, and, so writing, to refer somewhat to the past.

For the first three months after my arrival in China, and during the hostilities in the South, though charged to put myself in frank and unreserved communication with your excellency and Lord Elgin, I found myself in a position really of isolation. Instructed by my government, as you are aware, for I have every reason to believe a copy of my instructions was given to Count Sartiges, to avail myself of any opportunity by means of meditation, to terminate or avert actual or impending hostilities, I was deprived of all means of doing so by the perversity of the then imperial commissioner, who refused to see me, and thus frustrated all good offices. It is not worth my while to conjecture what would have been the result of an experiment at mediation, even if Yeh had solicited it. I made none, however, and only refer to this as illustrative of the solicitous feeling I had to be the means, however humble, of putting an end to what I believe we all regard as these deplorable hostilities. As to the "isolation" to which I as the representative of the United States felt myself condemned during the actual progress of hostilities, from the date of the blockade of the Canton river by Admiral Rigault de Genouilly on the 10th of December, to the restoration of peace by the notification of your excellency and Lord Elgin on the 6th February, I was willing to find ample reason for it in the necessities of a state of war, and your excellency will do me the justice to remember that I never sought in correspondence with you to depart from it or to intrude upon councils to which I was quite aware I could not be a party.

From this position I suppose I was entirely relieved by the communications made to me by your excellency and Lord Elgin, on the 4th February, and you do me no more than justice in saying that I entered and have adhered cordially to the concert of action which was there proposed; and I think you will do me the further justice, that until what your excellency seems to think was my separate action on Monday last (4th) every support was given by me to whatever measures Lord Elgin and your excellency suggested, that either you, we, or our respective governments could desire.

But at the same time your excellency will permit me to observe, for your frankness requires me to speak plainly, (*parler tout haut,*) that with the modified concert which was prescribed I was far from content. It is, I am quite aware, hardly consonant with good taste, even to seem to complain of a want of confidence among equals, nor should I do so, but for the fact of an undeserved inference, as it seems to me, that I had departed from a well understood concert between us. The moment that your excellency's notification of the 6th February announced to the world that hostile operations against China were suspended and treaty relations restored, I supposed that the distinction, well taken during actual war, between the representatives of the treaty powers was at end, and that there would be that free concert in the form of conference and consultation which is always most agreeable as it is the safest, and to which I could not but feel my country was entitled. Yet for reasons which no doubt were sufficient and into which I beg you to believe I do not pretend to inquire, a different course was and has been to this moment pursued and the concert from the date of the dispatches of February to those of April to the court of Pekin, has simply been the adoption of a course of action by the representatives of France and Great Britain, and a request to the Russian plenipotentiary and myself to follow it. Resolute that no accidental feeling on our part should interfere with a general line of conduct toward the Chinese authorities which our judgment approved, we have followed implicitly; and I beg to assure your excellency that no word has escaped me in correspondence with my own government revealing a state of feeling which would not have been made known to you now but for the friendly, though somewhat inculpatory tone of your last letter. Nor do I feel, and I have a strong desire to disabuse your excellency's mind on this point, that the course I have lately felt it my duty to adopt, is any departure from the concert I have so steadfastly cherished. It rather illustrates the evil of that sort of distant, half confidence which I have so much regretted.

I beg your excellency's attention to the actual state of recent facts. On the 23d April I received notes from your excellency and Lord Elgin, informing me that you proposed to send letters to Pekin allowing six more days from the 24th for the appointment of a duly accredited plenipotentiary to meet you at or near Takoo, a place within the mouth of the river, either on shore or on board one of your vessels. In this course I at once and cheerfully acquiesced, and was sorry that the very late hour at which I received your private note presented me from availing myself of the courteous offer of Lord Elgin and yourself to forward my dispatch by the gun-boat. I sent mine, as you are aware, through the friendly agency of Count Poutiatine. In my dispatch to Pekin, of which your excellency was at once furnished with a copy, I said that on the last day of the month (Friday, 30th) I meant to be at or near Takoo, hoping there to find a plenipotentiary. Such was my intention and such I believed to be yours; and it was my understanding that during those six days there was to be no change in our mutual relations, or in yours to the Chinese.

On Thursday the 29th, one day before the expiration of the time allowed to the Chinese, I learned accidentally from observations made by the officers on board this ship, that five or six English and French men-of-war had crossed the bar and anchored close to the Chinese batteries near Takoo. This was, I confess matter of surprise and regret to me, more perhaps, because it seemed to me to be a new revelation of the want of entire confidence, or rather of the separate action which I had so long deplored. My duty, however, was that of silence; and in maintaining it to follow the example set me, for your excellency will recollect that not one word passed between us from the 24th of April to the 1st of May, when I wrote to you what I may well describe as my anxious note of that day, except your note of the 28th and 29th, inclosing the letter of Tsung and Wú with its annotations.

With his excellency Count Poutiatine I had in that interval the most constant and unreserved intercourse, and I shall do him the greatest injustice did I fail to bear willing testimony to his earnest efforts at any sacrifice of personal convenience or official punctilio to induce the Chinese authorities to do what was right, and what he supposed you required. If I may venture to describe the prevalent sentiment which pervaded our conference, it was a sense of perplexity, and a strong regret that we were not apprised of the current state of things as affecting the acts of the other plenipotentiaries. Count Poutiatine had more than one personal interview with the Chinese officials, and I have every reason to believe what was designed, done, and said by and to him, was as unreservedly communicated to your excellency as it was to me.

Be this as it may, from the 23d to the 30th I remained in this ship. What communications passed between the First Commissioners Tsung-hièn and Wú and myself, the course I thought it my duty to take in sending back the first communication from Tau you are already apprised of.

I meant to treat it as a nullity and to go in near Takoo, as I had said I should, and in this decision I was more determined by the fact of the vessels-of-war having gone in the day before, and from my reasonable assumption that your excellency and Lord Elgin meant to go in too. If there is anything on the face of the correspondence or in our personal intercourse to authorize a different conclusion, it has escaped my recollection. This anticipation was strengthened by the receipt of a communication from, Tau on the morning of the 30th, in proper form, forwarded to me in a boat from the Audacieuse, and by the fact that the Chinese officers who brought it exhibited cards from your excellency and Lord Elgin, and informed me that Tau's letters to you had been received. I had a right to take for granted they were identical in terms with mine, and in the exercise of the best unassisted judgment I could form, mine was at least sufficiently satisfactory as to justify me in meeting the new commissioner. And here your excellency will permit me, in the same friendly unreserve which I assure you animates me, to observe another practical embarrassment resulting from the comparative estrangement to which Count Poutiatine and I have felt ourselves condemned; in the want of something like a standard of interpretation of those Chinese documents in which we are equally interested. Documents may be identical in words and yet differ widely when interpreted. I have some reason to think this has been the case, and nothing would have been more agreeable to me if I had supposed it would be acceptable than to put at your excellency's command any facilities I have, or to receive them in return. Thus uninformed and thus reasoning, I entered the river on the afternoon of the 30th. My letter to you of the 1st, described to you my disappointment at your then unexplained absence; the courteous urgency of the Chinese and my refusal to fix a time out of deference to the views of Lord Elgin and your excellency; unable to account for your absence, I had said to the Chinese that on Monday at the latest, I would fix the time for the interview, and much as I desired to conform my action to yours, having said so, I certainly did not feel at liberty, in consequence of the late revelations made to me on the evening of Sunday, (2d,) to say to the Chinese that I had changed my mind altogether, and would not meet them till a new scruple not originating with me had been removed. The fruit of my perplexity and of mature consideration was to keep the word I had given, and meet the commissioner. Your excellency will observe that I had no reason before to suspect that Tau's letter to you differed in terms from his to me, and that was not known to me till late in the evening of the 1st of May.

But it would be very unfair to attribute the course I took wholly to the silence of your excellency and Lord Elgin. My judgment differed then, as it does now, on the question of the expediency of personal conference and inquiry, before asking for the production of full powers. I doubt whether, even among western nations, pretending to great accuracy of forms, (though in this and all other matters of technical diplomacy, I defer to your excellency's greater knowledge and experience,) a preliminary demand as to the production of a plenipotentiary's powers would precede an interview or reception. Here, I am satisfied, no such condition precedent should be exacted; and thus thinking, deliberately and conscientiously, I was aware of nothing, even in the past friendly relations existing among us, to require me to yield that judgment. My adhering to it and acting on it, contrary to what it now appears were your excellency's wishes, is a new illustration of the evils of the limited confidence which has been allowed to exist.

I have thus frankly explained to your excellency the reasons which were operative to lead me to adopt the course I have pursued, and it will be a matter of extreme regret to me if they do not convince you that nothing was further from my mind than an intentional disregard of your wishes, or of any mode of concerted action you suppose was adopted. It may be, as your excellency intimates, that what you describe as my confidence, in the words of the imperial commissioner and his colleagues, may be misplaced, but if it is, I shall be content to bear the reproach of undue credulity, having the consciousness that, according to my unassisted judgment, I have done what little lies in my power to avert or postpone the shedding of blood in the unequal contest of the very strong with the very weak. A judgment on what I do, must, after all, be passed by my own countrymen, who have sent me here on an errand of peace.

Saying this, I beg to renew to your excellency the assurance of the great pleasure I shall have, in finding that, by this frank explanation of what I meant and have done, I have removed an erroneous impression from your mind, and of the high and sincere regard and distinguished consideration with which, I am, Monsieur le Baron, your excellency's obedient, humble servant,

WILLIAM B. REED.

His Excellency Monsieur le BARON GROS,
Commissioner Extraordinary and Embassador of
His Majesty the Emperor of the French in China.

2 *a.*

LEGATION OF THE UNITED STATES,
Antelope, May 11, 1858.

MONSIEUR LE BARON: I have the honor to inform you that I had another interview yesterday with the Chinese imperial commissioners, the result of which, I regret to say, was far from satisfactory. At my former interview, I promised to meet them again at the expiration of five days, if, in the meantime, they should furnish me from the archives at the capital a copy of the letter which, on the 10th of February, I addressed to the supreme council of state. A copy of that letter was sent to me on the 8th, (Saturday.)

My object in seeing the commissioners, aside from keeping the promise I had given them, was twofold:

1. To endeavor to persuade them by a candid and earnest expression of my own wishes, and of my conviction of the certain consequences of a refusal to comply with the requisition of your excellency and Lord Elgin, as to the production of powers, such as were held by Kiying and Ilipu, in 1842, and by Kiying in 1844. I regret to say that no impression seemed to be made by what I said, and that I have no doubt either that an absolute refusal will be sent, or the time allowed will expire without a word of reply to your excellency's demand. The high commissioner repeated all he had before said and written, as to his proximity to the court, and the inconsistency of such a delegation of power with the established rules of the Empire; adding at last the remarkable statement, of the truth of which you can judge as well as I, that if Kiying exhibited such powers, he must have forged them, and that he was degraded for what he did. I do not care to inquire where the falsehood is; from recent revelations my confidence in Kiying's good faith not being at all greater than what I have in his successor. All however that is material is, that the commissioners gave me distinctly to understand that the demand of the plenipotentiaries of France and Great Britain will not be complied with, and that he and his colleagues were prepared for the consequences of this decision.

With the view I had been willing to take of Tau's assumed powers, I had another object in my interview yesterday which was to ascertain, if possible, on what points he was, even in his own limited authority the same as he says Kiying really had, willing hereafter to negotiate.

With a very distinct understanding that it was but matter of preliminary inquiry, I had no difficulty in arriving at a result here also. To the suggestion of a resident minister at Pekin, or to any visit, periodical or otherwise, or to personal access to the court, and to opening the rivers and internal marts of China, an absolute refusal is given, even to the extent of not being willing to discuss it.

The points on which they expressed a willingness to treat, and which I believe could be embodied into a treaty, are:

1. Direct correspondence, by sealed communications, with the privy council—not only the receipt of such communications, but the acknowl-

edgement of them on terms of equality. In short, direct correspondence, in its most comprehensive form.

2. The immediate legalization and opening of all the ports where irregular trade is now carried on, and those named were Swatow, Chinchu, Taiwan, Fangshau, Wunchaw, and Chapoo. I think that a modification of duties might be treated of, though as I had no intention of doing more than ascertaining in a general way what hereafter they might be willing to discuss, I did not go into detail.

There was another incidental matter which was talked of in this interview—the proper mode of receiving the President's letter at the capital. I refused to hand it to the imperial commissioner until I should see the decree of the Emperor as to its mode of reception. It was promised to me, and this morning it has been sent. I inclose a copy, and need hardly say it is entirely unsatisfactory.

The subject of claims of citizens of the United States was also alluded to, as a matter about which I inquired if the commissioners felt themselves authorized hereafter to negotiate. They were not understood to deny their powers or willingness to treat of this, but the impression left on my mind was very clear that such claims, stated, as they were, in the most general way and to a moderate amount, would not be recognized. So distinct is this impression that it is my intention, by the earliest possible opportunity, to ask on this point new instructions from my government. I inclose to your excellency a copy of the note which it is my intention to-morrow to address to the high commissioners, from which you will see the final decision to which I have come; and I have every reason to hope that this incidental effort on my part to induce these officials to listen to reason, made by those they choose to regard as friends, will not be without its good results. Let those results be what they may in the immediate future, I am conscious of a sincere desire to defer the evil day of conflict, and to make more apparent to the Chinese government that it is a necessity created by themselves which reconciles me to what is about to occur.

I had the honor this morning to receive your excellency's letter of the 10th, for which I beg to thank you, and heartily reciprocate the kind feeling it expresses.

I have the honor to be, M. le Baron, with the highest consideration, your excellency's most obedient, humble servant,

WILLIAM B. REED.

His Excellency Monsieur le BARON GROS,
Commissioner Extraordinary and Embassador
of his Majesty the Emperor of the French in China.

A similar letter sent to Lord Elgin, omitting the last paragraph.

---

2 *b*.

LEGATION OF THE UNITED STATES,
Minnesota, May 13, 1858.

MY LORD: I find on conference with Mr. Williams, the secretary of legation and Chinese interpreter, who returned last evening from the river, that in my communication to your excellency of the 11th instant, I misstated the names of the ports which the Chinese authorities expressed a willingness to open to foreign trade. Those which really were named, are:

Hai-kau, the entrepot of Kiungcha-fu, in the island of Hainan;

Tienpeh and Châuchau-fu, (or Swatow,) in the province of Kwangtung;

Tsiuenchau-fu, in Fuhkien;

Tai-wan and Tan-schwui, in Formosa; and

Wanchau-fu, in Chehkiang.

I have no doubt these would be conceded without difficulty.

Mr. Williams, in delivering my last letter to the commissioners, had a long conversation with Tsien, the treasurer, who was deputed to meet him. So soon as the weather moderates, Mr. Williams will have the honor of waiting on your excellency and communicating the purport. It may interest you.

I have the honor to be, my lord, your excellency's most obedient servant,

WILLIAM B. REED.

His Excellency the Earl of Elgin and Kincardine,
Her Britannic Majesty's High Commissioner, &c., &c., &c.

A similar note was sent to Baron Gros, omitting the last paragraph.

---

2 *c*.

HER MAJESTY'S SHIP FURIOUS,
May 11, 1858.

SIR: I have had the honor to receive this evening your excellency's letter of this day's date, and beg to offer you my thanks for the very interesting information which it contains.

I have the honor to be, sir, your excellency's most humble, obedient servant,

ELGIN AND KINCARDINE.

His Excellency the Hon. W. B. REED, &c., &c., &c.

Exhibit 2.

[Translation.]

MISSION EXTRAORDINARY FROM FRANCE TO CHINA,
On board the Audacieuse, May 12, 1858.

SIR AND MINISTER: I received yesterday the dispatch which your excellency has done me the honor to write, to inform me of the result of the second interview you have had with the imperial commissioners recently appointed. I also equally acknowledge receipt of the documents annexed to the dispatch, and thank your excellency for this important communication. I have no need to say how much I regret the blindness and bad faith which the Chinese authorities have displayed in this matter.

Your excellency will find hereto annexed a translation of the answer which I have received from the same commissioners, whom I had asked to solicit from their government powers identical with those which Kiying received in 1842 and 1844. This answer is far from satisfactory, above all, after the declarations made to your excellency by the same commissioners as to their inclination to oppose a formal refusal to the requests of France and England.

In the serious circumstances which the attitude taken by the Chinese commissioners may induce, I shall soon have to come to a determination which my peculiar position commands; and whatever it may be, I shall have the honor of communicating it to your excellency as soon as possible.

I seize this occasion to renew to your excellency the assurance of my sentiments of high consideration.

BARON GROS.

His Excellency Mr. W. B. Reed,
Envoy Extraordinary and Minister Plenipotentiary of the United States of America to China, &c., &c.

Exhibit 2 d.

[Translation of translation from Chinese.]

ANSWER OF TAU TO BARON GROS.

May 10, 1858.

Tau, &c., &c., Tsung, &c., &c., Wú, &c., &c., make the following communication:

We have received a dispatch from your excellency in which you say to us that the Imperial Commissioners Kiying and Ilipu had received full powers from the august Emperor Tao Kwang to solve personally in conference (*de vive voix*) the differences which then existed between the two nations; and that you set a postponement of six days that we might ask from court full powers identical with those which then were given to those imperial commissioners.

What you say to us is proof of your prudent management of public affairs, but it is our duty to inform you that in China the title of *high functionary clothed with full powers* does not exist. The powers to treat upon opportune occasion which were given to the ex-Commissioners Kiying and Ilipu that they might conclude treaties were asked at that time; but such powers did not give them the right to treat freely and at their will. We, the high functionaries, having been expressly appointed by the august Emperor, have received from his Majesty a decree, which he says to us: "Tsung, the one, and the other, (Wú,) who have been appointed high imperial commissioners, may deliberate and treat of affairs, and Tau-ting-sian, occupying a more elevated position, has orders, by that even, to deliberate with them."

From the moment when the august orders of his Majesty authorized us to negotiate matters in litigation, we had powers like those of the two commissioners Kiying and Ilipu; and the questions we shall have to discuss will be treated with full justice and with entire impartiality for the welfare of both nations. To prove this, it is sufficient to remember that in the fourth year of Hein-fung, (1854,) in which the present Commissioner Tsung met at this place, with the second envoy of your noble nation and the envoy of England, to consider the exemption from payment of duties in arrear, the question treated of was submitted to the court, and after having received the approbation of the Emperor, could then be settled. And now having seen the dispatch you addressed to us, we have referred it to the court, and have received the imperial decree which prescribes to us conformity to orders which had been given to us to treat of affairs.

It is our duty, then, to address this reply to your excellency that you may understand the matter; and we pray you to have the goodness not to delay the affair, or to entertain doubts. We hope that you soon will please to indicate the day on which we can meet for deliberation.

Special dispatch addressed to Ko, &c., 27th day of third moon of the eighteenth year of Hein-fung, (May 10, 1858.)

True translation.

BARON GROS.

---

3 *a*.

MAY 7, 1858.

TAU, Governor General of Chihli; TSUNG, Superintendent of Granaries; and WÚ, Under Secretary of the Cabinet, hereby communicate on business:

We have to acknowedge your excellency's communication, in which you remark, "I am doing all in my power to avert hostilities, but [the imperal commissioners] must meet and deliberate in a proper spirit, &c.* We, the commissioners, having had the honor to receive his Majesty's commands to repair to Tientsin, and there to attend to and manage the demands of each nation, must necessarily carefully deliberate on those demands with justice and fairness. It is a matter of great satisfaction to us that we have now obtained your excellency's mediatory good offices, and consequently we ought to open negotiations upon those points which relate to the United States.

At the last interview you spoke to us respecting the letter from the

---

* This extract is abbreviated in an important point; the original dispatch reads thus: "I am doing all in my power to avert further hostilities; but unless the preliminary demands of the English and French ministers are met and acceded to in a proper spirit," &c., &c. The writers apparently wish to avoid the idea that they promise to accede to those demands, while referring to the rest of the sentence respecting the arrest of hostilities.

President, and we have now been instructed by a rescript from the throne that we have permission to receive it. Will your excellency accordingly prepare the letter and transmit it to us, with the translation, that we may respectfully hand up the same.

We also, herewith, inclose to your excellency a copy of the letter [which you] sent to the prime minister Yu, that you may examine the same.

An important communication sent to his excellency William B. Reed, envoy extraordinary and minister plenipotentiary of the United States in China.

Translated by S. W. WILLIAMS.

Mr. Reed to Tau.

ON BOARD THE MINNESOTA, *May* 7, 1858.

The undersigned, envoy extraordinary and minister plenipotentiary of the United States, informs his excellency Tau, &c., that, according to promise, he intends, if the weather permits, to be at the Takoo forts on Monday, the 10th instant, between 10 and 11 o'clock in the morning, then to resume his friendly interview with his excellency.

He is not yet officially informed whether his excellency has received from Pekin the papers he promised the undersigned to procure. If they have come, he hopes the imperial commissioner will notify him in writing of that fact, and send him copies of what he has received.

The moment the undersigned receives such official notification, he will send to his excellency the commissioner the points on which he desires to change the present treaty.

Having thus complied with all that he promised, the undersigned says to his excellency the commissioner that he shall expect, as a matter of friendship and justice, that his excellency shall produce, at the next meeting, his commission and powers, or the decree containing them, such as Kiying and Ilipu had in 1842, and Kiying had in 1844.

This the English and French demand under threats, and this the Americans, the faithful friends of China, have a right to look for. This is due to friendship.

The undersigned will remain on board his ship at the outer anchorage till Sunday evening.

W. B. REED.

MAY 8, 1858.

TAU, Governor General of Chihli; TSUNG, Superintendent of Granaries; with WÚ, Under Secretary of the Privy Council, herewith send a communication:

We have to acknowledge your excellency's communication, in which you inform us that, on the 10th instant, if the weather be favorable, you will come to an interview about 11 o'clock, a. m., for the purpose of friendly consultation, &c., &c.

We are gratified to learn from this new proof that your excellency still maintains your friendly and cordial regard. It is highly expedient that we should personally discuss all the points to be settled by us, and we accordingly request that the proposed interview may be held at the time specified, when we can confer together. We further request that the President's letter may be brought at the same time, in order that we may forward it to the court.

As is meet, we now forward this necessary note to his excellency William B. Reed, envoy extraordinary and minister plenipotentiary of the United States in China.

Translated by S. W. WILLIAMS.

MAY 10, 1858.

TAU, Governor General of Chihli; TSUNG, Superintendent of the Granaries; and WÚ, Under Secretary of the Cabinet, hereby communicate on business:

We have memorialized [the throne] respecting the letter sent from your country, and his Majesty is much pleased to learn that there is one. On the 5th instant his Majesty issued his rescript to the following effect:

"The national letter, (*i. e.* the President's,) which by regulation should have been given in to be forwarded from Canton, has now been brought to Tientsin. Tau-ting-siang and his colleagues were thereupon commissioned by ourself to attend to it, and they are now allowed to receive and forward the same, and to hand it up on behalf of the American minister, together with the translation, by which we may be able to understand it fully.

"This from the Emperor."

As is proper, we now respectfully copy the above, and communicate it to your excellency.

A necessary communication, addressed to his excellency William B. Reed, envoy extraordinary and minister plenipotentiary of the United States, in China.

Translated by S. W. WILLIAMS.

MAY 11, 1858.

The undersigned, envoy extraordinary and minister plenipotentiary of the United States of America, in China, makes this communication to his excellency Tau, imperial commissioner, &c., &c.

He does it with sincere regret, because it is the acknowledgment of a slowly-formed conviction that the high authorities of the Chinese government do not mean either to make those concessions which international necessities require, or to do that justice to the United States which is due to the friendship which has so long existed.

The undersigned has fully explained to their excellencies the importance he attaches to the proper reception and acknowledgment of the letter with which he is charged from the President of the United States to his Majesty the Emperor, and why, from the past experience of his country in this respect, he exacts a positive assurance, before it leaves his hands, that it will be safely forwarded and acknowledged on terms of equality. The imperial rescript sent to the undersigned to-day gives no such assurance, and is therefore unsatisfactory. He cannot forward the letter.

In his recent interviews with the high commissioners, the undersigned, in his sincere desire to avert hostilities, departed from the strict rules of form, and met them on their assurance that they had all the powers which their government could delegate, and which were needed for preliminary negotiations.

In his conversation yesterday, he ventured to inquire on what points they were willing to negotiate, and learned with much regret that the two to which the government of the United States attaches great, if not most importance—the residence or occasional visit of an accredited minister at the capital, and the free or even restricted navigation of the two great rivers of China—were not only, in the judgment of their excellencies, inadmissible, but could not even be discussed.

But it was with still greater regret that the undersigned was made aware that the just claims of his fellow-citizens, amounting relatively to a small sum, and open to the strictest scrutiny, for losses at Canton and elsewhere, were refused even the preliminary consideration he asked for them. This refusal he is bound at once to report to his government.

Having now done all that lies in his power to induce their excellencies and the government they represent to listen to friendly reasoning, the undersigned can do no more. The United States means still to be at peace with China, and her representative is at hand yet to render good offices; but he begs to be understood that his ability to avert trouble from the empire is already materially diminished, and that no responsibility for the future rests on him.

The undersigned renews the assurances of his distinguished consideration.

WILLIAM B. REED.

MAY 13, 1858.

TAU, Governor General of Chihli; TSUNG, Superintendent of the Granaries; with WÚ, under Secretary of the Cabinet, now make a communication:

We have received your excellency's dispatch, in which you speak of the proper manner of receiving the letter from the President, and also about the negotiations upon two important points, in order to maintain amicable relations.

With reference to the first-named point, we may remark that we have already memorialized and received his Majesty's pleasure, permitting us to send up the same for you. We accordingly requested your excellency to carefully transmit it to us, that we, on our part, may receive, and then as carefully send it up to the throne. Our august Sovereign is very much gratified to learn this, and there certainly will be a reply. Your honorable country has never been a dependency of China, and why, then, need you have undue apprehensions [on the subject]? When we have received this letter, and have sent it up to court, we shall, on obtaining the will, again make another communication to you.

In respect to the several points which your excellency asked for, and which we discussed at our recent interviews, we observe that those which are reasonable in themselves we will readily grant; for instance, the provision which you propose respecting the mode of reckoning tonnage-dues, by which a reduction is hereafter to be made, [on American ships], is a very great advantage to them, and in granting it China has not the least feeling of regret at the concession. Such an act on our part towards you must be regarded as highly friendly and courteous.

Your excellency now wishes further negotiation on two very important points: one of them is, that an accredited minister of the United States shall either reside in Pekin, or have the liberty of going there occasionally. We remark on this proposition, that there is no such law now in force, nor has ever existed. The consuls of the United States reside at the five ports, and if her minister have liberty to reside at, or occasionally visit Pekin, there is no business constantly requiring the presence of an officer there. However, lest some unpleasant feeling should arise between ourselves, and we should err or fail in our treatment of you, whereby the present friendly relations between us should be jeoparded, we request that the old regulation [in respect to this point] may be observed.

As to the question of vessels entering the two great rivers in China, we further remark that it is stipulated in the treaties made and agreed to during the reign of Tau-kwang that ships shall not go elsewhere than to the five ports therein mentioned. This regulation was made at that time, lest the stupid common people of this empire, who have no knowledge, and are ready for any unruly change, could not everywhere be restrained before trouble should arise. How much more now, as no long space of time has elapsed since, it is undesirable to substitute a new regulation so soon! and we accordingly request that the former one may remain in force.

In relation to the refusal of this government to make compensation for losses incurred at Canton and elsewhere, we reply: the fire in which that property was lost occurred through the difficulties caused by the English, and was not in consequence of anything done by the Chinese. In relation to other losses which merchants have suffered at various times by plunder and fire of their ships or goods, they ought, in compliance with the provisions of the treaty, to have laid the particulars before our officers. A long interval has since passed, and we have no documentary proof of the cases, and no means of ascertaining the clear truth concerning them.

If your excellency desires to secure further the amicable relations between our respective countries, and there are any other points which are likely to be of real advantage to them, we will not decline them; and now send this reply to your excellency. The present points, also, can be again brought up between us, when a time for it shall be agreed upon.

A necessary communication sent to his excellency W. B. Reed, envoy extraordinary and minister plenipotentiary of the United States, in China.

Translated by S. W. WILLIAMS.

Mr. Reed to Mr. Cass.

[Extracts.]

No. 18.] LEGATION OF THE UNITED STATES,
On board the Minnesota, Gulf of Pechele, May 21, 1858.

SIR: I regret to inform you that the hostilities which I have so earnestly labored to avert occurred yesterday; the allied naval forces of Great Britain and France having assaulted, and, after a brief but very resolute resistance, captured the Takoo ports. Before referring in detail to this incident, I desire to resume the narration of what has occurred since my last dispatch.

I then referred to a hope that there might be some concession on the part of the Chinese of the privilege of ministers at Pekin. It was founded on an informal communication, made in writing to the Russian minister, and by him communicated to the other plenipotentiaries, that the imperial commissioner intended to memorialize the throne on this very point, and that the answer might be expected in a day or two. Now, as these officials rarely venture to address the Emperor on matters about which his will is known to be formed, the very fact of the memorial going seemed to justify a hope. Both Lord Elgin and Baron Gros, especially the former, were inclined to be very hopeful of a favorable result.

In the interval, I determined, after full consideration, to cause the President's letter to be delivered to the imperial commissioner. Communication through an imperial commissioner is the mode recognized in the treaty, and was what I had claimed from Yeh in December last. Hew, the commissioner, was not only ready to receive the letter in person, but solicited it, and gave the most explicit assurance that it should be acknowledged and answered. I concluded, however, not desiring to multiply more ceremonial visits on shore, to send it, and for that purpose placed it in the hands of Captain Du Pont and Mr. Williams, who, accompanied by a large escort of officers, on the 18th, presented it in due form to his excellency the commissioner. It was received with marked respect, and a new, and I have every reason to think entirely sincere, assurance given that an answer would be sent. The secretary of legation availed himself of this opportunity to initiate an informal conference with Tsien, the treasurer of this province, and a high and confidential officer, on the subject of a revision of the treaty, from which, had it not been suddenly interrupted, I augured very good effects. The correspondence as to the President's letter accompanies this dispatch. (Inclosures Nos. 1 and 2.)

This, as I have said, was on the 18th, on which day I learned from Count Poutiatine that the Emperor had refused to admit foreign envoys at Pekin. (Inclosures Nos. 3 and 4.)

Early on the morning of the 19th I received from Baron Gros his communication (inclosures Nos. 5, *a*, *b*, *c*) informing me that it had been determined to take possession of the forts, if necessary, by force; that they would be summoned the next day, and if not surrendered within two hours, assaulted. Later in the day I received a similar communication from Lord Elgin. (Inclosures No. 6, *a*, *b*.) I answered these communications, and at the same time requested Mr. Williams to suspend the informal conference in which he was engaged. (Inclosure No. 7.) * * * * * * *

To the wishes and opinions of the English and French ministers, I am, of course, bound to yield no other deference than is dictated by my high personal regard, and their consonance with the policy and interests of my country. But the views of his excellency the Russian minister, who has, from first to last, steadily cöperated with me in my efforts at pacification, I am bound to regard with much more deference. His views are stated in his letter to Lord Elgin, of the 19th, which he sent me a copy of yesterday. (Inclosure No. 8, *a*, *b*.) Besides, another consideration is powerfully operative with me. The Chinese consider us as their friends, and do not wish us to withdraw. Less than an hour before the beginning of the bombardment, yesterday, a messenger came to Mr. Williams, then on board the Antelope, begging him to renew conference with them; and to-day, amid the fresh ruins of the forts, a Chinese officer of rank has visited the Russian minister and myself, soliciting further good offices on our part, and begging for our efforts to procure a suspension of offensive operations for three days, until the will of the Emperor be communicated since the events of yesterday were known.

These are inducements to us, as neutrals and friends, to remain and follow the other plenipotentiaries up the river, and to these inducements I am much inclined to yield. Whatever may be my final decision, I shall take care to do nothing that, by the severest criticism, shall be considered a departure from the well-ascertained policy of the government, or inconsistent with the course of individual action, which, from first to last, I have endeavored to pursue in China. * * * *

I have the honor to be, sir, your obedient servant,

WILLIAM B. REED.

Hon. LEWIS CASS,
Secretary of State, Washington.

Exhibit 1.

MAY 16, 1858.

TAU, Governor General of the Province of Chihli; TSUNG, Superintendent of the Granaries; with WÚ, an Under Secretary of the Privy Council, hereby send a communication:

We have already acknowledged your excellency's communication, in which you inquired how the letter from the President of the United

States would be received and forwarded. We then made the same known to his Majesty, and received permission for us to take and transmit the letter on your behalf, directing us still to await a reply.

We have now been honored by the imperial will as follows:

"The regulations of the Celestial Empire are for those countries which do not bring tribute to our court; that if a correspondence happens to arise between us and them, a fixed rule is to be observed; they are not to be treated with disdainful hauteur, but in the form in which their letter comes, so must the answer be returned from us. There is not the least cause for doubt or hesitation on their part.

"This from the Emperor."

As is proper, we respectfully copy his Majesty's rescript, and now send it for your excellency's information.

A necessary communication sent to his excellency William B. Reed, envoy extraordinary and minister plenipotentiary of the United States to China.

Translated by S. W. WILLIAMS.

Exhibit 2.

MAY 18, 1858.

The undersigned, envoy extraordinary and minister plenipotentiary of the United States of America, having received from their excellencies Tau, imperial commissioner and governor general of Chihli, Tsung, superintendent of the granaries, and Wú, under secretary of the cabinet, their replies of the 13th and 16th instant, in which [they] give a solemn assurance that a letter which the undersigned has from the President of the United States to his Majesty the Emperor of China will be received on terms of equality—the United States being no tributary of China, but a great and independent nation—and that there will be a reply, now has the honor to transmit the same to be sent to the Emperor. He sends it to their excellencies by one of the highest officers of his nation, who is directed to place it in the hands of his excellency Tau, the chief commissioner.

The undersigned deeply regrets the unfortunate hostilities which threaten to interrupt the friendly intercourse which he hoped to have with their excellencies. They are, he fears, inevitable.

WILLIAM B. REED.

Exhibit 3.

STEAMER AMERICA, IN THE RIVER PEIHO,
May 17, 1858.

SIR: The governor general, Tau, has just sent a mandarin to tell me that the Emperor refuses to admit foreign envoys to Pekin. I have communicated this intelligence to Lord Elgin and Baron Gross;

it makes them free to act as they think proper, and the hostilities, if they are not carried further than Takoo, may be necessary to produce a salutary effect on the court of Pekin.

With assurances of high consideration and esteem, I have the honor to be your excellency's most humble servant,

C. POUTIATINE.

His Excellency the Hon. W. B. REED,
Envoy Extraordinary, &c., &c., &c.

Exhibit 4.

LEGATION OF THE UNITED STATES,
On board the Minnesota, May 19, 1858.

MONSIEUR LE COMTE: Our repeated conversations and the frank intercommunication of opinion which we have had seem to render unnecessary any other than a formal acknowledgment of the receipt of your excellency's letter of the 17th, informing me of the decision of the Emperor as to the reception of foreign envoys at the capital. I deeply regret this result, leading, as I fear it must, to an interruption, by others, of the peaceful relations which we have so long sought to maintain between China and the western powers.

I beg to assure you that in consonance with my instructions and my own feelings I shall continue to act in entire concert with your excellency, our duty as pacificators I hope not being yet exhausted, so long as it is agreeable to you.

I have the honor to be, Monsieur le Comte, your excellency's humble servant,

W. B. REED.

His Excellency le Comte POUTIATINE,
Imperial Commissioner, &c., &c., &c.

Exhibit 5.

[Translation.]

MISSION EXTRAORDINARY OF FRANCE IN CHINA,
On board the Audacieuse, May 19, 1858.

MONSIEUR LE MINISTRE: I received, during the day before yesterday, the communication which his excellency the plenipotentiary of Russia did me the honor to address to me in order to inform me that the Emperor of China had rejected the proposition which had been made to him to admit temporarily foreign diplomatic agents at Pekin, and this annoying determination proves that the Chinese government is still far from understanding the perilous situation in which it is placed.

We have, however, believed, Lord Elgin and I, that all attempt for an arrangement ought not yet to be abandoned. The instructions of my government authorize me, if I should judge it opportune, to ascend, in concert with my colleagues, as high up the river Peiho as the navigability of its waters will permit, and, resolved no longer to lose an instant, I shall send to-morrow morning to the imperial commissioners the dispatch of which I annex a copy for your excellency. This will apprise them of the course we believe we ought to pursue, Lord Elgin and myself, and of which we spoke with your excellency during the fortuitous conference which had place yesterday on board the Audacieuse between the four plenipotentiaries, which will permit your excellency to take such decision as may appear suitable. Your excellency will easily comprehend that the occupation of the forts which command the entrance to the river, whether we can establish ourselves there amicably, with the consent of the Chinese authorities from whom it will be asked, or whether it will be needful to take them in case of refusal, is an indispensable preliminary operation before ascending further up. It would not be possible to advance up the river leaving behind one a port which it would be so easy to close. A summons from the admirals will then be sent to Tau at the same time as my dispatch, and a very short period of time will be granted for receiving a reply.

I here annex a copy of the summons. These voyages from Canton to Shanghai, from Shanghai to Peiho, and from Peiho still further off, are so many steps which bring us nearer to the capital, and add also to the pressure which we seek to exercise on the Chinese government. This forward movement will perhaps end in opening its eyes to the dangers which menace it, all the responsibility for which must fall back upon it if it persists in its blindness.

I avow, however to your excellency that I desire this more than I hope it.

Please to accept, Monsieur le Ministre, the assurances of the high consideration with which I have the honor to be your excellency's very humble and very obedient servant,

BARON GROS.

His Excellency W. B. Reed,
Envoy Extraordinary and Minister Plenipotentiary of the United States of America in China.

Exhibit 5 *b*.

[Translation.]

On board the Audacieuse,
May 20, 1858.

Baron Gros to the Imperial Commissioners Tau, Tsung, and Wú.

The undersigned received, some days ago, the letter which your excellencies did him the honor to write to him, in answer to that which he had addressed to them on the 5th of this month, on the subject of the powers with which they should have found themselves invested, to be in condition to treat with him.

This answer is not satisfactory; and the undersigned was about to close all communication with your excellencies, when, through the intervention of the Russian imperial commissioner, he received overtures which sufficed to give him hope that an amicable arrangement would at length take place.

By these propositions, the Chinese government seemed to be willing to consent to open some new ports to foreign commerce.

It should have occupied itself about the indemnities due to foreigners who suffered losses by the burning and pillage of the factories by the populace of Canton.

It should have protected in China the Christian religion, by granting liberty of conscience to the subjects of the Emperor, and permitting Christian missionaries to preach with safety, in all parts of the empire, that divine morality which tends to make men virtuous, and exhorts them to charity, to love for their fellows, and respect for the authority of the Emperor.

Finally, not being willing to consent to the permanent residence of foreign diplomatic agents at the capital, as is the practice among all civilized nations, it should have purposed to ask from the Emperor that these agents might, at least, at their own charge, go to Pekin, there to treat directly with the ministers of the Emperor upon affairs which might need their high intervention, when circumstances should have required it.

Confiding in the messages thus transmitted to him, on the part of their excellencies, the undersigned believed he might suspend reply until the moment when the last proposition, that relative to a clause which, above all others, was of a nature to reëstablish peace, and maintain it forever between the two nations, should have received a favorable solution. And, if this clause had been admitted, if the other propositions had been serious, the undersigned would, perhaps, have consented, on his side, to depart a little from his first demands. An amicable arrangement would have prevailed; and, after the ratification of the new treaty, the French troops would have evacuated Canton to reëmbark on their ships.

Unhappily, a fresh communication from Monsieur, the imperial commissioner of Russia, announces to the undersigned that the clause treated of has been rejected at Pekin; and thence he no longer dreams of the concessions which he might, perhaps, have made, and declares to your excellencies that he resumes all his rights, and can do no more than refer to the contents of his note of the 5th of this month, with this difference, however, that, not willing yet to abandon all hope, in place of suspending diplomatic action, as he had announced, he only causes it to be sustained by severe measures, which the blindness of the government forces him to take.

He has, therefore, the honor to inform the noble imperial commissioner that, to obey the orders of his government, he is again going to draw nearer to the capital of the empire, there to wait, that plenipotentiaries duly authorized to treat with him may come and join him where he shall be.

Article 30 of the treaty of Whampoa gives to French ships-of-war the right to enter all the ports of China; and the undersigned, using this right, is going to ascend the river Peiho, in concert with the admiral who commands the naval forces of France, which are at this moment in the Pechele, or are expected there, and which will not leave unpunished any insult offered to the flag of France.

May your excellencies listen seriously to the language which the undersigned and the admiral address to them this day. They are still friendly, although severe, because the Chinese government has forced us to come to that. But, on the least outrage committed against the flag of France, let the whole responsibility recoil on those who in their blindness shall have dared to make themselves guilty of it.

This communication is of great importance.

TAU, &c., TSUNG, &c., WÚ, &c.

True copy.

BARON GROS.

Exhibit 5 *c.*

[Translation.]

SUMMONS BY THE ADMIRALS.

MAY 20, 1858.

Their excellencies the embassadors of England and France, having taken the resolution to advance on the capital, to treat with the Chinese government, the admirals commanding the naval forces of France and England are obliged, to guarantee the safety of their excellencies, to require the imperial commissioner to put them in possession of the forts on both banks of the Peiho, and of the battery placed at the elbow of the river. If, in two hours, the forts are not delivered up to the admirals, they will be attacked and taken. If they are voluntarily delivered to the admirals, they engage, negotiations being finished, to restore them to the Chinese government, without destroying either the walls or the artillery.

True copy.

BARON GROS.

Exhibit 6 *a.*

HER MAJESTY'S SHIP FURIOUS,
Gulf of Pechele, May 19, 1858.

SIR: It is with very great regret that I have to inform your excellency that the result of the endeavors which I have made in conjunction with Baron Gros to satisfy myself as to the nature and extent of "Tau's powers," and the *bona fides* of the court of Pekin in appointing him to treat with me, has brought me to the conclusion that nothing but delay and disappointment are likely to result from an attempt to open negotiations with him at this place.

I need not recapitulate to your excellency the history of these endeavors, as you are already familiar with it, but I cannot refrain from expressing my acknowledgments to your excellency for the exertions which you have made to bring the Chinese authorities to more reasonable sentiments.

Deeply impressed, however, with the importance of settling the the differences now subsisting between Great Britain and China, and obtaining securities against their recurrence at the earliest possible period, I consider it to be my duty, before abandoning the attempt for the present, and applying to my government for fresh instructions, to make a further appeal to the court of Pekin from some point nearer to the capital.

This decision, which I have taken in concert with Baron Gros, is perfectly consistent with the course which I have hitherto followed in my endeavors to open negotiations with the Chinese government, and with the language of any successive communications to the court of Pekin, copies of all of which are in your excellency's hands.

It is proper, however, that I should inform your excellency that the commander-in-chief of the naval force of Great Britain in these seas, whose authority on such a point is of course conclusive with me, declines to permit the vessels under his command to ascend the river towards Tientsin while the forts at its mouth remain in the occupation of Chinese troops. He will therefore, as a preliminary measure, in concurrence with the commander-in-chief of the French naval force, summon the commander of the forts to deliver them temporarily into his hands, on the condition that they shall be returned to the Chinese government when the negotiations in which the plenipotentiaries are engaged shall have been satisfactorily concluded. Should this summons be disregarded, he will take them by force.

I have already had the honor of communicating to your excellency so fully in conversation the general views of policy by which I have been guided in determining on this mode of proceeding that I do not think it necessary to enter at length upon this branch of the subject upon the present occasion. It has been a matter of unfeigned gratification to me to believe that the sincerity of my desire to pursue a moderate course in my relations with the Chinese government has been appreciated by your excellency. I shall therefore close this letter with the assurance that, notwithstanding the greater stringency of the measures which the inaccessibility and impracticability of the court of Pekin impose on me in this instance, I shall present myself in the river or at Tientsin with the same earnest desire to arrive at a pacific settlement of existing differences and the same readiness to accept reasonable terms of accommodation by which I have been actuated in the successive endeavors to open negotiation with the Chinese government which I have already made in concert with your excellency.

I have the honor to inclose herewith the copy of a note which I propose to send to Tau at an early hour to-morrow.

I have the honor to be, sir, your excellency's most obedient, humble servant,

ELGIN AND KINCARDINE.

His Excellency W. B. Reed.

Exhibit 6 *b*.

HER MAJESTY'S SHIP FURIOUS,
May 20, 1858.

The undersigned had the honor to address a letter on the 6th instant to the Imperial Commissioner Tau.

The undersigned therein informed the commissioner that, being invested by her Britannic Majesty with plenipotentiary powers, he could not consent to treat with a representative of the Emperor of China, who did not hold from his Imperial Majesty corresponding authority as a negotiator.

The undersigned further inclosed to the commissioner in that communication the copy of a decree taken from the records, and bearing date the 27th July, 1842, in which the powers conferred by his late Majesty upon Kiying and Ilipu when he appointed them his commissioners to treat with Sir H. Pottinger were fully set forth; and he intimated to the commissioner that he had determined on according him a delay of six days to enable him to obtain powers similar to those granted to Kiying and Ilipu.

The undersigned at the same time took occasion to express his sincere hope that this additional evidence of his desire to avert the evil which persistence in an evasive policy could not fail sooner or later to entail on China might be duly appreciated by the imperial government.

Upon the 11th instant he received from the commissioners Tau, Tsung, and Wú, a reply to the above-mentioned letter.

Without dwelling on the contrast which the tone of this reply presents to that of the letters addressed in a similar case to Sir H. Pottinger, it is enough for the undersigned to observe that he can only draw from it the inference that his reasonable demand for the evidence of the sufficiency of the powers conferred by the Emperor on the high officer appointed to treat with him, has been refused by his Imperial Majesty.

The undersigned forebore for some days from taking the steps warranted by this refusal, in consequence of a friendly communication which he received from the plenipotentiary of Russia, and which led him still to hope that this deficiency in the plenipotentiary powers of the imperial commissioners might be, in some degree, remedied by instructions ample enough to enable him to treat upon the several subjects detailed in the letters of the undersigned to the chief secretary of state, Yu-ching, of the 11th of February. In this hope he has been disappointed. A later communication from Count Poutiatine has but strengthened his convicton of the futility of any further attempt to open negotiations at the mouth of the Peiho.

In pursuance, therefore, of an intention already announced in his letter of the 1st of April to the Chief Secretary Yu-ching, which, like its predecessor, has been left without reply, he has resolved to place himself in more immediate communication with the high officers of the imperial government at the capital. For this purpose he is about to move up the river towards Tientsin.

As a preliminary measure, it will be requisite that the forts in the mouth of the Peiho be placed in the hands of the commanders-in-chief of the allied force. Their excellencies will signify the time within which the imperial troops will be called on to evacuate these works. The forts once in possession of the allied force, the undersigned will ascend the river, trusting that the imperial government will, without further delay, admit the expediency of appointing a duly qualified representative to meet him.

ELGIN AND KINCARDINE.

Exhibit 7.

LEGATION OF THE UNITED STATES,
Minnesota, May 19, 1858.

MY LORD: I have to acknowledge the receipt of your excellency's dispatch of to-day, with its inclosures, and, with your excellency, deeply regret the necessity which compels you to adopt the course you have indicated. I avail myself of this opportunity to renew the assurance of my conviction of the sincerity of your excellency's desire to pursue throughout a moderate course in your relations with the Chinese government, and should hostilities yet be averted, as we all hope they may, I shall be most happy to unite with your excellency in a new and nearer appeal to the court of Pekin, and to continue that peaceful coöperation which my government so much desires, and which I need not add is most agreeable to me.

I have the honor to be, my lord, your excellency's most obedient, humble servant,

WILLIAM B. REED.

His Excellency the Earl of ELGIN AND KINCARDINE,
&c., &c., &c.

A similar note sent to Baron Gros.

Exhibit 8 *a*.

STEAMER AMERICA, IN THE RIVER PEIHO,
May 19, 1858.

MY DEAR SIR: In answer to the communication sent to me by Lord Elgin and Baron Gros, I forwarded to the first a note, the copy of which I inclose herewith for your perusal; and a similar one to Baron Gros.

I am, my dear sir, yours truly,

C. POUTIATINE.

His Excellency W. B. REED.

Exhibit 8 *b.*

STEAMER AMERICA IN THE RIVER PEIHO,
May 19, 1858.

MY LORD: I cannot but be grateful for the detailed communications that you did me the honor to forward to-day, as well for the acknowledgment of my late exertions in persuading the Chinese to yield to our general demands. Though these efforts proved unsuccessful, I am ready, as I have stated more than once, to follow your lordship up the river Peiho whenever you move in that direction, and to use again my endeavors, and give every moral support in conformity with my instructions, to promote a pacific arrangement of the present affairs in China.

I have the honor, &c.,

COUNT POUTIATINE.

His Excellency the Earl of ELGIN AND KINCARDINE.

Exhibit 9.

UNITED STATES LEGATION,
Minnesota, *May* 19, 1858.

SIR: I beg to inform you that I have this morning received official notices from their excellencies the French and English plenipontiaries, that to-morrow a final summons will be sent to the Chinese military commissioner to surrender temporarily the Takoo forts, and that on a failure to do so within two hours, they will be assaulted and taken.

You are aware that the chartered steamer Antelope, which I have used for this legation during the preliminary negotiations with the Chinese authorities in the river, is, with the Russian steamer America, at anchor within the bar, which she cannot recross at the present state of the tides. It seems to me very important, not only that the vessel should be as far as possible protected from accidental injury in the event of sudden hostilities, but that her officers and crew should be put under such control as to prevent any participation in a conflict in which we have no part whatever. I hope you will take measures to that end, and should you find it necesssary to exercise the control to which I have referred, through the agency of officers and men from this ship, I beg it to be understood, that under no circumstances (except what is most improbable, a wanton attack, imposing a necessity of actual self-defense) must there be any violation of our absolute neutrality. For these instructions, which I make in the most emphatic terms, I assume the whole responsibility.

I have the honor to be, sir, your most obedient servant,

WILLIAM B. REED.

Captain S. F. DU PONT,
United States steamship Minnesota.

Mr. Cass to Mr. Reed.

No. 13.] DEPARTMENT OF STATE,
Washington, August 17, 1858.

SIR: You will perceive from the inclosed copy of a note of the 12th instant, addressed to this department by Mr. De Fijaniere e Morao, the minister of Portugal accredited to this government, that his most faithful Majesty's government is desirous that its plenipotentiary in China should be invited to participate in the conferences and negotiations which are now going on between the diplomatic representatives of the treaty powers in that country and the Chinese authorities. I have accordingly to request that you will, so far as you can, carry out the wishes of the Portuguese government on the subject.

I am, sir, respectfully, your obedient servant,

LEWIS CASS.

WILLIAM B. REED, Esq., *&c.*, *&c.*, *&c.*

Mr. Reed to Mr. Cass.

No. 20.] LEGATION OF THE UNITED STATES,
Teintsin, June 2, 1858.

SIR: The opinion which I hazarded in one of my recent dispatches that an advance by military or other means on the capital would be a failure, has proved to be erroneous. There are now at anchor in front of this city, and at the confluence of the Grand canal and the river, seven armed steamers, some of them with a draft of water of eleven feet, none of which had any difficulty, except from the sinuosities of the stream in coming here. The distance from the bar to Teintsin by the river, as nearly as it can be computed, is sixty miles. The Russian steamer America, in which, through the kindness of Count Poutiatine, I made the passage, accomplished it at night, with one complete tide each way, in about twelve hours. The distance hence to Pekin by the road, is estimated at seventy miles. The English gun-boats advanced up the river about ten miles, but the water then entirely failed them.

Thus has the perverse refusal of the Chinese to treat effectually at the mouth of the river, dispelled another of the impostures which made their capital seem inaccessible, for you will bear in mind that Lord Macartney, in 1793, Lord Amherst, in 1816, and Mr. Gutslaff, who visited Teintsin in disguise, in 1831, came, or were brought in the craft of the country; and that everybody until now has acquiesced in the mistake that the bar and the shoals of the Peiho, made access thus far impossible. The English and French hydrographers are making full surveys of the river, and the effect will be, let the question of diplomatic residence at Pekin be decided as it may, that hereafter any serious difficulty at one of the ports can promptly be settled by a visit here in a light, draft steamer, and the question being brought directly to the attention of the imperial court.

I have the honor now to advise you of what has occurred since the date of dispatch, No. 18. On the morning of the 29th ultimo, I was formally apprised of the intention of the English and French plenipotentiaries to go to Teintsin, the river being reported by the admirals to be free from obstruction, and no signs of hostilities being detected. Baron Gros's note to this effect is appended. (Inclosure 6 *c*.) From Lord Elgin, I received a private note, in which he expressed a wish that all the plenipotentiaries should, as far as possible, continue to act in concert. I embarked on the evening of the same day on board the Russian steamer with Count Poutiatine, and we arrived here early on the morning of the 30th.

The brief correspondence that has since occurred with the Chinese authorities is unimportant, and is annexed to this dispatch. The material fact stated by it is, that two new plenipotentiaries are on their way from Pekin. They have not yet arrived.

The approach of this large force to a point where no foreign ship, or foreign flag, except when carried in submission was ever seen before, has produced great excitement and alarm. The last is rapidly subsiding, and the uneasy excitement is changed into stupid, and rather good humored curiosity. There is no sign of resentment, certainly none to us, the representatives of the peaceful powers. Business is very much suspended. The aspect of the neighboring country, as far as we have seen it in coming up the river, and in occasional walks on shore, is that of prosperous and well-cultured fertility. The impression made by all else is very sad on any one who wishes well to China. The symptoms patent to every eye, are those of a disintegrated community, official authority perverted and corrupted, and a vast and morally inert population submitting patiently to wrong, and in its decrepitude awakening no sympathy. The means of resistance to foreign aggression really amount to nothing, and never have been more clearly shown than in the secure position of the English and French here at this moment. Since the forts were taken, not an armed man, nor a piece of artillery has been seen.

I have the honor to be, sir, your obedient servant,

WILLIAM B. REED.

Hon. LEWIS CASS,
Secretary of State.

LEGATION OF THE UNITED STATES,
On board the Minnesota, Gulf of Pechele, May 25, 1858.

MY LORD: I have the honor to send to you the translation and copy of a communication sent to me last night by the imperial commissioners. Captain Du Pont, who brought it to me, says that a similar one was received by Count Poutiatine.

There seems a studied vagueness about the letter. The statement in it as to my remarks in the accidental interview on Friday 21st, on board the America, is unintelligible to me, as I did not open my lips. I shall send no reply.

I have the honor to be, my lord, your excellency's most obedient, humble servant,

WILLIAM B. REED.

His Excellency the EARL OF ELGIN AND KINCARDINE,
Her Britannic Majesty's High Commissioner, &c., &c., &c.

The same to Baron Gros.

MAY 22, 1858.

TAU, Governor General of the Province of Chihli; TSUNG, Superintendent of the Granaries; and WÚ, an Under Secretary of the Privy Council, herewith send a communication:

We have to state that we deputed a special messenger yesterday to repair to the place where your excellency was, there to inquire and collect information about the affairs of the two nations. From his report we ascertained that he saw your excellency, and your remarks as to your desire for a reconciliation fully exhibit your friendly wishes and good intentions. But hostilities having now commenced with those two nations, the points upon which we before memorialized must be again made known, that the imperial will may be requested thereon. When it is received we shall be able to attend to and arrange them in accordance thereto. The interval will be only a few days, and we will then dispatch a messenger to see your excellency, that you may repair to an interview, when we can consult together.

An important communication sent to his excellency W. B. Reed, envoy extraordinary and minister plenipotentiary of the United States of America in China.

HER MAJESTY'S SHIP FURIOUS,
Gulf of Pechele, May 25, 1858.

SIR: I beg to thank your excellency for the translation and copy of a communication from the imperial commissioners, which you have had the goodness to send me in your letter of this day's date.

I have the honor to be, sir, your excellency's most obedient servant,

ELGIN AND KINCARDINE.

His Excellency Hon. W. B. REED, *&c., &c.*

STEAMER AMERICA, *May* 25, 1858.

MY DEAR SIR: My communication from Tau and his colleagues appears to have the same vague character as yours. I spoke of it to the officer who brought the notes, and told him my opinion how it would be best for the commissioners to act in their present critical circumstances. The officer begged it should be put in writing, which was done in a memoir, without any address or signature. The substance of this memoir contained that the foreign plenipotentiaries will soon move to Tientsin, when proposals for negotiations ought to be done on the part of the Chinese without delay. The required full powers must be produced by the commissioners, with the consent of the government, to receive foreign envoys at Pekin. The court had nothing to fear from the appearance at the capital of four plenipotentiaries with small suites; whereas, in declining to allow this, it must be prepared to see the western powers forcing their way to Pekin.

Tau has lost his rank, but is not deprived of his functions. The Mongul prince Seu-Wang who fought with the rebels at Teintsin, is ordered to repair immediately to that fort with 30,000 troops. There remain but few small guns at Teintsin, and no resistance can be expected.

If you wish to communicate this to Lord Elgin and Baron Gros, will you have the goodness to explain to them, that, from the vague nature of this last communication from Tau, I thought it not worth while to apprise them of it officially.

With much respect, my dear sir, truly yours,

C. POUTIATINE.

Hon. W. B. REED,
Envoy Extraordinary, &c., &c., &c.

UNITED STATES SHIP MINNESOTA,
May 28, 1858.

The undersigned, envoy extraordinary and minister plenipotentiary of the United States, has the honor to acknowledge your excellency's communication of the 22d instant, which, he regrets to say, is very inconclusive and unsatisfactory. Friends ought to speak more clearly to each other. The undersigned is fully aware of the unfortunate incidents which, having interrupted his personal intercourse with your excellency, have in some measure accounted for the delay in answering the President's letter. He thinks, however, that considering the gravity and importance of the communication, that he has a right now to insist on an answer, which may be sent either directly to him, or by the intervention of his excellency the Russian minister. The undersigned therefore reminds your excellency of the solemn promise given that the President's letter should be answered on terms of equality, and insists on its fulfillment.

The undersigned, still anxious to render good offices to China, means to accompany his excellency the Russian minister on his nearer approach to the capital of his Imperial Majesty, or to some intermediate place where he may resume peaceful negotiations.

WILLIAM B. REED.

His Excellency TAU, (with colleagues,)
Imperial Commissioner, &c.

STEAMER AMERICA, *May* 28, 1858.

MY DEAR SIR: I will send your dispatch to the Chinese commissioners by the first opportunity I shall have. It seems difficult to explain why the allied plenipotentiaries are not moving up, when every reason ought to induce them to do it. We know that the admirals have found a safe way and were at Tientsin some three days ago. If you could persuade Lord Elgin and Baron Gros not to lose time, it would serve the interest of all.

I trust we shall have the pleasure of seeing you on board the America when we start up the river, and that you will not decline our hearty proposed though very modest hospitality.

I beg to be kindly remembered to Mr. Williams and your son, and remain, my dear sir, truly yours,

C. POUTIATINE.

His Excellency W. B. REED.

MAY 28, 1858.

TAU, Governor General of the Province of Chihli; TSUNG, Superintendent of Granaries; and WÚ, an Under Secretary of the Privy Council, herewith make a communication:

Respecting the matters at issue between ourselves and the English and French, your excellency having volunteered to speak of a reconciliation and amicable settlement, wherein was seen the probability of a harmonious agreement upon them, we were exceedingly pleased and put at ease. But now they have both come into the river, a procedure the results of which we cannot foresee. We, however, communicate with your excellency in the hope that you will have an interview with the high commissioners of those two nations, and come to an understanding on the points of a reconciliation with them, which will thus show the entire good feeling that exists between China and the United States.

We certainly will not retract our words.

His Excellency W. B. REED,
Envoy Extraordinary and Minister Plenipotentiary of the United States to China.

MAY 29, 1858.

TAU, Governor General of the Province of Chihli; TSUNG, Superintendent of the Granaries; and WÚ, an Under Secretary of the Privy Council, herewith send a communication:

We have this day been honored with the receipt of his Majesty's commands to the following effect: "Let Kweiliang, a cabinet minister, and Hwashana, president of the board of civil office, be appointed, and let them immediately depart by post to the mouth of the Tientsin (Peiho) river, to investigate affairs there. This from the Emperor."

We have accordingly respectfully copied out these imperial commands, and now send them to your excellency.

His Excellency W. B. REED,
Envoy Extraordinary and Minister Plenipotentiary of the United States to China.

MAY 30, 1858.

TAU, Governor General of the Province of Chihli: TSUNG, Superintendent of Granaries; and WÚ, an Under Secretary of the Privy Council, herewith send a communication:

We have to acknowledge your excellency's dispatch of the 28th instant, which we have fully examined. The letter of the President of the United States has already been sent up to court, and as we had previously been honored with the imperial command to do everything in the matter with courtesy, which we shall conform to, there certainly will be no mistake or disappointment. But the transmission of the reply to it has been delayed, and it will be necessary therefore to wait for its issue, when it will be in course transmitted to your excellency to be received with proper formality. This will still further exhibit our friendly good wishes.

As your excellency again makes the offer of your good offices in respect to the matters between us and the English and French, from which we fully perceive your good feelings, we request that you will have an understanding with the Russian minister when you both reach the intermediate place in the neighborhood, thus showing still further your amicable and peaceful intentions.

His Excellency W. B. REED,
Envoy Extraordinary and Minister Plenipotentiary of the United States to China.

Mr. Cass to Mr. Reed.

No. 14.] DEPARTMENT OF STATE,
Washington, September 3, 1858.

SIR: Your dispatches, from No. 3, of the 10th of November last, to No. 20, inclusive, have been received.

The President is gratified to find that, in carrying out your instructions, you have been able to preserve friendly relations with all the treaty powers, and that while, in connection with Count Poutiatine, you have faithfully endeavored to prevent unnecessary war, you have yet not been wanting in your support to the just demands upon China by England and France.

From what is stated in your No. 20, and from a dispatch received through the Atlantic telegraph, there is reason to believe that the Chinese have at length yielded to those demands, and that a treaty has before this time been agreed upon, which will confer important benefits upon the commerce of all nations. It is not doubted that you have been successful in obtaining for the United States full participation in all the advantages which may have been yielded to Great Britain and France. The authorities of China can hardly be less favorable to our demands, either as they respect commercial privileges or the payment of just claims of our citizens, because we have preserved a neutral position in the late hostilities, and have endeavored to save China itself from some of the worst consequences of war.

The President also observes with great satisfaction the courteous disposition which seems to have been at all times manifested by Admiral Poutiatine towards the minister of the United States, and especially the courtesy of that officer in affording you a passage to Tientsin, in the Russian steamer America. The President will not fail to convey to the Russian government, at an early period, his sense of this courtesy on the part of the Russian minister.

In transmitting the paper from Mr. Murphy, inclosed in my dispatch No. 10, nothing was further from my purpose than to sanction any statements whatever reflecting upon the official conduct of your predecessor, Doctor Parker. The suggestions of Mr. Murphy related to a subject of importance, and I thought it proper to bring them to your attention, in order that they might be fully considered.

I am, sir, respectfully, your obedient servant,

LEWIS CASS.

WILLIAM B. REED, Esq., *&c.*, *&c.*

Mr. Reed to Mr. Cass.

[Extract.]

No. 21.]

LEGATION OF THE UNITED STATES,
Tientsin, *June* 15, 1858.

SIR: I have the honor to resume the narrative of occurrences here, leading slowly, but I hope surely, to a successful negotiation. If it fails, it will be either through some new and unrevealed perversity on the part of the Chinese, or from the tone which the allied plenipotentiaries have, since their arrival here, thought it their duty to adopt.

On the 3d instant their excellencies Kweiliang and Hwashana communicated to me their arrival, and fixed a time for an interview. (Inclosures No. 1 *a*, No. 1.) They had previously informally desired a conference with all the plenipotentiaries, which, however, was very judiciously rejected by the English and French. In such course there would have been many practical difficulties, which could not be overlooked. Lord Elgin's interview took place on the 4th, Baron Gros's on the 6th, and mine on the morning of the 7th, the 5th being passed over as one of the unpropitious days of the Chinese calendar. Annexed to this dispatch (inclosures No. 2 *a*, No. 2 *a*, *c*, *d*, *e*) are the notes of these interviews, as communicated to me. My impression, as derived from other sources of information, is that the breaking off of the conference, especially by Lord Elgin, seemed to the Chinese rather more impetuous and abrupt than is revealed in their notes, and no personal intercourse has occurred since. The visits of the English and French ministers were made in considerable state, and with a large military escort.

On the morning of the 7th, accompanied by my suite, one or two officers of the squadron, and a small guard of marines from the Minnesota, I had an interview with the commissioners at the temple of Hai-kwang, about a mile beyond the city wall. My reception was in every way courteous and proper. Kweiliang, the senior commissioner, (the elder brother of the Governor General Eliang, who had an interview with Mr. Marshall, in 1853,) is an aged man, but both he and his associate, Hwashana, seemed to be very intelligent, and in all respects self-possessed. So soon as the compliments were over, I directed the interpreters to read them a paper, which, as embodying my views, I take the liberty of making part of this dispatch, and which was listened to with great attention:

"The minister of United States, having met their excellencies the imperial commissioners, appointed (as their communication, received a few days ago, expressly states) with full powers to negotiate with him, thinks it important, in view of the gravity and interest of the occasion, to state his views and the expectation of his government; and, in order that they may be well interpreted and understood, he has reduced them to writing, to be read to their excellencies. He begs for them earnest attention.

"1. He desires, in the first place, to see the decree by which the commissioners are appointed with full powers, and to have a copy of it; in return for which he is prepared to exhibit his powers, and to furnish a copy. In asking this, he does not mean to depart from the line of conduct which he prescribed for himself at Takoo, where he received in good faith the assurance of their excellencies, the late commissioners, that, according to the customs of the empire, absolute full powers are never granted, or, if granted, are, as is the case in the United States, subject, in their exercise, to revision by a higher authority. But the minister of the United States means to be treated, throughout, on precisely the same terms as those of England and France, and learning that copies of the powers of the imperial commissioners have been furnished (after the exhibition of the originals) to their excellencies the Russian minister, Baron Gros, and Lord Elgin, he expects and insists on the same thing.

"2. This being done, the Minister of the United States is prepared and anxious to resume the negotiations which were interrupted by the unfortunate hostilities at the Takoo forts, or to begin them anew, as may seem best to the imperial commissioners; but, being anxious to complete the performance of his duties, and to remain no longer than is absolutely necessary a witness to the difficulties with other nations, in which, as the Chinese authorities well know, he has no part—he expects to have a meeting every day, at the same hour, with their excellencies, till the new treaties shall be completed; or, if a different course be preferred, that the details of the proposed treaty shall be considered and discussed by one or two persons appointed on each side for that purpose; the result of such conferences to be reported at a meeting of the imperial commissioners and the minister of the United States, on Friday next, at 10 o'clock, a. m., if agreeable to their excellencies.

"3. Before stating in detail the propositions to be embodied in the new and revised treaty, the minister of the United States, meeting their excellencies the imperial commissioners for the first time, desires to say a few words as to the circumstances and objects of his visit to Tientsin. For them, he solicits earnest atention, and if there be anything in what he says unintelligible to their excellencies, he begs that questions may be asked, which he is prepared to answer.

"He begs to remind their excellencies that the United States have always been friends of China, and that never, either before or since the treaty of 1844, has there been the slightest interruption of friendly relation. When China has been in conflict with England or any other nation, the United States have continued its friend. When other nations have pressed China harshly, the United States have never added to the pressure, but, on the contrary, have always out of their ancient friendship, been willing to defer their just claims for redress.

"The United States differs from other western nations in this—that the fundamental law, that which is known as its Constitution, or most sacred law—prohibits it absolutely, even if disposed, (as it is not,) from acquiring colonies such as Hong Kong, or taking for permanent occupation any part of the territory of his Majesty the Emperor. The United States, therefore, neither will nor can occupy any portion of his Majesty's territory. Not only this, but the United States will view with extreme regret the seizure and occupation of more Chinese territory, by any of the European powers.

"The minister of the United States has the most positive assurances from his excellency the English minister, that no such occupation of territory is now contemplated by his government; but it is a spirit and tone of current warning that the minister of the United States says to the imperial commissioners that this resolution may soon be changed; and he implores them, for the sake of the integrity of the empire, to exert their best influence to bring about a speedy pacification. Be it as it may, the United States want no Chinese territory; will not seize it; and would not accept it if it were offered to them.

"The minister of the United States further begs to state to the imperial commissioners that England and France, more than a year ago, solicited his country to join in a hostile demonstration against China, such as is now in progress; but the United States, remembering their ancient friendship to China, refused to do so. He has nothing to do with hostilities now. The minister of the United States and the naval forces of his country were not present when Canton was taken. He saw, with deep regret, the hostilities at the Takoo forts.

"Thus, acting as a friend, he expects to be treated as a friend; for if friends are not treated better than enemies they soon become enemies, and the minister of the United States says distinctly and solemnly to the imperial commissioners that the United States being friends will not be content to be treated as if they were not friends.

"4. The minister of the United States came to China in November last. Until February he remained in the south hoping that peace would be restored. On the 10th February, he addressed a respectful letter to the supreme council of state at Pekin, stating his intention to go to Shanghai, and asking for the appointment of a plenipotentiary to meet him there for the purpose of peaceful negotiation. This, unfortunately, the government of his Majesty did not choose to do. The minister of the United States, among other things, selected Shanghai because Canton was in the possession of an enemy, and he could not negotiate there. Besides it is his determination, and he believes that of his government, that the legation of the United States shall ever again be permanently established in the south of China, or at any place further from the capital than Shanghai.

"5. No plenipotentiary coming to meet the minister of the United States at Shanghai though he remained there till the 13th April, he came to the north, to the Gulf of Pechele, as he said he would. What accused after his arrival near the mouth of the Pieho, he presumes is well known to their excellencies the imperial commissioners, and need not be repeated now. There, as everywhere, he sought to act the part of a friend of China. He told the late imperial commissioners what would be the effect of a refusal to make the preliminary concessions demanded of them; and it came to pass exactly as he foretold; and he now repeats to their excellencies the new commissioners the same words of warning, made more earnest by the results of the last few weeks, that unless there be speedy concession and pacification there will be new and more serious hostilities threatening the capital itself, and ultimatly the integrity of the empire.

"The minister of the United States, in conclusion, begs to say that his powers of mediation or rendering good offices, which he fears have always been overestimated are exhausted. He can best serve the Chinese now by testifying his regret at the continuance of hostilities, by going away and withdrawing the countenance his presence may be supposed to give to an elaborate campaign in China; but he will not go away until he concludes such a treaty as provides for the settlement of the just claims of his government, and gives him the express and solemn and renewed assurance that hereafter the United States shall have the same rights and privileges as other nations.

"It is in that spirit that he has prepared the project of a treaty which he is ready and anxious to present and discuss with the commissioners. If it is adopted as it now stands, or after mature and friendly consideration and modification it is signed and approved so that he can carry it back to his government, it is his intention to withdraw from this scene of disturbance, and until peace be restored to establish the legation of the United States elsewhere. If it is rejected, his course of action will be regulated by circumstances. He hopes it will be adopted, so that friendship may still exist between the United States and China.

"Their excellencies will observe that it is not his intention to intrude himself alone at the capital of the empire, or to ask for his fellow-citizen access to the rivers and territory generally of China, but to insist on the recognition for him and them of these rights, if hereafter they should be conceded to any other nations, either England, or Russia, or France. So reasonable a demand he hopes will be at once agreed to, and then the United States will be satisfied."

The credentials were then exhibited on both sides, and copies exchanged. (Inclosure No. 3.) The full powers, for which the allies were so scrupulous at the mouth of the river, and which they now accepted, are contained in the authority to the commissioners within certain limits "to do as they please." In answer to my inquiry whether the commissioners preferred *our* considering and discussing the project of a treaty or delegating it to others, they expressed a preference for the latter course. Mr. Williams was selected, on my part, and an officer of high rank, Chang, on the part of the Chinese. They have been in constant intercourse since; and I avail myself of this opportunity to express my great obligation to Mr. Williams and his interpreter, Mr. W. A. P. Martin, for their intelligent and devoted attention and efforts throughout. The formal minutes of the intercourse are annexed. (Inclosure No. 4 *a*.)

Late on the same day, I received a communication from Tau, the late commissioner, as to the Emperor's reply to the President's letter, (inclosure No. 5,) to which, however, having been informed that Tau had been superseded, I returned no answer beyond a verbal message, expressive of sympathy with his misfortunes.

Rumors were current, for several days, that Kiying, the former governor general at Canton, and the imperial commissioner who negotiated the various treaties of 1842 and 1844, and whose degradation had been long since believed and rumored, had been restored to power, and arrived at Tientsin; and, on the 9th instant, I received a note from him informing me of the fact, and that he should call on me in a few days. (Inclosure No. 6.) I had, of course, no question as to what I should do. It seemed to me a duty of personal courtesy and propriety to receive the visit thus tendered, whether Kiying had an official rank or not. He was an aged and eminent man, known in my country as such, and entitled to due consideration. I mention this only because a different course was pursued by Lord Elgin and Baron Gros, who refused to see or have any intercourse with him. I incline to think they rest their refusal on the facts revealed in the intercepted documents at Canton. The Russian minister, without any express concert between us, agreed with me.

I received Kiying at my residence with such honors as my limited means enabled me to pay him, and returned his visit. He bears the marks of extreme decrepitude, both bodily and, I think, intellectually, though he has much of the urbanity of manner for which he was celebrated. I am bound to say that the impression made on me by this interview was not very favorable, nor could I see that his visit to Tientsin was likely to produce any good result, my suspicion being that he had been sent here simply because he was reputed to have great influence with us, and that his inclination was to restore himself to imperial favor by exacting more than others. He is the first one who has said a word about ceremonial. He informed me that the Emperor's letter had arrived, and asked me very pointedly how I proposed to receive it. On my replying that I should receive it respectfully, as the letter of a great sovereign, and exactly as Tau had received the President's, he said that the President, however great, was but an earthly potentate, while his Emperor had divine attributes, was the Son of Heaven; that they regarded him as Heaven; and that he hoped I would receive his letter kneeling. You may imagine my answer to this; and the subject was at once dropped.

On the 10th I received letters from commissioners, formally announcing the arrival of the imperial answer. (Inclosure No. 7 *a*, 7 *b*, and 7 *c*.)

On the 11th, at noon, I had my second interview with the commissioners, and received the Emperor's letter in the manner described in the minutes annexed. (Inclosures No. 11 *a*, *b*, *c*, *d*.) Kiying was present, but took little part. He has since communicated to me his appointment as commissioner, (inclosure No. 12,) and, after doing so, suddenly left Tientsin, and has, it is said, gone to the capital. The reason for this is not known, or even conjectured.

The secretaries appointed to conduct preliminary discussion have been actively engaged for several days in considering the provisions of a new treaty. They are advancing satisfactorily, and I hope by this or the next mail to announce to you some result. The Russian treaty was signed on the 13th instant. Its exact provisions have not yet been made known; but Count Poutiatine promises me a copy in a day or two.

I am, as you may well suppose, very anxious for the end of pending discussions, the tedium and perplexity of which are very great. There is, too, a liability at all times to their being interrupted by the action of the belligerents. Troops are expected daily from the south, and on the arrival of the full reinforcements, I have no doubt, unless the Chinese yield, there will be the beginning of an elaborate campaign and a hostile march on Pekin. To that I shall not give any countenance; I can hardly imagine any will be expected. Should the Chinese, having made a treaty with any one nation, refuse to negotiate with me, or deny the United States an absolute equality of privilege with others, I shall promptly refer the matter to my own government that they may take what measure of redress they please. In the mean time, I shall persevere in a friendly and considerate course of policy towards them; treating their public men with the courtesy due to their position, and studiously abstaining from all cause of conflict with the people. I believe this course will be approved by the President.

I have, &c.,

WILLIAM B. REED.

Hon. Lewis Cass,
Secretary of State, Washington.

JUNE 3, 1858.

KWEILIANG, Cabinet Minister, Superintendent of the Board of Punishment, &c., with KWASHANA, President of the Board of Civil Office, Major General of the Bordered Blue Banner of the Army, &c., both of them Imperial Commissioners of the Ta Tsing empire, and invested with plenipotentiary powers to manage affairs, herewith send a communication:

We, having been honored by the commands to manage the affairs of the four nations, reached Tientsin on the 2d instant; and we now appoint the hour of 5 to 7 o'clock, a. m., on the 7th instant, for an interview with your excellency.

His Excellency W. B. REED,
Envoy Extraordinary and Minister
Plenipotentiary of the United States to China.

LEGATION OF THE UNITED STATES,
Tientsin, June 4, 1858.

The undersigned, envoy extraordinary and minister plenipotentiary of the United States to China, begs to acknowledge their excellencies' communication of the 3d instant, in which they announce their arrival and appoint a time for an interview, and will be happy to meet them on the 7th instant, at six o'clock, a. m. At this meeting the undersigned will be pleased to receive the reply of his Majesty to the letter of the President sometime since transmitted through his excellency Tau, governor general of this province, and which was promised by that dignitary.

WILLIAM B. REED.

KWEILIANG and HWASHANA,
Imperial Commissioners and Plenipotentiaries, &c., &c., &c.

TIENTSIN, *June* 7, 1858.

SIR: I beg to inclose for your excellency's information the copy of a memorandum, drawn up by Messrs. Wade and Lay, of what passed at an interview between the Chinese high commissioners and myself, held on the 4th instant.

I have the honor to be, sir, your excellency's most obedient, humble servant,

ELGIN AND KINCARDINE.

His Excellency the Hon. W. B. REED,
&c., &c., &c.

Memorandum of an interview held on the 4th of June, 1858, between his Excellency the Earl of Elgin, K. T., and the Chinese Commissioners Kweiliang and Hwashana:

After the usual compliments, Kweiliang opened the convention by saying that there had not been time to send a written answer to his lordship's letter of this morning, but that the commissioners could now communicate verbally with his lordship upon the subject of its contents.

His lordship remarked that it was matter of regret to him that no acknowledgment whatever had been returned by the chief secretary of state, Yu, to the repeated communications which his lordship had addressed to that functionary; the cards of their excellencies sent yesterday had, however, upon them characters signifying that they had received plenipotentiary powers, and his lordship had, therefore, not objected to come to the present interview.

Kweiliang stated that full powers, as we are in the habit of phrasing them, were not granted to Chinese, but that, to meet our wishes, the Emperor had inserted the word plenipotentiary, as we render it, in the decree which constituted their instructions, and under which himself and his colleagues were empowered by the Emperor to accede to what was practicable.

Lord Elgin's full powers was produced and shown to the commissioners, and a translation of it was handed to them.

Having read this, Kweiliang immediately remarked that it was not the custom of his country to give any special document of the nature of his lordship's full powers to any officers holding, as he and his colleagues did, a temporary appointment; that the commissioners had no seal as ministers plenipotentiary for the same reason; but they possessed a decree from the Emperor appointing them to their present post, which was produced.

Lord Elgin having heard the sense of it, said that he would take a copy of the decree away with him, and would leave the translation of his full power with the commissioners; but as their excellencies were not in possession of a document similar to the power held by him, and as the powers conferred by the decree just produced appeared limited, as compared with his own, he must take time to consider whether it was sufficient to warrant his entering upon the discussion of the different questions, attention to which had been so often pressed upon the imperial government since the 11th of February last, with their excellencies. He would now, therefore, take his leave, and they should hear from him again.

His lordship rose immediately, and the commissioners, after a few vain endeavors, by words and gesture, to retain him, accompanied him to his chair.

THOMAS WADE,
Chinese Secretary.
H. N. LAY,
Assistant Chinese Secretary.

LEGATION OF THE UNITED STATES,
Tientsin, June 5, 1858.

MY LORD: I beg to return my thanks for your excellency's communication of yesterday, with its inclosure, giving an account of the interview held on the 4th instant, with the Chinese commissioners, and have the honor to inclose to your excellency a memorandum of what took place at my interview with them.

I have the honor to be, my lord, your excellency's most obedient servant,

WILLIAM B. REED.

His Excellency the Earl of ELGIN AND KINCARDINE,
Her Britannic Majesty's High Commissioner in China, &c.

A similar note was also sent, with a copy of memorandum, to Baron Gros.

[Translation.]

MISSION EXTRAORDINARY FROM FRANCE TO CHINA,
Tientsin, June 7, 1858.

MONSIEUR LE MINISTRE: I have the honor to inform your excellency, that I had, on the 6th of this month, at 4 o'clock in the afternoon, an interview with the new imperial commissioners, and I hasten to send you the substance of what was said at this meeting; from it you will understand the attribute which I believe it to be my duty to take towards the new commissioners, whose powers are not identical with those which were given to Kiying.

Your excellency will perceive that, although the powers did not appear to me to be perfectly satisfactory, I nevertheless considered them as available if I should require a certainty that the government of Pekin sincerely desires to solve in a friendly manner, the questions pending with France, which the imperial commissioners declare they understand in their general purport.

I seize this occasion, Mr. Minister, to renew to you the assurance of the high consideration with which I have the honor to be, your excellency's very humble, and very obedient servant,

BARON GROS.

His Excellency W. B. REED,
Envoy Extraordinary and Minister Plenipotentiary of the United States of America to China, &c., &c.

[Translation.]

Note of the meeting of 6*th June.—Verification of full powers.*

TIENTSIN, *June* 6, 1858.

On the arrival of the French plenipotentiary at the public building where the imperial commissioners awaited him, and after the customary compliments and courtesies, the plenipotentiary of France, to whom the imperial commissioners had given precedence, thanked them for having been so good as to have sent to him a copy of their full powers, and then announced to them that he would submit to their inspection the original powers signed by the Emperor's own hands—powers of which he would give them an authenticated Chinese translation, which was immediately done.

The imperial commissioners, on their part, presented to the plenipotentiary of France the decree of the grand council made by order of the Emperor; and at the close of this sort of exchange of full powers, the plenipotentiary of France said to the imperial commissioners that although the full powers they had exhibited were not altogether satisfactory, he was nevertheless disposed to be content with them, provided he received, before the opening of the negotiations, unequivocal pledges of the sincerity of the good disposition of the Chinese government to determine seriously and satisfactorily to France the questions in dispute. Baron Gros afterwards said, that the imperial commissioners without doubt had knowledge of the reclamations presented by France, the principles of which had been specified in the various dispatches addressed to his excellency Yu, prime minister of the empire.

The Chinese commissioners having replied in an affirmative manner, the plenipotentiary of France added that the imperial commissioners could not be ignorant that it was his mission moreover, above all things, to reclaim from the Chinese government the punishment of the magistrate of the district of Si-sin-kien, who, in flagrant violation of the treaty solemnly concluded in 1844, between France and China, and ratified by the Emperor Tao Kwang, had put to death the Christian missionary Auguste Chapdelaine, an apostle of peace and charity, who only came to China to inculcate the practice of virtue.

The secretary of the Chinese mission, Py-hen, then sought to repeat the justification which had already been the object of the dispatches of the viceroy, Yeh, but he was made to remark that this assertion had no place here, and that it was more especially within the province of discussion at ulterior conferences. Py-hen received the interruption with intelligent tact, and finished by resting on the sincere desire of the imperial commissioners to arrive at a satisfactory and lasting solution of actually pending affairs. The plenipotentiary of France replied that he very anxiously desired that it might be so, and begged the imperial commissioners to be thoroughly persuaded that France had no views of ambition in regard to China; that she desired to respect her honor as well as her territory, and that he only desired to see peace and good accord reëstablished on durable bases between the two empires.

The plenipotentiary of France then rose and took leave of the two imperial commissioners.

BARON GROS.

A true copy.

JUNE 7, 1858.

TAU, a high officer of the Ta-Tsing Empire, and Governor General of the province of Chihli, herewith communicates on business:

I have already acknowledged the having a dispatch of your excellency, in which you stated your wish to receive the reply to the President's letter, and inclosed the same in a memorial, requesting directions. I have now to state that I was honored, on the 8th instant, with an imperial command to the following effect: "An answer is already prepared, and, ere long, will be forwarded to Tientsin, where it can be delivered as shall be found convenient. This from the Emperor." I have accordingly respectfully copied the above for the purpose, as I now do, of communicating it to your excellency.

His Excellency W. B. REED,

Envoy Extraordinary and Minister Plenipotentiary U. S. A.

JUNE 9, 1858.

KIYING, of the Imperial House, and an honorary Vice-President, herewith communicates on business:

I, Kiying, an honorary vice-president, having been appointed by the command of his Majesty to manage the affairs of all the nations, have arrived at this place, and will wait on you in one or two days, when I shall have the pleasure of wishing you the greatest happiness; and for this purpose previously send this communication.

His Excellency WILLIAM B. REED,

Envoy Extraordinary and Minister Plenipotentiary of the United States in China.

JUNE 9, 1858.

KWEILIANG and HWASHANA, Imperial Commissioners of the Ta-Tsing dynasty, invested with plenipotentiary powers, &c., herewith communicate on business:

The deputies of our two nations held a consultation yesterday at the Hai-Kwang temple upon the several articles of the treaty. Those whom we sent reported to us that we also should to-day take up its several stipulations, and carefully examine and decide upon them successively, in order to their equitable and secure arrangement, that thereby the future relations of our two nations may be settled in a friendly and harmonious manner.

We therefore request that the thirty-first article, which is wanting in this draft, may now be sent to us to be examined; and we further beg your excellency to allow the same deputies to meet again to-morrow, at the same place, at 2 o'clock, p. m., for the purpose of consulting together, provisionally arrange, and settle the articles. We deem it proper to mention that there are two articles in this draft numbered seven.

His Excellency WILLIAM B. REED,

Envoy Extraordinary, &c., of U. S. of America to China.

JUNE 10, 1858.

KWEILIANG and HWASHANA, Imperial Commissioners of the Ta-Tsing dynasty, invested with plenipotentiary powers, &c., &c., herewith communicate on business:

We have already acknowledged your excellency's communication respecting the receipt of the sealed reply to the President's letter, to which we have yet had no answer, though the messenger requested to be favored with one. The reply having now been received, we now appoint noon of the 11th instant, as before agreed on, and request your excellency to come to the Hai-Kwang temple to meet us, where we will then personally deliver it to you.

The deputies appointed by each party have a meeting for consultation to-day, on the treaty, and we again request, that after the Emperor's letter has been delivered, the consultations can be resumed.

His Excellency WILLIAM B. REED,
Envoy Extraordinary and Minister Plenipotentiary of the United States in China.

LEGATION OF THE UNITED STATES,
Tientsin, June 11, 1858.

The undersigned, envoy extraordinary and minister plenipotentiary of the United States to China, begs to acknowledge the three notes received from their excellencies, which he has fully examined.

That which you remark respecting the arrival of the Emperor's reply at Teintsin, and that you will deliver it to-day, at noon, at the Hai-Kwang temple, after which consultation can be resumed, is fully understood, and at the appointed hour I will be at the place to receive it, and then deliberate further upon the treaty, or else depute that to our agents.

With regard to the ceremony of receiving the reply, it may be according to that observed when the President's letter was received by the Governor General Tau, which will then be in conformity with the stipulation that there shall be the same etiquette observed by each party.

Their Excellencies KWEILIANG and HWASHANA, *&c., &c., &c.*

Memorandum of an interview between their Excellencies Mr. REED and KWEILIANG, HWASHANA, and KIYING, held at the Hai-Kwang Temple, June 11, 1858, at noon.

On reaching the entrance of the reception hall, Mr. Reed was met by the Chinese plenipotentiaries, who pointed out to him a table, screened by a yellow apron, on which the reply of the Emperor to the President's letter was resting on a frame, and inclosed in a cylinder ornamented with dragons. Kweiliang asked with what ceremony he would receive the letter, and when told with the same respect that Tau had received the President's, requested him to place both his hands on it, which when done in token of reception, the letter was handed to young Mr. Reed.

On taking their seats, Mr. Reed requested to see the powers of Kiying as plenipotentiary, if he was present in that capacity, for otherwise he could not be recognized; and a copy of the edict appointing him was promised to be sent after the interview. Reference was made to the progress of the negotiations upon the project of a treaty, and the arrangement was continued, of discussing it by deputies, until every point should be arranged. They were expecting to receive a special seal, as plenipotentiaries. They should be glad to have Mr. Reed remain at Tientsin.

Mr. Reed urged the commissioners to avoid further hostilities by concessions to the allies, and to do it soon; both the Russian plenipotentiary and himself were the friends of both, and earnestly desirous that there should be no further collision. Kweiliang expressed his thanks for the interest taken in their affairs, and said that a communication had to-day been sent to the English and French ministers respecting their demands. Mr. Reed referred to the letter he had received from them in the morning, and stated that he had sent the same to Lord Elgin. In future it would better comport with their own position and the honor due to Lord Elgin himself, as well as the other foreign minister here, for them to decline seeing subordinates. Hwashana assented to this view of the case, and they all consented to that plan as the most proper for all parties.

They said the seal would come within three or five days, for a special one had to be made for them. The deputies can settle all the points this afternoon probably. Chang and Pi-hen can, like Mr. Williams, speak with authority on points of treaty.

Mr. Reed again urged them to hasten the seals, and settle with the English and French. If his own treaty was signed, he should still remain at Tientsin; for, so long as there was peace, his duty and his wish was that all the western powers should coöperate as, thus far, they had done.

The rest of the interview, which was brief, was devoted to complimentary ceremonial of no moment.

NOTE.—The copy of the decree appointing Kiying a plenipotentiary has to-day, June 12, been sent to Mr. Reed, as well as information that the official seals have been received from the capital.

LEGATION OF THE UNITED STATES,
Tientsin, June 11, 1858.

MY LORD: I have the honor to send you the memorandum of my second interview with the imperial commissioners.

I am to have another interview on Wednesday next, at 11 o'clock.

I have the honor to be, my lord, your excellency's obedient, humble servant,

WILLIAM B. REED.

His Excellency the Earl of ELGIN AND KINCARDINE,
Her Britannic Majesty's High Commissioner, &c., &c., &c.

Similar note sent to Baron Gros.

TIENTSIN, *June* 14, 1858.

SIR: I have the honor to acknowledge the receipt of your excellency's letter of the 12th instant, inclosing the memorandum of your second interview with the imperial commissioners.

I have the honor to be, sir, your excellency's most obedient humble servant,

ELGIN AND KINCARDINE.

His Excellency the Hon. WILLIAM B. REED,
&c., &c., &c.

[Translation.]

MISSION EXTRAORDINARY OF FRANCE TO CHINA,
Tientsin, June 12, 1858.

MONSIEUR LE MINISTRE: I have just received the communication which your excellency has done me the honor to address to me, to give me a detailed account of the interview which you had, on the 11th of this month, with the imperial commissioners.

I thank your excellency for having had the goodness to make such communication, but I can only say to you that the communication which the Chinese plenipotentiaries announced to you that they had addressed to me on the subject of the demands of France has not reached me.

I have the honor to be, Monsieur le Ministre, your excellency's very humble and obedient servant,

BARON GROS.

His Excellency W. B. REED,
Envoy Extraordinary and Minister Plenipotentiary of the United States of America to China, &c., &c., &c.

JUNE 11, 1858.

KIYING, Imperial Commissioner of the Ta-Tsing empire, invested with plenipotentiary powers and an honorary Vice-President, herewith communicates on business:

The imperial commands have this day been received here, specially conferring on me joint plenipotentiary powers to act with Kweiliang and Hwashana.

His Excellency W. B. REED,
Envoy Extraordinary and Minister Plenipotentiary of the United States to China.

JUNE 12, 1858.

KWEILIANG, HWASHANA, and KIYING, Imperial Commissioners of the Ta-Tsing empire, invested with plenipotentiary powers, &c., &c., herewith communicate on business:

We were honored, on the 11th instant, with the imperial commands that the honorary Vice-President Kiying should exercise the functions of plenipotentiary, and we have respectfully copied the same, which we now send your excellency, that you may examine the same and put it on file:

"On the 11th instant we were honored by his Majesty's commands appointing Kiying joint and equal plenipotentiary with Kweiliang and Hwashana, and the same day the proper seal was issued for them to use. This from the Emperor."

His Excellency W. B. REED,
Envoy Extraordinary and Minister Plenipotentiary of the United States to China.

JUNE 13, 1858.

KWEILIANG, HWASHANA, and KIYING, Imperial Commissioners of the Ta-Tsing empire, and plenipotentiaries, &c., &c., herewith reply on business:

We have your excellency's communication of the 12th instant, in which you acknowledge having personally received the imperial letter which you will preserve with care. As that reply was sealed up, we ourselves did not dare to open it, and therefore are unable to furnish you with a copy. We expect that the deputies we have appointed will meet for consultation at 10, a. m., on Monday, the 14th, and that we ourselves can also have an interview at 11, a. m., on the 16th instant, where the treaty will be prepared and can be agreed to. The seal for our commission has been issued and received by us, so that we can apply it.

His Excellency W. B. REED,
Envoy Extraordinary and Minister Plenipotentiary of the United States to China.

I, the august EMPEROR, wish health to the President of the United States of America.

Having received with profound respect the commands of Heaven to sway with tender care the entire circuit of all lands, we regard the people everywhere, within and without the wide seas, with the same humane benevolence. Since the intercourse between us and them was settled by treaties more than ten years ago, nothing had occurred to disturb the peace until the English and French, last year, disregarding their treaty obligations, violated their obedience at Canton; but the ministers of the United States carefully observed the obligations of the treaty, and gave them no aid. We were much pleased and delighted at their conduct.

The minister of the United States has now handed up the letter under reply, on opening which the expressions of respectful request still further manifest the same friendly feeling and cordial sentiments. In it you desire that the minister of the United States may reside (i. e., as distinguished from "visit" or "sojourn") near our court; but there are many things connected with such an arrangement which cannot be effected without difficulty. Hitherto the foreign envoys who have repaired to Pekin, have all come from those kingdoms which bring tribute, but the United States is numbered among friendly (i. e., not tributary) nations; and if, on the arrival at court of her envoy, there should unluckily be any defect or untoward thing happen, (about ceremonies,) it might, we apprehend, seriously injure the present peaceful relation between our countries.

Moreover, the middle kingdom has no ministers of her own residing in other kingdoms, and an arrangement of this kind should be mutual.

The minister of the United States is now at Tientsin, where he is negotiating with our high officers, and their intercourse has been mutually agreeable. As soon as their deliberations are concluded, he should return to Canton to attend to the commercial duties of his office as usual. This will tend to secure and perpetuate the present friendly feelings between our countries, and we think you, the President himself, will be highly pleased with such an arrangement.

The Emperor's own seal.

HIEN FUNG 8th year, 4th month, 26th day, (June 7, 1858.)

Translated by S. WELLS WILLIAMS.

Mr. Reed to Mr. Cass.

No. 22.] LEGATION OF THE UNITED STATES,
June 18, 1858.

SIR: I have great pleasure in informing you that I have to-day signed a treaty and convention with the Chinese imperial commissioners. The departure of the mail boat within a few hours compels me to limit this dispatch to the mere annunciation of the fact. I shall send the treaty by the next mail steamer.

I have the honor to be, sir, your obedient servant,

WILLIAM B. REED.

Hon. LEWIS CASS,
Secretary of State, Washington.

Mr. Reed to Mr. Cass.

[Extracts.]

No. 23.] LEGATION OF THE UNITED STATES,
Tientsin, June 30, 1858.

SIR: I have the honor to forward to you, in charge of Mr. C. W. Bradley, whom I have appointed special bearer of dispatches, the treaty which, on the 18th instant, I signed with their excellencies the Chinese imperial commissioners, in the neighborhood of this city, and the original letter from his Majesty the Emperor of China to the President. The treaty was executed in quadruplicate, in Chinese and English. I send one in English sealed, and a Chinese copy, according to the usage here, signed but unsealed. I retain, for another opportunity, or for preservation here, an original of which the Chinese is sealed, and the English is unsealed. It may be well to retain this permanently in China, in order to its exhibition hereafter in case of difficulty here, especially now when the original treaty is to be deposited at the capital.

Referring you throughout to the correspondence with the imperial commissioners since the date of my dispatch, (No. 21,) and which is annexed, (inclosures 1 *a* to 1 *h*,) I proceed to explain the course of my negotiations, and the various difficulties which have presented themselves and been surmounted.

* * * * * * * *

The two great points of difficulty which presented themselves at the outset were the permanent residence of foreign ministers at Pekin, and the free navigation of the rivers. These, you will recollect, the commissioners at Takoo refused even to discuss. Here there was an entire willingness to listen, and once or twice a special reference for new instructions to Pekin, but throughout an apparently fixed resolution not to yield. This reluctance seemed to three of the plenipotentiaries of France, Russia, and myself, so invincible that at an early period of our discussions we saw it would be very wrong to persevere in the demand.

* * * * * * * *

The other point of difficulty was the free navigation of the rivers of China, and especially of the Yangtsekiang. In refusing this, the Chinese plenipotentiaries, and the court were, with me, as resolute as about the residence at Pekin. I confess, at the outset of my mission, and down to a very recent period, I felt a deep solicitude, expressed in many of my dispatches to you, to obtain this privilege, for I was and am still confident that the enterprise of my countrymen would find in the navigation of these streams material advantages of great value; but it is due to candor to say that observation of some of the results of commercial contact since I have been in China has very much abated my anxiety to open what are called new markets, and to increase the area of collision and corruption and oppression. My instructions were happily silent on this subject, and left me at liberty to act according to my discretion, and to do justice to the scruples and objections of the

Chinese. Besides, I could not but feel that their assertion of a right of absolute sovereignty over the rivers was one that I, least of all, had a right to question; and whilst I might wish to see them, as a matter of mere commercial interest, allow the foreigner to go and trade up their rivers at pleasure, yet they had a perfect right to refuse.

* * * * * * * *

I am compelled, from time to time in this dispatch, to refer to what, it is believed, are contained in the English and French treaties, though I desire this to be understood, as far as possible, as an exposition of my own conduct in the separate negotiation which I have conducted, and of the privileges which, unaided, I was enabled to secure. Of course, under the "most favored" clause, any privileges I have obtained may be enlarged by the operation of the other treaties; but I have every reason to think, on this point of intercourse with the interior of China, privileges, under limitation of passports and numbers, have been secured by them which our countrymen may not desire, and which I certainly did not wish to make matter of stipulation. So about the resident minister at Pekin; whilst the privilege will inure to us, if granted to the English, I can well conceive of conditions annexed to it, or responsibilities enfored by it, which may make it anything but desirable to us.

These being the difficulties and the facilities of my position here, I now desire, as briefly as possible, to state the new and modified provisions of the treaty I have succeeded in effecting, premising the following order of dates of the signatures of the different treaties: that with Russia was signed on the 13th, that of the United States on the 18th, with Great Britain on the 26th, and France on the 27th. It is but right that I should repeat here my obligations to his excellency Count Poutiatine, for his zealous coöperation with me from first to last. He was anxious to promote my views in every respect.

The signature of the new treaty puts an end entirely to the pretension of the Chinese, as stated in Yeh's correspondence last December, that in consequence of the peculiar phraseology of the treaty of Wang-hia, it was in substance a compact forever, and could only be modified on matters of inconsiderable import. The imperial commissioners never whispered this objection here, but went to work earnestly, and apparently in good faith, to make a new and revised treaty, exactly as if no such difficulty had been suggested. I have thought it best, observing how these people reason, to omit any limitation as to time in the new treaty. This leaves us at liberty to negotiate a change when the necessity arises, and you may depend on it, whether there is an express limitation or not in the treaty, the Chinese, in the first instance, will always object to change. The object of a limitation as to time is only of advantage as a matter of mutual obligation. The Chinese will never, of their own accord, ask for a change, and will be very apt to object whenever we do; so that a limitation of time would really only be a restriction on us.

The first article is a formal one. The concluding clause, providing for the mutual abstinence from offense and for good offices, originated, as may be inferred from its phraseology, with the Chinese plenipotentiaries. They were urgent about it. It may be that these promised good offices, instead of being repelled as they were by Yeh, may enure to the advantage of China in some future and perhaps not distant conflict, and I am confident it will be the wish of the United States to meet these expectations.

The second and third articles provide for the safe deposit at the capital and the official publication of the ratified treaties, and are very important. They render impossible the transfer or detention of this compact, with the imperial authority, to a distant and insecure part of the empire, as was the case before, and remove all doubts as to the promulgation of the treaty by imperial authority at the capital and in the provinces.

The fourth article gives to the United States the right of direct correspondence under sealed envelopes, the sacredness of which is expressly guaranteed, with the privy council, (*Nui Koh,*) at the capital. This right, as you will easily infer, may be a most important one, for a retrospect of the correspondence of all my predecessors shows that not a word they ever wrote is known to have reached the immediate counsellors of the Emperor, except by reports from governors-general and local authorities; and so persistent have the Chinese been in this, that no one of the communications addressed by the western plenipotentiaries to Pekin have been directly acknowledged. My belief is that the suppression was rather apparent than real, and that more information reached the capital than was supposed. But my predecessors never had the satisfaction of knowing it. This article puts an end to all this, and its willing adoption, following so soon on the letter of the Emperor to the President, gives every reason to believe that it will be honestly observed. The privy council is the most powerful of the official boards, and as such is the fit organ of correspondence with the highest diplomatic representative of the United States. Its duties, according to the imperial statutes, are "to deliberate on the government of the empire, proclaim abroad the imperial pleasure, regulate the canons of state together with the whole administration" of what they call "the great balance of power." What in other countries is performed by a prime minister, is in China done by this council. It is not the "Board of Kites," but superior to it, nor the *Li-fan-yuen,* or colonial office, having control of intercourse with tributary nations. If the permanent legation of the United States shall be, as I hope it will be, established at Shanghai, communications may be made directly to the privy council at the capital and answered in twenty days.

The fifth article stipulates under certain limitations, for the annual visit and sojourn of an American minister at Pekin. These limitations may be somewhat modified by the provisions of the other treaties, but as they are, I see no difficulty in agreeing to them. The details as to the arrangements to be made for the journey and residence of the minister at the capital were cordially assented to, and I have no doubt all facilities will be afforded by the Chinese authorities. The journey from Shanghai inland to the capital is, of course, an interesting one, though now much obstructed by the deflection of the Yellow river, and the want of water in the grand canal, but our recent experience in coming to this point, and the concurrent testimony of others show that any time from April to November, the capital is easily accessible by this route. I see no reason to anticipate, now that the treaty stipulation exists, any difficulty on the part of the Chinese. But I venture to express the hope there will be perfect good faith in the representative of the United States observing the limitations on this right of visit; I mean that it should only be made on important occasions, of which he must, of course, be the judge, and not be unnecessarily protracted. Mere curiosity, or the desire to gain some sort of illustration, will certainly not justify a visit, which, under the most favorable aspect, cannot but be repugnant to the prejudices of the Chinese. But on the other hand, when the important occasion does arise, I trust the exercise of the right will be demanded and insisted on, and, I repeat, I have not the least doubt it will be agreed to. In this spirit I assented to the article.

I may here state the reasons which are operative to induce me to agree in opinion with the other plenipotentiaries that this is not the time to assert the right. It is hardly necessary to say that a rational curiosity, and other motives would have been gratified by making this visit to the capital now. Aside from the fact that the treaty was not, and might not be immediately ratified, there are obvious reasons for deferring a visit. The imperial authorities feel deeply that in yielding this ancient prejudice, they have done so in the face of a powerful hostile force. The very concession is a crisis to them, and it is certainly not a magnanimous part to insist on its execution now. It has occurred to every one that the proper time for such a visit will be when the ratified treaty shall be returned, and the exchange be determined on. That exchange will constitute an occasion of sufficient importance to justify a demand for a visit to the capital. I hope it then will be made, and in the event of objection, which I do not anticipate, be resolutely insisted on. If the treaty be ratified by the President and Senate next winter, the exchange of ratifications may be made by my successor in the spring or summer of 1859, either separately or in conjunction with the representatives of the other western powers. I hope it will be done separately. From November to April, no embassy can conveniently approach or leave Pekin.

* * * * * * * *

The sixth article contains a stipulation providing for our having a permanent minister at Pekin, if one ever be allowed to any other nation. The Chinese plenipotentiaries most readily agreed to this. I thought it best beside a general "most favored clause," to insert a special stipulation for a resident minister, so that should the fears of the Chinese, and the presence of the military array now here at the last moment, induce the concession of permanent ministers, there should be no pretense for refusal to us.

The 7th is identical, excepting the insertion of the word "used," with the 30th article of the treaty of Wanghia, and provides for the terms of official intercourse of consuls, &c.

The 8th article, relating to the place where official interviews are to take place, is new, and is meant to obviate one of the difficulties which has given rise to the recent hostilities of Great Britain, by determining the places of personal intercourse.

The 9th article, regulating the access of national vessels, is a transcript of article 32 of the treaty of Wanghia, with a few verbal alterations, and the addition of the words "or for the advancement of science." It also contains a provision, as suggested by the Chinese plenipotentiaries, for the coöperation of American men-of-war in the suppression of that kind of coastwise piracy from which the commerce of this nation suffers so much. This provision, I may venture to say, will be a dead letter in its obligation on us, so long as our squadron on this coast consists of large vessels.

The 10th article corresponds generally with article 4 of the former treaty, with these exceptions: The exact relative rank of our consuls with intendents of circuits or prefects is defined, and a provision is made for the exequaturs of consuls. These have sometimes been vexatiously delayed, and it was better to make it a matter of express stipulation.

The 11th article combines the 19th and 21st articles of the treaty of Wanghia, with the additional stipulation that arrests, in order to trial, may be made either by American or Chinese officials.

I may make this article the subject of separate communication, but I cannot allow it to pass now without saying, in the most emphatic terms, that no greater wrong could be done to a weak nation, no clearer violation of the spirit or letter of a treaty, than claiming exemption from local law for our citizens who commit crime, and then failing to punish them ourselves. We extort from China "ex-territoriality," the amenability of guilty Americans to our law, and then we deny to our judicial officers the means of punishing them. There are consular courts in China to try American thieves and burglars and murderers, but there is not a single jail where the thief or burglar may be confined. Our consuls in this, as in many other particulars, have to appeal to English or French liberality, and it often happens that the penitentiary accommodations of England and France are inadequate to their own necessities, and the American culprit is discharged. Hence it follows that many claim the privilege of American citizenship, in order to have the benefit of this immunity, and every vagabond Englishman, or Irishman, or Scotchman, any one, who, speaking our language, can make out a *prima facie* claim to citizenship, commits crime according to his inclination, secure that if he is tried in the American courts there is no power of punishment. In the case of a murder, the provision of the act of Congress of 1848 is, that before the capital sentence can be carried into effect, the prisoner must be detained a year in custody. This, so long as the United States refuse or neglect to provide for the erection of prisons, gives to the worst crime the greatest privilege, and the wretch—and I regret to say there are many capable of this crime now haunting the coast—who commits a deliberate murder is sure of escape I consider the exaction of "ex-territoriality" from the Chinese, so long as the United States refuse or neglect to provide the means of punishment, an approbium of the worst kind. It is as bad as the cooly or the opium trade. Were it not that I have strong confidence that when this matter is fully understood Congress will apply the remedy, I should be ashamed to put my name to a treaty which asserts this boasted privilege of "ex-territoriality." I am not aware that I can find a more appropriate occasion to illustrate this enormity than here, and I therefore beg to recall to your attention a flagrant case of recent occurrence. In the early part of this year, a man named Jackson, claiming to be an American, was tried in the consular court of Ning-po, for an aggravated larceny, first drugging his victim, then robbing, and then attempting to murder him. The proof was ample. There was no prison at Ning-po, and the consul had no resource but to request Commander Saumarez, of her majesty's ship Cormorant, to take charge of the prisoner temporarily. He assented, and was rebuked by the senior naval officer on the station for having done so. The consul, after a time, sent the man to Shanghai, with a request that he might be confined in the English jail, (the legality of which custody being very doubtful.) The English consul, knowing the desperate character of the convict, refused to receive him. An appeal was made to the commander of the United States ship Mississippi, and he declined to have anything to do with consular adjudications. He was kept for a short time in the house of the marshal, and thence, without difficulty, escaped. This, I repeat, is the way in which the United States has heretofore observed her treaty obligation with China.

The 12th article contains a most important modification of the treaty of Wanghia, and one to which my attention was particularly directed by my instructions. The former treaty (article 17) provided for the interposition of the local authorities before the site of any leasehold property could be determined. The effect of this was to create an unnecessary embarrassment; for the officials, knowing that their previous consent was necessary, were always ready to interpose, and forbid the selection of a site which they or any interested or ill-disposed person wished to prevent. No such previous consent is now needed, and perfect freedom of individual contract is secured, and the authorities are only permitted to interfere when there is a direct appeal to them. This change is considered here of great advantage. The concluding provision of the article of the former treaty, which required the local authorities, in concert with the consuls, to define the limits beyond which it would not be lawful for the citizens of the United States to go, is omitted. There is no express prohibition of a citizen of the United States going anywhere in the neighborhood of the open ports, provided he engages in no unlawful trade in fraud of the revenue.

The 13th article combines the greater portion of articles 26 and 27 of the treaty of Wanghia, with material modifications. By the old treaty, the ship-wrecked mariner of the United States could only repair to the nearest of the five ports opened to commerce. He now can go to the nearest port whether open or not. The provision is added that in case of the collusion of local authorities in any robbery or piracy, there shall be a confiscation, by imperial order, of the property of the colluding official to repair the loss.

Article 14. To this article I beg to direct especial attention, as containing new commercial privileges, and the right to visit additional ports on the coast. When the negotiations were in progress at Takoo, the commissioners expressed a willingness to open all the ports where an irregular commerce existed. But here the new plenipotentiaries, acting on an unintelligible principle, eminently Chinese, receded from this, and while they allowed me the choice, limited it to two ports, and agreed to put in the article a special provision allowing citizens of the United States to trade at any port opened to other nations. The new ports opened to us by this treaty are Swatau, the great place for the export of sugar, and Tai-wan, in Formosa, in reference to which I beg to refer you to the report of Captain Simons, communicated to the Navy Department in ——— last. It is understood that the ports opened to all the other powers, and which, of course, are to us, are Nin-chwang, on the northeastern part of the Gulf of Pechele, in Manchuria; Tang-chau, on the Shautung promontory; Kiung-chau, in the island of Hainan, and Tau-shwin, in Formosa. These constitute, in the aggregate, the same number of ports as would have been conceded before the fall of the forts. It is believed by those familiar with the subject that the most available of the new ports are those named in our treaty, Swatau and Tai-wan. The whole number of ports on the coast open to American commerce will be eleven, instead of five.

In framing this article you will observe that access to the cities as well as the ports is given; thus removing an ambiguity which may be imputed to the former treaty. In my instructions I was directed not to unite in any effort to legalize the opium trade, and by a fair inference I was led to conclude that it was the wish of the government that the trade should not be legalized in any treaty, but be left to the prohibitory statutes of the Chinese. In the treaty of Wanghia, (Article 33,) dealing in opium was in terms prohibited to American citizens. In the new treaty I have omitted the word "opium," and left the trade to be dealt with as with that of any other article declared by law to be contraband. My reasons for this were twofold. In the first place, the retention of the word made the open defiance of the treaty more scandalous; and when, at every port, I found Americans dealing in opium freely and unreservedly, and at least one American built, but British owned steamer, with the American flag, plying regularly up and down the coast as a quick carrier of the poison, I felt that it was worse than a mockery to retain the specific prohibition, and much better to class opium in the general list of contraband. Another motive, also, influenced me. In one of the few interviews I have had with Lord Elgin, he expressed a strong wish that the word "opium" should be omitted in the American and Russian treaties. He seemed to think, and I thought with some reason, that it was a reflection on England, who derived a large revenue from the trade, and he assured me that if I would accede to this he would not attempt to legalize the trade by treaty, as he was instructed to do. (Dispatch of the Earl of Clarendon to Lord Elgin, April 20, 1857.) I confess this was an inducement to me, for I could not but believe, from the great indifference the Chinese commissioners at Takoo expressed on the subject, they might be easily persuaded to legalize the trade if the English insisted on it, and I thought Lord Elgin's half-expressed reluctance to comply with his instructions was very creditable to him, believing as I do that he feels a strong repugnance to this infamous traffic, and the connection of his government with it. Not having yet seen the English treaty, I am unable to say whether it contains any reference to it.

Article 15. This article corresponds generally with the 5th article of the treaty of Wanghia. The tariff of duties arranged by that treaty is adopted, as on the whole very moderate—the most so imposed by any nation that raises revenue on exports as well as imports. In this view I am confirmed by the fact that the Shanghai chamber of commerce, composed of English merchants whose interests on these subjects are identical with those of Americans, recently, in a formal report made to Lord Elgin, suggested no material diminution of the rates. It has been a favorite speculation in China that some great economical reform, extending, if not to the abolition of all duties on the coast, at least to that of export duties, should be embodied in the treaties now made. Such a revolution must be left to some very remote and more enlightened period. Certainly China is not prepared for it now. As to the transit duties said to be levied in the interior, it has been found impossible to determine where they are enforced and what they are. Whether they are the unauthorized exactions of corrupt officials, or levied by the authority of the government, cannot be ascertained. No treaty prohibition could be framed to reach them.

Article 16. By the treaty of Wanghia, a tonnage duty of five mace (75 cents) per ton of register was agreed to on vessels over one hundred and fifty tons. The English register ton is reckoned at fifty cubic feet, whilst ours is but forty. The apparent equality of the duty was, therefore, a discrimination to our advantage, which is obviated by the provision of the new treaty fixing the treaty at four mace (60 cents) per ton of forty cubic feet. The provision of the former treaty as to exemption from double tonnage is enlarged by the addition of the words "or being in ballast to purchase an entire or fill up an incomplete cargo."

I had a strong hope that I could persuade the Chinese plenipotentiaries to agree to a stipulation compelling the application of a portion of the tonnage duty to the improvement of navigation; but the difficulty may be appreciated when I state that their excellencies the commissioners frankly said that they did not know what a light-house or beacon was. The most that my peaceful persuasion could obtain was a stipulation, very vague I admit, that the subject of improvement of the river navigation should be considered by the local authorities.

Article 17 corresponds verbatim with article 8 of the former treaty regulating pilots, &c.

Article 18 is a consolidation of portions of articles 9 and 29 of the former treaty, as to surrender of mutineers and maintenance of order.

Article 19 is identical, excepting verbal corrections, with article 10 of the treaty. There is added to it a stipulation taken from the French treaty of 1844, providing for an appeal to the consul of any friendly power, or directly to the superintendent of customs, in case of a vacancy in the consulate of the United States.

Article 20, as to the adjustment of *ad valorem* duties, is the same as article 11 of the old treaty.

Article 21, as to the reëxportation, is the same as article 20 of the former treaty, with the addition of "foreign grain or rice brought into any port of China in a ship of the United States and not landed, may be reëxported without hindrance." Such a provision was rendered necessary by a difficulty recently at Shanghai, which led to great perplexity. I refer to that known as the "Spec" case, which was fully reported to the department, in September last.

Article 22, as to the medium of payment of duties, and the responsibility of consuls, contains new provisions of some moment. (See article 13, old treaty.)

In common with every one who has given any attention to matters of commercial interest in China, I was solicitous that some improvement should be effected in the currency, at least so far as the payment of duties influenced it. I have sought information from every source, and have received all sorts of suggestions, varying from those of the most intelligent merchants to the crudities which limited observation and no practical experience are so apt to generate. Had there been between the representatives of commercial nations the thorough concert which on such a point would be legitimate, perhaps some result in the way of suggestion to these impracticable people might have been reached. But what were considered greater objects of diplomatic interest absorbed attention, and down to this time I have not the most remote idea, what remedy, if any, the English plenipotentiary has suggested. At the conference of Takoo, I mentioned the subject to the imperial commissioners, but was met by the assurance, apparently sincere, that no coinage (beyond the wretched infinitesimal copper cash to which the people are accustomed) could be attempted by the imperial government, or with the habits of the people could succeed. It had been tried and failed entirely. The subject was presented by me in every form, but unavailingly. There was under these circumstances nothing to be done but to fall back upon an elementary principle, and agree that the standard should, as heretofore, be their own sycee or pure silver, and that foreign coins should be received at the current rate of exchange in comparison with that standard. In other words, that this sort of trade must regulate itself. It is doing so.

The Chinese plenipotentiaries, at one of the interviews, called my attention to the necessity of some treaty provision against consuls delivering ships' papers before the duties are paid, as you are aware, has been the case under the summary action of the former consuls at Fuh-chau and Canton. The English and American consuls had done this in 1853, and Mr. Jones, at Fuh-chau, in 1856, 1857. Desiring to act with entire good faith to the Chinese, I could not but admit that such consular action was an abuse of authority and ought not to be permitted; but at the same time, I was resolute that the consuls should in no sense be subject to the control or jurisdiction of the Chinese authorities, and that the withholding or surrendering the ship's papers should continue to be the act of our officers. The article was finally agreed to as it now stands, by which the consul is to be responsible to his own government, if he permits a ship to go without payment of duties. This will meet the case as it occurred at Fuh-chau, where the former consul let the ships go, not only without payment, even to him, of the duties, but without securing them; and at the last accounts, some portion of those due by British shippers were still unpaid. If, as with Chinese is always possible, some emergency arises, rendering necessary a detention of duties by proper authority, it may be done on *payment* by the shipper, and not on the mere faith of his promise, and thus the ultimate interest of the Chinese government be protected. A responsibility of the consul now exists by operation of law under his bond.

The 23d article, as to transhipment, is the same as article 14 of the old treaty with an improvement of phraseology, and a requisition of a "written" permit of transhipment. In the case of the "Spec," one of the difficulties was that the permit claimed was merely a verbal one.

The 24th article is the former provision (treaty of Wanghai, article 16) as to the recovery of debts due from and to citizens of the United States.

The 25th article, as to the free employment of teachers and linguists and their immunity, corresponds with the former provision, (article 18.)

The 26th article, as to neutrality and embargoes, is the article 22 of the former treaty adapted to the new ports.

The 27th article, as to rights of property, is article 25 of the old treaty.

The 28th article. The former treaty, (article 24,) in regulating the intercourse of citizens of the United States with the local Chinese authorities, required the submission of the communication, if in writing to the consul, that he might see that its tone was respectful. This is retained. But the provision requiring the Chinese to submit their communications for revision to the local authorities is modified. It never was practiced, and was quite unnecessary. The extortion of illegal fees is prohibited, and permission is given to peaceable persons to enter the consular courts in order to interpret.

The 29th article providing for the toleration of Christianity and the protection of Chinese converts. Though I may have occasion hereafter to address you particularly on this subject so soon as I am informed of the exact stipulations of the other treaties, I beg to say a word or two here in explanation of the form of this article. The recognition of both forms of Christian faith, professed by the Roman Catholic and Protestant churches, is rendered necessary by the fact that in the Chinese language different terms are used to describe them. The sign [Chinese characters] interpreted "the religion of the Lord of Heaven" is generally understood as applying only to the former, while [Chinese characters] or "religion of Jesus Christ" is applied to the latter. In the Chinese text of this treaty both characters are used and could only be rendered in English in the form I have adopted, and which I certainly should not otherwise have resorted to, accustomed as I am to regard them as part of a common faith. The recognition of that common faith, and the great principle on which it rests, and the immunity of its professors, whether native or American, are in the broadest terms, and that recognition is hailed here with entire contentment by the devoted men who are teaching the great doctrines of Christianity.

I cannot allow this occasion to pass without an incidental tribute to the missionary cause, as I observe it promoted by my own countrymen in China. Having no enthusiasm on the subject, I am bound to say that I consider the missionary element in China a great conservative and protecting principle. It is the only barrier between the unhesitating advance of commercial adventure and the not incongruous element of Chinese imbecile corruption. The missionary, according to my observation, is content to live under the treaty and the law it creates, or if, in his zeal, he chooses to go beyond it, he is content to take the risk without troubling his government to protect him in his exorbitance. But taking a lower and more practical view of the matter, I am bound to say further that the studies of the missionary and those connected with the missionary cause are essential to the interests of our country. Without them as interpreters, the public business could not be transacted. I could not but for their aid have advanced one step in the discharge of my duties here, or read or written or understood one word of correspondence or treaty stipulations. With them there has been no difficulty or embarrassment. It was the case also in 1844, when Mr. Cushing's interpreters and assistants were all from the same class; in 1853, with Mr. Marshall, and 1854, with Mr. McLane, Doctor Bridgeman, who was the principal assistant in all these public duties, still lives in an active exercise of his usefulness; and I am glad of the opportunity of expressing to him my thanks for incidental assistance, and constant and most valuable counsel. My principal interpreter for the spoken language of the north has been the Rev. W. A. P. Martin, of Indiana, of the Presbyterian board. There is not an American merchant in China (and I have heard of but one English) who can write or read a single sentence of Chinese, and the spoken language is the hideous compound that prevails at the open ports which has no single merit to recommend it, but suffices to convey the imperious mandates one universally hears to inferiors, or the mutual cravings of ordinary traffic. The missionary tries and succeeds in learning to speak Chinese, or in teaching the Chinese to speak English.

Fully appreciating all these obligations to the missionary cause, I was very anxious to introduce into the new treaty such a provision as would testify this obligation, and express what I believe to be the respectful sentiment of the Chinese themselves. To do so was not easy. The Chinese plenipotentiaries promptly acceded to the article as it now stands, which I believe is entirely satisfactory to the missionaries. They indeed went further and offered to insert a stipulation that a limited number of missionaries furnished with passports by the consuls and local authorities might travel, without their families, anywhere in China and preach Christian doctrines. To such a proposition I could not accede. I confess to a great repugnance to anything like a passport system. It would be impossible to agree to any limited number of missionaries to come from a country like ours, where there are so many forms of Christian faith. It would be equally inadmissible to deny to the American missionary the companionship of his family who, here, not only share his privations, but by their active coöperation contribute to his success. There are no American Roman Catholic missionaries that I am aware of in China. But, besides, there was a stronger objection; that obtaining such a privilege for missionaries would have involved the recognition of a distinction as to rights between missionaries and merchants and others which my judgment did not approve. In the Russian and probably French treaties, this privilege was accepted for obvious reasons, even with its limitations. I declined it on the grounds I have stated, and have reason to believe that the article in the treaty as it stands will give entire satisfaction to those directly interested, and insure the full protection needed.

The thirtieth article is that known as the "most favored clause," and I have endeavored to make it as comprehensive as language will permit. It covers political and social rights; it applies to privileges of commerce and navigation; it gives to the American merchant and missionary and traveler whatever any other nations gain, by solicitation or force, for theirs; and what is equally material, it was conceded by the Chinese with an alacrity which excluded all doubt as to their sincerity. There may be, and, as I have already said, it is probable there will be in the treaties with the other powers privileges conferred which the government and citizens of the United States may not choose to avail themselves of, but the choice will be absolutely with them.

The provision made for the ratification of the treaty differs from that on former occasions. It looks to the ratification by the Emperor forthwith, and it is understood that it may be expected immediately, or that there will be some equivalent form of acknowledgment for consideration. I recommend that the exchange of ratifications be at the capital, in the spring or summer of 1859.

I hesitate to add to this dispatch any further details of the negotiation thus concluded. But one incident, of peculiar interest, must be communicated. In my last dispatch, I mentioned the fact that Kiying had been accredited as joint imperial commissioner, had arrived in this city, and that I had an interview with him. A day or two afterwards, it was understood that he had returned to the capital, was arrested on his way, and had been brought to trial for some offense, not very intelligible, against the imperial authority. I annex to this dispatch a copy of the decree degrading him, and ordering his trial. (Inclosure 2.) Since that, it is known that he has been formally adjudged to death, but it is not ascertained positively whether the judgment has been executed or commuted into banishment. He has probably fallen a victim to some court intrigue, the ostensible reason for his punishment being that, through his agency, eighteen years ago, China was, in a measure, opened to foreigners. This, if true, is a sad revelation of the policy of this government. I beg further to inform you that, on the 19th instant, I returned to their excellencies the imperial commissioners the ratified copy of the treaty of Wanghia, which was found among Yeh's papers, at the time of his capture in Canton, in January last, and sent to me by the English and French ministers. I annex the correspondence on the subject. (Inclosures 3, 4.)

The subject of claims for our citizens, and the arrangement I have made for their liquidation, will be explained in a separate dispatch. I have limited this to a sigle topic.

Such is the treaty I have succeeded in negotiating, and which I now submit for the consideration of the President. I have the strongest confidence it will be approved. I shall be glad that, when it is submitted to the Senate, or at any other time the President shall think fit, every word of my correspondence, without the least reserve, shall accompany it. That correspondence faithfully records the course of events and their perplexities, from my first arrival in the midst of a war, to which the United States were not and were determined not to be parties, to this moment, when, after a very unsatisfactory concert, peace has been restored. It shows, too, that a resolute adherence to neutrality can be maintained. It illustrates various changes of opinion as to men and measures, which I have no disposition to disguise. The treaty which I send has been obtained by fair means, without the utterance of a threat, and with a distinct assurance from me, at every stage, that the United States had no warlike intentions. I should have thought myself and my country degraded by holding threatening language, when I knew that no coercion was intended.

* * * * * * * *

I have the honor to be, sir, your obedient servant,

WILLIAM B. REED.

Hon. LEWIS CASS,
Secretary of State.

* * * * * * * *

P. S. I find, on special reference to the act of Congress, that I have misstated the provision as to the detention for a year of a convict of a capital crime. Such detention, however, would be necessary, in case of the judgment being referred home for revision.

W. B. R.

JUNE 12, 1858.

The undersigned, envoy extraordinary and minister plenipotentiary of the United States, has had the honor to receive two communications informing him that his excellency Kiying has been appointed imperial commissioner and plenipotentiary in conjunction with their excellencies Kweiliang and Hwashana, and communicating the imperial decree giving him the necessary powers.

He has also the honor to inform their excellencies that he has now in his custody, and shall soon forward to Washington, the letter from his Majesty the Emperor to the President of the United States. Being a closed letter, he has no remarks to make on it, but if their excellencies have a copy of it he shall be glad to receive it.

The undersigned is happy to learn that the consultations of the agents appointed on both sides are advancing favorably. He hopes and desires that they may be resumed on Monday the 4th instant at 10 a. m., to-morrow being a sacred day of rest with Christian people. And, believing that they will soon be completed, he proposes to meet their excellencies the imperial commissioners on Wednesday the 16th instant at 11 o'clock, in due form to sign and seal the same if they be completed.

WILLIAM B. REED.

Their Excellencies KWEILIANG and HWASHANA, *&c.*, *&c.*

JUNE 15, 1858.

The undersigned, envoy extraordinary and minister plenipotentiary of the United States, having learned that the deputies appointed to arrange the details of the treaty have not yet quite completed their duties, and that his excellency Kweiliang is still laboring under illness, (which the undersigned very much regrets,) proposes to defer his interview with the imperial commissioners until Thursday at 6 p. m., when he hopes to sign the treaty.

The article regulating the visits to Pekin which was to-day referred to your excellencies is reasonable and must be adopted. If it is, the undersigned is willing to defer for the present the claims on the government of China. His great anxiety is for peace. If the article about visits to Pekin is not adopted as it stands, the undersigned reserves to himself the right at once to insist on the liquidation of their claims by the imperial government.

If convenient, and in view of the indisposition of Kweiliang, the undersigned will be glad to meet at some nearer place than the temple of Hai-Kwang. The Fung-shin temple is much nearer, but he will in this conform to your excellencies' wishes and convenience.

W. B. REED.

Their Excellencies KWEILIANG and HWASHANA, *&c.*, *&c.*

JUNE 16, 1858.

The undersigned, envoy extraordinary and minister plenipotentiary of the United States, has received the report of the deputies appointed to discuss the details of the treaty. He agrees to the modifications suggested with regard to the visit to Pekin and toleration of religion. He agrees to the article making consuls responsible for discharging ships without securing duties. He sends copies of the articles as he agrees to them. He regrets that the imperial commissioners will not consider and provide for the claims of citizens of the United States for losses at Canton, but he defers the consideration of them for the present, and if the same rule be applied to the claimants of other nations he is willing to discuss them with the commissioners at Canton.

In regard to the form of concluding the treaty, he does not yet know the form in which the Russian treaty has been signed, but he wishes the present one to conform in this respect to the previous treaty signed at Wanghia.

He proposes to meet their excellencies, as he said he would, to-morrow at 6 o'clock, either at the Hai-Kwang temple or at the residence of his excellency Kweiliang, or, if it is more agreeable, he will meet them for the purpose of signing on Friday at 10 o'clock. He hopes there will be no further delay.

WILLIAM B. REED.

Their Excellencies KWEILIANG and HWASHANA,
Imperial Commissioners and Plenipotentiaries, &c., &c.

JUNE 17, 1858.

KWEILIANG and HWASHANA, Imperial Commissioners and Plenipotentiaries of the Ta-Tsing Empire, &c., &c., herewith communicate on business:

The deputies who were appointed to deliberate on behalf of our respective countries on the articles of the treaty, having come to the end of their labors, we are on our side busily engaged in making a draft of the same. Accordingly we have decided to meet your excellency on the 18th instant, at 6 p. m., at the Hai-Kwang monastery, where we can sign the copies of this treaty, securing perpetual peace between our two countries. Appended are the slips containing the emendations of articles 22 and 29.

His Excellency WILLIAM B. REED,
Envoy Extraordinary and Minister Plenipotentiary
Of the United States of America to China.

The clause added to article 22, is as follows: "If the consul of the United States delivers the ship's papers to any vessel so that she leave the port before her duties are all paid, he shall be held responsible therefor."

ART. 29. "The sacred doctrines of Christianity, as professed by the Protestant and Roman Catholic churches, are recognized to be such as lead men to do good works, and hereafter all persons who peaceably preach and profess them shall be treated with kindness, and protected in their faith. No insult shall be offered or permitted, nor shall such persons be forbidden to propagate and practice their faith. Citizens of the United States may enter and travel in the country from the open ports to preach their doctrines. The consuls of the United States, after consultation with the local authorities along the coasts as to the proper number of persons so to be admitted to travel in the country, and ascertaining that persons applying for the same are missionaries and citizens of the United States, shall grant certificates to that effect; which shall be their protection."

The above is according to the form contained in the treaty with Russia, and together with the fifth article and the clause added to the twenty-second, are copied according to the forms sent us, and are all agreed to.

TIENTSIN, *June* 21, 1858.

KWEILIANG and HWASHANA, Imperial Commissioners and Plenipotentiaries of the Ta-Tsing Empire, &c., &c., herewith communicate on business:

On the 21st instant (to-day) the gentry and citizens here have petitioned us in a body, stating "that last night about 11 o'clock more than ten foreigners came into the Ho-tien and Tau streets, having fire-arms and knives in their hands, with which they cut and broke open the doors of a shop and carried off some clothes, killing a black dog, and leaving behind them a pistol and a painted board, each with foreign letters on them, and three plain silk handkerchiefs. The same night they broke open other houses, and this conduct has greatly alarmed the minds of all the inhabitants."

We have ourselves looked over the list of articles lost by the people, and seen the pistol and other things, so that there is no mistake about the matter; and herewith inform your excellency that you may ascertain to what nation the soldiers belong. We also earnestly request they may be restrained in future, that the present good feeling be preserved, and on no account be suffered to repeat such acts, lest we be prevented from bringing the present negotiations to a satisfactory conclusion. While we communicate this to each of the foreign ministers, we particularly request that your excellency will take the necessary steps for making it effectual.

His Excellency W. B. REED,
Envoy Extraordinary and Minister
Plenipotentiary of the United States to China.

JUNE 30, 1858.

KWEILIANG and HWASHANA, Imperial Commissioners and Plenipotentiaries of the Ta-Tsing Empire, &c., &c., herewith communicate on business:

On the 28th instant we memorialized his Majesty, informing him of the stipulations contained in the treaties of peace which we had signed and sealed with the ministers of the United States, Russia, England, and France, and begging him to examine them.

We have to-day been honored by the receipt of an imperial rescript dated the 29th instant, to the following effect:

"We have examined the memorial, and fully understand it. This from the Emperor."

We accordingly inform your excellency of the above, as is our duty.

His Excellency W. B. REED,
Envoy Extraordinary and Minister
Plenipotentiary United States America in China.

JUNE 19, 1858.

The undersigned, envoy extraordinary and minister plenipotentiary of the United States, makes this friendly communication to their excellencies the imperial commissioners:

In January last the undersigned received from their excellencies Lord Elgin and Baron Gros, the plenipotentiaries of England and France, a box containing the treaty between the United States and the Emperor of China, as signed at the village of Wanghia on the 3d of July, 1844, and ratified by the President of the United States, by and with the advice and consent of the Senate, and bearing the great seal of the United States, and the original exchange of ratifications at Pwan-Tang, near Canton, on the 31st December, 1845, by their excellencies Kiying, imperial commissioner, and James Biddle, commander-in-chief of the naval forces and acting minister and commissioner to China of the United States of America. These papers were found in the yamun of the Imperial Commissioner Yeh, at Canton.

The undersigned, when he received these papers, informed their excellencies the English and French plenipotentiaries that he should retain them till an opportunity presented itself of restoring them to the Chinese authorities. The time for this restoration has arrived, and the undersigned has instructed his secretary of legation, Mr. Williams, respectfully to place these papers in your excellencies' hands. The treaty of Wanghia is to a large extent superseded by the convention which the undersigned yesterday had the honor of signing with your excellencies, but it will always be a precious historical record, as that of the first written compact between two great nations of friendship which has never been, and the undersigned earnestly hopes never will be, seriously interrupted.

In restoring these documents to your excellencies the undersigned begs leave to observe that, had the treaty of Wanghia been deposited and kept at the capital, it would not have fallen into the hands of those who were temporarily engaged in hostilities with China. This cannot again happen, as the faith of his Majesty the Emperor is now pledged to the United States that hereafter these treaties shall be deposited and safely kept in charge of the privy council at the capital of the Emperor, where the undersigned sincerely hopes an enemy may never come.

The undersigned hopes to receive from your excellencies a written acknowledgment of the receipt of these documents, which he may send to the President of the United States.

W. B. REED.

Their Excellencies KWEILIANG and HWASHANA, *&c.*, *&c.*

JUNE 19, 1858.

KWEILIANG and HWASHANA, Imperial Commissioners and Plenipotentiaries of the Ta-Tsing Empire, &c., &c., herewith reply on business:

We have had the honor to receive at 4 o'clock this afternoon from the hands of Mr. Williams, the secretary of legation, whom your excellency has sent for the purpose, the original box containing all the documents relating to the old treaty signed at Wanghia, another proof of the friendly feelings existing on your part towards China. We shall most carefully retain them by us until we receive orders from court respecting their disposal, when they will be as carefully handed over to the safe-keeping of the privy council to be kept as a perpetual memorial.

His Excellency W. B. REED,
Envoy Extraordinary and Minister
Plenipotentiary of the United States in China.

LEGATION OF THE UNITED STATES,
Tientsin, June 19, 1858.

MY LORD: I have the honor to inform your excellency that on the 18th instant I signed a treaty on behalf of the United States with the Chinese imperial commissioners.

I shall have the honor to furnish your excellency with copies in English and Chinese of the treaty as soon as they can be prepared.

I have the honor to be, my lord, your excellency's obedient, humble servant,

WILLIAM B. REED,

His Excellency the Earl of ELGIN AND KINCARDINE,
H. B. M. High Commissioners, &c., &c., &c.

Similar note sent to Baron Gros and Count Poutiatine.

TIENTSIN, *June* 19, 1858.

SIR: I beg to acknowledge the receipt of your excellency's letter of this day's date, informing me that, on the part of the United States, you have signed a treaty with the Chinese imperial commissioners.

I have the honor to be, sir, your excellency's most obedient, humble servant,

ELGIN AND KINCARDINE.

His Excellency the Hon. W. B. REED,
&c., &c., &c.

[Translation.]

TIENTSIN, *June* 19, 1858.

MR. MINISTER: I have the honor to communicate herewith to your excellency a correct translation of the treaty concluded between Russia and China on the 1st (13th) of June, and I request you to be pleased to excuse me for not having sent it to you sooner, the dispatch of a courier to St. Petersburg having taken up all our time.

In the course of our previous communications and of our frequent conversations on a subject which interests us both to the same degree, I have already had occasion to make known to your excellency the various peculiarities connected with our new treaty with China, and I think I may be exempted from entering here into further details on this subject.

It it with the greatest satisfaction that I have received from your excellency the dispatch which announces to me the conclusion of the treaty between China and the United States of America, and I hasten to send you my most sincere congratulations on the happy termination of this affair.

Be pleased to accept, Mr. Minister, assurances of the very distinguished consideration with which I have the honor to be your excellency's very humble servant.

CT. POUTIATINE.

His Excellency Mr. REED,
Envoy Extraordinary and Minister Plenipotentiary, &c., &c., &c.

LEGATION OF THE UNITED STATES,
Tientsin, June 21, 1858.

MONSIEUR LE COMTE: I have the honor to acknowledge the receipt of your letter of the 19th, inclosing me a copy of the treaty negotiated by your excellency with the Chinese commissioners.

I now transmit to your excellency a copy in English of the treaty of the United States, and shall send one in Chinese so soon as it can be prepared. If possible, I shall be glad to have a copy of your treaty in Chinese.

Your excellency will observe that in my treaty there is no provision for liquidating the claims for loss of property, &c., at Canton. The Chinese authorities desired to refer them for settlement to the place where they occurred, and, with the distinct understanding that the rule should be equally applicable to all, I agreed to it. I understand your excellency has adopted the same rule with reference to the Russian factory property destroyed on the frontier.

I have the honor to be, Monsieur le Comte, your excellency's most obedient servant,

WILLIAM B. REED.

His Excellency Monsieur le Comte POUTIATINE,
Imperial Commissioner, &c., &c., &c.

LEGATION OF THE UNITED STATES,
Tientsin, June 21, 1858.

MY LORD: I have the honor to send you copies in English and Chinese of the treaty which, on the 18th instant, I signed with the imperial commissioners.

Your excellency will observe that no express provision is made for the adjustment and liquidation of the claims of American citizens for losses at Canton, the Chinese commissioners insisting that whatever responsibility existed should be enforced where the losses occurred. If, after all that has happened, the Chinese chose to invoke and insist on such a principle, I was not disposed to press the matter further, though I forbore only on the assurance voluntarily given to me that the same principle would be applied to all.

Anticipating this view of local responsibility, I advised my government, in January last, of what would probably occur, and I am in daily expectation of instructions on this point which will determine how and to what extent this local responsibility shall be enforced.

I only mention this to your excellency because, in the sketch of a treaty which I informally sent to you some weeks ago, a provision with regard to these claims was inserted, and I desire to inform your excellency why it was withdrawn.

I have the honor to be, my lord, your excellency's most obedient servant,

WILLIAM B. REED.

His Excellency the Earl of ELGIN AND KINCARDINE, *&c., &c., &c.*

A similar note was sent to Baron Gros.

TIENTSIN, *June* 22, 1858.

SIR: I beg to acknowledge the receipt of your letter of yesterday's date, inclosing copies in English and Chinese of the treaty which your excellency signed on the 18th instant with the imperial commissioners.

I have the honor to be, sir, your excellency's most obedient, humble servant,

ELGIN AND KINCARDINE.

His Excellency the Hon. W. B. REED, *&c.*, *&c.*, *&c.*

[Translation.]

EXTRAORDINARY MISSION OF FRANCE IN CHINA,
Tientsin, *June* 22, 1858.

MR. MINISTER: I received on the 19th of this month the letter which your excellency did me the honor to write to me on the same day for the purpose of announcing to me that, on the 18th, you had signed for the United States a treaty with the Chinese commissioners, and that you would send me a double copy, English and Chinese, of this treaty as soon as the two documents should be ready.

I hasten to announce to your excellency that this package reached me yesterday, together with the letter which your excellency was pleased to write to me on the 21st, and I thank you for that communication.

I have the honor to be, Mr. Minister, with high consideration, your excellency's very humble and very obedient servant,

BARON GROS.

His Excellency WILLIAM B. REED,
Envoy Extraordinary and Minister Plenipotentiary of the United States in China.

TIENTSIN, *June* 28, 1858.

SIR: I have the honor to inform your excellency that, on the 26th instant, I signed a treaty on behalf of Great Britain with the Chinese imperial commissioners.

I shall have the honor to furnish your excellency with a copy of this treaty as soon as it can be prepared.

I have the honor to be, sir, your excellency's most obedient, humble servant,

ELGIN AND KINCARDINE.

His Excellency the Hon. W. B. REED, *&c.*, *&c.*, *&c.*

Mr. Reed to Mr. Cass.

[Extracts.]

No. 24.]

LEGATION OF THE UNITED STATES,
Tientsin, July 1, 1858.

SIR: I have much pleasure in informing you that, besides the treaty which was recently signed, I have succeeded in effecting an arrangement for the prospective liquidation of the claims of American citizens for losses, &c., at and in the neighborhood of Canton.

* * * * * * * *

It was my duty to do my best to persuade the Chinese plenipotentiaries to agree to some provision for these claims. The correspondence will show that at Takoo, and in the early part of the negotiations here, the Chinese persevered in denying not only all responsibility on the part of the imperial government, but all power or inclination to control the local authorities at Canton. They assured me throughout that this was the case, and they should be obliged to apply the same rule to the English and French. Accepting this assurance, and, besides, not supposing myself at liberty to refuse to sign a treaty of general interest and obligation because claims for a relatively inconsiderable amount could not be provided for, I allowed the negotiations to proceed, taking care to make my acquiescence depend on the conduct of the Chinese to the belligerents. I found, on conference with Count Poutiatine, that the claims of his government for the destruction of property at a factory on the Siberian frontier were to be postponed in the same way, and with the same understanding the Russian and American treaties were signed.

No sooner was this done than I thought it best to have a distinct understanding with the commissioners on the subject, and I availed myself of the opportunity of what was meant to be a farewell visit to bring the matter of the claims directly to their view. The correspondence will show how it was at first received, and how naturally they resorted to what seemed to them the dexterous evasion of inferring the abandonment of the claims from my withdrawing the article from the rough draft of the treaty. This I at once corrected, and made them a proposition by which the gradual liquidation of these claims could be made without any acknowledgment of imperial responsibility, or any undue pressure on the resources of the government. To the claimants it is quite immaterial whence the payment comes, and I am satisfied, looking to the enormous and oppressive demands which the belligerents are about to make, that it would be bad policy and doubtful morality to press unduly this disorganized and bankrupt government. I have every reason besides to think that even those claims will be referrrd for ultimate settlement to Canton, and that something like a hypothecation of the commercial revenue will be made. Since the date of my last dispatch, I have seen the article of the French treaty on the subject of claims, and find it is all referred to Canton. The English and French, of course, have the advantage of holding that city as a pledge or material guarantee, but, as I informed you in a former dispatch, the revenue from customs there is ostensibly at least collected for the benefit of the Chinese.

Of course no one could say how long this might continue, and the plan occurred to me of procuring from the imperial commissioners, under their seals, an appropriation of a portion of their revenue to our benefit. By giving notice of such appropriation, as I have done, to the English and French, I have, to this extent, prevented any hypothecation to our disadvantage. I thought one fifth of the gross duties on goods in American bottoms and tonnage dues moderate and sufficient, my great object being not to press the government to desperate insolvency. With the extension of this to the revenue at Fuhchau and Shanghai every claimant should be satisfied. According to the best estimate now the claims, assuming them to amount to the sum stated in the agreement, will be liquidated in four or five years, but I cannot speak with entire precision, being separated from accurate statistical information.

To this the commissioners assented, and the agreement will be found in our several letters of the 22d, 23d, 24th, 25th, 26th, 27th, and 30th instant. (Inclosures 1 to 9.) I consider it, and mean to insist on it, as a perfect agreement and appropriation of the funds, subject to the one limitation that the aggregate amount is to be investigated, subject to the supervision of an officer specially appointed. That there should be such an investigation is manifestly proper. The United States would require it, even if the Chinese did not, and its result may be, and I sincerely hope will be, to reduce the amount.

I learn from Baron Gros that some arrangement of the same nature and in the same form is contemplated for the French indemnity, and this mode is preferred for the Chinese reason, that if such stipulations are put into a treaty and promulgated, it would disparage the negotiators in the popular mind.

Having procured this stipulation, which has been sealed with the same seal that was affixed to the treaty, (seals being momentous signs with Orientals,) the plan which I propose to adopt is this: to wait with entire good faith till business be restored at Canton, not necessarily till the restoration of the city, which may be deferred, but till revenue from customs shall be in full receipt, and then, under the authority of these stipulations of the imperial commissioners, to retain, if necessary, from the duties the proportion agreed upon, simultaneously at the three ports. At the same time, I shall invite and promote the thorough investigation of the amount by the local authorities. In enforcing this, I may need the presence of the squadron at the different ports, to assert our rights, not only against the Chinese, if they show a disposition to evade their obligation, but to show to other nations that our interests must be protected.

I hope this mode of action will meet with the approval of the Presi dent. It seems now to be well understood and willingly agreed to by the Chinese. It is a matter of great gratification to me that I have been enabled in this, also, to effect a peaceful arrangement, for I am satified that no other could be attempted here, and that the only alter native must be the coercion which I once thought would be inevitable Let me, however, be understood as distinctly saying, that whoeve begins or carries through the execution of this or any other arrangement, must do it with a steady hand.

I have the honor to be, sir, your obedient, humble servant,

WILLIAM B. REED.

JUNE 22.

The undersigned, envoy extraordinary and minister plenipotentiary of the United States, received this morning your excellencies letter of the 21st relating to an attack and depredation of some unknown sailors or soldiers on the property of citizens of Tientsin. The undersigned immediately directed inquiry made, and found that no one of his small escort of sailors and marines, or of the men on the chartered steamer which accompanies him, had anything to do with it; and it is hardly necessary for him to say that it would be a matter of extreme mortification to the undersigned if any person in the service of the United States should do any willful wrong to the inhabitants or authorities of Tientsin, whose whole conduct towards the undersigned, and those who accompany him, has been that of hospitable kindness.

The undersigned avails himself of this opportunity to beg that he may have another interview on business with their excellencies the imperial commissioners, or that the deputies who arranged the details of the treaty may again meet, if possible, to-day or to-morrow. His object is this:

In the discussion of the treaty, so happily concluded between the United States and China, the undersigned brought to the notice of your excellencies the subject of claims for indemnity for injuries done at Canton and in the south of China. Your excellencies reply, as contained in a memorandum given to Mr. Williams, was that the imperial government was not responsible for what was done at the outside province, but that the local authorities must make good any injuries their acts had occasioned. On the 16th of June the undersigned addressed a note to your excellencies in which he said: "He regrets that the imperial commissioners will not consider and provide for the claims of citizens of the United States for losses at Canton, but he defers the consideration of them for the present, and if the same rule be applied to the claimants of other nations, he is willing to discuss them with the commissioners at Canton."

To this decision he yet adheres, but he shall be glad to have this understanding put in a definite form, for he very frankly says to your excellencies, that if the claims for private pecuniary injury done to English or French be admitted to be binding on the imperial government, and not those of the United States, it will be a great wrong. He is quite willing if all are put on an equal footing to have it settled hereafter in the south, but he wishes to have it expressly agreed to. This is but justice to those who have been friends of China.

He desires to have this arranged as quickly as possible, as he is desirous to return at as early a period as possible to his ships at the outer anchorage.

W. B. REED.

Their Excellencies KWEILIANG and HWASHANA, *&c.*, *&c.*, *&c.*

JUNE 23, 1858.

KWEILIANG and HWASHANA, Imperial Commissioners and Plenipotentiaries of the Ta-Tsing Empire, &c., &c., herby reply:

We received your excellency's communication of yesterday about the affair of the robbery of the common people by some sailors, and are happy to learn that your excellency has good proof that none of the marines or sailors of the United States have had anything to do with it, and that orders had been issued that they should observe peaceful conduct in all their intercourse with our people; for which we tender our hearty thanks.

We receive the expression of your willingness to take out the article in the treaty about indemnity for claims, and when we had the last interview on the 18th instant, at the signing and sealing of the treaty, there was nothing said by either of us about any other topic, which also showed the belief we had about this point. At this commencement of the relations we have entered into the treaty we did not suppose your excellency was desirous to resume negotiations upon any subject, and this topic of indemnity for losses, which was taken out of the articles of the treaty, having been already settled between us, any arrangement which we may enter into with the English and French, about their claims can hardly be brought forward as a [precedent for] comparison.

His Excellency W. B. REED,
Envoy Extraordinary and Minister Plenipotentiary of the United States to China.

JUNE 23, 1858.

The undersigned, envoy extraordinary and minister plenipotentiary of the United States, has received the communication of your excellencies, and renews his request for an interview or for a meeting of the deputies.

It is not for the purpose of reopening negotiations, but in order to have a distinct understanding that the claims of American citizens shall be referred to Canton on exactly the same footing as the English. He will be satisfied to have this in writing.

W. B. REED.

Their Excellencies KWEILIANG AND HWASHANA,
&c., &c., &c.

JUNE 25, 1858.

KWEILIANG and HWASHANA, Imperial Commissioners and Plenipotentiaries of the Ta-Tsing Empire, &c., herewith reply:

At the interview held this morning, we received from his excellency W. B. Reed, the American minister, a written memorandum to the following effect:

"The present article about indemnity for losses must be considered as of the same force and virtue as if it was embodied in the treaty with the United States and formed a part of it. His Majesty the Emperor of the Ta-Tsing empire, acknowledging the complete neutrality of the United States in the hostilities which have occurred in the province of Kwangtung, and desirous to put her citizens on an equality with those of other nations, agrees that their claims for indemnity, to the amount of 600,000 taels, shall be liquidated by deducting one fifth of all the tonnage, import, and export duties which are paid by American ships at the three ports of Canton, Fuhchau, and Shanghai; and the sums thus accruing shall be applied to indemnify the losses suffered at Canton, Whampoa, and on the Island of Honan and thereabouts. The amount which shall be deducted each year by the consuls at those ports for this purpose shall be reported to the minister of the United States then in China; and the latter agrees to inform the high Chinese officers of the same every year, that they may know when the whole is entirely paid up."

We have now learned that this stipulation was withdrawn from the treaty before it was signed, and the reasons therefor; but, as we have no data by which to determine the amount of the claims, we refer that to the governor general at Canton to investigate and decide.

His Excellency W. B. REED,
Envoy Extraordinary and Minister Plenipotentiary of the United States.

Translated by

S. W. WILLIAMS.

LEGATION OF THE UNITED STATES,
Tientsin, June 26, 1858.

The undersigned has received the communication of their excellencies, relating to indemnity for American claims and the proper mode of their settlement, as follows:

(The preceding reply is here quoted entire.)

The undersigned understands that the reference to the governor general at Canton is that he may ascertain the precise amount of the claims, and that he shall inform the collectors at Canton, Fuhchau, and Shanghai, that, after business is resumed at Canton, one fifth of all the tonnage, import, and export duties paid by American ships at those ports, shall be deducted and applied to the payment of those claims; and that the governor general at Canton shall appoint a special officer to investigate them.

If this be the understanding of their excellencies, the undersigned will accept it unreservedly. He expects an immediate answer.

W. B. REED.

Their Excellencies KWEILIANG AND HWASHANA,
Imperial Commissioners, &c., &c., &c.

JUNE 27, 1858.

KWEILIANG and HWASHANA, Imperial Commissioners and Plenipotentiaries of the Ta-Tsing Empire, herewith reply:

We have to acknowledge the dispatch of the 26th instant, relating to the subject of indemnity of claims of American citizens to the extent of six hundred thousand taels. Your excellency deems the concluding sentence, [of our dispatch of the 25th instant,] viz: "that the governor-general shall investigate and decide," not to be clearly stated, and you request that the following addition may be made to it:

"That the reference to the governor general at Canton is that he may ascertain the precise amount of the claims, and that he shall inform the collectors at Fuhchau and Shanghai that, after business is resumed at Canton, one fifth of all the tonnage, import, and export duties paid by American ships at those three ports, shall be deducted and applied to the liquidation of these claims; and that the governor general shall appoint a special officer to investigate them."

We have examined the preceding proposition, and, as it appears to be a proper one, will accordingly communicate the same to his excellency the governor general at Canton, that he may carry its stipulations into effect and inform the collectors.

His Excellency WILLIAM B. REED,
Envoy Extraordinary and Minister Plenipotentiary of the United States in China.

Translated by S. W. WILLIAMS.

LEGATION OF THE UNITED STATES,
Tientsin, June 30, 1858.

The undersigned, envoy extraordinary and minister plenipotentiary, &c., &c., has the honor to acknowledge their excellencies' communications, of the 25th and 27th instants, in reference to the mode of liquidating the claims of citizens of the United States against the Chinese government, and has much pleasure in expressing his satisfaction with the arrangement now concluded, and which he has no reason to doubt will be carried out in good faith.

The negotiations proposed by the undersigned last year to his excellency the governor general at Canton, and begun at the mouth of this river, have now been brought to an amicable close, and he hopes that nothing may hereafter occur to disturb the friendly relations which exist between the governments and people of our respective countries.

* * * * * * * * *

W. B. REED.

Their Excellencies KWEILIANG AND HWASHANA,
Imperial Commissioners and Plenipotentiaries.

Mr. Reed to Mr. Cass.

No. 27.] LEGATION OF THE UNITED STATES,
Shanghai, July 13, 1858.

SIR: I have the honor to apprise you of my arrival here on the 11th instant, having left Tientsin on the 3d and the anchorage in the Gulf of Pechele on the 6th instant. Lord Elgin arrived here on the 12th. Baron Gros and Count Poutiatine are still in the north, though it is understood negotiations are amicably closed.

I yesterday received from Lord Elgin a copy of the British treaty, accompanied by a letter, which, with my answer, I now forward, (inclosures 1*a* and 1*b*,) and from which the President will see that whatever slight interruption of harmonious action may have occurred, the end is a restoration of entire friendly feeling between the representatives of western powers, and full justice to the exertions of all.

By the next mail I shall forward copies of the Russian, English, and French treaties, with such comments as, in my opinion, they may need.

I have the honor to be, sir, your obedient servant,

WILLIAM B. REED.

Hon. LEWIS CASS,
Secretary of State, Washington.

TIENTSIN, *July* 5, 1858.

SIR: I have the honor to inclose, for the information of your excellency, the copy of a treaty between Great Britain and China, signed on the 26th ultimo by me, on behalf of Great Britain, and by the imperial commissioners, Kweiliang and Hwashana, on behalf of China, and approved by a decree of which a copy was transmitted to me yesterday by the commissioners.

In communicating this document to your excellency, I venture to express the hope that the new arrangements with China, which we have been together engaged in effecting, will prove to be no less conducive to the interests of that empire than to those of the nations which have trading relations with it.

I have the honor to be, sir, your excellency's most obedient, humble servant,

ELGIN AND KINCARDINE.

His Excellency the Hon. W. B. REED, *&c., &c., &c.*

LEGATION OF THE UNITED STATES,
Shanghai, July 12, 1858.

MY LORD: I had the honor yesterday of receiving your excellency's letter, dated July 5, at Tientsin, and thank you for the copy in English of the treaty which, on the 26th ultimo, you signed, on behalf of Great Britain, with the imperial commissioners, Kweiliang and Hwashana.

I beg to assure your excellency that I cordially unite in the hope that the new arrangements with China, which we have been together engaged in effecting, will prove to be no less conducive to the interests of that empire than to those of the nations which have trading relations with it.

My countrymen, especially those engaged in commerce, have reason to thank your excellency for the enlarged privileges you have secured for subjects of Great Britain, and which, under the most favored clause, will enure to citizens of the United States. I am confident your excellency will feel with me the new responsibility which these enlarged privileges impose on all who derive benefit from them, and who will be placed in still closer contact with this peculiar and relatively helpless people. To my own government I have strongly represented the duty, which, in my judgment, devolves on it of enforcing on American citizens the obligation to regard not only the treaty stipulations, but the laws of the empire.

I beg further to say to your excellency that I have counseled the government at home to designate Shanghai as the place where the legation of the United States is hereafter permanently to be, and to direct the exercise of the right of occasional visit or longer sojourn at the capital with great reserve, and only on occasions of grave importance.

I have the honor to be, my lord, your excellency's obedient servant,

WILLIAM B. REED.

His Excellency the Earl of ELGIN AND KINCARDINE.

Mr. Cass to Mr. Reed.

No. 15.]

DEPARTMENT OF STATE,
Washington, October 16, 1858.

SIR: I have regularly acknowledged the receipt of your dispatches from time to time up to the 3d ultimo, the date of my last dispatch to you. I now have to acknowledge the receipt of your dispatches from No. 21 to No. 27, inclusive.

I congratulate you upon your negotiation of the treaty of Tientsin. The provisions of that treaty are judged to be quite as favorable to the United States as we had any just reason to expect.

In pursuance of the earnest desire you have expressed in some of your dispatches to this department, in regard to your return to the United States, I am directed by the President to signify to you, as I now do, his acquiescence in your wishes in that behalf, though he sincerely regrets that the country will lose your valuable services as minister to China.

I am, sir, respectfully, your obedient servant,

LEWIS CASS.

WILLIAM B. REED, Esq., *&c.*, *&c.*, *&c.*

Mr. Reed to Mr. Cass.

No. 28.] LEGATION OF THE UNITED STATES,
Shanghai, July 24, 1858.

SIR: I have great pleasure in sending to you the translation of a dispatch from their excellencies the imperial commissioners, with a decree from the Emperor absolutely ratifying the treaty which on the 18th ultimo was signed at Tientsin between the United States and China. Nothing now remains to be done but the ratification by the President, with the advice and consent of the Senate of the United States.

I congratulate you on this new proof of the good will of the imperial court, and on the conclusion of the important negotiations intrusted to me by the President.

I have the honor to forward two letters from the Russian and French ministers, and my reply, further illustrative of the friendly relations of the western powers.

On the 13th instant I received your dispatch (No. 11) dated 28th April, acknowledging the receipt of a large number of my dispatches, and informing me that the President had approved my conduct in uniting with the envoys of Great Britain, Russia, and France, in a peaceful appeal to the court at Pekin.

I have to request that dispatches may, as heretofore, be addressed to me at Hong Kong, and be sent by the way of Marseilles.

I have the honor to be, sir, your obedient servant,

WILLIAM B. REED.

Hon. LEWIS CASS,
Secretary of State.

Inclosure 1.

JULY 4, 1858.

KWEILIANG and HWASHANA, Imperial Commissioners and Plenipotentiaries of the Ta-Tsing Empire, herewith make a communication:

We have this day received a dispatch from court containing an imperial rescript, and having carefully made a copy of the same, we now have the honor to inclose it to your excellency for your information.

His Excellency W. B. REED,
Envoy Extraordinary and Minister Plenipotentiary of the United States to China.

[*Inclosure.*]

On the 3d of July, 1858, the following rescript was received from his Majesty:

"Kweiliang and his colleague have already presented for our exam ination copies of the treaties which they have negotiated and settled with the ministers of Great Britain, France, Russia, and the United States, and to which they have affixed their official seals. They have now further represented to us that the ministers of those nations desire to obtain the imperial ratification of those treaties; and we accordingly hereby declare that the treaties which our imperial commissioners have made known to us as having been settled with the ministers of Great Britain and France, and also with those of Russia and the United States, are all agreed to, and are to be carried into effect according to their provisions.

"This from the Emperor."

Inclosure 2.

TIENTSIN, *July* 6, 1858.

SIR: I have the honor to transmit to your excellency a packet from the Chinese commissioners, containing the full confirmation by the Emperor of China of the treaties signed by the four powers with China. It was sent to me on the 4th of July, and since then I had no opportunity of forwarding it to you sooner.

This confirmation has stopped all proceedings on the part of the English and French to threaten the Chinese government, and I am happy to say that most of their vessels have left Tientsin, and probably to-morrow it will be completely evacuated.

I am expecting the arrival of the America, and will also immediately leave this place for Japan.

At your desire, I inclose herewith a copy of our treaty in Chinese.

With assurances of high consideration and esteem, I have the honor to be, your excellency's most humble servant,

C. POUTIATINE.

His Excellency the Hon. W. B. REED,
Envoy Extraordinary and Minister Plenipotentiary,
&c., &c., &c.

Inclosure 3.

[Translation.]

SHANGHAI, *July* 20, 1858.

MR. MINISTER: I have the honor to send herewith to your excellency a copy of the Chinese text of the treaty which I signed at Tientsin with the imperial commissioners on the 27th of June last.

I have had the honor to déliver confidentially to your excellency a copy of the French text of the same treaty a few days after signing it, and your excellency has been pleased to permit me not to make the official delivery of it to you until I should likewise be able to send you the Chinese text which you desired to have.

I beg your excellency to be pleased to excuse the delay which has occurred in this transmission. In the main it was without inconvenience, and I claim a little indulgence for form.

It now only remains for me, Mr. Minister, to congratulate myself on the relations which have subsisted between us when we have had to act in concert in the negotiations that we had to follow, and everything causes me to hope that the happy result which we have obtained may lead to better days soon for the numerous communities of this vast empire, whose prosperity so warmly interests the policy of the Emperor's government as well as that of the government of which your excellency is the representative in these regions.

Be pleased to accept, I pray you, Mr. Minister, new assurances of the sentiments of high consideration with which I have the honor to be your very humble and very obedient servant,

BARON GROS.

His Excellency W. B. Reed,
Envoy Extraordinary and Minister Plenipotentiary of the United States of America in China.

Inclosure 4.

Legation of the United States,
Shanghai, July 24, 1858.

Monsieur le Baron: I have the honor to acknowledge your excellency's note of the 20th instant, inclosing a copy of the Chinese text of the treaty between France and China, signed at Teintsin on the 27th ultimo. I had already received and beg now to thank you for a copy of the French text.

I unite cordially in the hope that the treaty arrangements we have succeeded in making with the Chinese empire may largely promote the interests of its subjects generally, as well as those of the citizens of our respective countries who have commercial or other relations to the Chinese.

The concert of action which you are good enough to describe as having existed between us in the recent negotiations will be regarded by my government, as it has been by me, as the subject of sincere felicitation.

Begging you to accept the renewed assurances of my high consideration and sincere personal regard, I have the honor to be, Monsieur le Baron, your excellency's most obedient, humble servant,

WILLIAM B. REED.

His Excellency Monsieur le Baron Gros,
Commissioner Extraordinary and Embassador of His Majesty the Emperor of the French in China.

Mr. Reed to Mr. Cass.

No. 29.] LEGATION OF THE UNITED STATES,
On board the Minnesota, off Shanghia, July 29, 1858.

SIR: I now forward copies of the treaties signed on the 13th, 26th, and 27th ultimo by the ministers of Russia, Great Britain, and France, and beg to add a few remarks on such of the provisions of them as interest the United States and its citizens under our most favored clause. (Inclosures No. 1 *a*, 1 *b*, 1 *c*.)

I. DIPLOMATIC RELATIONS TO PEKIN.

The Russian, American, and French treaties contain a provision that, with more or less limitation, the ministers of each shall have the right to visit and sojourn at the capital, the permanent seat of the legation being elsewhere. In the Russian treaty, which was signed first in the order of time, one "of the ports open to commerce" is designated, and in the American, though there is nothing expressed, the understanding was the same. In the American and French treaties there are special provisions for community of privilege in case the Chinese grant to any other nation a resident minister. So that the decision as to whether we shall have permanent or occasional diplomatic relations at the capital is left absolutely with us.

I am at a loss to know why, on this important point, France and Great Britain being in the same position of semi-belligerent negotiators, the treaties were not the same. The British treaty, with the right of a residency, was signed twenty-four hours before the French treaty, and it is scarcely conceivable that so important a privilege was secretly obtained. The fairer inference is, that the French minister knew what his colleague meant to exact, but did not attach as much importance to the absolute privilege itself.

I repeat, however, that under the treaties as they now are framed, forming one system, the President must determine hereafter where the legation of the United States shall permanently be, and, doubting as I yet do on the subject, it seems to me the proper course will be to suspend an absolute determination till, on the exchange of ratifications at the capital, my successor shall be able to form a safe and final judgment. Even in the English treaty, you will observe, there is no absolute determination of the question whether there shall be a permanent or occasional legation at the capital. It is to be (Article III) at the option of the British government.

I have no doubt, however, what that decision will be, if Lord Elgin's counsels are followed by his government, and it is right that I should (since the same option rests with the President) fairly state the reasoning which has led him to the conclusion that constant intercourse with western officials at the capital is not only desirable but essential to the general interests and the safety of this empire. He thinks that all the difficulties which have heretofore occurred with western nations have arisen from the omission or denial of honest representation of facts to the imperial court by the local officers. They neither dare nor desire to tell the truth. The experience, too, it is alleged, everywhere but at Canton, with such men as Yeh and Seu is, that the personal contact of foreign with Chinese officials is salutary. There is no embarrassment in the relations to the taoutaes at the open ports or the governors or governor generals, and no difficulty in making them understand truth and feel the force of reasoning. Their conduct when they are at liberty to act shows that they may be thus influenced, but the moment they have to communicate with the capital or to ask for orders they become afraid to tell the truth, or to admit their own convictions of what is right.

Again, it is thought that a good influence may be exercised at the capital by invigorating the imperial authorities with a sense of their own power and what is due to themselves; that while contact with intelligent public men from the west may break down the absurd sentimental complacency of those surrounding the imperial center, it will make the court comprehend its real power and its duty to exercise it. As, for instance, one of the difficulties of the present state of things on the coast is, that there is an absolute immunity of the citizens of non-treaty powers. A Saxon, or Swede, or Dane, or Prussian does as he pleases. He defies law, commits crime with impunity, refuses the payment of duties or debts, and as the new treaties give unrestricted general right of access to the interior, he will be found following the footsteps, or close in the company, of the subject of the treaty powers, and carrying with him his immunities and his uncontrolled power of doing wrong. As matters now stand, the local authorities are too weak or corrupt, and the central power is too remote, to feel or to redress these wrongs; while nothing would be easier, it is assumed, than for the representatives of treaty powers, having direct access, to convince the Chinese government of their duty of repression, and that there is nothing to protect or give immunity to these outlaws. These are some of the many arguments plausibly urged in favor of such a permanent diplomatic establishment at Pekin as the provisions of the English treaty seem to contemplate, and I state them as intelligibly and as fairly as I can, in order that the question may be fully understood and properly decided by the President.

I have no doubt that such a reconstruction or invigoration of the central authority of this disorganized empire is hoped for as England thinks she has effected in Turkey; for it is very manifest from the terms of the new treaties that the rebellion, to which so great effects were once attributed, is regarded now as a mischievous convulsion that ought to be put an end to. The imperial power is to be sustained, and among the means of doing so is that which this treaty provides—a sort of diplomatic protectorate at the capital.

The objections, or rather, to speak more precisely, the doubts, which have occurred to me as to whether the American legation should be there located, were stated fully in a former dispatch. I renew my earnest suggestion that when the treaty shall be ratified, the minister of the United States shall proceed at once, either inland or by the Peiho river, to the capital.

II. ACCESS TO THE INTERIOR.

This is provided for in both the English and French treaties, and, of course, with its limitations, inures to us. The provision of the former is very comprehensive, for, with the limitation of requiring a passport, the form of which the consuls and not the Chinese are to determine, any foreigner may go anywhere in China "for pleasure, *or for purposes of trade*, and may hire vessels for the carriage of his baggage or *merchandise.*" No routes are specified; no limit to the character or amount of merchandise which may be taken into the interior, and there is nothing to prevent a foreigner—Englishman, Frenchman, Russian, or American—from unloading his ship load of cottons, or, if he happen to be unscrupulous, of opium, at Shanghai, or ——, when it shall be opened, and carrying it in one or a fleet of junks, or small craft steamers, to the frontiers of Thibet, or by the grand canal to Tientsin and Pekin, or, in short, anywhere, selling it as he goes along. But this is not all. He carries with him his "exterritoriality;" for the article which provides for his transit in the interior also provides for his immunity. "If," says the British treaty, "he shall commit any offense against the law, he shall be handed over to the nearest consul for punishment, but he must not be subjected to ill-usage in excess of necessary restraint." This rendered into plain language means that the foreigner who commits a rape or murder a thousand miles from the sea-board is to be gently restrained, and remitted to a consul for trial, necessarily at a remote point where testimony could hardly be obtained or relied on. These are the abuses and dangers which this new system of unlimited intercourse seems to foreshadow; but it would not be right or statesmanlike to shut one's eyes to other and better results from the opening of these secluded regions to a new and different civilization. No one can look at this immediate region, where, under the most favorable circumstances, this contact has been effected, without realizing its great advantages.

Here one can see the mutually respectful intercourse of the enlightened and honorable merchant of the west with the Chinese trader, or the entirely different but more interesting relation of the missionary with his pupils and the community generally, and the perfect and harmonious blending of the good elements of different national character. The great experiment is to be still further tried. The time has now come when, in the providence of God, and for His wise purposes, this great empire is to be opened, and whether it is to be to general or limited intercourse, the confidence I have that our countrymen will enjoy their full share of all the material advantages which it is supposed to secure, makes me the more clearly recognize the duties and dangers which accompany it.

The English and French plenipotentiaries think that they will find in a system of passports "which shall offer all desirable guarantees" adequate protection, and his excellency Baron Gros has invited my attention to it in the "projet of a protocol," which is to provide for it. I defer any remarks on the subject till my views shall be more matured, merely inclosing the brief papers that have passed between

Baron Gros and myself. (Inclosures No. 2 *a*, No. 2 *b*.) To make passports effective on American citizens in the way which is at all conformable to European usage, will require, it seems to me, the action of Congress. Before leaving China I shall have the honor of more fully explaining my views on this subject, though I shall in the interval omit no opportunity of conferring with the representatives of the other treaty powers so as to devise some lawful and practicable plan of protecting the Chinese from the unrestrained contact which has been forced upon them.

III. OPENING OF THE YANGTZE RIVER.

This privilege the British treaty secures, with the limitation that but one port, that of Chin-kiang, at the confluence of the river and the grand canal, is to be opened (and that a year hence) until the rebellion is at an end, when the two governments of England and China are to negotiate for three more ports between Hankow and the mouth of the river. In the French treaty Nankin is designated as an open port when it shall be recaptured from the rebels. Chin-kiang is now in the possession of the imperialists, and is likely to remain so. It may, therefore, be assumed, that a year hence the great river will be so far opened for the purposes of trade. As to the general advantages of this concession, it is not at all necessary for me to say anything. The best account of the navigation of the river and its capabilities will be found in the dispatches of Mr. McLane, who, in 1854, on board the United States ship Susquehanna, ascended it about fifty miles beyond Nanking. Hankow, the extreme point to which this arrangement prospectively applies, is about five hundred miles from the sea. Intelligent gentlemen, well acquainted with China, are of opinion that as a class of vessels such as steamers, with barges and schooners, will be needed for this navigation, there will be no sensible diminution of Shanghai trade, but rather that the free navigation of the river will leave Shanghai as the great maritime and distributing point.

IV. OPENING OF NEW PORTS.

The eleventh article of the British treaty creates, in all, eleven ports on the coast. Among the new ones are two in the Gulf of Pechele—Tang-chau, near the straits, an outlet of the great and fertile province of Shantung, and Ninchwang, in Manchuria.

This opens to lawful commerce a section of the coast of China fifteen hundred miles further north than it has yet been opened.

Aside from the specific advantages, whatever they may prove to be, of new ports, the extension of the right to trade from points as remote as Manchuria is from the Island of Hainan, from Ninchwang to Kiung-chau, one other is very obvious, that, with the reduction of tonnage dues, limitation of payment to once in four months, and right of reëxportation, it will transfer most of the coasting trade of China to foreign vessels, which are already preferred, on account of speed, safety from pirates, insurability, and cheapness. It is to be hoped that, with the diminution or annihilation of the junk trade on the coast, piracy will cease. Small American vessels, well commanded, as they generally are, will have advantage over all others.

V. COMMUTATION OF INTERNAL TRANSIT DUTIES.

The twenty-eighth article of the English treaty provides that, within four months from the signing of the treaty, (October 26, 1858,) all transit duties leviable on produce from the interior to the ports, or on imports from the coast to the interior, shall be ascertained and made public by authority, and that foreigners may clear goods from all such transit duties by a single payment on imports at the ports, or on produce at the custom-house or barrier nearest the place of production or purchase. This article, it is thought, will be very advantageous to foreign trade, if it becomes effective, and its effectiveness will soon be ascertained by the readiness or reluctance with which the Chinese dealers allow foreigners the face-value of the exemption or commutation certificate. If it appears in practice that produce bought by or for foreigners in the interior, and imports purchased of them on the seaboard, are subjected to no other taxes anywhere, or in any form than those specified in the published table, then such a trade will become a new and favorite branch of business, attractive to capitalists, because of its exemption from arbitrary and uncertain impositions, and of the protection and vigilance which the foreigner will be interested in bestowing on it.

These are the great privileges to which, by the operation of our most favored clauses, we are admitted, and which the coercive policy of Great Britain has been able to exact; for, after all, it was Great Britain, rather than France, which has taken the lead in the energetic course which has been adopted here. If, in the end, the good of unrestricted commerce overbalances the evil, and out of these new concessions and new points of contact no political entanglements arise, Lord Elgin will certainly deserve great credit for the steadiness with which, from first to last, he has kept these ends in view; and though, as you are well aware, I have had occasion more than once, in the course of negotiations here, to dissent from the course of reasoning which led him to certain measures, I should not do justice to myself or to him, now that these great results have been attained, if I were not to bear my willing testimony to the ability and energy which he has exhibited. It is matter of great gratification to me that the differences of opinion which have arisen, and the slight irritations which have followed such differences, (scarcely worth referring to,) have been controlled and moderated by discretion and good sense, and a sentiment of personal friendliness all round.

The only difficulty now remaining in the way of a general pacification and early restoration of trade, is the sad state of affairs at Canton, becoming worse every hour. There is utter desolation there, so far as industry and trade are affected. The army of occupation is almost besieged. Lord Elgin told me yesterday, and with expressions of regret very creditable to him, that the most reliable accounts describe Canton as more than half in ruins.

The braves are vexatiously hostile, not only picking off detatched parties in the city and suburbs, but actually attempting escalades of the walls. The direct consequence of this is constant and severe retaliation, which, when it is inflicted by the Freneh is very bloody. A few weeks ago, in consequence of a murderous attack made on a party of camp stragglers, the French commanding officers took possession of a street or neighborhood, marked off by measurement, and carefully guarded a number of houses, and then sent in armed parties with orders (executed with characteristic fidelity) to butcher every male inhabitant found within. A large number perished. The question now, I have every reason to believe, presents itself most painfully for the consideration of the British plenipotentiary, as to the best remedy for this. My own belief is, that nothing but an evacuation will do any good. The aspect of things at Canton, more deplorable every day, I need hardly say, satisfies me anew of the wisdom of that policy, which I have with all my heart endeavored under your instructions to pursue, of keeping steadily aloof from this wretched and bloody entanglement.

A hope is indulged (and I earnestly sympathize with it) that a new state of feeling may arise in the south when the news of the imperial ratification of the treaties reaches there. This will be so, unless the peculiar ferocity of the Cantonese has under local irritation got beyond control.

On the 24th instant, the governor general of this province addressed letters to the plenipotentiaries of the United States, Great Britain, and France, (inclosures No. 3, and 4,) informing us that their excellencies the Imperial Commissioners Kweiliang and Hwashana, with three other officers, were on their way towards Shanghai to meet us, and arrange the details of the revised tariff.

This is very important, as indicative of the views of the court, and its sincerity in carrying out the treaties. It is hoped when they arrive here, that some influence may be exercised by or through them by which the Canton difficulty may be settled. This, of course, belongs exclusively to the English and French plenipotentiaries.

I have the honor to be, sir, your obedient servant,

WILLIAM B. REED.

Hon. LEWIS CASS,
Secretary of State.

Inclosure 1 *a.*

[Translation of translation from the Russian.]

His Majesty the Emperor and Autocrat of all the Russias, and his Majesty the Emperor of China, holding it to be of the first necessity to define clearly the mutual relations between Russia and China, and to establish new regulations for the advantage of the two nations, have appointed, for such purpose, their plenipotentiaries, that is to say:

His Majesty the Emperor of all the Russias, his Aide-de-camp, General Vice-admiral Count Euphemius Poutiatine, Imperial Commissioner to China and Commander-in-chief of the Russian squadron in the Pacific ocean.

And his Majesty the Emperor of China for his empire the Dakiochi of the Oriental Section, Chief Director of the Tribunal of Criminal Justice, the High Functionary Kweiliang, and for his empire the President of the Tribunal of Inspection, Chief of Division of the Heavy Infantry of the Blue-fringed Banner, the High Functionary Hwashana.

The said plenipotentiaries, in virtue of the power which they have received from their respective governments, have agreed and concluded upon the following articles:

Article I.

The present treaty confirms afresh the peace and friendship which has existed through many years between his Majesty the Emperor of all the Russias and his Majesty the Emperor of China, and between their respective subjects.

Russian subjects who reside in China, and Chinese subjects who may be in Russia, shall constantly enjoy the protection of the governments of the two empires, as well for the safety of their persons as for their property.

Article II.

Henceforward communications between the supreme government of Russia and the supreme government of China shall not be made as heretofore up to this time, by the Senate on the one part and the tribunal Li-fan-yuan on the other; but the minister of foreign affairs of Russia shall be the person who will communicate with the senior member of the council of state, or the chief minister at Pekin. They shall treat on a footing of perfect equality. The ordinary correspondence of the personages above-mentioned shall be transmitted through the authorities on the frontiers of the two respective States. Communications of grave importance shall be carried to the capital by a person employed *ad hoc*, who shall be enabled to enter into verbal explanations with the members of the council of state and the chief minister. On his arrival, he shall transmit his dispatches through the medium of the tribunal of rites, (Lipon.)

Equality shall be observed likewise in the correspondence and interviews of envoys and ministers plenipotentiary of Russia with the members of the council of state, the ministers of the court of Pekin, and the governor general of frontier and maritime provinces; and in the relations between the governor general and between the authorities on the frontier of the two nations.

If the Russian government should judge it necessary to appoint a minister plenipotentiary to reside at one of the open ports of China, he shall treat in his personal relations and correspondence with the local Chinese authorities, and the ministers at Pekin, according to the general rules now recognized by all foreign States. The envoys of Russia may go to Pekin, passing either by Kiakta and Urga, or by Takoo, at the mouth of the Peiho, or by any other open port or city of China. After a preliminary notification, the Chinese government will immediately cause the necessary arrangements to be taken that the journey of the envoy and his suite may be prompt and comfortable. His reception at the capital shall be marked by the honors due to his rank; suitable residences shall be prepared, and all things necessary shall be supplied him.

All expenses occasioned by sending diplomatic missions from Russia to China shall be defrayed by the Russian government, and in no case become a charge on the Chinese government.

Article III.

Henceforward, commerce between Russia and China shall be carried on not only at the places designated on the frontier, but also by sea. Russian merchant vessels may traffic at the following ports: Shanghai, Ningpo, Foutchou-fu, Amoy, Canton, Tainon-fou, on the island of Formosa, Khioung-teheou-fou, on the island of Hainan.

Article IV.

In future, there shall be no limit placed by the two governments, as to the number of merchants or amount of capital engaged in the commerce. In maritime commerce and in all details which relate to it; that is to say, invoices of goods imported, payment of harbor dues, duties according to existing tariffs, &c., Russian subjects shall conform to the general rules established for foreign commerce in the ports of China.

All unlawful commerce which shall be carried on by Russians shall be punished by the confiscation of the merchandise landed, for the benefit of the Chinese government.

Article V.

The Russian government shall be at liberty to appoint consuls in the ports open to commerce. It may send thither vessels of war to maintain order for Russian subjects, and to give aid to the authority of the consul. The relations between the consul and the local authorities, the cession of ground suitable for the building of churches, of houses and stores, the purchase by Russians of lands from the Chinese, and all transactions which are of reference to the consul, shall be conducted in observance with the general rules of the Chinese government in business with foreigners.

Article VI.

If a Russian war or merchant vessel should be wrecked on the coast, the nearest Chinese authority shall at once give assistance to the crew, and shall take measures necessary for salvage of the vessel and cargo. It shall facilitate also the conveyance of the crew and cargo to the nearest port where there is a Russian consul, or an agent of a nation friendly to Russia, or to the frontier, if the shipwreck took place near it.

The Russian government will reimburse the costs occasioned by saving the crew and cargo.

In cases in which Russian war or merchant vessels may be under the necessity of making repairs or procuring fresh water and provisions, they may enter, on their route, ports not open to commerce and purchase what they need at prices amicably agreed on, and free from any obstacles interposed by the local authorities.

Article VII.

Any dispute between Russian and Chinese subjects in the open ports and cities shall be examined into by the Chinese authorities in concert with the Russian consul, or the agent who represents the authority of the Russian government at the place.

Russian subjects guilty of any offense or crime shall be judged according to Russian law. In like manner, Chinese subjects, for every crime or attempt against the person or property of a Russian, shall be tried and punished according to the laws of their country.

Russian subjects who shall have penetrated into the interior of China, and shall have there committed some crime or offense, shall be taken to the frontier, or to one of the open ports where a Russian consul may reside, to be tried and punished according to the Russian laws.

Article VIII.

The Chinese government having recognized the fact that the Christian doctrine promotes the establishment of order and peace among men, promises not to persecute its Christian subjects for the exercise of the duties of their religion ; they shall enjoy the protection accorded to all those who profess other creeds tolerated in the empire. The Chinese government, considering the Christian missionaries as worthy men who do not seek worldly advantages, will permit them to propagate Christianity amongst its subjects, and will not hinder them from moving about in the interior of the empire. A certain number of missionaries setting out from the open ports or cities shall be provided with passports, signed by the Russian authorities.

Article IX.

Those parts of the boundary between Russia and China which are not ascertained shall be examined, without delay, at the places themselves.

The two governments will appoint, for this purpose, deputies, who shall fix the line of demarcation, and shall conclude in relation thereto a convention, which shall be annexed as a separate article to the present treaty.

Maps and detailed descriptions of the frontier shall be afterwards prepared, and will serve as incontestable documents for future time.

Article X.

There shall no longer be a fixed term for the sojourn of the Russian ecclesiastical mission at Pekin. The members of such mission may, on the authorization of their government, return to their native country at any time. The vacancy may be filled by a new member.

The Chinese government shall no longer be at expense for maintaining the mission; all its expenses shall be at the charge of the Russian government.

The traveling expenses of members of the mission, of couriers, and of other persons who the Russian government may dispatch from Kiakta and the open ports of China, and *vice versa*, shall be paid by the Russian government. The Chinese local authorities are under obligations on their part to take the necessary measures that the journeys of all the persons above mentioned be speedy and convenient.

ARTICLE XI.

A regular post-service shall be established between Kiakta and Pekin, for communication between the two governments, as well as for the use of the Russian ecclesiastical mission at Pekin.

The Chinese courier shall be dispatched on a fixed day, once a month, from Pekin to Kiakta; and shall, in the space of fifteen days or less, deliver the official packets and letters at their place of destination.

Moreover, every three months, or four times a year, a convoy shall be dispatched at Kiakta for Pekin, and *vice versa*, for the transportation of all kinds of remittances and effects. This convoy shall make the journey in the period of one month. All the expenses occasioned by the establishment and upholding of these communications shall be paid, one half thereof by each government.

ARTICLE XII.

All privileges—political, commercial, or others—which shall hereafter be acquired by nations the most favored by the Chinese government, shall at the same time be extended to Russia, without needing any preliminary negotiation.

This treaty shall be ratified as of this date by the Emperor of China; and after it shall have been ratified by the Emperor of Russia, the exchange of ratifications shall be made at Pekin in one year, or sooner, if it can be done.

Copies in the Russian, Mantchou, and Chinese languages, bearing the signatures and seals of the plenipotentiaries of the two nations, are now exchanged, and the Mantchou text shall serve as the basis of interpretation of all the articles of the treaty, which shall be observed by the two high contracting parties faithfully and inviolably.

Done and signed in the city of Tientsin, the 13th of June, of the year 1858 after the birth of Jesus Christ, and in the fourth year of the reign of his majesty the Emperor Alexander II.

[SEAL.] COUNT EUPHEMIUS POUTIATINE.
[SEAL.] KWEILIANG,
HWASHANA.

True translation from the original.

BARON FR. OSTENSACKEN.

True copy.

S. WELLS WILLIAMS,
Secretary of Legation of the United States of America.

Inclosure 2 *a.*

[Translation.]

TIENTSIN, *June*, 1858.

The treaties of Tientsin between China, France, the United States of America, Great Britain, and Russia, being just signed, and the result they should produce, whether directly or by consequence, being inevitably the opening of the Chinese empire to the western nations, the attention of the four plenipotentiaries who signed them is naturally led to the danger which might result to people so gentle and apprehensive as those of the Celestial empire from a new order of things, which might facilitate the means of execution of enterprises by bold adventurers, or of excesses of all sorts, which it is for the honor and interest of the four western powers to prevent by all the means at their disposal.

It is, then, the duty of the four powers to guarantee China against her own weakness; and after having maturely reflected upon the best means to be employed to get at such results, the four plenipotentiaries have thought it to be found in giving a strong organization to the consular establishments of the four powers in China—establishments whose functions, sustained by extensive powers, would perhaps consist principally in protecting the timid and apprehensive people of China against the exactions of adventurers of all nations who should try to abuse the large concessions which the treaty secures to the four nations interested.

A good system of passports, identical with those established in Europe, should be adopted by the diplomatic and consular agents of the four powers in China.

The duration of the passports for presentation should be limited to six months or a year. They should not be issued by the diplomatic agents or consuls except to persons offering all the guarantees desirable, and the consuls should punish, without distinction, every infraction of established regulations, to which the bearer of the passport should bind himself in writing to submit.

No merchant, to whatever class he may belong, should be charged with consular functions; for experience has demonstrated that the influence which these functions necessarily give have been only too often employed to promote personal interests, to the detriment of right, or in opposition to rival interests.

The passports, printed in Chinese characters and in the language of the consul who may issue them, should be submitted to legalization both by the Chinese authority of the places where they may be issued as of the place of arrival and sojourn. They should be personal, bearing the signature of the bearer and that of the person who may be his surety; and they must never be collective.

Each of the four governments will have to decide to what extent it will authorize its agents in China to issue passports to foreigners not having treaties with the empire, and these passports should not be receivable by the bearers except on a formal condition undertaken by them to submit themselves to the authority as well as the jurisdiction of the consul who shall issue them on receiving suitable guarantees.

No passports shall be issued for cities and places occupied by the rebels. The missionaries, as well as merchants and travelers, should be provided with them.

These passports should not be given gratuitously, and the price paid to obtain them, and fixed in advance by common accord, should be used to cover the expenses of emission, and the surplus paid into the public chest of the city or place whence they are issued.

These chief rules seem to the four plenipotentiares to form the base for regulations to be adopted to give to China the guarantees which she needs in the first instance, so that she may not have to regret the concessions which she has made to the four contracting parties. It has been agreed between their plenipotentiaries that four copies of an act should be prepared to be sent to their respective governments, but to be submitted to their scrutiny merely as a simple informatory report.

In consequence, the four plenipotentiaries have signed this present document, agreed upon and reduced to writing by common consent, and have engaged to send it to their respective governments, who will take on this subject such determination as shall appear convenient to them.

Done at Tientsin in four copies, June 6, 1858.

BARON GROS.

Inclosure 2 *b*.

LEGATION OF THE UNITED STATES,
Shanghai, July 27, 1858.

The undersigned, envoy extraordinary and minister plenipotentiary of the United States of America, unites very cordially in the project of a protocol submitted for his consideration by his excellency the embassador of France, and which he learns has been agreed to without reserve by the ministers of the other western powers, who have signed treaties at Tientsin with the empire of China. He is very sensible of the danger to which the inhabitants of China may be exposed from unrestricted intercourse with foreigners, and very highly estimates the provident beneficence of the course suggested by his excellency Baron Gros. The undersigned, in giving his assent to the plan now suggested, is obliged, however, to do so with some limitations, which he now has the honor to state:

The jurisdiction of consuls over American citizens, in order to enforce penalties for traveling in the interior without passports, must be created and defined by an act of Congress, and no stipulation or agreement to submit to a jurisdiction can, in the opinion of the undersigned, effect the object. Such legislation, making it penal for any one to enter the country, especially for trade, without a compliance with such arrangements about passports as may be made, the undersigned will take the earliest opportunity of urging on his government.

The granting by an American consul of passports to others than American citizens is inadmissable; and here, also, in the opinion of the undersigned, the consent of a party taking a passport would confer no jurisdiction on a consular court.

The undersigned, as at present advised, is reluctant to recommend such a prohibition of "collective passports" as should prevent the issuing of one passport to an American citizen and his family. In the case of the Protestant missionaries in China, generally accompanied by their families, a requisition that each individual should have a passport would be attended with great inconvenience. Every adult male should, however, be so furnished.

By the existing statutes of the United States their consuls in China are already expressly prohibited from being in any way connected with trade.

With this explanation, and these reservations, which he hopes he has made intelligible, the undersigned repeats the expression of his entire concurrence in the views contained in the projet of a protocol signed by the representatives of France, Great Britain, and Russia, and desires to be considered as having united in the same.

Communicated, with the expression of my high consideration, to his excellency the embassador and high commissioner of his Majesty the Emperor of the French.

WILLIAM B. REED.

Inclosure 3.

JULY 24, 1858.

Ho, a Guardian of the Heir-Apparent, a President of the Board of War, and Governor General of the two Kiang Provinces, in the Ta-Tsing Empire, herewith sends a communication:

On the 22d instant a dispatch was received from the general council at Pekin, covering a copy of the following edict:

"On the 15th of July the privy council had the honor to receive the following rescript from the throne:

"Let Kweiliang, Hwashana, Képie, and Mingshen, be empowered to take the seal of imperial commissioners, and proceed by post to Suchau, in Kiangsu, where they can, in conjunction with Ho Kwei-tsing, consult upon and arrange all that is connected with the tariff and commercial matters. Let them also take with them such clerks and attachés as are necessary, who can also proceed by post. This from the Emperor."

I have learned that Kweiliang and his colleagues, in compliance with the above, have started, and will probably be at Suchau during the first decade of the next or seventh month, (August 9 or 19). The acting intendent of circuit at Shanghai, Sieh, has informed me that your excellency has already reached that place, and I therefore have had the above rescript carefully copied out, and now send it for your information. A necessary communication.

His Excellency WILLIAM B. REED,
Envoy Extraordinary and Minister Plenipotentiary of the United States to China.

Inclosure 4.

LEGATION OF THE UNITED STATES,
Shanghai, July 29, 1858.

The undersigned, envoy extraordinary and minister plenipotentiary of the United States to China, has the honor to acknowledge your excellency's communication of the 24th instant, in which you inform me that, on the 22d, you had received a dispatch from the general council covering a rescript of the 15th of July, sent by his Majesty to the privy council, and which had been copied by the same. The undersigned has much pleasure to learn that their excellencies Kweiliang and Hwashana, who negotiated the treaties of peace at Tientsin, have been appointed to arrange the details of the tariff and commercial regulations with your excellency and Képie and Mingshen, and he awaits at this place their arrival with much interest.

WILLIAM B. REED.

His Excellency HO KWEITSING,
Governor General of the Two Kiang, &c., &c., &c.

Inclosure 1 *c.*

[Translation.]

His Majesty the Emperor of the French and his Majesty the Emperor of China, the one and the other animated by the desire to put an end to the differences which have sprung up between the two empires, and willing to reëstablish and improve the relations of friendship, commerce, and navigation, which have existed between the two powers, as well in regulating the existence, favoring the development, and perpetuating the duration thereof, have resolved to conclude a new treaty, based on the common interest of the two countries, and have in consequence named as their plenipotentiaries—that is to say, his Majesty the Emperor of the French, the Sieur Jean Baptist Louis Baron Gros, Grand Officer of the Legion of Honor, Grand Cross of the Order of the Savior of Greece, Commander of the Order of the Conception of Portugal, &c., &c., &c.; and his Majesty the Emperor of China, Kweiliang, High Imperial Commissioner of the Dynasty Ta-Tsing, Grand Minister of the Oriental Palace, Director General of the Council of Justice, &c., &c., &c., and Hwashana, High Imperial Commissioner of the Dynasty Ta-Tsing, President of the Council of Finance, General of the Army China-Tartar of the Blue Bordered Banner, who, after having exchanged their full powers, which were found to be in good and due form, concluded upon the following articles:

ARTICLE I.

There shall be constant peace and lasting friendship between his Majesty the Emperor of the French and his Majesty the Emperor of

China, and also between the subjects of the two empires, without exception of person or place.

They shall all equally enjoy in the respective States of the high contracting parties full and entire protection for their persons and their property.

ARTICLE II.

To maintain the peace so happily reëstablished between the two empires, it has been agreed between the high contracting parties that, following the examples in practice among the western nations, diplomatic agents duly accredited by his Majesty the Emperor of the French near his Majesty the Emperor of China, may present themselves eventually in the capital of the empire when important affairs call them there.

It is agreed between the high contracting parties, that if one of the powers which have a treaty with China should obtain for its diplomatic agents the right to reside fixedly at Pekin, France shall immediately enjoy the right of which mention is above made.

Diplomatic agents shall reciprocally enjoy in their places of residence the privileges and immunities granted to them by the law of nations—that is to say, their persons, their families, their home, and their correspondence shall be inviolable; that they may take into their service such employés, couriers, interpreters, servants, &c., &c., as shall be necessary for them.

The expenses of every kind which the diplomatic missions of France to China may occasion shall be borne by the French government.

The diplomatic agents which it shall please his Majesty the Emperor of China to accredit near his Majesty the Emperor of the French shall be received in France with all the honors and all the prerogatives which are enjoyed by diplomatic agents of equal rank of other nations accredited at the court of his Majesty the Emperor of the French.

ARTICLE III.

The official communications of the French diplomatic and consular agents with the Chinese authorities shall be written in French, but shall be accompanied, to facilitate the service, by a Chinese translation as exact as possible, until the moment when the imperial government at Pekin, having interpreters to speak and write French correctly, the correspondence of diplomacy shall take place in that language on the part of the French agents, and in Chinese on the part of the functionaries of the empire. It is agreed that until then and in case of disagreement about the interpretation to be given to *the French text*, and *to the Chinese text*, upon the subject of the clauses concluded upon in advance in the conventions made by common consent, it shall be *the French text* which must prevail. This arrangement is applicable to the present treaty.

In the communications between the authorities of the two countries, it shall be always the original text, and not the translation, which shall be relied on.

Article IV.

Henceforth the official correspondence between the authorities and functionaries of the two countries shall be regulated according to the respective ranks and positions, and on the basis of the most absolute reciprocity. Such correspondence shall take place between the high French functionaries and the high Chinese functionaries, at the capital or elsewhere, by dispatch or communication, [Chinese characters;] between French functionaries of less grade and the high provincial authorities, for the first by exposé, [Chinese characters,] for the second by declaration, [Chinese characters;] between the subaltern officers of both nations, as is said above, on the footing of a perfect equality.

Merchants, and generally all persons not having an official character, will reciprocally use the formula, representation, [Chinese characters,] in all papers addressed to or intended for the information of the respective authorities.

Each time that a Frenchman shall have recourse to the Chinese authority, his representation must, in the first instance, be submitted to the consul, who, if it appears to him to be reasonable and properly drawn up, will give it due course, and who, if it be otherwise, will cause its tenor to be modified, or will refuse to transmit it. The Chinese, on their part, when they have to address the consulate, must follow an analagous proceeding with the Chinese authority, which shall act in the same manner.

Article V.

His Majesty the Emperor of the French may appoint consuls or consular agents at the seaports or rivers of the Chinese Empire, designated in article six of the present treaty, to serve as intermediaries between the Chinese authorities and the French merchants and subjects, and to watch over the strict observance of the regulations stipulated. These functionaries shall be treated with the consideration and respect which is their due. Their relations with the higher authorities shall be established on the footing of the most perfect equality. If they should have to complain of the procedure of said authority, they shall address themselves directly to the supreme authority of the place of their residence, and shall immediately give notice of it to the minister plenipotentiary of the Emperor.

In case of the absence of the French consul, French captains and merchants shall have the privilege of recourse to the consul of a friendly power; or if it be impossible to do that, they shall have recourse to the chief of the customs, who will attend to the means for securing to such captains and merchants the benefits of the present treaty.

Article VI.

Experience having shown that the opening of new ports to foreign commerce is a necessity of the times, it has been concluded upon, that the ports of Kiungtchaou and Tchaou-tchaou, in the province of Kwang tung; Taivan and Tanahwi, in the Island of Formosa, and province of Fukien; Tantchaou, in the province of Chantong; and Nankin, in the province of Kiang-nan, shall enjoy the same privileges as Canton, Shanghai, Ningpo, Amoy, and Fou-tcheou.

As to Nankin, the French agents in China shall not issue passports for that city to their countrymen until the rebels shall have been driven out therefrom by the imperial troops.

ARTICLE VII.

Frenchmen and their families may move to establish themselves, enter into commerce or industrial pursuits in perfect security and without hindrance of any kind, in the ports and cities of the Chinese empire situate on the maritime borders, and on the great rivers of which the enumeration is contained in the foregoing article.

They may freely travel from one to the other if furnished with passports; but they are formally prohibited from making on the coast clandestine purchases or sales on pain of confiscation of vessels and merchandise employed in such transactions, and such confiscation shall take effect for the benefit of the Chinese government, which shall however, before seizure and confiscation are legally pronounced, give notice to the French consul at the nearest port.

ARTICLE VIII.

Frenchmen who may wish to go to cities in the interior, or to ports which are not open to foreign vessels, may do so in perfect safety, provided they are furnished with passports, drawn in French and Chinese, legally issued by the diplomatic agents or consuls of France in China and visaed by the Chinese authorities.

In case of the loss of such passport, the Frenchman who shall be unable to present it when lawfully required to do so, must, if the Chinese authority of the place where he may be refuses to grant him permission to stay until he have time to ask for a new passport from the consul, be reconducted to the nearest consulate, without being suffered to be maltreated or insulted in any manner.

As was stipulated in ancient treaties, Frenchmen residing or in transit in ports open to foreign commerce may move about in their neighborhood without passports, and attend to their occupations as freely as people of the country, but they must not go beyond certain bounds, which shall be settled by agreement between the consul and local authorities.

French agents in China shall not issue passports to their countrymen, except for places where the rebels shall not be established at the time when the passport is asked for.

These passports shall not be issued by the French authorities to any persons who shall not offer them all the guarantees desirable.

ARTICLE IX.

All the changes introduced by common accord with one of the powers signers of treaties with China on the subject of ameliorations to be introduced into the tariff actually in force, or in that which will be at a later day, as also the customs, duties, tonnage of importation, of transit and of exportation shall be immediately applicable to commerce and to French merchants by the mere fact of their being put into practice.

Article X.

Every Frenchman who in conformity with article six of the present treaty shall arrive at one of the ports open to foreign commerce, may whatever be the length of his sojourn, hire houses and warehouses for the disposal of his merchandise, or hire land and build houses and warehouses thereon himself. Frenchmen may in like manner establish churches, hospitals, almshouses, schools, and cemeteries. To this end, the local authorities, after having arranged with the consul, will designate the quarters most suitable for the residence of Frenchmen, and the places where they may place the buildings before mentioned.

The terms for hiring and leasing shall be freely discussed between the parties interested, and regulated as far as may be by the average of local prices.

The Chinese authorities shall prevent their countrymen from surcharging or exacting exorbitant rates, and the consul will on his part take heed that the French use no violence or duress to force the consent of the proprietors. It is moreover well understood that the number of houses and extent of ground to be set apart to Frenchmen in the ports open to foreign commerce shall not be restricted, and shall be fixed according to the need and convenience of those having rights. If the Chinese desecrate or destroy the French churches or cemeteries, the guilty shall be punished with all the rigor of the law of the country.

Article XI.

Frenchmen in the ports open to foreign commerce may freely choose, and upon terms settled between the parties or with the intervention of the consuls only, compradors, interpreters, secretaries, laborers, boatmen, and domestics. They shall, besides, have the privilege of engaging educated men of the country to teach them to speak and write the Chinese language, and any other language or dialect in use in the empire, and also to be aided by them either in their writings or scientific or literary labors. They may equally teach any Chinese subject the language of their country, or foreign languages, and sell without hindrance French books, or purchase themselves all sorts of Chinese books.

Article XII.

Property of every kind belong to Frenchmen in the Chinese empire shall be considered by the Chinese as inviolable, and shall always be respected by them. The Chinese authorities shall not, although it occur, put an embargo on French vessels, or put them in requisition for any public or private service whatever.

Article XIII.

The Christian religion having for its essential object to lead men to virtue, the members of all Christian communications shall enjoy perfect security for their persons, properties, and the free exercise of the religious practice, and efficient protection shall be given to missionaries who may go peacefully into the interior of the country provided with the regular passports which have been spoken of in article eight.

No impediment shall be placed by the authorities of the Chinese empire to the right which is recognized in every individual in China to embrace Christianity if he chooses, and to follow its observances without being subject to any penalty to be inflicted on that account.

All that has heretofore been written, proclaimed, or published in China, by order of the government, against the Christian religion, is completely abrogated and without effect throughout all the provinces of the empire.

Article XIV.

No privileged association for commerce can henceforth be established in China, and the same shall be the case as to every coalition organized for the purpose of effecting any monopoly in commerce.

In case of any contravention of this article, the Chinese authorities will, upon the representation of the consul or consular agent, concert measures for breaking up such associations; the existence of which they will moreover strenuously endeavor to prevent by preliminary prohibitions, for the purpose of avoiding anything that may interfere with free competition.

Article XV.

When a French vessel shall arrive in the waters of one of the ports open to foreign commerce, she shall have the privilege of engaging such pilot as may suit her, for the purpose of taking her immediately into port; and, in like manner, when, after having defrayed all the legal charges, she be ready to make sail, shall not be refused pilots to take her out of port without hindrance or delay.

Every individual who desires to pursue the avocation of pilot for French vessels may, on the presentation of three certificates of captains of vessels, be commissioned by the French consul in like manner as that shall be done by other nations.

The remuneration paid to pilots shall be regulated according to equity for each port in particular, by the consul or consular agent, who will settle it suitably, having regard to distance and the circumstances of the navigation.

Article XVI.

As soon as the pilot shall have brought a French merchant vessel into port, the collector of the customs shall delegate one or two inspectors, who shall watch the vessel and prevent the practice of any fraud. These inspectors may, at their own convenience, remain on their own boat or remain on board the vessel.

The disbursement for their wages, provision, and keeping shall be a charge on the Chinese custom-house, and they may not demand any indemnity or restitution from the captains or consignees. Every infringement of this prohibition will be followed by a punishment proportionate to the amount of the exaction, which shall, moreover, be wholly replaced.

ARTICLE XVII.

Within the twenty-four hours which shall follow the arrival of a French merchant vessel in one of the ports open to foreign commerce, the captain, if he is not hindered by due cause, and in his default the supercargo or consignee, must repair to the French consulate and place in the hands of the consul the ship's papers, the bills of lading, and the manifest. Within the following twenty-four hours the consul must send to the chief of the customs a note in detail, giving the name of the vessel, the crew list, the legal tonnage of the vessel, and the nature of her cargo. If, in consequence of the neglect of the captain, the latter formality shall not have been complied with in the forty-eight hours after the arrival of the vessel, the captain shall be liable to a fine of fifty dollars a day for the delay, to the profit of the Chinese government. Said fine shall, in no case, exceed the sum of two hundred dollars. Immediately upon the reception of the note transmitted by the consulate, the collector of the customs shall deliver his permit to open the hatches. If the captain, before receiving the said permit, has opened the hatches and commenced discharging, it may be condemned to a fine of five hundred dollars, and the merchandise landed may be seized, all to the benefit of the Chinese government.

ARTICLE XVIII.

French captains and merchants may hire such kinds of lighters and boats as they may choose to carry merchandise and passengers, and the compensation to be paid for such lighterage shall be regulated as may be agreed between the parties concerned, free of interference by the Chinese authorities, and consequently without its guarantees in case of accident, fraud, or disappearance of such lighters. The number shall not be limited, and the monopoly shall not be conceded to any one soever, any more than that of porterage of merchandise on embarking or disembarking.

ARTICLE XIX.

Every time that a French merchant shall have goods to load or unload, he must first send a note in detail to the consul, or consular agent, who will immediately direct an interpreter recognized at the consulate to make communication to the collector of the customs, who will immediately deliver a permit to ship or discharge. The verification of the merchandise shall also be complied with in the manner most convenient, to avoid danger of loss to both parties.

The French merchant should be represented at the place of verification, (if he does not choose to be there himself,) by a person combining the proper qualifications, in order to attend to his interests at the time the verification is going on for the liquidation of duties; in default thereof any subsequent reclamation will be void and of no effect.

In what relates to merchandise, dutiable *ad valorem*, if the merchant cannot agree with the Chinese employé in fixing values, each party shall call two or three merchants charged to examine goods, and the highest price that shall be offered by any of them shall be held to constitute the true value of such merchandise.

Duties shall be estimated on net weight, in consequence the weight of the package and wrappers must be deducted. If the French merchant cannot agree with the Chinese officer in fixing the tare, each party shall selecct a certain number of cases and bales among those which are differed about; they shall then be weighed gross, then tared, and the mean tare of the packages weighed shall be taken as the tare of all the rest.

If during the course of the verification any difficulty should arise which cannot be settled, the French merchant may claim the intervention of the consul, who shall at once bring the question in controversy to the notice of the chief of the customs, and they two shall endeavor to come to an amicable arrangement; but the reclamation must take place within twenty-four hours; if not, it shall be without effect. While the result of the controversy is pending, the chief of the customs shall not enter its subject in his books, thus giving full latitude for the examination and solution of the difficulty.

Merchandise imported, which shall have sustained damage, shall be entitled to a reduction of duties proportionate to the depreciation. This shall be determined equitably, and, if necessary, by experts chosen on either part, as provided above for fixing duties *ad valorem*.

ARTICLE XX.

Every vessel which enters one of the ports of China, and which has not taken out a permit for discharging mentioned in article nineteen, may, within two days after her arrival, leave that port and go to another port without liability to pay tonnage dues or custom-house dues, provided she discharges them afterwards at the port where she may make sale of her merchandise.

ARTICLE XXI.

It is settled by common accord that the duties on imports shall be defrayed by French captains and merchants at once, and in proportion as they are landed and verified. Duties on exports shall be defrayed in like manner as goods are shipped. When the tonnage and customs duties owing by a French vessel shall have been wholly satisfied, the collector of the customs shall give a general acquittance, on the exhibition whereof the consul shall return the ship's papers to the captain, and permit him to set sail.

The collector of the customs shall designate one or more brokage-houses, which shall be authorized to receive the sum due from French merchants for account of the government, and the receipts of these brokage-houses, for all the payments which shall have been made to them, shall be held as acquittances from the Chinese government. These payments may be made in ingots, or in foreign money, the relative value of which to *sycee* silver shall be decided by agreement between the French consul, or consular agent, and the collectors of customs at the different ports, according to time, place, and circumstances.

Article XXII.

After the expiration of the two days mentioned in article twenty, and before beginning to discharge, each French merchant vessel shall fully discharge the tonnage dues so regulated: For vessels of 150 tons lawful measurement and above, at the rate of five maces (a half tael) the ton; for vessels measuring less than 150 tons, at the rate of one mace (one tenth tael) per ton. All retributions and surcharges previously imposed on arrival or departure are expressly done away, and shall not be replaced by any other.

On the payment of the duty aforesaid, the collector of the customs shall deliver to the captain or consignee a receipt, in form of certificate, stating that the tonnage duty has been fully paid, and, on exhibiting this certificate to the collector of the customs of every other port which it may please him to enter, the captain shall be dispensed from again paying for his vessel any tonnage duty; every French ship not being liable more than once on each of its voyages from a foreign country to China.

French barks, schooners, coasting-vessels, boats, decked or not, employed in carrying passengers, baggage, letters, provisions, and generally all things not liable to duties, are exempted from tonnage dues; if such vessels carry merchandise besides, they shall be rated in the list of vessels of measurement less than 150 tons, and shall pay at the rate of one tenth of a tael, (one mace,) per ton.

French merchants may always freight junks and other Chinese vessels, which shall not be liable to any tonnage dues.

Article XXIII.

All French merchandise, after having once paid in one of the ports of China, the customs duties ascertained by the tariff may be transported to the interior, without being subjected to any other supplementary charge than the payment of the duties of transit, according to the moderate rate at present in force, which duties shall not be susceptible of any future augmentation.

If any Chinese customs agents, contrary to the tenor of the present treaty, should exact unlawful retributions, or should enhance the amount of duties, they shall be punished according to the laws of the empire.

Article XXIV.

Every French vessel which enters at one of the ports open to foreign commerce, intending to discharge only part of its cargo, shall pay only the customs duties on the part discharged, and may carry the rest of its cargo to another port, and sell it there. The duties shall then be paid.

In a case where Frenchmen, after having paid duties at one port on merchandise, desire to reëxport it, and to go and sell it at another port, they shall notify the consul or consular agent of it. He, on his part, will inform the collector of the customs, who after having ascertained the identity of the merchandise, and the perfect integrity of the packages, will give to the applicants a declaration, attesting that the duties concerning said merchandise have been duly paid.

Provided with this declaration, French merchants on arrival at another port, will only have to present it through the consul to the collector of the customs, who will deliver to him for such portion of the cargo, without delay, and without charge, a landing permit free of duty, but if the authorities shall discover that there has been any fraud, or any contraband among the merchandise so reëxported, such shall, after proof, be confiscated to the use of the Chinese government.

Article XXV.

No transhipment of merchandise may take place without a special permit, and in case of urgency. If it becomes indispensable to do this, it must be referred to the consul, who will give a certificate, on view of which, the transhipment shall be authorized by the collector of the customs.

This officer may always delegate one employed in his administration to be present at the business.

Every unauthorized transhipment, except in case of danger by delay, will draw upon it confiscation to the use of the Chinese government of all the merchandise unlawfully transhipped.

Article XXVI.

In each of the ports open to foreign commerce, the collector of the customs shall himself receive, and shall deposit in the French consulate lawful scales for merchandise and money, as well as weights and measures in exact conformity with the weights and measures in use at the Canton custom-house, and distinguished with a stamp and seal establishing this conformity. These standards shall be the basis of all liquidations of duties, and of all payments to be made to the Chinese government. Resort shall be had to them, in cases of difference as to the weight and measure of merchandise, and it shall be settled according to the results they shall give.

Article XXVII.

The duties of import and export raised in China from French commerce shall be regulated in conformity with the tariff annexed to this treaty under the seal and signature of the respective plenipotentiaries. This tariff may be revised every seven years, to be reduced to harmony with the changes of value wrought by time on the products of the soil and industry of the two empires.

In consideration of the payment of these duties, the augmentation of which, during the course of seven years above mentionad, is expressly forbidden, and which no kind of charge or overrate whatever can make more heavy, the French shall be free to import into China from French or foreign ports, and in like way to export from China with any destination all sorts of merchandise, which shall not be on the day of the signing of the present treaty, and according to the classification of the tariff hereto annexed, the subject of formal prohibition or of special monopoly.

The Chinese government renouncing the privilege of augmenting hereafter the number of articles considered as contraband or as monolies, no modification can be made in the tariff, without a preliminary understanding with the French government, and its full and entire consent.

In regard to the tariff, as well as to every stipulation introduced or to be introduced into existing treaties, or which shall be ulteriorly concluded, it remains well and duly settled that the merchants, and in general all French citizens in China shall always and everywhere be entitled to the treatment of the most favored nation.

Article XXVIII.

The publication of a suitable and regulated tariff, taking away henceforth all excuse for contraband trade, it is not to be presumed that any act of that nature can be committed by French merchant ships in the ports of China. If it should be otherwise, all merchandise introduced by smuggling by French ships or merchants in those ports, whatever be their nature or value, as also all prohibited articles fraudulently landed, shall be seized by the local authority, and confiscated to the Chinese government. Besides, that may, if it pleases, prohibit the entrance into China of vessels taken in violation hereof, and compel them to depart immediately, after settling their accounts. If any foreign ship should fraudulently shelter itself under the flag of France, the French government will take the measures necessary for the repression of this abuse.

Article XXIX.

His Majesty the Emperor of the French may cause a vessel-of-war to be stationed in the principal ports of the empire when its presence shall be judged necessary to maintain good order and discipline among the crews of the merchant vessels, and to facilitate the exercise of the consular authority. All necessary measures shall be taken that the presence of these vessels-of-war may not bring on any inconvenience, and their commanders shall receive orders to cause the arrangements stipulated in article thirty-three, in respect to communications with the shore, and the discipline of the crews to be executed.

The vessels-of-war shall not be subjected to any duty.

Article XXX.

Every French vessel-of-war cruising for the protection of commerce shall be received as a friend and treated as such in all the ports of China where she may present herself. Such vessels may there procure the various things for recruit and reprovisioning which they may have need of, and if they have suffered damages may repair them, and purchase for this purpose necessary materials without the slightest hindrance.

It shall be so likewise for French merchant vessels which, in consequence of heavy damage, or any other cause, shall be forced to seek refuge in any port whatever in China.

If any of these vessels should be wrecked on the coast, the nearest Chinese authority, as soon as it shall be informed of it, shall forthwith give assistance to the crew; shall provide for its first need, and take prompt measures necessary for the salvage of the vessel and preservation of the cargo. Then it will give advice of all to the consul or consular agent the nearest in reach of the disaster, so that he, in concert with the competent authority, may devise means to restore the crew to their country, and to secure the remains of the vessel and cargo.

Article XXXI.

In case, when in course of time, China should enter into a war with another power, the circumstance shall cause no hindrance to the free commerce of France and China, or with the hostile nation. French ships may always, except in the case of effective blockades, pass to and fro without obstruction from the ports of the one to the ports of the other, and traffic as under ordinary circumstances, and import thereto or export therefrom all kinds of merchandise which are not prohibited.

Article XXXII.

If it should happen that seamen or other individuals should desert from vessels-of-war, or abscond from French merchant vessels, the Chinese authority, on the request of the consul, or in default thereof, of the captain, shall make every effort at once to discover and return into the hands of one or the other the above-mentioned deserters or fugitives.

Likewise, if Chinese deserters, or persons charged with crime, come for refuge to French houses, or on board a vessel belonging to Frenchmen, the local authority shall apply to the consul, who, on proof of the culpability of the parties charged, shall take immediately the measures necessary to effect their extradition. On the one side and the other all concealment and connivance shall be carefully avoided.

Article XXXIII.

When sailors shall go ashore, they shall be subjected to special rules of discipline, which shall be settled by the consul and communicated to the local authority, so as to prevent, as much as may be possible, any occasion for quarrel between the French sailors and the people of the country.

Article XXXIV.

In cases where French merchant vessels shall be attacked or plundered by pirates in places dependant on China, the civil and military authority at the nearest place, as soon as it shall be informed of the fact, shall actively pursue its authors, and neglect nothing which may cause their arrest and punishment according to the laws. The goods stolen, in whatever place and in whatever condition they may be found, shall be placed in the consul's hands, who shall charge himself with their restoration to those entitled to them.

If the guilty cannot be arrested, nor all the things stolen be recovered, the Chinese functionaries shall suffer the penalty imposed by law in such cases, but shall not be made pecuniarily responsible.

Article XXXV.

When a French subject shall have any cause of complaint, or some claim to present formally against a Chinaman, he must, in the first instance, explain his wrongs to the consul, who, after having examined the matter, will endeavor to arrange it amicably. So when a Chinaman shall have to complain of a Frenchman, the consul shall listen to his complaint with attention, and shall endeavor to effect an amicable arrangement. But if, in one or the other case, the thing is impossible, the consul shall request the assistance of the competent Chinese authorities, and the two, after having conjointly examined the affair, shall settle it according to equity.

Article XXXVI.

If henceforth French citizens shall suffer any damage, or be the objects of any insults or vexatious proceeding on the part of subjects of China, these shall be prosecuted by the local authority, which shall take the measures necessary to protect and defend the French; and with much greater cause, if the evil-doers, or any misled part of the populace, should attempt to plunder, destroy, or burn the houses and warehouses of the French, or any other establishment formed by them. The same authority, whether on request of the consul, or of its own motion, shall dispatch, in all haste, an armed force to disperse the mob, seize the guilty, and subject them to all the rigor of the law, without prejudice to prosecutions to be followed up by those who have a right to indemnity for losses endured.

Article XXXVII.

If the Chinese in future become debtors to French captains or merchants, and cause losses to them by fraud, or in any other manner, these latter shall no longer avail themselves of the solidarity which resulted from the old condition of things; they shall only be able to apply through the intermediation of their consuls to the local authority, who shall neglect nothing, after having examined the affair, to compel those complained of to fulfill their engagements according to the law of the country. But if the debtor cannot be found—if he is dead, or bankrupt, or if he has nothing left to pay with—the French merchants cannot call upon the Chinese authorities for guarantees.

In case of fraud or non-payment on the part of French merchants, the consul in the same manner shall lend aid to the claimants; without, however, himself or his government becoming in any manner responsible.

Article XXXVIII.

If unhappily, some strife or quarrel should arise between the French and Chinese, as well as in case where during the course of such quarrel one or more individuals may be killed or wounded, by fire-arms or otherwise, the Chinese shall be arrested by the Chinese authority, which shall take care to examine and punish them, if proper according to the law of the country.

As to the French, they shall be arrested by the action of the consul, and he shall take all the measures necessary for the delivery of the persons compromitted to the regular course of the French laws in the form and according to the provisions which may ultimately be adopted by the French government. The same course shall be pursued in all analogous cases, and not provided for in the present convention; the principle being that for the repression of crimes and offenses committed by them in China, Frenchmen shall always be ruled by French laws.

Article XXXIX.

Frenchmen in China, in all difficulties and controversies which may occur between themselves, shall also be subject to French jurisdiction. In case of difficulties happening between French and foreigners, it is well understood that the Chinese authorities shall not mix up in them in any manner; in likewise it shall not exercise any power over French vessels, they shall be subject only to the French authority and the captain.

Article XL.

If hereafter, the government of his Majesty the Emperor of the French may judge proper to apply modifications to some of the clauses of the present treaty, it shall be free, for that purpose, to open negotiations with the Chinese government after an interval of twelve years completed from the date of the exchange of ratifications. It is moreover understood that no obligation not expressly marked out in the present convention shall be imposed on consuls or consular agents, nor on their countrymen, whilst as it has been agreed, Frenchmen shall enjoy all the rights, privileges, immunities, and guarantees soever which may have been or shall be accorded by the Chinese government to other powers.

ARTICLE XLI.

His Majesty the Emperor of the French desiring to give to his Majesty the Emperor of China a proof of the sentiments by which he is animated, consents to stipulate in separate articles, having the same force and effect as if they were inscribed word for word in the present treaty, for the arrangements understood between the two governments on the subject of questions anterior to the events at Canton, and expenses occasioned thereby to the government of his Majesty the Emperor of the French.

ARTICLE XLII.

The ratification of the present treaty of friendship, commerce, and navigation shall be exchanged at Pekin within a year from the date of the signature hereof, or so soon as may be done by his Majesty the Emperor of the French, and by his Majesty the Emperor of China.

After the exchange of the ratifications, the treaty shall be made known to all the high authorities of the empire, in the provinces, and in the capital, so that its publicity may be well established.

In faith whereof the respective plenipotentiaries have signed the present treaty and affixed their seals.

Done at Teintsin, this twenty-seventh day of the month of June, in the year of grace one thousand eight hundred and fifty-eight, corresponding with the seventeenth day of the fifth moon of the eighth year of Hien-fung.

BARON GROS, [L. S.]
KWEILIANG. [L. S.]
HWASHANA.

True copy. BARON GROS.
True copy. S. WELLS WILLIAMS,
Secretary of Legation United States.

Inclosure 1 *b*.

TREATY.

Her Majesty the Queen of the United Kingdom of Great Britain and Ireland, and his Majesty the Emperor of China, being desirous to put an end to the existing misunderstanding between the two countries, and to place their relations on a more satisfactory footing in future, have resolved to proceed to a revision and improvement of the treaties existing between them, and for that purpose have named as their plenipotentiaries, that is to say:

Her Majesty the Queen of Great Britain and Ireland, the right honorable the Earl of Elgin and Kincardine, a peer of the United Kingdom, and Knight of the Most Ancient and Most Noble Order of the Thistle; and his Majesty the Emperor of China, the high commissioners, Kweiliang, a senior Chief Secretary of state, Captain General of the Plain White Banner of the Mauchee Banner Force, Superintendent General of the Administration of Criminal Law, and Hwashana, one of his Imperial Majesty's Expositors of the Classics, Mauchee President of the Office for the Regulation of the Civil Establishment, Captain General of the Bordered Blue Banner of the Chinese Banner Force, and Visitor of the Office of Interpretation.

Who, after having communicated to each other their respective full powers, and found them to be in good and due form, have agreed upon and concluded the following articles:

ARTICLE I.

The treaty of peace and amity between the two nations signed at Nankin on the 29th day of August, in the year 1842, is hereby renewed and confirmed.

The supplementary treaty and general regulations of trade having been amended and improved, and the substance of their provisions having been incorporated in this treaty, the said supplementary treaty and general regulations of trade are hereby abrogated.

ARTICLE II.

For the better preservation of harmony in future, her Majesty the Queen of Great Britain, and his Majesty the Emperor of China, mutually agree that in accordance with the universal practice of great and friendly nations, her Majesty the Queen may if she sees fit, appoint embassadors, ministers, or other diplomatic agents to the court of Pekin, and his Majesty the Emperor of China, may in like manner if he see fit, appoint embassadors, ministers, or other diplomatic agents to the court of St. James.

ARTICLE III.

His Majesty the Emperor of China hereby agrees that the embassador, minister, or other diplomatic agent so appointed by her Majesty the Queen of Great Britain, may reside with his family and establishment permanently at the capital, or may visit it occasionally, at the option of the British government. He shall not be called upon to perform any ceremony derogatory to him as representing the sovereign of an independent nation, on a footing of equality with that of China. On the other hand, he shall use the same forms of ceremony and respect to his Majesty the Emperor as are employed by the embassadors, ministers, or diplomatic agents of her Majesty towards the sovereigns of independent and equal European nations.

It is further agreed that her Majesty's government may acquire at Pekin a site for building, or may hire houses for the accommodation of her Majesty's mission, and that the Chinese government will assist it in so doing. Her Majesty's representative shall be at liberty to choose his own servants and attendants, who shall not be subjected to any kind of molestation whatever.

Any person guilty of disrespect or violence to her Majesty's representative, or to any member of his family or establishment, in deed or word, shall be severely punished.

Article IV.

It is further agreed that no obstacle of difficulty shall be made to the free movements of her Majesty's representative, and that he and the persons of his suite may come and go, and travel at their pleasure. He shall, moreover, have full liberty to send and receive his correspondence to, and from any point on the sea-coast that he may select; and his letters and effects shall be held sacred and inviolable. He may employ for their transmission special couriers, who shall meet with the same protection and facilities for traveling as the persons employed in carrying dispatches for the imperial government, and generally he shall enjoy the same privileges as are accorded to officers of the same rank by the usage and consent of western nations.

All expenses attending the diplomatic mission of Great Britain in China, shall be borne by the British government.

Article V.

His Majesty the Emperor of China agrees to nominate one of the secretaries of state, or a president of one of the boards, as the high officer with whom the embassador, minister, or other diplomatic agent of her Majesty the Queen, shall transact business, either personally or in writing, on a footing of perfect equality.

Article VI.

Her Majesty the Queen of Great Britain agrees that the privileges hereby secured, shall be enjoyed in her dominions by the embassador, minister, or diplomatic agents of the Emperor of China, accredited to the court of her Majesty.

Article VII.

Her Majesty the Queen may appoint one or more consuls in the dominions of the Emperor of China, and such consul or consuls shall be at liberty to reside in any of the open ports or cities of China as her Majesty the Queen may consider most expedient for the interest of British commerce.

They shall be treated with due respect by the Chinese authorities, and enjoy the same privileges and immunities as the consular officers of the most favored nations.

Consuls, or vice-consuls in charge, shall rank with intendants of circuits; vice-consuls, acting vice-consuls and interpreters, with prefects. They shall have access to the official residence of these officers, and communicate with them either personally or in writing, on a footing of equality, as the interests of the public service may require.

Article VIII.

The Christian religion as professed by Protestants or Roman Catholics inculcates the practice of virtue, and teaches man to do as he would be done by. Persons teaching or professing it, therefore, shall alike be entitled to the protection of the Chinese authorities, nor shall any such, peaceably pursuing their calling, and not offending against the law, be persecuted or interfered with.

Article IX.

British subjects are hereby authorized to travel, for their pleasure or for purposes of trade, to all parts of the interior, under passports which will be issued by their consuls and countersigned by the local authorities. These passports, if demanded, must be produced for examination in the localities passed through. If the passport be not irregular, the bearer will be allowed to proceed; and no opposition shall be offered to his hiring persons or hiring vessels for the carriage of his baggage or merchandise. If he be without a passport, or if he commit any offense against the law, he shall be handed over to the nearest consul for punishment, but he must not be subjected to any ill usage, in excess of necessary restraint. No passport need be applied for by persons going on excursions from the ports open to trade to a distance not exceeding one hundred *li*, and for a period not exceeding five days.

The provisions of this article do not apply to crews of ships, for the due restraint of whom regulations will be drawn up by the consul and the local authorities.

To Nankin, and other cities disturbed by persons in arms against the government, no passport shall be given until they shall have been recaptured.

Article X.

British merchant ships shall have authority to trade upon the great river, (Yangtsze.) The upper and lower valley of the river being, however, disturbed by outlaws, no port shall be for the present opened to trade, with the exception of Chin-kiang, which shall be opened in a year from the date of the signing of this treaty. So soon as peace shall have been restored, British vessels shall also be admitted to trade at such ports, as far as Hankow, not exceeding three in number, as the British minister, after consultation with the Chinese secretary of state, may determine shall be ports of entry and discharge.

Article XI.

In addition to the cities and towns of Canton, Amoy, Fuhchow, Ningpo, and Shanghai, opened by the treaty of Nankin, it is agreed that British subjects may frequent the cities and ports of Newchang, Zaugchow, Taiwan, (Formosa,) Chau-chow, (Swatow,) and Kiungchow, (Hainan.) They are permitted to carry on trade with whomsoever they please, and to proceed to and fro, at their pleasure, with their vessels and merchandise. They shall enjoy the same privileges, advantages, and immunities, at the said towns and ports, as they enjoy at the ports already open to trade, including the right of residence, of buying or renting houses, of leasing land therein, and of building churches, hospitals, and cemeteries.

Article XII.

British subjects, whether at the ports or at other places, desiring to build or open houses, warehouses, churches, hospitals, or burial grounds, shall make their arrangement for the land or buildings they require at the rates prevailing among the people, equitably and without exaction on either side.

Article XIII.

The Chinese government will place no restrictions whatever upon the employment, by British subjects, of Chinese subjects in any lawful capacity.

Article XIV.

British subjects may hire whatever boats they please for the transport of goods or passengers, and the sum to be paid for such boats shall be settled between the parties themselves, without the interference of the Chinese government. The number of these boats shall not be limited; nor shall a monopoly, in respect either of the boats or of the porters or coolies engaged in carrying the goods, be granted to any parties. If any smuggling takes place in them, the offenders will, of course, be punished according to law.

Article XV.

All questions in regard to rights, whether of property or person, arising between British subjects, shall be subject to the jurisdiction of the British authorities.

Article XVI.

Chinese subjects, who may be guilty of any criminal act towards British subjects, shall be arrested and punished by the Chinese authorities according to the laws of China.

British subjects, who may commit any crime, shall be tried and punished by the consul, or other public functionary authorized thereto, according to the laws of Great Britain.

Justice shall be equitably and impartially administered on both sides.

Article XVII.

A British subject, having reason to complain of a Chinese, must proceed to the consulate and state his grievance. The consul will inquire into the merits of the case, and do his utmost to arrange it amicably. In like manner, if a Chinese have reason to complain of a British subject, the consul shall no less listen to his complaint, and endeavor to settle it in a friendly manner. If disputes take place of such a nature that the consul cannot arrange them amicably, then he shall request the assistance of the Chinese authorities, that they may together examine into the merits of the case and decide it equitably.

Article XVIII.

The Chinese authorities shall at all times afford the fullest protection to the persons and property of British subjects, whenever these shall have been subjected to insult or violence. In all cases of incendiarism or robbery, the local authorities shall at once take the necessary steps for the recovery of the stolen property, the suppression of disorder, and the arrest of the guilty parties, whom they will punish according to the law.

Article XIX.

If any British merchant vessel, while within Chinese waters, be plundered by robbers or pirates, it shall be the duty of the Chinese authorities to use every endeavor to capture and punish the said robbers or pirates, and to recover the stolen property, that it may be handed over to the consul for restoration to the owner.

Article XX.

If any British vessel be at any time wrecked or stranded on the coast of China, or be compelled to take refuge in any port within the dominions of the Emperor of China, the Chinese authorities, on being apprised of the fact, shall immediately adopt measures for its relief and security; the persons on board shall receive friendly treatment, and shall be furnished, if necessary, with the means of conveyance to the nearest consular station.

Article XXI.

If criminals, subjects of China, shall take refuge in Hong Kong, or on board the British ships there, they shall, upon due requisition by the Chinese authorities, be searched for, and, on proof of their guilt, be delivered up. In like manner, if Chinese offenders take refuge in the houses or on board the vessels of British subjects at the open ports, they shall not be harbored or concealed, but shall be delivered up on due requisition by the Chinese authorities, addressed to the British consul.

Article XXII.

Should any Chinese subject fail to discharge debts incurred to a British subject, or should he fraudulently abscond, the Chinese authorities will do their utmost to affect his arrest and enforce recovery of the debts. The British authorities will likewise do their utmost to bring to justice any British subject fraudulently absconding or failing to discharge debts incurred by him to a Chinese subject.

Article XXIII.

Should natives of China who may repair to Hong Kong to trade, incur debts there, the recovery of such debts must be arranged for by the English courts of justice on the spot; but should the Chinese debtor abscond, and be known to have property, real or personal, within the Chinese territory, it shall be the duty of the Chinese authorities, on application by and in concert with the British consul, to do their utmost to see justice done between the parties.

Article XXIV.

It is agreed that British subjects shall pay on all merchandise imported or exported by them the duties prescribed by the tariff; but in no case shall they be called upon to pay other or higher duties than are required of the subjects of any other foreign nation.

Article XXV.

Import duties shall be considered payable on the landing of the goods, and duties of export on the shipment of the same.

Article XXVI.

Whereas, the tariff fixed by article ten of the treaty of Nankin, and which was estimated so as to impose on imports and exports a duty at about the rate of five per cent. *ad valorem*, has been found, by reason of the fall in value of various articles of merchandise therein enumerated, to impose a duty upon these considerably in excess of the rate originally assumed as above to be a fair rate, it is agreed that the said tariff shall be revised, and that as soon as the treaty shall have been signed, application shall be made to the Emperor of China to depute a high officer of the board of revenue, to meet at Shanghai officers deputed on behalf of the British government, to consider its revision together, so that the tariff, as revised, may come into operation immediately after the ratification of this treaty.

Article XXVII.

It is agreed that either of the high contracting parties to this treaty may demand a further revision of the tariff, and of the commercial articles of this treaty, at the end of ten years; but if no demand be made on either side within six months after the end of the first ten years, then the tariff shall remain in force for ten years more, reckoned from the end of the preceding ten years; and so it shall be at the end of each successive period of ten years.

Article XXVIII.

Whereas it was agreed, in Article 10 of the treaty of Nankin, that British imports, having paid the tariff duties, should be conveyed into the interior free of all further charges excepting a transit duty, the amount whereof was not to exceed a certain percentage on tariff value; and whereas, no accurate information having been furnished of the amount of such duty, British merchants have constantly complained that charges are suddenly and arbitrarily imposed by the provincial authorities as transit dues upon produce on its way to the foreign market, and on imports on their way into the interior, to the detriment of trade, it is agreed that, within four months from the signing of this treaty, at all ports now open to British trade, and, within a similar period, at all ports that may hereafter be opened, the authority appointed to superintend the collection of duties shall be obliged, upon application to the consul, to declare the amount of duties levyable on produce between the place of production and the port of shipment, and upon imports between the consular port in question and the inland markets named by the consul, and that a notification thereof shall be published in English and Chinese, for general information.

But it shall be at the option of any British subject desiring to convey produce purchased inland to a port, or to convey imports from a port to an inland market, to clear his goods of all transit duties by payment of a single charge. The amount of this charge shall be levyable on exports at the first barrier they may have to pass, or, on imports, at the port at which they are landed, and, on payment thereof, a certificate shall be issued which shall exempt the goods from all further inland charges whatsoever. It is further agreed that the amount of this charge shall be calculated, as nearly as possible, at the rate of two and a half per cent. *ad valorem*, and that it shall be fixed for each article at the conference to be held at Shanghai for the revision of the tariff.

It is distinctly understood that the payment of transit dues by commutation, or otherwise, shall in no way affect the tariff duties on imports or exports, which will continue to be levied separately and in full.

Article XXIX.

British merchant vessels of more than 150 tons burden shall be charged tonnage dues at the rate of four mace per ton; if of 150 tons, and under, they shall be charged at the rate of one mace per ton.

Any vessel clearing from any of the open ports of China for any other of the open ports, or for Hong Kong, shall be entitled, on application of the master, to a special certificate from the customs, on exhibition of which she shall be exempted from all further payment of tonnage dues in any open port of China for a period of four months, to be reckoned from the date of her port clearance.

Article XXX.

The master of any British merchant vessel may, within forty-eight hours after the arrival of his vessel, but not later, decide to depart without breaking bulk, in which case he will not be subject to pay tonnage dues. But tonnage dues shall be held due after the expiration of the said forty-eight hours. No other fees or charges, upon entry or departure, shall be levied.

Article XXXI.

No tonnage dues shall be payable on boats employed by British subjects in the conveyance of passengers, baggage, letters, articles of provision, or other articles not subject to duty, between any of the open ports. All cargo boats, however, conveying merchandise subject to duty, shall pay tonnage dues, once in six months, at the rate of four mace per register ton.

Article XXXII.

The consuls and superintendents of customs shall consult together regarding the erection of beacons or light-houses, and the distribution of buoys and light-ships, as occasion may require.

Article XXXIII.

Duties shall be paid to the bankers authorized by the Chinese government to receive the same in its behalf, either in sycee or in foreign money, according to the assay made at Canton on the 13th of July, 1843.

Article XXXIV.

Sets of standard weights and measures, prepared according to the standard issued to the Canton custom-house by the board of revenue, shall be delivered by the superintendent of customs to the consul at each port, to secure uniformity and prevent confusion.

Article XXXV.

Any British merchant vessel arriving at one of the open ports shall be at liberty to engage the services of a pilot to take her into port. In like manner, after she has discharged all legal dues and duties, and is ready to take her departure, she shall be allowed to select a pilot to conduct her out of port.

Article XXXVI.

Whenever a British merchant vessel shall arrive off one of the open ports, the superintendent of customs shall depute one or more customs officers to guard the ship. They shall either live in a boat of their own, or stay on board the ship, as may best suit their convenience. Their food and expenses shall be supplied them from the custom-house, and they shall not be entitled to any fees whatever from the master or consignee. Should they violate this regulation, they shall be punished proportionably to the amount exacted.

Article XXXVII.

Within twenty-four hours after arrival, the ship's papers, bills of lading, &c., shall be lodged in the hands of the consul, who will, within a further period of twenty-four hours, report to the superintendent of customs the name of the ship, her register, tonnage, and the nature of her cargo. If, owing to neglect on the part of the master, the above rule is not complied with within forty-eight hours after the ship's arrival, he shall be liable to a fine of fifty taels for every day's delay. The total amount of penalty, however, shall not exceed two hundred taels.

The master will be responsible for the correctness of the manifest, which shall contain a full and true account of the particulars of the cargo on board. For presenting a false manifest, he will subject himself to a fine of five hundred taels; but he will be allowed to correct, within twenty-four hours after delivery of it to the customs officers, any mistake he may discover in his manifest, without incurring this penalty.

Article XXXVIII.

After receiving from the consul the report in due form, the superintendent of customs shall grant the vessel a permit to open hatches. If the master shall open hatches, and begin to discharge any goods without such permission, he shall be fined five hundred taels, and the goods discharged shall be confiscated wholly.

Article XXXIX.

Any British merchant who has cargo to land or ship, must apply to the superintendent of customs for a special permit. Cargo landed or shipped without such permit will be liable to confiscation.

Article XL.

No transhipment from one vessel to another can be made without special permission, under pain of confiscation of the goods so transhipped.

Article XLI.

When all dues and duties shall have been paid, the superintendent of customs shall give a port clearance, and the consul shall then return the ship's papers, so that she may depart on her voyage.

Article XLII.

With respect to articles subject, according to the tariff, to *ad valorem* duty, if the British merchant cannot agree with the Chinese officer in fixing a value, then each party shall call two or three merchants to look at the goods, and the highest price at which any of these merchants would be willing to purchase them shall be assumed as the value of the goods.

Article XLIII.

Duties shall be charged upon the net weight of each article, making a deduction for the tare weight of congee, &c. To fix the tare on any article, such as tea, if the British merchant cannot agree with the custom-house officer, then each party shall choose so many chests out of every hundred, which being first weighed in gross, shall afterwards be tared, and the average tare upon these chests shall be assumed as the tare upon the whole, and upon this principle shall the tare be fixed upon all other goods in packages. If there should be any other points in dispute which cannot be settled, the British merchant may appeal to his consul, who will communicate the particulars of the case to the superintendent of customs, that it may be equitably arranged. But the appeal must be made within twenty-four hours, or it will not be attended to. While such points are still unsettled, the superintendent of customs shall postpone the insertion of the same in his books.

Article XLIV.

Upon all damaged goods a fair reduction of duties shall be allowed, proportionate to their deterioration. If any disputes arise, they shall be settled in the manner pointed out in the clause of this treaty having reference to articles which pay duty *ad valorem*.

Article XLV.

British merchants who may have imported merchandise into any of the open ports, and paid the duty thereon, if they desire to reëxport the same, shall be entitled to make application to the superintendent of customs, who, in order to prevent fraud on the revenue, shall cause examination to be made by suitable officers, to see that the duties paid on such goods, as entered in the custom-house books, corresponds with the representations made, and that the goods remain with their original marks unchanged; and he shall then make a memorandum on the port clearance of the goods, and of the amount of duties paid, and deliver the same to the merchant, and shall also certify the facts to the officers of customs of the other ports. All which being done, on the arrival in port of the vessel in which the goods are laden, everything being found on examination there to correspond, she shall be permitted to break bulk and land the said goods, without being subject to the payment of any additional duty thereon. But if, on such examination, the superintendent of customs shall detect any fraud on the revenue in the case, then the goods shall be subject to confiscation by the Chinese government.

British merchants desiring to reëxport duty-paid imports to a foreign country, shall be entitled, on complying with the same conditions as in the case of reëxportation to another port in China, to a drawback certificate, which shall be a valid tender to the customs in payment of import or export duties.

Foreign grain brought into any port of China in a British ship, if no part thereof has been landed, may be reëxported without hindrance.

Article XLVI.

The Chinese authorities at each port shall adopt the means they may judge most proper to prevent the revenue suffering from fraud or smuggling.

Article XLVII.

British merchant vessels are not entitled to resort to other than the ports of trade declared open by this treaty. They are not unlawfully to enter other ports in China, or to carry on clandestine trade along the coasts thereof. Any vessel violating this provision shall, with her cargo, be subject to confiscation by the Chinese government.

Article XLVIII.

If any British merchant vessel be concerned in smuggling, the goods, whatever their value or nature, shall be subject to confiscation by the Chinese authorities, and the ship may be prohibited from trading further, and sent away, as soon as her accounts shall have been adjusted and paid.

Article XLIX.

All penalties enforced or confiscations made under this treaty shall belong and be appropriated to the public service of the government of China.

Article L.

All official communications addressed by the diplomatic and consular agents of her Majesty the Queen to the Chinese authorities shall henceforth be written in English. They will for the present be accompanied by a Chinese version, but it is understood that in the event of there being any difference of meaning between the English and Chinese texts the English government will hold the sense as expressed in the English text to be the correct sense. This provision is to apply to the treaty now negotiated, the Chinese text of which has been carefully corrected by the English original.

ARTICLE LI.

It is agreed that henceforward the character (barbarian) shall not be applied to the government or subjects of her Britannic Majesty in any Chinese official document issued by the Chinese authorities, either in the capital or in the provinces.

ARTICLE LII.

British ships-of-war coming for no hostile purpose, or being in pursuit of pirates, shall be at liberty to visit all ports within the dominions of the Emperor of China, and shall receive every facility for the purchase of provisions, procuring water, and, if occasion require, for the making of repairs.

The commanders of such ships shall hold intercourse with the Chinese authorities on terms of equality and courtesy.

ARTICLE LIII.

In consideration of the injury sustained by native and foreign commerce from prevalence of piracy in the seas of China, the high contracting parties agree to concert measures for its suppression.

ARTICLE LIV.

The British government and its subjects are hereby confirmed in all privileges, immunities, and advantages conferred on them by previous treaties; and it is hereby expressly stipulated that the British government and its subjects will be allowed free and equal participation in all privileges, immunities, and advantages that may have been or may be hereafter granted by his Majesty the Emperor of China to the government or subjects of any other nation.

ARTICLE LV.

In evidence of her desire for the continuance of a friendly understanding her Majesty the Queen of Great Britain and Ireland consents to include in a separate article, which shall be in every respect of equal validity with the articles of this treaty, the conditions affecting indemnity for expenses incurred and losses sustained in the matter of the Canton question.

ARTICLE LVI.

The ratifications of this treaty under the hand of her Majesty the Queen of Great Britain and Ireland and of his Majesty the Emperor of China, respectively, shall be exchanged at Pekin within a year from this day of signature.

In token whereof the respective plenipotentiaries have signed and sealed this treaty.

Done at Tientsin, this 26th day of June, in the year of our Lord 1858, corresponding with the Chinese date the 16th day, 5th moon, of the 8th year of Hien-fung.

Seals and signatures.

True copy.

S. WELLS WILLIAMS,
Secretary of Legation United States of America.

Mr. Cass to Mr. Reed.

No. 16.]

DEPARTMENT OF STATE,
Washington, October 25, 1858.

SIR: I have to acknowledge the receipt of your dispatches Nos. 28 and 29, with your private letter of the 31st of July last, and to state that the suggestions therein contained shall be fully considered.

Lest the original may have failed to reach you, I inclose a duplicate of dispatch from this department No. 15, dated October 16, 1858, which acknowledges your dispatches from No. 21 to 27, inclusive.

I inclose also a copy of a note this day addressed to F. W. Pickens, minister of the United States at St. Petersburg, in which he is instructed to convey to the Russian government the President's sense of the courteous disposition at all times manifested by Count Poutiatine towards you, and especially the courtesy of that officer in affording you a passage to Tientsin in the Russian steamer America.

I am, sir, respectfully, your obedient servant,

LEWIS CASS.

WILLIAM B. REED, Esq., *&c., &c., &c.*

P. S. On the 2d of July last, Commodore Tattnall was ordered to send you home in the Minnesota by the way of the Cape of Good Hope. The Navy Department is of opinion that it would not be safe for that vessel to take you to Aden.

Mr. Reed to Mr. Cass.

No. 30.]

LEGATION OF THE UNITED STATES,
Shanghai, September 1, 1858.

SIR: After waiting until the 19th August, the latest period appointed for the arrival of the imperial commissioners, I addressed a letter to the governor general, informing him that I was still at Shanghai, and inquiring the reason for this delay. His reply, (inclosures 1 *a* and 1 *b*,) is annexed, from which you will see that the commissioners are not to arrive until October, though it is intimated that some subordinate officers are, in the meantime, to begin the proposed revision of the tariff. Doubts are entertained whether the imperial commissioners mean to come at all, and whether the whole scheme of action by officers of so high rank is not one of those inscrutable devices to attain some unintelligible result which Chinese public men are so fond of. I shall regret their failure to come, as it will prostrate the only reasonable hope of the peaceful adjustment of the Canton difficulty.

The last intelligence from that region is of the attack, by a combined military and naval force, on the town of Nantow, north of Hong Kong. The city was taken, pillaged, and, to a large extent destroyed. The loss of the English was considerable, especially of officers. This affair is but another symptom of the wretched condition of things in the south, lingering hostilities waged on both sides, necessarily with ferocity and pitiful results. In the meantime, trade is suspended, and the colonies of Macao and Hong Kong are suffering under all sorts of petty but most vexatious annoyances, such as the Chinese are adepts in inflicting. It is said, 40,000 Chinese traders, laborers, and servants have left Macao, (the aggregate being but 60,000,) and at Victoria it is very much the same thing. The United States ship Germantown is left at Whampoa to watch over the remnant of American prosperity and commerce.

Should the imperial commissioners not come to Shanghai, so as to effect a peaceful arrangement, and no reinforcement of troops arrive, I cannot look forward to any other than one of two results, the evacuation of Canton, or its retention as it is for an indefinite time. My own opinion is, that the only effectual remedy for existing and inevitable evil is evacuation. Baron Gros, who is still here, informed me, a day or two ago, that he is in daily expectation of the arrival of two thousand French troops at Canton, and that he is in favor of retaining possession of the city till the requisitions of the new treaties are complied with. Lord Elgin has not yet returned from Japan. He can, I think, hardly look for any English reinforcements till affairs in India are more completely settled.

I am awaiting his arrival, and that of Count Poutiatine, in order to ascertain, if possible, the result of their recent negotiations with the Japanese. By this mail, in charge of a special bearer of dispatches, goes the new treaty, which, on the 29th July, was signed by Mr. Harris, our consul general, with the Emperor of Japan. In a private letter received from Mr. Harris, I learn (and I mention this in case of any accidental delay of the courier in charge of the dispatches) that the treaty gives us a resident minister at Yedo; opens to trade five of the best harbors, and the cities of Ohosaka, Yedo, and Osaca; secures the free exercise of Christianity and missionary enterprise, with the right to build churches. The practice of trampling on the cross, as the symbol of Christianity, is forbidden. The currency is satisfactorily adjusted. For this success, Mr. Harris certainly deserves great credit. I have not seen the treaty, but believe I correctly describe it.

The English and Russian ministers knew nothing of the American treaty when they left Nagasaki for the Gulf of Yeddo.

Thus, have China and Japan been coincidently opened to the trade and policy of the West, and, so far as our agency is involved, without one drop of blood being shed or any unkind feeling created.

The current business of this legation has been without interest.

I beg again to call your attention to the subject of the traffic in coolies between China and the West Indies. Unless dispatches containing the views of the government on this subject are now on their way to me, I shall be obliged to leave China without knowing whether the measures of prevention to which I had recourse meet with the approval of the President or not. If they do, it is much to be regretted that the knowledge of the fact cannot be communicated to the unscrupulous men who are engaged in this infamous traffic, and a new warning be given. If they do not, then it would have been gratifying to me to know, at least, that I was sustained by the government in the view I take of the trade, even though no existing law can be found to apply to it.

The consul at Amoy, under date of the 19th July, says: "In relation to the cooly trade, I am happy to be able to report great decrease, I hope stop. There has been an attempt to load one vessel, the large British steamer Cleopatra, since my last. This was attended with much difficulty, and was, I suspect, only partially successful. The steamer was detained long in port, paying heavy demurrage, as coolies could not be obtained. Then a small steamer was chartered to go to Swatow, and tow up a lorcha filled with victims, said to have had two hundred on board. The lorcha was cast off tow, just outside of the entrance to Amoy, when the coolies rose, gained the mastery over those in charge, ran the lorcha on shore, plundered the vessel, and escaped. The parties engaged in the bringing of the coolies kept the matter so close, that it is not known whether any lives were lost or not. Reports were contradictory. After this, a larger steamer was chartered, (British,) at Macao or Hong Kong, and came to this, *via* Swatow, I conjecture, with coolies, for I have not obtained any certain knowledge of the case. Immediately after this, the Cleopatra sailed for Havana. This was in May, since which time, there has nothing transpired indicating any transactions in the cooly trade."

I regret to say later intelligence has reached me that a new impulse has been given to the trade, and that a number of American ships are now in China, and more are expected, to take large cargoes from Macao and Hong Kong to the Havana. I do not attribute, in any way, the increase of this business to the sudden stoppage of the passenger trade with California in consequence of the act of the legislature of that State, lately made known here, which will affect a very different description of emigrants. Such as can go thither, able and willing to pay their passage, and return, have no resemblance to the wretched cooly, who is decoyed and penned up in barracoons at Macao, and is stowed away between the decks of the English and American ships now engaged in the traffic.

In the views which I have expressed as to the cooly trade to the West Indies, I am conscious of no other impulse than that of ordinary sympathy with human suffering. There is an invariable law as to the fate of a large number of these poor creatures, on their way from the east to the west—disease, suicide, or death from barbarous treatment. As certain is their doom when they arrive—irredeemable slavery under the form of freedom. In its ultimate results, I believe this Asiatic slave trade is as bad, if not worse, than the African slave trade ever was; for the African may assimilate and is cared for. The Asiatic is kept isolated, so long as in numbers he is weak; and when the numbers become great, the isolation still continuing, there comes a certain and fatal struggle, in which the Asiatic, as the weakest, falls. It has been so in Java, in Luzon, in Borneo; so, before long, will it be in Cuba.

All that I have hoped for is that some measures shall be taken to prevent American ships from being used in this traffic.

I transmit, for the consideration of the President, a memorial lately addressed to me by the American ship-masters in this port, on a subject to which I have more than once addressed you—the necessity of prisons at the consular ports. (Inclosure 2.)

I have also the honor to forward (inclosure 3) the sketch of such an act of Congress as seems to me to be required by the provisions of the new treaty. I prefer a modification of the existing system, to which the consular agents are used, to any attempt at complete reorganization. This act so far changes the statute of 1848 as expressly to give the commissioner original jurisdiction in cases where a consul is either party or witness. As the law now is, a consul has no redress against an American citizen, and an American citizen has no redress against him.

I have the honor to be, sir, your obedient servant,

WILLIAM B. REED.

Hon. LEWIS CASS,
Secretary of State, Washington.

Inclosure 1 *a.*

SEPTEMBER 4, 1858.

The undersigned, envoy extraordinary and minister plenipotentiary of the United States to China, received a dispatch last month from your excellency, informing him that an imperial decree had been issued, directing Kweiliang, Hwashana, and others, to take the seal of imperial commissioners, and proceed to Kiangnan by post; and that your excellency supposed that they would reach Suchau by the first decade of the seven month.

The undersigned replied to this dispatch on the 29th ultimo, informing your excellency that out of respect to these distinguished officers, appointed by his Majesty the Emperor to consult with respect to commercial affairs in conjunction with your excellency, he would await their arrival on the day appointed. The first decade of the month has now expired without their arrival, and the undersigned is desirous to know how soon the arrival of their excellencies the imperial commissioners may be certainly looked for.

WILLIAM B. REED.

To his Excellency Ho,
Governor General of the Two Kiang Provinces, &c., &c., &c.

The 11th day of the 7th moon of the 8th year of Hien-fung, (August 19, 1858.)

Inclosure 1 *b*.

SEPTEMBER 4, 1858.

Ho, Governor-General of the Two Kiang Provinces, Guardian of the Heir Apparent, &c., &c., hereby sends a reply:

I had the honor, on the 23d instant, to receive a communication from your excellency, in which you remark as follows:

"I received a dispatch, in which your excellency informed me that an imperial decree had been received, directing Kweiliang, Hwashana, and others to proceed by post to Kiangsu. The first decade of the seventh moon has now expired without their arrival, and I am desirous to know when they will arrive at Shanghai," &c.

It is true that an imperial decree was received, as then stated; but subsequently, when the Imperial Commissioners Kweiliang and Hwashana were sending an answer to a dispatch from the British plenipotentiary to them, they stated to me at the same time that their departure from Pekin had been somewhat delayed by the illness of Kipu, and that an imperial decree had been issued ordering Twan, a civilian of the fifth rank, to be joined with the high officer Ming, and both of them to leave the capital on the 19th instant. It was further stated that, as they themselves had been ordered to attend to some matters of public business on their way down, they would not be able to travel by post regularly, but would endeavor to arrive by the end of the month ending October 6.

I have already directed the provincial judge, Sieh, to inform your excellency of these particulars; but it is proper for me to embody them also in this reply, which I now send for your information and guidance.

His Excellency W. B. REED,
Envoy Extraordinary and Minister Plenipotentiary of United States of America in China.

AUGUST 25, 1858.

Inclosure 2.

SEPTEMBER 4, 1858.

May it please your excellency, the undersigned, your memorialists, masters of American ships now lying in the port of Shanghai, respectfully represent:

Whereas, from the peculiar nature of the relations between the American and Chinese governments, the latter can take neither civil nor criminal jurisdiction over any citizen of the United States, whether seaman or resident; and in consequence thereof the United States consul has been invested by his government with extra judicial powers over all its citizens, and especially, and in addition to the usual consular power, over the seamen and masters of American ships.

And whereas, from the reasons aforesaid, the United States consul is not in a position to avail himself of the police force or prisons of the Chinese authorities in executing the penalties of the law, the undersigned beg leave to submit:

That it appears to them that the necessity for erecting a prison and instituting the means of punishing with hard labor or solitary confinement, or both, as the consular court may in its wisdom decree, is immediate and pressing, for the reasons following, to wit:

The consular court is now holding daily sittings, and scarcely a day passes that there is not a civil or criminal cause pending; and when, from the nature of the offense, the punishment should, in the opinion of the court, be severe, such as imprisonment and hard labor, and they find accordingly, it is the opinion of your memorialists that the result is a mockery, both of law and justice, simply because, in the absence of a man-of-war, which is not unfrequent, there is no prison, and no means of inflicting any material punishment; and after the sentence of the court has been read to the offending party, the consul has no alternative but to set at liberty the person whom the law has pronounced a criminal, to commit, if he pleases, further crime, with the most ridiculous impunity.

And again, when a case is pending between a master and a seaman, and fine or imprisonment is the punishment decreed, the offending party, if a master of a ship, is usually mulcted in pecuniary damages, which the consul has in his power to collect, to almost any amount; but if the offending party be a seaman the consul can neither recover the fine or inflict the imprisonment; and thus again are the ends of justice defeated; and not only this, but a positive injustice is done the shipmaster.

The British government, whose relations with the Chinese government, are identical with those between the latter and the American government, as your memorialists believe, have had a substantial and suitable building erected and used as a jail; and the proceedings of the British consular courts are, as your memorialists believe, as regular and effectual as the proceedings of any court of similar jurisdiction in the kingdom of Great Britain, notwithstanding the fact that the facility of access to the colonial courts of Hong Kong would seem to leave the British consul, if without the means of imprisonment or other punishment, in a comparatively unembarrassed position.

Your memorialists are well aware that the British consul has, as a matter of favor, granted to the American consul the use of the British jail when it was not crowded; but this is not always the case; and not unfrequently, as your memorialists believe, application from the American consul for the use of the jail has been refused—always, of course, in courteous terms—on the ground that the jail was already crowded.

But whether the British jail be crowded or vacant, your memorialists submit that it is a question whether a great nation like the United States of America should place itself in a position to receive, nay, to ask as a favor from a foreign nation that which its means are as ample as any other power on the face of the earth to furnish itself.

Your memorialists believe that your excellency cannot have failed to observed the necessity which they now urge as existing; and they beg that your excellency will take into consideration this their memorial, and at an early day urge upon the government some action in the premises.

And as in duty bound your memorialists will ever pray.

George N. Potter, master of ship Hotspur, of New York.
Prince Harding, master of ship Oscar, of Boston.
P. Bieir, master of ship Sancho Panza, of Boston.
Frederick Johnson, master of bark Kremlin, of Boston.
William H. Harrison, master of ship Bell Rock, of Boston.
Charle H. Odell, master of bark Quickstep, of Boston.
John Munro, master of bark Ann, of New York.
C. Coggins, master of ship Pampero, of New York.
Ernest Lane, master of ship Eureka, of New York.
John Sweeney, master of bark Lucky Star, of New York.
John Henry, master of ship Magnet, of Boston.
William Cole, formerly of ship Nabob.
William B. Preston, bark Lucky Star, New York.
John Baxter, ship Nabob.
Charles Gill, ship Emma.
James Higham, ship N. B. Palmer.

Hon. W. B. Reed,
Envoy Extraordinary and Minister Plenipotentiary of the United States to China.

Inclosure 3.

AN ACT to carry into effect certain provisions of the treaty with China.

Sec. 1. *Be it enacted*, That the act entitled "An act to carry into effect certain provisions in the treaties between the United States and China and the Ottoman Porte, giving certain judicial powers to ministers and consuls of the United States in those countries," passed the 11th day of August, 1848, except so far as it may be modified by the provisions of this act, be, and the same is hereby, renewed and declared to be applicable to the treaty signed at Tientsin on the 18th day of June, 1858, between China and the United States.

Sec. 2. That the jurisdiction of the commissioner or chief diplomatic officer in China, in all matters of civil redress or of crimes, shall be appellate, only to be exercised wherever the said commissioner may be, except in cases where a consular officer shall happen to be interested, either as a party or witness, in which case original jurisdiction is vested in the said commissioner.

Sec. 3. That the sum of ——— thousand dollars be appropriated for the purpose of erecting or hiring buildings, or parts of buildings, to be used as prisons for American convicts in China and paying keepers; the said sum to be applied and distributed under the authority of the commissioner or chief diplomatic officer in China.

Mr. Reed to Mr. Cass.

No. 31.] LEGATION OF THE UNITED STATES,
Shanghai, September 4, 1858.

SIR: I have the honor to forward to you by Mr. Paulding Tattnall, bearer of dispatches from the consul general at Simoda, a duplicate copy, certified by the secretary of legation, of the treaty between the United States and China, signed at Tientsin, on the 18th of June. The duplicate originals in English and Chinese will, for the present, be retained here.

As this is the last opportunity I shall have of communicating with you in time for the meeting of Congress, I beg leave to add a few remarks on the treaty itself, and its probable effect and operation, in addition to those which I have already made to you. They apply equally to the treaties made by the other western powers. They are necessarily in a certain sense speculative; and, I am quite aware, being admonished of it every moment that I pass here, how illusory speculation as to Chinese character and conduct is apt to be, still desiring the President to have before him the best views that even brief experience enables me to form, I think it my duty to express them.

If the inquiry be made how far we can depend on the fulfillment of the provisions of the treaties by the Chinese, no one will venture on more than general statements in reply. It is hardly worth while to go into any detail as to the differences in the moral, intellectual, and physical qualities and power of the parties to these compacts; and yet, in estimating the extent to which the Chinese government will carry out their provisons, it must be constantly borne in mind that this is a government where a sense of temporary expediency is much more the rule of action than what is understood as law and authoritative precedent. Each governor of a province has more or less legislative and executive functions, and is held responsible for the well-being of the territory committed to him; and so is each judge, intendent, prefect, and district magistrate under him; all these functionaries make as well as execute the laws within certain limits. More depends on the character and temper of the individual incumbent here than anywhere. If the governor general at Canton, in October, 1856, had changed places with the one at Fuhchau, it is quite possible that there would have been no disturbance at the former place.

The real nature of the Chinese government is a mixure of despotism and democracy, which is difficult to explain to those who have not seen its actual workings. The central government is supposed to be the irresponsible source of all power and authority; and its working officers, at the capital, labor together to maintain their position and influence in the remotest parts of the empire. But when one of their number is sent with proconsular powers to a distant province, he knows that the people are tenacious of their usages; and while they would like and expect to be protected, are not disposed to pay more than they are obliged for this protection. The ruler was once one of the people, and spent his early days as a private subject. He knows, too, that he can expect little help of money or men from the central government in case of insurrection; he must depend mainly on the resources of his jurisdiction, and endeavor to forward a large surplus revenue to Pekin, over and above *all* the local outlays for the civil, military, and naval services. A governor general or governor have similar powers in their particular provinces, to that which the Emperor has over the whole; but they have no responsibility for the condition of other provinces, and send nothing to them in case of trouble, unless ordered from court. Consequently, the provinces and departments do not have that bond of union which a practically powerful despotic government might, and this explains the comparative liberty the people possess, since the central power cannot concentrate its energy upon a single point, and thus reduce them at once, and thoroughly suppress revolt or discontent.

All this shows that when the central power in China makes a treaty with a foreign nation, it puts itself under obligations which it may be unable to carry into full effect from the integral weakness of its organization. It is to the credit of China, through its long existence, that it has based its principles of government upon the good administration of law and the protection of industry, and endeavored to obtain the best agents to carry out these purposes by subjecting them to a series of competitive examinations in the most moral works their literature affords. The excellence of the system has been proved by its long existence. No stream rises higher than its fountain, and we are all conscious that the moral perverseness of the Chinese cannot be removed or changed by mere human morality, however refined. This government is ridiculously weak if looked at in respect to the physical resources at its command to repel invasion or repress sedition, but it is strong in the passive regard the people have for their institutions, which survive even changes of dynasty.

The real authority is a kind of composition of forces, the tyranny of irresponsible despotic power, primary or delegated, acting against the license of ignorant democracy often goaded by poverty or misguided by sedition. In estimating the chances of the peaceable workings of a treaty with such a people and government, one hardly knows whether to fear most from their weakness when called on to repress, what is very apt always to occur, an attack upon a foreign vessel or individual, when it finds itself unable to satisfy the injured party, or to hope more from the good nature and peaceful habits of the mass of people. Cases of violence constantly occur among the people which the government never thinks of interfering with; the officers leave them to the gentry and headmen to settle among themselves, and the latter expect to do much to maintain the peace of their own region. Sometimes the power of the middle class of gentry sets the regular authorities at defiance, as is supposed to be the case now at Canton. In the dreadful insurrection about Canton in 1854–55, when it was estimated that more than half a million of inhabitants lost their lives by violence within twenty months in that single prefecture, the gentry coöperated with the government in suppressing the sedition. Yeh has been held up to opprobium by foreigners for his ruthless executions of the prisoners taken in that rising; but the people, who would have suffered by a rebel victory, better knew the deadly nature of the struggle, and did all in their power to arrest the disturbers of the public peace and deliver them over, after they had been tried and condemned to death by committees in every large town.

The assertion and maintenance of a principle is not to be expected among a people whose whole political system is one of expediency; who regard peace, no matter how obtained, the end and evidence of good government; and whose ideas of government are directed rather to the support of their rulers than defining their own rights. The Chinese, among pagan nations, deserve great consideration for the advances they have made in self-government, though much of the praise they have received has been from those who, having never lived among them, praised them unduly because they supposed they had reached a higher point of excellence even than some Christian or any Moslem nation. But those who come from western lands, where truth and integrity are held to be character itself, and supposing these descriptions to have some truth, are shocked at the flagrant violations of these cardinal virtues they meet in daily intercourse among the people, and perhaps place the race too low.

The treaties of Tientsin were signed by officers who had considerable knowledge of one of the practical results of the former treaties, viz: that the revenue had been greatly increased during the fourteen years of their operation, but who knew little of the character of foreigners. They supposed that trade was their main object in coming so near to the imperial court, and were ready to grant almost any mercantile privilege not incompatible with their independence; but they were ignorant of the resources, and afraid of the real designs of their visitors, and consequently closer political relations were not desired, chiefly from fear that they were only a pretext for something more. Judging others by themselves, and knowing what designs of conquest they would carry out, if possessed of the irresistible power seen in the hands of their visitors, they were loth to believe in the assertions made. The demand of the right of residence at Pekin for foreign ministers, for instance, seemed to them like seeking for a privilege which was not worth the trouble of such an array of force, and therefore that some ulterior designs were couched in it. Their own subjects had gone abroad and returned without embassadors to look after them. They went and came at their own risk. If they were treated well, it showed the humanity of foreign nations, and that those nations had at last learned something of the "benevolence of the sons of heaven." If they were treated ill, as was often the case, it only proved the barbarism of the foreigners, but did not call for interference on the part of the Emperor, who never took a thought about undutiful subjects who left their native land. This is the Chinese mode of reasoning on this point; and the success of the foreign ministers at Pekin in removing these misconceptions will vindicate the wisdom of the demand. On the whole, I think the officials of this empire, judging from the varied experience of my predecessors and myself, will be desirous to carry out the provisions of the treaty, if they find that remissness is likely to be noticed, and violations are fairly represented to them; but the impediments thrown in the way of audience and redress will be sufficiently vexatious.

One of the prolific sources of trouble in carrying out the stipulations of treaties is in another direction, viz: the difficulty of getting justice done to the Chinese when they are wronged by those who claim and obtain exterritoriality and exemption from all their laws. It results from the combined action of several causes. One is the difficulty of procuring such testimony as can reasonably be taken when the witnesses are Chinese, whose assertions must be received with doubt. Another is the loss of reputation in the little social community that clusters here, which would attach to a foreigner who should prosecute another for a crime committed against a native, or even bear witness against him for wrong done the latter. No native can arraign *any* foreigner in his own courts for crime; for not only is the principle of exterritoriality claimed by those who have, but by those who have no treaties, and even no consuls at the open ports; and he feels his helplessness when attempting to lay a criminal case before a consul.

A case in point may be cited. In July, 1856, the foreign community at Fuhchau was highly excited at the homicide of an American, who was killed in a street brawl among some of the townsfolk. The United States commissioner did all he could to urge the governor general to apprehend the offenders, and the criminal was arrested and and executed during the next year. About two months after the homicide, a passage-boat crossing the river some miles below the city, was fired into by an Englishman, under the apprehension that it was piratical, and a man killed. His body was brought to the door of the English consulate, and the demand for justice compounded for thirty dollars. The different management of the two cases, happening as they did about the same time, made an unfavorable impression on the minds of natives. It is not known that a foreigner has ever been executed for the murder of a Chinese, except in the colonies of Hong Kong and Macao; and the recurrence of cases like the above make an impression on the Chinese, and when repeated by lawless men who deem themselves free from all authority, they rise and revenge themselves, as was the case last year at Ningpo, where twenty-eight Portuguese were massacred by sailors who had long suffered from them or their countrymen.

With every desire to do justice to the native, the foreign minister or consul finds it very difficult to execute the laws of his own country upon the criminals who are brought before him. The English consuls have been able to do it more than any other, and their efforts tend to relieve the shortcomings of others, as the mass of natives make no distinction.

In respect, too, to this whole subject of wrongs and injuries by both sides, it should be mentioned that the best portion of the Chinese are well aware of the desperate character of the lower classes of their countrymen, and of the numerous aggressions, defalcations, and even murders, suffered by foreigners from them; so that a sort of rude balance of wrongs and benefits on both sides is struck in their minds with results varying according to accident and temperament.

There are now perhaps fifteen hundred foreigners resident at ports along this coast, and three times that number in the shipping there at a given time, all of whom are more or less under the cognizance of their consuls. If these gradually become scattered over the interior it will be difficult to follow them; and if they suffer from the natives or commit outrages it will be no easy matter to settle the wrong while it is fresh and evidence is available. Where the entire administration of law is loose and partial, foreigners begin soon to look upon all Chinese laws as deriving much of their sanction and justice from the degree of power that exists to inforce them. This weak government is therefore rendered weaker by those who should rather strengthen it, and who would do so if their interests lay in that direction.

This disregard for native law in the abstract has much of it grown out of the illegal traffic in opium. The history of this traffic, discreditable in every way, need not be reviewed; but there can be no doubt in the mind of an impartial observer that the understood impunity on the part of those who deal in this drug has the effect of weakening their respect for all laws, especially those of a fiscal character. So of other things. In some of the open ports a bargain is made by the importer of goods with the custom-house authorities, as to the amount of duties he shall pay on his cargo; and the export duties are settled in the same way by the native dealer. It would be abundantly easy for the local customs authorities to collect the full duties on all goods, if they had careful and honest agents. This state of things shows both their weakness and inefficiency, and how soon foreigners systematically take advantage of it. Indeed, no sooner does a careless officer allow an article to enter either free or under a nominal duty than the repetition of the admission a few times is likely to be construed into a precedent, even against the plainest construction of the tariff. If, however, on the other hand, the foreigner suffers a damage, or pays a higher duty than the strict letter of the tariff, he strenuously demands the rectification of the mistake. The native officials think, doubtless, that one might offset the other, for they often practice the same mode of judging in dealing with their own people. They oppress as far as they can, and the people resist to their utmost, and do maintain their own position against tyranny.

In carrying out the treaty much depends upon the conduct of foreigners in their daily intercourse with the Chinese. The respectable among them have a character for fulfilling their promises and paying liberally, which leads the natives to trust in them, and it is to be hoped this character will not be lost or seriously damaged, at least among the English-speaking portion of them. In case of wrong suffered, the Chinese rulers will be, as ever, usually desirous to smooth it over, hush it up, or let it pass; and their dislike to taking trouble about it, especially when considerable time has passed, and it happened in a distant region of the country, or under their predecessors, will require power to overcome it. Even the resident minister at Pekin may find the officers there as loth to attend to his complaints as he will find it difficult to execute justice on his countrymen for their misdoings. The Chinese do not wish to have trouble with foreigners, but their erroneous notions and perverse practice in dealing with them are almost sure to lead to it, while some consideration may be due to their general conduct in estimating this whole subject of intercourse. They say that they have no credit for the efforts they do make to act rightly towards them; and on one occasion they brought up the numerous cases in which they had kindly treated the French missionaries found in the country in violation of treaty, and taken them long journeys, as an offset to the harsh treatment of the one who was killed in Kwangsi. Their opinion has some grounds for it, but their own conceit, obstinacy, and misrepresentation, always stand very much in the way of their getting a fair judgment for themselves.

In short, the Chinese have so many features of justice, liberty, and civilization, in their social system and government, that we are led to expect all the results seen in western lands from the action of these qualities; but investigation shows that oppression, mendacity, and ignorance, so constantly neutralize what is excellent in theory and principle, that we begin to wonder how anything good remains, and why the whole system does not fall into ruin. The peaceful disposition, untiring industry, and democratic origin of the rulers, are doubtless the chief preservative elements.

In conclusion, I would estimate the value of these new treaties, in view of the relations they place China in to the great nations of the world, as compacts which will open other channels of intercourse with her people than those of trade. The safety of her government and institutions, during the long existence history gives them, has been owing very much to her isolation. Though she has been conquered by Tartars, that isolation has not been broken, as it is likely soon to be by the ingress of western enterprise, learning, and religion. It will be an interesting experiment to see how the millions of this pagan land will receive the diverse lessons, in every branch of human excellence and wickedness, they are likely to have set before them and enacted among them. It will also be a perilous experiment, and its conduct and consequences cannot fail to attract the attention of every friend of humanity. The contact of the Christian and Pagan world, now to be developed, must almost necessarily produce the destruction and absorption, or the elevation and strengthening, of the latter. It cannot remain as it is for any length of time. That contact with China assumes an importance and involves responsibilities that can neither be over estimated nor avoided.

Christianity has the power in itself to elevate and strengthen those nations which receive it; but the question here will be, whether the old system is to be totally demolished and then reconstructed, or whether it can be altered and renovated to adapt itself to new influences and institutions without undergoing the horrors of revolution.

There must be power at hand to show the Chinese the danger of violating the provisions of these treaties; but every well-wisher to the success of the great experiment now initiated should hope that some higher and steadier principle will regulate the exercise of power than has heretofore seemed to govern it. The two wars with which China has been afflicted, in 1839 and 1856, have been confessedly wars of injustice and wrong; or, in other words, they were instances of the unscrupulous application of power under the influence of a sordid or sudden impulse, and one effect has been to impress deeply upon these helpless heathens the idea that the power of western nations is at hand, not for purposes of protection or real justice, but as a sort of permanent threat that, if any material interest be interfered with, however illegitimate, this power will be ruthlessly used to their destruction. There is no stronger illustration of this than in the repugnance the Chinese have to deal with the subject of opium.

They fear (I incline to think they do not desire) to prohibit it, or seize it, or confiscate it, and I sometimes think they shrink from legalizing it and making it dutiable, less from any sense of duty to themselves, or regard to their countrymen, or fear of imperial authority, than from an ill-defined and not irrational apprehension that the great commercial monopolists here (not American houses) prefer the present unworthy state of things, and might resent a departure from it. It is idle to deny that these great houses, one of them it is said commanding large Parliamentary influence, have political influence here. They have defeated prohibition heretofore. They now dislike legalization, and in the wretched strife of these selfish interests the disgrace continues.

This is a pregnant instance of the effect of a long-continued abuse of power, which confounds all sense of right and wrong, and of obligation to comply with treaties or obey law.

Whether, in the proposed revision of the tariff—and no other mode is left—Lord Elgin means to endeavor in any way, either by efficient prohibition, or legalization with high duties, to dispose of this standing opprobium, I have no means of knowing. No better time could be than now, when the English government is about to assume the active responsibilities of the East India Company, including that of the forced growth and sale of opium, with its revenue of £5,000,000 sterling.

I refer to this subject now only as an incidental illustration of a general state of things here. Should it form any part of the proposed modification of the tariff, I shall have the honor, before leaving China, to address you specially on the subject.

The general result of such meditation as I have given the subject of the probable operation of the treaties as between the political contracting parties is hopeful. I believe the Chinese will comply with them. If they do, the nations of the west owe a sacred duty of expression on their own citizens, and a strict observance of law. If they do not, China should be made to feel that power is at hand to make them do what is right, and not, as I have said is often the case, to make them or tempt them to do wrong.

I have the honor to be, sir, your obedient servant,

WILLIAM B. REED.

Hon. Lewis Cass,
Secretary of State, Washington.

Mr. Reed to Mr. Cass.

No. 32.] LEGATION OF THE UNITED STATES,
On board the Minnesota, off Woosung, September 15, 1858.

SIR: I have the honor to acknowledge your dispatch, No. 12, dated Washington, June 25, with its inclosure. I beg you to thank the Secretary of the Navy for his prompt compliance with my wish as to returning to the United States in this ship, either by the way of Aden or the Cape of Good Hope. I shall avail myself of the leave to return in the month of December, or sooner, if the details of pending negotiation as to the tariffs can be arranged, and shall, of course, advise you of my movements. I know of no more appropriate occasion than this to repeat the expression of my sincere gratitude to the naval service in China for uniform kindness and consideration; and I attribute it very much to the precision with which our relations were defined, and to the eminent good sense of the officers in command. Nothing could be more harmonious and agreeable than has been our intercourse from first to last, and I refer to it, with great satisfaction, in contrast with the state of things of which most of my predecessors have reason to complain.

Little of interest has occurred since my last dispatch, unless it be the return from Japan of their excellencies the English and Russian ministers. They visited Yedo, resided for some days in the city, and signed each a treaty with the Japanese. The Russian treaty was signed before Lord Elgin arrived. It corresponds, Count Poutiatine informs me, with that of the United States; nor does the English treaty materially differ. I learn, unofficially, that its only new privileges are a five per cent. duty on cottons and woolens, (which I presume enures to us,) a revision of the treaty in five years, and that the treaty shall go into operation on the 1st instead of the 4th of July, 1859. Lord Elgin, in conversation, expresses himself as under great obligation to Mr. Harris for courtesy and assistance. I refer to these matters connected with Japan, thinking it probable you may not receive official intelligence directly thence for a long time.

The Russian minister, having completed the performance of his duties here, returns to Europe by the next steamer.

His excellency Baron Gros sailed for Japan on the 6th instant.

The arrangement of the details of the new tariff, to be determined on so soon as the imperial commissioners arrive, has been delegated to gentlemen familiar with commercial relations, and have been nearly completed. In these preliminary conferences, Mr. Williams, the secretary of legation, has represented the United States. So soon as the tariffs are concluded I shall have the honor to address you particularly on the subject, being of considerable interest to our fellow-citizens, merchants, and manufacturers.

From Canton the news is understood to be favorable. The governor general has issued a proclamation to the Chinese, in which he says: "I command you to pursue your usual callings and behave discreetly now that you know that peace has been declared at Tien-tsin, and that henceforward natives and foreigners shall be as friends. Tranquillity will be restored and trade, unhindered, will flow in its accustomed channels.''

Dated August 17, 1858.

I sincerely hope a pacification may soon take place.

It is in connection with the probable state of things in the south of China that your suggestion (in dispatch No. 12) as to the lease, for a long term of years, of an island in the Canton river requires on my part great consideration. I have two difficulties about it—one a conscientious doubt as to the policy of the United States beginning to acquire property of this kind in the East, (for a lease of a hundred years is equivalent to ownership,) and the other a still graver doubt as to the eligibility of such an acquisition anywhere in the south, or, indeed, anywhere except in this immediate neighborhood, for here, at or near the mouth of the great central river of China, must be the seat of commerce. Yielding any scruples I may have on the first point, and obeying your instructions, I shall at a proper season make the necessary inquiry and inform you of the result.

Permit me, in conclusion, to add a few earnest words on a subject in which I have no personal interest whatever, but which is of great importance in our future relations to this empire. I mean the manner in which my successor shall be accredited and equipped on the occasion of his first visit, as the bearer of the ratified treaty, to Pekin. It will be absolutely necessary for him to have the highest diplomatic rank known to our laws, the support and coöperation of the naval forces on this station, if, as is most probable, he shall approach the capital by the way of the Gulf of Pechele and the Peiho, and, further, the benefit of a liberal special appropriation to defray the necessary expenses of such a mission. Such an appropriation need not be very large. It is not designed, and will not of, course, be used, for any competition with the expensive ceremonial of European plenipotentiaries. But it is needed for the peculiar incidents and exactions of new travel and residence in the country. Without it, the American minister must be in mortifying dependence either on the Chinese, who, whatever construction they may put on the motives of those who receive it, are not wanting in a certain kind of liberality, or on the representatives of other powers, which is still less agreeable. It is needed for special interpreters, both foreign and Chinese, those who can write as well as speak the language. My limited experience and observation whilst at the mouth of the river and during the negotiation at Tien-tsin, satisfied me of the absolute necessity of what I now take the liberty of pressing on your attention. If the access and residence at the mysterious capital of this great empire be worth the effort just made by the nations of the west, surely the liberality of Congress will not be withheld in the proper equipment of the first mission of the United States.

I have the honor to be, sir, your obedient servant,

WILLIAM B. REED.

Hon. LEWIS CASS,
Secretary of State.

Mr. Reed to Mr. Cass.

No. 33.] LEGATION OF THE UNITED STATES,
Shanghai, October 21, 1858.

SIR: Availing myself of the leisure afforded by the delay of the imperial commissioners to come to Shanghai, I sailed on the 16th ultimo for Japan, and after a visit of rather more than a fortnight to Nagasaki, returned to the city on the 9th instant. The French plenipotentiary sailed for Yedo on the 6th September, but no intelligence has yet been received from him. He will, no doubt, on his return, bring dispatches from our consul general. We learned in Japan that the Emperor died at Yedo, on the 16th September. My visit to Nagasaki was full of interest. The transition there, at least, from a policy or habit of exclusion, to one of free and friendly intercourse, seemed easy and natural, and my relations to the people and the local authorities were in every way agreeable. I have also to acknowledge the courtesy and friendliness of Mr. Douker Curtius, the plenipotentiary of his Majesty the King of the Netherlands and his staff at Dezina.

Whatever may be the commercial advantages of opening such a port as Nagasaki, there is no question as to the political importance of the position as a place of most convenient resort and observation.

On my return here, I found that the imperial commissioners, the same high officers with whom I conducted the negotiations at Tientsin, and the governor general of this province, had arrived a few days previously. Lord Elgin was and is here, and had initiated a mode of discussion of the new tariff which was quite satisfactory to me, and with which, therefore, I have abstained from interfering. The commissioners, whether spontaneously or not, I am not prepared to say, have issued a proclamation announcing the treaties, a copy of which I inclose. (Exhibit 1.) Lord Elgin informed me, in conversation, that they have also agreed to memorialize the throne to dismiss Hwang, the governor general at Canton. My correspondence to this date with the commissioners I now inclose, (Exhibits 2, 3, 4, 5,) reserving all communications on the subject of the tariff in detail until some result shall be attained. I hope this will be before the departure of the next mail. This being completed, it is my intention to avail myself of the President's permission to return home by the way of Europe, where I hope to be in January. I shall sail in the Minnesota from Hong Kong about the 1st December.

Appended to this dispatch will be found copies of a series of very interesting papers given to me last week by Lord Elgin. They were found in one of the yamuns in Canton in January, but have never been shown to me till now, when they are only interesting—but in this point of view very much so—as throwing light on the character of the officials of this strange country, and the secrets of its past and probably of its present diplomacy. I beg to call your attention and that of the President to these papers, and also to the time when they are made known to me. Perhaps no stronger illustration could be given of the awkward and partial coöperation and semi-confidence of last summer than that such papers should have been in the hands of the allies, and yet not have been communicated to me. They relate largely to American affairs, and on that account, I should have seen them; but in other points of view they were important, at least one might suppose the allied plenipotentiaries would have thought so, as enabling me, in the difficult complication which arose, to regulate my conduct by a full and accurate knowledge of the whole truth as known to them. When I recall the transient irritability exhibited once or twice last summer by their excellencies the English and French ministers at the pacific and conciliatory course which I felt it my duty to pursue, I am still more at a loss to understand why these papers were withheld.

In one view, I am sincerely rejoiced that the inadvertence or intention to which I refer kept these papers from me. They are certainly the most painful revelations of the mendacity and treacherous habits of the high officials of this empire yet given to the world; they cannot be read without contemptuous resentment, and I have no such confidence in my own equanimity and self-control as to determine what might have been my inclination before and after the fall of the Taku forts had the contents of these papers been known to me. Nothing of course that the Chinese authorities, high or low, could say or write, would have materially influenced my course of action, under or without instructions; but had these papers been known to me, I am quite confident the moderate confidence I had in their professions would have been lessened, and my conciliatory tendencies not a little embarrassed. If it be, as I think it was, a mistake in the English and French ministers, concealing or omitting to communicate these things, it has not been without its good fruits in allowing my own peaceful inclinations to have full scope. I do not at all regret what was done or omitted last summer, but I deprecate any criticism on the course of the United States when, either intentionally or inconsiderately, information to which we were entitled in the friendly coöperation to which we supposed we were invited was withheld.

These papers are a series of reports made by various provincial officers, of the attempts at negotiation by Mr. McLane and Sir John Bowring, in 1854, as well in this neighborhood, with the viceroy Iliang, (who in 1853 had met Mr. Marshall,) as afterwards, when those gentlemen went to the Gulf of Pechele and attempted to visit Tientsin. What adds very much to the interest of these papers is, that they bear the autograph annotations of the Emperor himself, and are accompanied with his decrees, all of which were regularly sent to Yeh at Canton, to invigorate his obstinate repugnance to intercourse with foreigners. Some of these annotations and decrees are very curious, and will, no doubt, attract your attention.

In the memorial of Hu Nai-chau to the throne, dated 30th June, 1854, he ventured to say that if the foreign ministers should happen to propose any measure "positively beneficial to China," he might be disposed to grant it. This is indignantly italicised with the vermillion pencil, and for its utterance the writer was immediately degraded by the Emperor, and his successors admonished, in the decree of the 15th July, (for there seems to have been great promptitude in these means of repression,) that in case they had been duped into any concession "beneficial to China," they must at once repudiate it, and not be misled by such absurdity! Such revelations are very striking.

Aside from these matters, interesting generally to foreigners, there are many disclosures especially so to us. There is one, very illustrative of perverse ratiocination, and, at the same time, of the danger of allowing stipulations supposed to be immaterial, entering into treaties or other compacts with them. In the treaty of Wanghia there is a provision (Article 34) that no individual State of the United States can appoint or send a minister to China to call in question the provisions of the treaty. This, though utterly insignificant in its application to the United States, was, I have understood, inserted to gratify some whim of Keying, the negotiator of 1844. You will now observe, in several parts of these papers, that the Chinese put a very mischievous interpretation on this unmeaning clause, as preventing any alteration in the treaty itself. I am very glad I struck the clause out of the treaty of Tientsin, though, at the time, I was not aware of this misinterpretation. Unmeaning words are always troublesome.

I regret to say that I see nothing in these papers to countenance the belief that the Chinese take any very clear distinction between the United States and other nations; and the tone adopted to Mr. McLane may be regarded as especially offensive when it is remembered that it was through his agency the duty question at Shanghai was settled and a large amount of money paid into the local imperial treasury by American merchants, while not one dollar, to this day, has ever been paid by other nations.

The revelation generally is a very sad one. It unsettles confidence in the future. No one holding intercourse with their public men can have the least reliance on his words or acts being described with anything approaching to truthfulness. In one sense, it seems, the Emperor knows and directs everything. In another, he knows nothing. Spies at Canton report to him Sir John Bowring's alarm and perturbation lest a Russian fleet should take Hong Kong; and then the actual reality of the war is discredited, because, in the language of one of these papers, the English officials were at the time "jaunting it about China."

It is in this connection that I am free to say these papers have made an impression on my mind differing widely from those expressed in some of my previous dispatches.

The doubts heretofore expressed as to a permanent diplomatic residence at Pekin fade away in the very unpleasant light shed by these intercepted documents. There is, I am now convinced, no other security for anything like honest counsel reaching the imperial mind. No western diplomatic involvements (of which I confess I have a great dread) can so refract truth as always will the pernicious atmosphere which now surrounds the court; and I slowly and almost reluctantly yield to the conviction that, if American interests in China are worth protecting, it can only be done by direct representation at the capital.

One other impression is very distinctly made by these papers. They, in a great measure, justify the coercive policy pursued by the allies in the north. I do not think that Lord Elgin could have acted differenty on the assumption which such disclosures as these seem almost to authorize, that the rules of public law applicable to nations civilized and christianized cannot be made to apply here. I should have said and thought this earlier, had the confidence of the belligerent plenipotentiaries been less restricted and the whole truth told to us.

So soon as the tariff conferences are concluded, I shall communicate the results fully to you.

I have the honor to be, sir, your most obedient servant,

WILLIAM B. REED.

Hon. LEWIS CASS,
Secretary of State.

Exhibit 1.

PROCLAMATION OF KWEILIANG AND OTHERS, IMPERIAL COMMISSIONERS.

OCTOBER 9, 1858.

KWEILIANG, Chief Secretary of State, Superintendent of the Board of Punishment, &c., &c.; HWASHANA, President of the Board of Civil Office, &c.; MINGSHEN, high officer of the second grade belonging to the Household; and TWAN, a titular President and Member of the General Council, hereby issue their plain proclamation:

Whereas, China and the three countries of England, America, and France, having when we were at Tientsin negotiated and established the terms of an enduring peace, it is our duty, lest the fact should not be generally known to the gentry, merchants, and people, to issue a notification thereof.

Let it therefore be known to them and others at the ports, that China and these nations are now on the most friendly terms of enduring peace, and it is our earnest desire that all may enjoy pleasure and advantage therefrom. Let there be no disobedience on your part.

A proclamation for general information.

Exhibit 2.

KWEILIANG, ETC., TO MR. REED.

OCTOBER 16, 1858.

KWEILIANG, Chief Secretary of State, &c.; HWASHANA, President of the Board of Civil Office, &c.; Ho KWEI-TSING, Governor General of the two Kiang, &c.; and MINGSHEN, an officer of the second rank in the Household, &c., and TWAN, a titular Member of the General Council, herewith communicate on business:

We have to-day been personally informed by Sieh, acting intendant of the Su-Sung-tai circuit and provincial judge, that he yesterday received a dispatch from the American Consul Smith, informing him that your excellency had returned to Shanghai, on the 10th instant.

We, having received his Majesty's orders to consult upon and settle the details of the tariff, reached this city on the 5th instant. We designated Wang and Sieh, the provincial treasurer and judge, as our deputies to meet Mr. Olyphant and his colleagues on the part of the English. They have met from time to time, and report that they have deliberated on all the chief points. We now accordingly request your excellency immediately to appoint suitable persons to meet Wang and Sieh to discuss these affairs. When they have respectively reported upon their progress, we can decide upon the subject, and bring the whole to a conclusion.

His Excellency W. B. Reed,
United States Minister Plenipotentiary, &c.

Exhibit 3.

MR. REED TO KWEILIANG, ETC.

Legation of the United States,
Shanghai, October 21, 1858.

The undersigned, in answer to your excellencies' communication of the 16th instant, requesting him to appoint some one to confer with the representative of your excellency and Lord Elgin on the subject of the tariff, begs to say, that at this moment he does not think it expedient to do so, the consultation on the matter being, as he understands, nearly completed.

The undersigned is happy to learn from a communication of the 19th instant, that he shall soon have the pleasure of receiving a visit from your excellencies.

W. B. REED.

Kweiliang, Hwashana, Ho Kwei-Tsing, Mingshen, and Twan,
Imperial Commissioners, &c.

Exhibit 4.

MR. REED TO KWEILIANG, ETC.

Legation of the United States,
Shanghai, October 18, 1858.

The undersigned, envoy extraordinary and minister plenipontentiary of the United States to China, makes this respectful communication to their excellencies.

Having already informed them of his return to Shanghai, he will have great pleasure in receiving them, either at his temporary residence here, or on board the United States steam frigate Minnesota, now at anchor near Woosung, on any day and hour agreeable to their excellencies. He desires to renew with their excellencies those assurances of friendship and good will which were interchanged at Tientsin, and which matured in a treaty of amity and peace, which will, he hopes, long maintain the friendly relations now existing.

The undersigned has also to acknowledge the receipt of their excellencies' communication of the 16th instant on business, and will shortly have the honor to answer it.

The undersigned presents to their excellencies the assurance of his most distinguished consideration.

WILLIAM B. REED.

Exhibit 5.

KWEILIANG, ETC., TO MR. REED.

OCTOBER 19, 1858.

KWEILIANG, HWASHANA, HO KWEI-TSING, MINGSHEN, and TWAN, &c., &c., hereby send a reply:

We have the honor to acknowledge your excellency's dispatch of the 18th instant, in which you remark as follows:

"He desires to renew with their excellencies those assurances of friendship and good-will which were interchanged at Tientsin, and which matured in a treaty of peace and amity, which will, he hopes, long maintain the friendly relations now existing. He will have great pleasure in receiving them at his temporary residence here, on any day and hour agreeable to their excellencies," &c., &c.

From this, we clearly perceive your excellency's feelings of cordial good-will, at which we are much pleased, and while we shall have much pleasure in meeting as proposed, we beg a delay before appointing the time to go to your residence, and will send you a special communication upon the subject. For this purpose we now reply.

His Excellency WILLIAM B. REED,
Envoy Extraordinary and Minister Plenipotentiary of the United States to China.

Inclosure No. 6 *to Dispatch No.* 33, *October* 21, 1858.

Memorials and rescripts pertaining to the efforts of the British and American plenipotentiaries to obtain a revision of treaties, obtained in the office of Yeh, at the capture of Canton, in December, 1857.

HER MAJESTY'S SHIP FURIOUS,
[Mem.] *Shanghai, April* 10, 1858.

1. The papers of which the following are translations are part of the correspondence between the Emperor and his ministers concerned, upon the attempt made in 1854, by Sir John Bowring and the United States commissioner, Mr. McLane, to extend our trade and place our relations with China on a more satisfactory footing.

These documents were inclosed to Yeh, their imperial commissioner, for his information, accompanied by decrees for the guidance of himself and others. They may be divided into two sections—the first embracing the period before the expedition of the foreign ministers to the Peiho; and the second that after their arrival at the mouth of that river.

In order to a just estimate of the immovableness, either proper to or assumed by the court of Pekin, under circumstances which we have been elsewhere led to suppose occasioned it considerable embarrassment, we should recall the apparently desperate condition of things within the empire at the time the foreign ministers were in some sort menacing her from without, not only as in evidence at places distant from the capital, but as admitted and proclaimed by the government gazette.

Independently of the almost chronic disorders afflicting the far west provinces of China, the rebellion specially known as that of Tai-ping Wang had, in 1852, swept all before it, from Kwang-si, through Hu Nan and Hu Peh, to the Yang tsze Kiang, and down that stream, through every jurisdiction traversed by it, to Chin-Kiang, the point of its intersection by the grand canal. From this, as a center, a powerful detachment had made a rapid and successful movement north in the summer of 1853, maintaining itself within 80 miles of Pekin, on the borders of Tien-tsin Fu, until the spring of 1854; and, although then compelled to retire slowly upon Shau Tung, reinforced there by a large body of insurgents from the south. Rebellion was meanwhile closing round Canton; Kiangsi was disturbed, especially towards the north; and in Kiangsu the authorities, with difficulty holding their own before Chin Kiang and Nankin, had in their rear a separate and serious cause of alarm in the occupation of Shanghai by a gang of Canton and Fuh-Kien men, declaring for the Taiping party, and countenanced, if not supported, by foreigners, who, most incompatibly, according to imperialist notions, with their strong professions of neutrality, had more than once placed themselves in communication with the insurgent garrisons of Nankin and Chin Kiang. The provincial government could not but charge to the same account the constant misunderstandings on the subject of duties at Shanghai, resulting in non-payment of any for a considerable period of time, and the frequent collision of foreigners with the troops investing Shanghai, one of which had terminated in the seizure of a marine and the expulsion of the land force from its encampments.

This last affair had cost the governor, Hu Nai-chau, and intendant, Wû, otherwise Samqua, who was also superintendent of customs, their buttons of rank.

With the exception of the recovery of Amoy from a local gang of much the same claims to political *status* as the Shanghai rebels, and the very deliberate retreat, which the gazettes represented as a flight, of the Taiping northern corps from Chih Li into Shan Tung, every recent event, every announcement from its officers, whether conducting war or collecting revenue, should have added, according to our valuation of causes, to a conviction on the part of government that things were getting worse instead of better. Yet the correspondence here translated—which is much of it marked confidential, none of it published, none of it, consequently, designed to aid in keeping up appearances before the public—betrays, on the whole, far less of fear than of a sense of annoyance at the intrusive impertinence of the barbarian. He is mischievous and *méchant*, rather than dangerous, and the utmost he may declare himself about to attempt is never assumed by the Emperor to be beyond restraint by menace or remonstrance. The mere suggestion of conciliating him is reprobated as undignified, and concession, even in the forms of intercourse, is strictly prohibited. And this, although the authorities memorializing the throne, however much they may have otherwise modified the offence of failing to keep the barbarian more in hand, had certainly reported various of his acts, of which, even could it have heard the *pars altera*, the court of Pekin would have found it difficult to accept his justification, and which, as it stood advised, it could scarcely regard otherwise than as indicating an intention to make the most of the domestic troubles of the empire.

The conduct of the Chinese on this occasion may be somewhat explained by the observation that, although more or less bewildered by their uncertainty as to our particular object, they had faith in our adherence to the policy they lay to our charge, namely, of abandoning the chase as soon as we perceive that satisfaction of our demands is not to be obtained from them by entreaty or intimidation.

2. The *dramatis personæ* here appearing on the Chinese side are—

1st. Iliang, a Manchu, long governor general of the provinces of Kiangsu, Ngan Hwui, and Kiangsi, which together form the jurisdiction of the Liang Kiang, or Two Kiang. He has but very lately retired, and is now (April, 1858) replaced by Ho Kwei-tsing. The proper residence of this officer is Nankin, but rebellion has kept him for the last five years either at Soo-chow or Chang-chow.

2d. Hu Nai-chau, governor of Kiangsu, a man of high literary repute. He has four brothers, all of whom are equally distinguished. One of them, Hü Nai-tsi, was degraded during the early discussions on the opium traffic, for immorally recommending its legalization. Hü Nai-chau had been, at the time of this correspondence, for some months before Shanghai, vainly endeavoring to retake it from the rebels. The gossips of the camp did not put his abilities as an official at all above the Emperor's estimate of them.

3d. Kirhanga, a Manchu, and connected with the imperial family, who had come to Kiangsu in 1853 as an acting intendant, and in one twelve-month had risen, principally on the ruins of Hü Nai-chau, to be governor of the province. He was in immediate charge of military operations, to the conduct of which he was very incompetent. An attack, made by the French under Admiral Laguerre, having frightened the rebel garrison into abandonment of Shanghai, Kirhanga gathered all the laurels of its recapture. He was sent as high commissioner to command the force before Chin Kiang, and was there killed in 1855.

4th. Wû Kien-chang, otherwise known as Samqua, an ex-hong merchant of Canton, and thoroughly Cantonese in his ideas regarding foreign policy. The barbarian was a trading person to be kept within walls. Certain Canton and Fuh-Kien men, well-known members of an affiliated society, compelled him to take them into his pay as a bodyguard, and in a few days took the city of Shanghai in which he resided. He was at this time intendant of the circuit in which Shanghai stands, and superintendent of the customs. He contrived to make his superiors accept his statement that he was not within the city when it fell; the fact being that he had been for two days in the hands of his fellow-Cantonese, who then connived at his escape into the foreign settlement. His rank, which had cost him some £40,000, was eventually taken from him on the occasion of a collision between foreigners and the besieging force; and, on charges subsequently preferred against him of embezzlement and mal-administration, he was sentenced to severe punishment. His friends have brought him through, and he is now again an expectant of the office of intendant, with the honorary rank of commissioner of finance. He is cunning, but not able, either as a merchant or a public servant.

5th. Lau-wei-wau, Samqua's acting successor as intendant, and as determined an anti-barbarian, but a polished and, *à la Chinoise*, a well-educated Chinese, sagacious and capable. He has been recently degraded, to rise no more, for appropriating some £70,000 of public receipts, on which he had hoped to retire into private life.

6th. The members of the great council, literally the council of war, which is composed of the secretaries of state, presidents and vice-presidents of boards, and other metropolitan officials, selected specially by the Emperor, irrespectively of nationality, Manchu, Mongolian, or Chinese. Its functions are the preparation and transmission or promulgation of the Emperor's decisions, and the advising of his Majesty in all important matters of peace or war. Except when ordered to act as assessors, the members of the council appear to exercise no judicial functions. Their relation to the head of the state must be regarded as more intimate than in the case of any other court, confidential instructions occasionally passing through their hands without being communicated even to the *nui-koh*, or cabinet, the chiefs of which, however, before spoken of as secretaries of state, are, as has been observed, members of the great council. They have a separate hall of assembly, but according to the a certain number attend daily within the forbidden precinct of the palace, waiting to be called before the Emperor. This may happen once in the day, or more than once. A mat or cushion is placed for them to sit upon in the imperial presence—I believe their exclusive privilege—and they either submit drafts of decrees to be issued in the name of the Emperor, or, on occasion, receive his opinion in the autograph vermilion pencil upon the face of documents already before him. In the case of extra-metropolitan correspondence, at least, the original memorial appears always to be returned to the high officer from whom it came. It bears some notice in the vermilion pencil, for which some folds of blank paper are left at the close. When the copy is to be what we term a decree, it is drafted and copied on a separate sheet by the council, and then apparently submitted to the Emperor. One such document (that written in 1856 regarding Dr. Parker's rumored attempt to reopen the revision of treaty question) showed an erasure of one character by the vermilion pencil, and a substitution for it of another signifying "confidential." This is transmitted with the original memorial returned in a cover bearing the seal of the council, none of whose names appear in the note advising the officer addressed of their instructions to write to him.

THOMAS WADE,
Chinese Secretary.

I.

[Translation.]

Supplemental memorial of Hu Nai-Chau, *dated about the* 30*th June*, 1854.

Further, since the severe blow (lit. sore extermination) inflicted on them by the troops on the 5th moon, (23d June, 1854,) now seven days ago, the Shanghai rebels have lain perdu.

The bravest and most fighting rebels they have in the city, it appears, are from Chau-Chau.* Next are those from the department of Kwang-chau, (Canton,) and the men of Fuh-kien.

The squatters from the districts of Chuen-sha and Nau-hwui include also † people from Tung-au in Fuh-kien, (the district adjoining Amoy,) and from Ping-yang, in Cheh Kiang, who have left their homes for the sea-board flats of Chuen-sha and Nau-hwui. On these they had been used to support themselves by growing the *sháu-yü*, (a kind of potato,) but last year, when search was being made for the residue of the rebel gang already suppressed in that district, the inhabitants, erroneously conceiving that some were concealed in the huts of these people, set fire to them, and a thousand and more, thus left without a place of safety, went into Shanghai [prepared] to hold it for the rebels to the death.

Orders have been given to Sieh Ping, formerly acting magistrate of King-ki, to proceed to Chuen-sha and Nau-hwui, and, in concert with the sub-prefect and magistrate, to convene the upright and respectable gentry and literates of the place in question, and invite them to inform themselves thoroughly of the [former] positions of these squatters, and at the same time to notify to them that they will be permitted to tender their allegiance and return to their original districts to be good subjects for evermore. The squatters, hearing of this, have been breaking up, and coming out daily; and the men of Fuh-kien, Kwang Tung, and Ning-po as well, having heard the same report, continue to surrender themselves. There are chambers (committees) of [loyal persons representing] each of these provinces, the heads of which faithfully respond, [for such as do come out,] distinguishing which are to be sent away, and which detained [for service.]

Such matters properly belong to the supplementary arrangements consequent upon the recapture of the city, when it shall be taken; but, seeing that, were the rebels not to disperse until after the assault, the number who would resist would be great, and

---

* The Eastern Department of Kwang Tung.
† That is, besides natives of those districts.

the killed and wounded necessarily numerous in proportion, it is desirable that they should disperse before the assault. As there would in that case be fewer resisting, the number killed and wounded would also be small. It has been observed that on every occasion, for some time past, that an attack has been made with the firm determination of taking the city, its capture has been prevented by a sudden storm of rain; and it is possibly the purpose of Providence that the rebels should not resist our imposing force in great numbers, as the result would be the destruction of a large number of the innocent.

[The Emperor interlines in the vermilion pencil, "was there ever such * cant."] Being at present without the means of defraying their expenses home [your servant] does not venture to call on them to come out *en masse*. All he can do is to let them break up by degrees, and so weaken the strength [of the garrison.]

As regards the secret attack on the city, advantage will be taken of these dark moonless nights to observe at what point the besieged are most off their guard, and the mines will be pressed forward under the wall with all speed. A general attack will then be made on different points, and success, it is hoped, will be absolutely certain.

Tc. To come to another matter: Towards the end of the fifth moon, the English barbarians were very eager to drive away the Shanghai rebels; whither, the troops were not to ask. Their object was not comprehensible at the time. It has since been discovered that, according to the statement † of persons in the barbarian office on the Yang King Pang, (the foreign factories or consulates,) their chief [Sir John Bowring] had been informed of an attempt about to be made by the soldiers of Russia upon Hong Kong, the garrison of which place hardly amounted to a thousand men, a force insufficient, even with the assistance of the five ships brought by the [British] admiral, for its defence against the Russian troops, and that he wanted to complete his strength with the rebels, and to show a better front. ‡ As Kirhanga and the other officers did observe at the time that this chief appeared perturbed and excited, it would seem that the report was not altogether without foundation. The other day the English chief said himself that the steamer had brought news of a victory in Turkey and the capture of two Russian vessels, and he seemed to be at his ease.

Since Wû Kien-chang's § return to Shanghai from Kwan Shau, he has been day after day demanding of the English and American chiefs the duties received by them for him from the eighth moon of last year to the fifth of the present. (September, 1853, to July, 1854.) They say that they will be all forthcoming, but that Shanghai must be retaken before they can be paid in.

These chiefs also ask, "As it will be so much to the advantage of China to get rid of the rebels and to have the duties as well, why does your government persist in requiring the surrender of the criminals

* Lit. "What false humbugging notion equals this?" The word which qualifies the notion is one used especially of priests' stories told to gull the multitude, or the like; but there is almost as much stupidity implied by it as intention to deceive.

† Or, spies have since ascertained.

‡ Literally, strengthen the dignity of his army, or add to the awe that it should inspire.

§ Wû Kien-chang is Samqua.

who killed officials? Will it not delay the issue [you desire?]" They propose to insist on sending away in safety the whole of the leaders, great and small. *

A communication came yesterday from the English chief † proposing a conference on business, at the barbarian office, on the 9th of the moon, and your servant has written to agree to this. Not that, capricious and inconsistent as [he knows] these barbarians to be, he is going to exceed in concession; but that it is his duty, in every case, to weigh well the advantage and disadvantage of this or that order of proceeding, and *should there be any measure positively beneficial to China, and at the same time practicable, without violation of the law, he would assuredly not presume to abide in the smallest degree by standing prejudices.* ‡

The red-side junks from Kwang Tung are reported to have arrived at Wusung, and will of course be desired to hasten on to Chin Kiang. The expenses of these vessels, Yeh, governor general of the two Kwang, writes to promise shall be defrayed monthly from Kwang Tung.

Knowing the anxiety bestowed by your Majesty [on the matters herein detailed] your servant, as in duty bound, presents a supplementary memorial thereupon.

A respectful memorial.

Translated by

THOMAS WADE,
Chinese Secretary.

II.

Translation of the Imperial Decree commenting on Hu Nai-chau's timidity in dealing with the barbarians; on the intercourse of the latter with the rebels, and their unauthorized appearance in the interior. Yeh is to lecture them.

[Translation.]

Letter from the members of the Great Council to YEH, *Imperial Commissioner and Governor General of the Two Kwang.*

On the 13th of the 6th moon of the 4th year of Hien-fung, (7th July, 1854,) we had the honor to receive the following imperial decree.

---

*This is an allusion to certain communications upon the possibility of getting rid of the rebels through our means. The great imperialist difficulty was the pardon or connivance at the escape of two rebels who were concerned in the murder of the late magistrate of Shanghai. The rebels, on their part, were much too confident at this time to listen to offers of mediation.

†Sir John Bowring was still at Shanghai, and did receive Hu Nai-chau at the consulate.

‡He would feel it his duty not to hesitate about taking a line of his own. Literally, he would not dare in the least degree to retain the ready-made view, the *idée fixe*, not his own, but that of China, in respect of concession to the barbarian. The Emperor was by no means pleased with this deprecatory passage. The whole of the text *italicized* in the translation is scored with the vermilion pencil, and the conduct of Hu Nai-chau, as will be presently seen in another paper, was severely criticized by his Majesty.

"Iliang and his colleagues had been representing to us that the American barbarians wanted (or were about to sail up the Yangtsze Kiang, to have an interview with the governor general; and, according to a subsequent representation made by Kishen, the vessels of these barbarians did pass by way of Chin-Kiang, anchored off Pu-Káu, and subsequently off Kiva-chau, where they entered into close relations * with the rebels.

"The English barbarians, meanwhile, were offering every kind of hindrance atShanghai, [to the siege operations,] their malice going even greater lengths [than that of the Americans.] Our troops were in pursuit of the enemy, when, for no particular reason, they had the authority to fire on a Chá-chau militiaman, whom they wounded. Notwithstanding this, [though they were the aggressors,] they presented themselves at the headquarters [of the force] and demanded the surrender of the man who had returned the shot. They had further proposed to carry the Shanghai rebels elsewhere, or, if this were not acceded to, to proceed to Tientsin. Hu Nai-chau asked where they were going to take the rebels, and expressed his fears that they would create further disorder in some other province. He told them also that the two rebels guilty of the murder of officials must be surrendered to him. † The barbarians would not consent to this; so far from it, they sent a person to dictate a dispatch, which he was to write so worded as to make it appear that [on the occasion above named] the first fire had been delivered by his troops, for whose offense he was to apologize. ‡ If he did not write in these terms, it was added the camps should be attacked the following day. Most overbearing violence! The governor in question, apprehending that they [the English] were seeking a quarrel, and that trouble would come of it, did write in the terms prescribed, therein doing nothing short of providing a weapon against himself. ||

"For his cowardice and incompetence, we have taken his insignia of rank from Hu Nai-chau, but the affairs of Shanghai [rebel and foreign] are still unsettled. This mismanagement of them is truly deplorable.

"As regards [access to] the seaports of China, barbarians have never been authorized to visit any but the five open to trade. Of late, however, their vessels, in wanton defiance of law, have been proceeding, some to Chin-Kiang and some to Nankin, where they have been visiting the rebels—a manifest infraction of the treaty. With relations of peace and commerce between them and China, why do the barbarians hold intercourse with the rebels? It is certainly not in the spirit of friendly relations [so to do.] Then again, there is war upon the river. If barbarians [navigating it] were to be accidentally wounded by gun or musket, our troops could not be held answerable. Let Yeh Ming-chin set before the barbarian chiefs Bowring and Sterling,

* Literally went and came and made a league, or confederated with them.

† See paper I, note *, page 449.

‡ The militiaman in question did take a shot at one of the marines who was under arms for the protection of the foreign settlement during one of the many wretched fights between the Shanghai rebels and the besieging force. Admiral Sterling happened to be on the ground, and insisted on apology being made.

|| Literally presenting people the handle [of an offensive weapon.]

in peremptory language and plain terms, the risk [so incurred.] He will surely be able to stay their malice before it can develop itself.* It was but on the 16th of the 3d moon (14th April) that Bowring arrived in Kwang Tung; yet, on the 25th (15th?) of the 6th moon, he comes up to Shanghai with a ship-of-war, and on the 23d, detaches the barbarian chief Medhurst, with a steamer, to Chin-Kiang. How comes it, if they really have a war with Russia,† that [the English] can be jaunting it about China (or in the interior?) Everything shows that they are concealing a dangerous purpose. (Lit. A heart of woe, or danger.)

"Yeh Ming-chin has special charge of barbarian business. Let him enjoy [the English chief] to keep the treaty, and desire him to signify to the barbarians at Shanghai, that they are not to travel about as seems to them good; and let him (Yeh) declare authoritatively that at every port along the shores of the river (Yangtsze) there is a large force, and that if they are not amenable to [their chief's] control, and that life is taken by the act of our troops, the calamity thus brought upon themselves is not to be laid to our charge. This will make them aware that we do not regard the beginning of strife (the first blow) with alarm, and they will no longer venture on these demonstrations of daily increasing ferocity.‡ The governor general, we should imagine, will surely be enabled, by careful attention, so to lay his plans as to nip the danger in the bud.

"Let him at the same time lay his commands with equal earnestness upon the American and French barbarians. Let him also, from time to time, report to us whether there be any authentic intelligence of recent proceedings on the part of the Russians.

"Let copies of Hu Nai-chau's memorial and his two communications [with the barbarians] be furnished [to Yeh] for his information, and let this decree be hurried forward to him at the rate of six hundred *li* a day, with commands to him to attend to it. Respect this!"

In obedience to his Majesty's will this letter is sent.

Translated by THOMAS WADE,
Chinese Secretary.

NOTE.—Hawk-like, to spread [their wings].

NOTE.—It is remarkable that the docket of the above decree, which was issued in July, 1854, records its receipt on the 4th December, 1855. There is nothing to account for this. The words translated "hurried forward" are those of the form by which the greatest speed attainable by the courier office is meant to be insisted on.

T. W.

The communication touching treatment of foreign ministers from the government of China, contained in the decree of August, 1854, proves that the supercilious bearing of the Chinese Imperial Commis-

* Lit. Block the way of their malice in its budding.

† Lit. A difficulty. The declaration of war reached Shanghai by Sir James Sterling in June, 1854. Mr. Medhurst was sent to Nankin in the same month.

‡ They will not then venture with daily increasing extravagance.

sioner Yeh, was deliberate and performed under instructions. Therefore, it should become the duty of our government to insist on free and equal intercourse and to enforce it hereafter.

III.

Memorial of ILIANG, Governor General of the Two Kiang, reporting the visit of Mr. McLANE, United States Commissioner, and his success in dissuading Mr. McLANE from proceeding to the Peiho, dated about the 24th June, 1854:

[Translation.]

Your slave, Iliang, governor general of the Two Kiang, upon his knees addresses the throne.

The course pursued by him [in his reception of] the American chief, who had come to Kwanshau to pay his respects to him, he respectfully details in a confidential memorial, whereon, looking upwards, he prays for the sacred glance.

He has already had the honor, as it is recorded, to submit to the sacred glance a memorial, showing that a report had been sent up by Wú Kien-chang, intendant of the Su-sing-tai circuit, to the effect that the barbarian chief, McLane, of the United States of America, otherwise the American,* had come with two war steamers to Shanghai, and, after humbly† begging for an interview and tendering a communication, had gone up to Ningpo (Nankin?) and Chin-kiang, to look about him; and that your slave had thereon written to the proper authorities to be on their guard.

The magistrates of the districts of Tau-tu, Shang-yuen, Luh-hoh, Kiangpu, and Tang-tu have since reported that the above-mentioned barbarian vessels had visited Kiang-ning, (Nankin,) Ho-chau, and Wu-hu. They anchored, on their way back, at Tsiaú-spau, and a communication was forwarded to your slave, through the hands of the marine stationed off Chin-kiang, requesting him to meet [the writer] there.

Your slave replied that the Long river, (sc. the Yangtsze,) not being open to foreign trade, barbarian vessels had no right to stay there. If the chief desired to present a letter from his government in person, he should follow the precedent [furnished] last year by the case of Marshall; hasten back to Shanghai, and there wait till Wú Kien-chang should bring him to Kwan-shau to introduce him.

In obedient accordance with the above reply, the chief did presently turn back, and, having transferred himself to a native vessel, was brought, on the twenty-fifth of the fifth moon, (20th June,) to Kwan-shau by Wú Kien-chang, accompanied by his subordinates Lau Wei-wau, prefect of the Sung-kiangfu, and sub-prefect of maritime defenses.

---

* Mi-li-kin, the Canton pronunciation of American.

† As a person petitioning.

Your slave, having with him Pinghau, the acting prefect of Su-chaufu, long employed in that department, and thoroughly versed in business, had started from Su-chau on the 24th, and also arriving at Kwan-shau on the 25th, on the following day assembled the officials present in the public hall of Kwan-shau, and summoned* the chief to come forward and pay his respects. The chief's manner, it must be admitted,† was reverential. "Thanks to the favor," he said, "of his Celestial Majesty, by which the five ports are open to trade, we‡ have been enabled to steep ourselves in advantage. Of late years, however, the river communications have become impassable,|| and the losses hence sustained by the merchants have determined us to request that his Majesty be entreated graciously to permit us to trade along the Yangtsze Kiang. The merchandise we bring up the river, we will ourselves escort and protect. If [your excellency] will not do me the honor to make a representation for me to this effect to the throne, I shall be obliged to proceed to Tientsin."

Your slave told him authoritatively§ that the treaty under which the five ports were open to trade being that to which the imperial assent, as made known by decree, had been received with reference in the 24th year of Tâu Kwang, (1844,) it had become the duty of all alike, native and foreigner, officials and people, to observe it obediently [from that time forth] for evermore. It was besides clearly laid down in the treaty¶ that "no State shall hereafter send a minister to China to raise separate (or fresh) discussions." The request now preferred being at variance with the original treaty, could not well be conveyed to your Majesty. As to Tientsin, the Canton rebels had worked (had wormed or burrowed) their way across the Chih Li frontier. The people of the place become as a wall by the unanimity of their resolution, and, fighting boldly on the side of government,** had disciplined above 100,000 men. The rebels had several times attempted to reconnoiter, [their positions,] but had never carried their point. Were the barbarians so ill advised as to take their vessels thither, and the people, as might be apprehended, to be filled with misgiving, and to do them, as was possible, a mischief, it would not concern the [Chinese] government. The governor general of Chih Li, having no cognizance of barbarian affairs, would probably not grant the chief an interview; so that if he went to Tientsin, he would still gain nothing

---

* Called him up, as he would a party in a civil action, or a witness in any.

† Lit. The chief, in his adherence to forms, or in the forms he adhered to, was, notwithstanding, reverential; that is, notwithstanding the tone of his letters and his proceedings earlier noticed, we should say "was, I must say, respectful enough."

‡ There is nothing in the text to represent the pronoun; I assume him to speak for his nation.

|| Owing to the rebellion.

§ Told him as his official superior, commanded him, saying, &c.

¶ He quotes article 34 and last of the American treaty. I have translated the words as I believe Iliang meant the Emperor to understand them. In the original they represent the following English: "And no individual State *of the United States* can appoint or send a minister to China to call in question the provisions of the same." It suits Iliang to ignore the words italicized.

** Literally were hating as their authorities hated, and were courageous in fight. The population of the department rendered government important assistance by checking the advance of the rebels upon Pekin, in the winter of 1853–54. They never got beyond its western boundary.

by it. Several complete victories had been obtained over the rebels in the north. All those defeated, and hiding north of the [Yellow] river, had been exterminated. There could hardly fail to be peace presently. The water communications thereby reopened, trade would be sure to revive, and there would then be no need for discussing alterations and extensions.

The chief replied that he, too, was aware that the war in China was not over, and that this was the reason why he did not presume to give your sacred Majesty cause of anxiety, by proceeding direct to Tien-tsin; but it had been inserted in the treaty that a revision of this should be allowed after a lapse of twelve years, the expiry of which term was now not far distant. Several things were not as they should be. At Shanghai, for instance, the custom-house had been transferred to Wu-sung, and [its business was conducted under] other than the old regulations.* As plenipotentiary minister, he had full powers to do what might seem to him good. If the authorities of the Kiang provinces (Iliang, &c.) were not competent in matters affecting the old treaty, he had to request that application be made to your Majesty to send hither a minister of large powers, with whom he might bring negotiations to a definite issue.

Your slave told him authoritatively, that with reference to the treaty clause† respecting "inconsiderable modifications that may be found requisite in those parts [of the treaty] that relate to commerce and navigation," the twelve years ought first to expire, and readjustment then be fairly and equitably considered; that, in the words [representing] navigation,‡ passage up rivers or by land is in no way whatever included, while by "inconsiderable modifications," nothing is meant but that in the case of the five ports there should be, as occasion might require, a certain discussion of regulations it might be essential to adopt; not, certainly, that any great alteration should take place. It had been further most clearly laid down in a special article,‖ at the time that the treaty was made, that no vessel should enter any but the five ports, under penalty of confiscation of both vessel and cargo. The new custom-house at Wu-sung had been opened there for the time pending military operations at Shanghai, but was levying no extra duties whatever; and on the recapture of the city, which would be effected immediately, all the old [customs] arrangements would be restored. If foreign merchants had really any hardships to complain of, there was nothing to prevent a fair [statement of these] to the superintendent of maritime customs, and a satisfactory understanding with him thereupon.

[As to the appointment of a commissioner] in the administration of the Celestial Empire, the distance between the sovereign and his

---

* Mr. McLane's interpreter was a Canton Chinese, of whose powers I have a poor opinion. He has here, I suspect, caused a confusion of two things. A provisional custom-house had been opened on the 9th of February, 1854, on the Wu-Sung river, or, as we call it, the Su-Chau creek. The detection of the superintendent, Wu Kienchang, otherwise Samqua, in the act of clearing a foreign vessel by private arrangement, led to its suspension on the 21st of March. Samqua had, on that very day, opened two custom-houses *inland*, and it was against this breach of a treaty provision that Mr. McLane was remonstrating.

† Article 34 American treaty.

‡ The Chinese is "circumstances of the sea," or "sea details."

‖ Article 3 American treaty.

servants is too great to admit of such an officer as a plenipotentiary.* The imperial commissioner [stationed] in Kwang Tung for the superintendence of foreign affairs, (lit. the business of the different nations,) being in effect a minister sent [thither] by your Majesty, it would be importunity† to request anything further on this point.

The chief continuing to insist on what he had already urged, your slave set before him [the obligation of] good faith and justice; thrice and again he pointed out to him the right course to follow; from the third watch of the day till the seventh, ten hours and more. The chief debated no longer, but persisted in his entreaty, until, it being nearly sunset, he took his leave.

On the 27th he forwarded a duplicate of the letter of his government. It was much to the same effect as that presented by Marshall last year. It contained nothing whatever regarding permission to trade up the Yangtsze Kiang. He also handed in a communication in very obscure phraseology,‡ characters in which had been taken to signify what they did not properly mean. On the whole it differed nothing from the language he had employed, except in the addition that if, on representation made to the throne, he should be honored by [your Majesty's] assent to his requests, it would behoove him, of course, to assist China in completely removing her cause of disquiet;|| otherwise he should address his government and follow his own course, the government of China bearing the responsibility of its short-coming in the discharge of obligations§ recognized by itself, and he requested the abolition of the new custom-house at Shanghai.

It is the very humble opinion of your slave, that, inasmuch as the American barbarians, heretofore accounted so submissive, have taken advantage of the present conjuncture to press their demands, reliance is surely not be placed on their coöperation, though they promise it, in the restoration of order. The example set by these barbarians in the propositions they have brought forward will but too probably be followed, and to a more serious extent, by the English and French barbarians. "The Long river is the bound prescribed by Heaven;" to bring "a foreign race to dwell hard by" is to insure calamity in the time to come.¶

On the other hand, the English barbarians have been picking quarrels with the troops on several occasions of late. There is withal a story current that the Nankin rebels have worked their way to Ting-pa, and are disturbing that neighborhood, and men's ears and eyes are not to be stopped.** It might be bearing too hard on this chief, (McLane,)

---

* Lit. the ruler is exalted, the minister is humble, or low in rank; there is not at all a plenipotentiary minister.

† Lit: separately, or indistinct form, to make an important request, would not be correct.

‡ Tangled or knotted, like a bunch of cords tied at random together.

|| Lit: in planing or cutting smooth away the restless, viz: the rebels; I doubt that Mr. McLane offered to do more than mediate.

§ Lit: the fault of not exhausting its own [moral] policy, which, says a native assistant, dictates relations of courtesy and equality between the host and the stranger.

¶ Both the passages marked by inverted commas are quotations from historical writings. The first has special reference to what is now the Kiang Nan country in the time of the Three States, A. D. 150, and was used in argument against attempting invasion of a region provided with so impassable a barrier by nature. The second refers to events in Hu Nan about the time of Confucius.

** Foreigners will hear this.

(or it might drive him to extremity,) if, after having refused to make his requests the subject of a memorial, [your slave] were also to decline transmitting them [to the imperial commissioner.] And were he to go straight up the Long river, and there give full play to his malice, it might be found more difficult to hold him in than it would otherwise have been.

Having thrice and again reflected on his means, your slave saw no alternative but, in reverential obedience to the decree issued by your Majesty in the case of Marshall last year, to command him (the chief) to return to Canton and there abide the decision of Yeh Ming-chin; thus gaining time, which should be turned to account in keeping him within range; and further, to instruct Wú Kien-chang at once to make some satisfactory arrangement calculated to be durable, regarding the collection of duties at Shanghai, and so leave the different barbarians without grievance to allege.

If the red-side junks could be sent with all speed up the river, Chin-Kiang, Nankin, Kwa-chau, and Shanghai, might be recovered within a given time. Commerce would, as a consequence, resume its way, and the barbarians would then have no place to plant their bill, (no ground of complaint.)

Your slave, having sent an answer to [the chiefs'] communication, and in person commanded Wú Kien-chang to carry him back to Shanghai, and desire him to return to Canton, there to abide the decision of Yeh Ming-chin, and having forwarded copies of his correspondence and of the duplicate of the letter from his government to Yeh Ming-chin for his information, returned to Su-chau, accompanied by Ping-han, on the 29th of the moon, (June 23, 1854.)

The details of his proceedings it is his duty to embody in a respectful memorial, in order to a confidential representation of the truth. This, with copies of the duplicate of the letter of the American chiefs' government, and the correspondence between him and your slave, he submits for imperial perusal, prostrate, entreating that your sacred Majesty will glance thereon and make known your commands.

A respectful memorial.

Translated by THOMAS WADE,
Chinese Secretary.

IV.

Translation of the Imperial Decree approving of Iliang's conduct, as compared with that of Hu Nai-chau; any concessions made by whom to the barbarians are to be cancelled. Yeh alone is to deal with them.

[Translation.]

Letter from the members of the Great Council to YEH, Imperial Commissioner and Governor General of the Two Kwang; to I (Iliang) Governor General of the Two Kiang; and to KIH (Kirhanga), Governor of Kiangsu.

On the 21st of the 6th moon of the 4th year of Hien-fung, (July 15, 1854,) we had the honor to receive the following imperial decree:

"On learning how feebly Hu Nai-chau had conducted himself when the English chiefs were attempting to constrain him to act as seemed good to them, we issued a decree transferring [the case] to Yeh, with instructions to send orders to the barbarian chiefs in Kwang Tung, enjoining them to observe the treaty, and prohibit the barbarian merchants from proceeding into the interior.

"Iliang now reports that the American chief Robert McLane had paid his respects to him at Kwan Chau, and had presented a letter from his government and a communication from himself; that he tenaciously insisted on a revision* of the treaty in twelve years; wanted trade up the Yangtsze Kiang, alleging, at the same time, as matter of complaint, that the custom-house had been removed from Shanghai to Wu-sung, and requesting that it might be abolished. His own communication contained requests that did not appear in the letter of his government; and his conduct was otherwise presumptuous.

"Iliang wrote him a reply [in itself] correct.† He did nothing, it must be allowed, so undignified as Hu Nai-chau. It is to the governor general of the Two Kwang, however, that the administration of all things pertaining to commercial intercourse with [foreign] nations has always belonged. Let Iliang, therefore, now that he has transmitted copies of the letter from the government of the barbarian chief and of his correspondence with him to Yeh Ming-chin, desire him (the chief) to set out at once from Kwanshau for Kwang Tung, and not to indulge himself in long tarrying, [in Kiangsu,] lest he thereby hinder investigation and decision. It will be Yeh's duty to forestal his malice,‡ holding fast by the treaty, and addressing him authoritatively in peremptory language.

"From a succession of memorials received from Hu Nai-chau regarding the rebels and the English chief at Shanghai, the awkwardness and weakness‖ of his conduct becomes more and more apparent. He states that the chief had appointed a day for an interview with him, and that 'in any measure that might be of positive benefit to China, he will assuredly not presume in the least to abide by standing prejudices;' that is to say, in fact, that he has been perfectly prepared long since to make concessions. We have already degraded this governor, and we command Iliang and Kirhanga, in the event of his having been duped into any extravagant (or unlawful) engagement by the barbarians, to repudiate it utterly in plain language, and not to be misled by their absurdity. Let them at the same time desire them to proceed to Kwang Tung, and there abide the decision of Yeh Ming-chin.

"Let Kirhanga continue to lead our troops to the assault, and recover Shanghai without further delay. If the red-side junks shall have one and all reached Wu-sung, let Kirhanga hurry them forward, and communicate with Kishen and Hiang-Yung§ as to what disposi-

---

* Or modification, or accommodation.

† In accordance with reason or right—the natural principle of things.

‡ See note *, page 451.

‖ Weak enough to be gulled, and too weak to speak the truth.

§ Kishen is the mandarin whose name is well known to us in the last war as the negotiator of the first treaty with Captain Elliott. Hiang-Yung was a military man, high commissioner of civil war. The campaign expended both these men—Kishen at Kwachau by the mouth of the canal, and Hiang-Yung before Nankin.

tion of them will be best. The expenses of the force for the protection of Hu-Nan and the contingent brought up from its own jurisdiction by Tatsipu to suppress the rebellion, are matters of great urgency. Loh Pingchang (governor of Hu-Nan) represents that the treasury of Hu-Nan is short of money, and the country in a very forlorn condition, which is true; and of the adjoining provinces there are only Sz'Chuen and the Kwang that may be said, to a certain extent, to have recovered themselves. Let Yeh Ming-chin, without loss of time, set apart several tens of thousands of taels, taking them it matters not from what branch of the revenue, [of his jurisdiction,] and dispatch them by a sure hand. Let there be no delay in satisfying so important a requirement. Let copies of the memorial of Iliang and the supplementary memorial of Hu Nai-chau be sent him to read, and forward this at the rate of 600 *li* a day, with orders to him to attend to it. Respect this!"

In obedience to his Majesty's will this letter is sent.

Translated by THOMAS WADE,
Chinese Secretary.

V.

Memorial of ILIANG, Governor General of the Two Kiang, reporting the receipt of letters from Sir John Bowring; Mr. McLane's announcement of his intention to accompany that officer to the Peiho; and his own doubts as to the object of this visit, if, indeed, the mention of it be more than a ruse. Dated about the 20th August, 1854.

[Translation,]

Your slave, Iliang, upon his knees presents a memorial. He prays the sacred glance of your Majesty upon his respectful representation of the course he is pursuing in the conduct of barbarian business.

Upon the 6th of the 6th moon, (1st July, 1854,) your slave had the honor to report his journey to Kwanshau to give audience to the American chief, Robert McLane, and his refusal to grant the English chief, Bowring, the interview he had moved Wú-Kien-chang to solicit for him; such a request not being in conformity with the treaty, as it is recorded.

Upon the 21st of the 6th moon, (15th July,) Wú Kien-chang reported that Alcock, consul of the English barbarians, had forwarded a dispatch from Bowring to the effect that he wanted an interview. The dispatch he (Wú) transmitted. Your slave found it to state that under the commission he held from his government he was competent to meet any minister your Majesty might do him the honor to appoint to confer with him on business of importance. He had made most friendly overtures to the imperial commissioner in Kwang Tung, who [so far from responding in the same spirit] had, on the contrary, shown a want of due politeness in his reply.* There must now be an improvement in such relations, (or a greater liberality of treatment.) Should your Majesty do him the honor to appoint a high officer to discuss matters of equal interest to the Chinese and the foreigner, it would strengthen [the conditions of] peace and amity between them. The letter contained no request for an interview [with your slave.]

Your slave wrote, in reply, that the imperial commissioner for the administration of barbarian business in Kwang Tung, being in effect the minister [thereto] appointed by your Majesty, it would not be correct to trouble [the throne] with any additional request on the subject. There was nothing, either, that called for discussion at the present moment between China and the outer nations. How the imperial commissioner might have behaved towards him, it was not in [your slave's] power to say. But, to sum up, peace had endured a long time between China and the foreigner, and the obligations most to be regarded were those of good faith and justice. As to forms of politeness, the propriety of greater or less intimacy in these was really matter of public † opinion [in China.] When the chief took others to task on the score of politeness, it was to be presumed he knew how to behave politely himself; and so would not be raising questions [which he had no right to raise.]

This letter had been dispatched when Wú Kien-chang sent up a second letter from the American chief, Robert McLane, to the effect that as [your slave] had not done him the honor to submit to your Majesty his application for the appointment of a high officer to confer with him on questions in which China had a common interest with the United States, he had resolved to accompany the English chief to Tientsin, and [thence] communicate his wishes to your Majesty. On the Shanghai duty question his consul had been deputed to deliberate with the intendant of the Su-sung-tai circuit, (Wú Kien-chang or Samqua,) a satisfactory arrangement had been arrived at, and strict injunctions laid on the merchants of his nation to abide henceforth obediently by the treaty.

Your slave wrote to him to desist. The superintendence of trade at the five ports had always belonged to the imperial commissioner at Kwang Tung. Your slave was not imperial commissioner, nor had the chief handed up to him the original of the letter from his government. It would not, therefore, have been correct for him to address the throne on the subject, nor, consequently, in the course pursued by him, had any offense whatever been committed against the treaty. On every other matter he, (Iliang,) had given him the clearest instructions at their interview; the chief having [then] said that he did not ‡ presume to go to Tientsin, how could he be so inconsistent as, just twenty days later, to declare that he would accompany the English chief to Tientsin? Not only would [such a proceeding] be in non-accordance with what he had said before, but it was at variance, also, with the treaty. It became him, more than ever, now that the duty question had been discussed and brought to a satisfactory conclusion, and a com-

* Or paid him back with discourtesy, ignored *li*, the treatment due by man to man.

† They did not depend on the idiosyncracy of Yeh.

‡ Or, *would* not presume. There is nothing in either passage to mark exactly the word.

plete fulfillment of the treaty inculcated on his mercantile community, to continue as he had begun, and to make manifest the lasting durability of the good understanding between us, to the advantage, more or less, of his nation. Let him not go to Tientsin, but if there were questions absolutely requiring personal discussion, return to Canton and abide investigation and decision at the hands of the imperial commissioner. In the conduct of questions arising out of intercourse with foreign nations, the authorities of China rested entirely on the treaty. Things beyond the treaty they ignored, nor would they undertake the responsibility [attaching to them.]

This was written, and at the same time Wú Kien-chang was charged to point out to the chief authoritatively the advantage and disadvantage [of the two courses before him,] and to insure his taking the safe path. Further measures are deferred until Wú Kien-chang shall have sent up his reply.

It is, however, a standing device of the barbarian to make particular circumstances the plea of demands to be insisted on. Whatever these chiefs may insinuate (or whisper) against Yeh Ming-chin, it is evident that Yeh Ming-chin is he whom they are used to fear. They say they are going to Tientsin. This may be, notwithstanding, an assertion made to compel acquiesence in their demands. Your slave has commanded them with affectionate earnestness to stay, and the ships of their chiefs have not as yet departed. Still there is no certainty, so inconsistent and capricious is the barbarian character, that they will not, after all, sail north, and thereby attempt to constrain the imperial commissioner and the high provincial authorities of the coast jurisdictions.

Your slave has written expressly to Kweiliang, governor general of Chihli, that his establishment may be desired to be on the alert, and with coolness and secresy to prepare for the defense [of the province;] also to Yeh Ming-chin.

It is, further, his duty to embody the details of his present proceedings in a respectful memorial. He forwards it by post, and prostrate implores the sacred glance of your Majesty thereon.

A respectful memorial.

Translated by

THOMAS WADE,
Chinese Secretary.

VI.

Imperial Decree issued on the receipt of the foregoing. YEH is to prevent the barbarians from coming north, but he is to show them no greater politeness than is warranted by precedent. YEH appears to the Emperor misinformed about the war between England and Russia. His faith in it is not to throw him off his guard in dealing with England. Dated about 6th August, 1854.

[Translation.]

Letter from the Members of the Great Council to YEH, Governor General of the two Kwang.

On the 15th of the 7th moon of the 4th year of Hien-fung, (6th August, 1854,) we had the honor to receive the following imperial decree:

"On learning some time since that the chiefs of the English and American barbarians had been applying for interviews with the high authorities of Kiangsu, and attempting to constrain them to act as they pleased, we sent orders to Yeh Ming-chin to command these chiefs to obey the treaties, that so he might be enabled to nip their mischievous* [purpose] in the bud.

"Iliang now reports the receipt of a dispatch from the English chief, Bowring, complaining that when he was in Kwang Tung the imperial commissioner had met [his advances] with a want of politeness; also, of a dispatch from the American chief, Robert McLane, to the effect that he had determined to accompany the English chief to Tientsin.

"It is the nature of barbarians to be cunning and malicious. They perfectly understand that the entire administration of [foreign] trade centers in Kwang Tung, yet they rush† to the ports, insisting on the satisfaction of demands made with unreasonable extravagance. We have commanded Iliang to desire the chiefs to proceed to Kwang Tung, and there abide decision. Let Yeh Ming-chin, in obedience to our former decree, devise means of guiding them in the way they should go, and command them to continue steadily to observe the treaty. Let him on no account suffer them to be unlawfully (or unreasonably, extravagantly) playing the spy, on the ground that modifications [of the treaty are to be adopted] in twelve years. Let him tell them, also, that in consequence of the arrangements now being carried out for its defense [against the rebels] a force is assembled at the port of Tientsin as the clouds for number; that should the barbarians be so ill-advised as to come to it, injury may be done to their vessels, [in which case, so far from deriving any benefit from their visit] they will, on the contrary, have brought calamity on themselves.

"As to the forms to be observed by the governor general (Yeh) in his reception of the barbarian chiefs, let him religiously adhere to the old rules; not because of the application of these barbarians to be

* See above paper, note.

† The particle is used when something happens that should not, and unexpectedly; "away they go," &c.

treated somewhat more* liberally (or handsomely) is he to make any concession, no matter how small, lest it tend to dissipate their fears.†

"Yeh Ming-chin obtained information some time since that the Russian barbarians had declared war against the English barbarians, and had carried off merchant ships from Hong Kong; which events would make the latter barbarians look to themselves.‡ How then is it, that they are, on the contrary, making difficulties with China? The rumor [that reached Yeh's ears] was probably in great part untrue. The governor general (Yeh) must be more than usually careful in his management of this matter; the quarrel pending between these barbarians must on no account put him off his guard in any particular. Let him report by post the results of his late investigations, and the steps taken by him thereupon.

"The cities of Wu-chang and Han-yang, in Hu-Peh, will, it is hoped, be recovered immediately, but money for the pay of the troops is urgently needed. Let Yeh Ming-chin with all speed apply several myriads of taels [of the revenue of his jurisdiction] to this purpose, and appoint trusty officers to carry it, one following the other, to Yang Pei, for the supply of his camp. Let there not be a moment's delay.

"Send a copy of Iliang's dispatch [to Yeh] for his information, and hurry this forward to him at the rate of 600 *li* a day, with instructions to him to attend to it. Respect this!"

In obedience to the will of his Majesty, this letter is sent.

Translated by

THOMAS WADE,
Chinese Secretary.

Inclosure No. 7 to Dispatch No. 33, October 21, 1858.

SECOND MEMORANDUM.

Sir John Bowring and Mr. McLane, having failed to extract anything satisfactory from the Imperial Commissioner Yeh, or the authorities of Kiangsu, (the reports and comments on the correspondence with whom were included in Part I of this collection,) proceeded to the mouth of the Peiho, with the view of communicating directly with the court of Pekin, and reached their anchorage on the 15th October, 1854.

From the 16th October until the 10th November the ministers, or their secretaries, Mr. Medhurst and Dr. Parker, continued to meet or correspond with various officials of rank, with no result, however, beyond a promise that on three local questions, strictly within the scope of the old treaty, the chief authorities of the jurisdictions to

* See Iliang's report of Sir John Bowring's letter.

† Lit. Cause a relaxation of their heart of fear, of the fear in their hearts; a figure taken from a bowstring.

‡ Lit. Cautious, and so non-aggressive.

which these more properly belonged should be instructed to give equitable decisions. No allusion is made to the employment of force, except on the defensive. Tientsin was reinforced with 3,000 men, and the officers in charge of the coast were generally directed to be on the alert. No violence was apprehended from us, apparently, in the north, but it was thought not impossible we might join the rebels in the south if we were sent away with no answer at all to our petition. How little was to be granted was very early settled, and believing that with that little we should go home contented, the Chinese yielded a point of form, which we had fought for very stoutly, in the appointment of a plenipotentiary. Our delight at the announcement of his nomination appeared to them to justify the wisdom of the concession. It in no way affected the issue, as they had determined it, and, as it made the necessary message somewhat less disagreeable to us, it diminished our ostensible grounds of complaint. And so, having from the first been in possession of our demands, they carried the grand point, viz: that we can in no way have access to the Emperor, whom, by his desire, they maintained all along to be in ignorance of anything beyond the fact of our presence off the Peiho—a fact in itself abnormal and censurable; and that at Tientsin, (that is, at Takoo,) though for this once the announcement of our coming there did but recoil upon us in discourteous treatment, nothing definite was to be negotiated.

The bulk of our demands they looked upon as deliberately thrown in to swell our list, and the Shanghai duty question, which, without local knowledge and much fuller information, they could hardly have understood, they completely misapprehended. Our desire was that they should express some anxiety about the recovery of nearly a million of taels, for which the British and American consuls at Shanghai held promissory notes. Their impression was, that we desired to have this arrear remitted, and the Emperor does not seem to have thought a certain amount of liberality on this head unreasonable.

THOMAS WADE,
Chinese Secretary.

I.

Memorial of Wankien and Shwang-yui, of the 20th October, 1854. They cannot persuade the barbarians to return south, so recommend the appointment of the governor general of Chihli, or some other high officer, as commissioner to meet them.

[Translation.]

Your Majesty's slaves, Wankien, director general of the salt collectorate of Chang-lu, and Shwang-yui, general ocmmanding the Tientsin division [of the Chinese army of Chihli,] upon their knees, present a respectful memorial, being a confidential account of their reception of Medhurst and another, interpreters of the English and Americans, [and of their attempts] to persuade them to go in the right way; whereon, looking upward, they hope for the sacred glance.

They would humbly state, that the particulars of the interview with the English interpreter* Medhurst, and the American interpreter Parker, had with your slaves Shwang-yui and Tsien Hien-ho, intendant of Tientsin, on the 26th instant (October 17th) were immediately reported in full to your Majesty, as is on record.

On the 27th, your slave Wankien, and his colleagues together, had an interview with these barbarians in front of the fort. In reply to the question of your slave Wankien, why, as there is no [foreign] trade whatever at Tientsin, they had presumed to come there, the barbarian Medhurst stated that certain changes affecting trade had become necessary; they had been to Kwang Tung, and had requested an interview of the Governor General Yeh who had refused to see them; they had subsequently returned† to Shanghai, where they had seen the Governor Kih, (Kirhanga,) and informed him plainly that they were going to Tientsin. The Governor Kih, had again and again [endeavored to] prevent them, and had desired them to hand him the draft [of their propositions] presented before, in which case he might be enabled to submit it to the throne for them. Apprehensive of delays, they had come to the port of Tientsin, and [now] requested that application might be made to his Majesty the Emperor to allow Bowring and McLane, the envoys of their two nations, to meet the ministers of his Majesty in Pekin, to state the changes [needed] in the treaty. This would, without doubt, be greatly to the advantage of both Chinese and foreigner. Should representation of their requests be refused them, they would have no alternative but to return south with all speed, and report the result of their mission to their respective governments.‡ The treaty of peace, in short, that was to have lasted ten thousand‖ years, would in that case become waste paper.

Your slaves rejoined that, [in the first place,] they could not well, up here, be thoroughly acquainted with all the regulations of trade, these having been settled in time past in Kwang Tung. In the next, as the treaty of peace was for ten thousand years, it was of course a duty to show the deference due to it§ for evermore; how, then, could a request be preferred for modifying it? How, further, the twelve years' term of the Americans, not having yet expired, could negotiations be opened afresh?

Then, again, on their return to Shanghai, when Governor Kih had desired them to present their paper, that he might submit it to the throne, they ought to have handed it to him and waited further action on his part. What need was there for them to come to Tientsin importunately preferring requests? The proceeding to Pekin to state their case, as proposed by Bowring and McLane, was not only out of the question, but a measure which the memorialists¶ could not with propriety even submit for them to the throne.

---

* The term employed is that used at Canton for the native linguists, a very low order of employés.

† Both plenipotentiaries had been at Shanghai in the summer.

‡ Lit. the state king of their several States.

‖ The Chinese of Article —, in the treaty of Nankin.

§ To act in obedience to it, as sanctioned by the Emperor.

¶ The officer of the vigilance committee for the protection of Pekin and its vicinity against the rebels, in which capacity Wankien was acting at the time.

The barbarians added that trade at Tientsin was not what they were insisting on; the real reason of their application to go to Pekin was to complain of certain griefs too painful to be borne.

Referring to the memorials and correspondence of the authorities of Kiangsu on barbarian affairs, Kweiliang, the governor general of Chihli, had sent confidential instructions to Tsien Hien-ho, intendant of Tientsin, to desire the barbarians, should they come to Tientsin, to adhere strictly to the treaty.

Acting on these, your slaves exhorted them for several hours, trying every means to direct them in the way they should go, and employing in all they said an equal proportion of austerity and mildness, (lit., the hard and the soft.) The barbarians, however, with consistent disingenuousness, pertinaciously adhering to their request that representation be made to the throne, a special danger presented itself, viz: that unless some latitude (lit., tether) were allowed them, and a representation to the throne indulgently conceded them, these barbarians, although not presuming to dash up, [the river,] might sail away south and [instead of submitting] convert [their dismissal] into a ground of complaint. With the responsibility of an affair so important as the present resting upon them, your slaves dare not retain, be it ever so little, the standing prejudice, (*i. e.*, against any concession whatever.) The character of the barbarians is, notwithstanding, so extraordinarily malicious, that precaution against their advancing other irregular pretensions will still be indispensable.

It remains, therefore, for them frankly to set forth the truth, and prostrate to request your Majesty to declare for their guidance, whether or not a high officer shall be sent by your Majesty, or the governor general, Kweiliang, directed to proceed to Tientsin, to desire the barbarians to go back, and inform them to what place they are to proceed, there to abide investigation and decision, to the end that, with reverent obedience, they may return south.

Having written express to the governor general of Chihli, and repeated their commands to the officers of the land force, to keep watch and ward with strictness and secresy, it is further their duty to present their respectful memorial, whereon they request your Majesty's pleasure.

The reply, in the vermilion pencil, to the above was received on the 29th of 8th moon, (October 20, 1854.)

Translated by

THOMAS WADE,
Chinese Secretary.

II.

Postscript to the foregoing, suggesting that his Majesty should refer the barbarians to the high authorities of Kiangsu.

[Translation.]

SUPPLEMENTARY MEMORIAL OF WANKIEN.

Further, your slave Wankein finds it stated in the original memorial of Kirhanga, the governor of Kiangsu, that the chiefs of the three nations (England, France and America) had combined [or were acting together ;] whereas the ships that have arrived at the port of Takoo belong only to two nations, the English and American. It is stated, but whether truly or not there is no evidence to show, that the French barbarian vessel had come half way, when she was damaged by stress of weather. †

In the propositions brought forward by these barbarians at their interview, it was in most points the view of the one individual, Medhurst, that in general prevailed. The other three persons ‡ did no more than assent subsidiarily [to what he said.] To judge from appearances, Medhurst is much the most crafty. They aver that their end in coming to Tientsin on this occasion is the revision of the treaty and the exposition of grievous wrongs ; but there is no fathoming their minds, nor is it at all certain that they are not covering a mischievous purpose, their (real) object being to find a pretext for misunderstanding with us.

Yesterday they wanted to land for a walk, but your slave and his colleagues told them authoritatively that the Tientsin volunteers were very numerous, the population very fierce, and that should any misfortune thence come of their proceedings, [so far from its availing them anything,] the good understanding between us would on the contrary be affected. On this they at once desisted. Twenty soldiers have been stationed in a small boat alongside the barbarian vessels, || ostensibly for their protection, but really to watch their movements.

The nature of barbarians is, however, malicious and crafty. Were they obliged after their voyage, to return to Canton with nothing definitely settled, after making a long journey to no purpose, they would certainly be dissatisfied ; and when they sailed south, though they might not venture on any extravagant demonstration of violence, § it might not improbably occur to them to ally themselves secretly [with the rebels.]

Your slave has been very graciously treated by your Majesty, nor

---

* Acknowledged on the same day as the foregoing, in which it was, as is usual, most probably inclosed.

† The Jeanne d'Arc had grounded in the Yangtsze Kiang, and was in dock at Shanghai.

‡ Dr. Parker, secretary United States legation, and, I suppose, Lieutenant Grier, Royal Navy, and Lieutenant Carter, United States Navy.

|| Lying off Takoo.

§ Not dare with great extravagance hawk-like to spread [the wing,] or to make hawk-like swoops or flights.

dare he, in this autumn* of troubles, neglect to examine, and with heart unbiased, (or unpretending,) every means by which a satisfactory issue may be achieved. Barbarian ships have been in the habit of trading at Shanghai, and these barbarians themselves state that for the governor general and governor of the Kiang provinces they have always entertained the profoundest respect and deference. Might not your Majesty issue a commission to those two officers to inquire into and definitely dispose [of the barbarian question,] associating with them a high officer, perhaps, sent forward to assist in their deliberations? In this case, your slave could, with all respect, inform them that such was your Majesty's decree, and command them to return south, and there abide [further proceedings.] They would then be left without pretext of complaint, and might possibly be prevented from bringing forward any fresh propositions.

The opinion that is within range of his stolidity, your slave, in the rashness of his ignorance, bluntly declares, and, unequal to the excess of his trepidation, awaits your Majesty's commands.

A respectful memorial presented supplementarily by your slave,

WANKIEN.

The reply in the vermilion pencil was received Hien-fung, fourth year, eighth moon, 29th day. (October 20, 1854.)

Translated by

T. WADE,
Chinese Secretary.

III.

Confidential memorial of WANKIEN and SHWANG-YUI, acknowledged October 24, 1854. They had ascertained that the barbarian chiefs really were outside the bar; also that the object of their coming was to obtain modifications of the treaty. They had disputed the right to require these, and should now wait for Tsunglun's arrival.

[Translation.]

Your slave Wankien, director general of the salt-collectorate of the Chang-lu, and your slave Shwang-yui, general of the Tientsin division, upon their knees present a memorial.

They respectfully submit a confidential relation of their successive interviews with the barbarian Medhurst and others, and of the specious fallacies with which they strove to maintain their own ground while answering the queries put to them regarding the real object of their coming; and, looking upward, solicit thereon the sacred glance.

Your slaves had interviews with the English and American interpreters, Medhurst and Parker, on the 26th and 27th of the moon,

---

*A classical expression, like "the winter of our discontent," having reference to the time of year.

(October 17 and 18.) They inquired of them where the barbarian chiefs, Bowring and McLane, then were; and on their answering that they were lying below the bar waiting for further intelligence, your slaves detached a trusty military officer to observe. He found three steamers and one small sailing vessel anchored outside the bar, twenty *li* and more (some seven miles) distant from the forts. Had your slaves desired [the chiefs] to come in for an interview there would have been another barbarian vessel within the port;* but had they themselves gone out to see [the chiefs,] they feared that they should thus offend even more against the dignity [of China.] They had, therefore, two interviews with the barbarians, Medhurst and his colleague. On inquiring the real cause of their coming, Medhurst presented a draft of propositions, and Parker two volumes, one of which was identical with that already laid before Iliang, governor general of the two Kiang. Finding that the propositions in these were generally in the language of outrageous (or extravagant) absurdity too offensive† [to our notions] to be practicable, [your slaves] as in duty bound, rebuked them for their impropriety, and at once returned‡ [the papers] to them, not presuming to take on themselves to receive them. Their omission to mention this in the two memorials already presented to your Majesty was, indeed, an act of carelessness on the part of your slaves.

The council yesterday transmitted to them an imperial decree they had the honor to receive, in these words: "At their interview with them, Wankien and his colleagues must discomfit (lit. snap short) their deceit and arrogance, and foil their malicious sophistry."

With reverence they beheld how all-sufficienty your Majesty's instructions provide a support to your slaves in the duty intrusted to them. As they read the decree on their knees it was hard to describe their respect and gratitude.

In obedience to the commands received, they at once prescribed a time for an interview, but a northerly gale preventing the barbarian [chiefs from landing.] They had another interview with Medhurst and his colleague on the 30th, (21st October,) when they desired them to explain what really and truly was their object in coming. They again stated that it was in truth a modification of the treaty, goods being hardly saleable by reason of the disturbed state of the country; and they again presented the paper of propositions tendered before.

Your slaves went over it together, and stated the objections to each article, one by one. On the article, for instance, in which they require to establish themselves in any part of China they please, purchasing land, building dwellings, and opening warehouses, your slaves remarked authoritatively that even ships were not allowed to enter any but the five ports; how then could dwellings be built or warehouses set up in any other? The common people, besides, well knowing the severity of the law, would not venture illegally (or unauthorizedly, clandestinely) to sell land, though it were but an inch, to the outer barbarian.

---

* In addition to the lorcha Chusan and the United States tender F. Cooper.

† Lit. Obstructive, hindrances in the way we think right.

‡ Lit. Threw back, as a superior's usage is with an improper petition.

Next, as to the proposition to send a plenipotentiary to reside in the northern capital of China for the conduct of correspondence, your slaves observed authoritatively that under the original treaty, "no State was allowed to send officials* [to Pekin] on business so insignificant as that of trade;" what correspondence could there be to conduct? Yet more, the imperial precinct of the celestial dynasty is sacred ground, how could the outer barbarians be suffered to profane† it by their presence? All the above requests were outrageous and impertinent, utterly impracticable; it behooved us to leave them undiscussed.

Of the other changes of treaty applied for by them, the majority were conditions on their part only,‡ respecting the trade they required up the Yangtsze Kiang. Your slaves, following the general sense of Iliang's memorial, put down [all these notions] peremptorily, authoritatively declaring that in the original treaty no mention was made of permission to trade up the Yangtsze Kiang, and that the contravention of this provision was under treaty severely punishable. "Do you not know [asked your slaves] that, in the unmannerly application you are now making for a change of regulations, you violate [the obligations] of faith and justice you should religiously observe, and that it would therefore be next to impossible to give you permission to do [as you require?]"

There was also presented another paper in several articles, which, on inspection, was found to allege various grounds of complaint; difficulties were frequently put in the way of hiring houses of people at the five ports; the local officials did not secure the recovery of moneys due by merchants; cases of incendiarism, and robbery, and of piracy on the outer seas, in which appeal had been made to Chinese authorities, had been left to this hour unredressed. Further, Canton was invested [by rebels]; so was Shanghai. There was in consequence no market in the five ports for merchandise to the value of hundreds of thousands [of taels]; and as there was no authority with whom to discuss and arrange [these things,] they (the barbarians) had accordingly come north to complain.

Your slaves told them that, in the hiring of houses and similar matters, it must be left entirely to the people to give their consent or withhold it; no one, even though an official, could extort their consent. [As to debts] where money was really owing, did they mean to say that the authorities, when appealed to, did not entertain the suit, and take steps for recovery? As to robbery and piracy, the laws of China were very severe, the penalties against the local authorities [for not enforcing them] extremely grave; how should these fail, then zealously to make search for and seize [the delinquents?] At this place, however, there were no papers [connected with any case] to show in what place any injury [of the kind complained of] had been sustained, and where, consequently, proceedings were to be instituted, and the offense punished.

* This is the 34th article of the American treaty, "no State *of the United States*," &c. Iliang had misapplied it with somewhat similar dexterity. His memorial is referred to presently.

† Lit: The chariot [ways] of the celestial dynasty are important ground. How can it be suffered that the outer barbarians should defilingly enter therein?

‡ Coming from them, and regarding only their own interest.

As to Kwang Tung, there was intelligence of important successes in many parts of it; order would be immediately restored there, and merchants would then, of course, be enabled to trade as usual; there was no occasion for over-anxiety [on this head.]

This was authoritatively set before them in plain language. Again and again were they shown the right path. Medhurst and his colleague, unable to debate any longer, insisted pertinaciously that they were merely bearers of the letters they had brought; there must be an interview with their chiefs, Bowring and McLane, they said, before the different requests in their paper of negotiations, to all of which they had so earnestly besought assent, could be discussed and disposed of. If representation to the throne were denied them, they should acquaint their chiefs, who would return south.

Your slaves informed them they were ready to have an interview with Bowring and the other barbarian chief, on which Medhurst and the other declared that these could not well meet any one but a high officer sent from your Majesty. They tried every description of specious pretense to carry their point until it being sunset, the conference broke up.

They had spoken of going to Tung-chau,* on which it had been authoritatively set before them that, if they did venture to proceed, the authorities would not interfere, but that the volunteers of Tientsin amounted to upwards of a hundred thousand in number, united in heart; and if, as was probable, any harm were to be done to them on the road, it would not concern the authorities. Medhurst said: "We, too, have heard in the south to the repulse of the rebels who invaded Tientsin last year, by the volunteers;" and thereupon they desisted. Truly do they, in the words of your Majesty's decree, make false assertions to intimidate.

As Tsunglun will arrive at Tientsin immediately, it remains only for your slaves, in respectful obedience to your Majesty's commands, to consult together, and insure, by deliberation, the adoption of the best course to be [meanwhile] pursued, and to abide the deliberation and decision of the Governor General Kweiliang. Not, assuredly, dare they commit themselves, as by passive indifference, or by regarding only what is immediately before their eyes, to mar the fortunes of the moment.†

They have accordingly given orders to the troops and militia within the prefectural city (Tientsin) and without it, and at their several stations along the water communications, to keep watch and ward with strictness and secrecy. This done, they have, in concert with Tsien Hien-ho, the acting salt collector, to present a confidential memorial, respectfully drawn up, detailing the particulars of their second interview with these barbarians, the questions put to them regarding their object in coming, and the injunctions laid on them with affectionate earnestness.

They have to add that, in obedience to your Majesty's will, your slave Wankien did confidentially report to the Assistant High Commis-

* Within ten miles of Pekin.

† Lit. To spoil the opportunity; to influence the luck of things to evil.

sioner Sangkolinsin* the arrival of the barbarian ships in the port, and yesterday received a letter from him to the effect that he was sending Chang Tien-yuen, acting general-in-chief [of the Chinese army of Chihli], with 3,000 men, to the city of Tientsin, which they would reach immediately, to assist [the garrison] in its defense. Trading junks and rice junks are going in and out of the port of Takoo without hindrance. Officers have been sent to cruise and observe, without the knowledge of the barbarians, [all which particulars] it is the duty of your slaves to add to the foregoing relation. Prostrate they pray that your sacred Majesty will glance thereon, and issue your instructions. To this end, they respectfully memorialize.

On the 3d of the 9th moon, in the 4th year of Hien-fung, (October 24, 1854,) there was received the following reply, in the vermilion pencil:

"We have read the memorial. The falsehoods and clamorous bluster of the barbarians are transparent enough. They are not very skillful. As soon as Tsunglun comes, you must take friendly counsel with him, and devise some satisfactory arrangement of the matter. You will lose no time in reporting confidentially the arrival of any additional barbarian vessels, as well as any movement on the part of the barbarians. Respect this!"

Translated by THOMAS WADE, *Chinese Secretary.*

IV.

Confidential memorial of WANKIEN and SHWANG-YUI, of October 30, 1854. They had rejected at present, and returned an improper letter of the barbarians:

[Translation.]

Your slave Wankien, director general of the salt excise of Chang-lu, and Shwang-yui, general of the Tientsin division, on their knees present a memorial.

They respectfully present a confidential report upon the more recent proceedings of the barbarians, and communications received from them since, [the date of their last memorial,] and looking upward, pray for the sacred glance thereon.

Your slaves had dispatched their reply to the barbarians on the 5th day, (October 26th,) when in the watch called *shin*, (7–9 o'clock, a. m.,) Medhurst and Parker went out of port with about twenty persous. On the 6th day, (27th October,) in the same watch, they came into port, and returned to the vessel they had before been on board of. In the watch called *tsz*, (9–11, a. m.,) on the 7th, (28th October,) the barbarians delivered to the river patrol a dispatch to be forwarded to your

*A Mongolian prince of the highest order of imperial nobility, then associated with the commander-in-chief in operations against the rebels.

slaves, to whom they wanted at the same time to present thirty-six bottles of barbarian wine. This was stopped at once. They were not allowed to land the wine, and as some of the language in their communication was outrageous, and impertinent, [your slaves,] after duly consulting together, drew up a reply, and returned [threw back] the original, a fair copy of which, as well as of their letter, respectfully made, they tender with reverence for your imperial perusal.

The barbarians, however, maintained pertinaciously that they must have the honor of waiting for your Majesty's decree. Your slaves would not give any promise lightly, [on the other hand,] had they continued idly disputing, to use the words of the decree of your sacred Majesty, this business would never be brought to a termination. And having further information that the barbarians proposed to weigh anchor for the south on the 9th day, (29th October,) after deliberating thereon again and again, they wrote a reply, in which they made a slight allusion to, [the intended departure,] as an experiment to ascertain what their order of proceeding might be, [which discerned,] the course [of your slaves] might be shaped. There will be no difficulty in sending them off now at once, but the difficulty is to prevent them, when they shall have left this, from raising some fresh question or other elsewhere.

As soon as Tsunglun arrives in Tientsin, your slaves will deliberate further with him, and will contrive to have an interview with the barbarian chiefs, Bowring and the other. They trust, then, to succeed in effectually stopping these barbarians from playing they spy, and in bending their hearts to submission, thereby humbly to further the high purpose of the instructions again and again repeated by your Majesty.

Their respectful memorial, prepared in concert with Tsien Hien-ho, the acting collector of salt revenue, reporting the receipt of communications from Medhurst and his colleague, and [other] events of the last few days, they submit to your Majesty, and, prostrate, solicit the sacred glance of your Majesty thereon.

They beg leave to add that the barbarian vessel since come into port is one of the five steamers and others [already reported.] No fresh barbarian vessel has come in. The steamer is still anchored outside of the bar.

It is their duty to add these details to the foregoing. To this end they respectfully present this memorial.

On the 11th of the ninth moon of the fourth year of Hien-fung, (November 1, 1854,) the following reply in the vermilion pencil was received:

"We are informed of all that you have reported."

Translated by T. WADE,
Chinese Secretary.

V.

Postscript to the foregoing. WANKIEN has refused to see the barbarians MEDHURST and PARKER, because of the improper letter returned; they are penitent, and delighted at hearing of the approach of a Commissioner.

SUPPLEMENTAL MEMORIAL OF WANKIEN.

Further, in the watch called *shin* (4 p. m.) of the 8th instant, (29th October,) just as your slaves had dispatched their replies to Medhurst and the other, these barbarians requested an interview. Your slave, Wankien, declined to receive them, on the plea that certain expressions in their communication (*) had been offensive and impertinent; but your slave Shwang-yui, and your servant Tsien Hien-ho, went forward to meet them, and lectured them upon the obligations of duty.† Medhurst and Parker hung down their heads, having nothing to rejoin, and apologized for their error. They further observed that, as a high officer was to be at Tientsin immediately, to look into [the questions pending,] there would [now] be peace between us, and though they should die they should not care. ‡ They seemed greatly ashamed, and their language was most respectful.

Your slave, Shwang-yui, and his colleague, again told them authoritatively that, if the envoys Bowring and McLane were certain to come, an interview could be accorded them. Medhurst said: "The envoy of my nation would be wanting in politeness were he to decline the interview; let me go out of port to inform Bowring and his colleague, and return." The conference then broke up, and they departed.

The commandant of Takoo reported that in the watch called *yu*, (6– p. m.,) Medhurst and Parker had gone out of port in the lorcha, taking ten or more men with them. The port is shallow, and the weather is becoming cold with the north wind that has been blowing several days. These barbarians fear the cold, and are also alarmed about the ice. Their anxiety to go to the capital was clearly pretended—put on to make the most of the situation. They cannot certainly stay long. If, however, they could be bent to submission, and made to go back without any loop-hole left for a cause of quarrel, it being insisted on that they were to return south to arrange any slight modifications that may admit of discussion, the path prescribed by feeling and principle might be again pointed out to them, and they could not fail to follow it. To judge from appearances, they cannot well have any important demand to make here, nor will they venture to raise troubles elsewhere.

It is the duty of your slave to add to the foregoing this account of the subsequent interview with the barbarians on the day.

It was acknowledged on the 11th of the ninth moon, (November 1.)

Translated by

T. WADE,
Chinese Secretary.

---

* Already returned, as above shown.

† Lit. The great, or whole, or universal obligations; those incumbent on all men in all relations of life.

‡ They were so delighted at the appointment of a commissioner, they cared not what might become of themselves.

VI.

Confidential memorial of Tsunglun, Wankien, and Shwang-yui, of the 4th November, acknowledged on the 5th November, 1854. They have met the barbarian chiefs, and recommend the Emperor to allow them to refer the chiefs to the high authorities of some jurisdiction to which the treaty gives them access.

[Translation.]

Your slaves, Tsunglun, Wankien, and Shwang-yui, on their knees present a memorial. They respectfully present a confidential memorial, showing how they interrogated McLane and Bowring, the chiefs of the American and English barbarians, on their entering the port to pay them a visit, respecting the true cause of their coming hither, and detailing the steps taken by themselves upon deliberation; whereon, looking upward, they implore the sacred glance.

Your slaves would humbly state that the 13th (November 3) having been appointed for an interview with the barbarian chiefs, at noon on that day the two, McLane and Bowring, with a following of one hundred and sixty-seven barbarians, were brought into port in seven boats, and landed, accompanied by the interpreters, Medhurst and Parker. The barbarians advanced, every one armed, formed in file, and with a band playing, (or, with the music of drums.) Your slaves had had a blue tent pitched in front of the fort, and round this they planted troops in a continuous rank of soldiers; the officials, civil and military, divided into two wings, being drawn up in attendance to give substance to the spectacle, and present a duly imposing appearance. When the chiefs had come to the blue tent, they were immediately received by Tsunglun and his colleagues. All were then seated, each in his proper place.*

The barbarian chiefs, McLane and Bowring, were certainly very respectful in manner. They stated that they looked up with gratitude to his Majesty the Emperor for sending a minister to the port of Tientsin, to which they had come, and that it gave them (the envoys) inexpressible pleasure to meet him.

Your slave Tsunglun thereupon told them that Tientsin was properly not a place to which foreigners had a right to come; bearing in mind, however, their sea-voyage, he had consented to meet them. Anything they had to discuss they must truthfully declare, and if the matter lay within [the scope of] the treaty, and was at all reasonable, he would go into it with them.

McLane replied first: Since the original treaty was allowed† to come into operation, a long time had elapsed; the present state of things urgently called for alterations in it. He had been to Kwang Tung, but Yeh would not receive him; he had, therefore, come to Tientsin to intreat that steps might be taken in the matter. He presented at the same time the paper of propositions handed in before.

* That is, according to the courtesies regulating the intercourse between host and guest.
† Lit. Since we have had the honor to act, viz: under the sanction of the Emperor.

Its purport was much to the same intent as what has been again and again reported to your Majesty by your slave Wankien.

Your slave Tsunglun at once in plain words positively negatived the proposals therein set forth respecting the hire of dwellings, rent of lands, and establishment of warehouses in the interior, as well as the residence of a barbarian mission at Pekin for the conduct of correspondence.

The barbarian [McLane] had nothing to urge in reply. He said the paper before presented had not contained everything he had to say. If the minister now sent by your Majesty to Tientsin had powers sufficient, he would hand over a treaty in detail, containing the articles to which the United States so anxiously sought assent. If he (Tsunglun) had not the great powers necessary, further negotiation with him would be inexpedient.

Your slave Tsunglun authoritatively repeated, that public servants in our State do not pretend to plenipotentiary powers; in all things they wait for the command of their sovereign before they act; and that there has never been any such denomination [of officer] as plenipotentiary. "Now," he said, "if any one of the things which your United States so earnestly request be to the common advantage of both parties, or to the advantage of foreign nations, and of no prejudice to China, we can doubtless deliberate upon it, and arrangements can be made when it shall have been explained to his Majesty; but were I, his minister, so far to forget myself as to submit on your behalf [propositions] that were very offensive* to China, our Emperor would be sure to punish me for my irreverent obtrusiveness.† There can be no objection, however, to your producing what you have to propose. When we have read it we can discuss it with fairness, (or, on principles of justice.)"

The barbarian chief, McLane, on this, had a very long consultation with Bowring, Medhurst, and Parker; each [chief] then produced and presented a fair draft of the [proposed] modifications. Your slaves, Tsunglun and Wankien, perused them, and finding articles in them to contain matter in general prejudicial to large interests, and entailing consequences in no slight degree calamitous, [felt that] to bend the heart of the barbarians to submission, it would be necessary to disapprove and reject these with emphasis. But it was now near sunset, and their detention within the port would have involved the further trouble of making provision [for their stay.] Besides, on the part of England, it is Medhurst who interprets, and, as it was to be apprehended, so singularly ill disposed‡ is this barbarian, that he might not convey all that was said, it was deemed expedient to tell them authoritatively that several of the articles in their paper were inconsistent with the original treaty, and did not belong to the business of the five ports; that their requests were very outrageous and impertinent; but that, as their objectionableness could not be set before them in a moment, they must wait until the minister, (Tsunglun,) who would take home the papers for more attentive consideration, should write them a

*Or, obstructive; of great hindrance to. (See above.)
†This word includes the idea of profaning or defiling, as, "Fools rush in," &c.
‡Lit. Cunning and malicious.

reply. He would therein, article by article, negative all that was perfectly inadmissible. As regarded such matters as did admit of consultation, viz: adjustments [of the treaty] to meet alteration of circumstances, this was not a place for the transaction of barbarian business. He, the minister, had not the means of fully informing himself regarding the negotiation of the treaty at the time it was made, neither had he any documents to refer to. More impossible was it for him to give an opinion upon the customs duties, the conditions of this question being different in different places.

The proper course would be, doubtless, to lay the matter before the throne, and request his Majesty to give it in charge to the high authorities of the provinces concerned, on whom devolves the administration of barbarian business, to ascertain the provisions of the original treaty, and determine the matter on due consideration of the circumstances. Some slight advantage might then accrue to commerce of foreign nations, and the right and the wrong in the complaints [now preferred by them] would be easily distinguished.

The barbarian chiefs then asked on what day they might expect an answer respecting the [proposed] treaty now handed in.

Your slaves told them it would have to be carefully considered, article by article, and should be sent back on the 18th instant, (8th November.) The barbarians expressed themselves content, and, taking with them all whom they had brought on shore, left the port in the lorcha, and returned to their own ships.

The greater portion of the propositions of the barbarian chiefs, McLane and Bowring, your slaves find to be out of all reason; nor should they, by rights, presume to intrude them upon your sacred intelligence. Not venturing, however, on the other hand, in a matter of so grave importance, to do otherwise than frankly expose the truth, they respectfully forward, for your Majesty's perusal, a copy of these papers, presented by the Americans and English. As concerns the various outrageous demands put forward at the good will and pleasure of these barbarians, doubtless it were the part of your slaves to bestow their whole attention on a final (or judicial) decision of these, by injunctions to be just; by disapproving and rejecting their propositions, one by one; by peremptory refusal to close the way of their prying curiosity (or purpose of spying), of their insatiable desires. They ought not, indeed, to presume to trouble the sacred mind again. But, in the paper submitted [by the barbarians], there are various stipulations, in the matter of which, though it certainly does admit of discussion, the dignity [of the State] is nevertheless involved: the demand that there should be correspondence* with the high provincial authorities; that [official] interviews, when they occur, shall take place in the official residences of the authorities; that in collisions between Chinese and foreigners, both sides shall be heard by the authorities sitting together, and each party then punished by the government to which he may belong; also, that governors general shall receive barbarians on terms of equality; also, that [China] shall coöperate in

* Probably consular correspondence is meant. The treaty provision respecting it has been constantly ignored.

clearing the seas of pirates; and that proceedings shall be immediately instituted for the recovery of the property of which [certain] Englishmen have been defrauded by Chinese.

On the subject of the remaining sections, their proposal to pay duties in gold coin, their application for a gracious remission of arrears of duties, and the circulation of foreign silver and foreign coins, being things regarding the duties [as collected] in different places, it is not in the power of your slaves to inform themselves exactly; and were they without due consideration to enter on the discussion of these with the barbarians, they would probably, in their humble opinion, be misled by them.

To come [to the final arrangements to be made,] these chiefs went first to Kwang Tung. Yeh Mingchin refusing to see them, they returned to Shanghai; but though they there did meet Kirhanga, they were still without a means of humbly bringing to the notice of your sacred Majesty the requests which they had it at heart to prefer. They accordingly came straight to Tientsin; and it is shown by their words and looks that they are touched and gratified by the appointment of an officer to look into [their case.] Some of their proposed modifications of treaty, it is true, are outrageous and impertinent; yet if no single one were conceded, they would certainly return home crest-fallen and angry; and though they might not venture to break out at once into open violence, still the mist of the south (the rebellion) is not yet laid; and were they to commence some separate and secret machinations (or mischief,) the management of them would be a more delicate* matter [than at present.]

Now, from the absence here of any of the papers required for reference, inquiry into and disposal of such of the propositions of the barbarians as admit of discussion would involve a considerable delay; the frosts may set in in the twinkling of an eye; the barbarians dread the cold, and will certainly not wait long; still, as far as their intentions can be divined, it seems to be a point with their chiefs to wait for the expression of your Majesty's pleasure. It is doubtless for your Majesty to judge what means were best to keep them within range. Dare your slaves so far forget themselves as to be importunate? Still, having been charged by your Majesty to act independently † in the course adopted upon the inquiry they were commissioned to make, it becomes of course their duty to declare frankly the view taken by their dullness, whatever it may be.

[They must suggest then,] that selection be made of so many of the articles in the paper tendered by the barbarians as may be in reason admissible, and that these be handed over to the high provincial authorities in charge of barbarian affairs, with instructions to bestow all attention on their consideration, and to bring the inquiry to a satisfactory issue in accordance with what they shall find laid down in the original treaty; that the spirit of tenderness ‡ be made manifest.

On the propriety [of this course] your sacred Majesty will decide.

---

* Lit. The managing or arranging would be more thorny to the hand, or finger-pricking.

† Lit. Enjoined not to borrow from the bystander.

‡ The word is more specially used of tenderness to men from afar.

It is not that your slaves are presuming to allow the barbarians to coerce them, but that they do apprehend that, unless your Majesty vouchsafes them a path out of the strait in which they appear to be, they may fly to some inaccessible [position,] * and so render the affair interminable.

They have communicated to the Governor General Kweiliang the details of their interview with the barbarian chiefs, and their inquiry of these as to the real object of their coming. It is further their duty to submit respectfully to your Majesty a confidential memorial prepared after solemn deliberation with the Acting Salt Commissioner Tsien Hien-ho. Prostrate they solicit the sacred glance of your Majesty thereon.

They respectfully present their memorial, and pray your Majesty's pleasure.

[The council] had the honor to receive a reply, in the vermilion pencil, on the 15th day of the 9th moon, (November 5, 1854.)

Translated by

THOMAS WADE,
Chinese Secretary.

VII.

Postscript to the aforegoing, acknowledged on the 5th November, 1854.
The English are taking the lead in all this movement; they have been kept in the dark as to the Emperor's acquaintance with their proposals. They must be sent south, as before suggested; indifference affected about their further proceedings, and every precaution taken against them.

[Translation.]

SUPPLEMENTARY MEMORIAL OF TUNGLUN AND HIS COLLEAGUES.

Further: your slaves having received your Majesty's commands to administer barbarian business together, could they have so set the right before the barbarians as to prevent them going back from their engagements,† would they have dared to trouble your sacred Majesty with further matter of thought by the application which they respectfully make for a celestial decision.

The English barbarians are, however, full of insidious schemes, uncontrollably fierce and imperious. The American nation does no more than follow their direction. Every movement is the conception of the English. A perusal of the list of propositions presented by them shows that they are, in general, the views of a single self. They consist neither with right feeling nor principle. They have been mildly remonstrated with, but so crafty and slippery is their disposition that it is hard to set the right before them.

---

* The phrase employed is classical; an alliance with the rebels is what is supposed to be hinted at.

† Lit. Chopping and changing, going back and forward, accepting a decision and then repudiating it.

Your slaves, having duly taken counsel together, have resolved to point out to them what articles admit of discussion; and for discussion of these, whether important or otherwise, to refer them to one of the five open ports. The place to which they might prefer to proceed, your slaves would report to the throne; high authorities of the province in which it lies receiving instructions from your Majesty to consult together and make their disposition according to the particulars of the case as ascertained by them on investigation, and [on this decision] to oblige the barbarians to return and abide [the issue;] to reject the rest of their propositions one and all; and on a receipt of your Majesty's approval [of this course] to write them another letter for their instruction, and return them (lit. throw back) their paper of articles. Should they be willfully perverse, to take no notice of it, but to [be] more than ever active in preparing secretly for defense, and to wait spear in hand. With the right on our side and the wrong on theirs, it does not seem that they can have anything to allege against us. It is the nature of the *Man** and the *I*, while they dread the strong, to insult the weak. Without some display of power, they will not, perhaps, be deterred from their purpose of prying and spying, (lit. their heart of spying will not be awed.) It is proposed, in replying to them, to show a certain amount of indifference; thus to enhance the dignity of the State and annihilate their treacherous projects. The barbarians are in no ways to be informed that the paper of propositions tendered by them has been laid before the throne. They were told in the first instance that it was taken away to be studied more carefully; that on anything in it which might be of advantage to both sides, or in no way to the prejudice of either, your Majesty's pleasure would, after due deliberation, be requested for them; that the remainder would be negatived article by article, as being from their offensiveness and impertinence harmful and impracticable; and that the paper would be returned to them on the 18th, (November 8.) The barbarians have never been given to understand that a copy of it could have been submitted to your Majesty for perusal.

As in duty bound, they add this inclosure to the foregoing articles.

VIII.

Imperial Decree, approving the suggestions of Tsunglun and the tone he had adopted; reviews the barbarian propositions. November 5, 1854.

[Translation.]

On the 15th of the 9th moon of the 4th year of Hien-fung, (November 5, 1854,) was received the following imperial decree:

"Tsunglun and his colleagues have presented a memorial, showing that the barbarian chiefs of the American and English barbarians had

---

* The four barbarian races surrounding ancient China proper were, the Man, the I, the Jung, and the Tih. The second is now almost generic for races not Chinese.

come into port to visit them; that they had ascertained from them the object of their coming; also, the steps they (the memorialists) had agreed upon consultation to take.

"The tone taken by Tsunglun and his colleagues, in their interview with the chiefs, McLane and Bowring, certainly was dignified, and the suggestions of their supplementary memorial are tolerably complete. The propositions in the draft of modifications presented by these barbarians are outrageous and impertinent in the extreme, and must be rejected as improper, article by article, that their insatiate craving may be put an end to. As regards the question, for instance, of intercourse with the Chinese local authorities, certain forms were agreed to [when the treaty was] negotiated. Every high local officer has his jurisdiction to attend to; how should he so depreciate himself as to have interviews with the barbarians at every place they may come to?

"Then, in the hire or purchase of dwellings or building sites, and the transport of goods for sale, the old treaty must be abided by. It would, indeed, be difficult to let them build in any quarter they choose and travel where they please.

"The Yangtsze Kiang is properly not open to barbarian chiefs; and with fisheries on the sea, the working of mines on the coast, foreign trade has even less concern. What they want is, to be spying and appropriating at other places besides the five ports.

"In the payment of duties, heretofore, either sycee has been employed, or its equivalent in foreign silver. This is an authorized practice of long standing; the use of gold has never been mentioned, neither is gold ever tendered in payment of Chinese revenue (otherwise collected.)

"Still less reasonable is the proposition that merchandise shall be temporarily stored in government warehouses, under protection of the [foreign] merchants and the Chinese custom-house. [And when it is considered that the] capital is sacred, as being the imperial precinct, and that Tientsin adjoins the metropolitan territory, the proposition to station barbarians [in the one], and to trade [in the other], is yet greater folly; and Bowring's proposal to make opium dutiable, and to be admitted into the city of Canton, is a detestable inconsistency.*

"Of the remaining clauses, those of the American chief are the more seriously objectionable. They must be positively negatived in plain terms, that a stop may be put to these irregular demands.

"In the matter of collisions [or disputes] between our people and the barbarians, there is the old treaty to refer to. Inquiry shall be authorized as to whether or not any late decisions of the local authorities have been unjust, and the governors general and governors shall make investigation and equitably decide.

"At Shanghai, commerce has been embarrassed by the violence of the disorderly (or the rebels). The merchants have suffered from this cause, and want a remission of duties. We conciliate and restrain the native and the foreigner alike. We cherish the sentiment of tenderness to men from afar. Reduction or remission of duties to a certain

---

*The opium question was assumed to be dropped when the treaty was conceded, and the Canton question since the correspondence of 1849.

extent would not be difficult; but the proper proportions of such reductions must be considered and decided by the governors general and governors of the provinces concerned, when they shall have ascertained the facts. There not being, either, at Tientsin, any papers bearing on the alleged overcharge of two mace per pecul on tea in Kwang Tung, this question must be disposed of by the governor general of the Two Kwang.

"Into the three last questions, inquiry and decision thereon may be promised; but all the other propositions are to be rejected as improper. Let Tsunglun and his colleagues, then, affecting to act on their own opinion, set the right before them; and while they undertake to make representation on their behalf, command them, on the other hand, to return to Kwang Tung. If the barbarians obstinately refuse to return [thither,] they may be allowed to go to Shanghai, where Iliang and his colleague can make inquiry and take action accordingly. The barbarians may also be told that there is no analogy between Tientsin and the five ports; and that though, in this instance, representation of their wishes has been made as an indulgence, in consideration of the trouble they have had with the winds and the waves, if, inconsistent* and disobedient, they return at some future time to Tientsin, they cannot certainly be shown the same courtesy as on the present occasion. The paper of propositions presented by the barbarians is further to be thrown back to them.

"Tsunglun and his colleagues will lose no time in reporting to us whatever may follow upon their announcement to the barbarians that their propositions are disallowed; and they will, at the same time, take precaution against any mishap, with strictness and secrecy. Respect this!"

Translated by T. WADE,
Chinese Secretary.

IX.

Memorial of Tsunglun and his colleagues reporting the steps taken by them in obedience to the imperial decree of November 5, 1854. The barbarians doubt that any representation will be made to the throne; it is accordingly promised on the three questions; they seem to have had three points to carry, but to have advanced others for show; they have now gone south, and it would be well that the course pursued in their coming discussion with high provincial functionaries should disabuse them totally of the practicability of negotiations by way of Tientsin. Dated November 10, 1854.

[Translation.]

Your slaves, Tsunglun, Wankien, and Shwang-yui, on their knees present a memorial.

* Not abiding by the decision they now accept.

They pray the glance of your sacred Majesty upon their respectful memorial, showing how they had disapproved and rejected the modifications [of treaty] pressed for by the chiefs of the English and American barbarians; and reporting the receipt of communications, one from McLane and another from Bowring, and the departure of the two barbarians out of port.

Your slaves would humbly state that, on the 16th of the 9th moon, (November 6th,) they had the honor to receive through the council an imperial decree to this effect:

"Upon collisions between the people and barbarians there is the original treaty to refer to. Inquiry shall be authorized to ascertain whether justice has been done or not in their decisions of late by the local authorities, and the governors general and governors of the jurisdictions will deal equitably in the matter, &c. Respect this!"

We contemplated with reverence the sovereign purpose of your Majesty, who, by the even display of grace and dignity, would thus tranquillize and comfort the outer barbarians. The respectful emotion of your slaves, hereby provided with wherewithal to guide them, as they read the decree, was more than they could bear. As in duty bound they at once took counsel together, and [wrote] to reject as improper every one of the extravagant demands the barbarians had seen fit to bring forward, article by article; nor did they venture, while authorizing inquiry into the three [remaining] articles, to make any promise inconsiderately. In the communication they addressed to the barbarians they merely said "should any be open to discussion."

This letter was sent on the 18th instant, (November 8th,) and the same day Medhurst and Parker took it out of port. On the 20th a reply was received from each of the barbarian chiefs to the effect that, as the promise given did not extend to the whole of the propositions, there was no guarantee that representation [of any] would be made for them to the throne, and that they would go back and see the rulers of their States, that it might be decided whether the question be further proceeded with or not.

Your slaves, on this, wrote a reply, to be obeyed by these chiefs, to the effect that representation respecting the three questions that it had been decided were open to discussion should be made; that the tea duties were a Canton question; the arrears of duties a Shanghai question; and that it behooved them to return [whither they would;] whatever the place, the high authorities of the province would be sure to have had transmitted to them your Majesty's commands to investigate and decide.

This done, it was reported at noon by Hung-chikán, acting commodore of the Takoo station, that the two small barbarian vessels had weighed from their original anchorage in the watch called *tsz,* (9 to 10, a. m.,) on the 20th, and had stood out of port.

In the opinion of your slaves, the object of McLane and Bowring, the barbarian chiefs of America and England, in coming hither on this occasion, was, to judge from all the circumstances [of their visit]—their stay at Tientsin above twenty days, their application to have an audience of ministers in the capital—with a view to the modification of the existing treaty, and the redress of their complaints; failing this, to have a commissioner sent down to negotiate the settlement [of these questions;] so on till your slave Tsunglun did arrive in Tientsin, and had met these chiefs, when they presented a paper of demands, three of which, although all the articles have been singly disapproved of as improper, certainly are open to discussion. Their chief object [was to obtain consideration of] the arrear of duties at Shanghai, the over-charge on the tea duties at Canton, and trade up the Yangtsze Kiang. The remaining articles were mere talk (or lies) to produce an effect.

It would seem by their returning south, as they are now doing, that their success in obtaining a certain portion, though not the full amount, of what they made a voyage hither to ask for, will deter them from seeking cause of quarrel elsewhere (or otherwise.) Nevertheless, the singular inconsistency of these barbarians makes precaution against their insidious projects indispensable, and it becomes the duty [of your slaves] to request that your Majesty will command the governor general of the Two Kwang, the governor general of the Two Kiang, and the governor of Kiangsu, in the event of the barbarian ships of McLane and Bowring arriving [within their respective jurisdictions,] on the one hand to enforce the strictest vigilance, and on the other to consider with them the three questions of which discussion has been authorized, reporting the decisions arrived at to the throne, and at the same time to inform the barbarians that, when they came to Tientsin, the subjects your slaves agreed were open to discussion were laid by them before the throne; that they (the barbarians) may be made to understand that Tientsin is a place at which barbarian business is never transacted, and a recurrence of anything so untoward thus prevented for the future.

Your slaves are forwarding the draft of modifications presented by the barbarian chiefs, McLane and Bowring, to the high authorities of the Two Kwang and the Two Kiang, whom they also advise of the course determined by themselves. They have further respectfully to submit, for the perusal of your Majesty, fair copies of the reply, in which they disapproved and rejected the propositions of the barbarian chiefs, the reply to this received from the latter, and their rejoinders of the 20th instant, (November 10.)

They have to add that they have sent some trusty officers, civil and military, to see whether the small barbarian vessels, though they had left the port, had sailed south from below the bar. When these shall have returned to Takoo, and made their report of what they may ascertain to be the fact, your slaves will present another memorial. Meanwhile, they repeat their orders to the troops and officers to be strict and secret in their preparations for defense, nor to venture, be it ever so little, to relax their vigilance.

They are forwarding to the Governor General Kweiliang all particulars of their disapproval and rejection of the several articles in the paper of modifications they proposed, presented by the barbarian chiefs, of the reply received from them, and of the departure of their small vessels from the port.

It is further their duty respectfully to present a confidential memorial prepared by them, in concert with Tsien Hien-ho, the acting salt commissioner. Prostrate, they pray the sacred glance thereon. To this end they respectfully memorialize.

A reply in the vermilion pencil was received on the 22d of 9th moon 4th year of Hien-fung, (November 12, 1854.)

Translated by T. WADE.

X.

Postscript to the foregoing on the appearance of M. Kleczkowski, and his application for the release of a French missionary. Discussions regarding his reception, and doubts as to his real character.

SUPPLEMENTARY MEMORIAL OF TSUNGLUN AND HIS COLLEAGUES.

Further: when the barbarian chiefs, McLane and Bowring, were paying their visit on the 13th instant, (November 3,) after they had handed in their papers, [another] barbarian suddenly handed a red visiting-card to your slaves. This was the French assistant envoy, Kleczkowski.* He understood Chinese, and spoke it distinctly. He stated that the envoy of his government had not come himself, but had desired him to accompany the English and Americans to Tientsin, as they were going there for information. What the English and Amercans had come to negotiate about, or what modifications of the treaty they desired, he did not precisely understand. He said also that the treaty with his government was made in the 24th year of Tau-kwang, (1844,) just ten years ago; that his government was acting with the English and Americans, each party aiding the other. Kleczkowski had come with them merely to be able to report on their proceedings when he returned to the envoy of his government.

In reply to a further observation that he would come alone on the following day to discuss business with your slaves, Tsunglun and Wankien promised that he should be received by the general and the intendant; † and he withdrew with the rest of the barbarians.

On the 14th your slave, Shwang-yui, and your servant, Tsien Hien-ho, met Kleczkowski in front of the fort; but when they asked him his business, the barbarian refused to tell it. He would say no more than that it was of the most serious importance, and that he could not be more explicit unless he had an interview with your slave Tsunglun. The right path was again and again set before him, but he persisted in refusing to speak out. So full of cunning schemes is the barbarian character, that it was out of the power of your slaves to say whether this individual was really a Frenchman or an accomplice [of the others] disguised as one, to serve some new [or ulterior] purpose of treachery. An interview was not to be lightly accorded to him. After a consultation, [therefore,] your slave, Wankien, named a day

---

* He was present, I believe, as acting secretary of legation.

† M. Kleczkowski did not understand this limitation. When the commissioner did not appear on the following day, it was explained that it was because he was unwell.

for an interview with him. The barbarian obstinately persisted in refusing to accept the appointment; but of this your slaves took no notice. On the 16th, Kleczkowski handed to the marine force in charge of the river a letter [to the address of your slaves], the sense of which was not very clear, and with it a cover from the plenipotentiary of his government, addressed to the chief secretaries of state, Yuching and Choh Pingtien. As it would have been improper for your slaves to receive or forward this, they wrote to Kleczkowski, informing him that any business he had to discuss could be explained in an interview with the general and intendant; if the matter were very important, there was no objection to his saying what he had to say in a letter. This reply was sent to him, and the letter he had forwarded returned with it.

On the 20th, (November 10,) the barbarian forwarded another letter, which proved to be an application for the release of a missionary, he being a French barbarian, who had been seized in the district of Chau-chih, in Shensi. The rest of it was very outrageous and impertinent.

Your slaves wrote a reply to the barbarian, and have respectfully to submit, for the perusal of your Majesty, copies of Kleczkowski's letter and their reply to it.

They have the honor to present this supplementary memorial to your Majesty.

A reply in the vermilion pencil was received on the 22d day of the 9th moon of the 4th year of Hien-fung, (November 12, 1854.)

Translated by T. WADE,
Chinese Secretary.

XI.

Confidential circular to the high provincial authorities of Kwang Tung and Kiangsu, advising them of the course taken under instruction by Tsunglun. The barbarians, all intent on gain, are easily put off with partial concessions. The provincials are to carry out Tsunglun's policy, and to keep an eye on M. Kleczkowski. November 11, 1854.

[Translation.]

Confidential letter from the members of the Great Council to Yeh, Imperial Commissioner and Governor General of the Two Kiang; Iliang, Governor General of the Two Kiang, and Kirhanga, Governor of Kiangsu.

On the 27th of the 9th moon of the 4th year of Hien-fung, (11th November, 1854,) we had the honor to receive the following imperial decree:

"With reference to the memorial of Tsunglun and his colleagues, reporting that the vessels of the English and American barbarians have weighed anchor and stood out of port, as it is to be presumed that they will presently set their sails and return south, we have commanded Tsunglun and his colleagues to forward an exact account of all the steps taken by them at Tientsin to the chief provincial authorities in Kwang Tung and Kiangsu. On their coming north on this occasion, all the barbarians would speak of was the appointment of a commissioner; they would not declare for what purpose they had come, until Tsunglun and his colleagues did receive them; and, after the right way had again and again been set before them, they presented a number of requests, more than one of them objectionable by reason of their unreasonableness and impertinence. We confidentially instructed Tsunglun and his colleagues to disapprove and negative the whole of these, but to write a reply promising, as it were of their own motion, that three of the questions, viz: the misunderstandings between the people and the barbarians, the arrears of duties at Shanghai, and the tea duties in Kwang Tung, should, notwithstanding, be looked into and disposed of. The barbarians, continuing mistrustful, on the ground that no representation had been made to us, Tsunglun and his colleagues undertook to make one for them; [but] desired them to return south and abide [the promised] inquiry and decision.

"As it was on this reported that the barbarians had weighed anchor, it is to be assumed that they have returned southward; and that if they do not come to Shanghai, they will go back to Kwang Tung; their averment that they will return home for instructions from their governments being nothing more than another of their fictions.

"Let Yeh Ming-chin, Iliang, and Kirhanga patrol and watch with strictness and secrecy at every port [in their jurisdictions,] and if the barbarians return with fresh demands, inform them that Tsunglun and his colleagues have submitted to us every proposition that is at all reasonable, but that the arrears of duties is a Shanghai question, the tea duties a Kwang Tung question, and that the question of misunderstandings between the people and barbarians belongs generally to all the ports open to trade; that however possible it may have been to have representation [on these question] made for them at Tientsin, the decision of them there is impossible; and that it will, of course, be their duty, these questions having been committed to them by our commands, to be inquired into at Shanghai and in Kwang Tung, to dispose of the same with impartiality; that not only is the representation to us of the rest of their propositions impossible from Tientsin, but that the minister in charge of barbarian affairs dare not so forget himself as to bring such requests to our notice at all, and that were [any memorialist] so rash and unintelligent as to press their cause further,* he would but subject himself to severe punishment, while no advantage would accrue to the barbarian trade.

"Gain is all the barbarians study. All they are set upon while thus hurrying to and fro is trade and tariff.† A trifle of what they apply for under these heads accorded them, and, as a matter of course, they settle down into silence.‡ But their proposition to trade up the Yangtsze Kiang, as suggested in the memorial of Tsunglun and his colleagues, must be peremptorily negatived. Nor must the barbarians

* Lit. Make supplementary or continuous declaration.
† Lit. Duty business; they want more trade and less duties.
‡ Lit. Subsidingly, or acquiescently, they speak out.

be led to suppose that that idea was ever communicated to us, that so they may be to a certain extent deprived of any plea that they are still looking for decree or sanction from us [on the subject.]

"The governors general and governors concerned must, in every case, weigh well all circumstances, and so prosecute inquiry as to insure satisfactory decision. Let them lose no time in apprising us confidentially of the day on which [the barbarians] arrive at any port, and of the particulars of their reception of them.

"As to the appearance at Tientsin of the French barbarian, Kleczkowski, he made no mention of trade; but whether he was abstaining from the renewal of a discussion in which the English and Americans had exhausted all their art, or whether it is a fact that he did not come to Tientsin for such a purpose, Tsunglun and his colleagues will, of course, have succeeded in making him turn south, and the governors general and governors aforesaid will observe his movements from time to time, and devise means of keeping him in hand.

"Let them be supplied with copies of the memorial and supplement of this day's date from Tsunglun and his colleagues, and of the supplementary memorials of Tsunglun and Wankien of the 28th of the 8th moon, (October 19,) and of the 3d, 11th, and 15th of the 9th moon, (October 24th, November 1st and 5th,) in all seven papers, together with our confidential decree issued to Tsunglun and his colleagues on the 15th of the 9th moon, and forward this as a confidential decree to each of them for his information, at the rate of 600 *li.* a day. Respect his!"

In obedience to his Majesty's will we write.

Translated by

T. WADE, *Chinese Secretary.*

XII.

Postcript memorial of the high authorities of Kiangsu, apprising the court of the intention of the United States commissioner, Dr. Parker, to demand a revision of treaty; and of a like movement threatened by the other treaty powers. Written early in February, 1856.

[Translation.]

Iliang and Kirhanga, on their knees, present a memorial.

Further, on the 27th of the 12th moon of the 5th year of Hienfung, (February 3, 1856,) Lau Wei-san, provisional intendent of the Su-sung-tai circuit,* reported to your servant, Kirhanga, that the American consul, Fish, had forwarded a letter from Parker, barbarian chief of that nation, to the address of Kirhanga. It stated that the chief in question having received charge of the business of envoy (or commissioner) of his nation, had reached Kwang Tung; that he should

---

* The circuit composed of the prefectures of Suchau, Sung-kiang, and Tai-tsang, in which Shanghai is situated.

remain there a few months, until a man-of-war steamer of his nation should arrive; he would then proceed to Shanghai to reconsider the treaty.

A reply was at once written to him, to the effect that the examination and disposal of all matters whatever connected with the trade of the five ports, belonged properly to the imperial commissioner, governor general of the Two Kwang, on whose functions it was not possible for the government of Kiangsu to encroach, and that it behooved the barbarian to submit his title to [the proposed] negotiations to the governor general of the Two Kwang for his decision thereon, and not to give himself the unnecessary trouble of going back and forward.

Lau Wei-san also reports that the English barbarian inspector of customs, Li Tai-kwoh, (H. N. Lay,) had told him personally that every nation would certainly require a revision of its treaty, failing [concession of] which, there would probably be trouble; that in Kwang Tung the Governor General Yeh had carried his exclusiveness to such a pitch that no envoy of any nation would have further intercourse with him. He, the intendent, had in plain terms declared [such a proposition] utterly objectionable.

Your servants find that, when the envoys of the nations concerned passed through Shanghai, on their way back from Tientsin, in the winter of the 4th year of Hien-fung, (1854,) there was something said about their coming again in the 6th year (1856) to bring the questions under discussion to an issue. The American barbarians now take the initiative; the English barbarians then make their declaration by the mouth of the inspector. Their words, be it, are respectful and submissive, but their purpose at heart is to constrain by pressure. The whole thing is beyond penetration, and as the war in Kiangsu is not yet terminated, it becomes the duty [of the memorialists] to request your Majesty to send down instructions to Yeh Ming-chin, governor general of the Two Kwang, to endeavor to keep them within range, lest, by rushing up north, they add to the number of our drawbacks.

Orders have been given to the intendent of the Su-sung-tai circuit to keep them securely in hand, and secretly to take every precaution [against a movement.]

It is further the duty [of the memorialists] to address your Majesty confidentially in this supplementary memorial.

Prostrate, they pray your sacred glance and instructions thereon.

A respectful memorial.

Translated by

THOMAS WADE,
Chinese Secretary.

Mr. Reed to Mr. Cass.

No. 34.] LEGATION OF THE UNITED STATES,
Shanghai, October 22, 1858.

SIR: The current business of the legation is not important. The consulate at Macao has been vacated by the death of Mr. Rawle, and I have appointed Mr. Gideon Nye vice-consul, till the pleasure of the President be known.

Mr. W. L. G. Smith, the newly-appointed consul at this port, has just arrived and entered on his duties.

One of his first acts, rendered necessary by the absence of all means to pay jail expenses, has been to discharge all the American convicts in the British jail. They are now at large, ready for new outrages and new shame to their country and its representatives.

I do not feel at liberty to say another word about the cooly trade to the West Indies. The vice-consul at Macao informs me that the Spanish consul there has intimated his determination, under orders from home, to refuse any further attestation of contracts, the government having become alarmed at the increase and isolation of the Chinese in Cuba. He further informs me that, on this decision being made known, an individual described as the "Hon. George Lyall, one of the legislative council of Hong Kong," a large cooly dealer, and who was sometime since tried for a violation of the passenger act, remonstrated, and persuaded the consul general to ratify existing contracts. So the matter stands.

I recommend the appointment of consuls with salaries at some of the new ports opened by the treaties of Tientsin, especially Ninchwang, Tang-chau, and Swatau.

Sometime before I left Shanghai, a claim was brought to my attention by the American firm of Augustine Heard & Co., for a return of duties paid by mistake. I examined and had it brought at once to the attention of the intendent. It has since been satisfactorily adjusted, and with good feeling on all sides. The correspondence is annexed.

I inclose, also, a copy of a notification I have received of the blockade of the ports of Cochin China by a combined French and Spanish force. Little is known or surmised here of the object of this warlike operation.

I have the honor to be, sir, your obedient servant,

WILLIAM B. REED.

Hon. LEWIS CASS,
Secretary of State, Washington.

Inclosure 1.

LEGATION OF THE UNITED STATES,
Shanghai, August 28, 1858.

SIR: I have examined the papers submitted to me in the matter of the duties paid by Messrs. Augustine Heard & Co., on an invoice of land-otter skins, in March, 1857, and now communicate the decision which, in accordance with the suggestion of the Taoutae in his letter of the 15th instant, I have made.

I am entirely satisfied that the deduction of taels 360.2.5, part of the tonnage dues of the Golden West, was erroneous; and I must not be understood as approving of the course which seems to have been taken by Messrs. A. Heard & Co. with reference to the guarantee given on the clearing of the Channing. If it were necessary to refund that amount, paid under *this* mistake, before correcting the much mor serious one as to the otter skins, I should not hesitate to ask you to urge Messrs. A. Heard & Co. to return this amount. In the view, however, which I take of the whole case, such a repayment would be a mere form.

With regard to the skins, there can be no question that the duty paid by Messrs. A. Heard & Co. was paid under a mistake not of law, but of fact, and that the difference between the duty chargeable legally and that which was paid, (crediting the government with the tonnage dues allowed the Golden West,) is wrongfully in the local treasury. No time was lost in bringing this clear mistake of fact to the attention of the Taoutae; and I direct you to say to him that, in my opinion, the claim is perfectly just, and that my government will insist on its prompt liquidation.

I am, sir, respectfully yours,

WILLIAM B. REED.

GEORGE B. GLOVER, Esq.,
United States Vice-Consul.

Inclosure 2.

UNITED STATES CONSULATE,
Shanghai, September 20, 1858.

GENTLEMEN: I have the honor to inform you that the case of the otter skins per Rajah, has been settled by his excellency the Taoutae, as per extract from a communication on the subject, as follows: "In order to finish up this very disagreeable business, I will agree to Messrs. A. Heard & Co. paying one mace five candareens per skin on the otter skins, instead of one tael five mace, which will make the entire duty on the skins, taels 97.9.5."

The original amount paid by you being taels 97.9.5, there is to be deducted from this amount duty as above, say taels 97.9.5, as well as taels 360.2.5, tonnage dues of the Golden West, leaving a balance of taels 521.3.0 due you, for which amount I beg to inclose herewith chop, which will be received at the custom house in payment of duties, receipt of which please acknowledge.

I beg the honor to be, gentlemen, your obedient servant,

GEORGE B. GLOVER,
Acting United States Consul.

Messrs. AUGUSTINE HEARD & Co.

Inclosure 3.

SHANGHAI, *October* 14, 1858.

SIR: We have much pleasure in being able to inform you that our claim upon the Chinese government for excess of duties paid by us in error upon otter skins imported per steamer Rajah, has at length been satisfactorily settled.

This claim has been pending since May, 1857, and we would express to your excellency our sincere thanks for your active intervention in the premises, whereby so satisfactory an adjustment has been concluded.

We have the honor to remain, your excellency's most obedient servants,

AUGUSTINE HEARD & CO.

His Excellency WILLIAM B. REED,
Minister Plenipotentiary of the United States to China, &c.

Inclosure 4.

[Translation.]

BAY OF TOURANE, *September* 1, 1858.

The undersigned, Rear Admiral Commander-in-Chief of the French and Spanish forces ordered to obtain from the King of Cochin China indemnification of injuries which is due to the governments of France and Spain, and in virtue of the powers pertaining to me as commander-in-chief, declare—

From and after the first day of September, 1858, the bay and river of Tourane, and the port of Cham Callao are put in a state of effective blockade by the naval and military forces placed under my command.

Every vessel which shall attempt to violate this blockade, will be proceeded against according to international law and the treaties in force with neutral powers.

C. RIGAULT DE GENOUILLY.

MACAO, *February* 23, 1858.

True copy, KLECZKOWSKI,
Secretary ad interim of the Legation of France in China.

Inclosure 5.

[Translation.]

LEGATION OF FRANCE TO CHINA,
Macao, September 23, 1858.

SIR: I have just received, and have the honor to transmit, hereto annexed, to your excellency, in copy, the declaration of his excellency rear admiral the commander in-chief of the French and Spanish forces in Cochin China, relative to the establishment of an effective blockade of the bay and river of Tourane, as well as the port of Cham Callao.

I have the honor to be, sir, with great consideration, your excellency's very humble and obedient servant,

A. BOURBOULON.

His Excellency W. B. REED,
Minister Plenipotentiary of the United States of North America to China, &c., &c.

Mr. Reed to Mr. Cass.

[Extract.]

No. 35.]

LEGATION OF THE UNITED STATES,
Shanghai, November 5, 1858.

SIR: Since my last dispatch, I have had the honor to receive yours (No. 13) of the 17th August, inclosing a communication from the Portuguese minister, at Washington. In accordance with your instructions, I have written to his excellency the governor of Macao, (inclosure 1 *a*,) and hope to confer personally with him on my arrival at the south. It will be very conducive to the general interest, if treaties can be framed by China with all the commercial powers, great and small.

The tariff and regulations of trade are not yet completed, but negotiations are advancing happily, and I hope by the next mail to forward to you a supplementary convention on these subjects.

The English and French plenipotentiaries are still here, awaiting with me the result of the tariff consultations. Visits of friendly ceremony have been exchanged between the Chinese high commissioners and ourselves, they making the first visits.

* * * * * * * * *

Hon. LEWIS CASS,
Secretary of State.

LEGATION OF THE UNITED STATES,
Shanghai, November 3, 1858.

SIR: I have the honor to inform your excellency that, by the last mail, I received a dispatch from the Secretary of State of the United States, inclosing the copy of a note from his excellency M. de Figaniere é Morao, the minister of Portugal, at Washington, informing the Secretary that his most faithful Majesty's government in China desired that its plenipontentiary in China should be invited to participate in the conferences between the diplomatic representatives of the treaty powers and the Chinese authorities. The Secretary of State desires me, as far as I can, to carry out the wishes of the Portuguese government in this respect.

I beg to assure your excellency, that had these instructions reached me sooner, I should have had much pleasure in having had your assistance in the negotiations I have had with the Chinese plenipotentiaries; and obeying the directions of my government, and my personal inclinations, should have expressed this wish to you. There has, however, been no conference between the diplomatic representatives of the treaty powers jointly and the Chinese authorities. The United States has negotiated throughout separately, as have Great Britain, France, and Russia.

The negotiations are now happily concluded. I hope to sail hence on the 6th instant for Hong Kong, where, or at Macao, I shall be most happy to confer with your excellency, and to explain fully what has been accomplished.

I have the honor to be, sir, your excellency's most obedient servant,

WILLIAM B. REED.

His Excellency ISODORO F. GUIMARAÊS,
Governor of Macao, &c., &c.

Mr. Reed to Mr. Cass.

No. 36.]

LEGATION OF THE UNITED STATES,
Shanghai, November 9, 1858.

SIR: I forward, for the consideration and approval of the President, two supplementary conventions which I have signed with the Chinese imperial commissioners. In the signature of these treaties there were associated with Kweiliang and Hwashana, the plenipotentiaries at Tientsin, on the part of the Emperor, Ho Kwei-tsing, governor general of the two Kiang provinces, Mingshen, president of the ordinance office, and Twan, an under secretary, all specially deputed as imperial commissioners.

The treaties are twofold—one purely commercial, embodying a revised tariff and new regulations of trade and transit; the other finally adjusting the indemnities due to our citizens. I confine this dispatch to the commercial treaty.

As I informed you before my departure for Japan, the details of the new tariff had been referred to commissioners or deputies appointed to confer with the local revenue officers. With the exception of the leading articles of tea, silk, and opium, which were not to be considered by them, our representatives had little difficulty in coming to a satisfactory result, by which a general reduction of import and export duties was to be effected, and yet a due regard shown to the interests of the Chinese government. Indeed, such discriminations were soon suggested as, according to the best estimates, will increase its revenue. In these preliminary conferences I was represented by Mr. Williams, and Lord Elgin by Mr. Wade, men of experience and sound judgment, and entirely beyond or above the prevalent influence here, by which everything is thought right which is determined adversely to the Chinese.

I took the precaution, several months ago, to address a circular to all the accredited American mercantile houses in China, asking for information and suggestions as to changes in the tariff. The answers generally concurred in the opinion that the tariff of 1844 was a fair one, and that little modification was needed.

During my sojourn for more than two months at Shanghai, my attention was specially directed to the subject of the two great staples of China, tea and silk, on which, as you are aware, there is an export duty, and of opium, which forms a large element, indeed, a controlling one of the import trade. I invited information on these points, taking care not to direct my inquiries to any one class, but endeavoring to ascertain the candid, and, if possible, disinterested opinion of all—officials, merchants, and missionaries. Especially was this important in relation to opium. The result was less diversity of opinion than could have been expected. On one point there was no dissent, that any system would be better than that which now exists. When I say no dissent, I perhaps ought to be understood as saying no audible dissent, for it is perfectly well known here that those especially among the English and Parsees, whose machinery of smuggling is elaborate and complete, wish no change, being content with their monopoly of profitable and indecent violation of law. To defy or corrupt the Chinese officials is with them a normal state, and the transition to obedience to law is a painful process.

Amongst all others the accord of opinion was remarkable. I called upon the vice-consuls at Shanghai and Fuhchau for reports on the actual state of the trade, and I now forward the one which I have received. (Inclosure 1 *a.*) Coincidentally with this, I received from a leading American merchant in China, connected with the well-known house of Russell & Co., a communication on the same subject, which I also beg to forward, (inclosure 1 *c*,) with the expression of my slowly formed but fixed opinion, that it is the simple truth to say "that to neglect this topic is merely to postpone to some future day a subject whose difficulties are ever multiplying, and to maintain meanwhile an irregular traffic practically irrepressible, yet forbidden by law; tolerated and encouraged by the government bound to prevent it, and hurtful to those who conduct it, if not to the Chinese people." Such is the testimony of the American merchant. In a letter published within a few days by an eminent missionary, he says: "Some of the most intelligent and zealous missionaries laboring for the welfare of the Chinese, wearied and perplexed by the view of the sad collateral effects of a smuggling system almost virtually legalized by the indifference or corruption of the local mandarins, have deemed it expedient to succumb to an unavoidable evil, and to limit and check, by the regulation of a legalized custom-house tariff, the spread of a moral mischief now utterly beyond control." In this view, according to my observation, most honest men concur, that nominal prohibition is, in point of fact, encouragement; and that the only remaining chance of restraint is making the trade dutiable, and placing it under direct custom-house control.

The result of the closest meditation on this subject, as well as that of the tea and silk duties, was, that I should communicate frankly with the English plenipotentiary, and as the initiative as well as the ultimate responsibility was with him, for I could easily content myself with the existing tariff, bring them distinctly to his notice, suggesting an alternative course for his adoption, and assuring him of my readiness to acquiesce in any fair adjustment which the Chinese, without any compulsion or fear, might agree to. I have the honor to inclose the correspondence which passed between us, and beg to direct your attention to my letter of the 13th September, (inclosures 1 *b*, 1 *c*, 1 *d*, 1 *e*,) as the fullest exposition of my views on this subject.

It was not until my return from Japan that I received Lord Elgin's answer, and then it was, as I have stated in a former dispatch, that the conferences of the subordinate agents being renewed, I was desired by the imperial commissioner to join in them. This I declined, (aside from considerations of delay and inconvenience,) for the stronger reason that I did not wish that any representative of the United States should appear to the Chinese to have any agency, or appear to have any desire, in inducing them to relax their laws of contraband. I thought that Great Britain and China were the parties to settle this difficulty, and that the most which could be expected from me was to be silent, and act in entire good faith to Lord Elgin and the Chinese themselves.

The result has been that, in the British tariff, the Chinese have, of their own accord, agreed to make opium dutiable, or rather to transfer its duties from the local to the imperial treasury. It now pays to the local or provincial mandarins 24 taels, or about $35 per chest, a chest varying from 105 to 160 catties. Under the new system it will pay 30 taels, or $44 per pecul, or 100 catties. Besides, you will observe that, unlike other articles of import, which can be carried anywhere in the interior by foreigners at a transit duty not exceeding one half the impost, opium is especially made subject to any transit duty, however onerous, which the local authorities may choose to impose, and can only be taken into the interior by the Chinese themselves.

Such is the solution of this chronic difficulty which Lord Elgin has been able to effect. I have no reason to think that any compulsion was exercised or hinted at. He has to me expressly disavowed it. This has been accomplished by no agency of mine. In agreeing to it in a tariff, made in this respect by others, I have recognized an existing state of things which I could not modify. My disagreeing to it would not have arrested American participation in the trade, for under the most favored clause in our treaty, the American merchant would avail himself of the British tariff, and would care very little whether our treaty was silent or not about it. I trust the President will approve of the course I have taken, which I am satisfied is the only manly and statesmanlike one I could pursue, assuming, what cannot be seriously questioned, that an uniform tariff for the treaty powers is desirable.

I am more and more impressed every hour by the identity or rather community of the commercial interests of the west, and that nothing is more likely to defeat the true aims of American statesmanship here than a distempered jealousy of English or French progress, seeing, as I do, in the ports and markets of China, wherever English enterprise goes ours is quickly alongside of it; that every dollar Great Britain spends on its postal service or in maintaining its naval force is for our benefit; that for the material of every yard of cotton goods she circulates in this empire, her manufacturers must look to the United States and buy from us; and that even in the manufactured goods we compete fairly with her, and produce fabrics which I have seen piled up, and are readily sold in the shops of Tientsin, and are carried by junks into all the inlets of Pechele and Liantung. It is under these convictions that I have endeavored to conduct, throughout, the negotiations, especially the commercial ones, confided to me.

In urging a reduction of the export duty on tea, I confess I never was confident of success. The other duties, though specific, are founded on an approximation to a five per cent. *ad valorem*, (the rate contemplated by the former treaties,) and revised now only because there has been a fall in values generally. This is not the case with tea, the price, as I am informed, having varied little in a series of fifteen years.

Hence there is some reason for its being excepted. Besides, it must be remembered that before the tariffs of 1842–44, the export duty on tea was from seven to ten taels per pecul, or seven and eleven cents of our currency a pound. It is now two taels five mace per pecul, or about 2½ cents per pound—certainly not unreasonable, at least by contrast with the British import duty of 15*d.* sterling. There was another difficulty which especially embarrassed the European negotiators in any attempt to reduce the export duty on tea. If 5 per cent. *ad valorem* on teas would have worked a reduction, five per cent. *ad valorem* on silks would have been a large increase, and to that the French never would consent.

But that which, apart from these considerations, reconciled me to the existing duties on tea and silk, was the reduction of the transit duties. If this be effected, or even partial success attend the experiment, and internal transit taxes be reduced from a hundred per cent., as they often are, to half the export duty, or one tael five mace five candareens, ($2 50,) no one need complain of the export duty. Opinion is very much divided here as to whether a system so inveterate, and under Chinese institutions so essential, as transit taxes can be abandoned or overthrown by such an expression of Imperial will as a treaty contains. They are sometimes, no doubt, arbitrarily imposed. But, according to the Chinese system, every provincial government levies taxes as it pleases, to defray its own expenses; it has its treasury, custom-house, and local administration, and an interior province, such as Hupeh. A Kiangsi regards country produce or imported goods passing out or in its borders very much as the sea-board governments regard them when landed or exported, and levies its duties accordingly. What may be termed the nationality of China in these respects, is singularly feeble. All this local revenue system is to be at once broken up, and the whole transit duty, though by different modes, is to be collected and paid at the ports. This seems to me, if practicable, to be one of the most important features in the new treaties. If it succeeds tranquilly, no one can estimate its beneficial influence on trade. I am hopeful, but not sanguine. It will require, for a time at least, the invariable employment of foreign agents, and thus may endanger friendly political relations. It imposes most serious responsibility on consular and diplomatic representatives in providing for these dangers.

How important the success of this reduction of transit dues will be may be understood when it is recollected that, owing to their recent augmentation, and not at all to the value at the point of production, the price of teas at this port has, in the last half year, risen ten per cent. above the averages of the preceding three years, or from twenty-one taels five mace per pecul to thirty-two taels.

With regard to the tariff generally, I content myself with calling your attention to the fact that, on the kind of cotton goods which form the bulk of American imports, the duty is unaltered for pieces of forty yards, while it is reduced on pieces of thirty yards, and this too when, had a general five per cent. *ad valorem* been insisted on by the Chinese, owing to the rise of value in our manufactures, the duty would have been increased. This is one of the advantages from the American treaty of Tientsin being signed first. It enabled me to make my terms on the tariff. The revision is entirely satisfactory to our countrymen in China. They are confident there will be a large though gradual increase in the consumption of our heavy cotton fabrics, especially in the northern provinces, and along the rivers now directly opened to commerce. At the new port of Ninchwang, in the northern part of the Gulf of Pechele, if it be an available port, of which there are some doubts, the demand for the heavy American cotton fabrics ought to be large.

The regulations of trade appended to the tariff have been prepared with much care, and have my entire approval. A portion of them has reference to the continuance and extension of what is known in China as the "foreign inspectorate of Shanghai." It was originally instituted at the instance of most of the American and English merchants, with the approval of my predecessor, or Mr. McLane, Sir John Bowring, and M. de Bourboulon, the original design being that the intendant at Shanghai should appoint individuals, on the recommendation of the consuls of the treaty powers, to act as inspectors of customs. Although there was a temporary necessity for some measures to regularize the revenue at this new and important port, in creating it there was clearly an oversight of the principle which forbids the United States from aiding in the collection or administration of the Chinese revenue through officers in any way acting under its authority. For a long time the oath of the "American inspector" was taken before the United States consul, and filed among his archives as if he were an American officer. The first inspector was named by Mr. McLane or by the consul, at Mr. McLane's instance. The next and present inspector was named by Consul Murphy, and when, on a supposed vacancy, Dr. Parker recommended or nominated one, the intendant informed him he could not accept his nominee, because he had promised Mr. Murphy to keep the post open till a proper person could be sent by Mr. Murphy from America, whither he had gone. All this was clearly wrong, and since the act of 18th August, 1856, (section 19,) expressly illegal. One of my first acts on coming to China was (and this too without personal disparagement) to refuse to have any official correspondence with one who styled himself American foreign inspector. I have pursued this course throughout.

In the course of a year or less, the merchants who had, under some temporary exigency, urged this scheme on Mr. McLane, became dissatisfied. Those only who are familiar with the eccentricities of commercial reasoning, can explain the process which led the same individuals, who, in 1854 had earnestly recommended the plan, in 1855, to urge Mr. Parker to abrogate it. On reaching China, I was greeted with urgency to the same end, and I have had the greatest difficulty in persuading the gentlemen who complain of this inspectorate that, disavowing it altogether, and having no official relation to it, I had no power whatever to modify or abolish it.

But I was not the less bound to inquire into the justice of these complaints, so that, in any revision of the regulations of trade, I might persuade the Chinese to reform or abolish the inspectorate. I have done so with entire fairness; and I am bound to say that the trust delegated to these gentlemen has been honestly administered; that they have guarded the Chinese revenue most conscientiously; that they have been an obstacle to all sorts of high-handed and irregular action; and that no single well-founded complaint against them exists. This is the practical judgment I have formed, and I believe it to be that of every disinterested man in China.

When, therefore, the regulations of trade, agreed to by Great Britain and China, were presented to me, I was conscious of my ability to judge fairly the plan suggested, by which an uniform system of revenue administration should be extended to all the ports, and the right of the Chinese recognized, perhaps sanctioned, to employ citizens of the United States in their service, with a distinct disavowal of any agency, direct or indirect, of the government or its officers, consular or diplomatic. Lord Elgin was as anxious as I was to express this clearly; but he was earnest in the opinion that a foreign element was essential. This being the case, if, in the English treaty, there was a clause that the Chinese might employ an Englishman as inspector—and I had stricken out such a provision for the American—the conclusion would be inevitable, that it was to be altogether English, or English and French, and that Americans were to be excluded. This, of course, no one would desire, unless he is prepared to concede an English and French commercial protectorate on this coast. On full and careful consideration, I embodied the regulation in the treaty which I have signed.

The only other regulation which needs any explanation is that which prohibits the access of foreigners to the capital city of Pekin for the purposes of trade. When our negotiations were in progress at Tientsin, as to the visit and sojourn of an American minister at the capital, the Chinese desired to insert a provision that his residence should be designated and provided by them; in other words, as was quite apparent to Mr. Williams and others familiar with Chinese usages, that we should be received on the same footing as the Siamese, Anamese, and other tributaries, whose representatives are compelled to reside in a certain quarter or place provided for them, but who, when at the capital, have a right to trade. This was at once refused; and the Chinese commissioners were told that the American minister, if he came to the capital, would submit to no such restriction, and, of course, claimed no such privilege. They at once yielded; admitted that the United States were not in any way to be considered as a tributary; but expressed a strong desire for the insertion of a clause, (which implied no disparagement,) by which every one accompanying the minister should disclaim any design of trading. This is the history of the provision, as it stands in the treaty of Tientsin.

Lord Elgin informed me that, on his arrival at Shanghai, the imperial commissioners expressed so strong an apprehension of the effect on the government and the people of the resort of foreigners to Pekin for the purposes of general trade, that he did not feel at liberty to withhold his assent to a new restriction, especially as such a thing as trade at Pekin can scarcely be considered important by any one. I had as little difficulty in agreeing to it.

The other regulations as to free and prohibited goods, and the mode in which copper coin and grain are to be carried coastwise, explain themselves. Much importance is attached to them by the Chinese. In the tenth regulation, you will observe something very like a stipulation that the tonnage dues, or a portion of them, shall be applied to the maintenance of beacons and buoys and the improvement of harbors.

The whole correspondence connected with the tariff, as well as a very interesting communication addressed to me by the imperial commissioners, on commercial relations generally, and my answer, are annexed. (Inclosures 2 *a* to 2 *d*.)

I trust that this new arrangement of duties and regulations of trade will conduce to the interests of both nations.

I have the honor to be, sir, your obedient servant,

WILLIAM B. REED.

Hon. LEWIS CASS,
Secretary of State.

Index to Dispatch No. 36, *Shanghai, November* 9, 1838.

Inclosures.	From—	To—	Subject matter.	Date.
1*a*.	W. B. Reed...	G. B. Glover..	Making inquiries respecting mode of conducting opium trade..............	Aug. 9, 1858.
1*a*.	G. B. Glover..	W. B. Reed...	Details respecting opium trade at Shanghai..............................	Aug. 31, 1858.
1*b*.	W. B. Reed...	Lord Elgin....	Remarks and suggestions on important modifications in the tariff..	Sept. 13, 1858.
1*c*.	T. Walsh......	W. B. Reed...	Suggestions in favor of legalizing opium trade..............................	Aug. 28, 1858.
1*d*.	Lord Elgin....	W. B. Reed...	Showing the difficulties in the way of reducing the duty on tea—opium trade	Oct. 19, 1858.
1*e*.	W. B. Reed...	Lord Elgin....	Has declined to send deputies to meet Chinese............................	Oct. 20, 1858.
2*a*.	Kweiliang.....	W. B. Reed...	Proposing regulations for consuls, their granting flags to native boats, equality of officials....................	Nov. 5, 1858.
2*b*.	W. B. Reed...	Kweiliang	Suggests mode of action, how to regulate the flags on native boats...	Nov. 10, 1858.
2*c*.	Lord Elgin....	W. B. Reed...	Sends the tariff and regulations of trade	Nov. 6, 1858.
2*d*.	W. B. Reed...	Lord Elgin....	Accepts the tariff, &c.....................	Nov. 6, 1858.

Inclosure 1 *a.*

LEGATION OF THE UNITED STATES,
Shanghai, August 9, 1858.

SIR: I desire you to make me at your earliest convenience an official report on the subject of the importation of opium into the port of Shanghai, especially with reference to the following points:

1. What amount of opium was received at Shanghai and Woosung for the first six months of the year 1858, and how much was imported in American ships, specifying each and the owner, *or* on American account?

2. If you are able to furnish me the above information, or any part of it, I wish you to specify its sources, and whether the same be official or not.

3. If you are unable to furnish this information, then I will thank you to inform me what is the reason of such inability; and why, if the fact be so, the same detailed information cannot be procured with reference to opium as with reference to any other imported article.

4. Whether it forms any part of the duties of the office of the maritime customs, known as the foreign inspectorate, to supervise or take cognizance in any way of the import of opium at Woosung or at Shanghai, or whether this subject is expressly excluded from their supervision; and, if so, why?

5. Are there any statistical returns of the opium trade made or on file in the office of maritime customs?

6. Is the anchorage at Woosung under the jurisdiction, so far as custom regulations are involved, of the office of maritime customs?

7. Can a vessel loaded with American or European goods, paying duties, be discharged without a permit at Woosung or any where in its neighborhood?

8. What difference, in this respect, is there between the discharge of a vessel laden with opium and one laden with cotton or other goods of that description?

9. Is there a duty levied by Chinese authority on opium at Woosung or Shanghai; what is its amount; what express authority is there for it, and who collects it?

10. Are the officers of the maritime customs under any responsibility in the way of official oath or bond to the Chinese government or its officers; and, if so, what are its terms?

11. Are returns of the import of opium received by, or made to, any of the consular officers of the treaty powers at Shanghai?

12. Are there any vessels carrying the American flag engaged in the import of opium into Shanghai or Woosung; and, if so, furnish me with their names and owners?

13. If there are such vessels, be good enough to say to me whether in this case the provisions of the 10th article of the treaty of Wanghia are complied with, requiring the deposit with you of the ship's papers, including the manifest of her cargo, within forty-eight hours after she shall have cast anchor?

14. Are the forty-eight hours computed from the time of her casting anchor at Woosung, or from the time of her casting anchor at Shanghai; and, if so, does cargo discharge?

15. Are the papers of any American vessels now in your hands as consul which you have reason to believe are the papers of vessels engaged in the opium trade, or vessels really owned by other than Americans? If there be any such papers in your hands, be so good as to report them to me.

I have the honor to be, sir, your obedient servant,

WILLIAM B. REED.

G. B. GLOVER, Esq.,
United States Vice-Consul, Shanghai.

Inclosure 1 *a.*

UNITED STATES CONSULATE,
Shanghai, August 31, 1858.

SIR: I have the honor to acknowledge the receipt of your communication of the 9th instant, requesting information regarding the importation of opium into the port of Shanghai, in reply to which I beg to call your attention to the following answers, viz:

Answer to question 1. I am unable to inform you what amount of opium was received at Shanghai and Woosung for the first six months of the year 1858. I am also unable to inform you the amount imported in American ships, or on whose account opium is imported.

Answer to question 2. I am not able to furnish you with the required information.

Answer to question 3. The reason of my inability to furnish you with the information is, that the custom-house has no record of the amount of opium received at Woosung or Shanghai. The opium receiving ships at Woosung issue a circular to those interested in the opium trade, giving amount of imports and exports and stock on hand, but I have not a copy of one of these.

Answer to question 4. Opium is not reported at the custom-house, while all other articles of import are reported. The maritime inspectors inform me that they have never been instructed to take cognizance of the opium trade, and that an entire silence has always prevailed between the Chinese authorities and the maritime inspectors respecting the trade of opium. The reason of this is not stated.

Answer to question 5. There are no statistical returns of the opium trade made or on file in the office of the maritime customs.

Answer to question 6. The anchorage at Woosung is under the jurisdiction, so far as the custom regulations are involved, of the office of the maritime customs.

Answer to question 7. A vessel loaded with American or European goods, paying duties, cannot be discharged without a permit at Woosung, or anywhere in its neighborhood. The custom-house does not keep a regular force at Woosung, but occasionally the Chinese authorities send to Woosung Chinese watchmen to report if any smuggling is going on.

Answer to question 8. Opium is never taken cognizance of by any person that the maritime inspectors of the Chinese authorities may have at Woosung; and it is never reported at the custom-house that opium is landed at Woosung.

Answer to question 9. I am told by the Chinese dealers in opium that there is a duty of twenty-four taels a chest collected by mandarin boats (expressly appointed by a board of Chinese merchants at Shanghai for such purpose,) from the buyer of the opium, immediately on the delivery of the opium by the receiving ship at Woosung. The authority is supposed to come from the commissary at Soo-chow, who expends the same in purchasing munitions of war to destroy the rebels. The amount of duty so collected for the last six months is reported to be near $760,000. There are twelve Chinese boats cruising between Shanghai and Woosung, carrying a flag bearing the following characters, [Chinese characters,] which, being translated, mean "public committee for patriotic collections." Their province is to examine if any Chinese junks are smuggling opium.

Answer to question 10. The officers of the maritime customs are not under bond to the Chinese officers or to the Chinese government; the custom is for each inspector to take an oath before his respective consul, a Chinese copy of which oath I inclose herewith.

Answer to question 11. There are no returns made to any of the consular officers of the treaty powers by the maritime inspectors of the import of opium at Shanghai.

Answer to question 12. The steamers Yangtse and Antelope, carrying the American flag, are both said to have been engaged in bringing opium to Woosung. The steamer Yangtse at present stands in the name of Thomas Dearborn. The steamer Antelope, the last time her register was in the consulate, was in the name of R. B. Forbes.

Answer to question 13. These steamers always deposit their papers at the consulate within forty-eight hours after their arrival at Shanghai, and report being in ballast. As no oath is taken regarding the manifest, and as there is a regular custom-house inspector who boards these vessels on their arrival at Shanghai, to examine if they have any contraband goods, they do not deposit a manifest, although, when they bring cargo, such as rice, specie, or any other article, a manifest is produced.

Answer to question 14. The forty-eight hours are computed from the time of vessels casting anchor at Shanghai.

Answer to question 15. The papers of the American steamship Yangtse are now in my hands. I have mentioned before that I have reason to believe she is engaged in the transportation of opium.

I have the honor to be, &c.,

GEORGE B. GLOVER,
United States Vice-Consul, Shanghai.

His Excellency the Hon. W. B. REED,
Minister Plenipotentiary to China.

Inclosure 1 *b*.

LEGATION OF THE UNITED STATES,
United States ship Minnesota, September 13, 1858.

MY LORD: In the treaty between the United States and China, signed at Tientsin on the 18th June, it is provided, "that the tariff of duties to be paid by citizens of the United States on the export and import of goods from and into China shall be the same as was agreed upon at the treaty of Wanghia, except so far as it may be modified by treaties with other nations; it being expressly agreed that citizens of the United States shall never pay higher duties than those paid by the most favored nation."

In that signed subsequently by your excellency with the imperial commissioner, a provision is made having reference to a general revision of the tariff of duties on imports and exports, so as to approximate the impost as much as possible to an *ad valorem* rate of five per cent. The reason for this is declared to be the fall in the value of various articles of merchandise since the treaties of 1842, 1844, by which the rate of duties has been raised above the five per cent. It happens, however, that the main article of American manufactured goods used in China has appreciated since 1844, so that the rate fixed by the former treaty would be more favorable than a new *ad valorem* duty.

Still, properly estimating the advantage if not the necessity of something like a defined and equalized tariff, uniform in its provisions, for all commercial nations, and most especially interesting to Great Britain and the United States, I have requested the secretary of this legation to confer frankly and fully with the gentlemen understood to be deputed by your excellency, and the result of their consultation has been the sketch of a revised tariff to be submitted to the imperial commissioners, which I have carefully examined, and to which, with one or two modifications, which I shall presently have the honor to explain, I freely assent. I believe its terms will be generally satisfactory to my countrymen.

I am confident that had it been in our power to remodel the Chinese revenue system, your excellency would have agreed with me in endeavoring to procure a great reduction, if not total abolition of export duties. This, however, was out of the question. The aggregate revenue of the Chinese government for duties of all kinds is so meager and so inadequate to its necessities, and the system of export duties so familiar to them that it would have been idle to attempt. But now that a revision of details is to be made, I have indulged the hope that we should be able without detriment to the Chinese, to have somewhat abated the export duty, especially on tea, which, as you are aware, is and has been for many years imported free of duty into the United States; and on which, if I mistake not, the duty in Great Britain is in a process of reduction. There seems an incongruity, your excellency will permit me to observe, between the application of a general five per cent *ad valorem* rule to all other exports, and an acquiescence in an export duty at least of twelve per cent on average values. This is a very heavy tax on the European and American consumer. It is not easy to understand why tea and silk, the one of high and the other of low value should be excepted from the principle which the Chinese conceded in your treaty that five per cent. *ad valorem* was to be the value, unless it be meant as a boon to the Chinese.

I am quite aware that from another and most important clause in your treaty—the one reducing the transit duties to a rate not exceeding two and a half per cent. between the place of production and that of export—it is fair to assume that a great reduction will be effected in the cost of the article itself, and the hope is reasonable that the new treaty will very much reduce them. Still it is but an experiment, and with officials so ingenious in their devices of imposition as the Chinese, a doubtful one. In saying this your excellency will understand me as not meaning in any way to disparage a mode of action such as is provided in your treaty, (in regard to which I am very hopeful,) but as expressing a doubt as to the working of anything when applicable to a people such as this. Assuming, therefore, the possibility of the failure of the attempt to compel them to abandon the transit taxes, I beg to suggest to you the expediency of somewhat reducing the export duty on tea, and assimilating its rate to that on other exported articles.

But there is another matter of far greater interest, which, after full and anxious consideration, made more serious since I have been compelled to watch the operations of trade at this port during the last two months, I feel it my duty to bring before your excellency. I mean the opium question, which in its present condition is most mischievous in its relation to trade, and most discreditable to all parties, political and individual, which it taints.

In our brief conversations on this subject, at Tientsin, I frankly stated to your excellency what the views of the government of the United States were on this subject, and that I was instructed to inform the Chinese authorities, if the opportunity offered, that the United States did not seek for its citizens the legal establishment of the opium trade, and would not uphold them in any attempt to violate the laws of China by the introduction of the article into the country. I am not quite sure whether I mentioned to you, that on one occasion, at least, in my intercourse with the commissioners at the north, I did state these views to them; going even further, and assuring them that the United States would sustain any lawful attempt their government made to suppress this traffic. I have said something to the same effect to the Taoutae here, but in both instances the suggestion met with no response. The reluctance of the latter to talk on the subject, may be easily accounted for; but the indifference of those who more directly represented the Emperor, could only be explained on the ground either that it *was* indifference, or has been suggested by their fear, even to talk on a subject which they thought had once involved them in a war, and which might (so they reasoned) give them trouble again.

Be the reason what it may, I was unable to gain for the subject any consideration, and my deliberate judgment was and is that the trade must go on as it is, with all the mischief and disgrace, unless your excellency will undertake to adjust and regulate it.

At your excellency's instance, while the American treaty was in progress at Tientsin, I struck out from the draft the express prohibition of opium, which as you are aware, is in the treaty of Wanghia; and the reason for doing so, aside from my acquiescence in the views which your excellency suggested, was, that I was conscious that in its operation in China it was a dead letter, and as such, had only a place in the treaty for mischief. I beg to assure you that I do not at all regret my decision, and have reason to believe that what I did will be approved by my government. Opium *now* is expressly contraband. In the new treaties, for I understand them in this to correspond, it is contraband, or not, according to the laws of the Chinese government. Let me beg your excellency's attention to the actual state of things at this port—a type of others—a state of things with which I have been made painfully familiar, which I have sought to understand in all its bearings, and to which I refer in detail, not because it is unknown to you, but in explanation of the policy and necessity of the measures which I take the liberty of urging on your excellency.

It is not my intention to say a word as to the mischievous social or economical effects of the consumption of opium, about which I have little doubt there is some exaggeration, and of which, from personal observation, I have no means of judging. No one doubts it is very pernicious and demoralizing. But I am confident your excellency will agree with me that its evils as the basis of an illegal, connived at, and corrupting traffic, cannot be overstated. It is degrading alike to the producer, the importer, the official, whether foreign or Chinese, and the purchaser. This state of things, narrowing the question to this port of Shanghai, I understand to be this:

In the year 1857, it is said, upwards of 32,000 chests of East India opium, worth nearly $20,000,000, reached this port. It came either direct from Calcutta or Bombay, or by the way of Hong Kong, where it is an article of lawful trade, and where the sum of $33,960 is annually paid into the colonial treasury for the monopoly of dealing in it under a license. It comes to Shanghai in vessels of every nation, though, of course, as with other articles of trade, the bulk of it is in English and American ships. It so happens, and it is a matter of deep regret to me that it is so, that the most active opium business in any single ship is, at this moment, carried on in a steamer built in New York, nominally owned by an American, and carrying the American flag. I have endeavored to ascertain the aggregate amount imported hither in American bottoms; and as near as may be, I find it to be in American ships, counting the steamer Yangtse, to which I have referred, as over 6,300 chests, in English and others 25,700. It is brought as freely in the mail steamers as in any others. It is transferred at once to the ships known as opium hulks, anchored at Woosung, where it is carefully stored. These hulks, six in number, are under the English flag, though it is right to say that one of them is understood to be the property of an American house, and the depositary of much of the opium imported on American account.

This deposit has, as your excellency is well aware, all the discreditable features of a great smuggling transaction, except that of secrecy; for the scandal, if the trade were actually prohibited, is open and defiant. And yet the fact is that every chest of opium thus deposited is watched and guarded by boats belonging to the revenue service of

China; and on its discharge, is so designated as to secure in some way specific duty, (about twenty-four taels,) just as well ascertained as is the duty on every bale of English or American manufactures. Of these duties thus legitimated, and amounting, it is conjectured, to at least $1,000,000 per annum, no published return is made, no official or other regular statistical information afforded, except such as, I believe, the British consul makes; and an article which constitutes at this moment exactly one third of the import trade of Shanghai, is ignored as absolutely as if it did not exist.

I am at a loss to understand why this inconvenient masquerade, the English treaty being silent on the subject, and the Chinese laws virtually abandoned, is kept up. I am aware it has been suggested that the depositary of so valuable an article as opium should be at a distance from the city; but I cannot suppose there is a reason for the inconvenient and expensive contrivance now resorted to, and rather find one in the nominally unlawful and consciously discreditable character of the trade itself, and in the lingering desire on the part of some of the largest operators that it should continue on its present footing. The moment the opium is brought up and entered regularly at the custom-house, and the duty paid there as it is at Woosung, all the advantages which monopolists desire would be at an end, and the trade, let it be remembered, would not be in reality more legalized than it is now.

But, again, I beg your excellency's attention to another view of the matter, as affecting the character of the communities we represent. There is at this port a department of mercantile customs administered by three inspectors—English, American, and French—appointed by the intendant originally on the recommendation of the consuls of the three treaty powers. One of these gentlemen is employed, if I mistake not, on the present revision of the tariff, and all of them are persons of high respectability and fidelity in their peculiar trust. Their jurisdiction, as delegates of the Chinese authorities, extends below the anchorage of the hulks at Woosung, and over every description of imported merchandise, except opium, and over every ship that casts anchor within the river, except the ship that brings opium to Woosung, and goes away without coming to the city. In the printed returns of foreign commerce prepared by this department, and which, if complete, would be of great value in determining our relations to this empire, opium, forming, as I have said, one third, is omitted. All else is minutely included; and in a report made to me by the American vice-consul, it is stated that this subject has been expressly withdrawn from the cognizance of the foreign inspectors and reserved for the administration of the Taoutae himself, who receives the duties on opium, and remits the money to the authorities at Suchau. Whether this abstinence of what is familiarly known as the foreign inspectorate has always been as complete as it is now, I am not prepared to say, though the fact has been mentioned to me that during the war between Great Britain and Russia, while the exportation of saltpeter from Calcutta was prohibited, the Patna opium chests were regularly examined by the English and French inspectors, and thus this trade, legal and illegal, brought within their view. It is now, I admit, not within their province; and yet it can hardly be pretended that with an inspectorate, vigilant in all else in which England, France, and the United States are represented, the reproach of connivance at the traffic, if it be illegal, does not rest on them now.

I refer to this, and so I beg your excellency to understand me, not as indicating my willingness to assume any responsibility for the acts of the inspectors, or the administration of the Chinese custom-house generally, but as illustrating the discredit that is shed on everything and everybody by the present position of the opium trade.

In reference to the general effect on trade and revenue of the present state of things, I beg to refer your excellency to the inclosed communication, addressed to me by one of the most intelligent American merchants in Shanghai, which embodies views which I am sure will commend themselves to your excellency's attention. Whether we should concur in the remedy the writer suggests requires grave consideration; but of one thing I have no doubt—any course is better than that which is now pursued.

I have more than once understood your excellency to say that you had a strong, if not invincible repugnance, involved as Great Britain already was in hostilities at Canton, and having been compelled in the north to resort to the influence of threatened coercion, to introduce the subject of opium to the consideration of the Chinese authorities. Yet I am confident, unless the initiative is taken by your excellency, things must continue as they are with all their shame; and I appeal to your excellency's high sense of duty, so often and so strongly expressed, to this helpless though perverse people, whether we, the representatives of western and Christian nations, ought to consider our work done without some attempt to induce or compel an adjustment of the pernicious difficulty. In such an attempt I shall cordially unite.

But two courses are open for us to suggest and sustain—that of urging upon the Chinese authorities the active and thorough suppression of the trade by seizure and confiscation, with assurances that no assistance, direct or indirect, shall be given to parties, English or American, seeking to evade or resist the process; adding to this, what, if your excellency agrees with me as to the expediency of measures of repression, I am sure will be consonant with your personal conviction of what is right, the assurance of the disposition of your government to put a stop to the growth and export of opium from India.

I may be permitted to suggest that, perhaps, no more propitious moment for so decisive and philanthropic a measure could be found than now, when the privileges of the East India Company, and what may be termed its active responsibilities, including the receipt and administration of the opium revenue, are about to be transferred to the crown. I am confident my government would do ready justice to the high motives which would lead to such a course, and rejoice at the result.

Of effective prohibition, and this mainly through the inveterate appetite of the Chinese, I confess I am not sanguine; and I therefore more confidently, though not more earnestly, call your excellency's attention to the only other course open to us—the attempt to persuade the Chinese to put such high duties on the drug as will restrain the supply, regulate the import, and yet not stimulate some other form of smuggling, with or without the connivance of the Chinese. The economical arguments in favor of this course are so fully stated in the accompanying paper that I need not allude to them further.

In conclusion, I beg to assure your excellency that I am quite prepared to take my full share of the responsibility in sustaining either of the two courses I have ventured to suggest, and am sure your excellency will add new distinction to what you have already earned in reëstablishing commercial relations with China, by getting rid of this anomalous opprobium to all fair commerce.

I am compelled to put my views in the form of a communication to your excellency, for the reason that the treaty relations between the United States and China do not contemplate a revision of the tariff except through your action.

I avail myself of this opportunity to inform you that it is my intention to sail in a few days to Nagasaki, and to return to Shanghai about the first of October, in time to meet the imperial commissioners, should they adhere to their announced intention of coming south.

I have the honor to be, my lord, your excellency's obedient servant,

WILLIAM B. REED.

His Excellency the Earl of ELGIN AND KINCARDINE,
Her Britannic Majesty's High Commissioner in China, &c., &c.

Inclosure 1 *c.*

SHANGHAI, *August* 28, 1858.

SIR: In the treaties recently concluded at Tientsin, the opium trade appears to be ignored. As the approaching revision of the tariff may admit of reconsideration on this point, I propose to offer your excellency some reasons why so important a branch of foreign commerce with China should be more courageously treated:

1. Right or wrong, there is no doubt that this trade exerts a very great influence upon all foreign relations with China, and in any settlement affecting those relations is entitled to a prominent place.

To neglect it is merely to postpone to some future day a subject whose difficulties are ever multiplying, and to maintain meanwhile an irregular traffic practically irrepressible, yet forbidden by law, tolerated or encouraged by the governments bound to prevent it, and hurtful to those who conduct it, if not to the Chinese people.

2. The importance of the trade to our commerce will appear from the following statistics of the business of this port last year, viz:

Total exports of produce from Shanghai during 1847..Taels		33,444,000
Total exports of general merchandise from beyond the Cape of good Hope............Taels	7,044,400	
Total imports of general merchandise from east of the Cape................................	7,504,600	
		14,549,000
Total treasure imported, mostly from Europe..........		14,285,000
Total opium imported, 32,246 chests.....................		14,433,000
Total imports...Taels		43,267,000

The statistics of the other ports open to trade would exhibit a still larger percentage of opium imports as compared with all others. But I cannot obtain complete tables of their trade.

The whole importation of opium into China last year was, however, about 34,000 chests Malwa, and 36,000 chests Patna, of the aggregate value of about 35,000,000 taels.

3. Although this trade is contrary to treaty, and to Chinese law, yet it is carried on as openly as any other branch of commerce. The opium is derived from British India, where it pays a revenue to the government equal to fully twice the cost of production. Lord Dalhousie estimated this revenue for the year 1855–56, at £5,000,000 sterling, or about one sixth of the whole revenue of the company; and as this enormous sum is drawn entirely from foreign consumers, and levied with remarkable ease and certainty, it is not surprising that the Anglo-Indian government—a highly expensive administration in an exceedingly poor and very fully-taxed country—should encourage the trade which supplies it.

That it does so is known to all the world, and there is at present no sign of an intention to do otherwise.

4. The Chinese government appears to be as inclined to tolerate as the English government is to encourage the infraction of its laws about opium; for of late not only have no steps been taken to check the trade, but, at several of the ports, the imperial officers have publicly prescribed a specific duty on the article.

At this port there is a board of trade, commissioned by the Taoutae, which collects a duty of twenty-four taels on every chest landed, and, after deducting two taels a chest for expenses, remits the remainder to the provincial treasury at Soochow.

5. Nothing is better known than these facts. The foreign inspectors of customs, often annoyingly rigid on minor matters, offer no obstacle to the importation of opium, except the farcical one of forbidding its landing within the foreign quarter. At the anchorage, within a few miles of the town, the drug is discharged into station-ships in the broad daylight, and under the watchful cognizance of a Chinese revenue officer; and from these ships it is delivered to Chinese purchasers. These receipts and deliveries are made known as publicly as those of any lawful article of commerce.

Yet the foreign importer of opium is denounced as a smuggler, and, by treaty, his ship and cargo are held liable to confiscation.

6. But the absurdity of thus denouncing a trade so conducted, and playing so important a part in the commerce and revenue of great nations, is not greater than the injury done to the character of the merchants engaged in it.

There are very opposite opinions, held by very good men, as to the effects of the use of opium on the Chinese consumers of it, and doubtless many persons would decline to embark in the trade even if it were legalized. But there can be no two opinions as to the effect of smuggling, or the reputation of smuggling, upon the men concerned in it. Neither can there be any doubt that the necessity of taking expensive precautions against any sudden enforcement of the law, prevents free competition in the trade, and tends to confine it in the hands of large capitalists, who are therefore interested in retaining it under the ban of the law.

7. What has been said has had for its object the exposition of the unfairness and disadvantage of leaving the trade in its present anomalous condition.

I propose now to advert to some advantages likely to flow from legalizing it.

Taking the figures given under section 2, we find that the foreign trade of this port, in dutiable imports and exports, amounted in a year to about 48,000,000 taels. It will be an approximation to estimate the same trade of the other ports at 22,000,000 taels, making a total of about 70,000,000 taels a year.

Upon this the treaties allow the Chinese government to levy a port duty of five per cent., and an interior duty of about 2½ per cent., the united product of which may be estimated at 5,250,000 taels.

We may assume that, hereafter, this is all that the imperial treasury would annually derive from the foreign trade, and that it will probably prove a very inadequate sum for the necessities of the government. In such a case irregular exactions of various sorts are likely to be resorted to, just as they have been under the old treaties.

But if the opium trade were put under legal contribution at the same rate as other merchandise, the direct revenue to the treasury would be 2,625,000 taels more, and illegal exactions on other articles would probably be unnecessary. Indeed, the duty on opium might easily be increased so as to admit of a reduction on other duties; for there is no article imported into China upon which a high rate could be so surely levied or so seldom evaded. Even now, every chest is known to the public immediately on arrival, and as the Anglo-Indian government must take a strict account of all shipments from its territory, official returns of each could easily be obtained for the Chinese government.

8. There is, however, another consideration connected with this topic, which, while it might encourage your excellency to urge the legalization of the opium trade, might deter the British embassador from pursuing the same course.

This is, that the easy subjection of opium to a high duty might suggest to the Chinese government the feasibility of diminishing the consumption of the drug by this means. I have no doubt that this effect could be produced, since smuggling, except with the open connivance of the Chinese officials, might be made almost impossible, especially if the Indian government opposed it. For at high prices the consumption in China has always been less than at low prices. Thus, in 1854, the total consumption of Bengal opium was about 55,000 chests, at an average of 375 Mexican dollars each; in 1855, about 45,000 chests, at $450 each; in 1856, about 40,000 chests, at $500 each; and in 1857, about 36,000 chests, at $600 each.

Of Malwa the consumption has increased since 1854, probably in consequence of the diminished importation of the others, and prices of it have been steady at about 600 Mexican dollars per chest. The figures are: for 1855, 29,000 chests; for 1856, 33,000 chests; and for 1857, 34,000 chests.

It must be admitted, however, that China generally takes off the whole product of India, (less that sent to the Straits settlements,) so that the fluctuations in consumption may really have less to do with price than with supply.

But the fact that the Chinese already take most of the Indian crop is itself an argument for legalization, as proving that nothing but increased production can increase the import.

9. It is by no means certain that the Chinese government is so anxious to suppress the use of opium in its dominions as has been supposed. A prominent argument against it in 1839 was that it abstracted silver from the empire. But since 1853, when silver began again to flow into China, this argument has lost some of its force, and the toleration which the importation (and perhaps also the growth) of opium has since met may be the consequence of this flow of silver.

Even if the Emperor is sincerely hostile to the use of the drug, surely no western government, least of all the British government, could honorably oppose his using such lawful means to prevent it as the imposition of a high duty.

Yet it is to be feared that he will be deprived of this, in reality, his only means of suppression, if it is not offered to him. For the reluctance of his officers to approach the opium question without doubt arises from their conviction that England would resent or frustrate any efforts they might make to regulate or reduce the traffic.

I beg that these observations may engage your excellency's earnest attention, and that you will communicate anything that you may think valuable in them to the other plenipotentiaries prior to the revision of the tariff.

I remain, sir, your excellency's most obedient servant,

THOS. WALSH.

His Excellency WM. B. REED,
United States Minister.

Inclosure 1 *d.*

SHANGHAI, *October* 19, 1858.

SIR: It was not until after your excellency had left this place on your expedition to Japan that I received the very interesting and valuable letter on the subject of the Chinese tariff, which you did me the honor to address to me on the 13th ultimo. I have, accordingly, awaited your return before replying to it, as I had no means of communication with you during your absence. I trust that your excellency will now allow me to state that the frank and full manner in which you have been good enough to convey to me your opinions, and the able assistance afforded by the secretary of your legation to the gentlemen deputed by me to consider the details of the tariff, will materially aid me in my endeavors to bring the important questions at issue to a satisfactory settlement.

I so cordially assent to the views expressed by your excellency in reference to the opium trade, that I do not think it necessary to dwell on this part of your letter. I would only venture to observe on this head, that when I resolved not to press this matter upon the attention of the Chinese commissioners at Tientsin, I did so, not because I questioned the advantage which would accrue from the legalization of the traffic, but because I could not reconcile it to my sense of right to urge the imperial government to abandon its traditional policy in this respect under the kind of pressure which we were bringing to bear upon it at Tientsin.

The circumstances under which the question will come up for discussion in the conferences on the subject of the tariff, which are now being held at this place, are happily different, and I shall not fail to instruct the gentlemen who are acting for me on this occasion to call the attention of the officers of the Chinese government with whom they are negotiating to the considerations so ably stated in your letter. I have little doubt but that it will be found that legalization is the only available remedy for the evils which have attracted your excellency's notice, because I am confident that, even if the other difficulties to which you advert could be removed, it would be found practically impossible to suppress the traffic in an article so easily raised and transported, and the demand for which in the country is so great that, when the supply from some cause or another has fallen short, the price has, I am informed, even within the last few years, risen occasionally to upwards of $1,000 per chest, a sum exceeding, I should presume, five times the cost of production.

The subject of the tea duties presents certain peculiarities, and, in order that your excellency may clearly understand how I am situated in reference to it, it is necessary that I should trouble you with some details.

In the first place, the prime cost of tea has not fallen off since the first commenced treaties with China were framed. We can hardly, therefore, claim a reduction of the duty payable on this article on the plea of reverting to the rate established by those treaties. If, nevertheless, a clause providing for the revision of the tariff at this time had been inserted in all the treaties negotiated at Tientsin in June last, there would have been less difficulty in the matter.

We might have united in urging the Chinese commissioners to apply the principle of a five per cent. *ad valorem* duty—or rather of a specified duty fixed on that basis—indiscriminately to all articles, whether of import or export. The rigid application of the principle would, no doubt, in the great majority of cases, have resulted in a reduction of the duties now payable; but in some, as in that of silk, it would have led to an augmentation.

The existing tariff is, however, as your excellency knows, maintained by the terms of the American and French treaties. The French would probably rather adhere to it than accept a new one, which raised the duty on silk and lowered it on tea. I fear, therefore, that even if I could persuade the Chinese commissioners to carry out inflexibly the principle of a five per cent. duty in the amended British tariff, the result would be that under the most favored nation clause the tea merchants would look to the English treaty, the silk merchants to the French, for the duty which they were to pay on their respective exports; a system which would give rise to much confusion, and which would probably be regarded by the Chinese authorities as characterized by sharp practice, if not indifferent faith. The Chinese commissioners are alive to this risk, and have laid much stress upon it in resisting the arguments in favor of a reduction of the export duty on tea which have been urged upon them on my behalf.

And further, as your excellency very truly observes, the duty now payable on the export of tea is compounded of two elements, the inland, or transit, and the export duties. Your excellency puts the transit duty as now levied on tea at about one hundred per cent. on the value, the export duty at about twelve per cent. If this estimate be correct, it is obvious that the former is out of all proportion more onerous than the latter.

Moreover, the latter remains fixed. The former, as matters now stand, is practically susceptible of indefinite increase at the will of the mandarins. It may be a question, therefore, whether anything is gained by restricting the latter, unless the former be subjected to some limitation.

Under these circumstances, I have deemed it advisable that the gentlemen deputed by me to discuss the details of the tariff with the Chinese commissioners should, as regards the articles of tea, direct their attention principally to the regularization and limitation of the transit duty, although they will not fail to do what they can to secure a reduction of the export duty likewise.

I have the honor to be, sir, your excellency's most obedient, humble servant,

ELGIN AND KINCARDINE.

His Excellency W. B. Reed.

Inclosure 1 *e.*

Legation of the United States,
Shanghai, October 20, 1858.

My Lord: I acknowledge the receipt of your excellency's letter of the 19th, and beg to say, that if any suggestion of mine with reference to the tariff can be supposed to have weight with the Chinese authorities, I shall be most happy they should be communicated.

I am fully aware of the force of the reasoning against the chances of a reduction of the export duty on tea. It had occurred to my mind before; but it seems to me rather to apply to a reduction to a five per cent. basis than to an arbitrary reduction to some extent above that rate. Still, I shall be quite content if the reduction and precise ascertainment of the transit duties can be effected, and I am glad to infer from your excellency's letter that you are hopeful of such a result.

The imperial commissioners, a few days ago, addressed me a communication, inviting me to depute some one to meet the deputies appointed by yourself and them to perfect the tariff. Considerations of expediency have induced me to decline doing so. Under the terms of the treaty of Tientsin, of June 16, it would be in form irregular, and as the work was nearly done, and done after conference with Mr. Williams, I thought it better to decline the offer.

The moment I receive from your excellency or the imperial commissioners a copy of the tariff as agreed upon, I shall consider it, and determine in what way, if it meet my views, as I doubt not it will, the consent of the United States shall be given to it, so as to make it obligatory on its citizens.

I have the honor to be, my lord, your excellency's obedient servant,

WILLIAM B. REED.

His Excellency the Earl of ELGIN AND KINCARDINE,
&c., &c., &c.

Inclosure 2 a.

NOVEMBER 1, 1858.

KWEILIANG, HWASHANA, HO KWEI-TSING, MINGSHEN, and TWAN, Imperial Commissioners, &c., &c., herewith send a communication:

In the treaties concluded at Tientsin, it is provided that subjects of the treaty-making powers, when going into the interior of China must be provided with passports issued by and having the seals of their consuls. Each consul is to ascertain that the persons asking for these passports are honorable and upright men before issuing them. As it is of the highest importance that there should be no mistake on this point, we cannot refrain from addressing your excellencies (of the three treaty powers) upon the subject, and desiring you to come to a decision upon it, that no evils may ensue in its mode of operation. When you have done so, we hope to learn the result.

It is plain to us that the subjects of non-treaty powers should not be placed on the same footing as the subjects of those nations having treaties; but we, ourselves, being unacquainted with the usages of foreign nations in this respect, and unwilling of ourselves to lay down preventive regulations respecting issuing passports, desire first to receive the result of your deliberations before we act in the premises.

When persons belonging to either of the treaty powers disobey the laws, they are to be handed over to their respective consuls for trial and punishment; but the consuls of other nations are all merchants, and engaged in trade, having no control or restraint over their countrymen. Even these consuls themselves smuggle and commit other illegal acts. Such things are continually occurring, and if these consuls do not, and cannot restrain their countrymen, the results will be that the whole body of merchants will become more reckless, and evils multiply enormously among them.

We have anxiously deliberated on this subject, and come to the conclusion that all those nations ought to appoint consuls, whose special business shall be to atttend to the oversight of their countrymen; merchants ought no longer to act as consuls, for now they have only the name of such, and not the authority.

It is very important that consuls be appointed by the treaty powers to reside at all the ports newly opened to trade, there to exercise authority, and carry into effect the regulations. Many important duties devolve on the consuls, and we wish to speak of those officers candidly and frankly, for some of those of your respective nations have formerly and often acted in a manner calculated to impede and mar the harmony that existed between their nations and our own. They have acted perversely, without informing their own superiors, and willfully disregarding everything but their own opinions, have carried out their high-handed measures to the ruin of all cordial feeling.

We therefore earnestly request your excellencies to enjoin upon your consuls at the open ports that, when an altercation arises with the local authorities, and the two parties cannot agree, that both they and the native authorities are to refer the matter to their superiors for direction how to act. By following this rule, former evils will be avoided, and consuls not be able to do as they please, but he constrained to adhere to the treaties, and this will strengthen and perpetuate the harmony those compacts are designed to promote. The local authorities certainly have no desire to treat consuls disrespectfully, but the latter have frequently acted with rudeness and violence. This makes it desirable that plain rules for their official intercourse according to their respective ranks be laid down which will prevent all disputes.

The treaties now provide that a consul is of equal rank with an intendant of circuit; and the treaty with France stipulates "that the high officers [of that nation] shall correspond on equal terms with the high provincial dignitaries of China; but when those of an inferior rank have occasion to address the high provincial officers, they shall do so in the form of a representation, and the latter shall reply by a rescript, and all correspondence shall be conducted on the basis of mutual equality and reciprocal respect."

According to this article, the design is, that while a consul corresponds on equal terms with an intendant of circuit, a consul general should do so with the treasurer or judge of a province, as being of equal rank with him. If a rule like this be adopted, it will prevent all dispute on such points, and tend to a general harmony and good understanding.

Again, we have ascertained that various consuls at Shanghai have issued their own national flags to native boats, to the number of thirty and more, and the number is increasing, to the great inconvenience of public affairs. The masters of these boats are generally discontented men, unwilling quietly to attend to their own affairs, but who would not, if they had no such protection, dare, as they now do, to set the laws at defiance, screened by a foreign flag.

When the local authorities try to punish these offenders, they are unable to do so, for the miscreants act just as they please while they carry these flags. Outrage and lawlessness are, consequently, continually increasing, and there seems to be no limit to the evils flowing from this state of things. We fear, too, that it will be difficult to prevent the same practice at the other ports.

Conduct such as this, will, we apprehend, ere long, give rise to enormous wrongs and sufferings, and lead to disputes between our countries; and it is of the very highest importance that laws adequate to restrain and repress it be enforced. We have accordingly decided to ask your excellencies to enjoin upon the consuls of your nations, respectively, no longer to grant flags to native Chinese boats; and further, to request that those which have been granted to them be now withdrawn.

We will also ourselves issue our plain commands to the people, at the same time, for their guidance, announcing to them that any native who presumes to receive the flag of a foreign nation, and hoist it on his boat, will be regarded, on proof of the act, as a criminal, and be punished accordingly.

The preceding regulations will, we are of opinion, be for the best interests of the United States and of China, and, if adopted, conducive to our common welfare. We have, therefore, now communicated them to your excellency, and request you to consider them, and favor us with your reply. We have also sent a similar dispatch to each of the English and French ministers.

His Excellency WM. B. REED,
Envoy Extraordinary and Minister
Plenipotentiary of the United States to China.

Inclosure 2 b.

LEGATION OF THE UNITED STATES,
Shanghai, November 10, 1858.

The American minister has had the honor to receive the communication addressed to him by their excellencies the imperial commissioners, on the 5th instant, and has given to it careful and most respectful consideration. He highly estimates the friendly feeling which dictated it, and the eminently practical character of the inquiries and suggestions it makes. In the same spirit and with the aim of continuing the relations which have heretofore existed, he now replies to it.

The right of citizens of the United States to go into the interior of China is derivative, and is conferred by that clause of the treaty of Tientsin of the 18th June, which gives to the United States and its citizens all the privileges of the most favored nation. Being derivative, it must be exercised with all the limitations annexed to it, and one of those limitations is, that no one can enter the interior of China without a passport. This obligation rests on the United States as much as on Great Britain and on France, and shall be complied with. So soon as the treaty of Tientsin is ratified by the President of the United States with the advice and consent of the Senate, measures will, no doubt, be taken to prescribe a penalty to be inflicted by the consular authority on any one who enters China without a passport certifying to his citizenship, or having one, refuses to produce it. This the American minister will bring to the consideration of his government, and he does not doubt that it will at once make such provision as is needed to protect China and prevent the infraction of its laws by Americans.

As to placing the non-treaty powers of the west on the same footing as those nations which have treaties, the American minister, as the representative of a great and friendly treaty power, is alike sensible of the expediency of some change and the difficulty of effecting it.

He respectfully suggests, however, that the remedy is to a certain extent in the hands of the Chinese authorities. Let them, in the first instance, show a willingness to make treaties with such powers, small and great, as approach them for that purpose. Years ago, Spain asked to enter into treaty stipulations with China and was refused. This should not be now. At this moment Portugal has, it is understood, expressed the same wish.

It should be met in a proper spirit, and thus the non-treaty powers be reduced.

But even if things remain as they are, there is a remedy which the American minister respectfully suggests. By the received law of the west, and western nations will recognize it everywhere, no one can presume to act as consul, unless as such he is recognized and permitted to act by the government to which he is sent. If, therefore, any one is acting consul in China without such express recognition by the local, or provincial, or imperial authorities, he is acting without law, and in his assumed consular functions, is entitled to no protection. Let the Chinese authorities resolutely refuse to recognize these interloping officials. If they have done so, let them, as they have a perfect right to do, withdraw it. If an American acting as the consul of a non-treaty power uses this function for his benefit or protection as an American, let him be refused audience and be referred to his own consul who will always be respectfully listened to. If an American acting as such consul appeals to the local authorities for aid and redress for citizens of this non-treaty power, let him in humanity be kindly listened to; and if redress be given, let him understand why it is done, out of humanity, and not of right.

If these men calling themselves consuls, presume to enter or clear ships or transact business as such with the customs, let it be refused until they put themselves under treaty obligation, and if then they still resist or evade the laws, let the revenue officers, if need be, forcibly prevent it. This emergency will add force to the suggestion which, in a communication the American minister made to their excellencies Kweiliang and Hwashana, on the 30th of June, as to the importance of increasing the naval force of China, and the use of foreign ships and steamers.

As to consuls being engaged in trade, the American minister desires to say that it is now the law of his country that no one shall be consul who is engaged in trade.

The American minister deplores, as sincerely as your excellencies can do, any past misconduct of the consuls who have represented the United States in China, if such has occurred. By direction of the President, he has endeavored to put matters right, and hopes there will be no grounds of complaint hereafter. But, if there should, he begs to assure your excellencies, if it be brought to his knowledge, it shall be corrected; and if the proper authorities, on well-ascertained facts, withdraw the exequator from a consul misconducting himself, the American minister and his government will not complain.

The best redress for all these irregularities is the dignified and resolute, but, above all, moderate assertion by the Chinese authorities of their own rights.

The question of the relative rank of consuls general does not arise with the United States, which has no such officer in China.

The consul of the United States reports to the undersigned that he has granted no flags to Chinese boats, and, on examining the records, finds that none have been granted heretofore. The American minister has impressed on the consuls to abstain from any such practice.

In conclusion, on this topic, he respectfully suggests to your excellencies that something be attempted or done; and it would be a proper subject, it seems to him, for a memorial to the throne, so that the imperial will being known there should be uniform compliance, by which a national flag, the same everywhere, and easily identified, should be instituted, to be carried in some conspicuous place by every Chinese vessel, public or private. The United States compels its citizens to have such flag. So does every other nation in the west. Why, then, should not China, with her vast and unprotected commerce, do the same? There would then be means of distinguishing the honest trader from the pirate and robber, and less inducement to usurp or adopt foreign and spurious flags.

The American minister, soon about to depart to his country, leaving the discharge of his duties to a fit person hereafter to be designated, begs again to assure your excellencies of his most distinguished consideration, and further to remind your excellencies that the clause of the treaty of Tientsien, by which, in time of danger and impending conflict, the good officers of the United States were promised, is not an unmeaning one. The United States will always be ready peacefully to aid China. The United States expects, in return, a faithful compliance, to the very letter, of every engagement which China has made.

W. B. REED.

Inclosure 2 *c.*

SHANGHAI, *November* 6, 1858.

SIR: I have the honor to inclose herewith the draft of a tariff and accompanying regulations, as arranged between officers named by me, on the one part, and by the Chinese imperial commissioners on the other, in terms of the twentieth article of the British treaty of Tientsin.

In making this communication, I would beg leave to tender to your excellency my best thanks for the assistance which Mr. Williams has, by your desire, given to my deputies in the discharge of their duties, and for the kindness with which you have favored me with your opinion and advice when questions of difficulty have arisen, in the course of the discussions which have taken place on this subject.

I trust that it will be in your excellency's power to accept, on behalf of your government, this tariff and regulations, which are, in point of fact, the fruit of our joint labors. It would obviously be a hardship to the Chinese authorities, if there were an absence of uniformity in the tariffs recognized by our respective treaties; and I know too well your excellency's high sense of equity to doubt your desire to avert from them this source of embarrassment and misunderstanding.

I have the honor to be, sir, your excellency's most obedient, humble servant,

ELGIN AND KINCARDINE.

His Excellency Hon. W. B. Reed,
&c., &c., &c.

Inclosure 2 d.

Legation of the United States,
Shanghai, November 6, 1858.

My Lord: I have carefully examined the tariff and regulations which your excellency has done me the honor to send me, with most of the details of which I had already been made acquainted by Mr. Williams.

I accept it unreservedly, on the part of the United States, and propose formally to adopt it by a supplementary convention, a sketch of which I now inclose to your excellency. There will, in this way, be left no doubt of its obligation on citizens of the United States; and it has the further advantage that it will attest, in the most formal manner, what, with reference to some of the changes in the import system, is important—the willing assent of the imperial authorities to what is now done.

I am, therefore, prepared to sign a supplementary treaty, on the part of the United States.

I take the liberty of adding one other word in connection with this subject. Aside from my great obligation to your Chinese secretary, Mr. Wade, for his willing and most able assistance on all occasions when I have needed it, I beg to testify, through your excellency, my grateful sense of the kindness and cordial coöperation of Mr. Horatio N. Lay, who, though not, as I understood, connected with your excellency's staff, is a gentleman in whom, I am sure, you take an interest.

There are many reasons which will occur to your excellency why I should express my feelings on this subject, and thank Mr. Lay for the aid he has rendered me in this preliminary conference at Shanghai. No one can hereafter do more executive good in "moralizing" the commercial relations of this empire than Mr. Lay; and I sincerely trust, under no circumstances, may he be withdrawn from this distinguished function of rendering service to the Chinese, his own countrymen, and, according to my clear view of their true interests and duties, to mine.

I trust your excellency will pardon me for referring to matters aside from the proper subject of this note, but I have no other mode of expressing these views.

I reciprocate cordially the friendly feelings expressed by your excellency, and am confident that it will be a matter of great gratification to the President, and my countrymen generally, that the close of our diplomatic action in China has been so harmonious and agreeable.

I have the honor to be, my lord, your excellency's most obedient, humble servant,

WILLIAM B. REED.

His Excellency the Earl of ELGIN AND KINCARDINE,
&c., &c., &c.

Mr. Reed to Mr. Cass.

[Extract.]

No. 37.] LEGATION OF THE UNITED STATES,
Shanghai, November 10, 1858.

SIR: I desire to communicate to you some remarks explanatory of the convention signed at Shanghai for the final adjustment of claims of American citizens, which I have especial pleasure in forwarding, as the means of redressing the wrongs of a large body of our deserving countrymen.

When at Tientsin, I made an arrangement for the prospective liquidation of these claims, estimating their amount at 600,000 taels, or $840,000. I was compelled by the urgency of these Chinese plenipotentiaries, who seemed to have an ill-defined dread of making any more treaties, to leave it in the form of an agreement in correspondence, authenticated as far as possible by the seals of the commissioners, and which I thought, and still think, was sufficient to be ultimately obligatory. Still, as a sort of executory contract, it was not entirely satisfactory. Their acts might be disavowed, and when the time came at which the compact was to be enforced, the government of the United States might feel some hesitation in applying the coercion which, in the case of the violation of a clearly-expressed treaty obligation, would be properly applicable.

There were other difficulties about the execution of the contract as it originally stood. There was in it a provision, insisted on by the Chinese, that in the examination and adjudication of the claims, especially those at Canton, the governor general should be represented, and an officer be appointed to act for him. This necessarily involved delay, and with the Chinese probably something more. The claims were to be paid out of American duties at three ports, and no apportionment was made or time stated for its going into effect, except the uncertain one of a restoration of business at Canton. The commissioners, in their perplexity, seemed unwilling or unable to make these detailed stipulations. These were difficulties inherent to such a mode of adjustment as was adopted at Tientsin, of which I was fully sensible, and it was my intention to avail myself of the first opportunity to try and have them remedied.

That opportunity has presented itself at Shanghai, and I am happy to say all possible difficulty has been removed by reducing the agreement to the form of a treaty, dispensing with the necessity of Chinese revision of the claims, and precisely apportioning the duties among the three ports.

Nor has there been any great difficulty in effecting it, the Chinese plenipotentiaries showing no disposition to evade the agreement they had entered into at Tientsin, and being quite willing to arrange the details on reasonable grounds.

My first duty, not the less binding because it was a duty to the Chinese, was to revise the claims themselves, and ascertain whether, after giving credit for such as have in the mean time been settled and paid, (the Mermaid for instance,) and applying some clear principle of law, the aggregate could not be reduced. The amount assumed at Tientsin was an arbitrary one. In the estimate sent to the department in February last, the claims were stated at a maximum of $1,286,841 88, though with the suggestion that the probable amount to be insisted on would be about $660,000.

In order to arrive at a still more precise result, I called upon the claimants for a revised statement of their claims; for it was well understood that, in many cases where there had been a claim for a total loss, property had been restored or paid for by the Chinese. In many instances the requisition was complied with, and accurate statements made. In some the request was understood strangely enough to be an intimation that new and extravagant demands would be entertained; and all sorts of speculation and contingent claims were preferred—such, for example, as a vice-consul asking to be remunerated for fees that he might have made, and the captain of a steamer claiming the profits of a year to come. As a general thing, however, the claims were revised in a proper spirit, and were sensibly reduced by the claimants themselves. Still there were many of a contingent character.

To them it was necessary, even in forming my own judgment, to apply the well-settled principle of law that, in case of damages of this kind, the prime cost or value of the property lost and at the time of the loss, and in case of injury, the diminution in value by reason of the injury, with interest, affords the true measure. "This rule," it has been said by the Supreme Court of the United States, "may not secure a complete indemnity for all possible injuries, but it has certainty and general applicability to recommend it, and in almost all instances gives a fair and just recompense."

On a careful revision of all the evidence before me, I was satisfied I could materially reduce the amount to be demanded; and, after some friendly negotiation, it was fixed at 500,000 taels, or $700,000, which was accepted by the Chinese and apportioned precisely between the three ports. It seems reasonable that the larger proportion should be paid at Canton, where the mischief was done, and I agreed that it should be so, the more readily as the Chinese consented that the appropriation of the duties should begin at their new year, in February, and not be, at least at Shanghai and Fuh-chau, dependent on the restoration of trade at Canton. The interposition of a Chinese representative in adjudicating the claims was waived.

You will observe a provision in this treaty that the debentures which the Chinese government is to give, and which, in all probability, if there be no new interruption of commerce, will be equivalent to cash, are to be delivered to such person or persons for safe keeping as the chief diplomatic officer of the United States in China may direct. This the Chinese seemed to prefer to consular agency, though the latter is not expressly excluded. In the draft of a convention which I at first submitted to the commissioners at Shanghai, the sum stated was 525,000 taels, with a provision that in case of an excess beyond the claims and interest it should be refunded to the Chinese government. They preferred, however, the small sum without such provision, evidently thinking it was their best policy to get rid of the matter forever. The brief correspondence is annexed. (Inclosures 1, 2.)

This convention will, if ratified by the President, and carried into effect by the Chinese, (as I doubt not it will be,) liquidate every claim on China by citizens of the United States—principal and Chinese interest, at twelve per cent. per annum, calculated for the three years on most of the claims, and for a longer period on others—and among them one (that of the Rev. I. J. Roberts) as ancient as 1847, which occupied the attention and excited the sympathies of many of my predecessors. The rest of them have reference to the destruction of property at Canton and its neighborhood. This, too, has been effected without the utterance of a single harsh word.

I am not informed precisely what arrangement has been made for the liquidation of the English and French indemnities, amounting, it is supposed, in the aggregate, to about $6,000,000, though I have understood from Baron Gros that an arrangement similar to mine, of an issue of debentures, receivable in payment of all duties to the extent of one sixth, had been agreed to. I left Baron Gros at Shanghai. Lord Elgin went up the Yangtsze Kiang on the 8th instant.

I now ask your attention to some suggestions as to the practical operation of this adjustment, and to the necessity of some action by Congress. Its execution will, of course, devolve on my successor; but neither he nor you will, I presume, regard my views on this subject as intrusive or inappropriate.

In making any computation as to the time when the proceeds of the claim debentures will be realized, as well as to the amount, much depends on the complete resumption of trade at Canton. Shanghai duties admit of an easy estimate. The average of duties on American ships and their cargoes for the last three years has been about 600,000 taels. As this includes years of local disturbances in the south, when, perhaps, the trade of Shanghai was increased, it may be set down at

500,000 taels, and of course the claim debentures apportioned to that port will be exhausted in the course of next year. At Fuhchau it will probably be slower, and, assuming trade to begin at Canton, and that it will labor under difficulties, no greater sum can be expected there. A safe computation would therefore be, that in 1859, 200,000 taels may be realized, and the balance, which will be nearly all paid at Canton, in 1860 and 1861.

This being the case, and the debentures coming into circulation, though of course gradually, in February, 1859, the first step will be for my successor (or if he do not arrive, the chargé d'affaires) to select some safe depositary in China of the debentures and their proceeds, it may be for a moderate commission, to be determined on at the time of the deposit. I take for granted one of the large mercantile houses in China will be selected for this agency, and it may be desirable to select one not of a claimant, or the creditor of a claimant. In determining this, however, great discretion will be needed, for it is the interest of the claimants, especially the smaller ones not connected with trade, and whose cases are really the hardest, that the large commercial duty-paying houses here should concur to appreciate these debentures.

While this is in progress there will be time for Congress (and their attention should at once be called to it) to provide for the adjudication of the claims and a dividend among the claimants.

I am quite aware that the practice of the government heretofore has been to have the amount of indemnities remitted to the United States and distributed there. Such a course would be disastrous to the claimants resident in China, not only in consequence of the cost of remittance, but the expense of proof. There are, at least, two precedents for the course I recommend of an adjudication here. By the convention, signed in 1803, between France and the United States, when commissioners appointed by the ministers adjudicated certain claims in France, and the convention of 1852 with Great Britain, when the commissioners sat in London.

The plan I propose is this, that Congress shall authorize the appointment by the President of two citizens of the United States resident in China, who shall adjudicate all the claims of persons in China, and make a distribution ratably as the amounts are realized, being authorized to direct by their decrees whether the claimant shall receive his dividend in cash, or, at his option, in debentures at par. That the award of these commissioners shall be conclusive, or subject to appeal to the minister; and that for their services they shall be paid a moderate compensation, limited to two years at furthest.

I limit the powers of this commission to the cases of residents in China. In the tabular statement of claims which I have appended to this dispatch, you will, under the head of claims suspended, see two—No. 2, section 1, "the Caldera;" another, section 4, No. 3, "Ryder;" and one not numbered, that of A. Pierrepont Edwards—which I presume must be adjudicated at home.

The case of the Caldera is the claim of New York underwriters, whose original evidence is no doubt in the United States, and can be there most easily produced.

That of G. M. Ryder involves a question of law as to the rights of a claimant who had declared his intention when the injury was done, but not been certificated as a citizen, on which it will be necessary to have the views of the government.

And that of Mr. Edwards, which was a case of personal injury received by him as far back as 1841. When his claim was first brought to my notice, he was resident in America; but has since, I learn, died.

A sufficient sum can be reserved to cover these claims, all of which are more or less doubtful, and remitted in due season to the United States for distribution.

If they be recognized, and the principle of paying interest be adopted throughout, the fund will be exhausted. If they be disallowed, though interest be paid to all the other claimants, there will be a surplus at the disposition of the government. I append to this dispatch (Inclosure 3) a schedule of the claims as revised.

I am without any distinct information of the intention of the allies as to the occupation of Canton. Lord Elgin told me incidentally the other day that, until he received instructions from his government, after the arrival of the treaties, he was unable to form any positive opinion. I have no doubt of his extreme anxiety to get rid of Canton, and none that until it is absolutely evacuated by the military trade will not be entirely resumed. I have called upon the consul at Canton to report to me specially the exact condition of things; and, if his answer be received in season, shall forward it with this dispatch. One thing is very certain that the English will do nothing permanently to obstruct the export of tea.

* * * * * * * * *

I have the honor to be, sir, your obedient servant,

WILLIAM B. REED.

Hon. LEWIS CASS,
Secretary of State, Washington.

LEGATION OF THE UNITED STATES,
Shanghai, November 4, 1858.

The undersigned, envoy extraordinary and minister plenipotentiary of the United States of America, makes this respectful communication to their excellencies the imperial commissioners:

The undersigned thinks it a propitious time, in view of the presence of their excellencies, to bring to their attention the settlement of the American claims. At Tientsin their excellencies agreed that one fifth of the duties on American goods and ships at the ports of Canton, Shanghai, and Fuhchau, should be applied to the payment of their claims to an amount not exceeding 600,000 taels.

The undersigned proposes to their excellencies a plan for the immediate payment of these claims, by orders being at once given on the government bankers for the amount in the following proportions: one half at Canton, one third at Shanghai, and one sixth at Fuhchau. If this be done, the undersigned is willing to receive 525,000 taels in full discharge of all claims on the Chinese government. If not, he shall claim the execution of the former agreement to the full extent of 600,000 taels.

The undersigned has prepared a sketch of a proposed convention, which, on receiving your excellencies' reply, shall be immediately transmitted for inspection.

W. B. REED.

Their Excellencies KWEILIANG, HWASHANA, HO KWEITSING, MINGSHEN, and TWAN, *Imperial Commissioners, &c., &c., &c.*

NOVEMBER 6, 1858.

KWEILIANG, HWASHANA, HO KWEI-TSING, MINGSHEN, and TWAN, Imperial Commissioners, &c., &c., &c., herewith send their reply.

They have received your excellency's dispatch, in which you state that, as the claims of American citizens for indemnity for losses are not to exceed the sum of 600,000 taels, you propose a plan for their payment by orders given on the government bankers for the amount in the following proportions: one half at Canton, one third at Shanghai, and one sixth at Fuhchau; and that if this be done, you are willing to reduce the total amount of claims to 525,000 taels for all demands, &c. This proposition has been carefully examined by us; and we are also now engaged in examining the reclamations of the English and French for losses, and adjusting the manner of payment; but we acknowledge the consideration and kindness of your excellency in this matter, in that you have, of your own accord, reduced the first amount of claims, and now place the total at 525,000 taels. We have taken the matter into full consultation, and propose that, if a further reduction of 25,000 taels be made, fixing the total amount at 500,000 taels, their custom-house certificates can be issued at Canton, Shanghai, and Fuhchau, dating from the first day of our next year, (February 3, 1859,) which can be successively applied to the gradual payment of the entire sum. The custom-house at Canton shall pay 300,000 taels, and those of Shanghai and Fuhchau each 100,000.

If your excellency will reconsider this proposal, and draw out the scheme of a convention based upon it, and send it to us for examination, we then can arrange for an interview, at which the whole matter can be settled in accordance thereto. For this purpose we now send this reply.

His Excellency WILLIAM B. REED,
Envoy Extraordinary and Minister Plenipotentiary of the United States to China.

Inclosure 3.

Amended schedule of pecuniary claims of American citizens against the Chinese government, supplementary to the schedule inclosed in Dispatch No. 7, (February 1, 1858,) discriminating between the actual losses and the contingent and speculative claims granted on them.

Claimants and nature of claims.	Claims for actual losses allowed.	Speculative claims suspended.	Total allowed with interest.
Section 1.—Claims unsettled prior to October, 1856.			
1. Rev. I. J. Roberts, settled at 1,000 taels in 1847..	$1,400 00		
2. Rev. I. J. Roberts, for destruction in Canton in 1857	1,450 00		
3. Rev. R. S. Maclay, settled at Fuhchau in 1852...	213 46		
5. S. Drinker, balance of award in 1856	1,902 51		
		....	$4,965 97
Interest, at 12 per cent. per annum, three years and more	....	....	2,786 20
Total	....	....	7,752 17
Section 2.—Losses caused by bombardment of Canton by the English, October 29, 1856.			
1. Rev. Dyer Ball, books, furniture burned	$409 50		
2. Rev. John B. French, furniture burned	1,800 00		
3. Rev. C. F. Preston, furniture burned	774 00		
4. Rev. A. P. Happer, furniture burned	1,315 25		
5. Presbyterian Mission Board, school apparatus...	2,472 00		
		....	$6,770 75
Interest, at 12 per cent. per annum	....	....	2,437 47
Total	....	....	9,208 22
Section 3.—Losses caused by burning the foreign factories at Canton, December 14, 1856.			
1. O. H. Perry, furniture, silver ware, &c., burned.	$971 00		
2. Mission of American Board of Commissioners for Foreign Missions, printing office, &c.	17,598 00		
3. Medical Missionary Society, furniture	270 00		
4. S. W. Williams, type, furniture	5,700 00	$3,000 00	
5. Wetmore & Co., furniture, &c., boat	599 00		
6. W. W. Cryder, furniture	695 54	200 00	
7. S. Robertson, furniture	638 50		
8. King & Co., expenses of removing goods	2,000 00	33,391 10	
9. A. Heard & Co., house, furniture, demurrage...	15,395 00	30,760 15	
11. A. J. Case, clothing	1,200 00		
12. Russell & Co., furniture, demurrage	2,250 00	5,000 00	
13. T. Walsh, furniture, goods, commissions	3,503 00	4,995 82	
14. J. Read Smith, furniture	1,650 00		
15. H. S. Grew, furniture	400 00		
16. George Tyson, furniture	510 00		
22. George Tyson, as secretary of American Billiard Club	1,110 00		
18. W. C. Hunter, furniture, commissions, &c.	2,699 00	4,180 95	
19. Alvord & Co., furniture, commissions, &c	12,041 00	18,144 00	
24. James Purdon & Co., furniture	12,942 50		
James Purdon & Co., house in Canton	5,710 00		
James Purdon & Co., goods in warehouse	98,507 60		

INCLOSURE 3—Continued.

Claimants and nature of claims.	Claims for actual losses allowed.	Speculative claims suspended	Total allowed with interest.
24. James Purdon & Co., ginseng delivered, not paid for	$11,550 00		
James Purdon & Co., ginseng spoiled, 22 casks	9,930 00		
James Purdon & Co., various other claims, in all		$76,514 33	
25. Rev. C. W. Gaillard, furniture burned	822 40		
26. Rev. R. H. Graves, furniture burned	769 25		
27. Southern Baptist Mission, house, library	2,496 14		
29. Rev. D. Vrooman, furniture	200 00		
Hon. Humphrey Marshall, furniture	800 00		
Rev. Peter Parker, Chinese books	200 00		
			$213,157 93
Interest, at 12 per cent. for three years			76,736 85
Total		176,186 35	289,894 78
Section 4.—Losses at Whampoa, caused by Chinese, 1857.			
1. T. Hunt & Co., dock destroyed, fixtures	$80,000 00		
T. Hunt & Co., materials	53,020 19		
T. Hunt & Co., two floating dwellings	6,200 00		
T. Hunt & Co., schooner and cargo seized	4,648 00		
T. Hunt & Co., removal, damage, &c	9,010 00		
T. Hunt & Co., various other claims, in all		$111,094 32	
2. H. P. Blanchard		3,500 00	
James B. Endicott, timber	1,400 00		
4. F. Cady, house, goods, &c	19,817 00	9,000 00	
20. Steamer Willamette		14,227 00	
21. Smith & Lawrence		18,000 00	
Seamen's floating bethel destroyed	7,000 00		
			$181,095 19
Interest, at 12 per cent. for three years			65,194 26
Total		155,821 32	246,289 45

Summary of preceding schedule of claims.

Section 1. Totals of allowed claims and interest	$7,752 17
Section 2. Totals of allowed claims and interest	9,208 22
Section 3. Totals of allowed claims and interest	289,894 78
Section 4. Totals of allowed claims and interest	246,289 45
Total	554,144 62
Total of speculative claims	332,007 67

Additional claims not decided upon, nor entered in above.

Section 1, No. 2. Underwriters of Caldera	$100,000 00
M. Rooney, master of Caldera	4,750 00
Section 3, No. 10. P. L. Everett, unattested	6,500 00
No. 17. W. M. Robinett & Co	200,365 49
Section 4, No. 3. G. M. Ryder	14,128 00
A. H. P Edwards, for personal wrong suffered in 1841, amount not stated	
Total	325,743 49

Total of all claims now stated	$1,211,895 78
Amount stated in February 1, 1858, was	1,286,841 88

N. B.—The total of actual losses, including interest at 12 per cent. per annum, for three years on the above, is ... $554,144 62
Add Caldera's claim and interest ... 142,460 00

696,604 62

Two of the claimants (Messrs. W. M. Robinet and G. M. Ryder) have still to prove their citizenship, and their claims are therefore still undecided upon.

Sketch of an act to carry into effect the Convention between the United States and China, concluded at Shanghai on the 8th of November, 1858.

Sec. —. That the minister, or chief diplomatic officer of the United States in China, shall, so soon as the Chinese revenue officers issue the debentures or duty receipts provided for in the convention, select some proper depositary of the same in China, making such compensation as he shall think right, the said debentures or their proceeds being subject to the appropriation hereinafter provided.

Sec. —. That the President, by and with the advice and consent of the Senate, shall appoint two commissioners, who shall form a board in China to receive and examine all claims which may be presented to them under the same convention, according to the provisions of the same, the principles of justice and international law.

Sec. —. That the board so constituted shall meet at such time and place as shall be designated by the chief diplomatic officer in China, and within one year from the time of said meeting shall terminate their duties.

Sec. —. That the compensation of the said commissioners shall be $3,000 per annum; and the President of the United States is authorized to make such provision for the contingent expenses of the commission as shall appear to him necessary and proper, and the said salaries and expenses shall be paid out of any moneys in the treasury not otherwise appropriated.

Sec. —. That the said commissioners shall report to the chief diplomatic officer in China the several awards made by them, to be approved by him, a copy of which shall be by him transmitted to the depositary of the debentures or the proceeds as hereinbefore provided, who shall thereupon distribute in ratable proportion the said debentures, or their proceeds, according to the direction of the said diplomatic officer.

Sec. —. That so soon as the said commission shall be executed and completed, the records and documents, and all other papers in the possession of the commissioners relating to the same, shall be deposited in the office of the Secretary of State.

Mr. Reed to Mr. Cass.

No. 38.] LEGATION OF THE UNITED STATES,
On board the Minnesota, at sea, November 12, 1858.

SIR: His excellency Baron Gros has handed to me a copy of the treaty recently concluded on the part of the Emperor of the French with the Emperor of Japan, and I now have the honor to forward it to you.

Baron Gros did not go to Simoda after his visit to Yedo, and therefore had no opportunity of apprising Mr. Harris of his treaty.

Very little news that can be relied on has reached us from the French and Spanish expedition to Cochin China. The port of Turon has been taken, and is now occupied by the new allies; the Anamese have retired, maintaining a sort of feeble guerilla warfare, and disease is doing its deadly work among the French. The expedition is wholly in charge of military.

I have the honor to be, sir, your obedient servant,

WILLIAM B. REED.

Hon. LEWIS CASS,
Secretary of State, Washington.

[Translation.]

His Majesty the Emperor of the French and his Majesty the Emperor of Japan, wishing to establish between the two empires the most intimate and most friendly intercourse, and to facilitate the commercial relations between their respective subjects, have, in order to regulate the existence of these relations, to favor their development, and to perpetuate their duration, resolved to conclude a treaty of peace, friendship, and commerce, based on the reciprocal interest of the two countries; and, consequently, have appointed as their plenipotentiaries, to wit:

His Majesty the Emperor of the French, M. Jean Baptiste Louis, Baron Gros, Grand Officer of the Imperial Order of the Legion of Honor, &c., &c., &c.; and his Majesty the Emperor of Japan, Midzuno Tkigouno, Kami, Nagai Hguembano, Kami, Ynouie Schuianow, Kami, Hori Oribeno, Kami, Touashe Fuigouno, Kami, Kamaï Sakio, Kami—who, after communicating to each other their full powers, found in good and due form, have agreed upon the following articles:

ARTICLE I.

There shall be a perpetual peace and constant friendship between his Majesty the Emperor of the French, his heirs and successors, and his Majesty the Emperor of Japan, as also between the two empires, without exception of persons or places. Their subjects shall all equally enjoy in the respective states of the high contracting parties a full and complete protection for their persons and their property.

Article II.

His Majesty the Emperor of the French can appoint a diplomatic agent, who shall reside in the city of Yedo, and consuls or consular agents, who shall reside in the ports of Japan, which, in virtue of the present treaty, are opened to French commerce.

The diplomatic agent and the consul general of France in Japan shall have the right to travel freely in all parts of the empire.

His Majesty the Emperor of Japan can, on his part, send a diplomatic agent, who shall reside at Paris, and consuls or consular agents, who shall reside in the ports of the French empire.

The diplomatic agent and the consul general of Japan in France shall have the right to travel freely in all parts of the French empire.

Article III.

The cities and ports of Hakodadi, Kanagawa, and Nagasaki shall be open to French commerce and subjects on and after the 15th of August, 1859, and the cities and ports whose names follow shall be so at the periods hereinafter determined:

Nee-e-gata, or, if that city has not a port of suitable access, another port situated on the west coast of Nipon, shall be open on and after the 1st of January, 1860, and Hiogo on and after the 1st of January, 1863.

In all these cities and in their ports French subjects can reside permanently on the ground which shall be determined on for this purpose; and they shall have the right there to rent ground-plots and to buy houses, and can there build dwellings and warehouses, but no fortification or military post shall be there erected under pretext of building sheds or dwelling houses; and, in order to insure the faithful execution of this clause, the competent Japanese authorities shall have the right to inspect from time to time all the building works which shall be erected, altered, or repaired in those places.

The ground which the French subjects will occupy and upon which they can build their dwellings shall be determined by the French consul in concert with the competent Japanese authorities of each place; the same shall be the case in regard to port regulations, and, if the consul and the local authorities do not succeed in coming to an understanding on this subject, the question shall be submitted to the French diplomatic agent and to the Japanese authorities who shall conclude it by common agreement.

In like manner, in the places where the French subjects reside, there shall not be erected or placed by the Japanese authorities any wall, barrier, or inclosure, nor any other obstacle which can interrupt the free entrance to and departure from those places.

French subjects shall be at liberty to go whithersoever they please within the circuit formed by the bounds hereinafter designated.

From Kanagawa they can go as far as the river Locgo, which empties into the bay of Yedo, between Konasaki and Sinagawa, and in every other direction to a distance of ten rees (*ris.*)

From Hakodadi they can go to a distance of ten rees in all directions.

From Hiogo ten rees also in all directions, except towards Kioto, a city which cannot be approached, except at a distance of ten rees. The crews of French vessels which go to Hiogo cannot cross the river Inagava, which empties into the bay of Sessiu, between Hiogo and Osaca.

These distances shall be measured by land, commencing at the goyoso or yacousio of each of the above-named ports. The *ree* is equal to 3,910 metres.

At Nagasaki French subjects can go everywhere in the imperial province of the vicinity.

The bounds of Nee-e-gata, or of the port which may be substituted for it, shall be determined by the French diplomatic agent in concert with the competent authorities of Japan.

On and after the 1st of January, 1862, French subjects shall be authorized to reside in the city of Yedo, and on and after the 1st of January, 1863, in the city of Osaka, but only to carry on commerce there. In each of these two cities a suitable piece of ground whereon Frenchmen can rent houses shall be determined upon in concert with the Japanese government, and they shall also agree on boundaries around these cities, which Frenchmen are not to cross.

Article IV.

French subjects in Japan shall have the right to exercise freely their religion, and for this purpose they can there erect, on the ground intended for their residence, suitable edifices for their worship, such as churches, chapels, burial places, &c., &c., &c. The Japanese government has already abolished the use of practices which are insulting to Christianity.

Article V.

All differences which may arise among Frenchmen in relation to their rights, property, or persons, within the dominions of his Majesty the Emperor of Japan, shall be submitted to the jurisdiction of the constituted French authorities in the country.

Article VI.

Every Japanese who shall be guilty of any criminal act against a French subject shall be arrested and punished by the competent Japanese authorities in conformity to the laws of Japan.

French subjects who shall be guilty of any crime against Japanese, or against individuals belonging to other nations, shall be taken before the consul of France and punished in conformity to the laws of the French empire.

Justice shall be equitably and impartially administered on both sides.

Article VII.

Every French subject who shall have to complain against a Japanese, must go to the consulate of France, and there state his demand.

The consul shall examine whether it is well founded, and shall endeavor to settle the matter amicably. Likewise, if a Japanese has to complain of a French subject, the consul of France shall listen to him with attention, and shall endeavor to settle the matter amicably. If difficulties arise which cannot thus be removed by the consul, this officer shall have recourse to the competent Japanese authorities for assistance, in order that, in concert with them, the matter may be seriously inquired into and an equitable solution given to it.

Article VIII.

In all the ports of Japan open to commerce, French subjects shall be at liberty to import from their own country or from foreign ports, and there to sell, buy, and export to their own ports or to those of another country, every kind of goods which are not contraband, on paying the duties stipulated in the tariff annexed to the present treaty, and without having to sustain any other burden.

With the exception of munitions of war, which can only be sold to the Japanese government and to foreigners, Frenchmen can freely buy from Japanese and sell to them all articles which they may have to sell or buy, and this without the interference of any Japanese officer, whether so selling or so buying, or whether making or receiving payment in these transactions.

Every Japanese can buy, sell, keep, and make use of every article which shall be sold to him by French subjects.

The Japanese government shall offer no obstacle to Frenchmen resident in Japan taking into their service Japanese subjects, and employing them in any occupation which is not prohibited by the laws.

Article IX.

The articles regulating commerce annexed to the present treaty, shall be considered as forming an integral part thereof, and they shall likewise be obligatory on the two high contracting parties who have signed it.

The French diplomatic agent in Japan, in concert with the functionaries who may be designated for this purpose by the Japanese government, shall have power to establish in all the ports open to commerce the regulations which may be necessary to carry into effect the stipulations of the articles regulating commerce herewith annexed.

Article X.

The Japanese authorities in each port shall adopt such measures as may appear to them most suitable in order to prevent fraud and smuggling.

All the fines and confiscations imposed in consequence of infractions of the present treaty, and of the commercial relations thereto annexed, shall belong to the government of his Majesty the Emperor of Japan.

Article XI.

Every French merchant vessel arriving off one of the open ports of Japan shall be at liberty to take a pilot in order to enter the port, and likewise, when she shall have paid all costs and duties which may have been legally imposed on her, and she shall be ready to sail, she will be at liberty to take a pilot in order to leave the port.

Article XII.

Every French merchant who shall have imported goods into one of the open ports of Japan, and paid the duties exacted, can obtain from the principle officers of the Japanese custom-house a certificate showing that this payment has been made, and he will then be permitted to export his cargo into one of the other open ports of Japan without having to pay any additional duty of any kind.

Article XIII.

All the goods imported into the open ports of Japan by French subjects, and which shall have paid the duties established by this treaty, can be conveyed by Japanese into all parts of the empire, without having to pay any toll or any duty either of transit, excise, or of any other character.

Article XIV.

All foreign coin shall be a legal tender in Japan, and shall pass for the value of its weight compared with that of similar Japanese coin.

French subjects and Japanese subjects shall be at liberty to make use of Japanese or foreign coin in all payments which they may mutually have to make to each other.

As some time will elapse up to the period when the Japanese government will know exactly the value of foreign coin, the competent Japanese authorities shall furnish to French subjects, during the year following the opening of each port, Japanese coin in exchange of equal weight and of the same character as that which they shall give, and without their having to pay any premium for the new coinage.

Japanese coin of every kind, with the exception of that of copper, can be exported from Japan, as well as foreign gold and silver not coined.

Article XV.

If the principal officers of the Japanese customs should not be satisfied with the valuation given by the merchants to any of their goods, these functionaries can estimate their cost, and offer to buy them at the rate so fixed. If the owner refuses to accept the offer which shall have been made to him, he shall be required to pay to the superior authorities of the customs duties in proportion to this appraisement. If, on the contrary, the offer should be accepted, the price offered shall be immediately paid to the merchant without discount or diminution.

ARTICLE XVI.

If a French vessel should be wrecked or cast on the shores of the empire of Japan, or should be forced to seek refuge in some port of the dominions of his Majesty the Emperor of Japan, the competent Japanese authorities having knowledge of the fact shall immediately render to such vessel all possible assistance. The persons on board shall be treated with kindness, and means shall be furnished them, if this should be necessary, to proceed to the nearest French consulate.

ARTICLE XVII.

Supplies for the use of French vessels-of-war can be landed at Hanagawa, at Hakodadi, and at Nagasaki, and placed in warehouse on shore, under custody of a person employed by the French government, without having to pay duties; but if these supplies should be sold to Japanese or to foreigners, the purchaser shall pay to the competent Japanese authorities the amount of the duties which would be applicable to them.

ARTICLE XVIII.

If any Japanese should not pay what he owes to French subjects, or if he should fraudulently conceal himself, the competent Japanese authorities shall do everything in their power to bring him to justice, and to obtain from him the payment of his debt; and if any French subject should fraudulently conceal himself, or fail to pay his debts to a Japanese, the French authorities shall in like manner do all in their power to bring the delinquent to justice, and to compel him to pay what he may owe. Neither the French authorities nor the Japanese authorities shall be responsible for the payment of debts contracted by French or Japanese subjects.

ARTICLE XIX.

It is expressly stipulated that the French government and its subjects shall freely enjoy, reckoning from the day in which the present treaty shall be put in force, all the privileges, immunities, and advantages which have been, or which may hereafter be guarantied by his Majesty the Emperor of Japan to the government, or to the subjects of any other nation.

ARTICLE XX.

It is likewise agreed that each of the two high contracting parties, after having notified the other one year in advance, reckoning from the fifteenth of August, one thousand eight hundred and seventy-two, or after that period, can ask for a revision of the present treaty, in order to make in it the modifications or amendments which experience may have demonstrated to be necessary.

Article XXI.

Every official communication addressed by the diplomatic agent of his Majesty the Emperor of the French to the Japanese authorities shall be henceforward written in French. But in order to facilitate the prompt dispatch of business, these communications, as well as those from the consuls of France to Japan, shall be for a period of five years, reckoning from the date of signing the present treaty, accompanied by a Japanese translation.

Article XXII.

The present treaty of peace, friendship, and commerce shall be ratified by his Majesty the Emperor of the French, and by his Majesty the Emperor of Japan, and the exchange of these ratifications shall take place at Yedo within the year following the day of the signing.

It is agreed between the high contracting parties, that at the moment in which the treaty shall be signed, the French plenipotentiary shall give to the Japanese plenipotentiaries two drafts (*deux textes*) in French of the present treaty, as on their part, the Japanese plenipotentiaries shall give to the French plenipotentiary two drafts(*deux textes*) in Japanese. These four documents have the same sense and the same import, but for greater precision, it has been agreed that there shall be annexed to each of them a version in the Dutch language, which shall be an exact translation thereof, in consideration that on both sides this language can be easily understood, and it is likewise agreed that in case of a different interpretation being given to the same article in French and Japanese, the Dutch version shall then be relied on.

It is also agreed that the Dutch version shall not differ in any manner as to substance from the Dutch drafts, (*textes,*) which form part of the treaties recently concluded by Japan with the United States of America, England, and Russia. In case the exchange of ratifications should not have taken place before the fifteenth of August, one thousand eight hundred and fifty-nine, the present treaty, nevertheless, shall be carried into effect on and after that day.

In testimony whereof the respective plenipotentiaries have signed the present treaty, and to it have affixed their seals.

Done at Yedo, in four copies, on the ninth of October, one thousand eight hundred and fifty-eight, corresponding to the third day of the ninth month of the fifth year of the Nengo Anshei, (*Anchei,*) called the year of the horse.

The signatures follow.

[Translation.]

Commercial Regulations.

REGULATION I.

Within forty-eight hours following the arrival of a French vessel in one of the Japanese ports open to French commerce, the captain or commander of the vessel shall deliver at the Japanese custom-house the receipt of the consul of France, showing that all the ship's papers, bills of lading, &c., have been deposited with him, and the captain or commander shall then announce the entry of his vessel at the custom-house, by delivering a written declaration, which shall make known the name of the vessel and that of the port from which she proceeds, her tonnage, the name of her captain or commander, the names of the passengers, if there are any, and the number of persons who compose her crew. This declaration shall be certified to be true by the captain or commander, and shall be signed by him. He shall deposit at the same time a manifest of his cargo, indicating the number and the mark of the packages of which it is composed, their contents as detailed in the bills of lading, with the name of the person or persons to whom these packages are addressed. A list of the stores on board shall be annexed to the manifest. The captain or commander shall certify that this manifest contains the correct description of the whole cargo and of the vessel's stores, and he shall sign it with his name. If an error is discovered to have been committed in the manifest, it can be corrected within twenty-four hours (Sundays excepted) without occasioning the payment of any fine; but if an alteration or a tardy declaration should be made after that lapse of time, a fine of eighty-one francs shall be imposed on the delinquent.

All the goods not declared in the manifest shall pay double duty at the time of their landing. Every captain or commander of a French merchant vessel who shall neglect to declare the entry of his vessel at a Japanese custom-house within the time prescribed by this regulation, shall pay a fine of 324 francs for each day's delay in making the declaration.

REGULATION II.

The Japanese custom-house shall have the right to place its officers on board of every vessel which has entered the port, (ships-of-war excepted.) All these custom-house officers shall be treated with attention, and every facility which can be afforded them shall be given.

No goods shall be landed before sunrise nor after sunset without a special permit from the custom-house authorities, and the hatch and other passages of the vessel leading to the place where the cargo is contained shall be guarded by the Japanese custom-house officers, during the hours included between the setting and the rising of the sun, by means of seals on the locks or other fastenings; and if, without having permission therefor, any individual should open one of these passages which had been closed, or break the seals, locks, or other fastenings affixed by the Japanese custom-house officers, he shall be liable to a fine of 324 francs for each infraction.

All the goods which shall be landed from a vessel without having been lawfully declared at the Japanese custom-house as hereinbefore said, shall be confiscated, after examination made and proof obtained.

Packages of goods, arranged with the intention of defrauding the revenue of Japan by concealing articles of value, which are not declared in the manifest of entry, shall be confiscated.

If any French vessel should smuggle, or try to import goods into the ports of Japan which are yet closed, such goods shall be confiscated for the benefit of the Japanese government, and a fine of 5,400 francs shall be imposed upon the vessel for each offense.

Vessels which may need repairs can for this purpose land their cargoes without paying any duty. All the goods so landed shall be placed under custody of Japanese authorities, and all expenses incurred for storage, labor, and supervision, shall be paid for. But if a part of such cargo should be sold, the lawful duties must be paid on the part which shall have been disposed of. Cargoes can be transshipped to another vessel anchored in the same port without having to pay any duty; but every transhipment must be made under the supervision of the Japanese officers, after the custom-house authorities shall have had proof that the operation is performed in good faith, and when said authorities shall also have given permission to make the transhipment.

The importation of opium being prohibited, every French vessel arriving in Japan for the purpose of engaging in commerce there, and having more than three catties of opium on board, may see the surplus over this quantity confiscated and destroyed by the Japanese authorities; and every individual smuggling or trying to smuggle opium shall be liable to a fine of eighty-one francs for each catty of opium so smuggled.

Regulation III.

The owner or consignee of goods who shall wish to land them shall make declaration at the Japanese custom-house. This declaration shall be written, and shall contain the name of the person who shall make the importation, and that of the vessel having the goods on board, as well as the number and mark of the packages. The contents and value of each package shall be shown separately on the same sheet, and at the end of the declaration the value of all the goods which are comprised in the entry at the custom-house shall be added. On each declaration the owner or consignee shall certify, in writing, that it contains the actual value of the goods, and that he has not concealed anything in order to wrong the Japanese custom-house. The owner or consignee shall sign this certificate.

The invoice or invoices of goods so imported shall be presented to the custom-house authorities, and shall remain in their hands until said authorities shall have examined the goods mentioned in the declaration. The Japanese officers can verify one or several of these packages so declared, and for this purpose shall cause them to be transferred to the custom-house, if they so wish; but this examination must cause no expense to the importer, nor do any damage to the goods; and, after examining them, the Japanese shall replace these goods in the packages, and as near as possible in the condition in which they were in the first place. This examination shall be made without loss of time.

If any owner or importer of goods should perceive that they have been injured during the voyage of importation, before they have been delivered to him, he can notify the custom-house authorities of the injuries which have occurred, and such injured goods shall be appraised by two or by several competent and disinterested persons, who, after mature examination, shall issue a certificate making known the amount at so much per centum of the injuries which each package has sustained separately, describing it by its marks and numbers. This certificate shall be signed by the appraisers in presence of the custom-house officers, and the importer shall annex this certificate to his manifest, making the suitable deductions; but this fact shall not prevent the custom-house officers from appropriating to themselves these goods agreeably to the forms indicated in the fifteenth article of the present treaty to which these regulations are annexed.

When the duties shall have been paid, the owner shall receive authority to recover his goods, whether they are at the custom-house or are still on board the vessel. All the goods intended for exportation shall pass through the Japanese custom-houses before being conveyed on board. The declaration of entry shall be made in writing, and shall contain the name of the vessel on board of which they are to be exported, with the number of the packages, their marks, and a declaration of the value of their contents. The person who shall export these goods shall certify in writing that his declaration is a sincere statement of all the goods mentioned in it, and he shall sign it.

All goods which may be shipped on board of a vessel in order to be exported before passing through the custom-house, and all packages which contain prohibited articles, shall be seized by the Japanese government. It shall not be necessary for supplies intended for the use of French vessels, their crews, and passengers, nor for the articles of clothing of the passengers, to pass to the custom-house.

Regulation IV.

French vessels which want to be cleared by the custom-house shall notify it twenty-four hours in advance, and at the expiration of that term they shall receive their clearances; but, if they should be refused to them by the custom-house, the officers of this service must immediately inform the captain or consignee of the vessel, and make known to him the reasons for this refusal. They shall make the same declaration to the consul.

French vessels-of-war can freely enter the port and leave it without presenting any manifest. The custom-house and police officers shall not have the right of searching said vessels. As to French vessels which carry the mails, they must enter at the custom-house and be cleared on the same day, and they shall not be obliged to present any manifest except for the passengers and goods which they may have to land.

French whalers touching at a port for stores, and French vessels in distress, shall not be required to furnish a manifest of the cargo; but, if they wish afterwards to engage in commerce, they shall be obliged to give one, observing the formalities prescribed in the first regulation. The word vessel, (*bâtiment*,) wherever it occurs in this treaty and in its annex, shall always signify either a ship, a three-masted vessel, a bark, a brig, a schooner, a sloop, or a steam vessel.

Regulation V.

Every individual who shall sign a false declaration or a false certificate, with the intention of defrauding the revenue of Japan, shall pay a fine of 675 francs for each offense which he shall have committed.

Regulation VI.

No tonnage duty shall be collected from French vessels in the ports of Japan; but the following tolls shall be paid by them to the Japanese custom-house:

For the entry of a vessel, eighty-one francs.
For the clearance of a vessel, thirty-seven francs eighty centimes.
For each permit delivered, }
For each bill of health, } eight francs ten centimes.
For every other document, }

Regulation VII.

The duties to be paid to the Japanese government on all goods landed in this country will be in conformity to the following tariff:

Class 1.

All the articles contained in this class shall be free of duties: Gold and silver, coined or uncoined; clothing of every kind in use at the time; housekeeping utensils and printed books not intended to be sold, but being the property of persons coming to reside in Japan.

Class 2.

A duty of five per cent. shall be paid on the following articles: All materials used in building, rigging, repairing, or fitting out vessels; apparatus of every kind for whaling; salted provisions of all sorts; bread and similar commodities; living animals of every kind; coal; timber for building houses; rice, millet, steam machines, zinc, lead, tin, raw silk, cotton, and woolen stuffs.

Class 3.

A duty of thirty per cent. shall be paid on all intoxicating liquors, whether prepared by distillation, by fermentation, or in any other manner.

Class 4.

All goods not included in the foregoing classes shall pay a duty of twenty per cent.

All articles of Japanese production which are exported as cargo, shall pay a duty of five per cent., with the exception of coined gold and silver, and of copper in bars.

Rice and wheat harvested in Japan shall not be exported as cargo; but all French subjects residing in Japan, and French vessels, for their crews and passengers, may receive a sufficient supply of these stores.

Foreign grain brought into one of the open ports of Japan by a French vessel can be exported without impediment, if it has not been in part landed.

The Japanese government shall sell, from time to time, at public auction, a certain quantity of copper forming the surplus of what it produces.

Five years after the opening of the port of Kanagawa, the import and export duties may be modified if either of the two governments of France and Japan wish it.

Done at Yedo, in four copies, on the 9th of October, 1858, corresponding to the 3d day of the 9th month of the 5th year of the Nengo Anshei, (*Anchei*,) called the year of the horse.

Mr. Reed to Mr. Cass.

No. 39.] LEGATION OF THE UNITED STATES,
On board the Minnesota, Harbor of Hong Kong,
November 25, 1858.

SIR: I have the honor to inform you of my arrival here, having sailed from Shanghai on the 11th instant. It is my intention, availing myself of the permission of the President, to leave China so soon as this ship can be made ready for sea, which will probably be on the 8th proximo. I go in her as far as Bombay; thence taking the mail steamer for Europe.

I beg to forward to you a brief correspondence between Admiral Sir Michael Seymour and me, which will show to the President the very pleasant relations existing between us. I am indebted to Sir Michael Seymour for many acts of kindness.

I have the honor to be, sir, your obedient servant,

WILLIAM B. REED.

Hon. LEWIS CASS,
Secretary of State, Washington.

LEGATION OF THE UNITED STATES,
Minnesota, November 23, 1858.

SIR: Having understood that you had dispatched a vessel to make some examination of the Pratas shoal, I take the liberty of making an official inquiry of your excellency in relation to it. My object, I beg to assure you, is to convey to the President such information as a new proof of the liberal and enlightened policy of her Majesty's government in protecting and facilitating the commerce of all nations in these seas, and of the intelligent activity of her naval service.

I avail myself of this opportunity to announce to your excellency that it is my intention, by the permission of the President, to return to the United States shortly, leaving the duties of the legation in charge of Mr. Williams, as chargé d'affaires. I cannot leave China without making to you my sincere acknowledgements for the uniform courtesy and kindness I have received from your excellency, and all the officers of her Majesty's service under your command.

With assurances of the highest personal regard, and the most distinguished consideration, I have the honor to be, sir, your excellency's most obedient servant,

WILLIAM B. REED.

Rear Admiral Sir MICHAEL SEYMOUR, K. C. B.,
Her Majesty's ship Calcutta.

CALCUTTA, AT HONG KONG, *November*, 23 1858.

SIR: I have the honor to acknowledge the receipt of your excellency's letter of this date, making official inquiry of the object of my dispatching a vessel to the Pratas shoal, in order to convey to the President of the United States such information as a new proof of the liberal and enlightened policy of her Britannic Majesty's government in protecting and facilitating the commerce of all nations in these seas.

In reply, I have much pleasure in informing your excellency that, in the month of April last, in pursuance of orders from the lords commissioners of the admiralty, I dispatched Mr. Richards, the master in command of her Britannic Majesty's surveying vessel Saracen, to survey the Pratas shoal, with a view to select sites for the erection of one or more light-houses. This service was executed, and Mr. Richards, in his report, recommended three light-houses to be erected on the spots mentioned in his survey, which must be published by this time.

By the last packet, I received a dispatch from the admiralty, with an inclosure from the lords of the privy council for trade, requesting me to ascertain the depth of sand on the proposed sites, with a view to the erection of the light-houses, and this was the object of my yesterday dispatching the Cormorant to the Pratas, with an officer of royal engineers, to enable me to send home the requiredi nformation by the present mail packet.

I thank your excellency for the intimation of your intended departure from China, and for your kind mention of myself and the officers of the squadron under my command. I shall always regard with pleasure the period of our official intercourse, maintained throughout in a spirit of the utmost cordiality, and I highly appreciate the friendly feelings invariably displayed by the captains and officers of the United States squadron.

I beg to wish your excellency a favorable voyage to your own country, where, I have no doubt, your highly successful negotiations in these seas will be properly appreciated; and with much regard and high esteem, I have the honor to be, sir, your excellency's most obedient, humble servant,

M. SEYMOUR,
Rear Admiral and Commander-in-chief of her Britannic Majesty's Ships in China.

His Excellency the Hon. W. B. Reed,
United States Minister to China.

Mr. Williams to Mr. Cass.

[Extract.]

No. 1.] Legation of the United States,
Macao, January 14, 1859.

Sir: * * * * * * * *

The imperial commissioners still remain at Shanghai. On the occasion of announcing to them the departure of Mr. Reed, I referred to the recent convention signed with him respecting American claims, and asked them to notify the collectors of customs. Their answer is annexed. (Inclosures 1, 2, 3.) It is such a reply as has become familar to those conversant with Chinese official intercourse, never to be at a loss for a fact or a reason. I shall propose to them the form of a debenture certificate, and hold them to the fulfillment of the express terms of the convention. In any case, however, there would not be much money collected at present, if the commissioners did issue certificates, for the trade of the season, I am told, is nearly over, owing to the small supply of teas to be had. They may be of opinion that if the deduction be estimated from Chinese new year, the spirit of the compact is observed, though no money be paid over until it is likewise paid to the allies too. * * * * * *

I have the honor to be, your obedient servant,

S. WELLS WILLIAMS.

The Hon. Lewis Cass,
Secretary of State, Washington.

Mr. Williams to Mr. Smith.

Legation of the United States,
Macao, December 19, 1858.

Sir: I have to inform you that Mr. Reed took his depature in the Minnesota on the 8th instant, on his return to the United States, and that I have taken charge of the legation.

I inclose to your care a dispatch for the imperial commissioners, Kweiliang, Hwashana, and their associates, which I wish to have delivered to them as soon as it can be, with an intimation that their reply or any other communication they may have for me is to be forwarded through you. As soon as the preliminary arrangements are made, I shall inform you as to the mode in which the fifth part of the duties paid by American ships at the port of Shanghai are to be deducted after the third day of February next.

I remain, respectfully, your obedient servant,

S. WELLS WILLIAMS.

W. L. G. SMITH, Esq.,
United States Consul, Shanghai.

Mr. Reed to the Imperial Commissioners.

LEGATION OF THE UNITED STATES,
Minnesota, Hong Kong Harbor, December 8, 1858.

The undersigned, envoy extraordinary and minister plenipotentiary of the United States to China, having received instructions from his government permitting him to resign his official duties in China, and transfer the charge of the legation to Mr. S. W. Williams, *ad interim,* leaves this day in one of the national vessels of his country on his return. All business connected with the diplomatic relations of the government of the United States with that of China, and all communications which your excellencies may desire to make, should henceforth be directed to Mr. Williams, who has full powers to attend to them.

On the eve of his departure from China, the undersigned, referring to the convention which he entered into with your excellencies on the 8th ultimo, respecting compensation for the losses of American citizens, by which it was agreed that the sum of 500,000 taels should be paid in full for those claims, of which 300,000 are to be collected at Canton, and 100,000 at each of the ports of Shanghai and Fuhchau, by deducting one fifth from all the import, export, and tonnage duties paid by American ships, until those amounts had been made up, has personally instructed Mr. Williams to communicate these arrangements to the American consuls at those ports, and to inform them that they will begin to take effect on the 3d of February, 1859. He begs to remind your excellencies that that day is not far distant, and also takes the liberty to suggest that the Chinese officers at those three ports who have charge of the collection of foreign customs be instructed at an early day of the mode of carrying the convention into effect, that when the period arrives for it to go into operation, there will be no delay, hindrance, or dispute between them and the American consuls respecting the details.

The undersigned avails himself of this opportunity to wish your excellencies the possession of every happiness.

WILLIAM B. REED.

The Imperial Commissioners KWEILING, HWASHANA, HO KWEITZING, MINGSHEN, and TWAN, *&c., &c., &c.*

The Imperial Commissioners to Mr. Williams.

JANUARY 15, 1859.

KWEILIANG, a principal Secretary of State; HWASHANA, President of the Board of Civil Office; Ho KWEI-TSING, Governor General of the Two Kiang; MINGSHEN, of the Ordnance Office; and TWAN, a Secretary of the General Council, &c., &c., &c., hereby reply to the dispatch.

On the 3d instant, we had the honor to receive the dispatch of his excellency Mr. Reed, the late minister plenipotentiary of the United States in China, in which he informed us that he was on the point of weighing anchor to return to his own country, and that he had transferred the legation to Mr. S. W. Williams, as chargé d'affaires, who had full powers to attend to them. The arrangement is agreeable to us, and affords us much satisfaction.

In the dispatch under reply, the engagement by which one fifth of all the import, export, and tonnage duties on American ships are to be deducted, to the extent of 500,000 taels—one fifth of this sum to be collected at Shanghai, one fifth at Fuhchau, and the remaining three fifths at Canton—is referred to, and the wish expressed that the deduction may commence to take effect on the first of the next [Chinese] year.

To this observe that in the several treaties signed at Tientsin, it was stipulated that the plenipotentiaries of each country, including ourselves, should present them to their respective sovereigns for the purpose of getting the great seal affixed to them. After the ratifications are exchanged, a day can be set for their regulations and provisions to take effect.

We, his imperial commissioners, have consulted and agreed with [the American plenipotentiary?] at Shanghai, that a deduction be made from the duties, and extending over a number of years; but the whole matter must wait until the time during the next Chinese year, when the supplementary treaties containing the commercial regulations have been properly settled. They will then all be presented to his Imperial Majesty by memorial; and after approval, and the exchange of the ratifications of the new treaties, a day will be appointed for their provisions all going into effect.

Orders will then be issued straightway to the collectors of customs at Canton, Fuhchau, and Shanghai, to act in conformity to them; this will clearly show that China keeps the obligations she has entered into, and offers no delay, hindrance, or dispute, in their fulfillment; but until the new treaties have been promulged, the old commercial regulations be observed.

S. WELLS WILLIAMS,

Chargé d'Affaires ad interim of the United States in China.

Mr. Williams to Mr. Cass.

No. 2.] LEGATION OF THE UNITED STATES,
Macao, January 28, 1859.

SIR: * * * * * * * *

The inferences which may be drawn from the popular movements and combinations of the gentry and their followers, in respect to the general observance of the recent treaties, have induced me to refer to this trifling affair at Canton as an illustration of the difficulty which the government both at Pekin and in the provinces may find at times in compelling the observance and fulfillment of their unpopular stipulations. In dispatch No. 31, of September 4, 1858, this general subject was considered, and it is unnecessary to go over that ground again. The present instance, however, explains the inefficiency of the central authority; and the whole plan of operations last summer shows how at times it avails itself of popular feeling to effect its purposes, so that a short account of the whole movement will illustrate some of the features of Chinese polity, and may, perhaps, interest you.

One prominent characteristic, which distinguishes the Chinese government from other Asiatics, is its literary examinations for official candidates, whose eligibility for posts of power is based upon the principle that the persons best fitted for governing are those who are the best educated. This system was adopted and carried into operation under the Tang dynasty, during the eighth century, and, for more than a thousand years, has been one of the institutions of the empire—one which, amidst the internal wars and changes of dynasty, has been admitted and acted on as a fundamental political axiom. Two results have flowed from this high position given to literature, both of which explain, in part, the persistence of Chinese institutions—one is, that literary and peaceful pursuits have been elevated above warlike and military, and the subordination of the latter has gradually become so fixed, that all martial ambition is nullified, and the army itself has become almost a by-word among the people; the other is the cultivation of the democratic principle among all classes. One of the rules respecting the literary examinations, is that the highest honors in the state, below royalty, are open to the ambition of the lowest subject. The general standard of education is, by this stimulus, kept higher than it would otherwise be among the mass; and those who fit themselves to enter the examinations are, by their studies, placed above their original position, even if they never succeed to an office. A middle class of *literati* and gentry has thus been formed, an aristocracy of cultivated mind, which has gradually engrossed most of the popular power. The gentry are the possessors of most of the land, but in such sort that no one family, even in a single village, attains such a position of wealth and influence as to be able to oppress the people and set the laws or public opinion at defiance. On the contrary, it is for their interest and safety to please their neighbors; and they are expected to take the lead in matters of public welfare; represent the grievances of the people to the authorities; devise measures for their protection, in case of attack, or of punishment and repression in case of sedition; and raise funds for erecting or repairing public buildings or other works. It is their duty likewise to assist the officers of government in collecting the revenue, and lend their aid, if necessary, in arresting criminals. They have lists of families and hamlets, so that they soon ascertain where each person belonging to the village is to be found. The appointment of the village police, and management of funds raised for public purposes, are both very much in their hands; and, in this part of China, at least, many villages and towns have no officers appointed by the general government, all being elected by and among the inhabitants. There are, also, council-houses, where the gentry and elders of a circuit of villages meet together, from time to time, to consult on the public welfare of their region, or to confer with the higher authorities as to the proper measures to be taken in an emergency.

This system would promote the prosperity of the community to a high point, if the people themselves were peaceful and industrious, and the gentry kind and just. But China is a Pagan country; its people are, as a whole, ignorant, selfish, and cruel, and constantly at variance among themselves; its gentry and rich landholders oppressive and proud; and the supreme government merciless to exact and weak to defend. Yet, such is the inherent vitality of this democratic element in the body politic, by its operation producing an education of the people in self-government in their separate villages and communes, which accustoms them to their rights, that it has survived the most dreadful convulsions and insurrections, and preserved them from slavery and utter oppression.

In China, the legal taxation is light, and the returns, so far as we can learn, show that it is collected without resort to intimidation or military coercion, as is the case in many parts of Central and Western Asia. In times of peace, there is not more than the exigencies of the civil, military, and literary services ordinarily require, however; so that, in times of scarcity, war, or insurrection, extraordinary supplies must be raised. In case of an external war, the people do not feel the burden of the demand so much as when insurrection rears its gorgon head, and the whole country becomes involved in ruin; when its inhabitants, towns, villages, fields, crops, and stocks are pillaged, and trade, industry, life, all fall a prey to anarchy and rapine. Then no mercy is shown by either party.

In the insurrection which raged in the south of Canton province, in 1854 and 1855, it was estimated that more than half a million of *men* came to a violent end, or fled the country; and how many towns and villages were pillaged was unknown. The insurgents invested Canton itself, at one time, with more than three score thousand men. The governor general had only the resources in men and money of his own jurisdiction to depend upon to repress it; and, with the aid of the gentry and their constituencies, this was done, after an appalling loss of life, but it left the region in a deplorable state. However, after the storm had passed, every hamlet and village began to revive on the resources of men and means that were left.

The particular purpose of these remarks is, however, to show wherein the weakness of the general government consists; how difficult it is for it to carry out even beneficial measures, if they are unpopular, and the bearing which such a condition of things has on the fulfillment of the recent treaties. If this middle class of gentry and *literati* are decidedly averse to a line of policy or tenacious of a privilege, the imperial officers easily find some means of compromising the matter or give it up. They, themselves, came of the people, and know their feelings. They do all they can to maintain their power and keep the peace; and, at the same time, try, too, to go to the utmost safe limit of exaction to fill their own coffers from the individuals who come to their courts. It is these acts of oppression which goad the people to sedition, when the officials not unfrequently are put to death in their yamun. In China, as in other Asiatic governments, the rights and duties of both rulers and ruled are not defined; the *will* of the one or the other often rises above the law, and no one can be sure that it will not do so in every case. There is not much of what we call patriotism on either side; and the practice of government is a constant struggle between harsh and covetous officials and turbulent, ignorant subjects. It is the middle class which does so much to save both from destruction.

The question of entrance into the city of Canton will illustrate the relations between the parties. This point has been much discussed among foreigners, but whatever were its merits, based on the interpretation of the old treaties, the gentry of Canton resisted the entry of foreigners on purely personal grounds. They determined not to admit them inside the city because they disliked them; while the officers, who were all natives of other parts of the empire, were inclined, for peace sake, to allow it. The popular will was exhibited in 1843, when Sir Henry Pottinger demanded entrance, chiefly because it was granted at the other four ports, but Kiying was unable to bring the gentry over to his views. Sir John Davis found the determination stronger in 1847; and in 1849, when it was supposed that the English would force their way in, the people levied large bodies of volunteers to resist the expected attack. At this juncture, after Sir George Bonham had waived the right till it could be granted at a future period, the Emperor issued a rescript upon the matter, which exhibits the ideas of the Chinese upon the general subject in hand, and is here quoted:

"The purpose of walling cities is to protect the people; in the protection of the people lies the security of the State. When the people of Kwang Tung are unanimously determined against the admission of foreigners into the city, can an imperial injunction be laid on them by proclamation so to do, whether they will or no? It is not the power of the government of China to cross the wishes of the people out of deference to those of the men from afar; on the other hand, it behooves foreign nations to study the temper of the people, to the end that the capital of their merchants may work free from risk," &c.

And the Cantonese never have yielded, though their city is now in the hands of foreigners, to their admission within the city walls; though, in arguing the matter with them, few have tried to defend it.

A reference to the operations carried on against Canton last summer will further exhibit the working of this feature of the Chinese system. After Yeh had been taken prisoner at the capture of Canton, in December, 1857, all the defenses of the city and all its garrison were either destroyed or disarmed, and the allies kept armed possession. A new governor general arrived to take Yeh's place, but he was without troops or funds to march to regain the capital. Unable to occupy his office in Canton, and oversee the operations, they were confided to three influential persons among the gentry themselves. These three persons, named Lo, Lung, and Su, were appointed by imperial orders to take the control, and carry on hostilities on behalf of their sovereign. They circulated proclamations throughout this prefecture, calling upon all faithful subjects to join them, and subscribe in aid of their cause. The energy which they exhibited was great, but the results showed their weakness and inability to effect their object. They could annoy foreigners by withdrawing supplies and compelling their servants in Hong Kong, Macao, and Whampoa to leave their employ, under pains of imprisoning family and escheating property; they could hire men to murder sentries or foreigners walking the streets, or passing in boats; they could put a complete stop to business, and make a bravado of attacking the city, but they could not drive out the enemy.

On the announcement of the cessation of hostilities at the north, and the promulgation of the treaties of Tientsin by the governor general, they suspended hostilities, and disbanded most of their volunteers; but I am told that their authority to act is not yet rescinded, nor their forces entirely removed. The temporary possession of power, without most of its responsibilities, renders them, perhaps, inclined to find an excuse in the general unsettled state of the country for retaining all they can of it.

The people, too, who know that peace has been made, are not at all enthusiastic, and look upon them with suspicion, lest they attempt further aggressive acts, and raise more funds, which will involve them and not the gentry in trouble. The people are well convinced that their braves cannot resist foreign troops, and the recent dastardly flight of this body of 3,000 troops at Shih-tsing has thrown contempt on the whole force. The forbearance of the allies towards the villagers and boatmen has had a favorable effect in producing a change of feeling. It is to be hoped that no further rising will now take place in this region, though I think permanent peace cannot be looked for until the city of Canton is evacuated. The people regard its armed occupation as always likely to provoke trouble, and humiliating to their pride, and do not return to rebuild the desolate ruins which now look so dismal.

The result of the last two years has been to impoverish Canton, and reduce it from its position as a great commercial mart. The dislike of its citizens towards foreigners has been strengthened, and perhaps the English and French may deem it advisable to intrench their consulates in a fortified garrison, inside of the walls, in order to secure what they have obtained. One may well ask, in such a case, what is a treaty of peace worth which requires such guarantees? No foreign merchant wishes to reside in it, and there is nothing to invite his frequent visits. Still the policy of the Chinese government, which led it to seclude its imperial commissioner, who dealt with foreigners, behind these walls, has been broken down, never to be restored. An advance has been made, bearing with it, I hope, the good of this great mass of human beings, and opening channels for the introduction of better knowledge and morals, and government among them. The principle of conduct towards all foreign nations, which this government adopts, is isolation. "Keep them all at as great a distance as possible, and get into no quarrels with them, if it can be avoided," is their rule. It is quite a mistake to suppose that the rulers of China have any *regard* to one nation more than another; that they are more friendly, for instance, towards the Americans than towards the English; they may, perhaps, *fear* the English and Russians more than they do the Americans, but they would be glad if none of them ever came near them. With the people at the ports the case is different; but their rulers, whose ignorance, contempt, and fear of all foreign nations are about on a level, have everything to learn. One of the stipulations of the treaties, that of permission to travel the country, and become acquainted with the people in their homes, will allow access to the officials, too, and do much quietly to remove their ignorant hauteur, and show them they have nothing really to fear.

The imperial commissioners still remain at Shanghai, and it would be well if they could visit this province in company with Lord Elgin, when he returns.

* * * * * * * * *

I have the honor to be, sir, your very obedient servant,

S. WELLS WILLIAMS.

Hon. LEWIS CASS,
Secretary of State, Washington.

Mr. Williams to Mr. Cass.

[Extract.]

No. 3.] LEGATION OF THE UNITED STATES,
Canton, February 12, 1859.

SIR: * * * * * * * *

I have yet nothing definite to mention respecting the emission of the debenture certificates to be applied to the liquidation of American claims. The collector at this port says he has received no orders from the imperial commissioners to issue them, but the latter have agreed to the form of a certificate, which I proposed to them. I have not yet received an answer to my communication of the 5th ultimo, (a copy was sent you,) but hope to get it before the next mail, and the announcement of the necessary instructions having been transmitted to the collectors. I anticipate the usual hindrances in carrying this matter into operation, which attend almost everything of the sort among the Chinese, but have strong hopes that there will be no need of a resort to harsh measures to compel the commissioners to fulfill their obligations.

The imperial commissioners remain at the north, either at Shanghai, or Suchau, until one or other of the foreign plenipotentiaries return in the spring to proceed to Pekin, and exchange the ratifications of the treaties. The importance which the Emperor's government attaches to foreign relations appears in the retention of these high dignitaries as imperial commissioners for their management, although both of them still retain their posts at the capital, Kweiliang as prime minister, and Hwashana as president of the board of civil office; and this may also be taken as an evidence of its sincerity. It is to be hoped that the policy these two officials have done so much to initiate may not be rudely altered by the superior influence of their political opponents, who are still greatly in the majority.

I have the honor to be, sir, your obedient servant,

S. WELLS WILLIAMS.

Hon. LEWIS CASS,
Secretary of State, Washington.

Mr. Williams to Mr. Cass.

[Extract.]

No. 4.] LEGATION OF THE UNITED STATES,
Canton, February 25, 1859.

SIR:

* * * * * * * *

In the rejoinder of the imperial commissioners to the reply which I made to their communication of January 5, (copies of which are inclosed, 1, 2,) they state that they have sent their orders to the collectors of customs at the three ports; but none have yet been received at Canton. They were probably sent overland from Suchau by the usual government couriers, who are not unfrequently a month on their way. The collector at this port understands the plan, and will interpose no obstacle in carrying it out; but I am not so sure that some impediments may not arise in the working of the system from the mode of conducting business, which is such as to throw the responsibility of paying the duties at the custom-house on native produce entirely on the native dealers.

The collector at Shanghai is ready to issue them, and there will be no difficulty in collecting the proportion to be applied to the liquidation of the claims at that port. I have not heard from Fuhchau.

There is one sentence in the reply of Kweiliang and his associates which illustrates the laxity of this government and the want of harmony and vigor between its several parts so well, that I refer to it particularly. This is the intimation given that the fact of their having signed a convention with the United States minister for the settlement and liquidation of the claims of his countrymen had not been officially reported to the Emperor when they sent this reply to me, nearly three months afterwards. In our ignorance of much of the workings of this government, this delay cannot be satisfactorily explained; but the probability is that the expected reports of the several collectors to the board of revenue, stating that the American consuls at those ports had demanded one fifth of the duties on American shipping, stimulated the imperial commissioners to make their own report in anticipation, and explain the terms of the convention of last November. The incident shows, at least, what an unsound government we have to deal with, and how much ground there is for the suspicion of insincerity which rests upon everything its officers promise.

* * * * * * * *

I have the honor to be, with great respect, your obedient servant,

S. WELLS WILLIAMS.

Hon. LEWIS CASS,
Secretary of State.

Inclosure 1.

LEGATION OF THE UNITED STATES,
Macao, January 15, 1859.

The undersigned, chargé d'affaires of the United States *ad interim*, has the honor to acknowledge [the receipt of] your excellencies' reply of the 5th on the 12th instant.

In it you remark that, in the dispatch under reply, "the wish is expressed that the deduction on the duties may commence to take effect on the first of the next year." To this the undersigned has only to observe that, in the convention signed at Shanghai on the 8th of November, between the American minister and your excellencies, it is expressly agreed and stated that "the deductions shall commence on the first day of the next Chinese year." Why, then, do you now say that I wish to have the deduction commence on that day, when the contracting parties themselves stipulated and consented that it was to take effect?

It is also stated, in the dispatch now under reply, "that we, his imperial Majesty's commissioners, have consulted and agreed at Shanghai that a deduction be made from the duties extending over a number of years." Your excellency will find that there is no such expression in the convention; it is only declared that the collectors of customs at the said three ports shall issue debentures.

Furthermore, you remark "that the whole matter must wait until the time, during the next Chinese year, when the supplementary treaties containing the commercial regulations have been properly settled." The undersigned replies that both the original and supplementary treaties have all been definitively settled, though their ratifications have not been exchanged; the manner of making the deductions from the duties were also finally and plainly arranged at Shanghai, so that there can be no discussion, therefore, about further delay.

Lastly, it is asserted "that until the new treaties have been promulgated the old "commercial regulations must be observed." This remark seems to be quite unnecessary, for there is nothing in the convention itself of this purport; and it is surprising that the express stipulation of that compact respecting the date of its going into effect should thus be forgotten or ignored.

It is well known that the ratifications of the treaties of peace signed at Tientsin are to be exchanged within a year, but this convention relating to remuneration for losses indicates the day for its provisions to take effect. No alteration on this point can be allowed, and the necessity of transmitting orders to the respective collectors of customs, for their conformity thereto on the appointed day is manifest.

A copy of a proposed debenture certificate for the payment of duties is respectfully inclosed for the inspection and approval of your excellencies, or for such alterations as may be deemed advisable; and I shall look for its speedy return, that the matter in hand may be straightway carried into effect.

S. WELLS WILLIAMS,

Their Excellencies KWEILIANG, HWASHANA, HO KWEITSING, MINGSHEN, and TWAN, *Imperial Commissioners, &c., &c., &c.*

Inclosure 2.

JANUARY 25, 1859.

KWEILIANG, principal Secretary of State; and HWASHANA president of the Board of Civil Office; with HO KWEITSING, Governor General of the Two Kiang; MINGSHEN, a member of the Ordnance Department; and TWAN, employed in the General Council, the two former being Plenipotentiaries, and all Commissioners of his Imperial Majesty, hereby reply:

On the 22d instant we had the honor to receive your excellency's communication of the 19th, sent to us from Macao, in which you state "that the stipulations of the treaties which were signed at Tientsin and Shanghai require that the deductions are to commence to take effect from the first day of the next Chinese year; and that the necessity of immediately transmitting orders to this effect to the respective collectors of customs, for their conformity thereto on the appointed day, is therefore manifest." A draft of a proposed debenture certificate was also inclosed for such corrections as might be deemed necessary.

In reply, we beg to state that the arrangements made with [the plenipotentiaries of] each country respecting this matter were originally designed to be based on one plan, and to be carried into effect in a uniform manner; and it was on this ground that we based our previous reply in which we stated that the old commercial regulations must be observed [until the new treaties are promulged.]

But on receiving the dispatch now under reply, and at the same time reflecting on the good feeling existing between our respective nations, and desirous to perpetuate those amicable relations, we immediately memorialized the throne, stating that we had deliberated on the terms and had signed a convention, [for the liquidation of claims,] and that it was to go into effect on the next new year. We have also instructed the collectors of customs at Canton, Fuhchau, and Shanghai to obey their orders on receiving them, and carry out the provisions of the convention.

Two corrections are made in the form of the certificate sent to us. The phrase *wú fun yih kau tí* (one fifth to be deducted) is changed to *wú fun chí yih kau tí* (every fifth part deducted;) and the phrase *pei chàng* (liquidate, or reimburse the losses) is altered to *jin hwán* (agreed to give back.) The remainder of it is correct, and the same is now returned to your excellency.

S. WELLS WILLIAMS, Esq.,

Charge d'Affairés United States of America ad interim.

Mr. Williams to Mr. Cass.

[Extract.]

No. 5.] LEGATION OF THE UNITED STATES,

Canton, March 12, 1859.

SIR: * * * * * * * *

The collector of customs at Shanghai having declared that he was ready to issue debenture certificates to the value of 100,000 taels in 2,000 tickets, I have made an appointment of receivers at that port, and furnished them with such instructions as seemed necessary. (Inclosures 7, 8, 9, 10.) These instructions may require modification when the claims have been examined and adjudicated. In my reply to the imperial commissioners, (inclosure 11,) I have alluded to the most feasible mode of paying the indemnity money, by the customs authorities themselves redeeming the certificates at the departure of a ship to the extent of a fifth of her duties. This plan will be adopted at Shanghai, but I am not sanguine as to its success at the other ports. Chinese officials would find many reasons for retaining duties once paid into their hands, and some other plan must be considered as an alternative.

* * * * * * * * *

I have the honor to be, sir, your obedient servant,

S. WELLS WILLIAMS.

LEGATION OF THE UNITED STATES,

Canton, February 9, 1859.

MY LORD: I have the honor to inform you of the departure of his excellency W. B. Reed, on his return to the United States, in the United States ship Minnesota, *via* Bombay, on the 8th of December last, at which date the charge of this legation devolved on me *ad interim*.

I beg to inclose for the information of your excellency a copy in English and Chinese of the supplementary treaty of the tariff and the commercial regulations between the United States and China, signed at Shanghai on the 8th of November last by Mr. Reed and the imperial commissioners. I shall be pleased to receive a copy of that signed by your lordship with the latter functionaries on the same day, as the copy accompanying your excellency's dispatch of November 6 is described as the "draft of a tariff and regulations," and may have been incomplete.

At his departure, Mr. Reed desired me, at a convenient time, to mention to your excellency (though you may be already aware of it) that the kingdom of Sweden and Norway is also one of the western powers which have made treaties with China. It was signed at Canton March 20, 1847, between C. F. Liljevalch, on the part of the King of Sweden and Norway, and Kiying, on the part of the Emperor of China. The English version of this treaty is the same as that of the American treaty of Wanghia, except the necessary changes in the names of persons, dates, and places. I cannot ascertain that the ratifications were ever exchanged.

I have the honor to be, my lord, your excellency's most obedient servant,

S. WELLS WILLIAMS.

His Excellency the Earl of ELGIN AND KINCARDINE,
Her Britannic Majesty's High Commissioner, &c., &c.

FURIOUS, *Canton, February* 14, 1859.

SIR: I have the honor to acknowledge the receipt of your dispatch of the 9th instant, inclosing a copy in English and Chinese of the suplementary treaty of the tariff and commercial relations between the United States and China, and to inform you that a copy of the English tariff and commercial regulations will be forwarded to you as soon as it can be prepared.

I have the honor to be, sir, your most obedient, humble servant,

ELGIN AND KINCARDINE.

Dr. S. W. WILLIAMS, *&c., &c., &c.*

LEGATION OF THE UNITED STATES,
Macao, January 25, 1859.

SIR: I herewith send you an extract from the convention made at Shanghai on the 8th of November, 1858, between their excellencies the American minister and the imperial commissioners, respecting the liquidation of American claims, according to the terms of which the collector of customs at Shanghai is to issue debentures on the first day of the next Chinese year.

On the day specified, therefore, I wish you to apply to the collector of customs at Shanghai for these debentures, quoting the extract now sent, and state that you are ready to receive them according to the stipulations of the convention. On hearing that part or all of them are in your hands, I will appoint a receiver, and inform you.

In case the collector of customs does not issue them on the day specified, nor state an early date for so doing, I wish you to ascertain as accurately as you can, and keep a full account of the duties of all kinds paid by American ships to the Chinese government, which may leave the port after the 3d of February, proximo.

I remain, respectfully, your obedient servant,

S. WELLS WILLIAMS.

W. L. G. SMITH, Esq.,
United States Consul.

CONSULATE OF THE UNITED STATES,
Shanghai, February 17, 1859.

SIR: I have the honor to acknowledge the receipt of yours of the 25th ultimo, in relation to debenture notes, on the 4th instant, and in reply I have the honor to say that the Taoutae on the day before had informed me of the arrangement between the two governments, and requested me to have the notes prepared and sent to him according to the form which he sent, and he would then seal them and send them to me. I have, therefore, had two thousand printed, and shall send them to the Taoutae for him to number and seal; and as soon as he delivers them to me, numbered and sealed, I will inform you thereof, so that I may at once thereafter receive instructions from you to whom to deliver them. I received the sheets from the printer on yesterday, and paid him thirty taels for the same. To whom shall I look for payment of this expense?

The Taoutae is now absent at Soo-choo, and is expected to return in a few days. As soon as he returns, I shall send the notes to him to be numbered and sealed.

I inclose you one for your information.

I have the honor to be, your obedient servant,

W. L. G. SMITH,
United States Consul.

Hon. S. WELLS WILLIAMS,
Secretary of Legation, &c.

LEGATION OF THE UNITED STATES,
Canton, March 8, 1859.

SIR: I beg to acknowledge with thanks your communication of the 17th ultimo, and the copy of the debenture note inclosed therein. As the English version of the latter was a little different from that which had been previously agreed on with the imperial commissioners, I have had two thousand others printed here which will be delivered to you, sealed and numbered by the collector of customs, and the former ones are then to be destroyed.

On receiving them, I wish you to seal each of them with your consular seal as a precaution against counterfeiting, and then deliver them all to one of the partners of the American firm of Oliphant & Co., which house I have appointed to be the receivers of the same, taking a receipt therefor. In case any of the former certificates have already been redeemed for duties, the same number of these are to be returned to the collector of customs by the receivers on their receiving the money.

I will arrange for reimbursing the thirty taels expended by you in printing the former certificates.

I remain, your obedient servant,

S. WELLS WILLIAMS.

W. L. G. SMITH, Esq.,
United States Consul.

LEGATION OF THE UNITED SATETS,
Canton, March 8, 1859.

GENTLEMEN: I herewith transmit to you the appointment of receivers of the debenture certificates which will be issued by the collector of customs at Shanghai to the number of two thousand, of the value of fifty taels each, written in the English and Chinese languages, and stamped with his official seal. You will receive these certificates from the United States consul at Shanghai, who will also apply his consular seal as a precaution against simulation, and give him a receipt for the same. When you issue them, you will countersign and stamp them as a further security to the Chinese authorities of their genuineness.

The amounts collected from these debenture certificates are to be transmitted at least quarterly to the branch of your house in Hong Kong, for deposit in one of the banks at that place to the credit of the United States commissioner for the time being. The adjudication of the claims of American citizens against the Chinese government is for the present necessarily delayed until the action of the government at Washington is known; and these deposits will, therefore, remain until the decision on their claims is made known to the claimants. Your commission for acting as receivers must likewise be deferred until that action is known, by which time your experience will no doubt aid in deciding that point.

If it should be necessary to draw upon you directly for the money in your hands, or to issue orders for delivery of the debenture certificates to persons named therein, such drafts for money or certificates will have the seal of this legation.

I am, gentlemen, most respectfully, your obedient servant,

S. WELLS WILLIAMS.

Messrs. OLIPHANT & Co.,
Shanghai.

By virtue of the authority invested in me as the chief diplomatic officer of the United States of America in China, to carry into effect the provisions of a convention for the satisfaction of the claims of American citizens, made at Shanghai on the 8th of November, 1858, between their excellencies William B. Reed, minister plenipotentiary of the United States to China, and Kweiliang, Hwashana, Ho Kwei-tsing, Mingshen, and Twan, imperial commissioners of the Ta-Tsing empire, in which, among other things, it was agreed that debentures be issued by the collectors of customs at the three ports of Canton, Fuhchau and Shanghai, to be delivered to such persons as may be named by the chief diplomatic officer of the United States in China, be it known that I do hereby appoint Robert M. Oliphant, William W. Parker, Luman N. Hitchcock, A. B. Neilson, jr., Walter L. Purdie, Richard R. Tyers, and D. Oliphant Vail, Esquires, doing business at Canton, Fuhchau, and Shanghai, under the style and firm of Oliphant and Company, to be severally and collectively the receivers of the debentures issued by the collectors of customs at the aforesaid three ports, and of the moneys which may hereafter accrue from them.

In testimony whereof I have hereunto subscribed my name, and affixed the seal of the legation of the United States, at Canton, this 8th day of March, 1859.

S. WELLS WILLIAMS,
Chargé d'Affaires ad interim of the United States in China.

Done in triplicate.

LEGATION OF THE UNITED STATES,
Canton, March 12, 1859.

The undersigned, chargé d'affaires *ad interim* of the United States, has the honor to acknowledge the communications of their excellencies the imperial commissioners, of dates January 22d and February 15th, in the first of which they inform him that they have issued orders to the collectors of customs at Canton, Fuhchau, and Shanghai, to carry out the provisions of the convention for the satisfaction of claims.

The undersigned, however, begs to state, that while the collector of customs at Shanghai has acted in conformity to those orders, he is informed by the United States consuls at Canton and Fuhchan that the collectors at those ports, on the 5th and 17th ultimo, replied to their applications that they had not yet received orders from your excellencies to that effect. Nor up to this date have any instructions been received, nor has the delay been explained.

It has given much satisfaction to the undersigned to learn that the seals of the office of commissioner of foreign commerce, held by his excellency Hwang, governor general of the Two Kwang, have been transferred to Ho, governor general of the Two Kiang, who has been intrusted with the duties of that post.

Your excellencies have stated that his Majesty has already been memorialized respecting the convention which was agreed upon, and which is to be carried into effect for the satisfaction of claims; and the undersigned confidently expects that particular directions will be received by the several collectors of customs to act, so that upon all ships which may trade at the three ports under the American flag after the first day of the present Chinese year, whether the debenture certificates be issued now or later, one fifth of the duties may be deducted for this purpose.

S. WELLS WILLIAMS.

Their Excellencies KWEILIANG and HWASHANA, *Plenipotentiaries of the Ta-Tsing Empire*, with TWAN, *a Joint Imperial Commissioner.*

Mr. Williams to Mr. Cass.

[Extract.]

No. 6.] LEGATION OF THE UNITED STATES,
Macao, April 12, 1859.

SIR: In continuation of my last dispatch of the 12th ultimo, in which I inclosed the instructions given to the United States consul at Shanghai, as to the disposal of the debentures issued to him by the collector of customs at that port, with a copy of the commission appointing Messrs. Oliphant & Co. to be the receivers of the money accruing therefrom, I have now the honor to forward a copy of their acceptance of this trust (inclosure 1) under the regulations annexed to it. I have since been informed that they have made an arrangement with the inspector of customs at that port, to receive the fifth of the duties on American commerce, at the end of each month, and that the payments have already commenced.

I hope that the measures taken to prevent simulation of the certificates by stamping them three times, and the regulations which I have adopted for the security of the money until the claims are adjudicated, will meet with your approval. I inclose a printed copy of the debentures (inclosure 2) as they are now issued, the English version of which differs somewhat from the copy appended to the dispatch of the imperial commissioners, (dispatch No. 4, inclosure 2,) there having been a misunderstanding respecting the form.

From the report of the vice-consul at Fuhchau, you will perceive that the collection of the proportion of duties for the liquidation of claims has commenced at that port, the revenue officers having paid back the amount due on one ship which left port since Chinese new year. I had some missgivings as to the willingness of the officers there to refund duties once paid to them, and his letter has relieved me from some anxiety on this point. I have furnished Mr. Dunn with the printed certificates, and a few general instructions (inclosures 3, 4) to guide him, leaving him free to carry out the details in connection with the receivers as they can arrange between themselves and the collector of customs.

The consul at Canton informs me that the collector there has not received instructions from his superiors, but that, with his tacit consent, he (the consul) has retained the tonnage dues on one ship, the money to be passed to the credit of the claims. The Chinese are ready to issue and stamp the debentures, as soon as they get their orders. Mr. Perry has lately paid and received visits from the governor and other high functionaries at Canton, (inclosures 5, 6,) which shows how they are gradually conforming to their own new position. It may be observed, in explanation of the collector or hoppo, as he is here called, making visits in company with the governor of the province and the commander-in-chief of the Manchus, that he is at Canton of much higher grade than at any other port in China, being a Manchu appointed directly from the Emperor, and usually a member of his household. He farms the revenue at this port, and finds much difficulty now in collecting the stipulated sum and paying his establishment.

* * * * * * *

I have the honor to be, sir, your obedient servant,

S. WELLS WILLIAMS.

Hon. LEWIS CASS,
Secretary of State, Washington.

Inclosure 1.

SHANGHAI, *March* 25, 1859.

SIR: We have to acknowledge the receipt of your communication, dated 8th instant, inclosing a document whereby we are appointed receivers of the debenture certificates which will be issued by the collector of customs at this port.

Your instructions, in reference to the precautions to be adopted in issuing the certificates, will be duly attended to, as also those regarding the remittance of amounts collected.

We note that, should it be found necessary to draw upon us directly for money in our hands, or to issue orders for the delivery of certificates to persons named therein, such drafts for money or certificates will bear the seal of the United States legation.

We remain, sir, your obedient servants,

OLIPHANT & CO.

S. WELLS WILLIAMS, LL. D.
Chargé d'Affaires ad interim of the United States in China.

No. — Delivered to. Date.

DEBENTURE CERTIFICATE, No.

Collectorate of customs at the port of Fuhchau:

This is to certify, that in accordance with terms of a convention made between the United States of America and China, by which it agreed that one fifth of the duties levied on American ships and the goods carried in them, were to be deducted in order to be returned to American citizens; and further, that debenture certificates were to be issued by the collectors of customs to persons appointed by the chief diplomatic officer of the United States to receive them, this debenture, for the value of fifty taels, is hereby issued from the office of the collector of customs, at Fuhchau, to be received in payment of duties to that amount, at the same.

Issued on the 1st day of the 1st month, in the ninth year of the reign of Hien-fung, or February 3, 1859.

[Chinese characters.]

Inclosure 3.

CONSULATE OF THE UNITED STATES,
Fuhchau, March 23, 1859.

SIR: Since I last had the honor to address you, I have received from the haikwan at this port one fifth of the duties and dues of the American ship Ringleader. In the absence of any instructions from you, I have placed this amount on board of one of the receiving ships at the anchorage, where it will remain at a storage charge of one eighth per cent. per month until I receive your further directions in the matter.

I am under the impression that the one fifth duties can be collected at this port without recourse to the debenture certificates proposed; in fact, I anticipate much inconvenience in the use of the certificates, especially in the event of an American vessel coming consigned to a foreign (British) mercantile firm. Should my proposition coincide with the views of the legation, I have to request that I may be allowed to collect the duties from the custom-house direct, without using the proposed certificates.

The decree referred to in your last communication, I signed, as directed, and forwarded same to Ningpo.

I remain, very respectfully,

THOMAS DUNN,
United States Vice-Consul.

S. WELLS WILLIAMS, LL. D.,
Chargé d'Affaires, &c., &c.

Inclosure 4.

LEGATION OF THE UNITED STATES,
Macao, April 5, 1859.

SIR: I beg to acknowledge with thanks your reply of February 22, furnishing me with particulars respecting lorchas, and explaining the circumstances respecting three American citizens who were attacked last December, from which I am pleased to learn that my suppositions and inferences were erroneous.

I have also received your communication of the 23d ultimo, in which you inform me that the collector of customs at Fuhchau has already paid you the fifth of the duties and dues of the American ship Ringleader, and request that you may be allowed to collect the duties from the custom-house direct, without using the certificates.

I am much pleased to learn from this that the customs authorities at Fuhchau have received their orders from the superiors, and that the collection of the duties for the liquidation of claims has commenced so favorably. The use of the debentures will not, I think, interfere with the collection of the money from the custom-house direct, for they are merely the receipts agreed upon with the imperial commissioners, and I am inclined to think will be regarded by them as the authorized vouchers for the several collectors at the ports. By the terms of the convention, too, these officers are required to issue them.

On receiving the two thousand certificates now sent you, therefore, I wish you to have the collector at Fuhchau seal them with his official seal, and number them. On receiving them from him, I wish you to seal each one with your consular seal, as a measure of precaution, and then deliver the whole number to one of the partners of the American firm of Oliphant & Co., which house I have appointed to be the receivers, taking a receipt therefor.

When the fifth of the dues on a ship are to be paid, all that will be necessary then, will be for you to send to them as many certificates as the sum will cover, paying the money into their hands, and remitting the certificates to the collector. The receipts for the money already paid you should be given him in this manner, with an explanation of the reason, and I conceive the mode you propose is so nearly like it that there will be no difficulty. The sum that remains over short of fifty taels can be passed to his credit till the next ship departs. This plan requires no reference to shippers or consignees, further, perhaps, than to obtain a manifest or get an explanation, and your record of the amounts received from each ship will serve to verify the record of the receivers.

I remain, respectfully, your obedient servant,

S. WELLS WILLIAMS.

THOMAS DUNN, Esq.,
United States Vice-Consul.

Mr. Williams to Mr. Cass.

[Extract.]

No. 7.]

LEGATION OF THE UNITED STATES,
Macao, April 22, 1859.

SIR: I have the honor to acknowledge the receipt of your dispatches of the 24th and 26th of January, addressed to me as secretary of legation and Chinese interpreter, informing me of the appointment of W. Wallace Ward to the first named post, and giving directions respecting the form for drawing my salary in future.

Since the date of my dispatch of the 12th instant, I have received from the consul at Canton the statement of his reasons for retaining the tonnage dues of the American ship Minnehaha, that they might be placed to the credit of the claims, and the particulars of the visit of the collector to him, in consequence. The alternative of retaining the duties was mentioned to this officer in February, as one which might become necessary in case he did not issue the debentures soon, and his own evident desire to carry out the stipulations of the convention rather than have any trouble, convinces me that the fault of the delay does not rest with him.

I have approved Mr. Perry's proceedings, (inclosures 1, 2,) and given directions to Messrs. Oliphant & Co., the receivers at Canton, respecting the management of the certificates and disposition of the funds, similar to those sent to Shanghai. (Dispatch No. 5, inclosure 6.) The collection of the fifth of the duties on American commerce at Shanghai, Fuhchau, and Canton, to be applied to the liquidation of American claims on the Chinese government, is now arranged at them all, under such regulations as I have thought sufficient until they can be tested. The explanations respecting the plan which have already been laid before you, and the inclosures accompanying them, render further remark at this time unnecessary, and I shall be pleased to learn that the steps I have taken meet with your approval.

* * * * * * * * *

I have the honor, &c.

S. WELLS WILLIAMS.

Hon. Lewis Cass,
Secretary of State.

Mr. Perry to Mr. Williams.

[Extract.]

United States Consulate,
Canton, April 9, 1859.

Sir: I have the honor to inform you that, day before yesterday, the captain of the American ship Minnehaha applied to me to make application for the clearance of his vessel at the custom-house. As this vessel is a very large one, and the tonnage dues on the same amounted to a very large sum, viz: $1,295 76, and the captain being very well disposed to pay the amount directly into my hands, without reference to the custom-house, I determined to retain the money in my own hands, and under the same cover, addressed to the hoppo, requesting the clearance of the vessel, I inclosed a receipt for the amount, at the same time I sent him by the linguist, Archune, a verbal message to the effect that I had retained the amount of the vessel's tonnage dues, and had passed the same to the credit of the Chinese government, on account of the indemnity due by that government to the United States government, for losses sustained by American citizens at Canton. I also informed him that the hoppo at the ports of Shanghai and Fuh-chau had already commenced to pay their proportion.

The next morning he sent word that he would call upon me during the day. He arrived at about two o'clock.

After the usual exchange of civilities, I informed the hoppo the reasons I had for retaining the tonnage dues of the ship Minnehaha, viz: that the treaty signed on the 8th of November last stipulated that the fifth of all the American duties after the last Chinese new year should be paid to the United States government, or to such person as that government should direct; that two months had already elapsed, but not one dollar had yet been paid, although during that time I had required the American merchants to pay a large amount into the custom-house; that the Shanghai and Fuh-chau hoppos had already paid their proportion. He replied that he had received no instructions from his government to pay any money, and asked particularly whether I had forwarded his letter to Shanghai addressed to Kweiliang and others. I replied that I had.

He then stated that he had no objection to my retaining the tonnage dues on American vessels, but wished me to keep an account of the amount and give him a receipt for the same, which I promised to do. He also consented to furnish me with a statement of the amount of duties paid by American vessels.

During the conversation, he referred to the fact that the English and French had not yet commenced to collect their indemnity. I replied that that fact had nothing to do with the American claim. The hoppo is, I think, well disposed to do whatever is just and proper, but is embarrassed for want of instructions.

* * * * * * * * *

I have, &c.,

OLIVER H. PERRY,
United States Consul.

The Hon. S. WELLS WILLIAMS,
United States Chargé d'Affaires, &c., &c.

Mr. Williams to Mr. Perry.

LEGATION OF THE UNITED STATES,
Macao, April 19, 1859.

I have received your letter of the 9th instant, in which you state the reasons which induced you to retain the tonnage dues of the Minnehaha, and give the particulars of an interview held with the collector of customs on the 8th instant, at which he gave his private consent to your doing so pending the receipt of orders from his government which would authorize his official approval.

Considering that since you applied to him for the debentures, quite time enough has elapsed for him to have received such orders from his superiors as would enable him to carry out the convention for the liquidation of American claims, you have done properly in taking the initiative towards their collection. Until he informs you that he has those orders, you will continue to retain the duties on American ships, giving him receipts for all the moneys you thus receive.

For this purpose I now send you six thousand debenture certificates, each of the value of fifty taels, printed in the English and Chinese, and bound in twelve volumes. According to the terms of the convention of November 8, 1858, it is the duty of the collector to issue these, and I wish you to hand them to him that he may number and then stamp them with his seal of office before he returns them.

On receiving them you will stamp them with your consular seal, as a measure of precaution, and then deliver them all to Messrs. Oliphant & Co., whose partners I have appointed to be the receivers, taking a receipt therefor. They will stamp and countersign them when they issue them, and you can inform the collector that they have been appointed receivers in conformity with the provisions of the convention. The money which you have in hand you will pay Messrs. Oliphant & Co., and receive from them as many certificates as will equal it, as near as can be, and transmit the same to the collector. In succeeding cases, whenever the fifth of the duties on an American ship is paid to the receiver, either through you or directly, they will issue as many certificates as the sum will cover, passing the balance to the credit of the next payment. Your account of the amount received from each ship will serve to verify their record.

This plan of collection, by which the Chinese redeem the debentures, presents so few difficulties in comparison with your retaining the duties, or the shippers paying them in debentures, that I wish you to press it upon the superintendent of customs, as the only one which will prevent misunderstanding and trouble to those concerned, stating that it is already in operation in Shanghai and Fuhchau. You will assure him that while you have no alternative but to carry out the stipulation of the convention for the liquidation of these claims you wish to do so in the way most agreeable to him, which undoubtedly is for him to redeem debentures amounting to a fifth of the duties on every ship at its departure. I cannot suppose that he will long be without orders empowering him to act, and from what you remark of his willingness to cooperate, I hope you will not have to retain the duties on a second ship, and that he will pay over the proportion still due on the vessels which have left port since Chinese new year.

With respect to the collection of the fifth on the river steamers, I must leave it somewhat to your judgment. If the collector finds it difficult to estimate and settle the proportion on these vessels as he does on those landing at Whampoa, perhaps the payment into the receiver's hands of all that is collected by him from each steamer every fifth voyage will interfere least with its traffic, and simplify the matter, though a uniform system is the best, if you can carry it out.

I have strong hopes that, by the exercise of patience with firmness, you will be able to bring this plan of collection into operation at Canton.

I am, respectfully, your obedient servant,

S. WELLS WILLIAMS.

OLIVER H. PERRY, Esq.,
U. S. Consul at Canton.

Mr. Williams to Mr. Cass.

[Extract.]

No. 8.] LEGATION OF THE UNITED STATES,
Macao, May 4, 1859.

SIR: In my last dispatch of the 22d ultimo, I had the honor to inclose to you a letter from the consul at Canton, giving his reasons for retaining the tonnage dues of the ship Minnehaha, and my approval of the act when sending him the certificates to be used in collecting the indemnity. He has since informed me that the collector of customs has received his orders from the imperial commissioners, and has taken the certificates to his office to stamp and number them. Messrs. Oliphant & Co., of Canton, have likewise accepted the appointment of receivers, and have already one book in their possession containing 500 certificates, stamped with the seals of the collector and consul, which will enable them to commence their issue.

The orders from the imperial commissioners (inclosure 2) intimate that they had sent the collector at Canton (about the same time they wrote to me in January and February) instructions respecting the American claims; but these high officials are still disinclined to avail themselves of the coast steamers, preferring to send couriers overland, by which course they have, in this case, subjected their own officers at Canton and Fuhchau to annoying delay.

However, the stipulations of the convention for the liquidation of the American claims have now been complied with, and the plan adopted, of having the collectors at the three ports redeem the debenture certificates, is now in operation at them all, and I think in such a way that there will hereafter be no great difficulty in continuing it until the entire amount of 500,000 taels has been obtained. I am unable to inform you how much has been collected to this date; the consuls at Canton and Fuhchau report about $12,000 paid in, and I think more than that sum has been received at Shanghai.

The claimants are now very desirous to know when their claims are to be adjudicated, and whether they are to receive their money proportionally as it comes into the hands of the receivers, or otherwise; and I hope that, ere long, it will be possible to inform them, as some of them are in need of it. The funds are deposited in a bank at Hong Kong; but, in the uncertainty now existing, no arrangements can well be made for drawing interest upon them.

* * * * * * * *

I have the honor to be, sir, your obedient servant,

S. WELLS WILLIAMS.

Hon. LEWIS CASS,
Secretary of State.

Inclosure 1.

UNITED STATES CONSULATE,
Canton, April 22, 1859.

SIR: I have the honor to inclose herewith a copy, in Chinese, also a translation of the same made by the Rev. Mr. Bonney, of a document received by me from the hoppo. In this document he acknowledges to have received his instructions from the imperial commissioners about the return payment of one fifth of the duties.

You will perceive, on perusal of this document, that the return payment is not limited to American vessels, although the extract from the treaty that you sent me strictly confines it to American ships and goods shipped or exported in them.

On the 19th instant, I called upon the hoppo and had a long conversation with him about the debenture certificates. I carried one of the debenture books with me, which he retained and agreed to stamp with his official seal. He stated that he intended to have a book or books made somewhat similar, in order that he might be able to stamp one half on his book and one half on the certificate; this, he stated, was according to Chinese rule, and, in case of his removal or death, would render them more easily identified by his successor. He also agreed to put his seal in the middle of the certificate.

The hoppo called my attention to the fact that there might possibly be a fraction over or under, and wanted to know how it was to be paid in debenture certificates; that is to say, that the duties to be returned might amount to 110 taels; two certificates would only amount to 100, and three would amount to 150 taels, for which, of course, he would not receive three certificates, thus leaving ten taels in the hoppo's hands. I was a little puzzled what answer to make, but replied that I thought he could arrange that with the linguist. This is a question that must be settled, as otherwise the hoppo would be the gainer, in the case above suggested, of ten taels. I have, therefore, to request your instructions in the matter.

I think the great source of trouble will be to arrange about the payment of goods shipped by Chinamen on foreigners' account on what is called the "short-price" system, the seller paying the duties.

Since my interview with the hoppo, he has sent for three more of the books to have them sealed. He states that it is a very tedious business and will require time. I am to have another interview on Monday next, the 25th.

I beg leave to again call your attention to the great disability under which I labor for the want of an interpreter. Mr. Bonney certainly is always willing to assist me, but you can well imagine how disagreeable and unpleasant it is to me to be constantly calling on his willing and gratuitous services. Mr. Bonney has his own duties to perform. The government of the United States has made a new treaty with China which imposes extra duties on the consul at this port, which necessarily requires an interpreter to aid and assist him in carrying out our treaty obligations. Your long experience in China must have long ere this convinced you of the necessity of having an interpreter attached to this consulate at all times; how much more, therefore, when a large amount of money is to be collected under the new treaty, in which so many Americans are interested.

I have the honor to be, sir, your most obedient servant,

OLIVER H. PERRY,
United States Consul.

Hon. S. WELLS WILLIAMS,
United States Chargé d'Affaires.

Inclosure 2.

APRIL 17, 1859.

HĂNG, promoted by the Emperor to be a high officer in the household, and now charged with the maritime affairs of revenue in Canton, hereby sends a communication:

On the 14th instant, I had the honor to receive from the Imperial Commissioners Kweiliang, Hwashana, and Twan, a dispatch to the following effect:

"While at Shanghai we deliberated with the minister of the United States, and agreed with him respecting the manner of compensating the merchants of his country for their losses to the extent of 500,000 taels, stipulating that, after Chinese new year, one fifth of all the duties on imports and exports and tonnage dues were to be deducted for this purpose. On the 25th of January last, and on the 13th of February, we sent you these instructions by a special post, going 600 *li* daily; but lest those dispatches may have been delayed and not reached you in time, we have again had them copied out for you, and have to request your attention to them.

"Annexed is the paper sent you."

In my former communication you will find that, when I replied to you, I stated that it would be necessary for me to await the reception of orders from the imperial commissioners, and when they came I would immediately inform you that then this matter could be arranged in accordance thereto. They having now been received, I accordingly inform you of it, that we may together arrange the details. While sending this dispatch, I avail myself of the opportunity to wish you increasing prosperity.

A copy of the original instructions are annexed.

OLIVER H. PERRY, Esq.,
United States Consul.

Copy of dispatch.

* * * hereby send instructions.

We, having been honored by his Majesty's commands, came to Shanghai to arrange affairs relating to commerce and the tariff. We then made an engagement to reimburse the losses of the American merchants to the amount of 500,000 taels, commencing from Chinese new year, by deducting for this purpose one fifth of the duties paid on imports, exports, and tonnage dues, of which 300,000 taels are to be deducted at Canton, 100,000 at Fuhchau, and 100,000 at Shanghai. The agreement is, that, out of every 500 taels, 400 taels are to be received in cash, and debenture certificates are to be given for the proportion of 100 taels paid back, which are to be retained as evidence. The time in which the amounts are to be paid is not limited; but after they have been paid up, full duties are to be collected as before. These arrangements have been presented to the throne in a memorial, and distinct orders will likewise be given at the same time to the collectors at those ports for them to act in obedience thereto. These particulars are on record.

We now, therefore, send these orders for your observance. The manner of marking and stamping [the certificates,] numbering them in a series, and dividing them so that their registers shall match, in order that forgery and other modes of counterfeiting them may be prevented, we leave to your own judgment to decide and adopt, only requesting that you will report your proceedings in the matter to the board of revenue.

Inclosure 3.

LEGATION OF THE UNITED STATES,
Macao, April 28, 1859.

SIR: I have received your letter of the 22d instant and its inclosure, and am happy to learn from them that the collector has at last received authority to act in the collection of the claims-indemnity. The terms of the convention expressly limit the deduction of a fifth for liquidating these claims to the commerce in American ships; these documents do not propose to quote it verbally.

In my letter to you when sending the debentures, I stated that the receivers would pass whatever balance was paid them less than the value of a single debenture to the credit of the next payment, giving a temporary receipt for the same, to which I do not think the collector can have any reasonable objection. If you ascertain the total amount of duties paid by a ship from his office, he will of course be prepared to pay back one fifth to the receivers for account of the claims, after furnishing you with the data; but it will be well for you to verify this as much as lies in your power by examining the manifest. If you find that there is a discrepancy between the amounts, so great that you are sure there is some collusion or mistake, you will bring it to his notice. If he arranges with you to redeem the certificates, you cannot permit such violations of the convention; and the mode of doing business at Canton does not differ so much from that at Fuhchau, I think, as to render it very difficult to adopt the same plan at both places. The instructions of the imperial commissioners allow the collector liberty of action in such a matter, and you will then have no trouble with native or foreign shippers, who will pay their duties as they have heretofore done. I trust that he will also agree with you on some plan for estimating and collecting the proportion due on the traffic in the American river steamers, a point I referred to in my last.

In regard to stamping the certificates, so that their genuineness can be verified by collecting the ticket with its register, you must adopt the way which will best assure the collector of their authenticity. When he has redeemed 500 certificates, he can receive their registers back in the bound book; and if the receivers stamp or countersign them across the scroll before cutting them out, his object of verifying them without incurring the extra expense of printing a double set of debentures will be obtained.

I fully appreciate the difficulties under which you labor from not having an interpreter. I have represented to the department the increasing need there is for one to be appointed to aid you, and have hopes that you will ere long be provided.

I am, respectfully, your obedient servant,

S. WELLS WILLIAMS.

OLIVER H. PERRY, Esq.,
United States Consul.

Mr. Ward to Mr. Cass.

[Extract.]

No. 14.*] LEGATION OF THE UNITED STATES,
Shanghai, June 13, 1859.

SIR: I have the honor to inform you that, previous to my arrival in China, the Hon. F. W. A. Bruce having arrived in China, as the envoy extraordinary and minister plenipotentiary of her Britannic Majesty, on the 2d of May communicated his arrival to Mr. Williams, chargé d'affaires *ad interim*, and I herewith attach a copy of the correspondence, marked No. 1 *a*, 1 *b*.

Immediately on my arrival at Hong Kong, where I found Mr. Bruce, I communicated to him my appointment, and also that I had entered upon the duties of the office; and I annex a copy of my letter and his reply, marked 1 *c*, 1 *d*.

Learning that Monsieur de Bourboulon, envoy extraordinary and minister plenipotentiary of France, was at Macao, I gave him the same information; and herewith attach a copy of my letter to him and his reply, marked 1 *e*, 1 *f*.

As soon as Commodore Tatnall could procure a small steamer, in compliance with instructions received from the Secretary of the Navy, we left Hong Kong for Pekin, but, having learned that the commissioners who negotiated the treaty were at Shanghai, we called in at this port on our way. Immediately on my arrival here, I addressed a letter to the commissioners, announcing to them that it had pleased the President to appoint me envoy extraordinary and minister plenipotentiary to his Majesty the Emperor of China, and to intrust me with an autograph letter to be delivered to the Emperor in person, and that I was on my way to Pekin to perform that duty and to exchange the ratifications of the treaty made at Tientsin. A copy of my letter I hereto annex, marked 2 *a*. In the reply of the commissioners, a copy of which I hereto annex, (marked 2 *b*,) they expressed their inability to reach Tientsin for more than two months; alleged that

---

*Numbers 9, 10, 11, 12, and 13, are those dispatches sent by me to the department before reaching China, which were numbered 1 to 5.

they were the only persons authorized to exchange the treaty, and requested me to remain here until after the arrival of the ministers of England and France, and that they would then go north and make the arrangements for our reception; closing their communication with a request that I would give them an interview. I immediately replied that I could not understand or appreciate their reasoning for going north by the land journey, which would require two months, when they could go by sea and reach Pekin in almost as many days, and reminded them that the period fixed by the treaty within which the exchange must take place was rapidly approaching, and I appointed the 2d day of June for the proposed interview. I attach a copy of that letter and their reply, marked 2 *c*, 2 *d*. On the 2d of June I visited them at their residence in the city of Shanghai. I stated to them in that interview that the time mentioned in the American treaty expired on the 18th day of June, and I desired to know what arrangements they had made to carry this stipulation into effect. They admitted the fact, but said the duty of exchanging the treaty had been specially confided to them and no one else, and that they could not possibly reach Pekin by the 18th. They also alleged that as our right to visit Pekin was derived from the English treaty, it was proper they should go north first. I am somewhat embarrassed by the fact that no place is designated in our treaty where the exchange shall take place, whilst in the other treaties it is distinctly stated that they shall be exchanged at Pekin. If I insisted upon going to Pekin under the provisions of the American treaty, they replied I could only go according to its terms whenever I had business of importance to transact. My intention must then be communicated to the board of rights, &c. If I claimed to go under the most favored nation clause in our treaty, they replied that that right being derived from the English treaty, the ratification of that treaty should be first exchanged.

Upon receiving this last answer I asked them, do you intend to defer the exchange with me until that with the English minister has been accomplished? They replied, if the American treaty be first exchanged it must be done here. To which I replied that the President had ordered me to proceed to Pekin, there to exchange the ratification of the treaty, and I desired to know if the ratification should be exchanged here if I should then have the right to go to Pekin with the ministers of other nations? They answered I could go if I had business. I said I would not put it upon that contingency, but, if I desired to go, I should do so without inquiry into or statement of the nature of my business, and that I would go to Pekin with the minister of the first nation that went, or I would refuse to exchange the ratification of the treaty here. They then replied, that the copies of the treaties having the Emperor's signatures were all in Pekin, and that none of them could be exchanged within the year, that they must all be exchanged together. To this I assented, but stated to them that, as I had been instructed by the President to proceed without delay to the capital, there to exchange the ratification of the treaties, they must, in another reply to my last dispatch, distinctly state the three following propositions: 1st. That there had been no delay on my part in reaching China in ample time to exchange the ratification of the treaty of Pekin before the 18th of June, but that it was impossible to exchange the treaty within the time specified, because the copy with his Majesty's signature was at Pekin, and none of them could get there by the 18th instant. 2d. That I should go to Pekin with the minister of the first nation who should go there, and at that place exchange the ratification of the treaty. 3d. That the validity of all the provisions of the treaty with the United States should not be in the least impaired by this delay and overpassing of the limited time, but that it should have the same force as if the exchange had been made within the specified period. To this they assented; and the next day addressed me a communication fully embodying these propositions, a copy of which I hereto annex, marked 2 *e*. On the 5th of June I then replied to them, assenting to remain here until the arrival of the other ministers, but stated to them that the exchange of treaties having been tendered by me within the specified time, it must be regarded as having been exchanged *de jure* within that time; and all rights dependent thereon to have accrued, leaving the ceremony of exchange alone to take place at Pekin. A copy of that letter I hereto annex, marked 2 *f*. Immediately after sending in this dispatch Mr. Bruce and Monsieur de Bourboulon, the English and French ministers, arrived; and, on the 11th instant, I received from the commissioners another communication informing me that they have determined to leave for the capital on the 13th instant, that I might act accordingly. A copy of that communication I hereto annex, marked 2 *g*. Mr. Bruce has furnished me with a copy of his correspondence with the commissioners, which I hereto annex, marked 3 *a*, *b*, *c*, *d*. Since the receipt of that communication from Mr. Bruce, he has called upon me personally and exhibited to me the reply of the commissioners, a copy of which he is unable to furnish me in time for this mail. In that reply they say that they have sent a memorial to the Emperor to appoint other persons to exchange the ratifications, and to make arrangements for the English, French, and American ministers to go from Tientsin to Pekin.

They request Mr. Bruce to have his vessels anchored outside the bar of the Peiho river, and assure him that every courtesy will be extended to the representatives of the treaty powers. I shall leave on Thursday in the Powhatan, with the Toeywan, the chartered steamer, in tow for Tientsin; and, by the time I reach that point, I hope the necessary arrangements will have been made for my proceeding to Pekin without delay. * * * * * * * *

I have the honor to be, sir, your obedient servant,

JOHN E. WARD.

Hon. Lewis Cass,
Secretary of State, Washington,

Inclosure 1 *a.*

VICTORIA, HONG KONG,
May 2, 1859.

SIR: I have the honor to announce to you that her Britannic Majesty has been pleased to appoint me her envoy extraordinary and minister plenipotentiary to his Majesty the Emperor of China, and further, to give me her royal commission as superintendent of British trade in China, in virtue of which I have this day assumed the duties of my office.

I need not assure you of my ardent wish to preserve that cordiality and good understanding which have always characterized the relations of our respective governments, and those of their representatives in China, and which the identity of our interests in this country renders it so desirable to maintain unimpaired.

I have the honor to be, sir, your obedient, humble servant,

FREDERICK W. A. BRUCE.

S. WELLS WILLIAMS, Esq.,
&c., &c., &c.

Inclosure 1 *b.*

LEGATION OF THE UNITED STATES,
Macao, May 3, 1859.

SIR: I have the honor to acknowledge your excellency's communication of yesterday's date, in which you inform me that her Britannic Majesty has appointed you her envoy extraordinary and minister plenipotentiary to China, and that you have assumed the duties of superintendent of British trade in China.

I beg to congratulate your excellency on your arrival in China, charged with these important functions, and I most cordially reciprocate your excellency's wish that the good understanding which has heretofore existed between our respective governments and their representatives in China may continue to be maintained; and I cannot doubt that our harmony of action is calculated to have increasing influence on the welfare of this empire.

I have the honor to be, sir, your excellency's obedient servant,

S. WELLS WILLIAMS.

His Excellency the Hon. F. W. A. BRUCE, C. B.,
&c., &c., &c.

Inclosure 1 *c.*

LEGATION OF THE UNITED STATES,
U. S. Steamer Powhatan, Hong Kong Harbor, May 18, 1859.

SIR: I have the honor to inform your excellency that the President has been pleased to appoint me envoy extraordinary and minister plenipotentiary of the United States to China, and that I have entered upon the duties of that office.

It is hardly necessary for me to assure your excellency of the desire which I have that the friendly intercourse which has ever existed between our respective governments and their representatives in China for so long a period may be strengthened, and that the similarity of our objects in this empire may lead to harmony of action in whatever will conduce to the extension of freedom of intercourse with its rulers and their subjects.

With the expression of great personal regard, I have the honor to be, sir, your excellency's most obedient servant,

JOHN E. WARD.

His Excellency Hon. F. W. A. BRUCE, C. B.,
Envoy Extraordinary and Minister Plenipotentiary of Her Britannic Majesty in China.

Inclosure 1 *d.*

SHANGHAI, *June* 8, 1859.

SIR: I have the honor to acknowledge the receipt of your excellency's letter of the 18th ultimo, acquainting me with the fact of your appointment as envoy extraordinary and minister plenipotentiary of the United States to China.

Whilst offering to your excellency my best congratulations on your appointment, I cannot but express the sincere pleasure with which I have read the sentiments which accompanied its announcement.

I beg leave to assure your excellency that I gladly reëcho those sentiments, and that it will be my pleasing task to cement, to the best of my ability, the good relations happily existing between our respective governments on all questions of Chinese policy, convinced as I am that the main objects of freedom of intercourse and extension of trade which we seek in this empire can best be attained by unity of action and cordial coöperation.

I have the honor to be, sir, your excellency's most obedient, humble servant,

FREDERICK W. A. BRUCE.

His Excellency Hon. JOHN E. WARD,
&c., &c., &c.

Inclosure 1 *e.*

LEGATION OF THE UNITED STATES,
U. S. Steamer Powhatan, Hong Kong Harbor, May 18, 1859.

SIR: I have the honor to inform your excellency that the President has been pleased to appoint me envoy extraordinary and minister plenipotentiary of the United States to China, and that I have arrived and entered upon the duties of my office.

In communicating to your excellency, I beg to assure you of my earnest desire to continue the amicable relations which have ever characterized the intercourse between our respective governments and their representatives in China, and to coöperate in those peaceful plans which may best conduce to the extension of the friendly relations of western powers with this empire.

I look forward with pleasure to a personal acquaintance, and beg you to receive the assurance of the high consideration with which I have the honor to be, sir, your excellency's most obedient servant,

J. E. WARD.

His Excellency A. BOURBOULON,
Envoy Extraordinary and Minister Plenipotentiary of His Imperial Majesty in China.

Inclosure 1 *f.*

[Translation.]

LEGATION OF FRANCE IN CHINA,
Hong Kong, May 29, 1859.

SIR: I have the honor to acknowledge the reception of the letter which your excellency addressed to me on the 18th of this month, making known to me that it has pleased the President of the United States to appoint you envoy extraordinary and minister plenipotentiary of the United States in China, as well as your excellency's arrival in this country, and your entering into the exercise of your functions.

In thanking your excellency for this communication, and for the courteous and friendly assurances with which you have been so good as to accompany it, I request you to be persuaded of the lively desire which, on my part, I entertain for continuing with you the good and cordial relations which I have already been so happy as to maintain with three of your predecessors. This desire, sir, is with me still more increased by the conviction that the greatest harmony of views and of action between the representatives of the great powers of the west in this country, is the most efficacious means of speedily succeeding in establishing really, friendly, and reciprocally advantageous relations with its government.

Permit me to add, sir, that, in advance, I do not doubt that such an understanding, whether personally or in official connections, will be, for me, an easy task with such a colleague as I am sure to find in your excellency; and while waiting for an acquaintance, which I desire to render as early as possible, be so good as to accept the sentiments of high consideration with which I have the honor to be, sir, your very humble and very obedient servant,

A. BOURBOULON.

His Excellency Mr. J. E. WARD, &c., &c., &c.

Inclosure 2 a.

LEGATION OF THE UNITED STATES,
U. S. Ship Powhatan, off Weisung, May 28, 1859.

The undersigned has the honor to inform their excellencies the imperial commissioners, that the President has been pleased to appoint him envoy extraordinary and minister plenipotentiary of the United States to China, and that he is charged with an autograph letter from the President to his Majesty the Emperor, which he is now on his way to Pekin to deliver to him in person. The undersigned is also in possession of the ratified copy of the treaty signed at Tientsin, which he has been instructed to exchange at Pekin.

That this treaty will prove the basis of a lasting and friendly intercourse between our respective nations, and tend to establish those amicable relations which will be mutually advantageous to them, is what the undersigned most sincerely desires.

JOHN E. WARD.

Their Excellencies KWEILIANG, *Chief Secretary of State, &c., and* HWASHANA, *Superintendent of the Board of Civil Office, &c., Imperial Plenipotentiaries, and* TWAN, *a Minister attached to the General Council—all of them imperial commissioners.*

Inclosure 2 b.

MAY 30, 1859.

KWEILIANG, one of his Imperial Majesty's Secretaries of State, &c., &c., and HWASHANA, Superintendent of the Board of Civil Office, Imperial Plenipotentiaries; with Ho, Governor General of the Two Kiang Provinces, and TWAN, a Deputy in the service of the General Council, Imperial Commissioners, &c., &c., hereby send a reply:

We had the honor to receive your excellency's communication of the 28th instant this day. In it you inform us that the President has been pleased to appoint you envoy extraordinary and minister plenipotentiary of the United States to China, and that you are charged with an autograph letter from him, to be presented to his Majesty the Emperor, and have in your hands the ratified copy of the treaty signed at Tientsin, to be exchanged.

We beg to assure your excellency of our great satisfaction at this announcement; but as in our view the exchange of the ratifications of the treaty is a matter of high importance to both countries, it is undesirable that it be hastily done. We, ourselves, not having yet completed all our negotiations relating to the treaty negotiated with Lord Elgin, the late high commissioner of her Britannic Majesty, and placed everything on a well-understood and stable basis, have hitherto remained in Shanghai, without returning to Pekin.

Your excellency is now on your way to Tientsin, but we still remain in Shanghai; nor do we know when we can leave it for the north to go by land. It certainly cannot be with haste. Furthermore, we apprehend that the discommodities of the journey, and the contingencies of the weather, (when we do start,) will protract the time of arrival at Tientsin more than two months. Your excellency must therefore see very clearly that if you arrive at that city so early, while we are unable to hasten our departure, not only will no officer be there to receive you, but the duty of making the exchange of ratifications will still devolve on us. We also think, that as the summer heats there will be very great to wait through, it will be preferable for your excellency to delay awhile in Shanghai, before fixing the time to start.

We beg that you will appoint a day for an interview, at which we can deliberate upon the time for you to again continue your journey—a plan, which seems to us, likely to be more agreeable and safe. It is our belief that great carefulness should be taken that these important matters be arranged so as to secure their lasting and amicable action; and with this conviction, in the full assurance that your excellency, being profoundly acquainted with all public affairs, will coincide with our views, we now return this reply.

His Excellency JOHN E. WARD,
Envoy Extraordinary and Minister Plenipotentiary of the United States to China.

Inclosure 2 c.

UNITED STATES LEGATION,
Shanghai, June 1 1859.

The undersigned has this day received the communication of your excellencies, dated May 30, 1859, in which you have been pleased to say, "as the exchange of the ratification of the treaty is a matter of high importance to both countries, it is undesirable that it be hastily done."

It is from an appreciation of the vast importance of the exchange to both countries within the time prescribed by the treaty, that I am now here, ready and anxious to proceed to Pekin, there to have the exchange effected, on or before the 18th instant, according to the terms and provisions of the treaty.

I regret that I am able neither to appreciate the reasoning of your excellencies for the proposed delay, nor why you should in a matter of such vital importance determine to proceed by the land journey, to perform which, two months will be required, when the city of Pekin may be reached by another route in almost as many days. I feel assured that in a very short time your excellencies will be satisfied, that if "you have not yet completed your negotiations relating to the treaty made with Lord Elgin, the late high commissioner of her Britannic Majesty," that your own views will be best promoted by proceeding north without unnecessary delay.

It affords me great satisfaction to comply with the request of your excellencies for an interview. I will do myself the honor of calling upon you on Thursday next, the 2d instant, at five o'clock, p. m., when I trust that some arrangement may be made for my journey to Pekin, there to exchange the ratification of the treaty.

Their Excellencies KWEILIANG *and* HWASHANA,
And their associates HO, *and* TWAN, *Imperial Commissioners.*

Inclosure 2 d.

NOTE FROM KWEILIANG.

JUNE 2, 1859.

We have this moment received your excellency's dispatch of the 1st instant, and will accordingly be in readiness at the hour stated, at our temporary readiness, for the purpose of receiving you with the utmost respect. We avail ourselves of this opportunity to express the wish that the occasion may be a joyful one.

[Sent with the four commissioners' cards.]

Inclosure 2 e.

JUNE 3, 1859.

KWEILIANG, his Imperial Majesty's Secretary of State, &c., &c., and HWASHANA, President of the Board of Civil Office, Imperial Plenipotentiaries, with HO KWEI-TSING, Governor General of the Two Kiang and TWAN SHING-SHIH, all of them Imperial Commissioners, herewith send a communication:

We have already acknowledged a former dispatch of your excellency, in which we stated the extreme pleasure it has given us to learn that you have been designated by the President to come to China, and that you reached Shanghai on the 29th ultimo. We have also been still further gratified and assured in that you have done us the honor of making us a personal visit, at which we could converse upon points of public interest. From this, we learned that, as the time specified for exchanging the ratified treaties is so near, your excellency intended to proceed in a steamer to Tientsin, which can by that means be reached in the space of four or five days, and thus the period fixed for making the exchange would not be overpassed.

But it so happened that when the British high commissioner, Lord Elgin, returned to Canton last winter, we made an arrangement with him to wait at Shanghai until he came back, when the various matters still unsettled between us could be discussed, and placed upon a secure and well understood basis. We have accordingly tarried here till this time. We now learn that Lord Elgin has returned to England from Canton, and that his excellency Mr. Bruce, the newly appointed British minister to China, will reach this place in a very short time. We are, of course, obliged to await his arrival, and shall enter on the discussion and settlement of the points which are still to be arranged, and bring them to a conclusion as soon as possible. We shall then start for the north.

In relation to that journey, we think it will be necessary for us to follow the usages of our own country, and travel by the post, according to his Majesty's commands, and this will require fully two months or more to accomplish. On reaching Pekin, we will await the arrival of your excellency and the English and French ministers, and then at once exchange the ratifications of all those treaties, (*i. e.* the three here referred to,) which were negotiated last year, at Tientsin. In this manner the relations between the several parties to these compacts will be placed on a permanent and amicable footing, and all their provisions carried out to the common advantage of all.

If the ministers of Great Britain and France go to Pekin to exchange their treaties, your excellency, whose business is the same as theirs, can proceed thither at the same time. We are aware that it is definitely stated in the treaties negotiated at Tientsin last year, that copies of the same, ratified by the signatures of the sovereigns of all those countries, shall be exchanged within a year; but as that period is now nearly expired, it will make no difference when the ratifications are exchanged. Whenever this does take place it will be equally valid as if it had been done within the prescribed year.

We beg to apprize your excellency that we propose to call together on you to-morrow, the 4th instant, at two o'clock, p. m., at your residence, and therefore send this communication previously to inform you, at the same time tendering our respectful wishes that the day may be an agreeable one to you.

His Excellency JOHN E. WARD,
Envoy Extraordinary and Minister Plenipotentiary of the United States to China.

Inclosure 2 f.

LEGATION OF THE UNITED STATES,
Shanghai, June 5, 1859.

The undersigned, envoy extraordinary, &c., &c., has the honor to acknowledge the receipt of your excellencies' communication of the 3d instant, since which time he has also had the honor of a visit of friendship from you.

The undersigned acknowledges the force of the reasons upon which your excellencies have based the request that he would remain at Shanghai until the arrival of the other treaty ministers, and proceed north with them, that all the treaties might be exchanged at the same time and place.

In compliance with that request, the undersigned will remain at Shanghai until the arrival of the other ministers, and proceed with them to Pekin, where, as soon as possible, the "ceremony of exchange can take place."

To statesmen so renowned for their wisdom and experience, it can hardly be necessary to say that, as the undersigned is prepared to have the treaty exchanged within the specified time, and has tendered that exchange to your excellencies, the exchange must be regarded as having been made *de jure*, and that all rights dependent thereon have accrued, leaving the ceremony of exchange alone to take place after our arrival at Pekin.

Assuring your excellencies of the great pleasure I have enjoyed from my official and personal intercourse with you, and wishing you every happiness and prosperity, I send this reply.

JOHN E. WARD.

Their Excellencies KWEILIANG *and* HWASHANA, *Imperial Plenipotentiaries, with* HO KWEI-TSING *and* TWAN SHING-SHIH, *Imperial Commissioners, &c., &c.*

Inclosure 2 g.

JUNE 11, 1859.

KWEILIANG, His Imperial Majesty's Secretary of State, &c., and HWASHANA, President of the Board of Civil Office, Imperial Plenipotentiaries, with HO KWEI-TSING, Governor General of the two Kiang Provinces, and TWAN SHING-SHIH, &c., Imperial Commissioners, &c., herewith send a communication:

We have received your excellency's dispatch of the 5th instant, in which you refer to the exchange of the ratifications of the treaties of Tientsin, and to the interview we have had at your residence. We also observe in this dispatch, that to our request that your excellency would remain at Shanghai until the arrival of the ministers of Great Britain and France, after which you and they could go north together, and exchange the several treaties at the same place, you give your consent and agree to the proposition, and quote our remark, that the validity of the provisions of the treaty of Tientsin will be as unimpaired as if the ratifications had been exchanged within the prescribed year.

From this we clearly perceive, with the utmost satisfaction, your excellency's full understanding of all affairs of government, as well as your earnest desire to promote and exhibit whatever is kind and amicable. But we have now received dispatches from the British and French ministers since their arrival in Shanghai, in which they state that, as the time for exchanging their treaties is so near at hand, they cannot remain long in Shanghai. We have decided, therefore, to leave for the capital ourselves on the 13th instant, of which we now inform your excellency that you may act accordingly.

His Excellency JOHN E. WARD,
Envoy Extraordinary and Minister Plenipotentiary of the United States.

Inclosure 3 *a.*

SHANGHAI, *June* 12, 1859.

SIR: I have the honor to transmit herewith for your excellency's information copies of my correspondence with the imperial commissioners respecting the exchange of the ratifications of the treaty of Tientsin.

I have the honor to be, sir, your obedient, humble servant,

FREDERICK W. A. BRUCE.

His Excellency JOHN E. WARD, *&c.*, *&c.*, *&c.*

Inclosure 3 *b.*

[Received June 6, 1859.]

KWEILIANG, &c., HWASHANA, &c., HO, &c., Imperial Commissioners, &c., &c., make a communication.

It appears from the records that, on the twenty-second day of the twelfth moon of last year, (25th January, 1859,) a dispatch was received by the commissioners from the late British minister, Lord Elgin, in which there are the following words: "The undersigned has determined on proceeding to Canton to take certain steps, (or to act;) his business accomplished, in the course of some five or six weeks, he will name a time for his arrival at Shanghai, there to settle with the commissioners such questions as still remain to be discussed."*

In due course of time, on the twenty-sixth day of the second moon of the present year, (30th March, 1859,) the commissioners received a second letter, dated the twenty-ninth of the first moon, (8th March,) to the effect "that her Britannic Majesty has appointed the honorable Mr. Bruce to be her representative, &c., and that he would arrive in China shortly;" further stating that "the undersigned, now on the point of leaving China, must take leave on this his last opportunity of addressing them earnestly to impress [upon the commissioners] that the one essential to a continuance of friendly relations is the faithful observance of the treaty," &c., &c.

The commissioners, in consequence of Lord Elgin's earlier letter, in which he engaged to return to Shanghai for a conference with them, have been waiting for him, without moving, (lit. obstinately, persistently.) Lord Elgin has returned home; but Mr. Bruce, having received the commands of her Majesty to succeed him in the administration of all things essential, and now occupying, to the great satisfaction of the commissioners, a position identical with that of Lord Elgin, his predecessor, the proper course to be pursued is, doubtless, to appoint a day for a conference.

In faithful compliance with the engagement already entered into,

* This is a free retranslation of the Chinese, representing the English of Lord Elgin's dispatch, of which there is not a copy at hand.

and, as the period appointed for the exchange of the treaties is very near at hand, it is, of course, most expedient that all business which has to be considered should become the subject of consultation, and be proceeded with as early as possible.

A necesssary communication, addressed to Mr. Bruce, envoy extraordinary, &c., &c.

Hien-fung, ninth year, fourth moon, twenty-fifth day, (May 29, 1859.)

Translated by

THOMAS WADE,
Chinese Secretary.

Inclosure 3 *c.*

[Received June 6, 1859.]

KWEILIANG, &c., HWA, &c., HO, &c., TWAN, &c., Imperial Commissioners, make a communication.

It appears from the records that, on the thirteenth day of the twelfth moon of last year, (January 16, 1859,) the commissioners received from the late British minister, Lord Elgin, a communication to the effect that he was proceeding to Canton upon business, and would return to Shanghai in five or six weeks, to consider and dispose of all matters on which discussion was still pending.

Firmly persuaded of the good faith of Lord Elgin's words, the commissioners have been waiting for him several months. His lordship has now returned home; but, as Mr. Bruce has been commanded by her (Britannic) Majesty to replace him here, with plenipotentiary powers, his position is identical with that of his predecessor, Lord Elgin.

With Mr. Bruce's permission, the commissioners will state the questions which have been discussed with Lord Elgin, as well as those which remain to be discussed.

As regards admission into Pekin, the visit to Pekin, on this occasion, to exchange courtesies and treaties is exceptional, and when it is over, there is to be no permanent residence in the capital; some other place is to be chosen (for the minister) to reside at. These are the words of Lord Elgin's dispatch, the approval of which, by her Britannic Majesty, when Lord Elgin had the honor to receive it, was duly reported to his Imperial Majesty by the commissioners.

As regards the navigation of the river, (Yangtsze,) Lord Elgin has been himself to Hankan, to see the place for once. For the time to come, it will be safe and satisfactory that all arrangements be made, as, of course, they must be, in accordance with the treaty.*

As regards circulation in the interior, this, without doubt, on the principle laid down by Lord Elgin, viz: that any British subject of

---

* And consequently here.

respectability and good conduct should receive a passport from the local authorities, under which he may travel. This is perfectly fair. But inasmuch as China has no means of knowing what British subjects are respectable, it is still necessary that some good adequate means be devised (to this end,) that there may be no misgivings on either side.

As regards the city of Canton, Lord Elgin engaged to go further into this question when he should return to Shanghai; but, as his lordship has returned to England, it has not been possible to consider it with him. The time for the exchange of the treaties draws near. The treaties once exchanged, the relations between the two countries will be more friendly than ever. Added to this, as imperial commissioner for the management of the five ports, his Majesty the Emperor has already substituted the Governor General Ho, one of the commissioners,* for his predecessor, Hwang, by which appointment it is felt consultations on business, between China and foreign nations, will be much facilitated.† Everything is thus on a satisfactory footing. But as Canton is not yet restored, it would seem that no time should be lost in arriving at a satisfactory decision regarding it.

The commissioners will be greatly obliged to his excellency's replying specifically to them upon the above subjects, those which have been disposed of in discussion, and those which remain to be discussed.

A necessary communication, addressed to the honorable Mr. Bruce.

Hien-fung, quarter year, fourth moon, twenty-sixth day, (May 28, 1859.)

Translated by

THOMAS WADE,
Chinese Secretary.

Inclosure 3 d.

[Received June 6, 1859.]

KWEI, &c., HWA, &c., HO, &c., TWAN, &c., Imperial Commissioners, make a communication in reply;

On the 28th instant, (27th May, 1859,) the commissioners received Mr. Bruce's dispatch of the 14th instant, (16th May,) apprising them that her Britannic Majesty had done him the honor to appoint him her envoy extraordinary and minister plenipotentiary to the court of Pekin.

The commissioners were greatly gratified at this intelligence. They are of opinion, however, that an affair of so grave importance to both nations as an exchange of treaties cannot with propriety be hurried over. The commissioners, having the fullest confidence in his predecessor, Lord Elgin, when he engaged them to remain at Shanghai to

---

* And consequently here.

† This, I think, a regarding the extent to which our former relations are modified. The Chinese would prefer continuing to regard them as merely commercial, the Chinese superintendent of trade as foreign minister.

consider all matters not disposed of, were unable to return to Pekin, and if Mr. Bruce now proceed to Tientsin, the commissioners, having to travel north by land, cannot reckon upon arriving there so soon; indeed, taking into consideration the hindrance to be expected from the weather on their land journey, this will certainly occupy two months and more, as Mr. Bruce, they imagine, must be well aware.

As to the preparation of vessels, vehicles, &c., at Tientsin,* to which the letter under acknowledgment refers, and the selection of a building in proper order [for Mr. Bruce] to reside in, with the good understanding now subsisting between the two nations, the arrangements will be, of course, as liberal as it is suggested they should be.† But the commissioners cannot arrive in so short a time, nor can any of these things be done at a moment's notice.

There is another consideration. Not only will there be no one to receive Mr. Bruce at Tientsin, as it is impossible for the commissioners to be there against his arrival, but [there will be no one either to exchange the ratifications] the exchange of the treaties must be effected by the hands of the commissioners, and by their hands alone; no one can act as their substitute. And believing, consequently, that it would be better for Mr. Bruce to defer his departure from Shanghai for awhile than to be kept waiting at the other place, where, after midsummer, the heat is excessive, they feel bound to request him, in the first place, on his arrival at Shanghai, to name a day for an interview with them, and, in the second, to appoint some other time for proceeding. This seems to them would be the more satisfactory arrangement.

The commissioners are induced to put forward this proposition by the importance they attach to the question before them, and [their desire for] the establishment of friendly relations to endure for evermore.

Mr. Bruce's thorough acquaintance with the ways of the world (or the motives of men) is such that they feel sure he will appreciate their feelings, and they hope that he will at once reply to them.

A necessary communication addressed to the honorable Mr. Bruce, &c.

Hien-fung, ninth year, fourth moon, twenty-sixth day, (May 28, 1859.)

Translated by THOMAS WADE,
Chinese Secretary.

Inclosure 3 *e*.

The undersigned, &c., begs to acknowledge the receipt of the letter, addressed to him by their excellencies the imperial commissioners, Kweiliang, Hwashana, Ho Kweit-sing, and Twan Ching-shih, in reply to that sent by him to his excellency Kweiliang, chief secretary of state.

The undersigned must remind his excellency Kweiliang that the treaty of Tientsin, signed on the 26th June last, provides that the

---

* The suitable means of transmission spoken of in Mr. Bruce's letter of the ——.

† *Lit.*—It is certainly proper that according to this, or after this fashion, [China should be] liberal. There is a certain amount of patronage in the expression.

ratifications shall be exchanged at the capital within a year from that date, and the imperial commissioners themselves admit that on the 30th March last they were apprised by the Earl of Elgin that the undersigned was on his way to China for the purpose of fulfilling this engagement.

The commissioners were at the same time made aware that the Earl of Elgin was returning home, consequently that he would not revisit Shanghai. Notwithstanding this intelligence, they have thought proper to remain at Shanghai till within a month of the time appointed for the exchange of ratifications, alleging as a reason for so doing that various details connected with the execution of the treaty had been only in part discussed by the Earl of Elgin, while they at the same time declare that they are the only authorities by whom the exchange of the ratified treaties at Pekin could be effected.

They now write to inform the undersigned that their journey to Pekin will occupy above two months; that is to say, that they cannot reach the capital for upwards of a month after the day by treaty appointed; that there will be no one to receive the undersigned at Tientsin, and no one to exchange the ratifications at Pekin. They accordingly request the undersigned to delay his departure from Shanghai. The undersigned is determined that so far as it rests with him no stipulation of the treaty shall be violated. The exchange of the ratifications is a ceremony which records in the most solemn form that the new treaty is the rule henceforth to be observed in conducting the intercourse of the two nations; and as the treaty admits of no alteration or modification, the undersigned cannot allow that the period fixed for the exchange be made in any way dependent on arrangements necessary to carry certain of its details into execution.

It is with regret that the undersigned finds, at the outset of a mission sent by her Britannic Majesty as evidence of her desire for peaceful relations, that he is met, not as he had a right to expect, with a cordial and frank invitation to the capital, but with delays and hesitatations ill-calculated to cement a good understand. The undersigned will not, however, swerve in the least from the course he has laid down in his letter of the 18th ultimo. He is resolved to proceed forthwith to Pekin, there to exchange the ratifications of the treaty, and to deliver in person the letter intrusted to his charge by his gracious sovereign to his Imperial Majesty, to whom it is addressed, nor will he quit the capital until satisfied that effect will be given without reserve to every provision of the treaty of Tientsin.

The undersigned intends no discourtesy to the imperial commissioners, but he must, under the circumstances, decline positively any interview with them at this place. His resolution to proceed to Pekin without delay is inflexible.

It is at the same time his duty to warn his excellency Kweiliang that he is prepared to insist on a reception befitting the dignity of the nation he represents, and that any failure in this respect will be attended with the most serious consequences to the imperial government.

The undersigned avails himself of this opportunity, &c.

F. W. A. BRUCE.

His Excellency KWEILIANG,
Chief Secretary of State, &c., &c., &c.

Inclosure 3 *f*.

SHANGHAI, *June* 11, 1859.

The undersigned &c., had the honor to address a letter to the Chief Secretary of State Kweiliang, upon the 8th instant. He has received no reply to this, and he observes that neither his excellency nor his colleagues, the imperial commissioners, who have informed him that it is through their hands alone that the ratifications of the treaty can pass, are to all appearance making an effort to reach Pekin by the day on which it is by treaty agreed the ratifications shall be exchanged. He begs therefore to point out to them that there are lying in this harbor several steamers, one or two of them flying the Chinese flag, by the employment of which, it is perfectly within their power to accomplish their journey before the appointed time.

Admiral Hope, the naval commander-in-chief, has started for the Peiho with his squadron, charged to advise local authorities of the immediate approach of the undersigned and his colleague, Mr. de Bourboulon, the minister of France. The undersigned, before leaving Shanghai, begs again to impress upon his excellency Kweiliang that his proceeding is in strict accordance with the treaty provision, and he throws upon the Chinese government the entire responsibility of any consequences that may arise from its violation.

The undersigned avails &c., &c.,

F. W. A. BRUCE.

His Excellency KWEILIANG, *&c.*, *&c.*, *&c.*

Mr. Ward to Mr. Cass.

No. 15.]

UNITED STATES FRIGATE POWHATAN,
Off Peiho River, *July* 4, 1859.

SIR: I have the honor to inform you that since my last dispatch, I have received from Mr. Bruce a copy of the communication addressed to him by the imperial commissioners before leaving Shanghai, which is hereto annexed, (marked *a*.) In compliance with the invitation of the imperial commissioners, I left Shanghai on the morning of the 16th instant, in the steam frigate Powhatan, having in tow the steamboat Toeywan, chartered by the commodore, in which I expected to ascend the river as far as Tientsin. We arrived here on Tuesday morning, the 21st instant. For two days after my arrival the weather prevented my communicating with the shore.

On Thursday the British admiral called upon me and informed me that the mouth of the river had been obstructed with barriers so as to render its ascent impossible without their removal; that he had communicated with the shore, and informed them that the English and French ministers had arrived at the mouth of the river on their way to Pekin, and unless the obstructions were removed he should proceed to remove them himself; that they had informed him there was no officer there to receive them, and no one in the fort who could either read or write; that this was not the Peiho river, but that there was an entrance about ten miles to the north, and that in a few days some one would meet the ministers there.

To which the admiral informed me he had replied, that if the obstructions were not removed by Saturday, the 25th, he should on that morning commence their removal, the English and French ministers having requested him to open the door which had been closed upon them.

I frankly said to the admiral that my position was a very different one from that of the English and French ministers ; that their treaties were made whilst they were at war, and if any of their provisions had been violated, they might consider themselves as thrown back into the war which had been suspended by the treaties; that the American treaty was made whilst we were at peace with the Chinese, and that if any of its provisions were violated, my government was the proper judge of the remedy to be applied; but that I had been instructed by the President to go to Pekin ; that I should the next day cross the bar in the Toeywan and proceed until I was fired upon, when a new question would arise.

The next morning, Friday, the 24th, Commodore Tattnall with his flag lieutenant, and Captain Pearson went with me and my suite on board the Toeywan about 8 o'clock in the morning, and proceeded toward the river. After crossing the bar, and when within a half mile of the forts we run aground, the tide then falling very rapidly. The admiral immediately sent his flag-lieutenant and the gun-boat Plover, No. 86, to say that he expected to see us fired on every moment, and that when the tide fell, the boat would probably keel over, and to tender him the use of the gun-boat, requesting him to lift the American ensign at the peak and his own flag at the mizen-mast. The commodore declined to accept this kind offer, but said he would be glad of the services of the boat to pull him off. The effort was made and proved unsuccessful; the gun-boat left us and returned to her position in the line, which the admiral had commenced forming. About 2 o'clock, the flag-lieutenant of Commodore Tattnall, with Dr. Williams, Mr. Martin, and Mr. Atchison, the interpreters, went on shore to inform them that I was on board the steamer on my way to Pekin. The reply was, that we could not go by that river ; that there was no officer of my rank there ; that they could receive no communication whatever, not even a card; that they could neither read nor write; that they had heard that the Emperor had ordered the governor general to meet the ministers at what they called the north entrance of the river, which they said was ten miles distant, and that he had arrived there that day, and would have an interview with the English minister on the day following. They then returned to the steamer. About 8 o'clock in the evening, we fortunately succeeded in getting the steamer off. By that time, the admiral had formed a line with his ships. The commodore, fearing that a light moving about his vessel might be mistaken for signal in the admiral's squadron, ordered the steamer to drop below the line. About 12 o'clock we heard an explosion, which was the blowing up of the first barrier across the river, which was followed by two guns from the forts. The rest of the night everything was quiet. It was evident in the morning, from the position of the vessels, that the battle would be commenced sometime during the day. At a quarter before 3 o'clock, p. m., two of the gun-boats, one of them with the admiral's flag flying, commenced ascending the river, when the forts immediately opened upon them, and the battle had begun. About 5 o'clock, Commodore Tattnall having learned that the admiral was dangerously wounded, and had but three men capable of doing duty upon his flag-ship, and that he had sent down to a junk lying at our side for a reinforcement, but that the tide and wind were so strong against them that they could not be taken up in the small boats of the vessel, consulted with me as to the propriety of towing them up with the Toeywan. I told him, as neutrals, we had no right to interfere, or to render the slightest aid; but that we could not be regarded strictly as neutrals; that we were in company with the English not by my choice, because I had left Hong Kong so immediately after my arrival there, to avoid all complication with other powers; that I had been assailed in one of the Hong Kong papers; that on my arrival at Shanghai, the Chinese commissioners had insisted upon my waiting for the English and French, and coming with them; that we had been constantly receiving acts of kindness, inseparable from the position in which we were placed; that whilst we had no right to fire a gun in their defense or give them a man to aid in the attack, we ought to render the admiral the required assistance to relieve him from his position, and that his desire to tow up the boats, received not only my assent, but my unqualified approbation, and was in strict accordance with my own wishes. The boats were accordingly towed up by him, and during the heaviest part of the fire, he went in his open barge alongside the admiral's ship, not to assist him in the fight, but to give his sympathy to a wounded brother officer whom he saw about to suffer a most mortifying and unsuspected defeat. I regret to say that his cockswain was killed at his side just as he reached the admiral's ship, by a ball which sunk his boat, striking so near him and his flag-lieutenant as to throw them out of their seats, and for a while stunning the latter. Between six and seven o'clock in the evening, the commodore having rendered all the service in his power, the Toeywan came to anchor between the French gun-boat and the Coromandel. After remaining there as long as she could be of any service to those whom she towed up, she changed her position and came about a hundred yards below the French gun-boat, where she remained during the night, and about half past nine o'clock in the morning, the battle being over, and the admiral withdrawing his squadron, she took in tow two large launches loaded with the wounded, and carried them out to the vessel lying beyond the bar.

Determined to leave no effort untried to carry out the wishes of the President, I addressed, as soon as possible, a letter to the governor general of this province, who was said to be somewhere on the coast about twelve miles from the forts, and intrusted its delivery to Dr. Williams, Mr. Martin, Mr. Atchison, and Mr. W. Wallace Ward. The Toeywan left this anchorage on Wednesday, 29th ultimo, about 11 o'clock, a. m., with the parties bearing my letter, a copy of which is hereto annexed, (marked B.)

After going north along the coast about six miles, they discovered junks' masts over the land, and upon approaching within four miles of the coast, it then being high spring tide, and only ten feet water, and able to find no other channel where there was deeper water, they steamed again to the northward, and went five miles further north. Where the junks were seen, there was supposed to be a small stream of water.

This point was guarded by three forts, and there was a village in the neighborhood. It could not be approached any nearer for the want of water. About five miles north of the forts another village was seen, to which the Toeywan was enabled to approach within a mile and a half, having then nine feet at half tide. I herewith attach a tracing of the route of the Toeywan, marked C. As soon as the Toeywan came to anchor, Mr. Martin, one of the interpreters, Mr. Merchant, a midshipmen, and Mr. W. Wallace Ward, secretary of legation, went ashore in the boat of the Toeywan. At their approach all the villagers began to fly. They succeeded, however, in holding communication with two of the inhabitants, who stated that the governor general was at the forts at the mouth of the Peiho, and that they would deliver the letter to him. When told that the messengers were citizens of the United States of America, they said that they had never heard of that country. The messengers were warned that there was a large body of cavalry in the vicinity; that runners had been sent for them, and that they had better return to their boat without delay. Whilst conversing with the Chinese, a large body of well mounted cavalry appeared in sight, rapidly advancing upon them, and followed them to the water's edge.

On Saturday morning, about 8 o'clock, two junks came out to the Powhatan, bringing me a letter from the Taoutae, a copy of which, with my reply to it, I herewith annex, marked D 1, D 2. The interpreters understood from the bearer of the letter that the governor general would be on the coast, Tuesday the 5th, to furnish me with the means of conveyance to Pekin. The English and French ministers have broken off all negotiations, and are about to leave for Shanghai, which they are exceedingly anxious to have me do also; but the path of my duty seems to me to be very plain. I arrived here with the English and French ministers, not as an ally, but because the Chinese commissioners insisted upon my coming with them, and that my right to visit Pekin was derivative from the English treaty; which is true, unless, under the 5th article of our own treaty, I should desire to visit Pekin upon business of importance. I was determined, under the most favored nation clause, to go to Pekin, without reference to the importance of the business to be transacted, if the representative of any other nation went there. Both of the other ministers having now failed; in my effort to carry out the wishes of the President, I must look alone to the provisions of the American treaty. By the provisions of that treaty I am authorized to come to the mouth of the Peiho river, where I now am, and to notify the Chinese authorities, which I have done; and they are required to provide me with a means of conveyance to Pekin, when my visit there is upon business of importance. It only remains now to be seen whether they will comply with the stipulations of the treaty, or whether they will not make the pretext that the exchange of the treaty is not of a business of sufficient importance to authorize my visit to Pekin, as no place is designated in the treaty for the exchange, and that it may be made at any other place. I am satisfied that, under that or some other pretext, they will prevent my visiting Pekin. Their feelings now appear to be kindly enough to us, though I have no confidence in them. One of the junks, yesterday, brought out a liberal supply of fresh provisions, for which they would receive no pay; but Commodore Tattnall sent in return biscuits, pork, and whiskey, and distributed the fresh provisions among the sick and wounded of the English and French squadron.

As I cannot remain in China longer than the next spring, I respectfully request the President to have my recall sent to me so that I may leave China early in March next. I also respectfully request that permission may be granted me to return by the way of Europe, and spend a few months there with my family.

The French minister has informed me that he will leave to-morrow for Shanghai, and has kindly offered to take any communication there to be mailed, and as it is uncertain when I will have another opportunity, I send this dispatch before I am enabled to inform you of the result of the negotiation now pending in relation to my visit to Pekin, I can only give you the opinion heretofore expressed.

I have the honor to be, sir, your obedient servant,

JOHN E. WARD.

Hon. LEWIS CASS,
Secretary of State, Washington, D. C.

KWEI, HWA, HO, and TWAN, Imperial Commissioners, &c., make a communication in reply:

On receipt of Mr. Bruce's letter of the 8th instant, acquainting the commissioners that his determination to proceed forthwith to Pekin to exchange the ratifications of the treaty was unalterable, the commissioners, feeling that it would not be correct that the day appointed for that purpose, which was near at hand, should be passed, after due deliberation, decided that the only course open to them was to represent the matter fully to his Majesty the Emperor, and to request him to be pleased specially to select some high officer, who might proceed to Tientsin to make arrangements for Mr. Bruce's reception. Their memorial was sent forward at the rate of 600 *li* (200 miles) a day*, and would arrive, at the latest, in some eight or nine days at Pekin, so that it might be assumed that when Mr. Bruce and the ministers of France and America reached Tientsin, the imperial commissioner could not fail to have arrived as well; and so the exchange of treaties in Pekin would be effected by the time fixed for the purpose. The commissioners were in the act of addressing Mr. Bruce to the above effect when they received his second letter, dated the 11th instant,

* This is the form of words for the fastest rate of mail dispatch but one.

expressing a wish that they should proceed by steamer. They were not unaware that a steamer would be a most expeditious [means of conveyance,] but they have not received his Majesty's commands, [to avail themselves of it,] and they would on no account presume so to proceed on their own motion. Were they now to make the proposition the subject of a memorial, [so far from any advantageous result from such a course,] there would be, on the contrary, time lost in the marching and countermarching. It behooves them, therefore, in obedience to his Majesty's commands, to return post haste to the capital; as they have prayed his Majesty to detach a high officer to act as agent in the matter, Mr. Bruce will be certainly enabled to arrive at his destination by the time appointed. With the peaceful relations now established between the two nations, nothing will certainly be done that is not in conformity with the provisions of the treaty, and the commissioners accordingly pray Mr. Bruce at once to put away all misgiving on the subject. There is no need for him to feel any anxiety. They would wish that on his arrival at the mouth of the Tientsin river [the Peiho] he should anchor his vessels of war outside the bar, and then, without much baggage, and with a moderate retinue, proceed to the capital for the exchange of the treaties. His mission being a pacific one, [or, as he comes speaking peace,] his treatment by the government of China will not fail to be in every way most courteous; and it is the sincere wish of the commissioners that relations of friendship may be from this time forth consolidated, and that on each side confidence may be felt in the good faith and justice of the other.

A necessary communication addressed to the honorable F. Bruce, C. B., &c., &c., &c.

Hien-fung, 9th year, 5th moon, 12th day, (12th June, 1859.)

LEGATION OF THE UNITED STATES,
U. S. F. Powhatan, Mouth of the Peiho river, June 24, 1859.

The undersigned, envoy extraordinary and minister plenipotentiary of the United States, has the honor to announce to his excellency King, governor general of the province of Chihli, that he has arrived at the mouth of the Peiho river, the bearer of an autograph letter from the President of the United States to his Majesty the Emperor of China.

The undersigned has come charged with the most friendly messages from the President to his Majesty the Emperor. The undersigned is now here by the invitation of the Imperial Commissioners Kweiliang, Hwashana, Ho, and Twan, extended to him at Shanghai, to proceed to the capital, there to exchange the ratification of the treaty of Tientsin. By the fifth article of that treaty it is provided that suitable means and conveyance shall be furnished by the Chinese authorities for the journey of the minister of the United States from the mouth of the river Peiho to Pekin, and he now informs your excellencies of his arrival, that the necessary conveyances for the journey of himself and suite may be immediately prepared.

JOHN E. WARD.

JUNE 30, 1859.

SUN, Intendant of the Circuit of the Departments of Tientsin and Hokien, in the Province of Chihli, herewith sends a communication:

On the 29th instant, a dispatch was received from the American minister, by the way of the northern passage of the river, addressed to the governor general, from which it is understood that the ship bearing his excellency has anchored off the mouth of the Peiho, (or Tientsin river.)

The commands of his Imperial Majesty have already been received, directing the governor general and treasurer of this province to receive and conduct him to Pekin, there to exchange the ratifications of the treaty.

I now send a small present to the minister on board his ship, which I respectfully request him to accept.

His Excellency the AMERICAN MINISTER.

LEGATION OF THE UNITED STATES,
U. S. ship Powhatan, Gulf of Pechele, July 2, 1859.

SIR: I have been instructed by his excellency Mr. Ward to acknowledge the receipt of your communication of the 30th ultimo, and to thank you for the present which has been sent him.

He will be ready to meet his excellency the Governor General King at the northern entrance of the Peiho on the 5th instant; and I now request that you will previously send a messenger who is acquainted with the channel to conduct the steamer as near to that place as the depth of water will allow her to approach.

Respectfully, your obedient servant,

S. WELLS WILLIAMS.

SUN, *Intendant of Tientsin and Hokien Circuit.*

Mr. Ward to Mr. Cass.

No. 16.]

LEGATION OF THE UNITED STATES,
U. S. frigate Powhatan, off Peiho river, July 10, 1859.

SIR: I have the honor to inform you that on the 5th instant I received a communication from the governor general in reply to my communication, a copy of which I herewith annex, (marked *a.*) This communication having been received at too late an hour of the day to enable me to reach the place appointed for the meeting, I was compelled to fix the 8th as the day of our meeting. I herewith attach the correspondence, (marked 1 *b*, 2 *b*.) On the morning of the 8th, in complianc with the request of the governor general, I left the Powhatan in the Toeywan, accompanied by a very small escort. Commodore Tattnall kindly accompanied me in person. On reaching the mouth of the river we were met by junks, in which we were conveyed to the jetty. There was every demonstration of respect made for us. The governor general asked me almost as soon as I entered the room my opinion of the conduct of the English. To which I replied that I was pursuing what I considered the correct course under the provisions of the American treaty, and had no right to express any opinion upon the conduct of the ministers of other nations. I told him that to keep me in my ship off the coast, when I had been invited to come by their commissioners at Shanghai, was not respectful to the nation I represented, and must be so reported. He then asked me at what place I would prefer to remain until the arrival of the commissioners from Shanghai, which he said would be in the course of this month. I replied that the capital was the only place to which I would go. He then said he would memorialize the Emperor to be permitted to conduct me himself to Pekin if the commissioners did not arrive in ten days. To which I assented. He stated distinctly that the treaty was to be exchanged at Pekin, and yet I do not expect to go to Pekin. My impression is that they determined to break all the treaties so far as related to a visit to or residence in Pekin. That this policy was commenced by their insisting upon the English minister going in the way pointed out in the American treaty, which they knew he would not do, and that as soon as they have discovered that the English and French ministers have left this place, they will assume the ground taken at Shanghai, that the right of the American minister to go to Pekin to exchange the treaty is derivative from the English treaty, and that he must therefore wait until that right has been exercised by the English minister. Determined, however, to leave no effort untried to carry into effect the strongly-expressed wishes of the President, I shall remain here until a positive decision is wrung from them.

The English and French ministers have both left for Shanghai.

I have the honor to be, sir, your obedient servant,

JOHN E. WARD.

Hon. LEWIS CASS,

Secretary of State, Washington.

JULY 3, 1859.

HĂNGFUH, Governor General of the Province of Chihli and its Dependencies, a President of the Board of War, and a Deputy Censor in the Censurate, charged also with the Supervision of the Revenue and Commissariat Departments of the Province, herewith sends a communication:

On the 30th ultimo your excellency's communication was brought to me by way of Peh-tang, (or the northern entrance,) and from it I first learned that your ship had anchored off the coast. I have been honored with his Imperial Majesty's commands already, directing me and the treasurer of the province carefully to attend to the reception of all the foreign ministers at Peh-tang, and from that point to conduct them to the capital for the exchange of their treaties. This announcement I made to his excellency Mr. Bruce, the English minister, on the 25th ultimo, but I only received a short note in reply from the

Chinese secretary, Mr. Wade, stating that the dispatch could not be received from my messenger, as orders had already been given to the men-of-war to commence the battle. I cannot express my wonder and alarm when I heard this, for I supposed that the real intention of the English plenipotentiary in coming here was merely to proceed to Pekin to exchange the ratifications of his treaty, and not by any means to seek a quarrel. The works at Takoo have been erected by my government merely to protect and defend that locality, and without any sinister design whatever.

His Majesty's gracious commands had already been received by me, directing me, in conjunction with the treasurer, carefully to attend to every detail connected with the journey of all the foreign ministers to Pekin by way of Peh-tang; but the English plenipotentiary must needs determine to go by way of Takoo, and in breaking through all the obstructions placed there across the river, he has shown his intentions to disregard all restrictions. But [before doing so] the full merits of the question and all its bearings should have been openly discussed.

In your excellency's communication now under reply your intention of proceeding to the capital to exchange the treaty is clearly stated. I have already, in conference with the provincial treasurer, issued orders to the various local officers that carriages, horses, and coolies, with the post-houses, be all put in readiness for this service. But whether your excellency remains on board ship or lives on shore at Peh-tang, it will be necessary to await the arrival of the imperial Commissioners Kweiliang and Hwashana at Tientsin; for it is with them that your journey to court and the exchange of the treaty are all to be arranged. The relations between China and the United States have uniformly been friendly, and no cause of strife has ever existed between us. This nation has habitually treated other nations in a sincere and cordial manner, and therefore we (the governor general and treasurer) are under the strongest obligations to carry his Majesty's commands into full effect.

I was on the point of sealing this dispatch when the letter of Mr. Williams to the intendant of the circuit of Tientsin of the 2d instant was forwarded to me, from which I was much pleased to learn that your excellency had set the 5th instant for the day to have a personal interview at Peh-tang. As the water there is reported to be too shallow for the steamer to enter, I will at the time send the brevet captain Jin Lien-shing with boats to be in readiness to meet her, and conduct your excellency ashore to the meeting at Peh-tang. Our countries being on a friendly footing, I strongly request that a large escort be not brought, lest the inhabitants of the place be alarmed and excited; and, by doing so, the old established cordiality will be strengthened.

For this purpose I now send this communication, and beg that on coming to a decision your excellency will oblige me with a reply.

His Excellency John E. Ward,

Envoy Extraordinary and Minister Plenipotentiary of the U. S.

Translated by S. W. WILLIAMS.

LEGATION OF THE UNITED STATES,
U. S. frigate Powhatan, Gulf of Pechele, July 5, 1859.

The undersigned, envoy extraordinary and minister plenipotentiary of the United States, has the honor to acknowledge your excellency's dispatch of the 3d instant. In reply thereto, he begs to state that he will be happy to meet your excellency at Peh-tang on Friday, the 8th instant, at noon, attended by a small escort, and hopes that arrangements will there be made for himself and suite to be forwarded to Pekin. While at Shanghai, the Imperial Commissioners Kweiliang and Hwashana assured the undersigned that an officer would be here to meet him, and he therefore confidently expects that there will be no unnecessary delay in carrying these preparations into execution.

JOHN E. WARD.

His Excellency HĂNGFUH,
Governor General of the Province of Chihli, &c., &c., &c.

JULY 6, 1859.

HĂNGFUH, Governor General of the Province of Chihli and its Dependencies, &c., &c., herewith sends a communication:

I have the honor to acknowledge the receipt of your excellency's dispatch of yesterday's date, in which you inform me that you will come to Peh-tang on the 8th instant, at noon, to meet me at a personal interview. I will, in conformity to the provisions of the treaty, give instructions to the local magistrates to provide boats, and send them out to the bar at the mouth of the river to meet your excellency on that day, and conduct you to Peh-tang to the place of meeting.

In regard to the journey to Pekin, [it may be observed,] that, as his Majesty's commands have been issued to the effect that when the imperial commissioners Kweiliang and Hwashana return to Tientsin from Shanghai, they will meet and confer with your excellency, it is incumbent to await their arrival there; and when the time has been agreed on with them, it will become my duty, in conjunction with the provincial treasurer, to carry his Majesty's commands into effect, and provide carriages, coolies, post-houses, and everything which may be needed for the occasion.

His Excellency JOHN E. WARD,
Envoy Extraordinary and Minister Plenipotentiary of the United States to China.

Mr. Ward to Mr. Cass.

No. 17.] LEGATION OF THE UNITED STATES,
United States frigate Powhatan, August 20, 1859.

SIR: I have the honor to inform you that, on the 14th of July, I received a communication from the governor general and treasurer of the province of Chihli, informing me that they had been honored with his Majesty's commands permitting me to leave Peh-tang any day after the 19th July, on my journey to the capital. On the same day I replied to the communication, appointing the 20th July as the day of my departure. On the 15th July, I received another communication, calling my attention to that portion of the treaty in which it is stipulated that the United States shall employ its good offices to bring about an arrangement and settlement of any difficulties which may arise between the Chinese and other governments. On the 16th I replied, informing them that there was no stipulation in the treaty with which I would with more pleasure comply. I herewith attach copies of said communications, marked 1 *a*, 1 *b*, 1 *c*, 1 *d*.

I left the coast on the morning of the 20th, and arrived in Pekin on the evening of the 27th. On the 28th, I addressed a letter to the imperial commissioners, informing them of my arrival in Pekin, and of my readiness to pay my respects to them at such time and place as they should designate. On the 29th I received their reply, appointing the public hall in Kia-hiang-sze, and 11 o'clock on the morning of the 30th as the time and place of interview.

I herewith annex copies of the communications, marked 2 *a*, 2 *b*. On the morning of the 29th, Sich, the provincial judge, who acted as secretary of legation to the Chinese commissioners, called at the residence of the American legation to request that, at the interview, I should be accompanied only by the secretary of legation and the interpreters. In compliance with that request, on the morning of the 30th, I attended at the time and place appointed for the interview, accompanied by Doctor Williams, the interpreter of the legation, Mr. Wallace Ward, the secretary of legation, and Mr. Martin, whose familiarity with the mandarin dialect made his presence absolutely necessary; and I desire here to express my acknowledgments to him for the valuable services which he rendered to me as interpreter. We met, at the hall, the imperial commissioners and Sich, the secretary of legation. Immediately after our arrival the subject of an audience with his Majesty the Emperor of China was introduced, and I was told that an interview with his Majesty was absolutely necessary before any other business could be transacted in the capital, and that it would be necessary for me to practise the rites and ceremonies necessary to be observed for several days before the audience could take place. I replied that I should feel honored by an audience with his Majesty, and would observe all the rites and ceremonies necessary for an audience with the President of the United States, and no others; that I would neither kneel nor prostrate my person before his Majesty. They then asked me what I would do. I told them I would bow in the most respectful manner. They replied that without kneeling an audience would be impossible. I told them that an audience was not contemplated by the American treaty, and that I desired to exchange the treaty and to return as soon as possible to my ship, which could not remain off the coast much longer, as her supply of water, then almost exhausted, could not be replenished. They replied that, as we could come to no agreement during that interview in relation to the audience, they would return my visit in a few days and renew the discussion of the subject, repeating that the audience must take place before my business could be transacted in the capital. On the 1st of August I received a communication from them, appointing the 2d instant as the time when they would return my call, and renew the discussion of the subject. I replied on the same day, stating that I would be pleased to see them, and I herewith annex the correspondence, marked 3 *a*, 3 *b*. Before the hour arrived for their calling, Judge Sich called upon the interpreter and secretary of legation, and informed them that the Emperor insisted upon an audience with me, as he desired to be satisfied of the sincerity of my friendship, which he was disposed to doubt, as he had learned of the Toeywan having towed up the English boats to attack the forts, and that he also had an American prisoner, taken at that attack. This was reported to me by the interpreter, Mr. Martin, and I requested him to say in reply, that there could not be an American prisoner, for no Americans had landed; that, in relation to the Toeywan, I had always supposed that her towing up the troops was fully understood by the Chinese authorities; that the British admiral had, the day before, extended certain civilities to us, rendered necessary by the bad faith of the Chinese; that, in returning those courtesies, we not only desired no concealment, but had raised two flags instead of one, to avoid all misapprehension; and that, if my kneeling to his Majesty was necessary for an audience, it could never take place.

At the hour appointed the commissioners arrived at my lodgings; having, in the meantime, learned that an armed body of men was stationed about us when the commissioners proposed to enter upon the discussion of the audience, I told them it was necessary for them first to explain why soldiers were quartered about my lodgings. They assured me that it was only to preserve order and to keep off the Chinese crowd, which, but for the soldiers, would gather about us and be very annoying, but that any of my suite could leave the grounds and return as they pleased. At the same time they requested that the gentlemen would go out as little as possible until after the public business had been transacted. I then stated to them that, as my movements must be entirely free and untrammeled, the day of my departure from the capital must first be settled. Upon this point they hesitated, and said that was a matter to be submitted to the Emperor. I replied that his Majesty could not control my movements, and that without an assurance that my escort would be ready for me on any day I might designate, the discussion of all public matters must cease. They then assured me that my escort should be ready for me upon any day I might name, and I appointed the 11th of August, thus giving ample time for the transaction of all business. I found it necessary to be thus particular on the two points above stated to remove from the minds of some who had gone with me to Pekin as upon a pleasure party, and who might fancy themselves grievously wronged at the exercise of that caution which it has ever been the habit of the Chinese government to practice towards all strangers at their capital. It was my intention to deprive such persons of all excuse for misunderstanding. After these points had been settled, the subject of the audience was renewed and discussed for eight hours, when, still being unable to agree, the commissioners left me, saying they would, in a few days, send me a communication in relation to the exchange of the treaty. On the 5th of August I received a communication from the commissioners, to which I replied on the 6th. Copies of which I hereto attach marked 4 *a* and 4 *b*. On the same day I received another communication informing me that as I had declined to discuss further the subject of an audience with his Majesty, they would regard the presenting of the letter from the President in the same position; that it would not be suitable to exchange the treaties in Pekin, as there was no article which required the ratifications to be exchanged in the capital, and that I had remarked in Shanghai that it was immaterial where the ratifications were exchanged. I need not say that this last remark attributed to me was not true. When at Shanghai I urged upon them the necessity of exchanging the treaty within the time therein stated, which was about to expire, and they replied that as my going to Pekin to exchange the treaty was derivative from the English treaty, and not given in the American treaty, that I must therefore wait until the English have been to Pekin and exchanged their treaty. I replied to them, that rather than wait upon the movements of the English, I would exchange the treaty at Shanghai, provided I was allowed to go with the ministers of the first nations who visited Pekin, there to deliver the President's letter, and I was then told that the treaty was in Pekin. Although I did not feel authorized, upon the receipt of the last letter, to refuse to exchange the treaty out of Pekin, when there was no clause requiring it to be done there, and thus place the government in the dilemma either of commencing an expensive war, the termination of which could not be foreseen, or of tamely waiting with her treaty until, under the guns of other nations, it could be exchanged, my resolution was fixed, that unless the President's letter should be respectfully received in the capital, the treaty should not be exchanged by me, except under instructions, as I regarded the rejection of the letter an indignity to the Chief Magistrate of my country. The day after the receipt of this communication Judge Sich called upon the interpreter and secretary of legation and said he had been sent by the commissioners to say that, if I would request the appointment of an officer to receive the President's letter, and have the treaty exchanged north, both requests would be granted. I refused to make either request. He then admitted that the treaty had never yet received the seal of the Emperor, or been ratified by him; that the ministers had memorialized the Emperor to affix his seal to the treaty, and appoint a place for its exchange; that his Majesty had declined to answer the memorial, upon the ground that I had treated him with disrespect in refusing to comply with the terms given for an audience; that the ministers requested me, in my reply to their last communication, to say that if I should fail in rendering such respect to the Emperor as was consistent with the usages of my own country, it would be displeasing to the President. As this was strictly true, I could see no objection to embodying it in my reply, and therefore consented to do so. I herewith send copies of said communications, marked 5 *a* and 5 *b*. On the 9th of August I received another communication, informing me that the Emperor had appointed the commissioners to receive the President's letter, and inclosing me a copy of the imperial rescript, to which letter I replied the same day, assenting to the time and place appointed for the receipt of the President's letter, copies of which communications, with the imperial rescript, I herewith attach, marked 6 *a* and 6 *b*. I also received at the same time another communication from the commissioners, informing me that they had been honored with commands from the throne, directing them to apply the great seal to the treaty, and then to have the ratifications exchanged at the port of Peh-tang, a copy of which communication, with my reply, I herewith annex, marked 7 *a* and 7 *b*. In compliance with the arrangement made with the commissioners, at two o'clock on the 10th of August, accompanied by Dr. Williams, the interpreter of the legation, Mr. Wallace Ward, the secretary of the legation, and Mr. Martin, I went to the hall of Kia-hiang-sze, there to deliver the President's letter. The letter was handed by me to Kweiliang, the Emperor's prime minister, and the second man in the empire to the Emperor himself. It was received by him with every mark of respect—elevating it above his eyes, he placed it upon a table, under a guard of honor, until it could be conveyed to the Emperor. Having now no further business in the capital, and knowing the anxiety of Commodore Tattnall, both in relation to his scanty supply of water and the safety of his vessel, at her exposed anchorage, I requested that my escort should be ready for my departure at daylight in the morning, which request was granted, and on the morning of the 11th I left Pekin, with all my suite, for Peh-tang, where the exchange of the treaty was to be effected. On my arrival at Pei-tsang, I addressed a communication to the governor general of the province of Chihli, a copy of which, with his reply, I hereto annex, marked 8 *a* and 8 *b*.

I arrived at Peh-tang on the morning of the 16th of August, where I was received with every mark of respect, the military having turned out to receive me ; and where I was met by the governor general and treasurer of the province, and the exchange of the treaty immediately took place, and receipts were interchanged—a copy of which I herewith attach, marked 9 *a*. After the treaty had been exchanged, the governor general said that his Majesty had directed him, as a mark of his peculiar favor to me, to deliver to me an American prisoner, taken at the attack upon the forts. I replied, as no Americans had been landed, it was impossible that he could have an American prisoner. A young man was immediately introduced, and I was asked to question him. I insisted that the questions and answers should be interpreted by a Chinese mandarin, who spoke English, and not by Mr. Martin. I asked the man where he was born. He replied, in Canada. I asked him if he was a citizen of the United States. He said no ; he was a British subject. I asked him how he had come to the mouth of the Peiho river. He said, in an English gun-boat, and that he had told a lie on the Americans. It seems that he had represented himself as one of an American party, consisting of two hundred men, which had been landed to attack the forts, and I believe, up to that moment, the Emperor of China and all his officers had believed the story. The governor general and the treasurer expressed themselves as perfectly satisfied that the man had told what was not true, and that the Americans had landed no men to attack their forts. They both said to me, as we are now good friends, let us forget all that occurred at Takoo and not again refer to the subject; to which I assented. The governor general then said to me, the Emperor has ordered this man to be delivered to you, under the impression that he was an American citizen; we find that he is not; what will you do about receiving him? I said to him, he is a British subject, and your prisoner taken in war; as the American minister, I cannot act in the matter, the prisoner having no claim upon us for protection; if you will deliver him to me with a full knowledge of these facts, I will regard it as a personal favor, and will most gladly receive him on board the ship, and restore him to his countrymen at Shanghai. He said I could take him upon those terms, and send him aboard the Toeywan, then lying in the harbor. As soon after as possible we returned to the Powhatan, then lying at anchor about fifteen miles from the bar.

I must here express my acknowledgements to the Russian minister at Pekin, for his constant efforts to communicate with me, and to render me every service in his power. Although the jealousy of the Chinese government prevented any personal intercourse between us, and delayed our communications to each other, they could not prevent our mutual expression of good will. A copy of my correspondence with him I herewith annex, marked 10 *a*, 10 *b*, 10 *c*, 10 *d*, 10 *e*, 10 *f*, 10 *g*, 10 *h*, and 10 *i*.

I desire also to express my thanks to Flag-officer Tattnall, for the uniform kindness and courtesy with which I and my suite have been treated, and for the very efficient aid which I have at all times received from him in my efforts to exchange the treaty.

I have the honor to be, sir, your obedient servant,

JOHN E. WARD.

Hon. LEWIS CASS,
Secretary of State.

JULY 14, 1859.

HĂNGFUH, Governor General of the Province of Chihli and its Dependencies, &c., &c., with WAN, Treasurer of the same Province, herewith send a communication:

Referring to the personal interview which we had the honor to have with your excellency at Peh-Tang, on the 8th instant, at which the journey to Pekin for the purpose of exchanging the treaty was discussed, we then proposed to memorialize the throne jointly, and obtain express directions. We have now been honored with his Majesty's commands, permitting your excellency to leave Peh-tang any day after the 19th of this month, on your journey to the capital. You will there await the arrival of the Imperial Commissioners Kweiliang and Hwashana, with whom the ratifications of the treaty will be exchanged.

I (the governor general) have now designated Tsun-hau, an intendant of the inland transportation of the province, and a brevet commissioner of the Gabelle, with Chang Ping-toh, a lieutenant colonel of the central division at Siuen-heva, and a brevet general, to escort the American embassy to the metropolis and attend to all necessary details.

It has already been distinctly mentioned that there would be twenty (foreigners) in the party, together with ten (Chinese) writers and other assistants, making the whole company amount to thirty in all. We have jointly given directions to these two officers to prepare such carriages, horses, and boats as will be needed, to provide accommodations and all the supplies which will be required along the road from Peh-tang to Pekin, and attend to every particular connected with escorting the embassy.

We respectfully request your excellency to inform us of the day you decide on for your departure from Peh-tang to the capital, that we may jointly memorialize his Majesty in relation to the same, and at the same time issue the proper orders to these officers and all others who may be connected with these arrangements.

His Excellency JOHN E. WARD,
Envoy Extraordinary and Minister Plenipotentiary of the United States.

LEGATION OF THE UNITED STATEL,
United States ship Powhatan, Gulf of Pechele, July 14, 1859.

The undersigned, envoy extraordinary and minister plenipotentiary of the United States, has the honor to acknowledge the receipt of the dispatch from their excellencies the governor general and treasurer of the province of Chihli, of this day's date, in which they inform him respecting the arrangements made for his journey to the capital.

In reply, the undersigned begs to state that he will be ready to start on the 20th instant, unless prevented by the state of the weather; also, that his suite will consist, in all, of thirty persons, of whom twenty will be of his own company and ten of them native writers and others. He is satisfied with the officers appointed to be his escort, and expects that all the arrangements for the journey will be suitable.

JOHN E. WARD.

Their Excellencies HĂNGFUH and WAN,
Governor General and Treasurer of the Province of Chihli.

JULY 15, 1859.

HĂNGFUH, Governor General of the Province of Chihli and its Dependencies, &c. &c., with WAN, Treasurer of the same Province, herewith send a communication:

We had yesterday the honor to receive the dispatch of your excellency, in which you inform us that you have chosen the 20th instant to commence your journey to the capital to exchange the treaty; and we have accordingly issued the necessary orders to the officers deputed to escort the embassy and to the several local authorities along the way, that every preparation be made to facilitate the progress to the metropolis.

In the treaty of Tientsin, it is stipulated that when any matter arises between this and any other country, that the United States shall employ its good offices to bring about an arrangement and settlement of the difficulty. The English and French vessels are still anchored outside of the bar in the open sea, but we have no means of exchanging any communication with them, and we accordingly request your excellency to inform them for us respecting the recent events. The battle which occurred on the 25th ultimo, at Takoo, was really brought on by the English men-of-war forcing themselves up the mouth of the river, and not by any means from any provocation on our part. If their ships have any further (hostile) intentions, in consequence of the engagement which has already taken place, then the defenses at Takoo will quietly remain in preparation; but if aware of their own error, these nations are now ready to return to their former correct conduct, and wish to go to Pekin to exchange their treaties, then let their ministers proceed up to Peh-tang for preliminary arrangements. We, the governor general and treasurer, will then memorialize the throne for instructions as to the mode of arranging everything on an amicable basis, and how to dispose of the requests of the English and French plenipotentiaries, to the satisfaction of all.

In the hope that your excellency will favor us with a satisfactory reply, we now send this communication.

His Excellency JOHN E. WARD,

Envoy Extraordinary, &c., &c., of United States.

LEGATION OF THE UNITED STATES,
U. S. frigate Powhatan, Gulf of Pechele, July 16, 1859.

The undersigned, envoy extraordinary and minister plenipotentiary of the United States, has the honor to acknowledge the receipt of your excellencies' dispatch of yesterday's date, and begs to express his thanks for the courtesies extended to him, and for the satisfactory preparations made for his journey to the capital.

The undersigned is fully aware of the provisions of the treaty of Tientsin, whereby the United States is pledged to exert its good offices between China and other countries with which she may have differences, and there is no stipulation of the treaty with which the undersigned would more readily comply. When, on the 24th ultimo, he understood that a difficulty would probably arise between the English and French and Chinese, he entered the river in his tender, in the hope that he might do something to avert the impending battle, although the ratifications of the treaty had not then been exchanged. With this view, he attempted to open a communication with the fort at Takoo, and was sorry to learn that there was no officer there with whom he could communicate. Still, anxious to do all in his power to carry out these views, a pilot was asked for, who could take his vessel to Peh-tang, and he was told that none could be furnished. You are aware that it was only after great difficulty and some danger to his vessel that he was able to send his dispatch to your excellencies.

The undersigned refers to these matters now, simply to evince his strong desire in all respects to fulfill the stipulations of the treaty.

The English and French vessels have all now left their anchorage, the ministers and commanding officers have returned to Shanghai, and the undersigned is satisfied that no further hostilities will take place immediately. As soon as his own treaty has been exchanged, he will have an opportunity, after returning to Shanghai, to make known the views expressed in the letter under reply; and he begs to assure you that as soon as the right of a negotiator is given him by the exchange of those ratifications, he will use every effort in his power to adjust the difficulties which now so unhappily exist between China and England and France, and he hopes those efforts will prove successful.

The undersigned, with his suite, as heretofore stated, will anchor off Peh-tang, on the 19th, so as to be ready to start early the next morning. He sincerely trusts that when his mission has been accomplished, that the peace which has always existed between our respective countries may be fixed upon a firm and lasting basis, and the bonds of friendly intercourse be more strongly cemented.

JOHN E. WARD.

Their Excellencies HĂNGFUH and WAN,
The Governor General and Treasurer of Chihli, &c., &c., &c.

LEGATION OF THE UNITED STATES,
Pekin, July 28, 1859.

The undersigned (with titles) has the honor to inform their excellencies, the imperial commissioners, that he has arrived in Pekin, to which place he has come for the purpose of exchanging the ratifications of the treaty. If it be agreeable to the commissioners, he will pay his respects to them, at such time and place as they may designate.

JOHN E. WARD.

Their Excellencies KWEILIANG, HWASHANA, and TWAN,
Imperial Commissioners, &c., &c., &c.

JULY 29, 1859.

KWEILIANG and HWASHANA present their compliments to his excellency the American minister.

We yesterday received your communication, from which we were gratified to learn that your excellency had arrived at the capital on the 27th instant, after a pleasant and safe journey, upon which we are happy to offer our congratulations. We also learn that your excellency desires to have an interview, requesting us to designate the time and place for it. This we now do, and appoint it to be at the public hall in the Kia-hing-sze, at 11 o'clock on the morning of the 30th, where we shall both have the honor of awaiting your arrival.

For this purpose, we now send this note in reply, and avail ourselves of the opportunity to wish you every felicity.

AUGUST 1, 1859.

KWEILIANG and HWASHANA present their respects to his excellency the American minister.

They will, in company with Sich, the provincial judge, have the honor of returning his visit at 11 o'clock, on the 2d instant, when they can confer personally upon the several points under discussion, and therefore send this note beforehand, to inform him; at the same time expressing their best wishes for his daily happiness.

AUGUST 1, 1859.

The American minister presents his respects to their excellencies the imperial commissioners.

He has just received their note, from which he has learned that they propose to do him the honor of a visit to-morrow, at eleven o'clock, at his lodgings, and begs to assure them that he will be pleased to receive them at that hour, and offers them the expression of his wishes for their highest peace.

KWEILIANG, a Principal Secretary of State, and HWASHANA, President of the Board of Civil Office, &c., &c., Imperial Commissioners and Plenipotentiaries of the Ta-Tsing Empire, herewith send a communication:

Your excellency has now been in the capital several days, and though we have had a number of interviews, when we have consulted together upon the ceremonies to be observed at the audience with his Majesty the Emperor of China, we have not been able to come to any arrangement, owing to your firmly maintaining your own opinion; and we are quite at a loss to understand, therefore, for what purpose your excellency has come to Pekin.

You now say that it is needless further to discuss this matter; and as the treaty of Tientsin must be exchanged somewhere, where is it to be? We therefore request your excellency most carefully to think over all these points, and send a reply, in order that we may know what action to take.

His Excellency JOHN E. WARD,

Envoy Extraordinary, &c., &c., &c., of the U. S.

LEGATION OF THE UNITED STATES,

Pekin, August 6, 1859.

The undersigned (with titles) has the honor to acknowledge the receipt of your excellencies' communication of yesterday, in which you are pleased to say that you are quite at a loss to understand for what purpose he had come to Pekin.

The undersigned came to Pekin for two objects. He was the bearer of an autograph letter from the President of the United States to his Majesty the Emperor of China, and would have esteemed it a most distinguished honor to have been admitted into the presence of his Majesty and delivered the letter in person. It is not, as your excellencies remark, an obstinate maintainance of his own opinion which has prevented his compliance with the forms and ceremonies observed at an audience with his Majesty, but because those ceremonies are so much at variance with the laws, Constitution, and customs of his own country, that a compliance with them would have received the stern rebuke of the President, and been at once repudiated by him.

The undersigned does not mean here to discuss these questions, as he has already fully expressed his views to your excellencies; but he hoped that he would have been permitted to deliver this letter to his Majesty's ministers, which course he hoped would have been satisfactory to the Emperor of China, as it certainly would have been to the President of the United States. He would have fully appreciated the reasons of his Majesty for refusing to grant an audience, as his minister could not comply with the ceremonies to be observed, and was merely maintaining the usages of his country by declining it.

The undersigned also came to Pekin to exchange the ratifications of the treaty made last year at Tientsin, in accordance with the dispatch of their excellencies Hăngfuh and Wan, of the 14th ultimo, in which they inform him "they have been honored with his Majesty's commands, permitting him to leave Peh-tang any day after the 19th, on his journey to the capital, there to await the arrival of the imperial commissioners, Kweiliang and Hwashana; and on their reaching the city the ratifications of the treaty will be exchanged." From this, the undersigned certainly infers that the treaty ought to be exchanged either at the house of the American minister or at such other place as you may designate. He is prepared to meet you at any time and place which you may appoint, then and there to deliver to you the autograph letter of the President, to be transmitted by you to his Majesty, and to exchange the ratifications of the treaty, so that he may leave the city on the morning of the 11th, on his return to his ship, as has already been agreed upon.

JOHN E. WARD.

Their Excellencies KWEILIANG AND HWASHANA, *&c., &c.,*
Imperial Commissioners and Plenipotentiaries
of the Ta-Tsing Empire.

AUGUST 6, 1859.

KWEILIANG, a principal Secretary of State, and HWASHANA, President of the Board of Civil Offices, Imperial Commissioners and Plenipotentiaries of the Ta-Tsing empire, &c., &c., herewith send a reply:

We have just received your excellency's answer to our communication, in which you discuss the several points referred to in it, and we have fully considered what you say. You remark that it is needless any further to deliberate upon the subject of an audience with his Majesty; and we now also beg to observe that the proposition of presenting the letter from the President to be transmitted may likewise be regarded as in the same position, and need be no further discussed.

With respect to the exchange of the treaty, it will not be suitable to do it in Pekin, as there is no article which requires that the ratifications be exchanged in the capital. And further, at an interview held with your excellency at Shanghai, you remarked to us that it was immaterial where the ratifications were exchanged. We are now carefully deliberating as to the proper place for the exchange, and must respectfully request his Majesty to determine the locality. When his rescript has been received, we will inform your excellency, that arrangements may be made for carrying it into effect, and it is for this end that we now send you this reply.

His Excellency John E. Ward,
Envoy Extraordinary and Minister Plenipotentiary of the United States.

Legation of the United States,
Pekin, August 8, 1859.

The undersigned has the honor to acknowledge the receipt of your excellency's dispatch of the 6th instant, in which you inform him, that "as I remarked that it is needless any further to deliberate upon the subject of an audience with his Majesty, you also beg to observe that the proposition of presenting the letter from the President to be transmitted may likwise be regarded as in the same position and need be no further discussed. With respect to the exchange of the treaty, it will not be suitable to do it in Pekin, and you will respectfully request his Majesty to determine the locality, and inform him when the rescript has been received," &c., &c.

In thus dismissing these subjects, the undersigned has only to observe in the most explicit manner, that it has been from no want of respect to his Majesty, and with sincere regret, that he has found himself unable to comply with the ceremonies of an audience at his court. He not only entertains for the Emperor of China the highest respect, but if he should fail of rendering him every mark of respect not wholly inconsistent with the laws and usages of his own country, he would be sternly rebuked by the President, who he is well assured, entertains the greatest respect likewise for his Majesty.

The undersigned has deferred a reply to the communication of your excellencies until to-day, in expectation of receiving the imperial rescript, but does not think it proper any longer to defer this acknowledgement of your letter.

JOHN E. WARD.

Their Excellencies Kweiliang and Hwashana,
Imperial Commissioners, &c., &c.

AUGUST 9, 1859.

KWEILIANG, Principal Secretary of State, and HWASHANA, President of the Board of Civil Office, Imperial Commissioners and Plenipotentiaries of the Ta-Tsing Empire, &c., &c., herewith send a communication:

We yesterday had the honor to receive your excellency's dispatch, and beg to assure you of our great satisfaction and sincere pleasure at the expressions of respectful regard for his Imperial Majesty which it contains. We incorporated all the particulars of this and other dispatches received from you, and to-day respectfully submitted our statement to the imperial glance. We have now been honored by a decree from his Majesty, which we copy out for your excellency's information, that matters may be arranged conformably to the same.

We will ourselves be at our public hall at two p. m. to-morrow, where we will await the arrival of your excellency with the letter of the President, which we have been commanded to receive for transmission. We have also appointed proper officers to escort your excellency and suite, and they will be ready to leave the capital on the 11th instant.

Hereafter we will cherish the same feelings of respectful regard towards the President of the United States, which you have now made known towards our own Emperor, and these sentiments will be the expression of the friendly relations which should hereafter exist between our respective nations.

[One inclosure of the Imperial Rescript.]

On the 9th August, 1859, the privy council had the honor to receive the following rescript from the throne:

Last year several English ships came to the mouth of the Peiho, where they commenced a battle, and wounded our officers and troops, and, in consequence, we gave the strictest orders to Prince Sangkilinsin, of the Ghorchin tribe, to oversee the construction of defenses at Takoo and the mouth of the river.

The envoys of several nations having arrived to exchange their treaties, Kweiliang and Hwashana informed them at Shanghai that, as defenses had been constructed at Takoo, they must proceed on their journey by way of Peh-tang. But in the month of June, the English minister, Mr. Bruce, came to the mouth of the Peiho, and utterly disregarding his agreement with Kweiliang and Hwashana, and wished to force his way up into the Peiho, even if he destroyed all the defenses placed there. On the 24th June, the English vessels went up as far as the Kisin Reach, and blew up the iron chains placed there, but our men did not then join battle. The next day more than ten steamers pulled up perhaps a score of iron piles in the river; they also hoisted red flags as a challenge of battle.

The governor general of the province of Chihl, and others, whose duty it was, had already sent the intendant of Tientsin to inform the

English, and officers had proceeded to their ships to do so, but they were not received, for the English had already presumed to commence a cannonade on the forts. It was then that our forts began to use their artillery to repel them. Several of their vessels were much injured and sunk, and many hundreds of the foot companies which landed were killed. It is incontestible that the English brought this defeat on themselves. China did not break her faith.

At this juncture the American envoy, John E. Ward, in compliance with his engagement made with Kweiliang, came to Peh-tang in his ship, requesting that he might go up to Pekin, as he was the bearer of a letter from the President of the United States. Our permission was accordingly given for him to bring the letter up to the capital, where he arrived with it. This day the ministers, Kweiliang and Hwashana, have handed up the various dispatches received from the American minister for our examination, and from them it is to be clearly seen that his sentiments are exceedingly respectful and indicative of the utmost sincerity and truthfulness.

Let the letter which the envoy of the United States has brought be taken, and let Kweiliang and Hwashana be specially appointed to receive it for transmission to ourself. In regard to the exchange of the treaty, it would doubtless be proper to return to Shanghai to perform it, but when we reflect that the American envoy has already come over the seas so far for this purpose, we now specially direct that the great seal be affixed to the treaty, and it be delivered to Hăngfuh, the governor general, who is then to exchange the ratifications with the American minister at Peh-tang.

After this has been done, let lasting friendship and commerce continue between the two nations. This will show forth our great regard and kindness to people from afar, and clearly exhibit the deep respect we entertain for truth and justice.

Let Kweiliang and Hwashana make known these commands to the American minister, Mr. Ward. Respect this.

LEGATION OF THE UNITED STATES,
Pekin, August 10, 1859.

The undersigned, minister plenipotentiary of the United States to China, has the honor to acknowledge the receipt of their excellencies' dispatch of the 9th instant, inclosing a copy of an imperial rescript, in which they request him to meet them this day at two o'clock at their public hall, and there to hand them the letter from the President of the United States for transmission to his Majesty.

The undersigned begs to make known his gratification at this expression of willingness to receive the President's letter, and he will meet their excellencies at their public hall, with his previous suite, at the time specified. He is sure that this act will be regarded by the President as evincing the feelings of respect expressed in the imperial rescript.

JOHN E. WARD.

Their Excellencies KWEILIANG and HWASHANA,
Imperial Commissioners and Plenipotentiaries of the
Ta-Tsing Empire, &c., &c.

AUGUST 9, 1859.

KWEILIANG, Principal Secretary of State, &c., and HWASHANA, President of the Board of Civil Office, Imperial Commissioners and Plenipotentiaries of the Ta-Tsing Empire, &c., &c., herewith send a communication:

In compliance with the commands with which we have just been honored from the throne, we are to apply the great seal to the treaty, and then have its ratifications exchanged at the port of Peh-tang. When this has been done, it will follow that its regulations all come into effect and are to be followed.

But the commerce carried on at the open ports is not under the American flag alone; and as the English and French treaties are not yet definitively settled, it seems to be highly undesirable in all respects to have two modes of conducting the trade, lest serious difficulties arise in carrying it on. It has occurred to us, therefore, that it may be best to defer until the matters connected with those two nations are all finally adjusted, before acting on the new commercial regulations; but, as to what course may really be preferable to decide on in the premises, we are very desirous for your excellency to confer with Ho, the commissioner of foreign commerce, and so arrange the whole details that no serious obstacles may arise in the prosecution of the general trade. We think that you will also agree with us in this suggestion, and not be disinclined to follow it, and therefore now send this dispatch to inform you of our views, as we shall also state the same fully to his excellency Ho, that a full conference and arrangement may be made to general satisfaction. If this meets your views, we shall be happy to receive your excellency's reply.

His Excellency JOHN E. WARD,
Envoy Extraordinary and Minister Plenipotentiary
of the United States to China.

LEGATION OF THE UNITED STATES,
Pekin, August 10, 1859.

The undersigned, minister plenipotentiary of the United States, has the honor to acknowledge the receipt of your excellencies' communication of the 9th instant, in which you inform him that, in compliance with commands sent to you from the throne, you are to apply the great seal to the treaty, and then its ratifications are to be exchanged at Peh-tang.

The apprehension is also expressed, that as the English and French treaties are not yet definitively settled, two modes of conducting the trade at the open ports would produce serious impediments; and the opinion is given that it would be best to defer until the matters connected with those two nations are all finally adjusted, before acting on the new commercial regulations; but as to what may be the best mode of action in the premises, you desire me to confer with Ho, the commissioner of foreign commerce, and so arrange the whole details that no serious obstacles may arise in the prosecution of the general trade. It is certainly most desirable that, at all the open ports, there should be but one mode of carrying on commerce; and the undersigned will most cheerfully comply with the request now made, and confer with his excellency Ho, the commissioner of foreign commerce, with the view of arranging the details so that no obstacles arise in conducting the general trade.

JOHN E. WARD.

To their Excellencies KWEILIANG and HWASHANA,
Imperial Commissioners and Plenipotentiaries of the Ta-Tsing Empire, &c., &c., &c.

LEGATION OF THE UNITED STATES,
Peiho, August 13, 1859.

The undersigned, envoy extraordinary and minister plenipotentiary of the United States, has the honor to inform his excellency the governor general of Chihli, that his Majesty the Emperor, having appointed Peh-tang as the place for exchanging the ratifications of the American treaty, he is now on his way, and expects to arrive at that town on the morning of the 16th, and makes this communication to request his excellency to meet him there, and effect the exchange that day.

The undersigned makes this request because his ship has been so long upon the coast that her supply of water is low, and he is anxious not to detain her any longer than is absolutely necessary.

JOHN E. WARD.

HĂNGFUH, *Governor General of the Province of Chihli, and its Dependencies, &c., &c., &c.*

AUGUST 15, 1859.

HĂNGFUH, Governor General of the Province of Chihli and its Dependencies, a President of the Board of War, and a Deputy Censor, with charge of the Military Revenue and Inland Transportation Departments of the same Province, herewith sends a communication:

I have the honor to acknowledge the receipt of your excellency's communication, in which you inform me that you have left Pekin, and expect to reach Peh-tang on the morning of the 16th, for the purpose of exchanging the treaty.

I now send this reply to inform your excellency that I reached Peh-tang to-day, and shall have the honor here to await your arrival, and the treaty can be exchanged on the same day.

His Excellency JOHN E. WARD,
Envoy Extraordinary and Minister Plenipotentiary, of the United States.

The undersigned, John E. Ward, envoy extraordinary and minister plenipotentiary of the United States of America to China, and Hăng-fuh, governor general of the province of Chihli and its dependencies, a president of the Board of War, and having the supervision of the military revenue and inland navigation departments of the same province, with Wan-hi-uh, the treasurer of the province of Chihli, having met together for the purpose of exchanging the ratifications of the treaty of peace, amity, and commerce between the United States of America and the Ta-Tsing empire, concluded and signed at Tientsin on the 18th day of June, 1858, and the respective ratifications of the same having been carefully perused, the said exchange took place this day in the usual form.

In witness whereof, they have signed the present certificate of exchange, and have affixed thereto their seals and signatures, done at Peh-tang, in the province of Chihli, the 16th day of August, 1859, or the reign of Hien-fung 9th year, 7th month, 18th day.

JOHN E. WARD. [SEAL.]
HĂNGFUH. [SEAL.]
WAN-HI-UH. [SEAL.]

A true copy.

W. WALLACE WARD,
Secretary of Legation.

LEGATION OF THE UNITED STATES,
U. S. Frigate Powhatan, off Peiho river, July 6, 1859.

SIR: I have the honor to inform you that by a communication from his excellency F. W. Pickens, the minister from the government of the United States at St. Petersburg, addressed to General Lewis Cass, Secretary of State, I learn that you have been instructed by your government to grant to me all facilities in your power to advance to Pekin; and that, if I desired it, you would furnish me with all friendly aid and advice that could be afforded; and that, if, when I reached China, I would write you, you would do anything that the most friendly power could do under the circumstances, &c.

I am now at the mouth of the Peiho, anxious to reach Pekin as soon as possible, and would be greatly obliged for any advice or aid which it may be in your power to render.

I have the honor to be, sir, your obedient servant,

JOHN E. WARD.

His Excellency M. PEROWSKY,
Diplomatic Agent at Pekin for the Russian Government.

PEKIN, *July* 7, (19,) 1859.

SIR: Having arrived a few days since at Pekin to succeed the present Diplomatic Agent Perowsky, I have had the honor of receiving the dispatch of your excellency, addressed to my predecessor, dated from the Peiho, the 6th July. This dispatch did not reach me until last night.

Being provided with the same instructions which have been given to Mr. Perowsky, which mark out for me the agreeable duty of offering a friendly coöperation to the representative of the United States in China, at the time of my first interview with the Chinese ministers, I anticipated the wish expressed in your dispatch. Impressed with the feelings of the imperial cabinet with regard to the government represented by your excellency, I did not fail to announce to them that you would soon arrive in Pekin, insisting at the same time upon the necessity of receiving in a suitable manner and cordially the representative of a nation as great as that of the United States, and of cultivating the most friendly relations with him. Their evasive replies made me understand that the Emperor of China is exasperated against foreigners on account of the recent complications which have occurred unexpectedly in the Gulf of Pechele with the English, (from what they stated to me.)

At first, preparations had been made here to receive, for the ratifications of the treaties of Tientsin, the plenipotentiaries of America, of France, and of England. Lodgings had been arranged, by order of the Emperor, for the three embassies. But since then the news from the Peiho have arrived, throwing everything into confusion to such a point that the Chinese government would now desire to refuse the admission of the foreign legations, and even to exchange the ratifications.

I hope, nevertheless, that the conciliating attitude of the government of the United States will be at length appreciated as it deserves to be, and that you will succeed in attaining the object of your mission.

In placing entirely at the disposal of your excellency all the knowledge and information that I can afford you, I shall be delighted to render you every good office in my power.

I am, however, unable to hazard any opinion whatever relative to the measures it would be necessary for you to take to reach Pekin, before having received from you, sir, some positive information on what has recently taken place at Shanghai and at the Peiho, and without knowing the relations which you have held up to this day with the Chinese authorities, and your intentions for the future.

I hope, Mr. Minister, that the details, which you will be kind enough to communicate to me, will enable me fully to execute the desires of his Majesty the Emperor, and to attest once more the intimate character of the relations between the cabinet of St. Petersburg and the government of the United States.

Having caused the house destined to receive your excellency at Pekin to be visited to-day, I feel it my duty to inform you that, notwithstanding the care which has apparently been taken to fit it up, the lodgings, though spacious, are not very comfortable, and badly kept; entirely in the style of the country.

I profit by this occasion, sir, to beg you to have the kindness to send the packet, which I take the liberty of inclosing, to the captain of the first Russian vessel which shall come to the Gulf of Pechele.

Hoping soon to have the advantage of making your personal acquaintance, and not doubting that the most frank and cordial relations will soon be established between us, I have the honor to be your excellency's most obedient servant,

NICOLAS IGNATIEFF.

His Excellency Mr. WARD,
Envoy Extraordinary and Minister Plenipotentiary of the United States in China.

LEGATION OF THE UNITED STATES,
Pekin, July 28, 1859.

SIR: I have the honor to inform your excellency that I have arrived in Pekin, and would have availed myself of an earlier opportunity of delivering to you the inclosed papers, but that I have been waiting for an interview with the Chinese authorities, from whom I could learn how I was to be transported from one part of the city to the other. I do not feel authorized to withhold the documents inclosed from you any longer, as it may be important that you should receive them.

Your kind letter to me of the 7th (19th) instant, inclosing document No. 62, was delivered to me on my way to Pekin, and I deemed it wisest to retain it to my return to the mouth of the river, or until an earlier opportunity should be afforded you. I expect to leave Pekin as soon after the ratifications of the treaty have been exchanged as possible, and if the package has not then been sent, it will afford me great pleasure to take it, or any other communication which you may desire to send.

Hoping that I may soon have the pleasure of making your personal acquaintance, I have the honor to be your excellency's very humble servant,

JOHN E. WARD.

PEKIN, *July* 14, (24,) 1859.

SIR: One of the aid-de-camps of the Count Mouravieff Amunski, the Prince Dadeshkalian, arrived at Pekin the day before yesterday from Dager with dispatches to me. I shall send him back to-morrow *via* Gulf of Pechele and Shanghai; and desiring to be useful to your excellency as much as I can, I am very glad to offer to you this occasion for sending your dispatches by this way to America; therefore, this officer will wait for your dispatches till to-morrow evening, the 15th, (27th,) and I beg you to send them directly to me in the hotel of the Russian mission.

I should like to welcome your excellency in your new residence by the Prince Dadeshkalian himself, but the news I received about the measures taken by the Chinese upon the account of your sojourn in the capital of the Celestial Empire oblige me to give up my intention, in order to spare you annoyances with the Chinese authorities. The Chinese government has communicated to me that the American legation will not be authorized, till the ratifications of the treaty of the Tientsin, to circulate in the town, nor to receive any body of the Europeans; that even soldiers for that purpose would be placed at the entrance of the American hotel. I protested immediately against such illegal measures, but the Chinese ministers answered me that it cannot be otherwise, for such is the custom of their country, and an exception is made only for Russians who are a long time at Pekin. Thus, I limit myself, in order to avoid every sort of misunderstanding, to send only this letter to your excellency. I am sure that the energetic protestations of your excellency and mine will, in a short time, put an end to this embarrassing and insensate guardianship, and remove the numberless difficulties imagined by the Chinese government with the intention to prevent our relations. Any attempt made by the Want-chan court to hinder a perfect understandin g between us will be, certainly, a complete failure.

In hopes to have soon the pleasure to see you, notwithstanding all obstacles, I have the honor to be, sir, your obedient servant,

NICOLAS IGNATIEFF.

PEKIN, *July* 16, (28,) 1859.

General Ignatieff presents his compliments to his excellency John E. Ward, the minister of the government of the United States at Pekin, and has the honor to inform him that, having not yet received an answer to his letter of the 14th (26th) July, and dispatches from the American legation addressed to Shanghai, he has delayed the departure of Prince Dadeshkalian till this night. Prince Dadeshkalian had orders from Count Mouravieff Amunski to remain at Pekin only one day, but General Ignatieff has detained him four days for the purpose of having an opportunity of being useful to your excellency in forwarding your dispatches to Shanghai.

His Excellency JOHN E. WARD,
Envoy Extraordinary and Minister
Plenipotentiary of the United States. &c., &c.

LEGATION OF THE UNITED STATES,
Pekin, August 3, 1859.

SIR: I am extremely obliged to you for the very kind letters of the 14th (26th) and 16th (28th) ultimo, inclosing me a note from Count Mouravieff Amunski of the 9th, (21st,) which have this moment been received. Inclosed I take the liberty of sending you a letter of introduction which the count was kind enough to give me when I had the pleasure of meeting him at the mouth of the Peiho river. I had certainly hoped long ere this to have delivered it in person, but your letter fully explains to me the reasons why I have not been able to do so. I shall certainly avail myself of the earliest opportunity of seeing you;

although, if I should be compelled to leave Pekin without doing so, I hope you will understand and appreciate the reason. I have resolved that the present treatment shall be continued no longer, and if the treaty is not at once exchanged, I will demand my escort back to my ship, and upon their failure to comply with the demand, I shall leave the premises with the small escort I have, and let the Chinese government answer to my own for any consequences that may follow. I regret that your kind notes have been received after the departure of Prince Dadeshkalian to the mouth of the Peiho, so that I am unable to avail myself of your kind offer to convey my dispatches to Commodore Tattnall.

Still hoping that I may have the pleasure of seeing you soon, I have he honor to be, sir, your obedient servant,

JOHN E. WARD.

PEKIN, *July* 26, (*August* 7,) 1859.

SIR: I have received, yesterday, your kind letter of the 22d July, (August 3.)

The Chinese are aware of the aid which the Russians, living a long time at Pekin, would afford to the Americans, in giving every information, by their knowledge of the customs and proceedings of this peculiar country. Such is the principal reason for which they would not like to let us have a near intercourse; therefore, they have given to the American legation a house at a great distance from our own; therefore, they do not permit anybody to come to you, and do not remit to you my letters.

I have endeavored to do all that I could to deliver you from the guardianship which the Chinese authorities impose to all foreign representatives. I have at several times protested verbally and in writing against the absurd measures taken by the said authorities for preventing interviews between us. The Chinese told me, unconscionably, that they do not understand why I like so much to have communication with your excellency, when you do not say a word about this subject. At last, receiving no answer from your excellency to my letters, and suspecting that the Chinese do not tell the truth in saying that they have remitted to you my notes, the next day I profited of the first occasion for sending to the supreme council of state of the empire of China a protest against the above-mentioned measure, a copy of which I have the honor to inclose herewith for your excellency's information.

This protest obliges them, at least, to deliver you my notes of the 14th (26th) and 16th (28th) July.

The serious and decided attitude which your excellency has resolved to assume, will soon put an end to the present treatment, and oblige the Chinese to yield to all your demands; undoubtedly they cannot decline exchanging the ratifications of the treaty.

I am very sorry that till now I could not make your personal acquaintance, the more so as the letter of the Count Mouravieff Amounski rendered me most impatient to have the pleasure of meeting your excellency.

Supposing that news of Europe will interest you, I take the liberty to inclose twelve numbers of the "Times," which the last post running between Riahkta and Pekin brought us. If you wish to have the Nour. and the Journal de St. Petersburg, I would be delighted to put them to the disposition of your excellency.

I have the honor to be, sir, your obedient servant,

NICOLAS IGNATIEFF.

Communication from the Russian Plenipotentiary, the General Ignatieff, of the suite of his Majesty the Emperor of Russia, to the Supreme Council of State of the Empire of China:

The second article of the treaty of Tientsin stipulates that futurely Russian diplomatic agents shall not treat with the Lee-fan-Youan, but will communicate with the supreme council of state, observing a perfect equality.

Having, contrary to the treaty, received two days ago a paper from the Lee-fan-Youan, I desire it to be notified to the mentioned tribunal that it has no right to confer with me. In every case the tribunal ought not to engage in an idle correspondence, particularly when it is grounded on false reports of low functionaries. The subject of the said paper is most insignificant, and, besides that, nothing proves that the report made by the functionary of the Lao-Zuntan would not be erroneous. It is mentioned there of a Russian named Pirin, who perforce entered the house of the American legation. None of the officers belonging to my suite or of the members of the ecclesiastical mission have such a name. Russians live a long time at Pekin peacefully, are well acquainted with your customs, and never would have acted violently, particularly without reason. Russians never do so.

The plenipotentiaries Son and Tui announced to me at our conference the 23d of your sixth month that the Chinese government decided to hinder any communications with Europeans living at Pekin till the ratifications of the American treaty of Tientsin would be exchanged. Such measures have obliged me to protest immediately against them, and to make now the following observations:

We do nothing violently in your capital, being your neighbors and old friends; therefore only, and in order to avoid misunderstanding, I have not sent till now persons of my suite to the American legation, as I proposed to do at first, but I must *very seriously protest* against measures which hinder the American legation in having communication with Europeans. Such measures are absurd. To counteract the intercourse of foreign representatives is contrary to the ideas of every civilized nation; it is contrary to the laws of hospitality which are observed even by savages and brutal nomades, and, in this case, is even contrary to common sense, because Russia had always the most friendly and sincere relations with America as well as with China. What danger can you apprehend for your empire in tolerating communication between Americans and Russians? Preventing every intercourse between us, the Chinese government expressed only its mistrust to both.

At the mentioned conference I expressed my wish of sending somebody of my suit to the American legation directly after its arrival at Pekin, for complimenting the American embassador upon his arrival at the capital. The plenipotentiaries, Son and Tui, begged me to write rather a letter, and to give it up to the Chinese officially attached to our mission for conveying it. Therefore I wrote a letter and emitted it by the same official, desiring, as is the use between representatives of friendly nations, to have directly news of the American embassador, in order that I might announce to St. Petersburg his arrival in health at Pekin. In that letter I proposed to the American envoy to convey his dispatches to America with my courrier, whom I had the intention to send the next day to Peh-tang. Having waited four days and receiving no answer from the Americans, I was obliged to let the courrier leave Pekin, the 30th of your sixth moon, at noon. At the Gulf of Pechele he will meet with the Americans and bring them no news of this legation at Pekin, he will be obliged to tell them the true reason, and the Americans shall see that they cannot rely upon you, and how deceitful is the friendship of the Chinese government. Is it so that state affairs ought to be managed?

I desire that it would be immediately given by the supreme council of state the most positive orders for emitting my letters to the American embassador without delay, as well as his answers to me, and for removing all impediments to our personal communication.

The first day of the 7th month.

NICOLAS IGNATIEFF.

LEGATION OF THE UNITED STATES,
Pekin, August 10, (*July* 29,) 1858.

SIR: I have this moment received your very kind favor of August 7, (July 26,) and beg, in the warmest terms, to express to you my grateful acknowledgments for the kind feeling which you have manifested to me in every possible way since my arrival in Pekin.

What has induced the Chinese government to insist upon keeping us apart I cannot understand, unless it be to make Pekin as disagreeable to foreign ministers as possible. Immediately on my arrival in Pekin I expressed a strong desire to see you, but was told it could not be done until after the public business was dispatched. They have interrupted all communication between us, and forced upon me the necessity of fixing the day beyond which I would not remain at Pekin. That day is to-morrow, and I have received a letter informing me that my escort will be provided for me, so that I expect to leave here early in the morning. Although I have not been able to see you, I shall take with me a recollection of your kindness, and report it to my government. It will be one more link in the chain of friendship which already binds together the two governments.

They have refused to exchange the treaty in Pekin, upon the ground that there is no clause in the treaty requiring it to be exchanged here, which, unfortunately, is the fact. This refusal was based upon the ground that I had refused to comply with certain ceremonies necessary for an audience with the Emperor. Upon the same ground the receipt of the President's letter was refused, and if they had adhered to this, the treaty would not have been exchanged by me either in or out of Pekin; but last night I received a conciliatory letter from the commissioners, stating that the President's letter would be received this day at 2 o'clock, and that the treaty would be exchanged at Peh-tang. The letter was received to-day with every mark of respect by the prime minister, and I do not feel authorized to involve the two countries in war by insisting upon a right not given in the treaty. I shall, therefore, exchange the treaty at Peh-tang, and can only hope that when the Chinese learn to know us better they will be relieved of much of their suspicion, which is so annoying and so dangerous to the peace and harmony of the countries.

I am, of course, anxious to reach my ship, to relieve the admiral from the painful anxiety under which I know that he has for some time past been laboring.

With thanks for the papers which you have sent me, which I assure you were most acceptable, I have the honor to be, sir, your obedient servant,

JOHN E. WARD.

His Excellency General IGNATIEFF,
Envoy Extraordinary and Minister Plenipotentiary, &c., &c., &c.

Mr. Ward to Mr. Cass.

[Extracts.]

No. 18.] LEGATION OF THE UNITED STATES,
Shanghai, September 1, 1859.

SIR: I have the honor to inform you that, on my arrival at this place on the 22d ultimo, I received a communication from Mr. Wikoff, informing me that he was the bearer of the two conventions—one for the adjustment of claims, and the other for the regulation of trade between the United States and China—but that, too unwell to proceed on his journey, he had transferred them to the Peninsula and Oriental Company to deliver to me. This was not received by me until the 29th, when I also received your dispatches, Nos. 5, 6, and 7, with the inclosures. I remained at the north until Commodore Tattnall had but ten days' supply of water left, when we were obliged to leave. I regret that these two conventions were not forwarded to me in time to have the ratifications exchanged at the time and place of the exchange of the treaty of Tientsin. As you remark in your dispatch No. 5, these conventions are supplemental in their character to the treaty of Tientsin, and silent on the subject of the exchange of the ratifications. I do not think the exchange necessary; but such, I fear, is not the opinion of the Chinese authorities, for they proposed to make the exchange, which

I was unable to do, not having received the conventions. Immediately on their receipt, I addressed a letter to the governor general of this province, with whom I have agreed to correspond in relation to the details by which these new commercial regulations are to be carried into effect.

I have availed myself of the earliest opportunity of transmitting to Messrs. Roberts and Bradley the instructions of the department, given to them as commissioners to adjust the claims; and I have appointed Macao as the place of meeting, and the 10th of November as the time. Macao is the point at which all the evidence connected with these transactions may be most conveniently obtained, and the 10th of November is as early as it will be possible for me, with a proper regard for the public interests, to leave this part of China.

The disastrous result of the battle of the Peiho has done much to unsettle the condition of things in China. The whole manner and bearing of the Chinese population towards foreigners have been changed, and the people of this place have been, for weeks past, under the painful apprehension of an outbreak and an attack upon the foreign settlement.

* * * * * * * * *

I have not yet received the papers in the case of the Caldera, which, in dispatch No. 7, you said would be sent by the next mail. I am obliged to the department for the views which they have given me of that case. It will certainly command my most earnest and anxious attention.

I have the honor to be, sir, your obedient servant,

JOHN E. WARD.

Hon. LEWIS CASS,
Secretary of State, Washington.

Mr. Ward to Mr. Cass.

[Extract.]

No. 19.] LEGATION OF THE UNITED STATES,
Shanghai, September 17, 1859.

SIR: I have the honor to inform you that, since the date of my last dispatch, I have been endeavoring to have the treaty published in China, in compliance with the third article, that its provisions might be at once understood and obeyed by the people.

I would, without hesitation, have published the treaty, and directed our consuls to collect the tonnage dues according to its provisions, but that the mode by which it is to be proclaimed is pointed out in the treaty itself. I herewith attach my correspondence upon this subject with the governor general of this province, marked 1 *a*, 1 *b*, 1 *c*, 1 *d*, 1 *e*, and beg particularly to call your attention to my letter of the 14th September, marked 1 *e*, in which I have fully examined the reasons for delay in publishing the treaty advanced by the governor general. The effort for delay on the part of the Chinese government is in strict accordance with their usual proceedings, and I do not believe that the treaty will be published in China until it has been proclaimed in the United States, and instructions given that it shall be carried into effect. There is no reason why this should not be done, because it was distinctly understood in Pekin that I was to confer with the governor general of this province only in relation to the new commercial regulations made at Shanghai, November 8, 1858. This understanding was both in writing, and orally with Dr. Williams and Sech. In relation to the last-mentioned regulations, I was willing to confer with the governor general, because, until instructed otherwise by you, I should have been willing to have delayed those regulations until the affairs with the French and English had been settled. First, because by the fifteenth article of our treaty it is declared that "the tariff of duties to be paid by citizens of the United States on the export and import of goods from and into China shall be the same as was agreed upon at the treaty of Wanghia, *except so far as it may be modified by treaties with other nations.*" In the preamble to the new commercial regulations it is declared that "the assent of the United States of America is desired, and freely given, because, since the signature of the treaty, material modifications of the tariff, and other matters of detail connected with the treaty, had been made by Great Britain, France, and China. Now it did not then, and does not now, appear to me to be just to force these regulations into effect until the affairs of England and France have been properly adjusted. Second, because I do not think we would gain anything by enforcing these regulations. England would, under the most favored nation clause of our old treaty, immediately insist upon all the advantages derived from these regulations; and the relative position of England and the United States, as to the trade in China, is regarded by the merchants here as better under the old than the new regulations. Third, mindful of the policy of England and the United States towards China, and how widely they have differed, I have considered it wise for our government to admit that there should be but one mode of carrying on the trade in China, that all future advantages which England might hereafter obtain should at once accrue to us.

* * * * * * * * *

I have the honor to be, sir, your obedient servant,

JOHN E. WARD.

Hon. LEWIS CASS,
Secretary of State, Washington, D. C.

Inclosure 1 a.

LEGATION OF THE UNITED STATES,
Shanghai, August 27, 1859.

The undersigned, envoy extraordinary and minister plenipotentiary of the United States, begs to inform his excellency Ho, governor general of the Two Kiang, that during his sojourn at Pekin he held consultations with the Imperial Commissioners Kweiliang and Hwashana, and in consequence of those arrangements he exchanged the ratifications of the treaty of Tientsin, at Peh-tang, with Hăngfuh, the governor general, and Wan-hi-uh, the treasurer of Chihli, on the 16th of the present month, and passed certificates of the same. Its terms and provisions are therefore now in full force and effect.

The undersigned is therefore about to issue his proclamation to citizens of the United States, informing the merchants of the tonnage dues which are to be collected henceforth under the treaty, and he requests your excellency to instruct the proper officers at the five ports in respect to this matter, and also at the two ports of Chauchau, in Kwang Tung, and Taiwan, in Fuhkien, which are opened by the American treaty, that the stipulations of the new treaty are hereafter in force. He also desires that instructions be sent to the officers at those two ports to receive the consuls about to be appointed to proceed to them, and that they be properly respected in their public functions.

As it is very important to the interests of the United States and China that the new commercial regulations should be clearly understood by the people of both countries, and be enforced at all the ports at the same time, so that there shall be but one system, the undersigned requests your excellency to unite with him in a proclamation announcing these regulations and arranging the details without delay. This will conduce to the preservation of that friendship which now so happily exists between them.

JOHN E. WARD.

His Excellency Ho Kwei-tsing,
Governor General of the Two Kiang, and
Superintendent of Foreign Commerce, &c., &c.

Inclosure 1 *b*.

August 30, 1859.

Ho, Imperial Commissioner in charge of Foreign Commerce, Junior Guardian of the Heir-Apparent, a President of the Board of War, and Governor General of the Provinces of Kiangnan and Kiangsi, herewith sends a communication:

I yesterday had the honor to receive your excellency's dispatch, in which you state that, on the 16th instant, you exchanged the ratifications of the treaty of Tientsin at Peh-tang, with Hăngfuh, governor general, and Wan-hi-uh, the treasurer of the province of Chihli, and that you are therefore about to issue your proclamation to citizens of the United States, and to inform the merchants that the tonnage dues which are to be collected henceforth are to be in conformity to the new treaty. You also request me to instruct the proper officers at the five ports which are now open and the two newly opened by this treaty, viz: Chau-chau, in Kwang Tung, and Taiwan, in Fuhkien, in respect to this matter, that the stipulations and provisions of the new treaty are now in full force; and, further, to unite with you in a proclamation announcing these regulations to all the merchants at the open ports.

I have received already a dispatch from the high officers Hweiliang and Hwashana, in which they inform me that your excellency had already exchanged the treaty at Peh-tang. They further state that, inasmuch as the treaties with England and France were not yet definitively settled and in force, and as it would be very inconvenient to have two modes of carrying on the general trade at the open ports, they had written a communication to your excellency, in which they remark that it would be proper to delay until the affairs of the English and French nations had been finally settled before acting on the new commercial regulations; but the best mode of arranging this question was committed to your excellency and myself.

In your reply to that dispatch, the desirableness of having only one mode of conducting the foreign trade at the open ports is admitted, and you express a full willingness to consult with me respecting the manner of carrying it into effect. It gives me the utmost satisfaction to observe your excellency's thoughtfulness and earnest desire to promote and strengthen the amicable relations existing between all parties.

At present, however, the English and French treaties are not finally settled, and it seems to me that if the American trade is conducted according to the new treaty and regulations the general commerce will not be conducted according to the same rule, but, on the contrary, serious impediments will arise in its management. I would, therefore, request your excellency to delay until the treaties with England and France are finally settled, when the new commercial regulations can be adopted. I will then likewise send injunctions to the officers at the ports, and issue proclamations to the merchants for their observance. The whole trade will then be placed under one and the same rule. If your excellency still decides to issue a proclamation, I request that it be in conformity with the reasons and statements which have already been discussed, that no mistake or confusion arise.

Your excellency ever speaks the truth, and acts with a regard to the public good; and that you may perceive that my words are likewise in accordance with the facts of the case, I think it best to annex a copy of your reply to the imperial commissioners, dated the 10th of this month.

(Appended is a copy of Mr. Ward's reply to Kweiliang and Hwashana, with their note to Governor General Ho, transmitting it, with directions to act according to it.)

His Excellency JOHN E. WARD,
Envoy Extraordinary, &c., &c.

Inclosure 1 *c.*

LEGATION OF THE UNITED STATES,
Shanghai, September 5, 1859.

The undersigned, envoy extraordinary and minister plenipotentiary of the United States to China, has the honor to acknowledge the receipt of your excellency's dispatch of the 30th ultimo, which reached him to-day.

In his reply to the Imperial Commissioners Kweiliang and Hwashana, the undersigned did say that it was very desirable that the general trade at the open ports should be conducted according to one rule, and he expressed a willingness to consult with your excellency respecting the mode of carrying this plan into effect; but he has never consented that the provisions of the treaty with the United States, or the commercial regulations, should not be carried into effect before the settlement of the English and French treaties, nor can he give any such consent. It would be making his government dependent upon others. He desires to consult with your excellency respecting the best mode of carrying the new commercial regulations into effect; and with this view he earnestly requests that you will afford him an interview at Shanghai on the 15th instant, when this matter can be more fully discussed than it can be by letter.

The proclamation which the undersigned proposes to issue is simply to announce that the treaty has been exchanged and is in full force; and that, by article 16, the tonnage dues hereafter to be collected upon merchant vessels belonging to the United States will be at the rate of four mace per ton of forty cubic feet, &c., &c. He must insist that this provision be immediately accorded to all vessels belonging to his nation; and it was to prevent all confusion on this point that he requested your excellency to give the necessary instructions to the proper officers at the open ports, and he cannot doubt your willingness to comply, since it noways affects the trade with England and France.

By article 14, the ports of Chauchau and Taiwan are opened to American commerce, and citizens of the United States can reside there with their families. He desires with your excellency to fix an early day when the consuls of the United States will be received at these two ports, and that stipulation carried into effect. No good reason can be alleged for delay in so doing.

The undersigned, being most anxious in every way to promote good will and strengthen the harmony between the two nations, will delay further action until a reply is received from your excellency; but as he now remains at Shanghai only for the purpose of arranging these matters, and his public duties will require him to leave very soon for the south of China, he requests an immediate reply, designating a time when American consuls will be received at the two newly opened ports, and also sending instructions to the officers at all the ports that the tonnage dues upon American vessels hereafter be paid according to article 16 of the new treaty.

If your excellency can appoint an earlier day than the 15th instant to meet the undersigned at Shanghai, to discuss the manner of carrying the commercial regulations into effect, he will regard it as a favor.

JOHN E. WARD.

His Excellency Ho KWEITSING,
Imperial Commissioner in charge of
Foreign Commerce, &c., &c., &c.

Inclosure 1 d.

SEPTEMBER 10, 1859.

Ho, Imperial Commissioner, charged with the affairs of Foreign Commerce, &c., &c., herewith sends this reply:

I received your excellency's dispatch of the 5th instant on the 8th, and have carefully perused it.

It would appear, from the copy of the communication which the high ministers Kweiliang and Hwashana sent me, that it had been regarded as proper to delay until the affairs of the English and French were definitely settled before bringing the new commercial regulations into effect. Your excellency now desires, however, to appoint consuls, who shall proceed to the two ports of Chauchau and Taiwan, previous to this time; and (also proposes) that all American ships resorting to the open ports shall pay tonnage dues according to article 16 (of the new treaty.) This does not exactly correspond to what those high ministers have informed me, and it likewise differs somewhat from the expressions used in your excellency's own communication, when you speak of the necessity of there being a uniform mode of carrying on the general trade at the open ports.

As I cannot venture on alone taking the responsibility of acting in this matter, it will be necessary to lay the subject before the government, and request his Majesty's orders. When they reach me I will set a time for an interview; but I cannot now expedite my movements so as to meet you on the 15th instant.

His Excellency J. E. WARD,
Envoy Extraordinary and Minister Plenipotentiary of United States to China.

Inclosure 1 e.

LEGATION OF THE UNITED STATES,
Shanghai, September 14, 1859.

The undersigned, envoy extraordinary of the United States to China, has the honor to acknowledge your excellency's dispatch, of the 10th instant, which came this morning.

In the communication of the imperial commissioners, to which you allude, they expressly say: "When this has been done, (*i. e.* the treaty been exchanged,) it will follow that its regulations all come into effect, and are to be followed." They then speak of the general commerce carried on with China, and express the opinion that it would be highly undesirable to have two modes of conducting it. Now, they no doubt referred to the commercial regulations made at Shanghai, November 8, 1858; because they had admitted that all the stipulations of the treaty, when it was exchanged, must go into effect. These regulations, which were agreed upon subsequently, declare that they were made because the same had been made with England and France, and therefore it was desirable that they should all go into effect together.

There was reason in this request; and, although I had not the power to consent even to the postponement of this, I expressed a willingness to confer with you upon the subject, with a view of so arranging the details that no obstacles should arise in conducting the general trade

This I am still willing and desirous to do, and will meet your excellency at any time you may designate, between the 10th and 20th of October. There is, therefore, no discrepancy whatever between the expressions used in my communications to the imperial commissioners and to you. I shall return to Shanghai about the 10th proximo, but must again leave it on the 20th.

In relation to the stipulations of the treaty itself, I beg to call your excellency's attention to article 3, in which it is declared that, "in order that the people of the two countries may know and obey the provisions of this treaty, the United States of America agree, immediately on the exchange of ratifications, to proclaim the same and publish it by proclamation in the gazettes where the laws of the United States are published by authority; and his Majesty the Emperor of China, on the exchange of ratifications, agrees immediately to direct the publication of the same at the capital and by the governors of all the provinces." Now, if I wished, I have no right to alter this treaty, in a single particular; and I have been expecting since the exchange to learn that, in compliance with this provision, the government had directed the publication of the same at the capital, and by the governors of all the provinces. If this is not done, your excellency must see that embarrassments and difficulties will ensue, which may lead to the most serious consequences. The copy of the treaty ratified by his Majesty having been sent to Washington, will certainly be there proclaimed without delay, that its stipulations may be known and obeyed by the people. If not proclaimed in China, the citizens of the United States will consider themselves bound by one treaty and the Chinese by another, whereby it will be impossible for harmony to exist between the two nations.

I trust, therefore, on returning, that I shall learn that the treaty has been published in China, and that instructions have been sent to the officers at the open ports to collect the tonnage dues on American vessels, according to the provisions of article 16; and also what day, between the 10th and 20th proximo, you have designated for an interview to confer upon the new commercial relations.

The stipulations in articles 14 and 16, relating to the opening of the two ports of Chauchau and Taiwan, and to the rate of tonnage dues, have no connection with the English and French treaties, and can in no manner be made to depend on them, the American treaty having been made previously to those.

When the treaty is published in the United States, consuls will be appointed to both these ports, if not previously by me. Instructions will be given to the consuls at all the ports, that the tonnage dues on American vessels are to be collected according to it, and American merchants will not then pay any other rate. I anticipate this state of things, that your excellency may fully comprehend the result of your refusing or failing to instruct the local officers, without delay, to collect these tonnage dues at this rate, and designate a time when consuls will be received at the two new ports.

JOHN E. WARD.

His Excellency HO KWEI-TSING,
Imperial Commissioner charged with
the Affairs of Foreign Commerce.

www.ingramcontent.com/pod-product-compliance
Lightning Source LLC
LaVergne TN
LVHW021101110826
845150LV00001B/141

* 9 7 8 1 4 2 5 5 6 5 8 6 2 *